LOVE, MA٦

AND FAMILY

IN THE MIDDLE AGES

A READER

edited by

JACQUELINE MURRAY

broadview press

National Library of Canada Cataloguing in Publication Data

Main entry under title:
Love, marriage, and family in the Middle Ages: a reader

(Readings in medieval civilizations and cultures; 7)
Includes index.
ISBN 1-55111-104-7

1. Family — History — To 1500—Sources. 2. Marriage — History — To 1500—Sources. 3. Social history — Medieval, 500-1500—Sources. I. Murray, Jacqueline, 1953- . II. Series

HQ731.L68 2001   306.8'09'02   C2001-930763-2

Broadview Press Ltd. is an independent, international publishing house, incorporated in 1985.

North America:
P.O. Box 1243, Peterborough, Ontario, Canada K9J 7H5
3576 California Road, Orchard Park, NY 14127
TEL: (705) 743-8990; FAX: (705) 743-8353;
E-MAIL: customerservice@broadviewpress.com

United Kingdom: Thomas Lyster Ltd
Unit 9, Ormskirk Industrial Park
Old Boundary Way, Burscough Road
Ormskirk, Lancashire L39 2YW
TEL: (01695) 575112; FAX: (01695) 570120; E-mail: books@tlyster.co.uk

Australia: St. Clair Press, P.O. Box 287, Rozelle, NSW 2039
TEL: (02) 818-1942; FAX: (02) 418-1923

www.broadviewpress.com

Book design and composition by George Kirkpatrick.
PRINTED IN CANADA

In Memoriam
MICHAEL M. SHEEHAN
scholar, teacher, mentor

CONTENTS

INTRODUCTION

The Middle Ages is a society at once familiar and foreign. Its very familiarity can lull us into a false sense of knowing and trick us into overlooking the profound differences between our society and that of medieval people. This is especially true when we cast our eyes on apparently transhistorical phenomena such as the human experience of love, marriage, and family. These are shared experiences, yet they are also deeply rooted in the values and beliefs of specific times and places. Love, marriage, and family were interrelated in medieval society (as they are now) but this interrelationship was not always what we moderns might expect.

For medieval people the distinction between public and private was not as precise as it is now perceived to be. It is only when we examine the marital complications of the House of Windsor, or when we confront the challenge to conventional marriage posed by same-sex unions that we moderns encounter something of the tensions and urgency that surrounded love, marriage, and family in medieval society. For much of the early Middle Ages the structures of marriage and family were subject to the tectonic stresses of cultural and religious accommodation. Roman, Christian, and Germanic peoples, values, and beliefs converged in western and southern Europe. Theses and antitheses met and merged, and ultimately created new, distinctively medieval, syntheses which underlie much of western experience and inform much of western beliefs about love, marriage, and family into the twenty-first century. There was no one medieval synthesis that was seamless and unitary. Rather, a series of beliefs, values, and practices intersected, competed with, and accommodated each other.

Medieval views on love, marriage, and the family were complex and riddled with tensions and contradictions. Some of these can be expressed as binary oppositions. The understanding of marriage and family was informed by both secular and religious values. The family, after all, was the fundamental unit of society, and marriage was one of the primary means of extending social, economic, and political ties. Yet marriage was equally part of the order of salvation. It was one of the sacraments and a symbol of the profound unity between Christ and the church, between a man and a woman who became "two in one flesh." Secular society frequently viewed marriage as an expedient, subject to renegotiation with a change of circumstances. For the church, marriage, once contracted, was indissoluble, enduring unto death. The tensions between these two perspectives colored much of medieval discussion about marriage, but also influenced the lives and experiences of medieval people. Repudiation and divorce, coercion and consent were played out in people's lives and shaped the experiences of individuals and communities.

Many factors influenced how an individual experienced love, marriage, and the family. Men and women experienced marriage and family differently as patriarchal values constructed these relationships in terms of gender-based hierarchies. Men governed; women and other dependents were subordinate in theory, and frequently in practice. Demographic shifts, wars, and economic considerations all significantly influenced whom men and women married, or if they were even able to marry. Family structures, the economic factors governing marriage, and the relative autonomy of the individual were all shaped by considerations of class. Europe's elites, whether feudal or mercantile, found marriage a useful tool for forging political and economic alliances. Consequently, individual choice, for both men and women, was subordinate to the well-being of land and lineage. In this, church and secular society were at odds. The church championed the individual's right to choose a spouse and consent freely to marriage. After all, how could a sacrament be coerced? For more modest folk, economic constraints were more likely to influence the age at which they had the resources to marry, rather than to dictate their choice of spouse. This did not mean, however, that their choices were motivated more by romance than pragmatism.

Despite the interconnectedness of love, marriage, and the family, in medieval society they were not always considered inextricable. For twelfth-century proponents of courtly love, love was best directed outside of marriage. Similarly, church fathers condemned men who loved their wives "too ardently." While marriage was the only legitimate outlet for sexual desire, and for many people consummation was the *sine qua non* for an indissoluble union, the notion of a marriage free from carnal entanglements was considered an ideal. The church at once praised abstinent marriages and considered them vaguely scandalous. Similarly, while the procreation of children was one of the good ends of marriage, theological and canonical writers had remarkably little to say about the family and its internal dynamics. The relations between men and women were the focus of attention, whether it was sexual sins inside of marriage or out, or the nature and quality of marital consent. In the theoretical literature the conjugal couple remained at the center. Yet, in daily life, the dynamics of family members loomed large. Parents and children lived together and worked together; their relationship was enduring and mutually dependent.

This collection of primary documents seeks to illuminate love, marriage, and the family in the Middle Ages by complementing ideal with reality, theory with practice, secular with ecclesiastical. It acknowledges contradiction and competition between value systems. It endeavors to recognize both geographical and temporal differences and areas of medieval homogeneity. The selections include some of the standard and fundamental works for understanding medieval domestic life. Included, too, are the exceptions and anomalies.

Medieval society allowed for inconsistency and eccentricity while lauding cohesion and conformity. The more idiosyncratic documents have been included because they cast light on unusual situations or reveal new or different understandings of a topic. Some of these documents have been long available in standard English translations, while others are newly translated for the first time. The scholarly contributions of our late-nineteenth- and early twentieth-century predecessors also need to be acknowledged. I have relied on many of their translations of medieval sources. These have been revised and updated, partly to reflect our own idiom, partly to overcome their reticence. Earlier sensibilities often resulted in silent omission, abridgement or the obscuring of "racy" or sexually explicit material.

The usual caveats that govern the use of sources in translation pertain here as well. Translation is a form of historical interpretation. Generally, however, I have tried to avoid excesses of presentism. For example, although it may grate on modern ears, the medieval use of "man" to stand for "human being" has been retained. Medieval euphemisms, for example, "the carnal act," have been retained, while modern anachronisms, for example, "making love," have been avoided. Some medieval writers were less proficient in Latin than we might wish. Their awkwardness or turgid prose style is reflected in the translations.

The volume begins with a selection of documents representing the various influences that contributed to the medieval world view. This is followed by a series of thematic sections moving from love, through marriage, and into the family. Within each section the documents are presented chronologically, in order to allow for a sense of changing circumstances and contexts. The concluding section of documents focuses on those who dissented from the dominant ideology of Christendom: Jews, Muslims, and heretics. These groups influenced Christians and were influenced in return. Despite Christendom's hegemony in the medieval west, the medievals were aware of peoples with differing views of these fundamental institutions.

Love, marriage, family: these are inherent in the experience of human life. Often assumed to be natural, they are profoundly shaped by society and its values. The individual's experience of life, the intensity of its rewards or the depths of its disappointments, are all influenced to some degree by love, marriage, and family. This collection of documents presents something of the richness and texture of medieval life, but it can only provide a tantalizing sample. It is hoped that readers will be sufficiently intrigued to read further and that they will come to respect and learn from this period, which underlies our modern world and the complex values we have inherited from the past.

★ ★ ★

I am truly grateful to my colleagues for their patience and their continuing interest when circumstances prevented me from completing a project long ago begun. The remarkably helpful and cheerful people of Broadview Press have done much to encourage and facilitate the appearance of this volume. In particular, Don LePan has been particularly gracious, and Barbara Conolly and Betsy Struthers have brought to bear their efficiency and acumen in ways that will never be fully appreciated. Like so much in publishing, if one's work is done well it is invisible to the outside observer. The Pontifical Institute of Mediaeval Studies (Toronto) and its excellent library continue to be an intellectual haven for medievalists. Caroline Suma and Sheila Campbell provided me with invaluable assistance.

A number of people have provided advice, insight, and encouragement as I prepared this volume. I am indebted indeed to Shannon McSheffrey, Robert L. A. Clark, and Paul Dutton for generously allowing me to include their original translations. Laura Gardner has been an indispensable collaborator from the beginning. Abigail Young continues to inspire me with her love of Latin. Leslie Howsam and Susan Riggs were there every step of the way. Paul Dutton is the epitome of a colleague and a consummate editor. Finally, Michael Sheehan continues to cast his shadow over all that I do. My debt to him is immense.

CHAPTER ONE:

FOUNDATIONS AND INFLUENCES

The values and practices that formed the foundations and exercised influence over love, marriage, and the family in the Middle Ages were inherited from a variety of sources. In particular, medieval beliefs were the result of a complex interweaving of Roman law, Germanic customs, and Judeo-Christian religious beliefs. From the first through the fifth centuries, there occurred a process of accommodation and transformation in western Europe, as peoples of different beliefs and values learned how to live side by side. Gradually, the laws of the Romans and their new Germanic neighbors influenced each other. Similarly, as Christianity evolved from the religion of a persecuted minority to the official state religion, its adherents needed to find ways to mediate their beliefs to the majority of common folk, of both Roman and Germanic descent. How these various peoples with their diverse legal systems, religious beliefs, and customary practices gradually evolved into a distinctly medieval culture and society is a fascinating process. Together they merged to form the foundations of medieval society.

1. THE BIBLICAL FOUNDATIONS

Many of the medieval ideas and values underlying marriage, its nature and purpose, were based on the teachings of Hebrew and Christian scripture. The very purpose of marriage and the ideal relationship between the spouses were set out when God created Eve in the Garden of Eden. Christian writers also re-evaluated marriage in the light of their new circumstances. The various teachings medieval people inherited presented numerous contradictions. Marriage was a necessary state of life, ordained by God in paradise and confirmed by Jesus' miracle at the wedding in Cana. Numerous rules established who was eligible to marry, with prohibitions against consanguinity, affinity, and incest being established early on. So, too, the married couple was perceived to be in a mutually dependent and sanctified union, yet one that was hierarchical and based on female subordination. The teachings of the Apostle Paul were of particular importance in the development of a Christian understanding of marriage. Like many of his contemporaries, Paul valued celibacy as a higher state of life than marriage with its attendant sexual activity. Nevertheless, Paul did present marriage as an honorable estate. As well, Paul also presented husbands and wives as playing complementary roles, although the relationship was clearly hierarchical and based on women's subordination and obedience. At the same time, scripture also presented marriage as a union based on love and as playing a positive role in human life.

Source: *The Holy Bible,* Douay Reims Version (Baltimore: John Murphy, 1899; rpt. Rockford, IL: Tan Books, 1971), pp. 6-7, 26, 105, 127, 191-93, 222, 230, 265; modernized.

The Institution of Marriage in Paradise, Genesis 2:7-8, 18-25

7. And the Lord God formed man from the slime of the earth and breathed into his face the breath of life, and man became a living soul.

8. And the Lord God had planted a paradise of pleasure from the beginning in which he placed man whom he had formed.

18. And the Lord God said: it is not good for man to be alone. Let us make a helper for him.

19. And the Lord God having formed out of the ground all the beasts of the earth and all the birds of the air, brought them to Adam to see what he would call them, for whatever Adam called any living creature, that is its name.

20. And Adam called all the beasts by their names, and all the birds of the air, and all cattle of the field; but for Adam no helper like himself was found.

21. Then the Lord God cast a deep sleep upon Adam. And when he was fast asleep, he took one of his ribs and replaced it with flesh.

22. And the Lord God built the rib which he took from Adam into a woman and brought her to Adam.

23. And Adam said: This now is bone of my bones and flesh of my flesh; she shall be called woman because she was taken out of man.

24. That is why a man shall leave father and mother and shall cling to his wife and they shall be two in one flesh.

25. And they were both naked: that is, Adam and his wife, and they were not ashamed.

The Regulation of Marriage in Ancient Jewish Law, Leviticus 18:5-23

5. Keep my laws and my judgments, which if a man does, he shall live in them. I am the Lord.

6. No man shall approach a woman who is near kin to him to uncover her nakedness. I am the Lord.

7. You shall not uncover the nakedness of your father or the nakedness of your mother. She is your mother; you shall not uncover her nakedness.

8. You shall not uncover the nakedness of your father's wife, for it is the nakedness of your father.

9. You shall not uncover the nakedness of your sister by father or by mother, whether born at home or abroad.

10. You shall not uncover the nakedness of your son's daughter, or your daughter's daughter because it is your own nakedness.

11. You shall not uncover the nakedness of your father's wife's daughter, whom she bore to your father and who is your sister.

12. You shall not uncover the nakedness of your father's sister because she is the flesh of your father.

13. You shall not uncover the nakedness of your mother's sister because she is your mother's flesh.

14. You shall not uncover the nakedness of your father's brother. Neither shall you approach his wife who is joined to you by affinity.

15. You shall not uncover the nakedness of your daughter-in-law because she is your son's wife; neither shall you discover her shame.

16. You shall not uncover the nakedness of your brother's wife because it is the nakedness of your brother.

17. You shall not uncover the nakedness of your wife and her daughter. You shall not take her son's daughter or her daughter's daughter, to discover her shame because they are her flesh and such copulation is incest.

18. You shall not take your wife's sister for a harlot, to rival her; neither shall you discover her nakedness, while your wife is still living.

19. You shall not approach a woman having her flowers [menstrual period]; neither shall you uncover her nakedness.

20. You shall not lie with your neighbor's wife nor be defiled with mingling of seed.

21. You shall not give any of your seed to be consecrated to the idol Moloch nor defile the name of your God. I am the Lord.

22. You shall not lie with man as with woman because it is an abomination.

23. You shall not copulate with any beast; neither shall you be defiled with it. A woman shall not lie down with a beast nor copulate with it because it is a heinous crime.

In Praise of Marriage, Ecclesiasticus 40:18-23

18. The life of a laborer who is content with what he has shall be sweet and in it you shall find a treasure.

19. Children and the building of a city shall establish a name but a blameless wife shall be counted above them both.

20. Wine and music rejoice the heart but the love of wisdom is above them both.

21. The flute and the psaltery make a sweet melody but a pleasant tongue is above them both.

22. Your eye desires favor and beauty but more than these green sown fields.

23. A friend and companion meeting together in season but above them both is a wife with her husband.

The Indissolubility of Christian Marriage, Matthew 19:3-12

3. And there came to him the Pharisees tempting him and saying: Is it lawful for a man to put away his wife for every cause?

4. Answering, he said to them: Have you not read that he who made man from the beginning "Made them male and female?" And he said:

5. "That is why a man shall leave father and mother and shall cling to his wife and they shall be two in one flesh."

6. Therefore now they are not two but one flesh. What therefore God has joined together, let no man put asunder.

7. They said to him: Why then did Moses command to give a bill of divorce and to put away?

8. He said to them: Because Moses, by reason of the hardness of your heart, permitted you to put away your wives, but from the beginning it was not so.

9. And I say to you, that whosoever shall put away his wife, except it be for fornication, and shall marry another, commits adultery; and he that shall marry her that is put away, commits adultery.

10. His disciples said to him: If that is the case with husband and wife, it is not expedient to marry.

11. He said to them: All men take not this word, but they to whom it is given.

12. For there are eunuchs who were born so from their mother's womb, and there are eunuchs who were made so by men, and there are eunuchs who have made themselves eunuchs for the kingdom of heaven. He that can take, let him take it.

The Marriage Feast at Cana, John 2:1-11

1. And on the third day, there was a marriage in Cana in Galilee and the mother of Jesus was there.

2. And Jesus and his disciples were also invited to the marriage.

3. And the wine failing, the mother of Jesus said to him: They have no wine.

4. And Jesus said to her: Woman, what is that to me and to you? My hour is not yet come.

5. His mother said to the waiters: Do whatever he tells you.

6. Now there were set there six waterpots of stone, according to the manner of the purifying of the Jews, containing two or three measures apiece.

7. Jesus said to them: Fill the waterpots with water. And they filled them up to the brim.

8. And Jesus said to them: Draw some out now, and carry it to the chief steward of the feast. And they carried it.

9. And the chief steward tasted the water made wine, and did not know where it came from, but the waiters knew who had drawn the water. The chief steward called the bridegroom

10. And said to him: Everyone at first serves good wine and when everyone has drunk well then that which is worse. But you have kept the good wine until now.

11. This beginning of miracles Jesus performed in Cana in Galilee and manifested his glory and his disciples believed in him.

Paul on Marriage and Celibacy, 1 Corinthians 7

1. Now concerning the things about which you wrote to me: It is good for a man not to touch a woman.

2. But for fear of fornication, let every man have his own wife, and let every woman have her own husband.

3. Let the husband render the debt to his wife and the wife also similarly to her husband.

4. The wife does not have power over her own body, but the husband. And in like manner the husband also does not have power of his own body, but the wife.

5. Do not defraud one another, except, perhaps, by consent, for a time that you may give yourselves to prayer; and come together again, lest satan tempt you for your incontinency.

6. But I say this as an indulgence, not as a commandment.

7. For I should like all men to be as I am myself; but everyone has his own gift from God, one after this manner and another after that.

8. But I say to the unmarried and to the widows: it is good for them if they so continue, even as I.

9. But if they do not contain themselves, let them marry. For it is better to marry than to be burnt.

10. But to them that are married, not I but the Lord commands, that the wife not separate from her husband.

11. And if she separate, that she remain unmarried or be reconciled to her husband. And let not the husband put away his wife.

12. To the rest I speak, not the Lord. If any brother has a wife that does not believe, and she consents to dwell with him, let him not put her away.

13. And if any woman has a husband that does not believe, and he consents to dwell with her, let her not put away her husband.

14. For the unbelieving husband is sanctified by the believing wife; and the unbelieving wife is sanctified by the believing husband. Otherwise your children would be unclean but now they are holy.

15. But if the unbeliever departs, let him depart. For a brother or sister is not under servitude in such cases. But God has called us in peace.

16. For how do you know, O wife, whether you shall save your husband? Or how do you know, O husband, whether you shall save your wife?

17. But as the Lord has distributed to everyone, as God has called every one, so let him walk: and so in all churches I teach.

18. Is any man called, having been circumcised? Let him not procure uncircumcision. Is any man called being uncircumcised? Let him not be circumcised.

19. Circumcision is nothing and uncircumcision is nothing, but the observance of the commandments of God.

20. Let every man abide in the same calling in which he was called.

21. Were you called, being a bondsman? Care not for it; but if you are made free, rather use it.

22. For he that is called in the Lord, being a bondsman, is the freeman of the

Lord. Likewise he that is called, being free, is the bondsman of Christ.

23. You are bought with a price; be not made the bondslaves of men.

24. Brothers, let every man, wherever he was called, there abide with God.

25. Now concerning virgins, I have no commandment from the Lord; but I give counsel, as having obtained mercy from the Lord, to be faithful.

26. I think therefore that this is good for the present necessity, that it is good for a man to be so.

27. Are you bound to a wife? Seek not to be loosed. Are you free from a wife? Seek not a wife.

28. But if you take a wife, you have not sinned. And if a virgin marry, she has not sinned. Nevertheless, such people shall have tribulation of the flesh. But I spare you.

29. This therefore I say, brothers; the time is short. It remains, that they also who have wives, should be as if they had none;

30. And they that weep, as though they wept not; and they that rejoice, as if they rejoiced not; and they that buy, as though they possessed not;

31. And they that use this world, as if they used it not: for the fashion of this world passes away.

32. But I would have you to be without solicitude. He that is without a wife is solicitous for the things that belong to the Lord; how he may please God.

33. But he that has a wife, is solicitous for the things of the world; how he may please his wife: and he is divided.

34. And the unmarried woman and the virgin think about the things of the Lord, that she may be holy both in body and in spirit. But she that is married thinks about the things of the world; how she may please her husband.

35. And this I say for your benefit, not to lay a snare for you but for that which is decent and which may give you power to attend upon the Lord without impediment.

36. But if anyone think that he seems dishonored with regard to his virgin, because she is above the age, and it must be so, let him do what he will. He does not sin if she marries.

37. For he that is determined, being steadfast in his heart, having no necessity, but having power over his own will, and has judged this in his heart, to keep his virgin, does well.

38. Therefore, both he that gives his virgin in marriage does well and he that does not give her does better.

39. A woman is bound by the law as long as her husband lives, but if her husband dies, she is at liberty: let her marry whom she will, only in the Lord.

40. But more blessed shall she be, if she remains so, according to my counsel and I think that I also have the spirit of God.

The Hierarchical Arrangement of Marriage and Family

Ephesians 5:21-33

21. Be subject one to another, in the fear of Christ.

22. Let women be subject to their husbands, as to the Lord,

23. Because the husband is the head of the wife, as Christ is the head of the church. He is the savior of his body.

24. Therefore as the church is subject to Christ, so also let the wives be subject to their husbands in all things.

25. Husbands, love your wives, as Christ also loved the church and delivered himself up for it

26. That he might sanctify it, cleansing it by the bathing of water in the word of life,

27. That he might present to himself a glorious church, not having spot or wrinkle or any such thing, but that it should be holy and without blemish.

28. So also ought men to love their wives as their own bodies. He that loves his wife, loves himself.

29. For no man ever hated his own flesh but nourishes and cherishes it as also Christ does the church

30. Because we are members of his body, of his flesh, and of his bones.

31. "For this cause shall a man leave his father and mother and shall cling to his wife and they shall be two in one flesh."

32. This is a great sacrament; but I speak in Christ and in the church.

33. Nevertheless let every one of you in particular love his wife as himself: and let the wife fear her husband.

Colossians 3:18-22

18. Wives, be subject to your husbands, as it is proper in the Lord.

19. Husbands, love your wives, and be not bitter towards them.

20. Children, obey your parents in all things, for this is well pleasing to the Lord.

21. Fathers, provoke not your children to indignation, lest they be discouraged.

22. Servants, obey in all things your masters according to the flesh, not serving to the eye, as pleasing men, but in simplicity of heart, fearing God.

1 Peter 3:1-7

1. In like manner also let wives be subject to their husbands that if any do not believe the word, they may be won without the word, by the conversation of their wives.

2. Consider your chaste conversation with fear.

3. Whose adorning let it not be the outward plaiting of the hair or the wearing of gold or the putting on of apparel,

4. But in the hidden being of the heart, in the incorruptibility of a quiet and a meek spirit which is rich in the sight of God.

5. For after this manner up to now the holy women also, who trusted in God, adorned themselves, being in subjection to their own husbands

6. As Sara obeyed Abraham, calling him lord; whose daughters you are, doing well, and not fearing any disturbance.

7. You husbands, likewise dwelling with them according to knowledge, giving honor to the female as to the weaker vessel, and as to the co-heirs of the grace of life, that your prayers be not hindered.

How is the relationship between husband and wife characterized in Genesis and Ecclesiasticus? How does the vision presented in Ephesians, Colossians, and 1 Peter differ? What was the ultimate significance of the metaphor that husband and wife "are two in one flesh"? What did the apostles think about Jesus' teaching? What does the miracle at Cana signify? Why did Paul believe that people should marry? Why did he think that celibacy was superior to marriage? What is the intent of the regulations set out in Leviticus?

2. THE GERMANIC FOUNDATIONS

The Germania *was written by the Roman historian Tacitus in 98 C.E. In it Tacitus describes the culture and values of the Germanic tribes who lived beyond the northern and eastern borders of the Roman Empire. By the third century the Germanic peoples began to filter into the empire, a process that accelerated in the fourth and fifth centuries with huge movements of tribes westwards. The Germanic peoples brought their own culture and beliefs with them and these exerted a significant influence on the development of medieval society. Tacitus provides an idealized view of Germanic society because one of his goals was to praise the morality of the so-called barbarians as a means to criticize what he perceived to be the increased laxity and decadence of the Romans. Thus Tacitus presents a description of a highly organized patriarchal society which adhered to strict discipline and moral principles. Nevertheless, despite Tacitus' polemical nature, the* Germania *does provide an early glimpse into Germanic culture and society.*

Source: Trans. Alfred John Church and William Jackson Brodribb, *The Complete Works of Tacitus* (New York: Modern Library, 1942), pp. 712-13, 717-21.

7. They choose their kings by birth, their generals for merit. These kings have not unlimited or arbitrary power, and the generals do more by example than by authority. If they are energetic, if they are conspicuous, if they fight in the front, they lead because they are admired. But to reprimand, to imprison, even to flog, is permitted to the priests alone, and that not as a punishment, or at the general's bidding, but, as it were, by the mandate of the god whom they believe to inspire the warrior. They also carry with them into battle certain figures and images taken from their sacred groves. And what most stimulates their courage is, that their squadrons or battalions, instead of being formed by chance or by a fortuitous gathering, are composed of families and clans. Close by them, too, are those dearest to them, so that they hear the shrieks of women, the cries of infants. They are to every man the most sacred witnesses of his bravery — they are his most generous applauders. The soldier brings his wounds to his mother and wife, who shrink not from counting or even demanding them and who administer both food and encouragement to the combatants.

8. Tradition says that armies already wavering and giving way have been rallied by women who, with earnest entreaties and bosoms laid bare, have vividly represented the horrors of captivity, which the Germans fear with such extreme dread on behalf of their women, that the strongest tie by which a state can be bound is the being required to give, among the number of hostages, maidens of noble birth. They even believe that the sex has a certain sanctity and prescience, and they do not despise their counsels, or make light of their answers. In Vespasians's days we saw Veleda, long regarded by many as a divinity. In former times, too, they venerated Aurinia, and many other women, but

not with servile flatteries, or with sham deification....

17. They all wrap themselves in a cloak which is fastened with a clasp, or, if this is not forthcoming, with a thorn, leaving the rest of their persons bare. They pass whole days on the hearth by the fire. The wealthiest are distinguished by a dress which is not flowing, like that of the Sarmatae and Parthia, but is tight, and exhibits each limb. They also wear the skins of wild beasts; the tribes on the Rhine and Danube in a careless fashion, those of the interior with more elegance, as not obtaining other clothing by commerce. These select certain animals, the hides of which they strip off and vary them with the spotted skins of beasts, the produce of the outer ocean, and of seas unknown to us. The women have the same dress as the men, except that they generally wrap themselves in linen garments, which they embroider with purple, and do not lengthen out the upper part of their clothing into sleeves. The upper and lower arm is thus bare, and the nearest part of the bosom is also exposed.

18. Their marriage code, however, is strict, and indeed no part of their manners is more praiseworthy. Almost alone among barbarians they are content with one wife, except a very few among them, and these not from sensuality, but because their noble birth procures for them many offers of alliance. The wife does not bring a dower to the husband, but the husband to the wife. The parents and relatives are present, and pass judgment on the marriage-gifts, gifts not meant to suit a woman's taste, nor such as a bride would deck herself with, but oxen, a caparisoned steed, a shield, a lance, and a sword. With these presents the wife is espoused, and she herself in her turn brings her husband a gift of arms. This they count their strongest bond of union, these their sacred mysteries, these their gods of marriage. Lest the woman should think herself to stand apart from aspirations after noble deeds and from the perils of war, she is reminded by the ceremony which inaugurates marriage that she is her husband's partner in toil and danger, destined to suffer and to dare with him alike both in peace and in war. The yoked oxen, the harnessed steed, the gift of arms, proclaim this fact. She must live and die with the feeling that she is receiving what she must hand down to her children neither tarnished nor depreciated, what future daughters-in-law may receive, and may be so passed on to her grandchildren.

19. Thus with their virtue protected they live uncorrupted by the allurements of public shows or the stimulant of feastings. Clandestine correspondence is equally unknown to men and women. Very rare for so numerous a population is adultery, the punishment for which is prompt, and in the husband's power. Having cut off the hair of the adulteress and stripped her naked, he expels her from the house in the presence of her kinsfolk, and then flogs her through the whole village. The loss of chastity meets with no indulgence; neither beauty, youth, nor wealth will procure the culprit a husband. No one in

Germany laughs at vice, nor do they call it the fashion to corrupt and to be corrupted. Still better is the condition of those states in which only maidens are given in marriage, and where the hopes and expectations of a bride are then finally terminated. They receive one husband, as having one body and one life, that they may have no thoughts beyond, no further-reaching desires, that they may love not so much the husband as the married state. To limit the number of their children or to destroy any of their subsequent offspring is accounted infamous, and good habits are here more effectual than good laws elsewhere.

20. In every household the children, naked and filthy, grow up with those stout frames and limbs which we so much admire. Every mother suckles her own offspring, and never entrusts it to servants and nurses. The master is not distinguished from the slave by being brought up with greater delicacy. Both live amid the same flocks and lie on the same ground till the freeborn are distinguished by age and recognized merit. The young men marry late, and their vigor is thus unimpaired. Nor are the maidens hurried into marriage; the same age and a similar stature is required; well-matched and vigorous they wed, and the offspring reproduce the strength of the parents. Sister's sons are held in as much esteem by their uncles as by their fathers; indeed, some regard the relation as even more sacred and binding, and prefer it in receiving hostages, thinking thus to secure a stronger hold on the affections and a wider bond for the family. But every man's own children are his heirs and successors, and there are no wills. Should there be no issue, the next succession to the property are his brothers and his uncles on either side. The more relatives he has, the more numerous his connections, the more honored is his old age; nor are there any advantages in childlessness.

21. It is a duty among them to adopt the feuds as well as the friendships of a father or a kinsman.

These feuds are not implacable; even homicide is expiated by the payment of a certain number of cattle and of sheep, and the satisfaction is accepted by the entire family, greatly to the advantage of the state, since feuds are dangerous in proportion to a people's freedom.

No nation indulges more profusely in entertainments and hospitality. To exclude any human being from their roof is thought impious; every German, according to his means, receives his guest with a well-furnished table. When his supplies are exhausted, he who was but now the host becomes the guide and companion to further hospitality, and without invitation they go to the next house. It matters not; they are entertained with like cordiality. No one distinguishes between an acquaintance and a stranger, as regards the rights of hospitality. It is usual to give the departing guest whatever he may ask for, and a present in return is asked with as little hesitation. They are greatly charmed with gifts, but they expect no return for what they give, nor feel any obligation for what they receive.

22. On waking from sleep, which they generally prolong to a late hour of the day, they take a bath, most often of warm water, which suits a country where winter is the longest of the seasons. After their bath they take their meal, each having a separate seat and table of his own. Then they go armed to business, or no less often to their festal meetings. To pass an entire day and night in drinking disgraces no one. Their quarrels, as might be expected with intoxicated people, are seldom fought out with mere abuse, but commonly with wounds and bloodshed. Yet it is at their feasts that they generally consult on the reconciliation of enemies, on the forming of matrimonial alliances, on the choice of chiefs, finally even on peace and war, for they think that at no time is the mind more open to simplicity of purpose or more warmed to noble aspirations. A race without either natural or acquired cunning, they disclose their hidden thoughts in the freedom of the festivity. Thus the sentiments of all having been discovered and laid bare, the discussion is renewed on the following day, and from each occasion its own peculiar advantage is derived. They deliberate when they have no power to dissemble; they resolve when error is impossible.

23. A liquor for drinking is made out of barley or other grain, and fermented into a certain resemblance to wine. The dwellers on the river-bank also buy wine. Their food is of a simple kind, consisting of wild-fruit, fresh game, and curdled milk. They satisfy their hunger without elaborate preparation and without delicacies. In quenching their thirst they are not equally moderate. If you indulge their love of drinking by supplying them with as much as they desire, they will be overcome by their own vices as easily as by the arms of an enemy.

24. One and the same kind of spectacle is always exhibited at every gathering. Naked youths who practice the sport bound in the dance amid swords and lances that threaten their lives. Experience gives them skill, and skill again gives grace; profit or pay are out of the question; however reckless their pastime, its reward is the pleasure of the spectators. Strangely enough they make games of hazard a serious occupation even when sober, and so venturesome are they about gaining or losing, that, when every other resource has failed, on the last and final throw they stake the freedom of their own persons. The loser goes into voluntary slavery; though the younger and stronger, he suffers himself to be bound and sold. Such is their stubborn persistency in a bad practice; they themselves call it honor. Slaves of this kind the owners part with in the way of commerce, and also to relieve themselves from the scandal of such a victory.

25. The other slaves are not employed after our manner with distinct domestic duties assigned to them, but each one has the management of a house

and home of his own. The master requires from the slave a certain quantity of grain, of cattle, and of clothing, as he would from a tenant, and this is the limit of subjection. All other household functions are discharged by the wife and children. To strike a slave or to punish him with bonds or with hard labor is a rare occurrence. They often kill them, not in enforcing strict discipline, but on the impulse of passion, as they would an enemy, only it is done with impunity. The freedmen do not rank much above the slaves, and are seldom of any weight in the family, never in the state, with the exception of those tribes which are ruled by kings. There indeed they rise above the freeborn and the noble; elsewhere the inferiority of the freedman marks the freedom of the state.

26. Of lending money on interest and increasing it by compound interest they know nothing—a more effectual safeguard than if it were prohibited.

Land proportioned to the number of inhabitants is occupied by the whole community in turn, and afterwards divided among them according to rank. A wide expanse of plains makes the partition easy. They till fresh fields every year, and they have still more land than enough; with the richness and extent of their soil, they do not laboriously exert themselves in planting orchards, enclosing meadows and watering gardens. Corn is the only produce required from the earth; hence even the year itself is not divided by them into as many seasons as with us. Winter, spring, and summer have both a meaning and a name; the name and blessings of autumn are alike unknown.

27. In their funerals there is no pomp; they simply observe the custom of burning the bodies of illustrious men with certain kinds of wood. They do not heap garments or spices on the funeral pile. The arms of the dead man and in some cases his horse are consigned to the fire. A turf mound forms the tomb. Monuments with their lofty elaborate splendor they reject as oppressive to the dead. Tears and lamentations they soon dismiss; grief and sorrow but slowly. It is thought becoming for women to bewail, for men to remember, the dead.

Why does the presence of women inspire Germanic men in battle? What is significant about their style of dress? Who practices polygamy and why? What kind of gifts are given at marriage? Who gives them to whom? How does Tacitus describe the spouses and the nature and quality of their relationship? What were the main features of Germanic morality? Did these values pertain equally to men and women?

3. THEOLOGICAL FOUNDATIONS: AUGUSTINE, *ON THE GOOD OF MARRIAGE*

St. Augustine (354-430), bishop of Hippo, was one of the most important theologians of the fourth century. He wrote his famous treatise On the Good of Marriage *(De bono conjugali) in 401. It was written in response to what were then considered the heretical teachings of a rival theologian, Jovinian, who had claimed that marriage and virginity were states of life of equal merit. These ideas were harshly condemned by orthodox theologians who taught that a life of virginity was far superior to married life. Augustine provided an important and more moderate perspective. In his treatise he examined the nature and quality of marriage and the role it played in the life of the faithful. Carefully basing his arguments on the teachings of St. Paul, Augustine argued persuasively that sexual intercourse between married persons was not always sinful, and indeed could be meritorious. He set out the three pillars or goods of marriage: faith, children, and sacrament. These became the foundation for subsequent medieval explorations of the nature of marriage and its role in human life. In this treatise, Augustine also firmly established other principles that would guide the church's understanding of marriage and human sexuality. Of particular importance was his insistence on monogamy and indissolubility, the central importance of the conjugal debt, and his condemnation of adultery, fornication, and unnatural sex acts. Augustine's conclusion that marriage and chastity were both meritorious did much to mitigate the much harsher evaluation of marriage developed by his contemporary Jerome. It was Augustine's views that formed the foundation of the medieval theology of marriage.*

Source: Trans. Charles T. Wilcox in Augustine, *Treatises on Marriage and Other Subjects*, Fathers of the Church, 27 (New York: Fathers of the Church, 1955), pp. 12-14, 16-17, 19-20, 24-26, 31, 33; reprinted with permission.

3. This is what we now say, that according to the present condition of birth and death, which we know and in which we were created, the marriage of male and female is something good. This union divine Scripture so commands that it is not permitted a woman who has been dismissed by her husband to marry again, as long as her husband lives, nor is it permitted a man who has been dismissed by his wife to marry again, unless she who left has died. Therefore, regarding the good of marriage, which even the Lord confirmed in the gospel, not only because he forbade the dismissal of a wife except for fornication, but also because he came to the marriage when invited, there is merit in inquiring why it is a good.

This does not seem to me to be a good solely because of the procreation of children, but also because of the natural companionship between the two sexes. Otherwise, we would not speak of marriage in the case of old people, especially if they had either lost their children or had begotten none at all. But, in a good marriage, although one of many years, even if the ardor of youth has

This is a nineteenth-century drawing of Augustine, bishop of Hippo, one of the most important of the early church fathers. His theology of marriage and sexuality influenced the subsequent teaching of the church and dominated Christian values throughout the Middle Ages.

cooled between man and woman, the order of charity still flourishes between husband and wife. They are better in proportion as they begin the earlier to refrain by mutual consent from sexual intercourse, not that it would afterwards happen of necessity that they would not be able to do what they wished, but that it would be a matter of praise that they had refused beforehand what they were able to do. If, then, there is observed that promise of respect and of services due to each other by either sex, even though both members weaken in health and become almost corpse-like, the chastity of souls rightly joined together continues the purer, the more it has been proved, and the more secure, the more it has been calmed.

Marriage has also this good, that carnal or youthful incontinence, even if it is bad, is turned to the honorable task of begetting children, so that marital intercourse makes something good out of the evil of lust. Finally, the concupiscence of the flesh, which parental affection tempers, is repressed and becomes inflamed more modestly. For a kind of dignity prevails when, as husband and wife they unite in the marriage act, they think of themselves as mother and father.

4. There is the added fact that, in the very debt which married persons owe each other, even if they demand its payment somewhat intemperately and incontinently, they owe fidelity equally to each other. And to this fidelity the apostle has attributed so much right that he called it power, when he said: "The wife has not authority over her body, but the husband; the husband likewise has not authority over his body, but the wife." But the violation of this fidelity is called adultery, when, either by the instigation of one's own lust or by consent of the lust of another, there is intercourse with another contrary to the marriage compact. And so the fidelity is broken which even in material and base things is a great good of the soul; and so it is certain that it ought to be preferred even to the health of the body wherein his life is contained. For, although a small amount of straw as compared to much gold is as nothing, fidelity, when it is kept pure in a matter of straw, as in a matter of gold, is not of less importance on this account because it is kept in a matter of less value....

6. There are also men incontinent to such a degree that they do not spare their wives even when pregnant. Whatever immodest, shameful, and sordid acts the married commit with each other are the sins of the married persons themselves, not the fault of marriage.

Furthermore, in the more immoderate demand of the carnal debt, which the apostle enjoined on them not as a command but conceded as a favor, to have sexual intercourse even without the purpose of procreation, although evil habits impel them to such intercourse, marriage protects them from adultery and fornication. For this is not permitted because of the marriage, but because of the marriage it is pardoned. Therefore, married people owe each other not only the fidelity of sexual intercourse for the purpose of procreating children—and this is the first association of the human race in this mortal life—but also the mutual service, in a certain measure of sustaining each other's weakness, for the avoidance of illicit intercourse, so that, even if perpetual continence is pleasing to one of them, he may not follow this urge except with the consent of the other. In this case, "The wife has not authority over her body, but the husband; the husband likewise has not authority over his body, but the wife." So, let them not deny either to each other, what the man seeks from matrimony and the woman from her husband, not for the sake of having children but because of weakness and incontinence, lest in this way they fall into damnable seductions through the temptations of satan because of the incontinence of both or of one of them.

In marriage, intercourse for the purpose of generation has no fault attached to it, but for the purpose of satisfying concupiscence, provided with a spouse, because of the marriage fidelity, it is a venial sin; adultery or fornication, however, is a mortal sin. And so, continence from all intercourse is certainly better than marital intercourse itself which takes place for the sake of begetting children.

"Let marriage be held in honor with all, and let the marriage bed be undefiled." We do not call marriage a good in this sense, that in comparison with fornication it is a good; otherwise, there will be two evils, one of which is worse. Or even fornication will be a good because adultery is worse—since violation of another's marriage is worse than associating with a prostitute. Or adultery will be a good because incest is worse—since intercourse with one's mother is worse than lying with another's wife—and so on, until we come to those things about which, as the apostle says: "It is shameful even to speak." All will be good in comparison with that which is worse. But who would doubt that this is false? Therefore, marriage and fornication are not two evils, the second of which is worse; but marriage and continence are two goods, the second of which is better. Just so, your temporal health and sickness are not two evils, the second of which is worse; but your health and immortality are two goods, the second of which is better....

11. The intercourse necessary for generation is without fault and it alone belongs to marriage. The intercourse that goes beyond this necessity no longer obeys reason but passion. Still, not to demand this intercourse but to render it to a spouse, lest he sin mortally by fornication, concerns the married person. But, if both are subject to such concupiscence, they do something that manifestly does not belong to marriage. However, if in their union they love what is proper rather than what is improper, that is, what belongs to marriage rather than that which does not, this is granted to them with the apostle as an authority. They do not have a marriage that encourages this crime, but one that inter-

cedes for them, if they do not turn away from themselves the mercy of God, either by not abstaining on certain days so as to be free for prayers, and by this abstinence as by their fasts they put their prayers in a favorable light, or by changing the natural use into that which is contrary to nature, which is all the more damnable in a spouse.

12. For, although the natural use, when it goes beyond the marriage rights, that is, beyond the need for procreation, is pardonable in a wife but damnable in a prostitute, that use which is against nature is abominable in a prostitute but more abominable in a wife. For, the decree of the creator and the right order of the creature are of such force that, even though there is an excess in the things that have been granted to be used, this is much more tolerable than a single or rare deviation in those things which have not been granted. Therefore, the immoderation of a spouse in a matter that is permitted is to be tolerated lest lust may break forth into something that has not been granted. So it is that, however demanding one is as regards his wife, he sins much less than one who commits fornication even most rarely.

But, when the husband wishes to use the member of his wife which has not been given for this purpose, the wife is more shameful if she permits this to take place with herself rather than with another woman. The crown of marriage, then, is the chastity of procreation and faithfulness in rendering the carnal debt. This is the province of marriage, this is what the apostle defended from all blame by saying: "But if you take a wife, you have not sinned. And if a virgin marries, she does not sin" and "Let him do what he will; he does not sin, if she should marry." The somewhat immoderate departure in demanding the debt from the one or the other sex is given as a concession because of those things which he mentioned before....

15. Once, however, marriage is entered upon in the City [that is, church] of our God, where also from the first union of the two human beings marriage bears a kind of sacred bond, it can be dissolved in no way except by the death of one of the parties. The bond of marriage remains, even if offspring, for which the marriage was entered upon, should not follow because of a clear case of sterility, so that it is not lawful for married people who know they will not have any children to separate and to unite with others even for the sake of having children. If they do unite, they commit adultery with the ones with whom they join themselves, for they remain married people....

19. Therefore, as many women as there are now, to whom it is said: "If they do not have self-control, let them marry," are not to be compared even to the holy women who married then. Marriage itself among all races is for the one purpose of procreating children, whatever will be their station and character afterwards; marriage was instituted for this purpose, so that children might be born properly and decently.

How did the Lord confirm that marriage was good? What aspects of marriage did Augustine identify as good? Why is companionship a necessary good? How did Augustine characterize chastity within marriage? How can sexual intercourse be dignified? How does marriage alter the nature and consequences of sexual intercourse? Why does Augustine say that one spouse cannot refuse to have intercourse with the other? When is sexual intercourse blameless? a venial sin? a mortal sin? How are "natural use" and "use contrary to nature" distinguished? When can a marriage end?

4. THEOLOGICAL FOUNDATIONS: AUGUSTINE ON MARRIAGE AS A SOCIAL INSTITUTION

Augustine and his fellow fathers of the church, St. Jerome and St. Ambrose, played an important role in developing and disseminating orthodox theology in a period in which heresies flourished and multiplied and Roman and Germanic customs governing marriage and family were coming into conflict with the teachings of Christianity. In this selection from Augustine's monumental work, The City of God, *the great theologian sets out the rationale for prohibiting marriage between near relations and instead advocates the practice of exogamy.*

Source: Trans. Gerald G. Walsh and Grace Monahan in Augustine, *The City of God*, Fathers of the Church, 14 (New York: Fathers of the Church, 1952), pp. 450–54; reprinted with permission.

The City of God, Book 15, Ch. 16

The first of all marriages was that between the man made out of dust and his mate who had issued from his side. After that, the continuance and increase of the human race demanded births from the union of males and females, even though there were no other human beings except those born of the first two parents. That is why the men took their sisters for wives.

But, of course, just as this is the best thing to do when natural necessity compels it, it becomes all the more wicked when moral obligation condemns it. This can be proved as follows. The supreme human law is love and this law is best respected when men, who both desire and ought to live in harmony, so bind themselves by the bonds of social relationships that no one man monopolizes more than one relationship, and many different relationships are distributed as widely as possible, so that a common social life of the greatest number may best be fostered. Take the two relationships which are implied by the words, "father" and "father-in-law." Now, when a person has one man for a father and a second for his father-in-law, love can reign over a larger number. Adam, however, was obliged to monopolize in his single person this double relationship of love to his sons and daughters when, as brothers and sisters, they became husbands and wives. So, too, Eve, his wife, played the double role of mother and mother-in-law to her children of either sex, whereas, had there been two women available, one to be mother and the other to be mother-in-law, there would have been more strands in the bond of social love. So, too, a sister who had to become a wife was the bearer in her single person of two relationships of love. If these had been borne by two different persons, one a sister and the other a wife, then a greater number of persons would have had a share in the love of kinship. But there was then no possibility for this increase, since the only human beings were the brothers and sisters born of the first two parents.

But, as soon as, with an increased population, it became possible for men to choose wives who were not their sisters, they were bound by the law of love to do so. Thus, once there was no necessity for the old arrangement, it ceased to have any moral validity. The reason is that the grandchildren of the first pair could now choose cousins for their wives, and, if they continued to marry sisters, then not merely two but three relationships of love which ought to be distributed would have been concentrated in a single person, in disregard for the duty of each to respect the right of love to have itself diffused, so that one love may hold together as many persons as possible. For, in this case, one person would be in relation to his own children—to a brother and sister become a man and wife—not only as father and father-in-law but also as uncle; and his sister-wife, in relation to his and her children, would be mother and aunt and mother-in-law; and the children of a brother and sister would be in relation to one another not only as brothers and sisters, and husbands and wives, but also as cousins. Now, instead of concentrating three relationships in a single person, there could have been nine relationships of love diffused over nine persons, so that a man could have been linked in love to one person as his sister, to another as his wife, to a third as his cousin, to a fourth as his father, to a fifth as his uncle, to a sixth as his father-in-law, to a seventh as his mother, to an eighth as his aunt, and to a ninth as his mother-in-law. Thus, the love which holds kindred together, instead of being narrowed to a few, could have opened its arms to embrace a greater number of people spread over a far wider area.

Now that the human race has increased and multiplied, we find this law of love well observed even among the pagan worshipers of many and false gods. There are, indeed, occasional perversions of law which allow brothers and sisters to marry, yet by custom men's lives are so much better than these laws that such license is utterly repudiated; so that, allowable as it was in the very earliest ages to marry one's sister, the practice is today just as abominated as though it could never have been permitted. In general, custom has great power both in provoking and preventing the play of human passion. In this matter, custom keeps concupiscence in bounds and, therefore, any detraction from or destruction of custom is branded as criminal. Thus, unjust as it is to encroach, out of greed, on another's property, it is still more wicked to transgress, out of lust, the limits of established morals. In fact, I have noticed how rarely custom allows even in our days what is permissible in law, namely, marriages between first cousins, who are the nearest in consanguinity after brothers and sisters. The divine law has not forbidden this nor, so far, has human law. Nevertheless, custom has disapproved of something that is right, simply because it is too near to what is wrong. After all, a marriage with a cousin looks almost like one with a sister; because, by custom, cousins who are so closely related are called brothers and sisters; and they almost are so.

It is true that our ancestors had a religious regard for kinship and, being afraid that it might be lessened and lost in the course of successive generations, they tried to hold on to it by the bond of marriage and, as it were, to call it back before it got too far away. So it was that, when the world was fully populated and there was no more marrying of sisters or half-sisters, people still preferred to marry within their own clan. No one, however, can doubt that the modern attitude toward the marriage even of cousins is morally sounder. First, there is the argument I have already outlined, namely, that it is socially right to multiply and distribute relationships of love and wrong to have one person needlessly monopolizing two relationships which could be distributed to two persons and thus increase the community of kinship. There is also the argument from that indefinably precious modesty of our human nature which makes even the purest of parents to blush over the element of lust in the generative act and which bridles this desire when a double respect is due to a partner by reason of close consanguinity....

What was the necessary nature of marriage among the children of Adam and Eve? Why did Augustine criticize it? Relate this to the selections from Leviticus in document 1. What did the "law of love" require regarding marriage? Why? Why did Augustine believe that love ought to be diffused? How did Augustine use pagan practices, customs, and human nature to explain and support his conclusions?

5. LEGAL FOUNDATIONS: THE BURGUNDIAN LAWS

The steady movement of Germanic peoples into the Roman Empire characterized the period between the middle of the third and the middle of the sixth centuries. The Germanic tribes brought with them a distinct set of cultural and legal norms governing marriage and family life. Contact between Roman and Germanic peoples, living side by side, led to intermarriage and a consequent process of cultural accommodation. Roman and Germanic legal systems influenced and modified each other and gradually merged. The Burgundians were among the earliest Germanic peoples to settle in the western empire, establishing a federated kingdom west of the Rhine river as early as 413 C.E. Gundobad, who was king from 474 to 516 when the Burgundian kingdom was at its largest, began the codification of Burgundian law. Given that the Burgundians had lived alongside the Romans for some time, their law code attempted to accommodate the legal needs of both peoples. The extent of the influence of Roman society on the Burgundians is reflected by the fact the code was originally written in Latin. It was one of the most influential of all the Germanic law codes and was used as late as the ninth century.

Source: Trans. Katherine Fischer Drew, *The Burgundian Code: Book of Constitutions or Law of Gundobad* (Philadelphia: University of Pennsylvania Press, 1972), pp. 17, 31-33, 40-41, 44-46, 50-52, 54-55, 58-61, 64-68, 70-73, 74-75, 78-80, 82, 85, 92; reprinted with permission.

1. In the name of God in the second year of the reign of our lord the most glorious king Gundobad, this book concerning laws past and present, and to be preserved throughout all future time, has been issued on the fourth day before the Kalends of April [March 29] at Lyons....

12. Of the Stealing of Girls

1. If anyone shall steal a girl, let him be compelled to pay the price set for such a girl ninefold, and let him pay a fine to the amount of twelve solidi.

2. If a girl who has been seized returns uncorrupted to her parents, let the abductor compound six times the wergeld of the girl; moreover, let the fine be set at twelve solidi.

3. But if the abductor does not have the means to make the above-mentioned payment, let him be given over to the parents of the girl that they may have the power of doing to him whatever they choose.

4. If indeed, the girl seeks the man of her own will and comes to his house, and he has intercourse with her, let him pay her marriage price threefold; if moreover, she returns uncorrupted to her home, let her return with all blame removed from him.

5. If indeed a Roman girl, without the consent or knowledge of her parents, unites in marriage with a Burgundian, let her know she will have none of the property of her parents....

14. Of Succession

1. Among Burgundians we wish it to be observed that if anyone does not leave a son, let a daughter succeed to the inheritance of the father and mother in place of the son.

2. If by chance the dead leave neither son nor daughter, let the inheritance go to the sisters or nearest relatives.

3. It is pleasing that it be contained in the present law that if a woman having a husband dies without children, the husband of the dead wife may not demand back the marriage price (*pretium*) which had been given for her.

4. Likewise, let neither the woman nor the relatives of the woman seek back that which a woman pays when she comes to her husband if the husband dies without children.

5. Concerning those women who are vowed to God and remain in chastity, we order that if they have two brothers they receive a third portion of the inheritance of the father, that is, of that land which the father, possessing by the right of *sors* (allotment), left at the time of his death. Likewise, if she has four or five brothers, let her receive the portion due to her.

6. If moreover she has but one brother, let not a half, but a third part go to her on the condition that, after the death of her who is a woman and a nun, whatever she possesses in usufruct from her father's property shall go to the nearest relatives, and she will have no power of transferring anything therefrom, unless perhaps from her mother's goods, that is, from her clothing or things of the cell (*rescellulae*), or what she has acquired by her own labor.

7. We decree that this should be observed only by those whose fathers have not given them portions; but if they shall have received from their father a place where they can live, let them have full freedom of disposing of it at their will....

24. Of Burgundian Women Entering A Second or Third Marriage

1. If any Burgundian woman, as is the custom, enters a second or third marriage after the death of her husband, and she has children by each husband, let her possess the marriage gift (*donatio nuptialis*) in usufruct while she lives; after her death, let what his father gave her be given to each son, with the further provision that the mother has the power neither of giving, selling, or transferring any of the things which she received in the marriage gift.

2. If by chance the woman has no children, after her death let her relatives receive half of whatever has come to her by way of marriage gift, and let the relatives of the dead husband who was the donor receive half.

3. But if perchance children shall have been born and they shall have died after the death of their father, we command that the inheritance of the husband or children belong wholly to the mother. Moreover, after the death of the mother, we decree that what she holds in usufruct by inheritance from her children shall belong to the legal heirs of her children. Also we command that she protect the property of her children dying intestate.

4. If any son has given his mother something by will or by gift, let the mother have the power of doing whatever she wishes therewith; if she dies intestate, let the relatives of the woman claim the inheritance as their possession.

5. If any Burgundian has sons (children?) to whom he has given their portions, let him have the power of giving or selling that which he has reserved for himself to whomever he wishes....

30. Of Women Violated

1. Whatever native freeman does violence to a maidservant, and force can be proved, let him pay twelve solidi to him to whom the maidservant belongs.

2. If a slave does this, let him receive a hundred fifty blows....

33. Of Injuries Which Are Suffered By Women

1. If any native freewoman has her hair cut off and is humiliated without cause (when innocent) by any native freeman in her home or on the road, and this can be proved with witnesses, let the doer of the deed pay her twelve solidi, and let the amount of the fine be twelve solidi.

2. If this was done to a freedwoman, let him pay her six solidi.

3. If this was done to a maidservant, let him pay her three solidi, and let the amount of the fine be three solidi.

4. If this injury (shame, disgrace) is inflicted by a slave on a native freewoman, let him receive two hundred blows; if a freedwoman, let him receive a hundred blows; if a maidservant, let him receive seventy-five blows.

5. If indeed the woman whose injury we have ordered to be punished in this manner commits fornication voluntarily (i.e., if she yields), let nothing be sought for the injury suffered.

34. Of Divorces

1. If any woman leaves (puts aside) her husband to whom she is legally married, let her be smothered in mire.

2. If anyone wishes to put away [repudiate or divorce] his wife without cause, let him give her another payment such as he gave for her marriage price, and let the amount of the fine be twelve solidi.

3. If by chance a man wishes to put away his wife, and is able to prove one of these three crimes against her, that is, adultery, witchcraft, or violation of graves, let him have full right to put her away: and let the judge pronounce the sentence of the law against her, just as should be done against criminals.

4. But if she admits none of these three crimes, let no man be permitted to put away his wife for any other crime. But if he chooses, he may go away from the home, leaving all household property behind, and his wife with their children may possess the property of her husband.

35. Of the Punishment of Slaves Who Commit a Criminal Assault on Freeborn Women

1. If any slave does violence to a native freewoman, and if she complains and is clearly able to prove this, let the slave be killed for the crime committed.

2. If indeed a native free girl unites voluntarily with a slave, we order both to be killed.

3. But if the relatives of the girl do not wish to punish their own relative, let the girl be deprived of her free status and delivered into servitude to the king.

36. Of Incestuous Adultery

If anyone has been taken in adultery with his relative or with his wife's sister, let him be compelled to pay her wergeld, according to her status, to him who is the nearest relative of the woman with whom he committed adultery; and let the amount of the fine be twelve solidi. Further, we order the adulteress to be placed in servitude to the king....

42. Of the Inheritance of Those Who Die Without Children

1. Although we have ordered many things in former laws concerning the inheritance of those who die without children, nevertheless after considering the matter thoroughly, we perceive it to be just that some of those things which were ordered before should be corrected. Therefore we decree in the present constitution that if a woman whose husband has died without children

has not taken her vows a second time, let her possess securely a third of all the property of her husband to the day of her death; with the further provision that after her death, all will revert to the legitimate heirs of her husband.

2. Let that remain in effect which has been stated previously concerning the morning gift (*morgengeba, morginegiva*) [a gift from husband to wife given the morning after the marriage was consummated]. For if she wishes to marry within a year from the time of the death of her first husband, let her have full right to do so, but let her give up that third part of the property which she had been permitted to possess. However, if she wishes to take a husband after a year or two have passed, let her give up all as has been stated above which she received from her first husband, and let the heirs in whose portion the inheritance of her former husband belongs receive the price which must be paid for her (second) marriage.

Given in council at Amberieux, September 3rd (501), Abienus *vir clarissimus* [a man of greatest dignity] being consul.

44. Of the Adultery of Girls and Widows

1. If the daughter of any native Burgundian before she is given in marriage unites herself secretly and disgracefully in adultery with either barbarian or Roman, and if afterward she brings a complaint, and the act is established as charged, let him who has been accused of her corruption, and as has been said, is convicted with certain proof, suffer no defamation of character (*calumnia*) upon payment of fifteen solidi. She, indeed, defeated in her purpose by the vileness of her conduct, shall sustain the disgrace of lost chastity.

2. But if a widow who has not been sought, but rather overcome by desire, unites with anyone, and she bursts forth in an accusing voice, let her not receive the stated number of solidi, and we order that she, demanding marriage thus, be not awarded to him to whom she joined herself in such a disgraceful manner, because it is just that she, defeated by her vile conduct, is worthy of neither matrimony nor reward....

47. Of the Condemnation of Thieves, of Their Wives, and of Their Children

1. Although in former laws it has been established by what means the crimes of robbers should be repressed, nevertheless, because so far neither by corporal punishments nor by losses of property has it been possible to bring an end to the cruel acts of robbers, we decree in the present law: if any native freeman,

barbarian as well as Roman, or a person of any nation dwelling within the provinces of our kingdom, takes horses or oxen in theft, and his wife does not immediately reveal the committed crime, let her husband be killed, and let her also be deprived of her liberty and given in servitude without delay to him against whom the deed was committed; because it cannot be doubted, and is often discovered, that such women are sharers in the crimes of their husbands.

2. Also regarding the children of such persons, let this punishment be followed according to law: if any of these at the time at which the theft has been committed has passed the fourteenth year of age, in accordance with the fact that the mother has been condemned by previous judgment to the loss of her liberty, let him, too, be placed in perpetual subjection under the dominion (*dominium*) of that man against whom the theft is proved to have been committed, since he knows about the committed crime beyond doubt if he has attained the stated number of years of age.

3. However, those children of criminals who are found within the tenth (fourteenth) year of age at the time of the perpetrated crime shall not be condemned to lose their liberty. Because just as at such a tender age they do not have knowledge or understanding of the crime committed by their father, so they cannot be blamed, nor shall they sustain the previous judgment concerning their freedom; and the children who were innocent may claim the allotment of property (*sors*) and personal possessions (*facultas*) of their parents.

4. Concerning the thefts and crimes of slaves, let that form of punishment be followed which is contained in the code of the ancient law....

51. Of Those Who Do Not Give Their Sons The Portions of Their Property Due To Them

1. Although these things have been observed from of old among our people, that a father should divide his property equally by law among his sons, nevertheless we have ordered in a law established now for a long time that this practice be observed, and we have added this useful counsel to fathers that a father should have freedom to do what he wishes with that which belongs to his own portion.

But because in a recent controversy it became clear that a certain Athila had passed over the provisions of the old enactments and displayed insubordination to these most useful precepts of law and had not given his son the portion due to him but had transferred his property to other persons through illegal written title since he had wished nothing therefrom to belong to his son, and that no one may follow a bad example in this manner, we order that what he has done contrary to law shall have no legal force, and we add that all his property shall be possessed by his son. It is also the purpose of our judgment to cut off the disobedience of the transgressor, so that the justice of the general precept will be inscribed in the laws and retained.

On this account we have ordered in matters of this sort that the law be observed which was promulgated long ago to the effect that any man who will not hand over portions of his property legally belonging to his sons may do nothing adverse or prejudicial to them in writing, and if he does so, it shall be invalid.

2. Nevertheless, it is pleasing that this rule be defined thus with the force of law, that a son shall have full power of doing what he wishes with the portion he receives, with the further provision that if he dies without heirs and the decrees of fate permit his father to survive, and if he has made no gift from the property legally belonging to him during his lifetime and left no will, then his father may claim the succession to these portions in question. However, the father shall have no power of alienating them and when he has died the property of their dead brother will pass to the remaining sons.

3. The mother's ornaments and vestments belong to the daughters without any right to share on the part of the brother or brothers; further, let this legal principle be observed concerning those ornaments and vestments in the case of girls whose mothers die intestate. But if the mother shall have made any disposal of her own ornaments and vestments, there shall be no cause for action thereafter.

4. But if an unmarried girl who has sisters dies, and she has not declared her wish in writing or in the presence of witnesses, let her portion after her death belong to her sisters and, as has been stated, let her brothers have no share therein.

5. However if the girl dies and does not have a blood sister, and no clear disposition has been made concerning her property, let her brothers become her heirs.

52. Of Betrothed Women Who, Incited by Desire, Go to Consort with Others

1. Howsoever often such cases arise concerning which none of the preceding laws have established provisions, it is fitting that the ambiguity of the matter be removed so that the judgment set forth shall receive the strength of perpetual law, and the special case shall have general application.

2. Since the deserts of a criminal case which is pending between Fredegisil, our sword-bearer on the one side, and Balthamodus together with Aunegild on the other, have been heard and considered, we give an opinion which punishes this recent crime and imposes a method of restraint for the future.

3. And since Aunegild, after the death of her first husband, retaining her

own legal competence, promised herself, not only with the consent of her parents, but also with her own desire and will, to the above-mentioned Fredegisil, and since she had received the greater part of the wedding price which her betrothed had paid, she broke her pledged faith, having been aroused by the ardor of her desire for Balthamodus. Furthermore, she not only violated her vows, but repeated her customary shameful union, and on account of this, she ought to atone for such a crime and such a violation of her free status not otherwise than with the pouring forth of her own blood. Nevertheless we command, placing reverence for these holy days before public punishment, that Aunegild, deprived of honor by human and divine judgment, should pay her wergeld, that is three hundred solidi, to Fredegisil under compulsion.

4. Nor do we remove merited condemnation from Balthamodus who presumed to receive a woman due in marriage to another man, for his case deserves death. But in consideration of the holy days, we recall our sentence for his execution, under the condition that he should be compelled to pay his wergeld of one hundred fifty solidi to that Fredegisil unless he offers evident (public) oaths with eleven others in which he affirms that at that time in which he was united with the above-mentioned Aunegild as if by the right of marriage, he was unaware that she was pledged to Fredegisil. But if he shall have so sworn, let him suffer neither loss nor punishment.

5. In truth we command that the judgment set forth in this case be established to remain the law forever, and lest the moderation of the composition now permitted encourage anyone hereafter to commit a deed of such great crime, we command that whosoever incurs the guilt of such a deed not only may sustain the loss of his property, but also may be punished by the loss of his life. For it is preferable that the multitude be corrected by the condemnation of a few rather than that the appearance of unsuitable moderation introduce a pretext which may contribute to the license of delinquency.

Given on the 29th of March (517) at Lyons, Agapitus being consul.

53. Of the Inheritance of Sons Who, After the Death of Their Father, Die Intestate, While Their Mother Still Survives

1. It has been permitted now for a long time as set forth and established in previous law, that if, a father being dead, his son dies without a will and the mother still lives, she shall possess the substance (usufruct) of the son's property during the rest of her life, and after her death the nearest relatives of the son coming from the father's side shall receive all those properties of which we speak. However, discussing this case more thoroughly with the nobles of our people (*obtimates populi nostri*), we direct attention to the fact that the nature of this afore-mentioned law causes no less of loss and discord than of advantage to

the heirs since they disagree among themselves over the various contradictions involved in the contest. As a result, on the one hand, the slowness of acquiring inheritance gives offense, and on the other the loss of property causes anxiety. Therefore it seems more just that the bonds of the above-mentioned condition should be relaxed under circumstances whereby the case will not be delayed, but ended.

2. Therefore we order, that, just as a similar case was concluded by our decision, since the contrary decrees of the fates often shift under these circumstances, a legal division of the remaining property shall be made on an equal basis immediately between the mother of the deceased son, if there be no daughter, and his nearest relatives as we mentioned above, with the further provision that each of them may have the power according to law of doing what he pleases with the half received. For surely it is more desirable that the cases should terminate immediately to the welfare of the parties concerned rather than that anyone should gain an advantage because of any delay in point of time....

56. Of Slaves Bought in Alamannia

1. If anyone buys back another's slave in Alamannia, either let his master pay his price (wergeld) or let him who redeems him have the slave; furthermore we order this to be observed henceforth from the present time.

2. Also if a native freeman has been redeemed at his own request, let him return his price (wergeld) to the buyer.

57. Of Freedmen of the Burgundians Who Do Not Have the Privilege of Departing

A freedman of a Burgundian who has not given his master twelve solidi as is the custom so that he may have the privilege of departing whither he wishes, and who has not received his third from the Romans (i.e., from the Roman property owners) must be treated as a member of his master's household....

59. Of Grandchildren

If the father is dead, let a grandchild with all his possessions be given over to the supervision and care of the grandfather if his mother has decided upon a second marriage. Moreover, if she fails to remarry because she has chosen chastity, let her children with all their property remain in her care (custody) and power....

61. Of Women Who Willingly Seek Union With a Man

Whatever woman, barbarian by nation, enters into union with a man willingly and secretly, let her wedding price be paid in fee simple to her relatives; and he to whom she has been joined in an adulterous union may be united afterward in marriage to another if he wishes.

62. Of Only Sons

1. Let an only son, if his father is dead, leave a third part of his property for the use of his mother, provided nevertheless she does not take another husband; for if she enters another marriage, let her lose all.

2. Nevertheless, let her use her wedding gift (*dos*) which she received from her husband, as long as she lives, and let the ownership be reserved for the son.

Given on the tenth day of June, in the second year of our lord the king (517)....

65. Of Widows from Whom the Debts of Their Husbands Are Sought

1. If any widow has sons, and if she and her sons have made a cession of the goods of the deceased husband, let them suffer no suit for recovery nor further claim on account of his debts.

2. If indeed they assume the inheritance, let them also pay the paternal debt.

66. Of Girls Without Fathers and Mothers Who Are Given in Marriage

1. If a girl is given in marriage and has neither father nor brothers, but only an uncle and sisters, let the uncle receive a third part of the *wittimon* [marriage portion], and let the sisters know they may claim another third.

2. If indeed she is without father or brothers, and she receives a husband, it is pleasing that the mother receive a third part of the *wittimon* [marriage portion], and the nearest relatives another third.

3. If she does not have a mother, let her sisters receive that third....

68. Of Adultery

1. If adulterers are discovered, let the man and woman be killed.

2. This must be observed: either let him (the injured party) kill both of them, or if he kills only one of them, let him pay the wergeld of that one according to that customary wergeld which has been established in earlier laws.

69. Of the Wedding Gift (*Wittimon*)

1. If a woman enters upon a second marriage, let her *wittimon* be claimed by the nearest relatives of the first husband.

2. If indeed she wishes to take a third husband, let the *wittimon* which the husband gives go to the woman....

74. Of Widows and Their Children

1. Indeed it has been established in general in a law stated in earlier times that if a woman whose husband has died childless does not enter into a second marriage, she may claim a third of his inheritance for her own use throughout her lifetime; but now after considering more carefully with the nobles (*obtimates*) of our people all these matters set forth under this same title, it pleases us to limit the general application of the above-mentioned law.

Wherefore we order that any such widow, concerning whom we speak, may receive a portion of the inheritance of her husband if she has not already obtained property from her father or mother, or if her husband has not given her any portion of his property by means of which she can live.

2. If any woman whose husband has died does not take vows to a second husband, or does not wish her sons, now grown, to live with her, she may accordingly divide the property of the dead husband with them. If she has one son only, let her obtain the above-mentioned third; if there are two or three or four or more sons, let her receive a fourth part; nevertheless after her death, let the property return to the sons.

3. If anyone enters a second marriage after the death of his first wife by whom he had children, and has children also by this second wife, and if he then dies, the rule should be observed that his widow shall not hold that anything must be given to her from the portion of her stepchildren, but let her receive the portion designated above from the property inherited by her own children.

75. Of an Inheritance Divided Between Nephew and Aunt

1. It is fitting that those suits which are not shown to have been regulated by prior decrees should be settled by the equity of a newly stated (*prolatae*) law, so that the heirs may not remain ignorant of the order of procedure in this present matter of the succession, and so that a competent instruction for judges may not be lacking.

Therefore if a son whose father is still living has a son, and if he (the son) dies leaving a sister, the father just mentioned should bestow the portion of his property due to his son in this manner. From that amount of property which belongs to him at his own death (i.e., from that half of the entire property which he retained for himself after dividing with his son), he shall make no special bequest to grandson and daughter, but half shall be kept for the portion of the minor party from the paternal inheritance, while the other half of the property shall be divided equally between the grandson and daughter (who stand in the relation to one another of nephew and aunt).

2. But if the son with whose posterity this law deals shall possess all things undivided with his father, on his death let one half go to the portion of the grandson, while the other half should be divided in equal parts between the daughter and grandson.

3. And that no motive of litigation may be left unremoved from this same title, whether there are one or two or more daughters, we command that the statement of law be observed which we set forth above, that is, that half (of the undivided property left after the grandson had received half, i.e., his father's share, of the total) be acquired by the daughters, half by the grandson or grandsons from the son.

4. If indeed as has been said, the father has died, and the son leaves no male heirs, but a daughter only, and the sisters of her father (i.e., the above son) are still living, the law establishes the rule for claiming the title of inheritance as follows: the amount of the father's portion must be set aside (for the daughter), while the other half (i.e., her grandfather's portion) shall legally belong to the aunts mentioned above, nor let it be thought that any of their half may be claimed by the daughter (the only heir of the son)....

78. Of the Succession of Inheritance

1. Upon careful consideration of these matters, we have established that if a father shall have divided his allotment (*sors*) with his sons and afterward it happens a son dies childless while his father is still living, the father may claim the use of the entire portion by the law of usufruct in accordance with the son's wish. But upon the father's death, let him divide between sons and grandsons so that all fatherless grandsons sprung from any one son shall obtain such a portion as their father would have had.

2. Further, let that portion which the father had retained (for himself after the) division among his sons be left to the surviving sons, and let the grandsons not succeed to that share.

3. Nevertheless the present law pertains to male heirs only....

85. Of Wards

1. If a mother wishes to assume guardianship (*tutela*), no other relationship (*parentela*) shall be placed before her.

2. But if indeed there is no mother, then the nearest relative shall assume the

property of the minor under the condition that to the degree that his own property is increased, the property of the minor should also be increased to his advantage; nor is it permitted to waste or alienate any of it.

3. If indeed anyone presumes to take any of the property of minors, as has been said, let him return it in simple from his own property; also if a minor party is involved in a suit, let that person answer who has his wardship.

86. Of the Marriage Ornaments (*Malahereda*)

1. If a father leaves daughters, and while living, wishes to give the marriage ornaments (*malahereda*), let him give to whom he pleases, with the consequence that no one may seek their return to his daughters.

2. If the father shall have asked that the marriage portion (*wittimon*) not be sought, let his wish be disregarded; but, as a former law has stated, let the nearest relative receive it; with the further provision that the girl will obtain a third part of the ornaments (of the marriage portion) which the relative has received.

87. Of Contracts Entered Into By Minors

1. We believe that the following provision should be made concerning the age minors (for their protection), that they shall not be permitted to have the liberty of making sales or bequests before fifteen years of age. And if they have been cheated because of their infancy, let none of it be valid. Thus what they have done before the fifteenth year of age, they may have the power of retracting within another fifteen years if they wish.

2. But if they have not retracted it within the stated time, let it be permanent and remain valid.

88. Of Emancipation

Since the title of emancipation takes precedence over the law of possession, great care must be exercised in such matters. And therefore it should be observed, that if anyone wishes to manumit a slave, he may do so by giving him his liberty through a legally competent document; or if anyone wishes to give freedom to a bondservant without a written document, let the manumission thus conferred be confirmed with the witness of not less than five or seven native freemen, because it is not fitting to present a smaller number of witnesses than is required when the manumission is in written form....

92. Of Women Whose Hair Has Been Cut Off in Their Own Courtyard

1. If any native freeman presumes to cut off the hair of a native freewoman in her courtyard, we order that he pay thirty solidi to the woman, and let the fine be twelve solidi.

2. But if the woman has gone forth from her courtyard to fight, and her hair has been cut off or she has received wounds, let it be her fault because she has gone forth from her home; and let nothing be sought from him who struck her or cut her hair.

3. If he has done this to a maidservant in her courtyard, let him pay six solidi to the maidservant, and let the fine be two solidi.

4. If a slave presumes to do this to a native freewoman, let him be handed over to death and let nothing be sought from the master of the slave.

5. But if the master of the slave wishes to redeem him from death, we order that he redeem the slave with ten solidi.

6. Also we order that after the slave has been handed over to the master by the judge, let him receive a hundred blows, so that afterward he will do injury to no one nor bring loss to his master....

100. Of Women Who Go to Their Husbands Voluntarily

If any woman, Burgundian or Roman, gives herself voluntarily in marriage to a husband, we order that the husband have the property of that woman; just as he has power over her, so also over her property and all her possessions.

101. Of the Marriage Price (*Wittimon*)

1. If any Burgundian of the highest (*optimas*) or middle class (*mediocris*) unites with the daughter of another (probably of the same class) without her father's consent, we order that such a noble make a triple payment of one hundred fifty solidi to the father whose daughter he took, if he took her without stating his intentions in advance or seeking his consent; and let the fine be thirty-six solidi.

2. Indeed if one of the lower class (*leudes*) has presumed to do this (i.e., has married one of his own class without her father's consent), let him likewise make a triple payment, that is, forty-five solidi; and let the fine be twelve solidi.

Additional Enactments

20. An Edict Concerning Foundlings

Sigismund, king of the Burgundians.

Since we have learned at the worthy and laudable suggestion of that venerable man Bishop Gimellus that exposed children whom compassion would cause to be taken in are neglected because those who would shelter the foundlings fear that they would be taken from them by legal charges (*calumnians intencio*), and so because of lagging compassion the souls of these children perish wretchedly; wherefore, having been moved by the just suggestion which has been raised in this case by our father of holy memory, we decree by this proclamation and the provisions of the present edict and we state in this declaration of our law that in this matter the rules of the Roman law be observed among Romans and let such litigation as has arisen between Burgundians and Romans be concluded as has been established by us; however those cases of this kind which have been completed before the date of this present edict shall in no wise be changed, and the status of pending business is to be governed by the laws mentioned; establishing however that no one may hereafter dare to impose penalties contrary to this salutary precept.

Given on March 8 (516) in the consulship of Petrus.

How do these laws show the intermingling of Roman, Germanic, and Christian values? What factors influenced the severity of the punishment for abduction? What were the significant features of Burgundian laws of inheritance? How did the social status of victim and perpetrator influence punishments for the same crime? When can a man divorce his wife? a wife her husband? How and with what conditions were widows protected? What does the case of Aunegild reveal about the nature of betrothal? How do a widow's status, rights, and responsibilities alter if she marries? What was the significance of cutting of a woman's hair? What role did the women's consent play in an agreement to marry? her parents' consent? Which was more important?

parents concent
more impt

6. LEGAL FOUNDATIONS: ANGLO-SAXON LAWS

Anglo-Saxon England presents a slightly different situation from that on the continent. Separated by the English Channel, the island was never as thoroughly Romanized as was continental Europe, nor did it experience the dramatic Germanic migrations to the same degree. It was not until the late fifth and early sixth centuries that the Anglo-Saxons first invaded and then settled on the island. Without an enduring Roman presence, the Angles and Saxons were less subject to the process of cultural accommodation and retained their language and customs intact. It was only in the late seventh century, moreover, that Christianity was widely embraced and began to influence and modify the Germanic basis of Anglo-Saxon customs governing marriage and family life. While early Anglo-Saxon laws reflect their pre-Christian origins, later laws show the influence of Christian values on secular society. In contrast with the Germanic laws from the continent, Anglo-Saxon law was not influenced by the presence of Roman neighbors. These laws, promulgated by King Canute in the early eleventh century, were originally written in Old English (Anglo-Saxon).

Source: Trans. A.J. Robertson, *The Laws of the Kings of England from Edmund to Henry I* (Cambridge: Cambridge University Press, 1925), pp. 155, 163, 173, 177, 201, 203, 209, 211-13, 215; reprinted with permission.

The Laws of Canute, I

This is the ordinance which King Canute, king of all England and king of the Danes, determined upon with the advice of his Councillors, to the glory of God and for the furtherance of his own royal authority and for his [people's] benefit; and that was during the holy Christmas season at Winchester.

1. The first provision is, that above all else they would ever love and honor one God, and unanimously uphold one Christian faith, and love King Canute with due fidelity....

6. And we desire that men of every estate readily submit to the duty which befits them.

6a. And most of all the servants of God — bishops and abbots, monks and nuns, canons, and women under religious vows — shall submit to their duty and live according to their rule, and day and night frequently and often call upon Christ, and zealously intercede for all Christian people.

§1. And we pray and enjoin all the servants of God, and priests above all, to obey God and practice celibacy and guard themselves from the wrath of God and from the raging fire which blazes in hell.

§2. They know full well that they have no right to marry.

§2a. And he who will turn from marriage and observe celibacy shall obtain the favor of God, and as worldly honor he shall enjoy the privileges of a thegn.

§3. All Christian men likewise through the fear of God shall strictly avoid illicit unions and duly observe the laws of the church.

7. And we instruct and pray and enjoin, in the name of God, that no Christian man shall ever marry among his own kin within six degrees of relationship, or with the widow of a man as nearly related to him as that, or with a near relative of his first wife's.

§1. And no Christian man shall ever marry his god-mother or a professed nun or a divorced woman.

§2. And he shall never commit adultery anywhere.

§3. And he shall have no more wives than one, and that shall be his wedded wife, and he who seeks to observe God's law aright and to save his soul from hell-fire shall remain with the one as long as she lives....

24. And we enjoin that foul lasciviousness and illicit unions and every [kind of] adultery be zealously abhorred.

The Laws of Canute, 2

4. And we enjoin that the purification of the land in every part shall be diligently undertaken, and that evil deeds shall everywhere be put to an end.

Wizards

4a. If wizards or sorcerers, those who secretly compass death, or prostitutes be met with anywhere in the land, they shall be zealously driven out of this land or utterly destroyed in the land, unless they cease from their wickedness and make amends to the utmost of their ability.

§1. We enjoin that apostates and those who are cast out from the fellowship of God and of men shall depart from the land, unless they submit and make amends to the utmost of their ability.

§2. And thieves and robbers shall forthwith be made an end of, unless they desist.

6. Murderers and perjurers, injurers of the clergy and adulterers shall submit and make amends or depart with their sins from their native land....

50. Concerning adultery

If anyone commits adultery, he shall make amends according to the nature of the offence.

§1. It is wicked adultery for a pious man to commit fornication with an unmarried woman, and much worse [for him to do so] with the wife of another man or with any woman who has taken religious vows.

51. Concerning incest

If anyone commits incest, he shall make amends according to the degree of relationship [between them], either by the payment of wergeld or of a fine, or by the forfeiture of all his possessions.

§1. The cases are not alike if incest is committed with a sister or with a distant relation.

52. Concerning widows

If anyone does violence to a widow, he shall make amends by the payment of his wergeld.

§1. Maidens

If anyone does violence to a maiden he shall make amends by the payment of his wergeld.

53. No woman shall commit adultery

If, while her husband is still alive, a woman commits adultery with another man and it is discovered, she shall bring disgrace upon herself, and her lawful husband shall have all that she possesses, and she shall then lose both her nose and her ears.

§1. And if a charge is brought and the attempt to refute it fails, the decision shall rest with the bishop, and his judgment shall be strict.

54. If a married man commits adultery with his own slave, he shall lose her and make amends for himself both to God and to men.

§1. And if anyone has a lawful wife and also a concubine, no priest shall perform for him any of the offices which must be performed for a Christian man, until he desists and makes amends as thoroughly as the bishop shall direct him, and ever afterwards desists from such [evil-doing].

55. Foreigners, if they will not regularize their unions, shall be driven from the land with their possessions, and shall depart in sin....

70. Concerning heriots

If a man departs from this life intestate, whether through negligence or through sudden death, his lord shall take no more from his property than his legal heriot [a fine, usually the best horse, due to the lord, from a deceased tenant's property].

§1. But, according to his direction, the property shall be very strictly divided among his wife and children and near kinsmen, each according to the share which belongs to him.

71. Heriots shall be fixed with due regard to the rank of the person for whom they are paid.

71a. An earl's heriot.

The heriot of an earl, as is fitting, shall be eight horses, four saddled and four unsaddled, and four helmets and four byrnies and eight spears and as many shields and four swords and 200 mancuses of gold.

§1. The heriot of a king's thegn.

And further, the heriots of king's thegns who stand in immediate relation to him shall be four horses, two saddled and two unsaddled, and two swords and four spears and as many shields and helmets and byrnies and 50 mancuses of gold.

§2. The heriot of another thegn.

And the heriot of ordinary thegns shall be a horse and its trappings and his weapons or his *healsfang* in Wessex, and in Mercia 2 pounds, and in East Anglia 2 pounds.

§3. And among the Danes the heriot of a king's thegn who possesses rights of jurisdiction shall be 4 pounds.

§4. And if he stands in a more intimate relationship to the king, it shall be two horses, one saddled and the other unsaddled, and one sword and two spears and two shields and 50 mancuses of gold.

§5. And for the man who is inferior in wealth and position the heriot shall be 2 pounds.

72. And when a householder has dwelt all his time free from claims and charges, his wife and children shall dwell [on the same property] unmolested by litigation.

§1. And if the householder had been cited before his death, then his heirs shall answer the charge, as he himself would have done, had he been alive.

73. Concerning widows, that they remain for a year without a husband

And every widow shall remain twelve months without a husband, and she shall afterwards choose what she herself desires.

73a. And if then, within the space of the year, she chooses a husband, she shall lose her morning-gift and all the property which she had from her first husband, and his nearest relatives shall take the land and the property which she had held.

§1. And he (the second husband) shall forfeit his wergeld to the king or to the lord to whom it has been granted.

§2. And although she has been married by force, she shall lose her possessions, unless she is willing to leave the man and return home and never afterwards be his.

§3. And no widow shall be too hastily consecrated as a nun.

§4. And every widow shall pay the heriots within twelve months without incurring a fine, if it has not been convenient for her to pay earlier.

74. And no woman or maiden shall ever be forced to marry a man whom she dislikes, nor shall she be given for money, except the suitor desires of his own freewill to give something....

76. Concerning stolen goods.
If anyone carries stolen goods home to his cottage and is detected, the law is that he (the owner) shall have what he has tracked.

§1. And unless the goods had been put under the wife's lock and key, she shall be clear [of any charge of complicity].

§1a. But it is her duty to guard the keys of the following—her storeroom and her chest and her cupboard. If the goods have been put in any of these, she shall be held guilty.

§1b. But no wife can forbid her husband to deposit anything that he desires in his cottage.

§2. It has been the custom up till now for grasping persons to treat a child which lay in the cradle, even though it had never tasted food, as being guilty as though it were fully intelligent.

§3. But I strictly forbid such a thing henceforth, and likewise very many things which are hateful to God.

How do the values underlying the prohibition of adultery in Anglo-Saxon law differ from those in Burgundian law? Where else do Christian values influence the law? Why were widows required to delay remarriage? What was the relationship between husband and wife reflected in the laws governing theft?

have to do w/ marriage—
adultery
laws?

7. PASTORAL FOUNDATIONS: THE PENITENTIAL OF THEODORE

Penitentials were written in the early Middle Ages, in particular between the sixth and tenth centuries. They appeared first in Ireland and England and, somewhat later, on the continent. Penitentials were intended to assist confessors to administer confession and assign penances appropriate to each sin. They provide tariffs or lists of sins and penances which allow modern readers to understand the kinds of activities the early medieval church considered sinful and the relative seriousness of each sin. Penitentials were frequently criticized for not being consistent: the seriousness of sins could differ widely between manuals. The selections here are from the penitential attributed to Theodore, archbishop of Canterbury, which dates from the late seventh century.

Source: Trans. J. Murray from *Die Bussordnungen der abendländischen Kirche*, ed. F.W.H. Wasserschleben (Halle: Ch. Graeger, 1851), 185-87, 197-200, 213-17.

Book I

Chapter 2. Concerning Fornication

§1. If anyone fornicates with a virgin let him do penance for one year; if with a married woman let him do penance for four years, two of these entirely, during the other two years in three periods of forty days and for three days a week.

§2. It is judged that he who often fornicates with a man or with an animal should do penance for ten years.

§3. Likewise, elsewhere it is judged that he who has coitus with animals should do penance for fifteen years.

§4. Let him who has coitus with a man, after he is twenty years old, do penance for fifteen years.

§5. If he fornicates with a man let him do penance for ten years.

§6. Let sodomites do penance for seven years and the effeminate the same as an adulteress.

§7. Likewise, let him who commits this masculine crime once do penance for four years. But if he does it habitually, let him do fifteen years, as St. Basil says; but if he cannot bear it, one year as for a woman. If he is a boy, two years for the first time, four years if it was repeated.

§8. If he commits a sex act between the thighs one year, or three periods of forty days.

§9. If he pollutes himself, let him do penance for forty days.

§10. Let him who desires to fornicate but is not able do penance for forty days or for twenty.

§11. Let boys who fornicate with each other be judged so that they are whipped.

§12. If a woman fornicates with a woman, let her do penance for three years.

§13. If she has coitus alone with herself [masturbates], let her do the same.

§14. There is one penance for widows and young girls; she who has a husband warrants a greater penance if she fornicates.

§15. Let him who ejaculates semen into the mouth do penance for seven years; this is the worst of evils. It has also been judged otherwise, that both of them do penance to the end of their lives or for fifteen years, or as stated above, for seven years.

§16. If he fornicates with his mother, let him do penance for fifteen years and never change [his clothes] except on Sundays. But this so wicked incest is similarly spoken of in another way, so that he shall do penance for seven years with perpetual pilgrimage.

§17. Let him who fornicates with his sister do penance for fifteen years in the same fashion as is stated above concerning a mother. But elsewhere he also confirmed in a canon the penance as twelve years, whence it is not out of line that the fifteen years that were written, apply to the mother.

§18. The first canon judged that he who fornicates often should do penance for ten years, the second canon seven years, but on account of human weakness upon consideration they advised he do penance for three years.

§19. If a brother fornicates with a natural brother through the union of the flesh, let him abstain from all kinds of flesh for fifteen years.

§20. If a mother imitates fornication with her young son, let her abstain from meat for three years and let her fast one day a week until vespers.

§21. Let him who amuses himself by thinking about fornication do penance until the imagination is subdued.

§22. Let him who loves a woman in his mind seek mercy from God. If he has spoken to her about love and friendship, but was not accepted by her, let him do penance for seven days.

Chapter 14. Concerning the Penance of Married People in Particular

§1. In a first marriage the priest ought to sing the mass and bless them both and afterward let them stay away from the church for thirty days. Having done this, let them do penance for forty days and stay away from prayers, and afterwards let them take communion, bringing an offering.

§2. Let the person twice-married do penance for one year; let him abstain from meat on Wednesdays and Fridays and during the three periods of forty days, although he shall not repudiate his wife.

§3. Let him who has married three times or more, that is a fourth or fifth or sixth marriage or more, abstain from meat for seven years on Wednesdays and Fridays and during the three periods of forty days, however, he shall not repudiate his wife. Basil decided this, but according to the canon he should do penance for four years.

§4. If any man finds his wife committing adultery and does not wish to repudiate her, but has had her in matrimonial relations up to then, let him do penance for two years two days a week and observe the religious periods of fasting; or, for as long as she shall do penance, let him abstain from matrimonial relations with her, because she has committed adultery.

§5. If any man or woman, having vowed virginity, is joined in marriage, let him not be repudiated, but let him do penance for three years.

§6. Foolish vows and those that cannot be performed, are to be set aside.

§7. It is not allowed for a woman to make a vow without her husband's consent; but if she should make a vow, it can be set aside, and let her do penance according to the judgment of the priest.

§8. Let him who repudiates his wife and marries another woman do penance with tribulation for seven years, or a lighter penance for fifteen years.

§9. Let him who defiles his neighbor's wife, abstaining from relations with his own wife, fast on two days a week and during the three seasons of forty days for three years.

§10. If she were a virgin, let him do penance for one year without meat or wine and mead.

§11. If he defiled a girl consecrated to God, let him do penance for three years, as we stated above, whether or not a child is born of her.

§12. If she was a slave, let him free her and let him fast for six months.

§13. If a wife should separate from her husband, let her do one year of penance if she returns to him undefiled, otherwise, for three years. If he has married another woman let him do penance for one year.

§14. Let an adulterous woman do penance for seven years. And this matter is discussed in the same fashion in the canon.

§15. Let a woman who joins herself to another in the manner of fornication, do penance for three year, just like a fornicator. So, also, let her do penance who mixes her husband's semen in food so that by this means she may receive more love.

§16. Let a wife who, as a remedy, tastes her husband's blood, fast for forty days, more or less.

§17. Moreover, women, either nuns nor laywomen, shall not enter a church nor take communion during their menstrual periods. If they should presume to do this, let them fast for three weeks.

§18. Similarly, let them do penance who enter a church before being purified after giving birth, that is for forty days.

§19. But let him who has sexual intercourse at these times do penance for twenty days.

§20. Let him who has sexual intercourse on Sunday seek forgiveness from God and do penance for either one, two, or three days.

§21. If a man should have sexual intercourse with his wife from behind, let him do penance for forty days.

§22. If he should have anal intercourse, he ought to do the same penance as he who has intercourse with animals.

§23. If he has coitus with her during her menstrual period, let him fast forty days.

§24. Let women who effect an abortion before the fetus has a soul do penance for one year or for three periods of forty days or for forty days, according the nature of their guilt. And if it is later, that is more than forty days after insemination, let them do penance for murder, that is for three years on Wednesdays and Fridays and in the three seasons of forty days. According to the canons this is judged punishable by ten years.

§25. If a mother kills her child, if she commits murder, let her do penance for fifteen years and never change [her clothes] except on Sundays.

§26. If a poor woman kills her child, let her do penance for seven years. In the canon it says she should do penance for ten years if it is murder.

§27. Let a woman who conceives and kills her child in the womb before forty days [have elapsed] do penance for one year, but if it is after forty days, let her do penance as a murderer.

§28. If an infant is ill and is pagan and been committed to a priest [for baptism], if it should die [unbaptised] let the priest be deposed.

§29. If parents are negligent let them do penance for one year, and if a three year old dies without baptism, let the father and mother do penance for three years....

§30. It is advised that he who kills his unbaptised child should do penance for seven years, although in the canons it says ten years.

Book 2

Chapter 12. Concerning Questions Pertaining to Marriage

§1. Let them who are married abstain from sexual intercourse for three nights before they receive communion.

§2. Let a man abstain from his wife for forty days before Easter until Easter week. Concerning this the apostle said: "So that you are free for prayer."

§3. When a woman conceives she ought to abstain from her husband for three months before the birth and after during the time of purgation, that is for forty days and nights, whether she has given birth to a male or female child.

§4. Also, before a woman gives birth, it is allowed to her to receive communion.

§5. If someone's wife should fornicate, he is allowed to dismiss her and marry another, that is, if the man dismisses his wife on account of fornication, if she was his first wife, it is permissible that he marries another. But, if she wishes to do penance for her sin, after five years she may marry another husband.

§6. A woman is not allowed to dismiss her husband, even if he is a fornicator, unless perhaps, to enter a monastery. Basil decided this.

§7. A legal marriage cannot be dissolved without the consent of both spouses.

§8. According to the Greeks, either may give the other permission to enter the service of God in a monastery and be married to it, if it is a first marriage. However, this is not canonical. Moreover, it is not permitted in a second or third marriage while the husband or wife is still alive.

§9. If a husband makes himself a slave through theft or fornication or some other sin, if she has not been married before, the wife has the ability to take another husband after one year although this is not allowed for the twice married.

§10. When a woman dies it is permissible for a man to marry another woman after a month; when a man dies it is permissible for a woman to take another husband after a year.

§11. If a woman is an adulteress and her husband does not want to live with her, if she wants to enter a monastery, let her retain a quarter of her inheritance; if she does not want to, let her have nothing.

§12. Any woman who commits adultery is in her husband's power, if he wants to be reconciled with an adulterous woman. If he reconciles, her punishment does not concern the clergy but pertains to her own husband.

§13. When a man and woman are joined in matrimony, if he wants to serve God and she does not, or she wishes to and he does not, or if one or the other is ill, they may nevertheless be separated by mutual consent.

§14. A woman who vows that after her husband's death she will not marry another, and when he dies she wrongfully marries again, and, moved by penitence, wants to fulfil her vow, it is in the power of her husband whether or not she may fulfil it.

§15. Therefore, Theodore gave to one woman, who confessed such a vow after eleven years, permission to cohabit with her husband.

§16. And if anyone of secular condition should make a vow without the consent of the bishop, the bishop himself has the power to change the intention if he wishes.

§17. A legitimate marriage is allowed equally during the day or at night, as is written: "Yours is the day and yours is the night."

§18 If a pagan man repudiates his pagan wife, after baptism it will be in his power to have her or not have her [as his wife].

§19. In the same way, if one of them is baptized and the other pagan, just as the apostle says: "If the unbeliever leaves, let him leave." Therefore, if his wife is an unbeliever and a pagan and cannot be converted, let her be repudiated.

§20. If a woman deserts her husband, despising him and not wishing to return and be reconciled with him, after five years, with the bishop's consent, he is allowed to marry another.

§21. If she has been thrown into captivity by force and cannot be redeemed, he is able to marry another after a year.

§22. Again, if she is taken into captivity, let her husband wait five years; and the woman, as well, if such a thing happened to her husband.

§23. Therefore, if a man should marry another woman let him accept back the first when she returns from captivity, repudiating the later one. Similarly, so shall the woman as we stated above, if such a thing happened to her husband.

§24. If an enemy carries off someone's wife and he is unable to get possession of her again, he is allowed to take another; it is better to do this than to fornicate.

§25. If, after this, that wife returns to him again, she ought not to be received by him, if he has married another. But she may take another husband for herself, if she has only had one before. The same judgment stands in the case of slaves from overseas.

§26. According to the Greeks, it is permissible to marry within the third degree of carnal relationship, as it is written in the law, according to the Romans, in the fifth degree. However, they do not dissolve a marriage in the fourth degree after it has taken place. Therefore, let them marry within the fifth degree; let them not be separated if they are in the fourth degree; in the third degree, let them be separated.

§27. However, it is not permissible to marry the wife of another man, after his death, if he was related within the third degree.

§28. Equally, a man is joined in matrimony to those who are related to him by blood and to the blood relatives of his wife after her death.

§29. Also, two brothers are able to marry two sisters and a father and son [can marry] a mother and daughter.

§30. Let a husband who sleeps with his wife wash himself before entering a church.

§31. Also, a husband ought not to see his wife nude.

§32. If someone has a union or a marriage which is not licit, nevertheless, it is allowed for him to eat the food that he has, because the prophet said: "The earth is the Lord's and its plenty."

§33. If a man and women are joined together in marriage, and afterwards the woman says that the man is not able to have intercourse with her, if anyone can prove this to be true, she may marry another.

§34. A betrothed girl is not allowed to be given to another man by her parents, unless she absolutely resists, however, she is allowed to enter a monastery should she wish.

§35. But if a betrothed girl does not want to cohabit with the man to whom she is betrothed, let the money which he gave for her be returned to him and a third part added to it. If, however, it is he who refuses, let him lose the money which he gave for her.

§36. A girl of eighteen years of age has the power of her own body.

§37. A boy is in the power of his father up to the age of fifteen, then he is able to make himself a monk. But a girl of sixteen or seventeen years old, who before was in the power of her parents, [can enter religious life]. After this age, it is not permissible for a father to give a girl in marriage against her will.

13. Concerning Male and Female Slaves

§1. A father has the power to hand over his seven year old son into slavery if he is forced by necessity; thereafter he does not have the power without his son's consent.

§2. A person of fourteen years of age is able to make himself a slave.

§3. It is not permissible for a person to take away money from his slave, which the slave acquired by his own labor.

§4. If a master joins a male and female slave together in marriage and afterwards the man or woman is freed, if the one who is in servitude cannot be redeemed, the one who has been freed may marry a free person.

§5. If a free man takes a slave woman in marriage, he does not have the right to repudiate her, if before they were married by mutual consent.

§6. If someone purchases a pregnant woman who was free, the child borne of her is free.

§7. If someone should free a pregnant slave woman, the child she gives birth to will be in servitude.

What kinds of penance are prescribed? What kinds of sexual acts are considered to be serious sins? What circumstances might influence the relative seriousness of a given sin?

When and why should people refrain from going to church? When are women treated differently from men? How did a person's age affect the seriousness of a sin? What examples show the continuing influence of pre-Christian practices or beliefs?

CHAPTER TWO:

LOVE AND ITS DANGERS

Medieval people had various complex ideas about love, most of which differed markedly from modern notions of romantic love. Love could include the honor one owed to parents, the compassion and charity one directed to the less fortunate, or the loyalty and integrity due to friends, comrades at arms, and lords. Familial love could encompass the pride one felt in an exalted lineage, obedience to elders, or the sacrifice of individual desires for the well-being of the extended kin group.

The relationship between a man and a woman, too, could be characterized as love, but this kind of love could have a variety of contradictory aspects. Marital love was predicated on a hierarchical relationship between spouses; wives were to be subordinate and obedient, husbands kind, but they were also expected to discipline their wives.

A third notion of love, similar to a modern sense of romantic love, was promoted by the courtly love movement. This kind of love was expected to be passionate and, ideally, chaste. Courtly men were to worship their beloved from afar and perform deeds of bravery and loyalty as proof of their devotion. Love was also viewed as dangerous: erotic love and sexual passion were signs of weakness and the inability of reason to control the flesh; adultery and fornication were considered mortal sins. Yet medieval people did fall in love. Moved by passionate love they flirted, eloped, and committed adultery.

For much of the Middle Ages, there was a chasm separating love and marriage; the former pertained to the individual and was characterized by passion, while the latter encompassed society, kin, and duty. Fortunate were those who were able to unite these in their lives.

8. A BIBLICAL CELEBRATION OF LOVE

One of the most moving and passionate depictions of the love between men and women is that found in The Song of Songs, *also known as* The Song of Solomon. *This love poem, ascribed to the famous King Solomon, was incorporated into Hebrew Scripture. The poem, written as a dialogue, depicts the passionate, even erotic, longing of a man and woman and can be read as a celebration of sexual love and physical desire. From a very early date, however, both Jewish and then Christian exegetes and theologians chose to interpret* The Song of Songs *as an allegory, especially of God's love for the church, or for the individual soul. Hence, the soul's longing for God and God's desire for the soul were reciprocal. While intellectuals may have tried to temper the meaning of this work, there is no mistaking the passionate eroticism and the delight in the physical love between a man and a woman. This book, then, provided medieval people with a language for passionate, sexual love, despite the efforts of churchmen to imbue it with abstract theological meaning.*

Source: *The Holy Bible,* Douay Rheims Version (Baltimore: John Murphy, 1899; rpt. Rockford, IL: Tan Books, 1971), pp. 691-96; modernized.

The Song of Songs

Chapter 1

1. Let him kiss me with the kiss of his mouth: for your breasts are better than wine,

2. Smelling sweet of the best ointments. Your name is oil poured out: therefore young maidens have loved you.

3. Draw me: we will run after you to the aroma of your ointments. The king has brought me into his storerooms: we will be glad and rejoice in you, remembering your breasts more than wine: the righteous love you.

4. I am black but beautiful, O daughters of Jerusalem, like the tents of Cedar, like the curtains of Solomon.

5. Do not examine me because I am brown, because the sun has altered my color: my mother's sons have fought against me, they have made me the keeper in the vineyards: my vineyard I have not kept.

6. Show me, O you whom my soul loves, where you pasture your flocks, where you rest at midday, lest I begin to wander after the flocks of your companions.

7. If you yourself do not know, O fairest among women, go forth, and follow the steps of the flocks, and feed your kids beside the shepherds' tents.

8. To my cavalry, in Pharaoh's chariots, I have compared you, O my love.

9. Your cheeks are beautiful like the turtledove's, your neck like jewels.

10. We will make you chains of gold, inlaid with silver.

11. While the king was lying on his bed, my spikenard gave off its scent.

12. To me my beloved is a bundle of myrrh, he shall lie between my breasts.

13. To me my beloved is a cluster of cypress, in the vineyards of Engaddi.

14. Behold you are beautiful, O my love, behold you are beautiful, your eyes are like those of doves.

15. Behold you are beautiful, my beloved, and lovely. Our bed is covered with flowers.

16. The beams of our houses are of cedar, our rafters of cypress trees.

Chapter 2

1. I am the flower of the field, and the lily of the valleys.

2. Like the lily among thorns, so is my love among the daughters.

3. Like the apple tree among the trees of the woods, so is my beloved among the sons. I sat down under his shadow, whom I desired: and his fruit was sweet to my taste.

4. He brought me into the wine cellar, he set love over me.

5. Sustain me with flowers, encompass me with apples: because I languish with love.

6. His left hand is under my head, and his right hand shall embrace me.

7. I adjure you, O daughters of Jerusalem, by the deer, and the stags of the fields, that you do not stir up, nor make the beloved awaken, until she please.

8. The voice of my beloved, behold he comes leaping upon the mountains, skipping over the hills.

9. My beloved is like a deer, or a young stag. Behold he stands behind our wall, looking through the windows, looking through the lattice.

10. Behold my beloved speaks to me: Arise, make haste, my love, my dove, my beautiful one, and come.

11. For winter is now past, the rain is over and gone.

12. The flowers have appeared in our land, the time of pruning has arrived: the voice of the turtledove is heard in our land:

13. The fig tree has put forth her green figs: the vines in flower yield their sweet smell. Arise, my love, my beautiful one, and come:

14. My dove in the clefts of the rock, in the hollow places of the wall, show me your face, let your voice sound in my ears: for your voice is sweet, and your face comely.

15. Catch us the little foxes that destroy the vines: for our vineyard has flourished.

16. My beloved is mine, and I am his who pastures his flocks among the lilies.

17. Until the day breaks, and the shadows retire. Return: my beloved, be like a deer, or a young stag upon the mountains of Bether.

Chapter 3

1. In my bed by night I sought him whom my soul loves: I sought him, and did not find him.

2. I will rise, and will go about the city: in the streets and the broad ways I will seek him whom my soul loves: I sought him, and I did not find him.

3. The watchmen who guard the city, found me: Have you seen him, whom my soul loves?

4. When I had passed by them a little ways, I found him whom my soul loves: I held him: and I will not let him go, until I bring him into my mother's house, and into the chamber of her that bore me.

5. I adjure you, O daughters of Jerusalem, by the deer and the stags of the fields, that you stir not up, nor awaken my beloved, until she please.

6. Who is she that goes up from the desert, like a pillar of smoke of aromatical spices, of myrrh, and frankincense, and of all the powders of the perfumer?

7. Behold sixty valiant men of the most valiant of Israel, surrounded the bed of Solomon.

8. All holding swords, and most expert in war: every man's sword upon his thigh, because of fears in the night.

9. King Solomon has made him a litter from the wood of Lebanon:

10. Its pillars he made of silver, the back of gold, the seat of purple: the middle he covered with charity for the daughters of Jerusalem.

11. Go forth, you daughters of Sion, and see king Solomon in the diadem, with which his mother crowned him on the day of his wedding, and on the day of the joy of his heart.

Chapter 4

1. How beautiful you are, my love, how beautiful you are! Your eyes are doves' eyes, besides what is hidden within. Your hair is like a flock of goats, which come up from mount Gilead.

2. Your teeth are like flocks of sheep, that are shorn, which come up from the washing, all with twins, and none among them is barren.

3. Your lips are like a scarlet garland: and your speech sweet. Your cheeks are like a piece of a pomegranate, besides that which lies hidden within.

4. Your neck is like the tower of David, which is built with bulwarks: a thousand bucklers hang upon it, all the armor of valiant men.

5. Your two breasts are like two young fawns that are twins, which feed among the lilies.

6. Until the day breaks, and the shadows retire, I will go to the mountains of myrrh, and to the hill of frankincense.

7. You are all fair, O my love, and there is not a stain on you.

8. Come from Lebanon, my bride, come from Lebanon, come: you will be crowned from the top of Amana, from the top of Senir and Hermon, from the dens of the lions, from the mountains of the leopards.

9. You have wounded my heart, my sister, my bride, you have wounded my heart with one of your eyes, and with one hair of your neck.

10. How beautiful are your breasts, my sister, my bride! your breasts are more beautiful than wine, and the sweet smell of your ointments above all aromatical spices.

11. Your lips, my bride, are like a dripping honeycomb, honey and milk are under your tongue; and the smell of your garments, is like the smell of frankincense.

12. My sister, my bride, is a garden enclosed, a garden enclosed, a fountain sealed.

13. Your plants are a paradise of pomegranates with the fruits of the orchard. Cypress with spikenard.

14. Spikenard and saffron, sweet cane and cinnamon, with all the trees of Lebanon, myrrh and aloes with all the chief perfumes.

15. The fountain of gardens: the well of living waters, which run with a strong stream from Lebanon.

16. Arise, O north wind, and come, O south wind, blow through my garden and let its aromatical spices flow.

Chapter 5

1. Let my beloved come into his garden, and eat the fruit of his apple trees. I am come into my garden, O my sister, my bride, I have gathered my myrrh with my aromatical spices: I have eaten the honeycomb with my honey, I have drunk my wine with my milk: eat, O friends, and drink, and be inebriated, my dearly beloved.

2. I sleep, and my heart is awake: the voice of my beloved is knocking: Open to me, my sister, my love, my dove, my unblemished one: for my head is full of dew, and my locks with the drops of the night.

3. I have put off my garment, how shall I put it on? I have washed my feet, how shall I defile them?

4. My beloved put his hand through the key hole, and my belly trembled at his touch.

5. I arose to open my beloved: my hands dripped with myrrh, and my fingers were full of the choicest myrrh.

6. I opened the lock of my door to my beloved: but he had turned aside and was gone. My soul melted when he spoke: I sought him and found him not: I called and he did not answer me.

7. The watchmen that go about the city found me: they struck me: and wounded me: the watchmen of the walls took away my veil from me.

8. I adjure you, O daughters of Jerusalem, if you find my beloved, that you tell him that I languish with love.

9. What is your beloved more than any other, O most beautiful among women? what is your beloved more than any other, that you have so adjured us?

10. My beloved is white and ruddy, chosen out of thousands.

11. His head is like the finest gold: his locks like branches of palm trees, black as a raven.

12. His eyes are like doves upon brooks of waters, which are washed with milk, and sit beside the plentiful streams.

13. His cheeks are like beds of aromatical spices set by the perfumers. His lips are like lilies dripping choice myrrh.

14. His hands are wrought as of gold, full of hyacinths. His belly is like ivory set with sapphires.

15. His legs are like pillars of marble, that are set upon bases of gold. His form is like Lebanon, excellent like the cedars.

16. His throat most sweet and he is all lovely: such is my beloved, and he is my friend, O daughters of Jerusalem.

17. Where has your beloved gone, O most beautiful among women? Where has your beloved turned aside and we will seek him with you?

Chapter 6

1. My beloved has gone down into his garden, to the bed of aromatical spices, to pasture his flock in the gardens, and to gather lilies.

2. I am beloved's, and my beloved is mine, who pastures his flock among the lilies.

3. You are beautiful, O my love, sweet and comely as Jerusalem: terrible as an army set in array.

4. Turn your eyes away from me, for they have made me flee. Your hair is like a flock of goats, that appear from Gilead.

5. Your teeth are like a flock of sheep, which come up from the washing, all with twins, and none among them is barren.

6. Your cheeks are like the bark of a pomegranate, beside what is hidden within you.

7. There are sixty queens, and eighty concubines and young maidens without number.

8. One is my dove, my perfect one is but one, she is the only one of her mother, the chosen of her that bore her. The daughters saw her and declared her most blessed: the queens and concubines, and they praised her.

9. Who is she that comes forth like the morning rising, fair as the moon, bright as the sun, terrible as an army set in array?

10. I went down into the garden of nuts to see the fruits of the valleys, and to look if the vineyard had flourished and the pomegranates had bloomed.

11. I knew not: my soul troubled me about the chariots of Aminadab.

12. Return, return, O Shulammite: return, return that we may look at you.

Chapter 7

1. What will you see in the Shulammite but the dance of the camps? How beautiful are your steps in your shoes, O prince's daughter! The joints of your thighs are like jewels that are made by the hand of a skillful workman.

2. Your navel is like a round bowl never lacking drink. Your belly is like a heap of wheat, circled with lilies.

3. Your two breasts are like two young fawns that are twins.

4. Your neck is like a tower of ivory. Your eyes like the fishpools in Heshebon, which are by the gate of the daughter of the multitude. Your nose is like the tower of Lebanon, that looks toward Damascus.

5. Your head is like Carmel: and the hairs of your head like the purple of the king bound in braids.

6. How beautiful you are, and how comely, my dearest, in delights!

7. Your stature is like a palm tree, and your breasts are like clusters of grapes.

8. I said: I will go up into the palm tree and will take hold of the fruit there: and your breasts shall be like the clusters of the vine and the scent of your mouth like apples.

9. Your throat is like the best wine, worthy for my beloved to drink, and for his lips and his teeth to caress.

10. I am beloved's, and his desire is towards me.

11. Come, my beloved, let us go forth into the field, let us abide in the villages.

12. Let us get up early to go to the vineyards, let us see if the vineyards

flourish, if the flowers are ready to bring forth fruits, if the pomegranates flourish: there I will give you my breasts.

13. The mandrakes give off a scent. On our gates are all fruits: the new and the old, my beloved, I have kept for you.

Chapter 8

1. Who shall give you to me as for my brother, sucking the breasts of my mother, that I may find you without, and kiss you, and now no man may despise me?

2. I will take hold of you, and bring you into my mother's house: there you shall teach me, and I will give you a cup of spiced wine and juice from my pomegranates.

3. His left hand under my head and his right hand shall embrace me.

4. I adjure you, O daughters of Jerusalem, that you stir not up nor awaken my love until she please.

5. Who is this that comes up from the desert, flowing with delights, leaning upon her beloved? Under the apple tree I raised you up: there your mother was corrupted, there she that gave birth to you was violated.

6. Put me as a seal upon your heart, as a seal upon your arm, for love is strong as death, jealousy as hard as hell, the lamps thereof are of fire and flames.

7. Many waters cannot quench love, neither can the floods drown it: if a man should give all the substance of his house for love, he shall despise it as nothing.

8. Our sister is little, and has no breasts. What shall we do for our sister on the day when she is spoken for?

9. If she is a wall let us build upon it bulwarks of silver: if she is a door, let us join it together with boards of cedar.

10. I am a wall and my breasts are like a tower since I am become in his presence like one finding peace.

11. The peaceable had a vineyard, in that which has people: he let out the vineyard to keepers, each one offered for its fruit a thousand pieces of silver.

12. My vineyard is before me. A thousand are for you, the peaceable, and two hundred for them that keep its fruit.

13. You that dwell in the gardens, the friends listen: make me hear your voice.

14. Flee away, O my beloved, and be like the deer, and the young stag upon the mountains of aromatical spices.

What metaphors are used to describe the woman? The man? How could these images be used in a theological way?

9. THE BIBLICAL REGULATION OF SEXUAL BEHAVIOR

The exercise of human sexuality was an area of great conflict for medieval theologians. Despite the positive view of physical love found in The Song of Songs, *and despite God's command to Adam and Eve to "go forth and multiply" (Gen. 1:28), most ecclesiastical writers had a negative and suspicious view of human sexuality and love. Marriage and sexual intercourse might be acceptable and even necessary for the propagation of the human race, but they were necessary evils to be tolerated rather than promoted. Based on a passage from* Tobias, *medieval moralists exhorted married couples to observe a period of sexual abstinence immediately after their nuptials, as a way of separating the sacredness of the mutual vows from the profane act of consummation. While sexual activity could be tolerated in marriage, it was considered a sin outside it. The Apostle Paul summarized the inherent evil of extramarital and other alternative forms of sexual expression, linking such acts with serious sins and rebellion against God.*

Source: *The Holy Bible,* Douay Rheims Version (Baltimore: John Murphy, 1899; rpt. Rockford, IL: Tan Books, 1971), pp. 171, 191, 519; modernized.

An Exhortation to Chastity on the Wedding Night, Tobias 8:1-10

1. And after they had eaten, they brought the young man in to her.

2. And Tobias, remembering the angel's word, took out of his bag part of the liver and laid it upon the burning coals.

3. Then the angel Raphael took the devil and bound him in the desert of upper Egypt.

4. Then Tobias exhorted the virgin and said to her: Sara, arise, and let us pray to God today and tomorrow and the next day: because for these three nights we are joined to God, and when the third night is over, we will be in our own wedlock.

5. For we are the children of saints and we must not be married like heathens that do not know God.

6. So they both arose, and prayed earnestly together that health might be given to them,

7. And Tobias said: Lord God of our fathers, may the heavens and the earth and the sea and the fountains and the rivers and all your creatures that are in them, bless you.

8. You made Adam out of the slime of the earth and gave to him Eve as a helper.

9. And now, Lord, you know, that it is not because of lust that I am taking my sister as my wife, but only for the love of posterity, in which your name may be blessed for ever and ever.

10. Sara also said: Have mercy on us, O Lord, have mercy on us, and let us grow old both together in health.

Paul's Sexual Prohibitions, Romans 1:21-32

21. Because when they knew God, they have not glorified him as God or given thanks; but became vain in their thoughts, and their foolish heart was darkened.

22. For professing themselves to be wise, they became fools.

23. And they changed the glory of the incorruptible God into the likeness of the image of corruptible man and of the birds and of fourfooted beasts and of creeping things.

24. Therefore God gave them up to the desires of their heart, to uncleanness, to dishonor their own bodies among themselves.

25. Who changed the truth of God into a lie and worshipped and served the creature rather than the Creator, who is blessed for ever. Amen.

26. For this reason God delivered them up to shameful passions. For their women changed the natural use into that use which is against nature.

27. And, in like manner, the men also, leaving the natural use of women, have burned in their desires for one another, men committing filthy acts with men, and receiving in themselves the recompense which was due to their error.

28. And as they liked not to have God in their knowledge, God delivered them up to a reprobate sense, to do those things which are not appropriate;

29. Being filled with every iniquity, malice, fornication, avarice, wickedness, full of envy, murder, controversy, deceit, malignity, whisperers,

30. Detractors, haters of God, contumelious, proud, haughty, inventors of evil things, disobedient to parents,

31. Foolish, dissolute, without affection, without fidelity, without mercy.

32. Who, having known the justice of God, did not understand that they who do such things, are worthy of death; and not only they that do them, but they also that consent to them that do them.

1 Corinthians 6:9-20

9. Do you not know that the unjust shall not possess the kingdom of God? Do not err: neither fornicators nor idolators nor adulterers

10. Nor the effeminate nor those who have sexual intercourse with men, nor thieves, nor the covetous, nor drunkards, nor cursers, nor extortioners, shall possess the kingdom of God.

11. And such some of you were; but you are washed, but you are sanctified,

but you are justified in the name of our Lord Jesus Christ, and the Spirit of our God.

12. All things are lawful to me, but all things are not expedient. All things are lawful to me, but I will not be brought under the power of any.

13. Meat is for the belly, and the belly for meat; but God shall destroy both of them: but the body is not for fornication, but for the Lord, and the Lord for the body.

14. Now God has raised up the Lord, and will raise us up also by his power.

15. Do you not know that your bodies are the members of Christ? Shall I then take the members of Christ and make them the members of a prostitute? Never.

16. Do you not know that he who is joined to a prostitute is made one body with her? It is said, "for they shall be two in one flesh."

17. But he who is joined to the Lord, is in one spirit with him.

18. Flee fornication. Every sin that a man commits, is outside the body; but he that commits fornication, sins against his own body.

19. Do you not know that your body is the temple of the Holy Ghost, who is in you, whom you have from God; and you are not your own?

20. For you are brought with a great price. Glorify and bear God in your body.

According to Tobias, what distinguishes the marriage of believers and non-believers? According to Paul, how do those who worship idols behave? Why is sexual activity to be avoided?

10. THE MARRIAGE OF THORSTEINN AND SPES

Icelandic sagas provide an important point of entry into the values and mode of life of the pre-modern Scandinavian peoples. Sagas contain both historical and legendary accounts of people who lived and events that occurred during the period of great Scandinavian expansion in the ninth through eleventh centuries. Sagas were a fluid genre based on oral tradition and consequently they changed and modified over time. It was only when sagas were written down that they lost this oral nature and became static. This selection from Grettir's Saga *was written down about 1325, but describes events reputed to have occurred in the ninth century. Consequently, the saga describes people and events that occurred in pre-Christian, Norse society. However, the story also reflects the values and beliefs of the Christianized society in which it was written down. Thus, the saga shows something of how Christian beliefs were layered over the culture and social practices of a story about an earlier pre-Christian period. This hybridity accounts for some aspects of the story that appear contradictory or surprising. The story of Thorsteinn and Spes contains passion, adultery, and betrayal, divorce countenanced by ecclesiastical authorities, love and loyalty, and, ultimately, repentance.*

Source: G.A. Hight, trans., *The Saga of Grettir the Strong* (London: Dent, 1913), pp. 223-38, modernized.

Chapter 87. The Lady Spes

There was a very distinguished lady in that town, the owner of a large establishment, very rich and highly born. Her name was Spes. Her husband's name was Sigurd; he too was wealthy, but of lower birth than she was. She had been married to him for his money. There was not much love between them, and the marriage was thought an unhappy one. She was very proud, and had much dignity.

One evening, when Thorsteinn was diverting himself, she happened to pass along the street near the dungeon and heard singing so sweet that she declared she had never heard the like. She was walking with several retainers, and told them to go in and find out who it was that had such a magnificent voice. They called out and asked who was there in such close confinement. Thorsteinn told his name. Spes said: "Are you as good at other things as you are at singing?" He said there was not much in that. "What have you done," she asked, "that they should torture you here to death?" He said he had killed a man and avenged his brother, "but I have no witness to prove it," he said, "so I have been put here unless someone comes to release me, of which there seems little hope, since I have no relations here." "It would be a great loss if you were killed," she said. "Was your brother then a man of such renown, he whom you avenged?" Thorsteinn said he was half as good a man again as himself. She asked what token there was of that. Then Thorsteinn spoke this verse:

> "Goddess of rings! No eight could meet him,
> or gain the sword from his vanquished hand.
> Brave was Grettir; his foemen doughty
> severed the hand of the ruler of ships."

Those who understood the song declared that it told of great nobility. When she heard that she asked, "Will you receive your life at my hands if the choice is offered you?" "Indeed I will," he said, "if this companion of mine sitting here is released along with me. If not, we must both remain sitting here together." She answered: "I think you are more worth paying for than he is." "However that may be," he said, "either we both of us come out from here together or neither of us comes out."

So she went to the Varangians' quarters and asked for the release of Thorsteinn, offering money. They agreed. With her interest and her wealth she brought it about that both of them were released. Directly Thorsteinn came out of the dungeon, he went to pay his respects to the lady Spes. She welcomed him and kept him there secretly. From time to time he went campaigning with the Varangians, and was distinguished for his courage in all their engagements.

Chapter 88. The Adventures of Thorsteinn and Spes

At that time Harald the son of Sigurd was in Constantinople, and Thorsteinn became friendly with him. Thorsteinn was now a very great personage, for Spes kept him well supplied with money, and they became very attached to one another. She was a great admirer of his skill. Her expenses were very great because she tried to keep up many friends. Her husband noticed a great change in her character and her behavior, and especially that she had become very extravagant. Treasures of gold and other property which were in her keeping disappeared. One day her husband Sigurd spoke with her and said that he was much surprised at her conduct. "You pay no attention to our affairs," he said, "and squander money in many ways. You seem as if you were in a dream, and never wish to be where I am. I am certain something is going on."

She replied, "I told you as I told my kinsmen when we married that I meant to be my own mistress in all matters which concern myself; that is why I do not spare your money. Or is there anything more than this that you wish to speak about with me? Do you accuse me of anything shameful?"

He said, "I am not without my suspicions that you are keeping some man whom you prefer to me."

"I do not know," she said, "that there would be very much in that; and yet certainly there is no truth in what you say. I will not speak with you alone if you bring such improper accusations against me."

He dropped the subject for the time. She and Thorsteinn continued to carry on as before, and were not very heedful of the talk of evil-minded people; they relied upon their wits and her popularity. They were often sitting together and diverting themselves.

One evening when they were sitting in an upper room in which her treasures were kept, she asked Thorsteinn to sing something, and thinking that her husband was, as usual, sitting at drink she fastened the door. When he had sung for a time there was a banging at the door, and someone called to them to open it. It was her husband with a number of his followers. The lady had opened a large chest to show Thorsteinn the treasures. When she knew who was outside she refused to open the door, and said to Thorsteinn, "Quickly! Jump into the chest and keep very quiet."

He did so. She locked the chest and sat upon it. Her husband then entered, having forced his way in.

She said, "What are you coming here for with all this uproar? Are there robbers after you?"

He said, "Now it is well that you yourself give proof of what you are. Where is the man who was letting his voice run on so grandly? No doubt you think his voice is better than mine."

"No man is a fool if he keeps silence," she said, "that applies to you. You think yourself very cunning, and would like to fasten your lies on to me, as in this case. Well, if you have spoken the truth, find the man. He will not escape through the walls or the roof."

He searched all through the room and found nothing.

"Why don't you take him," she said, "if you are so certain?"

He was silent and did not know how he could have been deceived. He asked his men whether or not they had heard what he heard, but when they saw that the lady was displeased, there was nothing to be got out of them; they said that one was often mistaken about sounds. He then went away, not doubting that he knew the truth, though he could not find the man. After that he ceased for some time to pry into his wife's concerns.

On another occasion, much later, Thorsteinn and Spes were sitting in a storeroom where dresses were kept which belonged to them, both made up and in the piece. She showed many of the cloths to Thorsteinn and spread them out. When they were least expecting it, her husband came up with a troop of men and broke into the room. While they were forcing their way in she covered Thorsteinn up with a bundle of clothes and leaned against the heap when they entered.

"Do you again deny," he said, "that there was a man here with you? There are those present here now who saw you both."

She told him not to be so violent. "You will not fail to catch him now," she said. "Only leave me in peace and do not push me about."

They searched the room, but finding nothing had to give it up.

"It is always good to have better proofs than people suppose. It was only to be expected that you would not find what was not there. Now, my husband, will you admit your folly and free me from this slanderous accusation?"

"By no means will I free you," he said, "for I know that what I have accused you of is true, and it will cost you an effort to free yourself of the charge."

She said she was quite ready to do that, and therewith they parted.

After this Thorsteinn remained entirely with the Varangians. Men say that he acted by the advice of Harald the son of Sigurd, and it is thought that they would not have got out of it as they did if they had not made use of him and his wits.

After a time Sigurd gave out that he was about to go abroad on some business. His wife did not try to dissuade him. When he was gone Thorsteinn came to Spes and they were always together. Her house was built on the very edge of the sea and there were some of the rooms under which the sea flowed.

Spes and Thorsteinn always sat here. There was a small trap-door in the floor, known to no one but these two, and it was kept open in case of its being wanted in a hurry.

Sigurd, it must be told, did not go away, but concealed himself so as to be able to watch his wife's doings. One evening when they were sitting unconcernedly in the room over the sea and enjoying themselves, in came her husband with a party of men, taking them by surprise. He had taken some of the men to the window of the room that they might see whether it was not as he had said. They all said that he had spoken truly, and that it must have been so too on the former occasions. Then they rushed into the room.

On hearing the noise Spes said to Thorsteinn, "You must go down here whatever it costs. Give me some sign that you have got away from the house."

He promised that he would, and descended through the floor. The lady closed the trap-door with her foot, and it fell back into its place so that no one could see any mark of the floor having been touched. Sigurd entered the room with his men, searched, and of course found nothing. The room was uninhabited and there was no furniture in it, but only the bare floor and a bed, on which the lady was sitting and twirling her fingers. She paid little attention to them and seemed as if their business did not concern her. Sigurd thought it altogether ridiculous and asked his followers if they had not seen the man. They declared that they had seen him most assuredly.

The lady said, "Now we may say as the proverb has it, 'All good things are in threes.' This is your case, Sigurd. Three times you have disturbed me, if I remember rightly; and now are you any the wiser than you were in the beginning?"

"This time I am not alone to tell the story," he said. "For all that, you will have to clear yourself, for on no terms will I allow your shameful deeds to go unpunished."

"It seems," she said, "that you require the very thing which I would myself propose. It will please me well to show the falsehood of this accusation, which has been so thoroughly aired that I shall be disgraced if I cannot refute it."

"At the same time," he said, "you will have to deny that you have expended my money and my property."

She replied, "At the time when I clear myself I will refute all the matters which you brought against me, and you may consider how it will all end. I mean to go at once, tomorrow morning, before the bishop that he may grant me full compurgation from this charge."

Her husband was satisfied with this and went away with his men.

In the meantime, Thorsteinn had swum away from the house and landed at a convenient place, where he got a firebrand and held it aloft, so that it could be seen from the lady's house. She stayed long outside in the evening and the night, for she was anxious to know whether Thorsteinn had reached the land. When she saw the light she knew that he had landed, for that was the signal which they had agreed upon.

The next morning, Spes proposed to her husband that they should speak with the bishop on their matter. This he was quite ready to do, so they went before the bishop and Sigurd repeated his accusation. The bishop asked whether she had ever been accused of misbehavior before, but nobody had heard of such a thing. Then he asked upon what evidence this charge was brought against her, and Sigurd produced the men who had seen her sitting in a room with the door locked and a man with her. Her husband said that this was ground enough for supposing that the man meant to seduce her.

The bishop said that she might very well purge herself from this accusation of she so desired. She replied that she desired it very much. "I hope," she said, "that I shall have many women to swear for me on this charge."

The form of the oath which she was to swear was then communicated to her and the day for the compurgation fixed. She returned home and was quite happy. She and Thorsteinn met and laid their plans.

Chapter 89. The Ordeal

The day now arrived when Spes was to make the oath. She invited all her friends and relations, and appeared in the finest clothes that she possessed, with many a fine lady in her train. It was raining heavily and the roads were flooded; on the way to the church there was a swamp to be passed. When Spes came with her company to the swamp there was a great crowd on the high road, and a multitude of poor people asking for alms, for all who knew her thought it a duty to give her a greeting and wish her well because of the kindnesses which they had often received from her. Among these poor people there was a beggar, very large of stature and with a long beard. The women halted at the swamp; being people of high rank they did not like to cross the dirty slough. The big beggar, seeing that Spes was better dressed than the other ladies, said to her, "Good lady, have the condescension to allow me to carry you over the swamp. It is the duty of us beggars to serve you in whatever way we can."

"How can you carry me," she said, "when you can scarcely carry yourself?"

"Nevertheless, it would be a great condescension. I cannot offer you more than I have, and you will prosper the better in other things for having had no pride with a poor man."

"Know then for a certainty," she said, "that if you do not carry me properly the skin shall be flayed from your back."

"Gladly will I venture upon that," he said, and waded out into the stream. She pretended not to like very much being carried by him; nevertheless, she got upon his back. He staggered along very slowly, using two crutches, and when they reached the middle he was reeling in every direction. She told him to pull himself together. "If you drop me here," she said, "it shall be the worst journey that you ever made."

The poor wretch gathered up all his strength and still went on. By dint of a valiant effort he had all but reached the shore when he struck his foot against something and fell forwards, projecting her on to the bank, while he himself fell into the mire up to his armpits. There, as he lay, he put out his hands, not on her clothes, but on her legs. She sprang up cursing and said she always suffered ill from low vagabonds. "It would only be right that you should have a good beating," she said, "were I not ashamed to beat such a miserable creature as you are."

He said, "Unequal is the lot of man. I thought to earn some benefit and to receive alms from you, and you only give me abuse and insult without any reward." And he pretended to be very much disgusted. Many felt pity for him, but she said he was a very cunning rascal. When they all began to beg for him she took out her purse, wherein was many a gold penny. She shook out the money, saying, "Take that, fellow! It would not be right that you should go unpaid for all my scoldings. You are now paid for what you have done."

He gathered up the money and thanked her for her liberality. Spes then went to the church, which was full of people. Sigurd proceeded with energy and told her to clear herself of the charge which he had brought against her.

"I pay no heed to your accusation," she said, "but I want to know what man it was whom you pretend to have seen in the room with me, because there is always some proper man near me; there is nothing to be ashamed of in that. But this I will swear, that to no man have I given money and that by no man has my body been defiled except by my husband and by that beggar, who put his muddy hands upon my thigh today when I was carried over the ditch."

Many then were satisfied and declared that her oath was perfectly good and that she was in no way disgraced by a man having touched her unwittingly. She said she had to tell the story just as it happened, and then she swore the oath in the words appointed for her. Many said that she would be observing the saying that "nothing should be omitted from an oath." But she replied that wise men would hold that there was no cause for suspicion. Then her relations began to talk with her and said that such lies should not be told about her and go unpunished, for they said it was an offence punishable with death if a woman were proved to have been unfaithful to her husband. So Spes asked the bishop to divorce her from Sigurd, saying that she would not endure the lies which he had told. Her kinsmen supported her, and with their help her request was granted. Sigurd got little of the property and had to leave the country. So it happened, as usual, that the weaker had to bow, nor could he accomplish anything although the right was on his side. Spes took all the money and was held in high esteem, but when men came to consider her oath they thought it was not altogether above suspicion, and they concluded that very skillful men had composed the Latin formula for her. They discovered that the beggar who carried her was Thorsteinn Dromund. But Sigurd got no redress.

Chapter 90. Thorsteinn and Spes Return to Norway

While the affair was being talked about, Thorsteinn Dromund remained with the Varangians, where he was held in such high estimation that his prowess was considered to be beyond that of nearly every man who had come to them. Harald the son of Sigurd especially did him honor, and claimed kinship with him; it was supposed to have been by his advice that Thorsteinn had acted.

Soon after Sigurd was driven from the country, Thorsteinn proposed marriage to Spes; she was quite agreeable, but referred it to her kinsmen. There were family meetings and all agreed that she herself ought to decide. Matters were settled between them; their union was most prosperous and they had

plenty of money. Thorsteinn was considered lucky to have got out of his difficulties in such a way. After they had lived together for two years in Constantinople, Thorsteinn told her that he would like to visit his property once more
in Norway. She said he should do as he pleased, and he then sold his property
so as to have some ready money. They left the country with a good company
of followers and sailed all the way to Norway. Thorsteinn's kinsmen welcomed
them both, and soon saw that Spes was both generous and noble; accordingly,
she quickly became very popular. They had three children, and remained on
their property very well contented with their condition.

The king of Norway was at that time Magnus the Good. Thorsteinn soon
went to meet him, and was well received because of the fame which he had
earned through having avenged Grettir the Strong. Scarcely an example was
known of a man from Iceland having been avenged in Constantinople, except-
ing Grettir, the son of Asmund. It is said that Thorsteinn entered his body-
guard. Thorsteinn remained nine years in Norway, both he and his wife being
in high honor. After that, King Harald the son of Sigurd returned from Constantinople, and King Magnus gave him half of Norway. Both kings were
together in Norway for a time. After Magnus's death some who had been his
friends were less contented, for he was beloved of all, but Harald was not easy
to get on with, since he was hard and severe. Thorsteinn Dromund then began
to grow old, but was still very vigorous. Sixteen winters had now passed since
the death of Grettir.

Chapter 91. Absolution in Rome

There were many who urged Thorsteinn to visit King Harald and become his
man, but he would not. Spes said to him, "I would not want you to go to
Harald, Thorsteinn, for a larger debt remains unpaid to another King, to which
we must now turn our thoughts. Our youth is now passed; we are both
becoming old, and we have lived more according to our desires than to
Christian doctrine or with regard for righteousness. Now I know that neither
kinsmen nor wealth may pay this debt, if we do not pay it ourselves. I would
wish, therefore, that we now change our way of life and leave the country to go
to Rome. I have hope that I shall be absolved from my sin."

Thorsteinn answered, "The matter of which you speak is as well known to
me as it is to you. It is right that you should rule now, and most seemly, since
you allowed me to rule when our matter was much less hopeful. And so it shall
be now in all that you say."

This resolve of theirs took people by surprise. Thorsteinn was then two
years past sixty-five, but still vigorous in all that he undertook. He summoned
all his kinsmen and connections to him and told them his plans. The wiser

men approved of his resolve, while holding his departure a great misfortune for themselves. Thorsteinn said there was no certainty of his return. He said,

"I wish now to thank you all for the care of my goods which you took while I was absent. Now I ask you to take over my children along with my property and to bring them up in your own ways; for I have now reached such an age that even if I live there is much doubt about whether I shall return. Manage all that I leave behind as if I should never return to Norway."

The people answered that matters would be more easily managed if his wife remained to look after them.

She answered, "I left my own country and came from Mikligard with Thorsteinn. I bade farewell to my kinsmen and my possessions, because I wished that one fate should befall us both. And now it has seemed pleasant to me here, but I have no desire to remain in Norway or in these northern lands after he has departed. There has always been good-will between us and no dissension. Now, we must both depart together; for we ourselves know best about many things which have happened since we first met."

When they had thus dealt with their own condition, Thorsteinn appointed certain imperial men to divide his property in two parts. Thorsteinn's kinsmen took over the half which was to go to the children, and brought them up with their father's relations. They became in time men of the utmost valor, and many of their descendants are the Vik. Thorsteinn and Spes divided their share, giving some to the church for the good of their souls and keeping some for themselves. So they set off for Rome, bearing the good wishes of many with them.

Chapter 92. The End of Thorsteinn and Spes

They traveled then the whole way to Rome, and appeared before him who was appointed to hear confessions. They related all that had happened, all the cunning tricks wherewith they had achieved their union. They submitted with humility to the penances laid upon them, and by reason of their having voluntarily turned their hearts to desire absolution from their sins, without any pressure from the elders of the church, their penance was lightened so far as it was possible, and they were gently admonished to arrange their lives with wisdom for the well-being of their souls, and, after receiving absolution in full, to live henceforward in purity. They were declared to have acted wisely and well.

Then the lady Spes said, "Now, I think it has gone well; and now we have not suffered only misfortune together. It may be that foolish people will follow the example of our former lives. Let us now end in such way that we may be an example to the good. We will come to an agreement with some men skilled in building to erect for each of us a stone retreat; thus may we atone for all offences which we have committed against God."

So Thorsteinn advanced money to stone-masons and such other persons as might be needed, that they might not be without the means of subsistence. When these works were completed and all matters were settled, a fitting time was chosen for them to part company with each other, each to live alone, in order more surely to partake of the eternal life in another world. They remained each in their own retreat, living as long as it pleased God to spare them, and thus ending their lives.

Most people consider Thorsteinn Dromund and Spes to have been most fortunate in escaping from the difficulties which they had fallen into. None of their children or posterity are mentioned as having come to Iceland.

Why was Spes's marriage to Sigurd unhappy? Why did Spes go to the bishop? How did Spes prove her innocence? On what grounds was Spes granted a divorce? Why was the marriage between Thorsteinn and Spes a happy one? Why did Thorsteinn and Spes go to Rome? How did the couple end their days? Why? Which parts show later attempts to Christianize an older, pre-Christian story?

11. CHARLEMAGNE'S DAUGHTER AND HER LOVER

In his biography of Charlemagne, Einhard presented the king as a loving father, but one who refused to allow his daughters to marry. He probably wished to avoid (even if Einhard feigns ignorance of the dynastic strategy at work) having his daughters marry Frankish nobles who could then establish legitimate royal lines that would over time rival his own. As even Einhard knew, this led to scandals at court, for the king had many daughters and granddaughters but even more courtiers. Indeed, Charlemagne's daughter Bertha did have a lasting relationship with the courtier Angilbert (the lay abbot of St-Riquier after 790) that produced two sons, the historian Nithard and his brother Hartnid.

The story of the love affair at the king's winter palace, which is reported in the twelfth-century Lorsch Chronicle, *is however historically garbled. At the monastery of Lorsch the story was connected to Einhard and his wife Emma and was used to account for the extensive properties Einhard held and granted to the monastery. Bertha was the daughter of Charlemagne who had the most famous affair at court, but her sister Rotrude was the one who had once been betrothed to a Byzantine prince. Nevertheless, it is likely that the story of some real event lies at the base of this legend and that in it we can see something of the oft-forgotten nature of Charlemagne's dynamic court and its sexual politics.*

Source: Trans. Paul Edward Dutton, *Charlemagne's Courtier: the Complete Einhard* (Peterborough: Broadview Press, 1998), pp.28-29; reprinted with permission.

Einhard, *The Life of Charlemagne*, 19

[Charles] believed that his children, both his daughters and his sons, should be educated, first in the liberal arts, which he himself had studied. Then, he saw to it that when the boys had reached the right age they were trained to ride in the Frankish fashion, to fight, and to hunt. But he ordered his daughters to learn how to work with wool, how to spin and weave it, so that they might not grow dull from inactivity and [instead might] learn to value work and virtuous activity.

Out of all these children he lost only two sons and one daughter before he himself died: Charles, his eldest son [who died in 811], Pepin, whom he had set up as king of Italy [died in 810], and Rotrude, his eldest daughter, who [in 781] was engaged to Constantine, emperor of the Greeks [she died in 810]. Pepin left behind only one surviving son, Bernard [who died in 818], but five daughters: Adelhaid, Atula, Gundrada, Berthaid, and Theoderada. The king displayed a special token of affection toward his [grandchildren], since when his son

[Pepin] died he saw to it that his grandson [Bernard] succeeded his father [as king of Italy] and he arranged for his granddaughters to be raised alongside his own daughters. Despite the surpassing greatness [of his spirit], he was deeply disturbed by the deaths of his sons and daughter, and his affection [toward his children], which was just as strong [a part of his character], drove him to tears.

When he was informed [in 796] of the death of Hadrian, the Roman pontiff, he cried so much that it was as if he had lost a brother or a deeply loved son, for he had thought of him as a special friend. [Charles] was, by nature, a good friend, for he made friends easily and firmly held on to them. Indeed, he treated with the greatest respect those he had bound closely to himself in a relationship of this sort.

He was so attentive to raising his sons and daughters, that when he was home he always ate his meals with them and when he traveled he always took them with him, his sons riding beside him, while his daughters followed behind. A special rearguard of his men was appointed to watch over them. Although his daughters were extremely beautiful women and were deeply loved by him, it is strange to have to report that he never wanted to give any of them away in marriage to anyone, whether it be to a Frankish noble or to a foreigner. Instead he kept them close beside him at home until his death, saying that he could not stand to be parted from their company. Although he was otherwise happy, this situation [that is, the affairs of his daughters] caused him no end of trouble. But he always acted as if there was no suspicion of any sexual scandal on their part or that any such rumor had already spread far and wide.

Love at the Carolingian Court

Source: Trans. Paul Edward Dutton, from *Chronicon Laureshamense*, ed. K.A.F. Pertz, in *Monumenta Germaniae Historica: Scriptores*, vol.21 (Hannover: Hahn, 1869), pp. 357-59; printed with permission.

Let us briefly report, just as it was remembered by our predecessors, how the cell of Michelstadt was added to [our] monastery of Lorsch by the venerable Einhard during the time of that very pious ruler [Louis the Pious]. For it is a thing worthy to be known and wondered at, and supplies a clear example of the nature and greatness of [Charles's] imperial excellence for in it he displayed piety toward his subjects, generosity toward the devoted, and clemency toward the excesses of others.

This man Einhard was the archchaplain and scribe of Emperor Charles. While serving with much praise at the royal court, he was treasured by all, but loved even more fervently by Emma, the emperor's daughter, who had been pledged to the king of the Greeks. As time passed, their love grew stronger day by day, but fear and royal disapproval held them back, so that they did not enter into the dangerous task of meeting. But [as Virgil says], "Passionate love overcomes everything."

Finally, since the illustrious man was burning with an incurable love and dared not speak to the virgin through a go-between, he worked up his courage and came secretly during the night to the girl's bedroom. He knocked quietly as though about to relay a royal message to the young girl and was allowed to enter. Everything changed at once when he was alone with her. He spoke intimately to her and exchanged caresses, and satisfied his desire for love.

With dawn coming on, he wanted to return while all was still quiet to his own place, but he discovered that a great deal of snow had fallen unexpectedly during the night. He was afraid to go outside lest his male footprints betray him. With both of them aware of their situation and full of anxiety and fear, he was forced to stay inside. Full of worry they were wavering back and forth about what to do, when finally that fine young girl—made bold by her love—conceived a plan. She would bend down and lift him [onto her shoulders], and carry him before dawn came to his own abode; then, after depositing him, she would come back by carefully walking in her own footprints.

But that night by God's plan (as it is believed) the emperor couldn't sleep. He rose at first light and looking outside he saw his daughter at some distance from the palace staggering with difficulty beneath her heavy load; and he saw her, after she had deposited her package, run quickly back again. The emperor watched all of this in great amazement and was struck with both wonder and sadness, but he did not think that it could have occurred without divine dispensation. He kept silent for the time being about what he had seen.

But Einhard knew that it could not be hidden from his lord king for long and finally in this tricky spot he came up with a plan and approached the emperor. On bended knee he asked to be released [from his service], claiming that the rewards for his great and constant service were insufficient. When the emperor heard all this he kept quiet, giving no indication [that he knew] of the incident or its outcome. Then he assured him that he would before too long respond to his request.

He ordered the chief counselors of his kingdom and other summoned aides to gather at once. So it happened that a magnificent gathering of dignitaries assembled. He told them that his imperial majesty had been greatly wounded and harmed by the shameful intercourse (*copulatio*) of his daughter and the scribe, and because of it he was deeply perturbed. The gathering was overcome with astonishment and set to discussing the magnitude and unheard of nature of the incident; the king laid out for them what had occurred and what he knew from his own observation. He asked for their advice and judgment about this matter. But being of different minds among themselves, they believed different things and gave firm and various judgments against one who would presume to do such a thing: some, saying what first occurred to them, judged that he should be punished without warning, others that he ought to be sent into exile, others that he should be ruined in some other way. But some of them were gentler and wiser and deliberated among themselves and gently suggested to the king that, just as it was right for him to investigate the matter, it was also right for him to assess it based on the wisdom gathered from heaven [Scripture] for him.

The king weighed the truth presented to him by each and he considered which of the many opinions was the strongest and ought to be followed. Then he spoke to them: "You should know that human beings are subject to various misfortunes and [also] that it frequently happens that some things that begin badly have a good outcome. For that reason you should not despair about this matter, which by its unusual and serious nature overwhelmed [even] my mind; rather remain pious in expectation and hope for divine providence, which never fails in its disposition and which even knows how to employ evil things for a good end. For that reason I shall not exact punishment from my scribe for so lamentable an act, because that would only work to increase rather than lessen my daughter's disgrace. Hence, we think it fitting, more worthy and praiseworthy for the glory of our empire, that, with the permission of [my daughter] having been given, I join them in matrimony and return the luster of honesty to a disgraceful act." When the judgment of the king was heard incomparable joy broke forth and the greatness and gentleness of his mind was highly praised.

Einhard, having been ordered to appear, came forward; the king unexpectedly greeted him and spoke calmly to him: "A short while ago you complained to us that I had not rewarded your service with due royal munificence. But, to tell the truth, your negligence was mostly to blame for this, since although I alone bear so many and such great responsibilities, nevertheless if I had known of your desire, I would have rewarded your service with fitting honor. But, in order not to detain you with a lengthy sermon, I shall answer your complaint with the most generous gift [possible] and so that I may be sure that you will remain faithful to me as before and well-disposed hereafter, I give to you in legal marriage my daughter, your porteress, who was entirely ready and willing to serve as your transport on high [not long ago]."

Right away, after a command from the king, his daughter with a great crowd of people was brought forth. She, with her face all ablush, was given by the hand of her father into the hand of that Einhard along with a plentiful dowry of land, gold and silver, and other precious goods. The most pious emperor Louis, after the death of his father, granted them his own properties of Michelstadt and Mulinheim, which is now called Seligenstadt.

What was the nature of Charlemagne's family? Why were his daughters guarded even while out riding with their father? How did family values define Charlemagne's relations with friends? How did the story of Bertha and Angilbert, if indeed it had its roots in a real tryst, become so garbled over time? Does the story defy or reinforce Christian values? Why is the story so filled with property and service issues?

12. THE IDEOLOGY OF COURTLY LOVE

One of the most enduring themes found in the literature of the high Middle Ages is that of courtly love. In the late twelfth and thirteenth centuries in particular, the ideology of courtly love flourished in the literature emanating from courtly society. One of the most significant statements of the meaning, parameters, and rules governing courtly love is that of Andreas Capellanus (Andrew the Chaplain, fl. ca. 1170-1190) in his renowned The Art of Courtly Love *(De amore). Courtly love literature flourished in southern France and was patronized by the famous Eleanor of Aquitaine and her daughter, Marie, countess of Champagne. Indeed, Andreas may have been familiar with Marie's court.* The Art of Courtly Love *drew heavily on Ovid's* Ars amatoria *but adopted the style of a scholastic treatise rather than a lyric poem. Allegedly written to help young Walter navigate the tricky waters of courtly love, the treatise sets out the nature and goals of love, as appropriate for people of differing social status. There is an ongoing debate about the historicity of courtly love and whether, in fact, it could have existed outside of literary convention. The ideology of courtly love was frankly erotic, adulterous, and subversive in a way that threatened the very fabric of noble society and the moral framework established by the church. Nevertheless, courtly love exerted a tremendous influence on medieval literature and contributed to an enduring vision of romance.*

Source: Trans. John Jay Parry in Andreas Capellanus, *The Art of Courtly Love* (New York: Columbia University Press, 1990), pp. 27-36, 141-50; reprinted with permission.

I am greatly impelled by the continual urging of my love for you, my revered friend Walter, to make known by word of mouth and to teach you by my writings the way in which a state of love between two lovers may be kept unharmed and likewise how those who do not love may get rid of the darts of Venus that are fixed in their hearts. You tell me that you are a new recruit of Love, and, having recently been wounded by an arrow of his, you do not know how to manage your horse's reins properly and you cannot find any cure for yourself. How serious this is and how it troubles my soul no words of mine can make clear to you. For I know, having learned from experience, that it does not do the man who owes obedience to Venus's service any good to give careful thought to anything except how he may always be doing something that will entangle him more firmly in his chains; he thinks he has nothing good except what may wholly please his love. Therefore, although it does not seem expedient to devote oneself to things of this kind or fitting for any prudent man to engage in this kind of hunting, nevertheless, because of the affection I have for you I can by no means refuse your request; because I know clearer than day that after you have learned the art of love your progress in it will be more cautious, in so far as I can I shall comply with your desire.

Book One. Introduction to the Treatise on Love

We must first consider what love is, whence it gets its name, what the effect of love is, between what persons love may exist, how it may be acquired, retained, increased, decreased, and ended, what are the signs that one's love is returned, and what one of the lovers ought to do if the other is unfaithful.

Chapter 1. What Love Is

Love is a certain inborn suffering derived from the sight of and excessive meditation upon the beauty of the opposite sex, which causes each one to wish above all things the embraces of the other and by common desire to carry out all of love's precepts in the other's embrace.

That love is suffering is easy to see, for before the love becomes equally balanced on both sides there is no torment greater, since the lover is always in fear that his love may not gain its desire and that he is wasting his efforts. He fears, too, that rumors of it may get abroad, and he fears everything that might harm it in any way, for before things are perfected a slight disturbance often spoils them. If he is a poor man, he also fears that the woman may scorn his poverty; if he is ugly, he fears that she may despise his lack of beauty or may give her love to a more handsome man; if he is rich, he fears that his parsimony in the past may stand in his way. To tell the truth, no one can number the fears of one single lover. This kind of love, then, is a suffering which is felt by only one of the persons and may be called "single love." But even after both are in love the fears that arise are just as great, for each of the lovers fears that what he has acquired with so much effort may be lost through the effort of someone else, which is certainly much worse for a man than if, having no hope, he sees that his efforts are accomplishing nothing, for it is worse to lose the things you are seeking than to be deprived of a gain you merely hope for. The lover fears, too, that he may offend his loved one in some way; indeed he fears so many things that it would be difficult to tell them.

That this suffering is inborn I shall show you clearly, because if you will look at the truth and distinguish carefully you will see that it does not arise out of any action; only from the reflection of the mind upon what it sees does this suffering come. For when a man sees some woman fit for love and shaped according to his taste, he begins at once to lust after her in his heart; then the more he thinks about her the more he burns with love, until he comes to a fuller meditation. Presently he begins to think about the fashioning of the woman and to differentiate her limbs, to think about what she does, and to pry into the secrets of her body, and he desires to put each part of it to the fullest use. Then after he has come to this complete meditation, love cannot hold the reins, but he proceeds at once to action; straightway he strives to get a helper and to find an intermediary. He begins to plan how he may find favor with her, and he begins to seek a place and a time opportune for talking; he looks upon a brief hour as a very long year, because he cannot do anything fast enough to suit his eager mind. It is well known that many things happen to him in this manner. This inborn suffering comes, therefore, from seeing and meditating. Not every kind of meditation can be the cause of love, an excessive one is required; for a restrained thought does not, as a rule, return to the mind, and so love cannot arise from it.

Chapter 2. Between What Persons Love May Exist

Now, in love you should note first of all that love cannot exist except between persons of opposite sexes. Between two men or two women love can find no place, for we see that two persons of the same sex are not at all fitted for giving each other the exchanges of love or for practicing the acts natural to it. Whatever nature forbids, love is ashamed to accept.

Every attempt of a lover tends toward the enjoyment of the embraces of her whom he loves; he thinks about it continually, for he hopes that with her he may fulfill all the mandates of love — that is, those things which we find in treatises on the subject. Therefore in the sight of a lover nothing can be compared to the act of love, and a true lover would rather be deprived of all his money and of everything that the human mind can imagine as indispensable to life rather than be without love, either hoped for or attained. For what under heaven can a man possess or own for which he would undergo so many perils as we continually see lovers submit to of their own free will? We see them despise death and fear no threats, scatter their wealth abroad and come to great poverty. Yet a wise lover does not throw away wealth as a prodigal spender usually does, but he plans his expenditures from the beginning in accordance with the size of his patrimony; for when a man comes to poverty and want he begins to go along with his face downcast and to be tortured by many thoughts, and all joyousness leaves him. And when that goes, melancholy comes straightway to take its place, and wrath claims a place in him; so he begins to act in a changed manner toward his beloved and to appear frightful to her, and the things that cause love to increase begin to fail. Therefore love begins to grow less, for love is always either decreasing or increasing. I know from my own experience that when poverty comes in, the things that nourished love begin to leave, because "poverty has nothing with which to feed its love."

But I do not tell you this, my friend, with the idea of indicating by what I say that you should follow avarice, which, as all agree, cannot remain in the same dwelling with love, but to show you that you should by all means avoid prodigality and should embrace generosity with both arms. Note, too, that

LOVE, MARRIAGE, & FAMILY IN THE MIDDLE AGES: A READER

nothing which a lover gets from his beloved is pleasing unless she gives it of her own free will.

Chapter 3. Where Love Gets Its Name

Love gets its name (*amor*) from the word for hook (*amus*), which means "to capture" or "to be captured," for he who is in love is captured in the chains of desire and wishes to capture someone else with his hook. Just as a skillful fisherman tries to attract fishes by his bait and to capture them on his crooked hook, so the man who is a captive of love tries to attract another person by his allurements and exerts all his efforts to unite two different hearts with an intangible bond, or if they are already united he tries to keep them so forever.

Chapter 4. What the Effect of Love Is

Now it is the effect of love that a true lover cannot be degraded with any avarice. Love causes a rough and uncouth man to be distinguished for his handsomeness; it can endow a man even of the humblest birth with nobility of character; it blesses the proud with humility; and the man in love becomes accustomed to performing many services gracefully for everyone. O what a wonderful thing is love, which makes a man shine with so many virtues and teaches everyone, no matter who he is, so many good traits of character! There is another thing about love that we should not praise in few words: it adorns a man, so to speak, with the virtue of chastity, because he who shines with the light of one love can hardly think of embracing another woman, even a beautiful one. For when he thinks deeply of his beloved the sight of any other woman seems to his mind rough and rude.

I wish you therefore to keep always in mind, Walter my friend, that if love were so fair as always to bring his sailors into the quiet port after they had been soaked by many tempests, I would bind myself to serve him forever. But because he is in the habit of carrying an unjust weight in his hand, I do not have full confidence in him any more than I do in a judge whom men suspect. And so for the present I refuse to submit to his judgment, because "he often leaves his sailors in the mighty waves." But why love, at times, does not use fair weights I shall show you more fully elsewhere in this treatise.

Chapter 5. What Persons Are Fit For Love

We must now see what persons are fit to bear the arms of love. You should know that everyone of sound mind who is capable of doing the work of Venus may be wounded by one of Love's arrows unless prevented by age, or blindness, or excess of passion. Age is a bar, because after the sixtieth year in a man and the fiftieth in a woman, although one may have intercourse his passion cannot develop into love; because at that age the natural heat begins to lose its force, and the natural moisture is greatly increased, which leads a man into various difficulties and troubles him with various ailments, and there are no consolations in the world for him except food and drink. Similarly, a girl under the age of twelve and a boy before the fourteenth year do not serve in love's army. However, I say and insist that before his eighteenth year a man cannot be a true lover, because up to that age he is overcome with embarrassment over any little thing, which not only interferes with the perfecting of love, but even destroys it if it is well perfected. But we find another even more powerful reason, which is that before this age a man has no constancy, but is changeable in every way, for such a tender age cannot think about the mysteries of love's realm. Why love should kindle in a woman at an earlier age than in a man I shall perhaps show you elsewhere.

Blindness is a bar to love, because a blind man cannot see anything upon which his mind can reflect immoderately, and so love cannot arise in him, as I have already shown. But I admit that this is true only of the acquiring of love, for I do not deny that a love which a man acquires before his blindness may last after he becomes blind.

An excess of passion is a bar to love, because there are men who are slaves to such passionate desire that they cannot be held in the bonds of love — men who, after they have thought long about some woman or even enjoyed her, when they see another woman straightway desire her embraces, and they forget about the services they have received from their first love and they feel no gratitude for them. Men of this kind lust after every woman they see; their love is like that of a shameless dog. They should rather, I believe, be compared to asses, for they are moved only by that low nature which shows that men are on the level of the other animals rather than by that true nature which sets us apart from all the other animals by the difference of reason. Of such lovers I shall speak elsewhere.

Chapter 6. In What Manner Love May Be Acquired, and in How Many Ways

It remains next to be seen in what ways love may be acquired. The teaching of some people is said to be that there are five means by which it may be acquired: a beautiful figure, excellence of character, extreme readiness of speech, great wealth, and the readiness with which one grants that which is sought. But we hold that love may be acquired only by the first three, and we think that the last two ought to be banished completely from Love's court, as I shall show you when I come to the proper place in my system.

A beautiful figure wins love with very little effort, especially when the lover who is sought is simple, for a simple lover thinks that there is nothing to look for in one's beloved besides a beautiful figure and face and a body well cared for. I do not particularly blame the love of such people, but neither do I have much approval for it, because love between uncautious and unskilled lovers cannot long be concealed, and so from the first it fails to increase. For when love is revealed, it does not help the lover's worth, but brands his reputation with evil rumors and often causes him grief. Love between such lovers seldom lasts; but if sometimes it should endure it cannot indulge in its former solaces, because when the girl's chaperone hears the rumors, she becomes suspicious and watches her more carefully and gives her no opportunities to talk, and it makes the man's relatives more careful and watchful, and so serious unfriendliness arises. In such cases, when love cannot have its solaces, it increases beyond all measure and drives the lovers to lamenting their terrible torments, because "we strive for what is forbidden and always want what is denied us."

A wise woman will therefore seek as a lover a man of praiseworthy character—not one who anoints himself all over like a woman or makes a rite of the care of the body, for it does not go with a masculine figure to adorn oneself in womanly fashion or to be devoted to the care of the body. It was people like this the admirable Ovid meant when he said,

> Let young men who are decked out like women stay far away from me,
> A manly form wants to be cared for within moderate limits.

Likewise, if you see a woman too heavily rouged you will not be taken in by her beauty unless you have already discovered that she is good company besides, since a woman who puts all her reliance on her rouge usually doesn't have any particular gifts of character. As I said about men, so with women—I believe you should not seek for beauty so much as for excellence of character. Be careful therefore, Walter, not to be taken in by the empty beauty of women, because a woman is apt to be so clever and such a ready talker that after you have begun to enjoy the gifts you get from her you will not find it easy to escape loving her. A person of good character draws the love of another person of the same kind, for a well-instructed lover, man or woman, does not reject an ugly lover if the character within is good. A man who proves to be honorable and prudent cannot easily go astray in love's path or cause distress to his beloved. If a wise woman selects as her lover a wise man, she can very easily keep her love hidden forever; she can teach a wise lover to be even wiser, and if he isn't so wise she can restrain him and make him careful. A woman, like a man, should not seek for beauty or care of the person or high birth, for "beauty never pleases if it lacks goodness," and it is excellence of character alone which blesses a man with true nobility and makes him flourish in ruddy beauty. For since all of us human beings are derived originally from the same stock and all naturally claim the same ancestor, it was not beauty or care of the body or even abundance of possessions, but excellence of character alone which first made a distinction of nobility among men and led to the difference of class. Many there are, however, who trace their descent from these same first nobles, but have degenerated and gone in the other direction. The converse of this proposition is likewise true.

Character alone, then, is worthy of the crown of love. Many times fluency of speech will incline to love the hearts of those who do not love, for an elaborate line of talk on the part of the lover usually sets love's arrows a-flying and creates a presumption in favor of the excellent character of the speaker. How this may be I shall try to show you as briefly as I can.

To this end I shall first explain to you that one woman belongs to the middle class, a second to the simple nobility, and a third to the higher nobility. So it is with men: one is of the middle class, another of the nobility, a third of the higher nobility, and a fourth of the very highest nobility. What I mean by a woman of the middle class is clear enough to you; a noblewoman is one descended from a vavasor or a lord, or is the wife of one of these, while a woman of the higher nobility is descended from great lords. The same rules apply to men, except that a man married to a woman of higher or lower rank than himself does not change his rank. A married woman changes her status to match that of her husband, but a man can never change his nobility by marriage. In addition, among men we find one rank more than among women, since there is a man more noble than any of these, that is, the clerk.

Chapter 7. The Love of the Clergy

Now, since in the preceding sections we have dealt with three classes of men: namely, commoners, simple nobility, and the higher nobility, and we recall mentioning at the beginning of the discussion the noblest class of all—that is, the clergy—let us speak briefly concerning their love affairs and see where the men of this fourth class get their nobility. Now the clerk is considered to be of the most noble class by virtue of his sacred calling, a nobility which we agree comes from God's bosom and is granted to him by the divine will, as God tells us himself when he says, "He that touches you touches me," and "He that touches you, touches the apple of my eye." But so far as this nobility goes, a clerk cannot look for love, for on the strength of it he ought not devote himself to the works of love but is bound to renounce absolutely all the delights of the flesh and to keep himself free from all bodily filth, unspotted for the Lord whose service, according to our belief, he has taken upon him. A clerk's nobility, therefore, is not derived from his ancestors, nor can the secular power deprive him of it, but by God's grace alone, as we know, is it granted, and by his gift is it given, and by God alone may the privileges of this kind of nobility be annulled if his commands are violated. So it is very clear that a clerk, so far as concerns the distinction of this clerical nobility, cannot love, and thus it would be improper for me to treat of his love according to the dignity of this rank and the nobility of the order. A clerk ought therefore to be a stranger to every act of love and to put aside all uncleanness of body, or he will deserve to be deprived of this special nobility granted him by God. But since hardly anyone ever lives without carnal sin, and since the life of the clergy is, because of the continual idleness and the great abundance of food, naturally more liable to temptations of the body than that of any other men, if any clerk should wish to enter into the lists of Love let him speak and apply himself to Love's service in accordance with the rank or standing of his parents, as we have already fully explained in regard to the different ranks of men.

Chapter 8. The Love of Nuns

You may be interested enough to ask what we have to say regarding the love of nuns. What we say is that their solaces must be absolutely avoided just as though they were a pestilence of the soul, because from them comes the great wrath of our heavenly Father and the civil authorities are greatly stirred up and threaten the most severe punishments, and by all of this we become infamous among men and our good reputation is destroyed. Even Love's commandment warns us not to choose for our love any woman whom we may not properly seek to marry. And if anybody should think so little of himself and of both laws as to seek for the love of a nun, he would deserve to be despised by everybody and he ought to be avoided as an abominable beast. There is no reason to have any doubt about the faith of a man who for the sake of one act of momentary delight would not fear to subject himself to the death penalty and would have no shame about becoming a scandal to God and men. We should therefore condemn absolutely the love of nuns and reject their solaces just as though they carried the plague. We do not say this with the idea that one cannot love a nun, but because by such love body and soul are condemned to death. Therefore we do not want you to know any words that may be used to solicit them. For one time when we had a chance to speak to a certain nun we spoke so well on the art, not being ignorant of the art of soliciting nuns, that we forced her to assent to our desire; we were smitten with what we may call mental blindness, and wholly forgetting what was seemly (since "no lover ever sees what is seemly" and also "Love does not see anything well, he sees every-thing with his blind eye") we straightway began to be violently attracted by her beauty and captured by her pleasant conversation. But in the meantime we realized the madness that was carrying us away, and with a great effort roused ourselves up from the deadly sleep. And although we consider ourselves very expert in the art of love and well instructed in its cure, we were barely able to avoid her pestilential snares and escape without contamination of the flesh. Be careful therefore, Walter, about seeking lonely places with nuns or looking for opportunities to talk with them, for if one of them should think that the place was suitable for wanton dalliance, she would have no hesitation in granting you what you desire and preparing for you burning solaces, and you could hardly escape that worst of crimes, engaging in the work of Venus. For if the charm of such women forced us, who are experienced in every trick and esteemed for our knowledge of the art of love, to waver, how can your inexperienced youth prevent it? Therefore you should avoid a love of this kind, my friend.

Chapter 9. Love Got with Money

Now let us see whether real love can be got with money or any other gift. Real love comes only from the affection of the heart and is granted out of pure grace and genuine liberality, and this most precious gift of love cannot be paid for at any set price or be cheapened by a matter of money. If any woman is so possessed with a feeling of avarice as to give herself to a lover for the sake of pay, let no one consider her a lover, but rather a counterfeiter of love, who ought to join those shameful women in the brothel. Indeed the wantonness of such women is more polluted than the passion of harlots who ply their trade openly, for they do what one expects them to, and they deceive no one since their intentions are perfectly obvious. But those others who pretend to be fine ladies of the very best breeding force men to languish for love of them, and under the false veil of affection they gleefully rob of all their wealth those who have been smitten by Cupid's arrow. Men are deceived by their fallacious looks, outwitted by their crafty beckonings, and impelled by their clever and deceitful demands; they are kept busy giving them as many good things as they can, and they get more pleasure out of what they give away than from what they keep for their own use. These women have all sorts of ways of asking for things, and so long as they see that a man can respond to their greedy desire for gifts, they say that he is their adored lover, and they never cease to drain away his property or ruin him by their constant demands. But when his substance is gone and his patrimony is exhausted they despise and hate him and cast him aside like an unproductive bee, and then they begin to appear in their real colors. Any man who would seek for the love of women like these ought to be classed with shameless dogs and deserves no help from anybody. It ought therefore to be clear to everyone that the love which seeks for rewards should not be called love by anybody, but rather shameful harlotry and greedy wantonness, which no man's property can satisfy, nor can anybody's generosity mitigate it in the least by giving these women money. Anyone who has a firm manly character ought to exert himself to keep away from the allurements of women like these and to avoid their dangerous frauds. For a woman who is really in love always rejects and hates gifts from her lover, and devotes her efforts to increasing his wealth so that he may always have something he can give away and thereby increase his good name; she does not expect anything from him except the sweet solaces of the flesh and that her fame may increase among all men because he praises her. For a woman thinks that anything that her lover gives to others for her sake and for the sake of acquiring praise benefits her. Even though a woman is in need of a great many things, if she is really in love she thinks it a very serious thing to lessen her lover's property; but the lover, for his part, ought never to permit her to suffer for lack of anything if he can be of any assistance. It is a great disgrace for a lover to allow his beloved to be in need of anything when he himself has plenty. It is never held to the discredit of a woman if in a time of urgent need she accepts gifts from her lover and takes full advantage of his generosity. But when a woman has plenty of money it is enough that for her sake her lover gives gifts to others so far as is seemly.

A woman who you know desires money in return for her love should be looked upon as a deadly enemy, and you should be careful to avoid her like a venomous animal that strikes with its tail and fawns with its mouth. If you are so driven by wantonness of the body that you want to seek paid women, it would be better for you to do business with the women who openly loiter in the brothels and sell their bodies for a small price than to be robbed of your property, under the fiction of love, by some woman who pretends to be a lady, but acts like a strumpet. In such a business he is said to drive the best bargain who gets what he wants at the lowest price, and you get a thing more cheaply when it is offered for sale than when the buyer asks the other to sell. Alas, we grieve because we see the honorable name of ladies profaned by meretricious actions! Therefore let all worthy ladies take up arms when they see their rights usurped by unworthy women, and let them be zealous to avenge such infamous conduct, lest such a ruinous example spread further through the world.

Therefore do not let the distinguished but false outward show of a woman deceive you, or the ancestry of a degenerate woman, whose first enticements are sweeter than any honey, but whose last prove more bitter than gall or wormwood. Whenever you notice a woman reminding you how generous someone else was in showering gifts upon his beloved, or hear her praise someone else's jewelry, or complain that some of her things have been pawned, or, under some pretext or other, ask for a piece of jewelry, you must take good care to guard yourself against her wiles, for she doesn't want to be loved, but to draw money out of you. If nothing else could convince you of the truth of this, the rule of Love which says that love and avarice cannot dwell in the same abode would prove it. For if love does not come from the pure pleasure of giving and is not given without payment, it is not love, but a lying and profane imitation of it.

But although such an agreeable love can rarely be found, because the craving for money debases many women, you should strive with all your might to find a loved one whose faithfulness to you will not be changed if great poverty or misfortune should come upon you. For if you fall in love with a woman who is deceitful and desirous of being made rich, you can never gain her love, but she will deceive you by her foxy tricks; because when for the sake of what she can get out of you she makes you false signs of love, she will be giving you only a breath of empty air, while she leads you on to give her presents. And then your dearest possession will seem very little to give in return for one of those expensive, deceitful nods, and so, taken in by a clever woman, you will be forced to sail to the coast of poverty and will be in all respects an object of contempt. All men throughout the world agree that there is nothing so contemptible as for a man to waste his substance on the work of the flesh and the solace of Venus, and what sort of love it is that is granted for a price can be very clear to you from this book. Therefore, my friend, you should always follow this maxim: whenever you have reason to believe that a woman is interested in piling up the coin, be careful to avoid her in the very beginning and not to involve yourself at all in her snares. For if you try to fall in with what she says in order to find out what her real intention is, you will find yourself foiled by your own plan, because no amount of searching will reveal how she feels and what she means to do until the leech is full of blood and leaves you only half alive with all the blood of your wealth drained off. A wise man's best efforts can hardly find out what is beneath the guile of a deceitful lady-love, for she knows how to color her frauds by so many arts and with so much cleverness that the faithful lover is rarely clever enough to see through them. The ability of a greedy woman is greater than that of the ancient enemy [that is, satan] was when by his shrewdness he cleverly perverted the mind of our first parent. Therefore you should use all your cleverness to see that you are not tripped up by the snares of such a woman, because a woman of that kind does not want to love, but to revel in your wealth. If we wanted to devote ourselves to the reform of such women and to call to mind their lives and their deeds, our span of life would be spent before there was any lack in the abundance of material to write about. We do not say these things with the desire of running down honorable women, but because we want to expose the lives of those who do not blush to bring disgrace upon the military service of a host of honorable women by the way they act, and to profane this service under the pretense of love. God forbid that we should ever wish, or be able, to cast a slur upon the deeds of honorable women, or to run them down in the least in this little book of ours, because it is through them that all the world is induced to do good deeds, the rich increase in wealth, abundant provision is made for the needs of the poor, and the avaricious are brought back again to the path of rectitude and learn the way of generosity. Indeed, since women are able to confer praise, they give the occasion for doing all the good things that are done in the world. Now, Walter, if by continual reading you learn those things which we are telling you with such splendid brevity, it is not likely that you will be overreached by the tricks of a deceitful woman.

Chapter 10. The Easy Attainment of One's Object

Let us see next whether if one attains one's object easily it may lead to love. First we must see what we mean by attaining it easily. We may say it is easily attained when a woman, under the impulse of carnal passion, readily gives herself to a man who asks her and will easily do the same to another who asks, feeling no trace of love when the deed is done, but accepting no pay for it. Do not fall into the toils of such a woman, because you cannot win her love no matter how hard you try. This kind of woman has so much of the spirit of Venus in her that she cannot confine herself to the love of any one man, but she desires to sate her lust with many. Therefore it is idle for you to seek her love unless you know that you are so potent at Venus's trade that you can satisfy her; that would be harder for you to do than to dry up the oceans, so we think that there is good reason for you to have nothing to do with her love. Although you may enjoy her embraces as fully as you wish, her solaces will cause you intolerable pain and will give rise to many woes for you. You can never know, until you have been through it, how bitter will be your grief when, as lovers will, you want to believe that you are the only one to enjoy her solaces, but you know that she has gratified the passion of another man and made you share her with him. From what we have said it should be perfectly clear to you that where you find it easy to attain your desire you may be sure there is no love; for when a woman is so passionate that she cannot confine herself to one man, but desires to gratify the passion of many, there love can find no place at all. For true love joins the hearts of two persons with so great a feeling of delight that they cannot desire to embrace anybody else; on the contrary they take care to avoid the solaces of everybody else as though they were horrible things, and they keep themselves for each other. This readiness to grant requests is, we say, the same thing in women as overvoluptuousness in men—a thing which all agree should be a total stranger in the court of Love. For he who is so tormented by carnal passion that he cannot embrace anyone in heart-felt love, but basely lusts after every woman he sees, is not called a lover but a counterfeiter of love and a pretender, and he is lower than a shameless dog. Indeed the man who is so wanton that he cannot confine himself to the love of one woman deserves to be considered an impetuous ass. It will therefore be clear to you that you are bound to avoid an overabundance of passion and that you ought not to seek the love of a woman who you know will grant easily what you seek.

Chapter 11. The Love of Peasants

But lest you should consider that what we have already said about the love of the middle class applies also to farmers, we will add a little about their love. We say that it rarely happens that we find farmers serving in Love's court, but naturally, like a horse or a mule, they give themselves up to the work of Venus, as nature's urging teaches them to do. For a farmer hard labor and the uninterrupted solaces of plough and mattock are sufficient. And even if it should happen at times, though rarely, that contrary to their nature they are stirred up by Cupid's arrows, it is not expedient that they should be instructed in the theory of love, lest while they are devoting themselves to conduct which is not natural to them the kindly farms which are usually made fruitful by their efforts may through lack of cultivation prove useless to us. And if you should, by some chance, fall in love with some of their women, be careful to puff them up with lots of praise and then, when you find a convenient place, do not hesitate to take what you seek and to embrace them by force. For you can hardly soften their outward inflexibility so far that they will grant you their embraces quietly or permit you to have the solaces you desire unless first you use a little compulsion as a convenient cure for their shyness. We do not say these things, however, because we want to persuade you to love such women, but only so that, if through lack of caution you should be driven to love them, you may know, in brief compass, what to do.

Chapter 12. The Love of Prostitutes

Now in case anybody should ask how we feel about the love of prostitutes we say that they are all to be shunned absolutely, because it is most shameful to have dealings with them, and with them one almost always falls into the sin of lewdness. Besides, a prostitute seldom gives herself to anyone until she has been given a present that pleases her. Even if it should happen once in a while that a woman of this kind does fall in love, all agree that her love is harmful to men, because all wise men frown upon having familiar intercourse with prostitutes, and to do so spoils anybody's good name. Therefore we have no desire to explain to you the way to gain their love, because whatever the feeling that makes them give themselves to a suitor they always do so without much urging, so you don't need to ask for instructions on this point.

What role do sight, the mind, and reflection play in love? Where does love exist? Why is it impossible for love to exist between people of the same sex? What kind of people are suitable for love? What is the difference for clerics and for nuns to love? What role does physical beauty play in love? What are the economic relations between lovers? the physical relations? What ideas and values about women dominate in the discussion? How do age and social status affect one's ability to love? How does the author define nobility? What does he say about love between people of different social ranks? What areas of the discussion betray a double standard of conduct?

13. TROUBADOUR LOVE POETRY

The development of a trend toward highly idealized courtly love can, in large part, be attributed to the troubadour poets. The troubadours flourished in the last half of the twelfth century but their influence extended through the thirteenth century and beyond. The troubadours wrote their songs in Old Provençal, to be sung at the courts of the great lords. They were initially found in southern France and northern Spain and Italy, but their influence rapidly spread across Europe, helped by patrons such as Eleanor of Aquitaine, who brought troubadours with her from Provence to the courts of the kings of France and England. The following two songs (cansos) were written by Bernart de Ventadorn (ca. 1145-1180), one of the best known and most frequently imitated of the troubadours. Bernart's songs are remarkable for their language, images, and emotions. As was typical of troubadour lyrics, they were written in the first person, purporting to convey the poet's own story.

Source: Trans. Samuel N. Rosenberg, Margaret Switten, and Gérard Le Vot, *Songs of the Troubadours and Trouvères* (New York: Garland, 1998), pp. 64-65, 68-69; reprinted with permission.

It is No Marvel that I Sing

It is no marvel that I sing
Better than any other singer,
For my heart draws me more towards love
And I am better made for its command.
Heart and body, knowledge and sense,
Force and power have I placed in it.
The rein so leads me towards love
That elsewhere I do not turn my attention.

He is certainly dead who feels not of love
Within his heart the sweet taste.
And what is the use of living without merit
Except to annoy people?
May God not so hate me
That I may live a day or a month
After I am guilty of being a nuisance
Or have no desire of love.

In good faith and without deceit
I love the fairest and the best;
From the heart I sigh and from the eyes weep
Because I love her so much it brings me pain.

What more can I do if Love seizes me,
And the prison in which it has put me
No key can open except mercy,
And I find no mercy there?

This love wounds me so gently
In the heart with a sweet savor;
A hundred times a day I die of grief,
And revive with joy another hundred.
Truly my anguish is of fine appearance.
And my anguish is worth more than any good;
And since my anguish seems so good to me,
Good will be the reward after suffering.

Ah God, if only one could distinguish
True lovers from among the false,
And if only slanderers and deceivers
Wore horns on their foreheads.
All the gold and silver in the world
I would have given, if I had it,
Provided my lady might know
How truly I love her.

When I see her, it certainly shows
In my eyes, my face, my color,
For I tremble with fear
Like the leaf in the wind.
I haven't the judgment of a child,
So overwhelmed am I by love,
And toward a man who is thus vanquished,
A lady could show great pity.

Fair lady, I ask you nothing
Except that you take me as your servant,
For I will serve you as a good lord,
Whatever the reward.
See me now at your command,
Noble figure, humble, gay and courtly.
You are not a bear or a lion
That you would kill me if I give myself to you.

A nineteenth-century depiction of a trouvère writing love songs.

To my *Cortes*, wherever she is,
I send the song, and never may it grieve her
That I have been away so long.

When I See the Lark Beating

When I see the lark beating
His wings, for joy, against the sun's ray
Until he forgets to fly and lets himself fall
For the sweetness which goes to his heart,
Alas! such great envy comes over me
Of those whom I see rejoicing,
I marvel that at once
My heart does not melt from desire.

Alas! I thought I knew so much
About love, and I know so little!
For I cannot keep myself from loving

Her from whom I shall have no good.
She has stolen my heart, and stolen my self,
And herself and all the world;
And when she took herself away, she left me nothing
Except desire and a longing heart.

Never have I had power over myself
Or belonged to myself from the very hour
That she let me see into her eyes,
Into a mirror that pleases me greatly.
Mirror, since I mirrored myself in you,
Deep sighs have slain me;
I have destroyed myself just as the beautiful
Narcissus destroyed himself in the fountain.

I despair of ladies;
No more will I trust them;
And just as I used to defend them
Now I shall abandon them.
Since I see that none aids me
Against her who destroys and confounds me,
I fear and distrust them all,
For well I know that they are all alike.

In this, she surely shows herself to be a woman,
My lady; that is why I reproach her.
For she does not want what one ought to want,
And what one forbids her, she does.
I have fallen into ill favor,
And I have indeed acted like the fool on the bridge;
And I do not know why this happens to me,
Unless I tried to climb too high.

Mercy is lost, truly,
And I never knew it,
For she, who ought to have most of it,
Has none, and where shall I seek it?
Ah! how terrible it appears, to one looking at her,
That this poor, love-sick wretch,
Who will never have good without her,
She allows to perish, without helping him.

Since with my lady nothing avails me,
Neither prayers nor pity nor the rights I have,
And since to her it is no pleasure
That I love her, never shall I tell her again.
Thus I leave her and give up.
She has slain me, and by death I shall answer,
And I go away, since she does not retain me,
Wretched, into exile, I know not where.

Tristan, you will have nothing more from me,
For I depart, wretched, I know not where.
I forsake and give up singing,
And I hide myself from joy and love.

What is the role of suffering in love? How does love influence or change the poet? How does the poet characterize the lady? What does he want from her? What are the features of a love relationship? How do these poems reflect the ideology of courtly love?

14. GOLIARDIC LOVE SONGS

The Goliards were the wandering students who roamed northern Europe in the twelfth and thirteenth centuries, moving from town to town, university to university. These students were characterized as the followers of the fictional Golias. Although nominally clerics, the students were best known for gambling, drinking, and riotous behavior. Given their education, it is not surprising that goliard poetry was written in Latin. However, despite the use of the language of education and scholarship, goliard poetry was irreverent and satirical, promoting the joys of drink, dice, and sexual liaisons. While the names of some of the goliard poets are known, most of the songs circulated anonymously. Many were collected together and the title given to them in one Bavarian manuscript, the Carmina Burana, *has now come to epitomize the wild and carefree life of medieval students. These songs, and their vision of amorous relations between men and women, are far removed from the contemporary songs by the troubadours.*

Source: Trans. George F. Whicher, *The Goliard Poets: Medieval Latin Songs and Satires* (Norfolk, CT.: New Directions, 1949), pp. 163-65, 190-93, 219; reprinted with permission.

Fealty To Venus

Janus rounds the year at full,
Spring announces summer's coming;
The sun's bright wain, with hot hoofs drumming,
Rolls in the region of the Bull
Beyond the Ram's domain.

Love conquers all—the proud, the fierce:
There is no mail Love cannot pierce.

Then put regrets away!
Sweet joys, we own your sway:
Venus keeps holiday
With all her pupils.
Mirth is the patrimony
Of those who serve Dione:
Then laugh and banish scruples.

While I still wore Wisdom's colors,
I was fain with Venus' scholars
At her school to make repair,
But of all the maidens there

Only one I saw was fair,
Featly formed, with Helen's features,
Most goddess-like of mortal creatures,
Full of charms that strike the eye,
But loveliest in her modesty.

Unique is my passion
For one so unique:
A fire of new fashion
That never turns ashen —
Its rage is not weak.
And where could one seek
A girl more magnanimous,
Free from all animus,
Lovely and lovable,
Full of docility
Joined to stability
Firm and immovable?

To see her joys
Delights me best;
Were I her choice,
Then truly I'd be blest.

Love overcomes both great and small,
Love rules, for Love is lord of all.

Boy Cupid, spare a boy!
And, Venus, grant me joy:
Keep my fire
Mounting higher,
Let it not die, the flame I foster,
Nor let her prove a Daphne, over coy,
For me to love like Phoebus when I've lost her.

Once, long since, Wisdom was my god;
Now Love, I yield, I kiss thy rod.

Flowering Time

The time draws near for flowers to spring,
Birds appear and sing and sing,
Earth now comforts everything.
Ah, my dear! well I see
Love has little joy for me.

Not to think of, not to tell—
For a while I hid my fear,
And I loved, I loved too well.
Now my fault must all be clear,
For I feel my body swell;
Childbed and its pangs are near.

For this my mother rates me,
For this my father hates me;
Both do their best to hurt me.
I sit at home outlawed,
I dare not stir abroad,
Nor anywhere divert me.

When in the street I venture out,
People stare that meet me
As if a monster walked about.
Each notes my shape, and judges;
One man another nudges,
And no one cares to greet me.

Nudging elbow so loose-jointed,
Finger always my way pointed,
Am I such a holy show?
Wagging head and curling lip,
Death's too good for me, *you* know,
Just because of one small slip.

Where shall I go, I alone,
I a byword now become
In the mouths of all and some?
What more can I know of grieving
Since my own true love is leaving

Till the storm be overblown?

From my father's countenance
He has fled to farthest France,
Leaving me alone to face
All the gibes, all the disgrace.
In despair I could die,
And I cry and cry and cry.

Sweet Fire Within

The time is ripe for pleasure,
O maidens, leave your chores,
Come, squire them to the revels,
You lusty bachelors.

Sing O, sing O, as forth I go,
From top to toe so blooming!
Fresh fires are all consuming:
A new, new love is dooming
My total overthrow.

The nightingale, O listen!
Melodiously yearns,
And long the cadence echoes ....
The fire within me burns.

She is the flower of maidens
On whom my love is set,
A rose, a queen of roses;
Often our eyes have met.

Could I but win her promise,
There I could find content;
But should her lips refuse me,
O worse than banishment!

Her maiden charms entice me
To take my joy of her;
Her innocence forbids me
To make a toy of her.

O nightingale, be silent,
A moment stint your woe,
That my heart's canticle of love
May rise and overflow.

For winter now is ended,
The season grim and gray,
And the new zest of springtime
Disposes man to play.

Then, darling, come—have pity!
My joy—O grant it soon.
Come to me, come, my pretty,
For want of you I swoon.

What does the poet want from the woman he loves? What are the consequences of love for the woman?

15. VERNACULAR SONGS OF LOVE

French Love Songs

These anonymous love songs were written in the vernacular in France in the twelfth and thirteenth centuries. They are of a more popular origin than those written by the troubadours or the goliard poets. Consequently, they illustrate ideas about love and courtship found among the average people rather than the troubadours' carefully crafted idealization of love or the irony of the goliards. These lyrics also provide insights into daily life and allow glimpses of how courtships might have been conducted and marriages arranged.

Source: Trans. Claude Colleer Abbott, *Early Mediaeval French Lyrics* (London: Constable, 1932), pp. 29, 31, 33, 63, 71, 73; reprinted with permission.

> Spinning, fair Amelot began to sing
> Lone in her room, her love remembering,
> And named her love aloud as she did sing;
> Careless she was, her mother listening.
> *'God, to Garin marry me,*
> *My sweet lover.*

> Your lover verily am I, Garin,
> I love you always, and have always loved
> So deep that wanting you I marry none;
> Maiden I'll live for all my days to run.
> *God, to Garin marry me,*
> *My sweet lover.*

> I slay myself if other he shall be
> Or I shall do what loving counsels me;
> If not Garin, or this or that 'twill be.
> God banish all these woes, and give him me.
> *God, to Garin marry me,*
> *My sweet lover.*

> Pity this maiden, God, O pity me,
> Let Garin my espoused husband be.
> I kill myself should other wed with me,
> And to die thus would shame me wretchedly.'
> *God, to Garin marry me,*
> *My sweet lover.*

Her mother enters, sits in front of her —
'Girl, choose for husband' — so she counsels her —
'Either Count Henri or the duke Gerairt.'
'Mother, i'faith, from here I would not stir.
God, to Garin marry me,
My sweet lover.

Mother, truly, to marry I have doubt:
That is a bargain many weep about,
For should he love me not, and my love's out,
With him to shame and sorrow I'll be vowed.
God, to Garin marry me,
My sweet lover.

This marriage is a text none dares gainsay
Nor will repentance wash the bond away,
It must be suffered, be it dark or gay;
Who weds amiss, she treads a dolorous way.'
God, to Garin marry me,
My sweet lover.

'Fie daughter, oft your father's angered grim
Because of it.' 'Mother, 'tis grievous sin.
You hate me when you strive so sharp to win
My wedding, and to drive me from my kin.'
God, to Garin marry me,
My sweet lover.

When Amelot heard what her mother said,
How that her father wished to see her wed,
Then tears she silently began to shed
And uttered once a cry; her heart was dead.
God, to Garin marry me,
My sweet lover.

Down by her mother Amelot swooning slid;
God, how her mother's heart was sad of it!
Weeping, her daughter tenderly she kissed,
Coaxed her with soothing words to stand uprist.
God, to Garin marry me,
My sweet lover.

The mother sees her child with grief bested;
Nobly she murmurs, 'Girl, be comforted.
Garin you love, with Garin you shall wed
So help me God, his worth is not gainsaid.'
God, to Garin marry me,
My sweet lover.

Her mother sends command Garin the bold,
Gives him great wealth of silver and fine gold,
Soon his lord Lancelin's fair leave is told,
And lover and beloved are fast consoled.
Amelot won Garin so
Her sweet lover.

* * *

'Twas Tuesday we went playing
In a wood beside Béthune,
My love and I lone straying
All night beneath the moon,
Until dawn broke
And the lark awoke
Singing, 'Lover, let us go.'
And he whispered low
'It is not day,
My sweetheart smooth and white;
Love bid me stay!
The lark has lied.'

Then he drew closer next me
And I was no way prim;
A good three times he kissed me
I more than once kissed him
First wooed me now,
And we wished to vow
This night should be five score
And he should sigh no more
'It is not day,
My sweetheart smooth and white;
Love bid me stay!
The lark has lied.'

* * *

The pleasant pangs that stir my heart,
How shall I cure them?

The villein never goes to buy
At market, nor to bargain sly,
But for to keep his wife in eye
Lest any horn him.
The pleasant pangs that stir my heart,
How shall I cure them?

Villein, because you treat me ill,
Because your rancid breath must kill
Henceforth your love and my love will
Divided journey.
The pleasant pangs that stir my heart,
How shall I cure them?

Villein, and did you think to hold
Both lady fair and fortune bold?
Your portion is a penance cold,
The joy my lover's.
God in my heart the sweet pangs dart,
How shall I cure them?

* * *

My lover dear, I tell it you,
Our enemies say things untrue.

Because I am a dark haired may,
A damsel dark, a damsel young,
I was not born to say men nay
And make a many shifts at love.
The slanderers have injured us
Speaking of us two thus and thus.
My lover dear, I tell it you,
Our enemies say things untrue.

My husband, he may threaten me,
And say that he will beat me too;
Whatever he may do to me
My heart will never perjure you,
But I will love you day and night
As lady should her loyal knight.
My lover dear, I tell it you,
Our enemies say things untrue.

German Love Songs

The influence of the troubadours and the values of courtly love spread across Europe. In the late twelfth and thirteenth centuries, the Minnesingers (love-singers) flourished in Germanic lands, especially in Bavaria. The most notable Minnesinger was the brilliant lyricist Walter von der Vogelweide (ca. 1170-1230). In particular, his Under the Lindentree *has had an enduring influence.*

Source: Trans. Michael Benedikt, "Under the Lindentree," and Kenneth Oliver, "When the Flowers up Through the Grass are Springing," in *Mediaeval Age: Specimens of European Poetry from the Ninth to the Fifteenth Century*, ed. Angel Flores (London: J.M. Dent and Sons, 1963), pp. 142, 144; reprinted with permission.

Under the Lindentree

Under the lindentree
on the heather
there our bed for two was
and there too
you may find blossoms grasses
picked together
in a clearing of a wood
tandaradei!
the nightingale sang sweetly.

I came walking
over the field:
my love was already there.
Then I was received
with the words "Noble lady!"
It will always make me happy.
Did he kiss me? He gave me thousands!
tandaradei!

O look at my red mouth.
He had made
very beautifully
a soft bed out of flowers.
Anybody who comes by there
knowlingly
may smile to himself.
For by the upset roses he may see
tandaradei!
where my head lay.

If anyone were to know
how he lay with me
(may God forbid it!), I'd feel such shame.
What we did together
may no one ever know
except us two
one small bird excepted
tandaradei!
and it can keep a secret.

When the Flowers Up Through the Grass Are Springing

When the flowers up through the grass are springing,
with laughter to the playful sun replying
upon some early morning when it's May;
and the little birds are also singing —
each to give his very best is trying:
What pleasure can compare with such a day?
There's half a Paradise in this.
And shall we name what comparable is?
Then I will say what seemed to be
still better, as it will again when sight of it is granted me.

When a proper, high-born, lovely lady,
nicely dressed, and with her hair bound neatly,
for entertainment goes among the crowd;
not alone she goes, but gracious, haughty,
looking about her here and there discreetly,
as sun among the stars, so she stands out: —
then all its wonder let May bring;

A nineteenth-century depiction of *Minnesingers*. These writers and musicians wrote and popularized love lyrics in German-speaking areas of medieval Europe.

where else is such a lovely thing
as her inspiring form and dress?
From all the flowers we turn away to gaze
upon her loveliness.

Well! Now then, would you see yourself what truth is?
To spring's festivities let us be going,
for May, with all its powers, is in our sight;

Look on the spring, on ladies fair, where youth is,
note whether one the greater joy's bestowing—
see whether I have made my choice aright.
Woe be to him who bade me choose:
to take the one, the other lose—
and yet how quickly I my choice would make!
Sir May, you'll be transformed to March before the ladies
I forsake.

Iberian Love Songs

The Iberian Peninsula, too, was influenced by the troubadours and courtly love. In the thirteenth and fourteenth centuries, particularly in the areas of Galicia and Portugal, writers began to compose vernacular poetry. Some imitated the troubadour cansos, *although new and different genres emerged, including the* cantigas de amigo *(women's poetry), which featured a girl longing for her absent lover or seeking advice from her mother or sister. Particularly adept at this genre was Pero Meogo (Peter the Monk), who flourished in the middle of the thirteenth century.*

Source: Trans. Jean R. Longland in *Mediaeval Age: Specimens of European Poetry from the Ninth to the Fifteenth Century*, ed. Angel Flores (London: J.M. Dent and Sons, 1963), pp. 179-80.

Forlorn Is My Suitor, Mother

—Forlorn is my suitor, mother,
for love has felled him here
and wounded him as the huntsman
wounds the mountain deer.

Forlorn is my suitor, mother,
for love has shot its dart
and wounded him as the huntsman
wounds the mountain hart.

And if his wound goes deeper,
he will sail and die at sea.
This is what will happen
if he cannot hope for me.

—Take good care, my daughter;
I had a suitor too

who feigned such hopeless passion,
my virtue to pursue.

Take good care, my daughter;
a suitor I had too
who feigned such hopeless passion,
my virtue to undo.

Mother I Beg of You

Mother, I beg of you
that you will tell me true:
will my lover dare
to speak while you are there?

He has sent a message to me
and I would like to see:
will my lover dare
to speak while you are there?

I will go and meet him near
the drinking pool of the deer:
will my lover dare
to speak while you are there?

For Fear of You, Mother, That Is Why

For fear of you, mother, that is why
to my promised lover I will lie,
and he will rage if I do not go.

I promised I would meet him near
the drinking pool of the mountain deer,
and he will rage if I do not go.

To lie to him I have no desire,
but for dread of you I will be a liar,
and he will rage if I do not go.

No desire to lie have I
but for fear of you I will have to lie,
and he will rage if I do not go.

What is the relationship between love and marriage? What role did parents play in courtship? in marriage? To what extent do the songs reflect religious values and the church's moral code? How can this be explained? Are there noticeable differences in the sentiments expressed in the poems from different national traditions?

16. ADULTEROUS LOVE: THE STORY OF *EQUITAN*

Marie de France was the first French woman known to have written poetry. Despite signing her poems, little is known about Marie herself and her life. Her poems circulated in the courts of northern Europe in the late twelfth century. Marie brought a specifically feminine perspective to her material, a perspective that sets her work apart from male writers who took courtly love as their subject matter. Her Lais *are short poems which frequently tell stories that explore the crises and complications of love. They specifically highlight issues of sexuality, passion, and fidelity.*

Equitan *presents a didactic and moralistic exploration of the adulterous underpinnings of the courtly love tradition. Exposing courtly love's foundation on betrayal between husband and wife and between men bound by oaths of loyalty, Marie shows unsympathetic characters reaping their just rewards.*

Source: Trans. Robert Hanning and Joan Ferrante, *The Lais of Marie de France* (Durham, NC.: Labyrinth Press, 1978), pp. 60-69; reprinted with permission.

Equitan

Most noble barons
were those Bretons of Brittany.
In the old days they were accustomed, out of bravery,
courtliness, and nobility,
to create *lais* from the adventures they heard,
adventures that had befallen all sorts of people;
they did this as a memorial,
so that men should not forget them.
They made one that I heard —
it should never be forgotten —
about Equitan, a most courtly man,
the lord of Nauns, a magistrate and king.

Equitan was a man of great worth,
dearly loved in his own land.
He loved sport and lovemaking;
and so he kept a body of knights in his service.
Whoever indulges in love without sense or moderation
recklessly endangers his life;
such is the nature of love
that no one involved with it can keep his head.

Equitan had a seneschal,
a good knight, brave and loyal,
who took care of his land for him,
governed and administered it.
Unless the king was making war,
he would never, no matter what the emergency,
neglect his hunting,
his hawking, or his other amusements.
This seneschal took a wife
through whom great harm later came to the land.
She was a beautiful woman
of fine breeding,
with an attractive form and figure.
Nature took pains in putting her together:
bright eyes in a lovely face,
a pretty mouth and a well-shaped nose.
She hadn't an equal in the entire kingdom.
The king often heard her praised.
He frequently sent his greetings to her,
presents as well;
without having seen her, he wanted her,
so he spoke to her as soon as he could.
For his private amusement
he went hunting in the countryside
where the seneschal dwelt;
in the castle, where the lady also lived,
the king took lodging for the night
after he had finished the day's sport.
He now had a good chance to speak to the wife,
to reveal to her his worth, his desires.
He found her refined and clever,
with a beautiful body and face,
and a pleasing, cheerful demeanor.
Love drafted him into his service:
he shot an arrow at the king
that opened a great wound in the heart,
where Love had aimed and fixed it.
Neither good sense nor understanding were of use to the king now;
love for the woman so overcame him
that he became sad and depressed.
Now he has to give in to love completely;

he can't defend himself at all.
That night he can't sleep or even rest,
instead he blames and scolds himself:
"Alas," he says, "what destiny
led me to these parts?
Because I have seen this woman
pain has struck at my heart,
my whole body shivers.
I think I have no choice but to love her—
yet if I love her, I'm doing wrong;
she's the wife of my seneschal.
I owe him the same faith and love
that I want him to give me.
If, by some means, he found out about this
I know how much it would upset him.
Still, it would be a lot worse
if I went mad out of concern for him.
It would be a shame for such a beautiful woman
not to have a lover!
What would become of her finer qualities
if she didn't nourish them by a secret love?
There isn't a man in the world
who wouldn't be vastly improved if she loved him.
And if the seneschal should hear of the affair,
he oughtn't be too crushed by it;
he certainly can't hold her all by himself,
and I'm happy to share the burden with him!"
When he had said all that, he sighed,
and lay in bed thinking.
After a while, he spoke again: "Why
am I do distressed and frightened?
I still don't even know
if she will take me as her lover;
but I'll know soon!
If she should feel the way I do,
I'd soon be free of this agony.
God! It's still so long till morning!
I can't get any rest,
it's been forever since I went to bed."
The king stayed awake until daybreak;
he could hardly wait for it.

He rose and went hunting,
but he soon turned back
saying that he was worn out.
He returns to his room and lies down.
The seneschal is saddened by this;
he doesn't know what's bothering the king,
what's making him shiver;
in fact, his wife is the reason for it.
The king, to get some relief and some pleasure,
sends for the wife to come speak with him.
He revealed his desire to her,
letting her know that he was dying because of her;
that it lay in her power to comfort him
or to let him die.
"My lord," the woman said to him,
"I must have some time to think;
this is so new to me,
I have no idea what to say.
You're a king of high nobility,
and I'm not at all of such fortune
that you should single me out
to have a love affair with.
If you get what you want from me,
I have no doubt about it:
you'll soon get tired of me,
and I'll be far worse off than before.
If I should love you
and satisfy your desire,
love wouldn't be shared equally
between the two of us.
Because you're a powerful king
and my husband is your vassal,
I'm sure you believe
your rank entitles you to my love.
Love is worthless if it's not mutual.
A poor but loyal man is worth more —
if he also possesses good sense and virtue —
and his love brings greater joy
than the love of a prince or a king
who has no loyalty in him.
Anyone who aims higher in love

than his own wealth entitles him to
will be frightened by every little thing that occurs.
The rich man, however, is confident
that no one will steal a mistress away
whose favor he obtains by his authority over her."
Equitan answered her,
"Please, my lady! Don't say such things!
No one could consider himself noble
(rather, he'd be haggling like a tradesman)
who, for the sake of wealth or a big fief,
would take pains to win someone of low repute.
There's no woman in the world—if she's smart,
refined, and of noble character,
and if she places a high enough value on her love
that she isn't inconstant—
whom a rich prince in his palace
wouldn't yearn for
and love well and truly,
even if she'd nothing but the shirt on her back.
Whoever is inconstant in love
and gives himself up to treachery
is mocked and deceived in the end;
I've seen it happen many times like that.
It's no surprise when someone loses out
who deserves to because of his behavior.
My dear lady, I'm offering myself to you!
Don't think of me as your king,
but as your vassal and your lover.
I tell you, I promise you
I'll do whatever you want.
Don't let me die on your account!
You be the lord and I'll be the servant—
you be the proud one and I'll be the beggar!"
The king pleaded with her,
begged her so often for mercy,
that she promised him her love
and granted him possession of her body.
Then they exchanged rings,
and promised themselves to each other.
They kept their promises and loved each other well;
they died for this in the end.

Their affair lasted a long time,
without anyone hearing of it.
At the times set for their meetings,
when they were to speak together at the king's palace,
the king informed his followers
that he wanted to be bled privately.
The doors of his chamber were closed,
and no one was so daring,
if the king didn't summon him,
that he would ever enter there.
Meanwhile, the seneschal held court
and heard pleas and complaints.
The king loved the seneschal's wife for a long time,
had no desire for any other woman;
he didn't want to marry,
and never allowed the subject to be raised.
His people held this against him,
and the seneschal's wife
heard about it often; this worried her,
and she was afraid she would lose him.
So when she next had the chance to speak to him —
when she should have been full of joy,
kissing and embracing him
and having a good time with him —
she burst into tears, making a big scene.
The king asked
what the matter was,
and the lady answered,
"My lord, I'm crying because of our love,
which has brought me to great sorrow:
you're going to take a wife, some king's daughter,
and you will get rid of me;
I've heard all about it, I know it's true.
And — alas! — what will become of me?
On your account I must now face death,
for I have no other comfort than you."
The king spoke lovingly to her:
"Dear love, don't be afraid!
I promise I'll never take a wife,
never leave you for another.
Believe me, this is the truth:

If your husband were dead,
I'd make you my lady and my queen;
no one could stop me."
The lady thanked him,
said she was very grateful to him;
if he would assure her
that he wouldn't leave her for someone else,
she would quickly undertake
to do away with her lord.
It would be easy to arrange
if he were willing to help her.
He agreed to do so;
there was nothing she could demand of him
that he wouldn't do, if he possibly could,
whether it turned out well or badly.
"My lord," she says, "please
come hunting in the forest,
out in the country where I live.
Stay awhile at my husband's castle;
you can be bled there,
and on the third day after that, take a bath.
My lord will be bled with you
and will bathe with you as well;
make it clear to him—and don't relent—
that he must keep you company!
I'll have the baths heated
and the two tubs brought in;
his will be so boiling hot
that no man on earth
could escape being horribly scalded
as soon as he sat down in it.
When he's scalded to death,
send for his men and yours;
then you can show them exactly how
he suddenly died in his bath."
The king promised her
that he'd do just as she wished.
Less than three months later,
the king went out into the countryside to hunt.
He had himself bled to ward off illness,
and his seneschal bled with him.

On the third day, he said he wanted to bathe;
the seneschal was happy to comply.
"Bathe with me," said the king,
and the seneschal replied, "Willingly."
The wife had the baths heated,
the two tubs brought;
next to the bed, according to plan,
she had them both set down.
Then she had boiling water brought
for the seneschal's tub.
The good man got up
and went outside to relax for a moment.
His wife came to speak to the king
and he pulled her down beside him;
they lay down on her husband's bed
and began to enjoy themselves.
They lay there together.
Because the tub was right before them,
they set a guard at the bedroom door;
a maidservant was to keep watch there.
Suddenly the seneschal returned,
and knocked on the door; the girl held it closed.
He struck it so violently
that he forced it open.
There he discovered the king and his own wife
lying in each other's arms.
The king looked up and saw him coming;
to hide his villainy
he jumped into the tub feet first,
stark naked.
He didn't stop to think what he was doing.
And there he was scalded to death,
caught in his own evil trap,
while the seneschal remained safe and sound.
The seneschal could see very well
what had happened to the king.
He grabbed his wife at once
and thrust her head first into the tub.
Thus both died,
the king first, the wife after him.
Whoever wants to hear some sound advice

can profit from this example:
he who plans evil for another
may have that evil rebound back on him.
It all happened just as I've told you.
The Bretons made a *lai* about it,
about Equitan, his fate,
and the woman who loved him so much.

What aspects of the ideology of courtly love are found in this story? How does Equitan justify his adulterous thoughts? How do issues of differing rank and social status influence the plot? How does the understanding of this difference vary according to whether one is a man or a woman? How does the story of Equitan undercut other images of courtly love?

17. A DEBATE ABOUT LOVE AND MARRIAGE: *THE OWL AND THE NIGHTINGALE*

The poem The Owl and the Nightingale, *written some time in the late twelfth century in English, presents a debate between two birds, each representing a different value system. It is considered to be the best early English poem of a didactic nature. It is not known who wrote it although perhaps the author was Master Nicholas, whom the birds choose to be their judge. The poem was most likely written during the reign of King Henry II, as part of the vernacular culture that flourished at his court.*

In the poem, the Nightingale represents the ideas found in contemporary courtly love literature. In contrast, the Owl presents the conventional morality of the church. The debate highlights three main topics. The first two focus on religious attitudes and questions pertaining to fortune and astrology; the third and most important section of the poem is a debate on love and marriage. The Owl, representing traditional morality, criticizes adultery and praises monogamous marriage. The Nightingale, on the other hand, presents the more frivolous, secular perspective that excuses, if not condones courtly love and extramarital affairs. The ideas in the poem may reflect a certain tension that existed in society between these two value systems. The Owl is not uncompromisingly doctrinaire, however, and she roundly condemns bad husbands and displays remarkable understanding for neglected wives. On her part, the Nightingale rejects adultery, while presenting a sympathetic view of women in love. Thus, there is in the poem a move toward reconciling the two disparate perspectives on love. In the end, after each bird has made her case, the poem breaks off, leaving the reader to decide which argument is more persuasive.

Source: Trans. J.W.H. Atkins, *The Owl and the Nightingale* (Cambridge: University of Cambridge Press, 1922), pp. 152, 155, 169-78; modernized; reprinted with permission.

In a remote part of a certain valley I heard an Owl and a Nightingale hold a great debate. Their dispute was stern and strenuous and stubborn: quiet at times, then loud again. Each bird raged against the other, uttering many a malicious thought: each one spoke of the other's character the worst things that she could devise. But above all, they made their complaints of each other's singing: and this they did in downright terms.

The Nightingale began the pleading, in the corner of a copse, seated on a twig that was rich with blossom, in a close thick hedge with reeds and sedge entangled. Rejoicing she sang with many a trill and quaver, so that her notes seemed to come from harp or pipe—from harp or pipe, not from living throat.

Near by there stood an old tree-stump, where the Owl was accustomed to sing her "hours." It was all overgrown with ivy, and was the dwelling-place of the Owl....

"But," said the Owl: "Who is there to settle our difference? Who can and will give lawful judgment?" "I know well," the Nightingale answered, "of that there need be no discussion. Master Nicholas of Guildford is the man: for he is wise and cautious of speech, prudent as well in giving judgment, and an enemy to vice of every kind. Then, too, he has taste in matters of song: he knows who sings well, and who sings badly. He can distinguish the wrong from the right, the things of darkness from things of the light."

The Owl for a time pondered on this, and at length she replied as follows: "I am willing that he should judge: for although somewhat wild in days gone by—fond of the nightingales, and other creatures, too, gentle and neat—I know that now his ardor is cooled. He will not be fooled by you, so that, for old time's sake, he may prefer your cause to mine. You are unable so to please him, that for your sake he will utter false judgment. Now he is settled and steady of mind: follies for him have no attraction. He delights no longer in flighty ways: he will adopt the course that is straight." ...

The Owl was now angry, ready for strife: and after this speech she rolled her eyes. "You say that you guard the dwellings of men where there are leaves and flowers that are fair: and where two lovers lie in bed, well protected in each other's arms. Once you sang—I know well where—near to a dwelling. You told the lady of unlawful love: and, with song high and low, you taught her to indulge a shameful and evil passion. Her lord, soon seeing how things were, set bird-lime and snares, and many other things in order to capture you: and quickly you came to the casement. You were caught in a trap: your shins paid you out: and the doom decreed was none other than that you should be torn asunder by wild horses. Try again, then, if you can, to seduce either wife or maid: your singing, indeed, may prove so successful, that you shall flutter helplessly in a snare!"

The Nightingale, on hearing this, would have attacked with sword and spear, had she but been a man: but since she could do nothing better, she took as her weapon her prudent tongue. "He fights well who talks well," so the song runs: and to her tongue she looked for help. "He fights well who talks well," as Alfred said.

"What!" exclaimed the Nightingale, "do you say this to put me to shame? But the husband in the end had the worst of it. He was so jealous of his wife, that, to save his life, he could not bear to see a man speak with her, but his heart would break. He therefore locked her up in a certain dwelling—to her, a harsh and bitter treatment. And I had pity and compassion for her: I felt sorry for her trouble, and amused her with my singing as much as I could, singing early and singing long. And that was why the knight was angry with me: he hated me out of sheer spite. He thrust on me his own disgrace, but it all turned to his own injury. King Henry got to know of this—may Christ have mercy on his soul! Then did he outlaw the knight, who, through sheer spite and envy foul, had behaved so badly in that good king's land, as to have the little bird taken and condemned to death. That was an honor to all my kind: for the knight immediately forfeited his happiness, and paid a fine of a hundred pounds. And, ever since, my birds have lived unharmed: they have lived in happiness and in joy, and have been of good cheer—as well they might. Thus was I so well avenged, that, ever since then, I speak more boldly; for since it happened so on one occasion, I am the blither ever more. And now I can sing wherever I want: nor dare any man annoy me. But as for you, you miserable thing! you ghastly object! you cannot find, you don't know of, a single hollow tree in which to hide and so save your skin. For girls and boys, masters and men, all are keen on hurting you. If they but see you sitting quiet, they put stones in their pockets, and they pelt you, and ill-treat you, and break your ugly bones to pieces. If you are knocked over, or perhaps, shot, then for the first time you are useful. For then you are hung upon a stick: and with your grim and baggy body, and that hideous neck of yours, you protect the cornfields from all animals. Alive and full-blooded, you are useless: but as a scarecrow, you are excellent. For where new seeds have been sown, there neither hedge-sparrow nor goldfinch, rook nor crow will ever venture, if your carcass hangs by. And where trees shall bloom in the spring-time, and young seeds burst forth and grow, there no bird dares venture to pluck them, if you are hanging overhead. All your life you are sordid and vile: you are useless except when dead. Now, indeed, you know the truth, that in life your appearance is frightening: even when you are hanging dead, the birds that before cried out against you, still remain in terror of you. And rightly, too, are men hostile to you: for you always sing of their troubles. All that you sing, early or late, has to do with the misfortunes of men: and after you have cried out at night, men are mortally afraid of you. You sing where someone is going to die: you foretell some disaster. You sing before the loss of property, or at the ruin of a friend. Or else you foretell a house burning down, an invasion, or the pursuit of a thief. You also predict a cattle-plague, that neighbors will suffer much distress, that a wife, again, shall lose her husband: or you prophesy strife and disputes. Always you sing of the troubles of men: through these they become both sad and miserable. Never at anytime do you sing except of some disaster or other. And this is the reason why you are shunned, why you are pelted and beaten with sticks and with stones, with turf and clods, so that no way of escape is left open for you. Bad luck to such a herald among men, who is ever proclaiming futile secrets, bringing continually unwelcome tidings, and always telling of unlucky things! May the wrath of God Almighty and of all decent folk descend upon him!"

The Owl lost no time in making a rejoinder, stern and vigorous. "What!" she exclaimed, "are you of priestly rank? Or do you excommunicate, not being ordained? For the priestly office you are surely performing. I am not aware that you were ever a priest: I doubt if you can really sing mass, though you know much of the church's curse. It is because of your ancient malice that you have cursed me this second time: and to this curse I can easily reply. 'Go to!' as the carter said. Why do you twit me with my foreknowledge, my understanding, and my power? For most certainly I have much wisdom and am acquainted with all that the future holds. I have foreknowledge of famine and invasion: and I know if men are to have long life. I know, too, whether a wife shall lose her husband: also where malice and vengeance shall be rife. I can tell who is fated to be hanged or to come to some other vile end: and if men come together in battle, I am aware which side will be beaten. I know, also, if a pestilence is to fall on the cattle and whether the wild beasts shall lie still in death. I know if trees shall bear their blossom, if the cornfields also shall yield their increase. I can predict the burning of houses: whether men shall run afoot or proudly ride, I know if ships will founder at sea, and if snow shall bind the earth with harsh fetters. And I know much more as well. I am well skilled in bookish lore: I know more of Holy Writ than I will tell you, for I go often to church and learn much wisdom. I know all the symbolic meanings, and many other things as well. If a man is to undergo the hue-and-cry, I know all about it before it happens. And so, because of my great knowledge, often I sit, sad at heart and perturbed: for when I see trouble approaching men, I cry aloud lustily, bidding them to be wary and to look out for themselves. For Alfred said a wise thing which all men should treasure: 'If you see (trouble) before it comes, it is robbed of almost all its force.' And violent blows become weaker, if one but cautiously takes heed of them; just as an arrow shall miss if you see it fly from the string. For then you may well flinch and jump aside, if you see it heading for you. If any man has fallen into disgrace, why shall he blame me for his trouble? For although I see his trouble coming, it is not my fault that it comes. Or again, if you should see some blind man or other, who, unable to walk straight, pursues his erratic course to a ditch, and falling in it, is covered with mud, do you suppose, although I see it all, that it happens any sooner because of me? And so it is with my foreknowledge: for when I am perched upon my bough, I know and discern very clearly, that on someone trouble is straightway coming. Shall he, therefore, who knows nothing of it, put the blame on me because I know? Shall he upbraid me for his misfortune, simply because I am wiser than he? When I see that some trouble is coming, I call out lustily, bidding men earnestly to be on their guard, because a cruel disaster approaches. But though I exclaim both loudly and quietly, it all comes about by the will of God. Why will men therefore complain about me, even though I annoy them with the truths I tell? For though I warn them all year round, the trouble is no nearer on that account. But to them I sing because I wish them to know, that when my hooting reaches their ears, some misfortune is close at hand. For no man can be sure that he is exempt from the prospect and the fear of approaching trouble, even though he cannot see it. Alfred therefore said very wisely, and his words were gospel truth, that 'every man, the better off he is, the better he must look after himself.' And again: 'Let no man trust too much to his wealth, though he be rich: for there is nothing so hot that it does not grow cool, nothing so white that it does not soil, nothing so beloved that it does not become hateful, nothing so merry that it does not become angry. But everything is not eternal, and all worldly happiness, must pass away.' Now you may clearly see that talk is foolish; for all that you say to my shame, reflects on you to your undoing. However things go, in every bout, you trip yourself up by your own tricks. All that you say to put me to shame, adds to my honor in the end. Unless you make a better beginning, you will win nothing but disgrace for yourself."

The Nightingale, meanwhile, sat still and sighed: anxious was she—and with good reason—seeing how the Owl had spoken and managed her case. She was anxious and much puzzled as to what her reply should be: but nevertheless she collected her thoughts. "What!" she exclaimed, "Owl! are you mad? You are boasting of a strange wisdom, and you were ignorant from where it came, unless it came to you by witchcraft. And of witchcraft, you wretch, you must cleanse yourself, if you are anxious to remain among men: otherwise you must flee the country. For all those, who were skilled in witchcraft, were cursed in the past by the mouth of the priest: as you are still, since you have never forsaken witchcraft. I told you this a short while ago: and you asked in scornful tone, if I were an ordained priest. But it is so common to curse you, that were no priest to be found in the land, you would still be an outlaw. For every child calls you vile, and every man, a despicable owl. I have heard—and true it is—that he who knows rightly what things are coming, as you say is true of you, must be well versed in astrology. But what do you know of the stars, you miserable creature! except that you see of them from afar?—as many a beast and man do, who know nothing about such matters. An ape, for instance, may gaze on a book, turn its pages, and close it again: but it is unable, all the same, to make head or tail of what is written. And though in a similar fashion you gaze at the stars, you are still none the wiser for it. And yet, you vile thing! you chide and reproach me viciously for singing near the dwellings of men and for teaching their wives to break their vows. You lie for certain, you loathsome thing! Wedlock was never harmed by me. Yet I sing and declaim, where ladies and fair maidens be: and true is it also that of love I sing. For a virtuous wife

may, in her married state, love her own husband far better than any philan-
derer: and a maid may take a lover without loss of honor, with true affection
loving him to whom she grants her favor. Such love as this I teach and commend: this is the sense of all my utterances. But if a wife is weak of will—for
women are soft-hearted by nature—so that through the wiles of a fool, who
eagerly entreats her with many a sad sigh, she happens to go astray and do
wrong on occasion, shall I in that case be held to blame? If women love in
foolish ways, am I to be scolded for their misdeeds? Though a woman be bent
on a secret love, I cannot nevertheless refrain from singing. A woman may
frolic as she will—either honestly or viciously: and as a result of my song, she
may do as she will—either well or badly. For there is nothing in the wide
world so good that it may not do evil if turned to wrong uses. Gold and silver,
for instance, are always valuable: yet with them may be bought adultery and
other such crimes. Weapons, again, are useful in keeping the peace: yet men
with them are unlawfully slain in lands where thieves make use of them. And
so it is with my singing: though it be chaste, it may yet be abused and connected with foolish and evil deeds. But must you, wretched creature, speak evil
of love? Of whatever kind it may be, all love is pure between man and woman,
unless it be stolen: for them it is impure and also corrupt. May the wrath of the
Holy Cross descend upon those who thus transgress the laws of nature! Strange
is it that they do not go mad. Yet, indeed, they do: for mad are they who go to
brood without a nest. Woman is but frail of body: and since carnal lust is hard
to crush, it is no wonder that it persists. But though fleshly lusts make women
err, they are not all completely lost, who trip at the stumbling-block of the
flesh. For many a woman, who has gone wrong, rises again out of the slough.
Nor are all sins quite the same: they are, indeed, of two different kinds. One is
the fruit of carnal lust: the other, of the spiritual nature. For whereas the flesh
leads men to drunkenness, to sloth and also to wantonness, the spirit goes
wrong through malice and anger, and through the joy felt at another's shame. It
also longs for more and more, having little regard for mercy and grace: and,
ascending on high through haughtiness, it proudly disdains what is below. Tell
me truly, if you can, which is worse, the flesh or the spirit? You may answer, if
you will, that the flesh is the less evil: for many a man is pure of body, who in
his heart is of devilish nature. No man must therefore cry out at a woman,
upbraiding her for the lusts of the flesh: but such may he blame for wantonness
as indulge in the greater sin of pride. Yet if through my singing I cause wife or
maid to fall in love, I would defend the cause of the maid—if you can grasp
my meaning correctly. Listen now and I'll tell you why—the reason complete
from beginning to end. If a maid loves secretly, she stumbles and falls according
to nature: for though she frolic for a time, she has not gone very far astray.
From her sin she may escape lawfully through the rites of the church, and

afterwards have her lover as husband, free from all questioning: and to him she may go in the full light of day, whom before she had received under cover of darkness. A young maid knows nothing about such things: her young blood leads her astray, and some foolish fellow entices her to evil with all the tricks at his command. He comes and goes, he commands and entreats: he pays her attention, then neglects her, and thus he woos her often and persistently. How can the girl help but go wrong? She never knew what things were: and so she thought to experiment, and learn for certain of the sport that tames high spirits. And when I see the dawn expression which love gives to the young maid, I cannot refrain, out of sheer pity, from singing to her some song of cheer. Thus do I teach them by my singing, that love of this kind does not last long. For my song is but short-lived: and love merely alights upon such girls: it soon passes, and the hot passion quickly subsides. With them I sing for a while: I begin high and end low: and after a time, I cease completely. The maid knows, when I have finished, that love is just like my singing: for it is but a brief excitement that soon comes and soon goes. The girl through me understands things: and her naïvety is turned to wisdom. She sees clearly from my song, that unbridled love does not last long. But I want you to know that I find hateful the lapses of wives. And if a married woman will take heed of me, she will see that I do not sing in the breeding season. Though marriage bonds may seem to be harsh, yet a wife should ignore the teaching of fools. And to me it appears most astounding, how a man could find it in his heart to wrong another's wife. For it means one of two alternatives; there can be no other possibility. Either, on the one hand, the husband is worthy; or else he is feeble and of no account. If he is honored and courageous, no man, who is wise, will wish to shame him, especially through his wife: for he will stand in awe of the good man's anger, and the payment of that penalty which shall deprive him of future longings. And even if that terror is not present, yet it is wicked and senseless in a high degree, to injure in this way a worthy man by alluring his partner away from him. If, on the other hand, the husband is ineffectual, and feeble as well, in all his relations, how could there exist any affection whatsoever, when such a boor makes love to her? How can there be any sort of love, when he lies in bed with her? From this you are able to see clearly, that in one case there is sorrow, in the other, disgrace, as a result of stealing another man's wife. For if the man of courage is her husband, you can look out for trouble when lying by her side. And if the husband be good for nothing, what pleasure can be derived from the deed? If you remember who is her bed-fellow, you may pay for her favors with loathing. I do not know how any man with self-respect may after that make advances to her. If he but thinks by whom he lay, all his love will immediately vanish."

The Owl was glad to hear these words: for she thought that the Nightingale, through arguing well to begin with, had in the end come to grief. And so she exclaimed, "Now do I see that maidens are your special interest: You take their side, defending them and praising them beyond all reason. The married women turn to me: to me they make their complaints: for it happens, often and frequently, that man and wife are at odds. Therefore, that man is guilty of sin, who takes delight in loose living: who spends on a woman all the money he has, making love to one without claim on him, and leaving at home his lawful wife, with bare walls and an empty house, leaving her, too, but thinly clad and poorly fed, without food and without clothing. And when he comes home to his wife again, she dare not utter a single word: he storms and shouts like a madman—and this is all the kindness he brings. All that she does merely annoys him: all that she says is utterly wrong. And often when she does nothing amiss, her reward is a blow from his fist in her teeth. There is no man living who cannot send wrong his wife by such treatment. Such a one may be so often maltreated, that on occasion she may consult her own pleasure. God knows! she cannot help it even if she makes a cuckold of him. For it happens, time and again, that the wife is tender and gentle, fair of face and of good figure: and this but makes it the more unjust that he should shower his love on one who is not worth a hair of her head. And men of this sort are very plentiful, so that a wife is unable to behave properly. Nor may any man speak to her: for he thinks that she is at any moment about to betray him, if she so much as looks at a man or speaks sweetly to him. And so he puts her under lock and key, as a result of which, marriage ties are often broken. For if she is brought to such a pass, she does what before she had not thought of. Accursed be he who talks too much, if such wives proceed to avenge themselves. Concerning this matter, wives complain to me: and sadly enough they grieve me. My heart, indeed, is almost breaking when I see their great distress. With them I weep bitter tears, and pray that Christ shall have mercy on them, so that he may quickly succor the wife, and send to her a better husband. And, moreover, I can tell you this, that to what I have said, you shall find no answer, even to save your skin: for all your talking shall now be futile. Full many a merchant and many a knight loves and cherishes his wife properly; as does many a husband-man too. And then the goodwife behaves accordingly, rendering him service at bed and at board, with gentle deeds and kindly words, anxiously striving how to please him. The husband goes away among other people, bent on supplying the needs of them both: and then is the goodwife sad at heart, because of her husband's anxious journeyings. She sits-a-sighing, full of sad longings, and with sore vexation at her heart. Because of her husband she spends troubled days and watchful nights: and time appears to move slowly to her, for every step seems like a mile. While others around her lie sound asleep, I alone am listening outside the house: for well do I know her sad heart, and I sing at night for her benefit. And for her sake I turn my song partly into mourning. Thus I take a share of her sorrow, and that is why she welcomes me. I give to her what help I can, because she tries to do what is right. But you have greatly angered me, so that my heart is almost crushed, and I can speak only with difficulty. And yet I will continue to press my case. You say that I am hateful to men, that every man is angry with me, and, attacking me with stones and sticks, they beat me and break me all to pieces: and, moreover, when they have slain me, that they hang me high upon their hedges to scare away magpies and also crows, from the seeds that are sown nearby. Though this is true, it is also true that I render them service; for them indeed I shed my blood. I do them good by my death — which for you is very difficult. For although you lie dead and shriveling up, your death nevertheless serves no purpose. I know not in the least what use you are: for you are only a miserable creature. But if the life is shot out of me, yet even so I may do some good. I can be fastened to a small stick in the thick-set of a wood, so that man can attract and capture little birds, and thus obtain through my help roast meat for his food. But neither alive nor dead have you been useful to man. I do not know why you rear your young: neither living nor dead are they any good."

The Nightingale heard what had been said; and hopping onto a twig in blossom, she perched herself higher than before. "Owl!" she said, "now take good heed. I will plead with you no further, since here your usual lore has failed you. You boast that you are hated by men, that every creature is angry with you, and with yells and shouts you bewail that you are accursed. You say that boys catch you and hang you high upon a stick: that they also pluck you and shake you to pieces: while some of them make a scarecrow out of you. To me it seems that you forfeit the game: for you are boasting of your own shame. You appear to be surrendering, for you boast of your own disgrace." When she had spoken, the Nightingale alighted in a lovely spot: and after having tuned her voice, she sang so sweetly and so clearly, that both far and near her song was heard. And therefore presently to her came thrush and throstle and woodpecker, and other birds as well, both great and small. And since they assumed that she had beaten the Owl, they also cried aloud and sang many a tune. In just the same way does one cry shame on the gambler who plays at dice and loses the game.

The Owl, on hearing this, immediately exclaimed: "Have you indeed summoned an army? And do you, wretched creature, wish to fight with me? No! no! you are not strong enough for that. What are they crying who have thus come here? I think you are bringing an army against me. But you all shall learn, before you fly away, what is the strength of my particular tribe. For all

This nineteenth-century depiction idealizes medieval courtly society. Images such as these have contributed to a romaticized view of the Middle Ages.

with hooked bills and claws sharp and crooked, all belong to my own race, and would come if I but asked them. The cock himself, that valiant warrior, he must naturally side with me; for we both have voices clear, and both sit under the clouds at night. If I but raise the hue-and-cry against you, I shall bring up so mighty a host that your pride shall have a fall. I care not a straw for you all! Nor shall there be left by evening one wretched feather among you all. But it was agreed by us both when we came here, that we should abide by that decision, which lawful judgment would give to us. Do you then wish to break this agreement? Judgment, I presume, seems too hard for you: and since you dare not await the verdict, you wish, wretched creature, now to fight and quarrel! Yet I would give you all this piece of advice, before raising the hue-and-cry against you, that you should put an end to your fighting, and fly away quickly and at once. For there is no one among you so brave as to endure the sight of my face." Thus with great boldness the Owl spoke: for although she would not have gone so quickly after her host, yet she wished to reply in these terms. For many a man, feeble enough with spear and shield, yet can cause his foe in the field to sweat out of sheer cowardice; so brave are his words, his countenance so frightening. The Wren, however, because of her skill in singing, came in the morning to the help of the Nightingale: for though her voice was but small, she had a throat that was good and shrill, and her songs were a source of pleasure to many. Moreover she was considered a bird most wise, for although she had not been bred in the woodland, she was brought up among the race of men, and from them she derived her wisdom. She could speak wherever she pleased—before the king if she wished. "Listen!" she said, "and let me speak! What! do you wish to break the peace, and to put the king to this disgrace? But he is neither dead nor infirm; and to both of you shall come trouble and shame, if in his land you commit a breach of the peace. Therefore, finish and come to an agreement! Proceed at once to hear judgment; and let the verdict end this debate, as was arranged at an earlier stage."

"I am quite willing," said the Nightingale, "but not, Mistress Wren, because of your argument, but on account of my own law-abiding nature. I do not want lawlessness to win in the end: nor am I afraid of any judgment. I have promised—true it is—that Master Nicholas, with his wisdom, should be our judge; and I still hope that he will act. But where should we be able to find him?" The Wren replied, as she sat in her lime-tree, "What! Don't you know where he lives? He lives at Portisham, a place in Dorset, in an outlet near the sea: and there he delivers many lawful judgments, he composes and writes many wise sayings, and indeed through his sayings and also his writings things are better even in Scotland! To seek him out is an easy task, for he has but one dwelling—much to the shame of the bishops, and of all who have heard of him and his work. Why will they not arrange in their own interests, that he should frequently be with them, teaching them out of his store of wisdom? Why not give him livings in several places, so that he might often be at their service?"

"Certainly," said the Owl, "that is quite true. These great men are much to blame, in passing over this excellent man—so well instructed in many things—and in bestowing livings indiscriminately, while they hold him in but light esteem. Towards their own kin they are more generous: they grant livings to little children. Thus their good sense shall convict them of error, in that Master Nicholas still suffers neglect. But let us however go now to him, for with him our judgment is ready."

"Yes, let us do so," said the Nightingale, "but who is there to present our statement, and to speak before this judge of ours?"

"On that point," replied the Owl, "I can set your mind at ease: for I can repeat every word from beginning to end: and if perhaps I seem to go wrong, you can protest and pull me up." And having thus spoken, they went on their way without any supporters, until they arrived at Portisham. But as to how they fared in the matter of judgment, I can tell you nothing: this is the end of this particular story.

Why does the Owl accuse the Nightingale of leading women astray? What kind of love is pure? impure? Why is the secret love of the maiden less serious? Why are wives sometimes driven to adultery? What is the view of men presented in the debate? of women? How is marriage characterized?

18. ABELARD AND HELOISE

Peter Abelard (ca. 1079-ca. 1142), arguably the greatest philosopher of the twelfth century, was renowned for his learning and charismatic personality. While teaching at the cathedral school in Paris, he was hired to tutor Heloise (ca. 1099-ca. 1164), twenty years younger and the most learned woman of her day. Abelard's autobiographical Letter of Consolation to a Friend (Historia Calamitatum) *provides an account of the couple's ill-fated relationship from meeting to consummation, through discovery, culminating in separation and entry into religious life. The story of Abelard and Heloise is often viewed as a tragic story of great love, although some historians have queried the coercive and domineering aspects of Abelard's attentions and how freely Heloise entered this relationship. There is no doubt, however, about the enduring nature of Heloise's love for Abelard. Her diatribe against marriage reveals the ambivalence with which the institution was regarded, especially in learned circles of the day.*

Source: Trans. J.T. Muckle, *The Story of Abelard's Adversities* (Toronto: Pontifical Institute of Mediaeval Studies, 1964), pp. 26-40; reprinted with permission.

There lived in Paris a maiden named Heloise, the niece of a canon named Fulbert, who from his deep love for her was eager to have her advanced in all literary pursuits possible. She was a lady of no mean appearance while in literary excellence she was the first. And as the gift of letters is rare among women, so it had gained favor for her and made her the most renowned woman in the whole kingdom.

I considered all the qualities which usually inspire lovers and decided she was just the one for me to join in love. I felt that this would be very easy to accomplish; I then enjoyed such renown and was so outstanding for my charm of youth that I feared no repulse by any woman whom I should deign to favor with my love. And I felt that this maiden would all the more readily yield to me as I knew she possessed and cherished a knowledge of letters; thereby we, though separated, could through interchange of missives live in each other's presence and, by writing more boldly than conversation permits, we could constantly engage in pleasant talks.

And so, all on fire with love for her, I sought opportunity to enable me to make her familiar with me by private and daily association, the more easily to win her over. To effect this, through the intervention of some friends, I arranged with her uncle to receive me at his own price into his home which was near my school on the pretext that the care of my household greatly interfered with my studies and proved too heavy a financial burden. He was a very avaricious man and also most anxious that his niece advance in her literary studies. Because of these two traits, I easily gained his assent and got what I desired since he was all eager for the money and considered that his niece would profit from my teaching. On this latter point he strongly urged me beyond my fondest hopes, acceding to my wishes and furthering my love. He put his niece entirely under my control that whenever I was free upon returning from school I might devote myself night and day to teaching her, telling me to use pressure if I found her remiss. I was astonished at his simplicity in this matter and would have been no more astounded if he had been giving over a tender lamb to a ravenous wolf. For when he handed her over to me not only to teach but to discipline, what else was he doing but giving free rein to my designs, and opportunity, even if I were not seeking it, easily to subdue her by threats and stripes if blandishments did not work? Two factors especially kept him from suspecting any wrongdoing, namely his fondness for his niece and my own reputation in the past for chastity.

What was the result? We were first together in one house and then one in mind. Under the pretext of work we made ourselves entirely free for love and the pursuit of her studies provided the secret privacy which love desired. We opened our books but more words of love than of the lesson asserted themselves. There was more kissing than teaching; my hands found themselves at her breasts more often than on the book. Love brought us to gaze into each other's eyes more than reading kept them on the text. And the better to prevent suspicion, I sometimes struck her not through anger or vexation but from love and affection which were beyond the sweetness of every ointment. No sign of love was omitted by us in our ardor and whatever unusual love could devise, that was added too. And the more such delights were new to us, the more ardently we indulged in them, and the less did we experience satiety. And the more these pleasures engaged me, the less time I had for philosophy and the less attention I gave to my school. It became wearisome for me to go there and equally hard to stay when I was using nightly vigils for love and the days for study. I became negligent and indifferent in my lectures so that nothing I said stemmed from my talent but I repeated everything from rote. I came simply to say again what had been said long ago and, if I composed any verses, the theme was of love and not of the secrets of philosophy. Many of these songs, as you yourself know, are still popular in various places and sung by people of like tastes. It is not easy even to realize the sadness, the expressed regrets and sorrow of my students when they saw the preoccupation and disturbance of my mind with such things.

Such a course could have escaped the notice of very few and of no one at all, I feel, except the man most disgraced by such base conduct, I mean the uncle of the maiden. When it was suggested to him at times by some, he could not believe it on account of his extreme love of his niece noted above and of my well-known chastity in the past. For it is hard for us to suspect those we love and the taint of suspicion of evil cannot exist along with strong affection. As St. Jerome says in his letter to Sabinianus:

"We are usually the last to know of the scandal in our own household and the sins of our wife and children remain hidden from us although they are the common gossip of the neighbors."

But at length we come to find out and recognize it and what is common knowledge cannot easily be kept from just one person.

And in the course of several months that is what happened with regard to us. Imagine his bitter sorrow when her uncle found it out. Imagine the grief of us lovers at being separated; how I was filled with shame and remorse over the maiden's trouble. Imagine the sadness which flooded her soul from my sense of shame. Neither one of us complained of our own trials or bewailed our own misfortune but those of the other. The bodily separation became a strong link to bind our hearts together and our love became the more inflamed, denied opportunity. But shame gradually disappeared and made us more shameless and it became less as acts became easier. What the poet tells us of Mars and Venus caught in the act happened also to us. For not long afterwards the girl noticed that she was pregnant and she wrote me about it with great exultation and asked what I thought should be done. One night, when her uncle was away, I secretly took her from his house, as we had arranged, and had her taken directly to my native place. There she stayed with my sister until she gave birth to a boy whom she named Astralabe.

Upon his return, her uncle almost went mad and no one could appreciate except from experience the anguish which wrenched him or the shame he felt. He did not know what to do to me or by what plan he could waylay me. He was very much afraid that, if he maimed or killed me, his dear niece would pay for it in my native place. He could not get hold of me and coerce me anywhere against my will especially since I was very much on my guard for I had no doubt that he would quickly attack me if he could or dared to. After a while I began to sympathize with him in his extreme anxiety and blamed myself for the deceit which love had wrought which was, as it were, a base betrayal. I went to see him and, begging forgiveness, promised to make whatever amends he decided on. I told him that whoever had felt the force of love or recalled to what a crash women from the beginning have brought even the greatest men would not be surprised at my fall. And further to appease him, I made an offer beyond his fondest hopes to make satisfaction by marrying her whom I had defiled, provided this be done secretly so that my reputation would not be damaged. He agreed both by his own word and kiss of peace and by that of his backers. He thereby became on good terms with me which was what I asked but he did it only the more easily to betray me.

I straightaway returned to my native land and brought back my beloved to marry her. She disapproved of the plan and tried to dissuade me from it on two counts, the risk involved and the disgrace I should incur. She stated with an oath that her uncle could never be placated by such satisfaction, as we afterwards found out. What glory, she asked, would she derive from me since she would bring me to disgrace and humiliate both of us alike. What punishment would the world demand of her if she deprived it of such a shining light? What curses, what loss to the church, what weeping among philosophers would ensue from our marriage; how disgraceful, how lamentable would it be, if I, whom nature had produced for all, should devote myself to a woman and submit to such baseness! She utterly abhorred such a marriage which would prove a disgrace and a burden to me. She pointed out both the loss of my reputation and the hardships of marriage, which latter the apostle exhorts us to avoid when he says:

"Art thou freed from a wife? Do not seek a wife. But if thou takest a wife, thou has not sinned. And if a virgin marry, she has not sinned. Yet such will have tribulation of the flesh. But I spare you that … I would have you free from care, etc." [1 Cor. 7.27, 28, 32].

But if I would not heed the advice of the apostle and the exhortations of the saints on the great burden of marriage, she said, I should at least listen to the philosophers and pay attention to what has been written by them or of them on this matter. The saints in general have carefully done this to rebuke us. One instance is St. Jerome in his first book *Against Jovinianus* when he recalls how Theophrastus carefully set forth in great detail the unbearable troubles and constant cares of marriage and confirmed by patent proofs his declaration that a philosopher should not marry and concludes his reasons based on the exhortation of philosophers by saying: "When Theophrastus so reasons … what Christian should not blush, etc.?" And again in the same work St. Jerome goes on:

"When Cicero, after divorcing Terentia, was requested by Hirtius to marry his sister, he emphatically declined saying that he could not devote himself to a wife and philosophy alike."

He did not say simply "to devote himself" but added "alike," not wishing to do anything which would compete with his zeal for philosophy.

To say no more about the hindrance to the study of philosophy, she went on, consider the status of the dignified life. What could there be in common between scholars and wetnurses, writing desks and cradles, books, writing tablets and distaffs, styles, pens and spindles? Or who is there who is bent on sacred or philosophical reflection who could bear the wailing of babies, the silly lullabies of nurses to quiet them, the noisy horde of servants, both male and female; who could endure the constant degrading defilement of infants?

You will say that the rich can do it whose palaces or mansions have private rooms, and who with their wealth do not feel expense and are not troubled with daily anxieties. But I answer that the status of philosophers is not that of millionaires and of those who, engrossed in riches and entangled in worldly cares, will have no time for sacred or philosophical studies.

And so it is true to say that the great philosophers of old utterly despising the world fled rather than retired from it and renounced all pleasures that they might repose in the embrace of philosophy alone. The greatest of them, Seneca, says in instructing Lucilius:

> "You are not to pursue philosophy simply in your free time. Everything else is to be given up that we may devote ourselves to it for no length of time is long enough … It makes little difference whether you give up or interrupt the study of philosophy for, once it is interrupted, it does not abide … We must resist occupations which are not simply to be regulated but avoided."

What those among us who truly bear the name of monks endure for love of God, that they, the esteemed philosophers among the pagans, endured for love of philosophy. For among every people, whether Jew, Gentile, or Christian, there have always been some who were outstanding for their faith and uprightness of life and who cut themselves off from the rank and file by their distinguished chastity and abstinence. Among the Jews of old there were the Nazarenes who consecrated themselves to the Lord according to the Law. And there were also the sons of the Prophets, the followers of Elias and Eliseus who, as St. Jerome witnesses, are called monks in the Old Testament. Later on there were three classes of philosophers whom Josephus distinguishes in his *Antiquities* calling some Pharisees, others Sadducees, still others Essenes. Among us there are the monks who imitate the common life of the apostles or the earlier life of solitude of John the Baptist. And among the Gentiles, as we have mentioned, there are the philosophers. For the term wisdom or philosophy was used to refer not so much to acquisition of knowledge as to a religious life as we learn from the first use of it and from the testimony of the saints themselves.

In line with this, St. Augustine in the eighth book of his *City of God* distinguishes the classes of philosophers:

> "The Italians had Pythagoras of Samos as the founder of their school who, it is said, first used the term philosophy. For before him, anyone who appeared to be outstanding by a praiseworthy manner of life was called a sage. But when he was asked what his profession was, he answered that he was a philosopher, that is to say, one who pursues and

loves wisdom; it seemed to him that to say that such a one was already a wise man would be the height of arrogance."

And so in this passage where he says "appeared to be outstanding by a praiseworthy manner of life, etc.," he clearly shows that the wise men, that is, the philosophers, among the Gentiles were so called in praise of their life rather than of their knowledge. How temperately and chastely they lived is not for me to adduce from instances lest I appear to teach Minerva herself.

Now, she continued, if lay people and pagans so lived, men who were bound by no religious profession, what should you, a cleric and canon, do to avoid preferring base pleasure to sacred duties lest such a Charybdis drag you down headlong and you shamelessly and irrevocably swamp yourself in such obscenities. And if you do not regard the privilege of cleric, at least uphold the dignity of philosopher. If you despise reverence for God, let the love of uprightness at least restrain your shamelessness. Recall that Socrates had a wife, and the degrading incident by which he atoned for this defilement of philosophy to put others on their guard by his experience. Jerome himself in his first book *Against Jovinianus* brings this out when writing of Socrates:

"Once, after he had withstood numberless words of invective which Xanthippe hurled against him from the upper story, she threw some filthy water down upon him; Socrates wiped his head and exclaimed: 'I knew that a shower would follow such rumblings'."

Heloise went on to point out what a risk it would be for me to take her back and that it would be dearer to her and more honorable to me to be called my lover than my wife so that her charm alone would keep me for her, not the force of a nuptial bond; she also stated that the joys of our meeting after separation would be the more delightful as they were rare. When she could not divert me from my mad scheme by such arguments of exhortation and discussion and could not bear to offend me, she sighed deeply and in tears ended her final appeal as follows: "If we do this, one fate finally awaits us: we shall both be ruined and sorrow will thereby pierce our hearts equal in intensity to the love with which they are now aflame." And, as all the world knows, she was possessed of the spirit of prophecy in this statement.

And so when the infant was born we entrusted it to my sister and returned secretly to Paris. After a few days, we spent a night in a secret vigil of prayer in a church and early on the following day we were joined by the nuptial blessing in the presence of her uncle and some of his and our friends. We straightaway separated and left secretly. After that we saw each other only rarely and then on the quiet, hiding by dissimulation what we had done.

But her uncle and the members of his household seeking solace for his disgrace began to make our marriage public and thereby to break the word they had given regarding it. Heloise on her part cursed and swore that it was a lie. Her uncle became strongly aroused and kept heaping abuse upon her. When I found this out, I sent her to the convent of nuns in a town near Paris called Argenteuil where as a young girl she had been brought up and received instruction. I had a religious habit, all except the veil, made for her and had her vested in it.

When her uncle and his kinsmen heard this they considered that now I had fooled them and that by making her a nun I wanted easily to get rid of her. They became strongly incensed against me and formed a conspiracy. One night when I was sound asleep in an inner room of my lodgings, by bribing my attendant they wrought vengeance upon me in a cruel and shameful manner and one which the world with great astonishment abhorred, namely, they cut off the organs by which I had committed the deed which they deplored. They immediately fled but two of them were caught and had their eyes put out and were castrated; one of these was my servant already mentioned who while in my service was brought by greed to betray me.

When morning came, the whole city flocked to me and it is hard, yes impossible, to describe the astonishment which stunned them, the wailing they uttered, the shouting which irritated me and the moaning which upset me. The clerics and especially my students by their excessive lamentation and wailing pained me so that I endured more from their expressions of sympathy than from the suffering caused by the mutilation. I felt the embarrassment more than the wound and the shame was harder to bear than the pain. I fell to thinking how great had been my renown and in how easy and base a way this had been brought low and utterly destroyed; how by a just judgment of God I had been afflicted in that part of my body by which I had sinned; how just was the betrayal by which he whom I had first betrayed paid me back; how my rivals would extol such a fair retribution; how great would be the sorrow and lasting grief which my mutilation would cause my parents and friends; with what speed the news of this extraordinary mark of disgrace would spread throughout the world; what course could I follow; how could I face the public to be pointed at by all with a finger of scorn, to be insulted by every tongue and to become a monstrosity and a spectacle to all the world.

This also caused me no little confusion that according to the letter of the Law, which kills, God so abominated eunuchs that men who had their testicles cut off or bruised were forbidden as offensive and unclean to enter a congregation and in sacrifice animals of like character were utterly rejected (Lev. 22):

"You shall not offer to the Lord any beast that hath the testicles bruised or crushed or cut and taken away (Deut. 23): An eunuch, whose testicles are broken or cut away or yard cut off shall not enter into the church of the Lord."

Filled as I was with such remorse, it was, I confess, confusion springing from shame rather than devotion the result of conversion, which drove me to the refuge of monastic cloister. Heloise meanwhile at my order had consented to take the veil and entered the convent. Both of us alike took the holy habit, I in the abbey of St. Denis, she in the convent at Argenteuil mentioned above. I recall that many of her sympathizers tried to keep her, young as she was, from submitting to the yoke of monastic rule as an intolerable punishment. But it was in vain. Amid tears and sighs she broke forth as best she could into the famous complaint of Cornelia:

> "O mighty husband, too good for such a wife, had Fortune such power over one so great? Why am I guilty of marrying you, if I was to bring you misery? Now accept the penalty—a penalty I willingly pay."

And while uttering these lines she hastened to the altar and straightway took from it the veil blessed by the bishop and bound herself in the presence of all to religious life.

The exposure of their love affair, Abelard's castration, and their subsequent entry into the cloister did not spell the end of Abelard and Heloise's relationship. They continued to correspond and their later letters reflect their thoughts about their passionate relationship and the nature of love and sexuality more generally. Heloise's letters are particularly important as they provide an authentic female perspective on love and sexuality, one that reflects her personal experience. They capture some of Heloise's passion and intelligence and show her to be an active participant rather than the passive creation of Abelard.

Source: Trans. Betty Radice, *The Letters of Abelard and Heloise* (Harmondsworth: Penguin Books, 1975), pp. 113-18, 133-34, 145-48; reprinted with permission.

Letter 1. Heloise to Abelard

...You know, beloved, as the whole world knows, how much I have lost in you, how at one wretched stroke of fortune that supreme act of flagrant treachery robbed me of my very self in robbing me of you; and how my sorrow for my loss is nothing compared with what I feel for the manner in which I lost you. Surely the greater the cause for grief the greater the need for the help of consolation, and this no one can bring but you; you are the sole cause of my sorrow, and you alone can grant me the grace of consolation. You alone have the power to make me sad, to bring me happiness or comfort; you alone have so great a debt to repay me, particularly now when I have carried out all your orders so implicitly that when I was powerless to oppose you in anything, I found strength at your command to destroy myself. I did more, strange to say — my love rose to such heights of madness that it robbed itself of what it most desired beyond hope of recovery, when immediately at your bidding I changed my clothing along with my mind, in order to prove you the sole possessor of my body and my will alike. God knows I never sought anything in you except yourself; I wanted simply you, nothing of yours. I looked for no marriage-bond, no marriage portion, and it was not my own pleasures and wishes I sought to gratify, as you well know, but yours. The name of wife may seem more sacred or more binding, but sweeter for me will always be the word mistress, or, if you will permit me, that of concubine or whore. I believed that the more I humbled myself on your account, the more gratitude I should win from you, and also the less damage I should do to the brightness of your reputation.

You yourself on your own account did not altogether forget this in the letter of consolation I have spoken of which you wrote to a friend; there you thought fit to set out some of the reasons I gave in trying to dissuade you from binding us together in an ill-starred marriage. But you kept silent about most of my arguments for preferring love to wedlock and freedom to chains. God is my witness that if Augustus, emperor of the whole world, thought fit to honor me with marriage and conferred all the earth on me to possess for ever, it would be dearer and more honorable to me to be called not his empress but your whore.

For a man's worth does not rest on his wealth or power; these depend on fortune, but worth on his merits. And a woman should realize that if she marries a rich man more readily than a poor one, and desires her husband more for his possessions than for himself, she is offering herself for sale. Certainly any woman who comes to marry through desires of this kind deserves wages, not gratitude, for clearly her mind is on the man's property, not himself, and she would be ready to prostitute herself to a richer man, if she could. This is evident from the argument put forward in the dialogue of Aeschines Socraticus by the learned Aspasia to Xenophon and his wife. When she had expounded it in an effort to bring about a reconciliation between them, she ended with these words: "Unless you come to believe that there is no better man nor worthier woman on earth you will always still be looking for what you judge the best thing of all — to be the husband of the best of wives and the wife of the best of husbands."

These are saintly words which are more than philosophic; indeed, they deserve the name of wisdom, not philosophy. It is a holy error and a blessed delusion between man and wife, when perfect love can keep the ties of marriage unbroken not so much through bodily continence as chastity of spirit. But what error permitted other women, plain truth permitted me, and what they thought of their husbands, the world in general believed, or rather, knew to be true of yourself; so that my love for you was the more genuine for being further removed from error. What king or philosopher could match your fame? What district, town, or village did not long to see you? When you appeared in public, who did not hurry to catch a glimpse of you, or crane his neck and strain his eyes to follow your departure? Every wife, every young girl desired you in absence and was on fire in your presence; queens and great ladies envied me my joys and my bed.

You had besides, I admit, two special gifts whereby to win at once the heart of any woman—your gifts for composing verse and song, in which we know other philosophers have rarely been successful. This was for you no more than a diversion, a recreation from the labors of your philosophic work, but you left many love-songs and verses which won wide popularity for the charm of their words and tunes and kept your name continually on everyone's lips. The beauty of the airs ensured that even the unlettered did not forget you; more than anything this made women sigh for love of you. And as most of these songs told of our love, they soon made me widely known and roused the envy of many women against me. For your manhood was adorned by every grace of mind and body, and among the women who envied me then, could there be one now who does not feel compelled by my misfortune to sympathize with my loss of such joys? Who is there who was once my enemy, whether man or woman, who is not moved now by the compassion which is my due? Wholly guilty though I am, I am also, as you know, wholly innocent. It is not the deed but the intention of the doer which makes the crime, and justice should weigh not what was done but the spirit in which it is done. What my intention towards you has always been, you alone who have known it can judge. I submit all to your scrutiny, yield to your testimony in all things.

Tell me one thing, if you can. Why, after our entry into religion, which was your decision alone, have I been so neglected and forgotten by you that I have neither a word from you when you are here to give me strength nor the consolation of a letter in absence? Tell me, I say, if you can—or I will tell you what I think and indeed the world suspects. It was desire, not affection which bound you to me, the flame of lust rather than love. So when the end came to what you desired, any show of feeling you used to make went with it. This is not merely my own opinion, beloved, it is everyone's. There is nothing personal or private about it; it is the general view which is widely held. I only wish that it *were* mine alone, and that the love you professed could find someone to defend it and so comfort me in my grief for a while. I wish I could think of some explanation which would excuse you and somehow cover up the way you hold me cheap.

I beg you then to listen to what I ask—you will see that it is a small favor which you can easily grant. While I am denied your presence, give me at least through your words—of which you have enough and to spare—some sweet semblance of yourself. It is no use my hoping for generosity in deeds if you are grudging in words. Up to now I had thought I deserved much of you, seeing that I carried out everything for your sake and continue up to the present moment in complete obedience to you. It was not any sense of vocation which brought me as a young girl to accept the austerities of the cloister, but your bidding alone, and if I deserve no gratitude from you, you may judge for yourself how my labors are in vain. I can expect no reward for this from God, for it is certain that I have done nothing as yet for love of him. When you hurried towards God I followed you, indeed, I went first to take the veil—perhaps you were thinking how Lot's wife turned back when you made me put on the religious habit and take my vows before you gave yourself to God.

Your lack of trust in me over this one thing, I confess, overwhelmed me with grief and shame. I would have had no hesitation, God knows, in following you or going ahead at your bidding to the flames of hell. My heart was not in me but with you, and now, even more, if it is not with you it is nowhere; truly, without you it cannot exist. See that it fares well with you, I beg, as it will if it finds you kind, if you give grace in return for grace, small for great, words for deeds. If only your love had less confidence in me, my dear, so that you would be more concerned on my behalf! But as it is, the more I have made you feel secure in me, the more I have to bear with your neglect.

Remember, I implore you, what I have done, and think how much you owe me. While I enjoyed with you the pleasures of the flesh, many were uncertain whether I was prompted by love or lust; but now the end is proof of the beginning. I have finally denied myself every pleasure in obedience to your will, kept nothing for myself except to prove that now, even more, I am yours. Consider then your injustice, if when I deserve more you give me less, or rather, nothing at all, especially when it is a small thing I ask of you and one you could so easily grant. And so, in the name of God to whom you have dedicated yourself, I beg you to restore your presence to me in the way you can—by writing me some word of comfort, so that in this at least I may find increased strength and readiness to serve God. When in the past you sought me out for sinful pleasures your letters came to me thick and fast, and your many songs put your Heloise on everyone's lips, so that every street and house echoed with my name. Is it not far better now to summon me to God than it was then to satisfy our lust? I beg you, think what you owe me, give ear to my pleas, and I will finish a long letter with a brief ending: farewell, my only love.

Letter 3. Heloise to Abelard

... In my case, the pleasures of lovers which we shared have been too sweet—they can never displease me, and can scarcely be banished from my thoughts. Wherever I turn they are always there before my eyes, bringing with them awakened longings and fantasies which will not even let me sleep. Even during the celebration of the Mass, when our prayers should be purer, lewd visions of those pleasures take such a hold upon my unhappy soul that my thoughts are on their wantonness instead of on prayers. I should be groaning over the sins I have committed, but I can only sigh for what I have lost. Everything we did and also the times and places are stamped on my heart along with your image, so that I live through it all again with you. Even in sleep I know no respite. Sometimes my thoughts are betrayed in a movement of my body, or they break out in an unguarded word. In my utter wretchedness, that cry from a suffering soul could well be mine: "Miserable creature that I am, who is there to rescue me out of the body doomed to this death?" Would that in truth I could go on: "The grace of God through Jesus Christ our Lord." This grace, my dearest, came upon you unsought—a single wound of the body by freeing you from these torments has healed many wounds in your soul. Where God may seem to you an adversary he has in fact proved himself kind: like an honest doctor who does not shrink from giving pain if it will bring about a cure. But for me, youth and passion and experience of pleasures which were so delightful intensify the torments of the flesh and longings of desire, and the assault is the more overwhelming as the nature they attack is the weaker.

Men call me chaste; they do not know the hypocrite I am. They consider purity of the flesh a virtue, though virtue belongs not to the body but to the soul. I can win praise in the eyes of men but deserve none before God, who searches our hearts and loins and sees in our darkness. I am judged religious at a time when there is little in religion which is not hypocrisy, when whoever does not offend the opinions of men receives the highest praise. And yet perhaps there is some merit and it is somehow acceptable to God, if a person whatever his intention gives no offence to the church in his outward behavior, does not blaspheme the name of the Lord in the hearing of unbelievers nor disgrace the Order of his profession amongst the worldly. And this too is a gift of God's grace and comes through his bounty—not only to do good but to abstain from evil—though the latter is vain if the former does not follow from it, as it is written: "Turn from evil and do good." Both are vain if not done for love of God.

Letter 4. Abelard to Heloise

… However, it may relieve the bitterness of your grief if I prove that this came upon us justly, as well as to our advantage, and that God's punishment was more properly directed against us when we were married than when we were living in sin. After our marriage, when you were living in the cloister with the nuns at Argenteuil and I came one day to visit you privately, you know what my uncontrollable desire did with you there, actually in a corner of the refectory, since we had nowhere else to go. I repeat, you know how shamelessly we behaved on that occasion in so hallowed a place, dedicated to the most holy Virgin. Even if our other shameful behavior was ended, this alone would deserve far heavier punishment. Need I recall our previous fornication and the wanton impurities which preceded our marriage, or my supreme act of betrayal, when I deceived your uncle about you so disgracefully, at a time when I was continuously living with him in his own house? Who would not judge me justly betrayed by the man whom I had first shamelessly betrayed? Do you think that the momentary pain of that wound is sufficient punishment for such crimes? Or rather, that so great an advantage was fitting for such great wickedness? What wound do you suppose would satisfy God's justice for the profanation such as I described of a place so sacred to his own Mother? Surely, unless I am much mistaken, not that wound which was wholly beneficial was intended as a punishment for this, but rather the daily unending torment I now endure….

You know the depths of shame to which my unbridled lust had consigned our bodies, until no reverence for decency or for God even during the days of Our Lord's Passion, or of the greater sacraments could keep me from wallowing in this mire. Even when you were unwilling, resisted to the utmost of your power and tried to dissuade me, as yours was the weaker nature I often forced you to consent with threats and blows. So intense were the fires of lust which bound me to you that I set those wretched, obscene pleasures, which we blush even to name, above God as above myself; nor would it seem that divine mercy could have taken action except by forbidding me these pleasures altogether, without future hope. And so it was wholly just and merciful, although by means of the supreme treachery of your uncle, for me to be reduced in that part of my body which was the seat of lust and sole reason for those desires, so that I could increase in many ways; in order that this member should justly be punished for all its wrongdoing in us, expiate in suffering the sins committed for its amusement, and cut me off from the slough of filth in which I had been wholly immersed in mind as in body. Only thus could I become more fit to approach the holy altars, now that no contagion of carnal impurity would ever again call me from them. How mercifully did he want me to suffer so much only in that member, the privation of which would also further the salvation of my soul without defiling my body nor preventing any performance of my duties! Indeed, it would make me readier to perform whatever can be honorably done by setting me wholly free from the heavy yoke of carnal desire....

Why was the fact that Heloise was learned important to their relationship? What information does the treatise provide about the sexual dimensions of love? Who was responsible for the affair? How does Abelard shift responsibility for the affair? What were the arguments against marriage? Why did Heloise believe it was preferable to be a lover than a wife? Why was castration both a suitable revenge and a profound disgrace? How are love and desire or lust distinguishable? What were Heloise's views of her relationship with Abelard? How did they differ from Abelard's views? What did Heloise want? What did Abelard offer her?

19. PAOLO AND FRANCESCA

The great Italian poet Dante Alighieri (1265-1321) wrote the Divine Comedy *(1314)*
as a journey through hell, purgatory, and heaven. As Dante journeyed through hell with
his guide, the poet Virgil, he greeted the suffering souls who explained their sins to him;
these were frequently famous people from the past, or those who were prominent in his
own day. Each circle of hell was reserved for a different sin, the progressively more serious
being placed lower down. In the first circle of hell, he encountered the tortured souls of
people who had loved too much in the worldly rather than spiritual sense. Among them
were the souls of the ill-fated lovers, Francesca de Rimini and Paolo Malatesta. About
1275, in a union of political expediency, Francesca was married to Paolo's brother in a
ceremony in which Paolo acted as his brother's proxy. The couple fell in love and contin-
ued their affair despite both being married to others. Sometime between 1283 and 1286,
Francesca's husband found the couple in each other's arms and killed them both on the
spot, as was his right according to both prevailing secular law and contemporary morality.
As adulterers, Dante had no choice but to place the lovers in hell, yet clearly he also felt
compassion for them, suggesting that their love was so enduring it would last an eternity,
even if in eternal damnation.

Source: Trans. Charles S. Singleton in Dante Alighieri, *The Divine Comedy*, vol. 1, *Inferno* (Princeton: Princeton University Press, 1970), pp. 73, 75, 77; reprinted with permission.

Inferno: Canto 5

Thus I descended from the first circle into the second, which girds less space,
and so much greater woe that it goads to wailing. There stands Minos, horrible
and snarling: upon the entrance he examines their offenses, and judges and dis-
patches them according as he entwines. I mean that when the ill-begotten soul
comes before him, it confesses all; and that discerner of sins sees which shall be
its place in Hell, then girds himself with his tail as many times as the grades he
wills that it be sent down. Always before him stands a crowd of them; they go,
each in his turn, to the judgment; they tell, and hear, and then are hurled
below.

"O you who come to the abode of pain," said Minos to me, when he saw
me, pausing in the act of that great office, "beware how you enter and in whom
you trust; let not the breadth of the entrance deceive you!" And my leader to
him, "Why do you too cry out? Do not hinder his fated going: thus is it willed
there where that can be done which is willed; and ask no more."

Now the doleful notes begin to reach me; now I am come where much
wailing smites me. I came into a place mute of all light, which bellows like the
sea in a tempest when it is assailed by warring winds. The hellish hurricane,

never resting, sweeps along the spirits with its rapine; whirling and smiting, it torments them. When they arrive before the ruin, there the shrieks, the moans, the lamentations; there they curse the divine power. I learned that to such torment are condemned the carnal sinners, who subject reason to desire.

And as their wings bear the starlings along in the cold season, in wide, dense flocks, so does that blast the sinful spirits; hither, thither, downward, upward, it drives them. No hope of less pain, not to say of rest, ever comforts them. And as the cranes go chanting their lays, making a long line of themselves in the air, so I saw shades come, uttering wails, borne by that strife; wherefore I said, "Master, who are these people that are so lashed by the black air?"

"The first of these of whom you wish to know," he said to me then, "was empress of many tongues. She was so given to lechery that she made lust licit in her law, to take away the blame she had incurred. She is Semiramis, of whom we read that she succeeded Ninus and had been his wife: she held the land the Sultan rules. The next is she who slew herself for love and broke faith to the ashes of Sichaeus; next is wanton Cleopatra. See Helen, for whom so many years of ill revolved; and see the great Achilles, who fought at the last with love. See Paris, Tristan," and more than a thousand shades whom love had parted from our life he showed me, pointing them out and naming them.

When I heard my teacher name the ladies and the knights of old, pity overcame me and I was as one bewildered. "Poet," I began, "willingly would I speak with those two that go together and seem to be so light upon the wind."

And he to me, "You shall see when they are nearer to us; and do you entreat them then by that love which leads them, and they will come."

As soon as the wind bends them to us, I raised my voice, "O wearied souls! come speak with us, if Another forbid it not."

As doves called by desire, with wings raised and steady, come through the air, borne by their will to their sweet nest, so did these issue from the troop where Dido is, coming to us through the malignant air, such force had my compassionate cry.

"O living creature, gracious and benign, that go through the black air visiting us who stained the world with blood, if the king of the universe were friendly to us, we would pray him for your peace, since you have pity on our perverse ill. Of that which it pleases you to hear and to speak, we will hear and speak with you, while the wind, as now, is silent for us.

"The city where I was born lies on that shore where the Po descends to be at peace with its followers. Love, which is quickly kindled in a gentle heart, seized this one for the fair form that was taken from me—and the way of it afflicts me still. Love, which absolves no loved one from loving, seized me so strongly with delight in him, that, as you see, it does not leave me even now. Love brought us to one death: Caina awaits him who quenched our life."

These words were borne to us from them. And when I heard those afflicted souls I bowed my head and held it bowed until the poet said to me, "What are you thinking of."

When I answered, I began, "Alas! How many sweet thoughts, what great desire, brought them to the woeful pass!"

Then I turned again to them, and I began, "Francesca, your torments make me weep for grief and pity; but tell me, in the time of the sweet sighs, by what and how did Love grant you to know the dubious desires?"

And she to me, "There is no greater sorrow than to recall, in wretchedness, the happy time; and this your teacher knows. But if you have such great desire to know the first root of our love, I will tell as one who weeps and tells. One day, for pastime, we read of Lancelot, how love constrained him; we were alone, suspecting nothing. Several times that reading urged our eyes to meet and took the color from our faces, but one moment alone it was that overcame us. When we read how the longed-for smile was kissed by so great a lover, this one, who never shall be parted from me, kissed my mouth all trembling. A Gallehault [panderer] was the book and he who wrote it; that day we read no farther in it."

While the one spirit said this, the other wept, so that for pity I swooned, as if in death, and fell as a dead body falls.

What is the nature of love portrayed by Dante? Why was reading romantic stories dangerous? How do Paolo and Francesca suffer? How does the poet feel?

20. EDWARD III'S LOVE FOR THE COUNTESS OF SALISBURY (1342)

Although the literature of courtly love permitted, even idealized, the adulterous love of a knight for a lady, for real men and women the situation was quite different. A double standard governed the conduct of each sex. While men might engage in numerous sexual liaisons, whether or not they were married, it was much more dangerous for women to do so. The rigid standards of morality imposed upon aristocratic women, in particular, were intended to safeguard the lineage and ensure the legitimacy of heirs. Yet women were subjected to pressure to engage in extramarital affairs. Such pressure, especially if it came from a king or other social superior, was difficult to resist. The chaste matron walked a fine line between preserving her chastity and maintaining her fidelity to her husband, while at the same time not offending a powerful man who, if rebuffed, could exact a harsh revenge. Jean Froissart reported the case of Edward III, king of England, and his infatuation with the countess of Salisbury, the wife of one of his vassals.

Source: Trans. John Bourchier and Lord Berners in Jean Froissart, *The Chronicle of Froissart*, vol. 1 (London: David Nutt, 1901), pp. 193–95; revised.

The same day that the Scots departed from Wark Castle King Edward arrived with his army, about noon, and came to the same place that the Scots had stayed. He was furious to find the Scots gone because he had come in such haste that his men and horses were exhausted. Then he ordered the army to pitch their camp for the night and said that he would go to see the castle and the noble lady who held it, for he had not seen her since before her marriage. And as soon as the king had disarmed, he took with him ten or twelve knights and went to the castle to greet the countess of Salisbury and to assess the damage done by the Scots' attack and the defense against it.

As soon as the lady knew of the king's arrival she opened the gates and went out to meet him dressed so richly that every man marveled at her beauty and could not stop regarding her nobility and the graciousness of her words and demeanor. When she came to the king, she curtsied down to the ground, thanking him for his support, and led him into the castle to entertain him as well as she could. Everyone watched her with wonder. The king himself could not stop gazing at her and thought that he had never before seen so noble or fair a lady. His heart was stricken by a spark of love that endured for a long time afterward. He thought no lady in the world was so worthy to be loved as she.

Thus they entered the castle, hand in hand. The lady led him first into the hall and afterward into his room, which was richly furnished. The king stared at the lady so much that she was embarrassed. At last he went to the window and leaned against it and fell into revery. The lady went about making the lords and knights who were there comfortable and ordered the hall prepared for dinner.

When she had arranged everything, cheerfully she returned to the king, who was still deep in thought. She said, "Dear sir, why are you so thoughtful? If it please your grace, it does not suit you. Rather, you should be cheerful and good humored, given that you have chased away your enemies, who dared to attack you. Let other men contemplate for the time being."

Then the king said, "Ah, dear lady, know in truth that since I entered the castle, a thought has come to mind that I cannot help but ponder, nor can I tell what will result from it, but I cannot push it aside."

"Ah, sir," said the lady, " you ought always to be in good humor and feast with your people. God has helped you in your endeavors and has given you such great gifts that you are the most feared and honored prince in all Christendom. If the king of Scotland has done you any harm you can right it when you like, as you have done on other occasions. Sir, stop your brooding and come to the hall, if you please. Your dinner is ready."

"Ah, fair lady," said the king, "There are other things deep in my heart that you know nothing about. Truly, your sweet nature, perfect wisdom, good grace, nobility, and exquisite beauty have so surprised my heart that I cannot help but love you, and without your love I will die."

Then the lady said, "Ah, right noble prince, for God's sake do not mock or tempt me. I cannot believe that what you say is true, nor that so noble a prince as you would consider dishonoring me or my lord, my husband, who is so valiant a knight and has served you so faithfully, and is now in prison on your account. Certainly, sir, you would earn no praise and gain nothing by this. I have never had so much as a thought for any man, nor, will it please God, that I ever will. If I had any such intention, your grace not only ought to blame me but also ought to punish my body by dismemberment, as is just."

Then the lady departed from the king, and went into the hall to supervise the dinner. Then she returned again to the king and brought some of his knights with her, and said, "Sir, if it please you to come into the hall, your knights are waiting for you to wash. You have fasted too long."

Then the king went into the hall and washed and sat down with his lords, and with the lady as well. The king ate sparingly. He sat still thinking and gazed at the lady whenever he could. His knights were confused by his sadness because he was not accustomed to be moody. Some thought it was because the Scots had escaped.

All that day the king lingered there and did not know what to do. Sometimes he blamed himself since honor and truth prohibited him from setting his heart on such a course, dishonoring such a lady and so loyal a knight as her husband, who had always served him well and faithfully. Other times love so constrained him that its power overwhelmed honor and truth. Thus the king debated with himself all that day and night. In the morning he arose and gathered his army to pursue the Scots and chase them from his realm.

Then he took leave of the countess, saying, "My dear lady, I commend you to God until I return again, and asking you to reconsider what you have said to me."

"Noble prince," said the lady, "May God the Father guide you and drive all evil thoughts from your mind. Sir, I am, and always will be, ready to serve you in a way that will reflect well on your honor and mine."

The king then departed, ashamed. He then followed the Scots until he arrived at the city of Berwick. He camped about four leagues from the forest of Jedworth, where King David and his army had halted, harboring in the wilderness. The king of England lingered there for three days, to see if the Scots would venture out to fight. During these three days there were various skirmishes between the two parties, and numerous were killed, captured, or wounded. Sir William Douglas, in particular, damaged the English. He bore arms of azure and silver, with three red stars.

The Chess Game

While the king's infatuation with the countess of Salisbury is well attested, the account of their game of chess did not appear in all versions of Froissart's Chronicle, *nor is it found in modern editions. This vignette, nevertheless, provides useful insights into how aristocratic men and women might conduct a flirtation. Chess, while a popular game, in this instance also serves as a metaphor for the maneuvering between the king and countess. The game occurred during the day, while the king tarried in the castle contemplating what he should do about his infatuation with the countess.*

Source: Trans. W.P. Ker in "The Chess Game," in Jean Froissart, *The Chronicle of Froissart*, vol. 1, ed. John Borchier and Lord Berners (London: David Nutt, 1901), pp. lxxii–lxxv; revised.

After dinner the tables were removed. Then the king sent Lord Reynold Chobham and Lord Richard Stamford to the retinue who were lodged near the castle to find out how they were faring and to instruct them to begin preparations because he wished to follow the Scots. He ordered that they should send the carriages and munitions on ahead and said he would join them by evening. He ordered the earl of Pembroke to muster a rearguard composed of five hundred men with lances, who should wait until he joined them. The rest of the army could ride on ahead. The two barons did as he commanded.

The king remained in the castle with the countess. He hoped that before his departure she would give him a more agreeable response than she had yet. So he called for chess, and the lady ordered it brought in. Then the king asked the lady to play with him, and she agreed happily because she wished to entertain him as well as she could. And that was her duty, because the king had done her a good service by raising the Scots' siege of the castle. And she was also obligated because the king was her right and natural lord to whom she owed fealty and homage.

At the beginning of the game of chess, the king, who wished that the lady might win something of his, laughingly challenged her and said, "Madam, what will be your stake in the game?" She answered, "And yours, sir?" Then the king put down on the board a beautiful ring with a large ruby that he wore. Then the countess said, "Sir, sir, I have no ring as rich as yours." "Madam," said the king, "put down whatever you have, and do not be so concerned about its value." Then, to please the king, the countess drew from her finger a light ring of gold of no great value.

And they played chess together, the lady with all the ability and skill she could, so that the king would not think she was too simple or ignorant. The king, however, deliberately played poorly, and would not play as well as he was able. There was hardly a pause between moves, but the king stared so hard at the lady that she was very embarrassed, and made mistakes in her moves. And when the king saw that she had lost a pawn or a knight or another piece, he would also lose one to restore the lady's game.

They played on until at last the king lost, and was checkmated with a bishop. Then the lady rose and called for the wine and sweets because it seemed the king was about to leave. She took her ring and put it on her finger and wanted the king to take his back also. She gave it to him, saying, "Sir, it is not appropriate that in my house I should take anything of yours, but rather you should take something of mine." "No, madam," said the king, "since the game has caused it to be so. You may be sure that if I had won, I would have taken something of yours." The countess would not urge the king further, but went to one of her damsels and gave her the ring and said, "When you see that the king has gone out and has taken leave of me, and is about to mount his horse, go to him and give him back his ring again, courteously. Tell him that I will certainly not keep it because it is not mine." And the damsel answered that she would do so.

At this point the wine and sweets were brought in. The king would not take any before the lady, nor the lady before him, and there was a great debate between them, all in fun. Finally, it was agreed, to make it short, that they would begin at the same time. After this, and when all the king's knights had drunk, the king took leave of the lady and said to her aloud, so that no one should comment upon it, "Madam, you remain in your house, and I will go to follow my enemies." At these words the lady curtsied low before the king. And the king took her by the hand and pressed it a little, for his pleasure, as a sign of love. The king waited until the knights and damsels were busy saying goodbye to one another. Then he came forward again to say two words privately: "My dear lady, I commend you to God until I return again, asking you to change your mind about the decision you have given me." "My dear lord," answered the lady, "God the Father glorious be your guide, and banish all base and dishonorable thoughts from your mind, because I am and always shall be ready to serve you to your honor and mine."

Then the king left the room, and the countess as well, and she accompanied him to the hall where his palfrey was. Then the king said that he would not mount while the lady was there. So, to speed things along, the countess said her final goodbyes and took leave of the king and his knights, and returned to her private rooms with her maidens. When the king was about to mount, the damsel whom the countess had instructed came to the king and knelt. When the king saw her, he quickly helped her up, thinking she was going to speak about another matter than she did. Then she said, "My lord, here is the ring which my lady returns to you. She begs you not to consider this a discourtesy, because she does not wish to keep it. You have done so much for her in other ways that she is bound, she says, to be your servant always." When the king heard the damsel and saw that she had his ring, and was told about the countess's wish and excuse, he was amazed. Nevertheless, he make up his mind

This nineteenth-century drawing of a chess game is based on a medieval illustration. Chess was a popular game with both men and women of the nobility.

quickly and, in order that the ring would remain in that house, as he had intended, he answered briefly (since a long speech was unnecessary) and said, "Mistress, since your lady does not like the little gain that she won from me, let it remain in your possession." Then he mounted quickly and rode out of the castle to the lawn where his knights were, and found the earl of Pembroke waiting for him with more than five hundred soldiers. Then they all set out together and followed the army.

The damsel returned and reported the king's answer, and gave back the ring that the king had lost at chess. But the countess would not accept it, and claimed she had no right to it: the king had given it to the damsel; let her take it and she was welcome to it. So the king's ring was left with the damsel.

What qualities in the countess of Salisbury caused the king to fall in love? How did the countess counter the king's advances? How did the king behave when he was in love? Why was the countess anxious not to keep the king's ring?

21. THE PASTON FAMILY ON LOVE AND MARRIAGE

The correspondence of the Paston family is a remarkable source for information about daily life in the late Middle Ages. The Pastons were a gentry family in Norfolk in the fifteenth century. Their economic pursuits and legal cases meant that the Paston men frequently traveled far from home, while the Paston women supervised the estates. Consequently, family members generated a voluminous amount of correspondence which has fortunately survived. The information about courtship and marriage contained in these letters is invaluable. It reveals that women were expected to be passive and accept the matches that were arranged on their behalf, with an eye to the greater good of the whole family. The correspondence also illustrates what could happen when women rebelled. The first two letters discuss the situation of Elizabeth Paston who, at twenty, was offered in marriage to Stephen Scrope, a wealthy fifty-year-old. Elizabeth resisted the match at considerable personal cost. She eventually agreed, but in the end the marriage did not occur. The other significant union was the love match between Margery Paston and the family steward, Richard Calle. The fact that Margery and Richard exchanged their vows secretly and privately and their union was valid and indissoluble indicates that the laity were well aware of the church's teaching on marriage. The outrage of Margery's family, especially her formidable mother Margaret, is understandable as not only did Margery defy her parents but her downward marriage could have harmed the family's social standing. Margery's marriage may have prevailed, but Margaret never completely forgave her daughter. Richard Calle, however, did retain his position as the Pastons' steward.

Source: Trans. J. Murray from *The Paston Letters*, ed. James Gairdner (Westminster: A. Constable, 1896), vol. 2, pp. 108–11; vol. 5, pp. 25–28, 37–40.

Agnes Paston to John Paston I (not after 1449)

Son, I greet you well with God's blessing and mine and to let you know that my cousin [Elizabeth] Clere wrote to me that she has spoken with [Stephen] Scrope after he had been with me at Norwich, and told her what hospitality I had given him, and he said to her he very much liked the reception I gave him.

He told my cousin Clere that unless you gave him a warm reception and comforting words at London, he would speak no more of the matter.

My cousin Clere thinks that it would be folly to forsake him unless you knew of another as good or better; and I have consulted your sister and I've never found her so willing toward anyone as she is to him, if it be the case that his land stands clear.

I sent you a letter by Braunton for silk and about this matter before my cousin Clere wrote to me, which was written on the Wednesday right after Midsummer Day.

Sir Harry Inglose is very busy regarding Scrope on behalf of one of his daughters.

I pray you not to forget to bring me my money from Horwelbury when you come from London, either all of it or the greater part....

I can no more but almighty God be our good Lord, who has you always in his keeping. Written at Oxnead in great haste on the Saturday after Midsummer.

By your mother, Agnes Paston

Elizabeth Clere to John Paston I (not after 1449)

Let this letter be delivered to my cousin, John Paston.

Trusty and well-beloved cousin, I commend me to you, desiring to hear about your welfare and that your affairs are going well, for which I pray that God send you his pleasure to ease your heart.

Cousin, I am letting you know that Scrope has been in this area to see my cousin your sister, and he has spoken with my cousin your mother. And she desires that he show you the indentures made between the knight that has married his daughter and him, whether, if Scrope were married and fortunate enough to have children, the children would inherit his land or his daughter who is married.

Cousin, for this reason pay careful attention to his indentures, for he is glad to show them to you or to whomever you will assign. And he said to me that he is the last in the line of his livelihood, which is 350 marks or better, as Watkin Shipdham says, for he has taken account of his livelihood a number of times. And Scrope said to me that if he marries and has a son and heir, his daughter that is married should have 50 marks from his estate and no more. Therefore, cousin, it seems to me that he would be good for my cousin, your sister, unless you can find her a better one. And if you can get her a better match, I would advise you to arrange it in as short a time as you possibly can, for she has never been in such great sorrow as she is nowadays. She may not speak with any man, whosoever comes, nor may she see or speak with my man, nor with her mother's servants, unless she insinuates something other than what she means. And since Easter she has, for the most part, been beaten once or twice a week, and sometimes twice on one day, and her head was broken in two or three places. On this account, cousin, she has sent Friar Newton to me in great secrecy, and has asked me to send to you a letter about her burdens, and ask you to be her good brother, as her trust is in you. And she says, if you can see by his documentation that his children and she may inherit, and she will have a reasonable jointure, that she has heard so much about his birth and condition that, if you wish, she will have him, whether or not her mother wishes it, notwithstanding that she has been told he is a simple person. She says that men shall have more esteem for her if she obeys him as she ought to do.

Cousin, I am told there is a good man in your Inn whose father died recently. And if you think he would be better for her than Scrope, it would be a good effort. And give Scrope a good answer so that he is not put off until you are sure of a better match. For he said to me when he was with me, unless he had some reassuring answer from you he would not pursue this matter any longer, because he might not see my cousin your sister and he says he might have seen her if she had been better than she is, and it demeans him that her mother does not approve, and so I have sent my cousin your mother word. Therefore, cousin, think about this matter, for sorrow often causes women to afflict themselves more than they would otherwise, and if that is her case, I know well that you would be sorry. Cousin, I ask you to burn this letter so that your men nor any other man should see it, for if my cousin your mother knew that I had sent this letter to you she would never love me. I write no more to you at this time, but the Holy Ghost keep you. Written in haste on St. Peter's Day, by candle light.

By your cousin, Elizabeth Clere.

Richard Calle to Margery Paston (1469)

My own lady and mistress, and before God my very true wife, with a heart full of sorrow I recommend me to you, as one that cannot be merry, nor shall be until it be otherwise with us than it now is. For this life that we now lead is neither pleasing to God nor to the world, considering the great bond of matrimony that is between us, and also the great love that has been, and I trust is still between us, and on my part has never been greater. On this account I beseech almighty God to comfort us as soon as it pleases him, for we who ought by right to be together are torn apart; it seems to me that it is a thousand years since I spoke with you. I would rather be with you than have all the goods in the world. Alas, alas, good lady, consider little them and what they do to keep us apart. Four times in the year they who obstruct matrimony are cursed. It causes many men to reflect inwardly who have a great conscience in matters other than matrimony. But, lady, suffer as you must and make merry as you can, for certainly, lady, in the long run God will from his righteousness help his servants who mean well and wish to live according to his laws, etc.

I understand, lady, that you have had as much sorrow for me as any gentle-woman has had in the world. I wish to God that all the sorrow that you have had rested upon me, so that you would be free of it. For certainly, lady, it is like death for me to hear that you are being treated otherwise than you ought to be. This is a painful life that we lead. I cannot live thus without it being a great displeasure to God.

Also, I would like you to know that I had sent you a letter from London by my lad, and he told me he was not allowed to speak with you, and was made to wait there for you a long time. He told me that John Thresher came to him in your name and said that you sent him to my lad for a letter or a token which I should have sent you. But he didn't trust him and he would not deliver anything to him. After that he brought him a ring, saying that you sent it to him, commanding him that he should deliver the letter or token to him, which I have affirmed by my lad was not sent by you, but was sent by my mistress and on Sir James Gloys' advice. Alas, what do they intend? I suppose that they consider us not to be pledged together. And if they think that I am amazed, for then they are not well advised, remembering the plainness with which I broke the matter to my mistress at the very beginning, and I suppose by you as well, if you did as you ought to have done by right. And if you have done the contrary, as I have been informed you have done, you did it neither from conscience nor to God's pleasure, unless you did it from fear and to please for the time those who were around you. And if you did so for this reason it was a reasonable cause, considering the great and unbearable demands you had, and the many untrue tales being told you about me, which God knows I was never guilty of.

My lad told me that my mistress your mother asked him if he had brought any letter to you, and she insinuated many other things to him. Among all the others she said to him, that I would not tell her about it at the beginning but she supposed I would at the end. And as to that, God knows she knew of it first from me and no other. I do not know what her ladyship means, for upon my word there is no gentlewoman alive whom my heart cherishes more than her, nor is more loathe to displease, except only your person, which by right I ought to cherish and love best, for I am bound to you by the law of God, and so I will do while I am alive, whatsoever results from it. I suppose if you told them plainly the truth they would not damn their souls for us. Although I tell them the truth, they will not believe me as well as they will you. And therefore, good lady, at the reverence of God be plain to them and tell the truth. And if they will be no means agree to it, it will be between God, the devil, and them, and the peril that we should be in, I beg God that it may lie on them and not upon us. I am grieving and sorry to remember their disposition. God send them grace to guide all things well, as well as I wish they did. God be their guide, and send them peace and rest, etc.

I marvel greatly that they should take this matter so hard, as I understand they do, remembering that it is a situation that cannot be remedied. My desire on behalf of everyone is for it to be thought there is no obstacle against it and also that their honor is not in your marriage; it is in their own marriage, which I pray God send them such as may be to their honor and pleasing to God, and to ease their hearts, for otherwise it would be a great pity. Mistress, I am afraid to write to you, for I understand you have shown my letters that I have sent you previously, but I ask you to let no one see this letter. As soon as you have read it, let it be burned for I wish that no man should see it in any way. You have had no letters from me for these two years, nor will I send you any more. Therefore I send this whole matter to your wisdom. Almighty Jesus preserve, keep, and give you your heart's desire, which I know well to be God's pleasure, etc.

This letter was written with as great pain as was anything I ever wrote, I think, in my whole life, for in good faith I have been sick and am not yet very well recovered, God amend it, etc.

Margaret Paston to John Paston II (10 or 11 September 1469)

I greet you well and send you God's blessing and mine, letting you know that last Thursday my mother and I were with my Lord [bishop] of Norwich, and asked him to do no more in the matter concerning you sister until you and my brother and others who were your father's executors might be here together, for they have authority over her as well as I. And he said plainly that he had been required so often to examine her that he could not, nor would not, delay it longer. And he charged me on pain of anathema that she should not be delayed but that she should appear before him the next day. And I said plainly that I would neither bring her nor send her, and then he said that he would send for her himself, and ordered that she should be free to come when he sent for her. And he said by his oath that he would be as sorry for her if she wasn't doing well as he would be if she were his very near kin, both for my mother's sake and mine, and other of her friends, for he understood well that her behavior had pricked our hearts sorely.

My mother and I informed him that we could never understand her saying by any words she had ever had with him, that either of them were bound to the other, but that they both might choose. Then he said that he would say this to her as well as he could, before he examined her. And so various people told me that he spoke about this as well and plainly as if she had been near to him, which words are too long to write about at this time. Hereafter you shall know that and who were the advocates in this. The chancellor was not so guilty in this as I thought he had been.

On Friday the bishop sent for her by Ashfield and another who were very sorry for her behavior. And the bishop spoke to her plainly and reminded her of her birth, who her kin and friends were, and would continue to have if she were ruled and guided by them, and what rebuke and shame and loss it would be to her if she were not guided by them and on that account she would be forsaking any good or help or comfort she might have from them. And he said that he had heard that she loved a man that her friends were not pleased she should have. Therefore he asked her to be careful what she did and he said he would understand whether or not the words she had said to him made a marriage. And she repeated what she had said, and said boldly that if those words did not make it certain, she would make it more certain before she left there. For she said that she thought in her conscience that she was bound, whatever the words were. These lewd words grieve me and her grandmother as much as all the others. And the bishop and the chancellor both said that neither I nor any of her friends would receive her.

And then Calle was examined apart, by himself, to see if her words and his were in accord, and the time and the place where it had happened. And then the bishop said that he supposed that there might be other things found against him that might allow it to be stopped. Therefore, he said he would not be too hasty to give his judgment on the matter and said that he would bind it over until the Wednesday or Thursday after Michaelmas, and so it is delayed. They would have preferred to have their will confirmed in haste, but the bishop said that he would not do otherwise than he had said.

I was with my mother at her place when Margery was examined and when I heard about her behavior I ordered my servants that she should not be received into my house. I had given her warning that she might have been prudent to be gracious. She was brought back to my place to be received, and Sir James Gloys told those who brought her that I had instructed them all that she should not be received. And so my Lord of Norwich has placed her at Roger Best's, to stay there until the aforesaid day, God knows against his will and his wife's, but evil will happen if they dare to do otherwise. I am sorry that they are encumbered with her, yet I am better off that she is there for the time than if she were in another place, because of the sobriety and good character of he and his wife, because she shall not be permitted to play the brothel there. I ask and require you not to take it too sorrowfully, for I know well that it cuts near to your heart, and so it does to mine and to others'. But remember, as I do, that with her we have lost but a wretch, and so take it less to heart. If she had been good, whatever she had done, it would not have been as it is, for if he were dead at this moment, she would never be in my heart as she was. As for the divorce that you wrote to me about, I suppose what you meant, but I order you upon my blessing that you do not do, nor arrange another to do, what should offend God and your conscience. For if you do it, or arrange for it to be done, God will take vengeance on that account, and you would put yourself and others in great jeopardy. Know well that she shall sorely repent of her lewdness hereafter, and I pray God she be required to. I ask you, for my heart's ease, to be of good cheer in all things. I trust God shall help well, and I pray God do so in all our affairs. I want you to take heed if there was any case made before the court of Canterbury about the aforesaid lewd matter.

TWO: LOVE AND ITS DANGERS

What were the financial considerations pertaining to the proposed marriage between Scrope and Elizabeth Paston? How were rebellious daughters regarded and treated? Who was involved in the marriage negotiations? How was Margery Paston treated by her mother? What was the bishop of Norwich's main concern in his interrogations? Why did Margaret characterize Margery's actions as "lewd"?

163

22. PROSECUTIONS AND PUNISHMENTS FOR SEXUAL MISCONDUCT

Throughout the Middle Ages adultery was proscribed, especially for women, according to secular law, canon law, and popular custom. The church insisted that all sexual activity outside marriage was sinful and, without proper penance, could imperil an individual's salvation. Secular courts were influenced by older attitudes that considered a wife to be her husband's property. Consequently, adultery was theft by one man of another's property. According to popular values, adultery and other wanton behavior disgraced the whole family. These ideas had a remarkable endurance over the centuries.

Adultery in the Merovingian World

Allegations of adultery were serious because they dishonored all of a woman's family. Consequently, women and their families were at pains to prove their innocence. As in this episode, appeals could go to the highest levels and the quarrels result in bloodshed.

Source: Trans. Lewis Thorpe in Gregory of Tours, *The History of the Franks* (Harmondsworth: Penguin, 1974), pp. 294-95; reprinted with permission.

Book 5. 32. In Paris a woman who had left her husband was accused by a number of people of living with another man. The husband's relations went to the woman's father and said: "Either you must prove your daughter's innocence or else let her die, for we cannot permit her adultery to bring disgrace upon our family." "I know that my daughter is completely innocent," answered the father. "There is no truth at all in this rumor which is being spread by malicious people. I will prove her innocence by an oath and so stop the accusation going any farther." "If she really is innocent," they replied, "swear an oath to that effect on the tomb of St. Denis, the martyr." "I will certainly do so," said her father. Having agreed to this, they went off together to the holy martyr's church. The father raised his hands over the altar and swore that his daughter was not guilty. The husband's supporters declared that he had perjured himself. An argument ensued, in which they all drew their swords, rushed at each other and started killing each other in front of the altar. These men were of noble birth and among the leaders of Chilperic's court. Many received sword-wounds, the holy church was spattered with human blood, the portals were pierced with swords and javelins, and weapons were drawn in senseless anger at the very tomb of St. Denis. Peace was restored with great difficulty, but services could not be held in the church until what had happened was brought to the notice of the king. Both parties rushed off to court, but Chilperic refused to exonerate any of them. He sent them to the local bishop with orders that only if they were found not guilty were they to be admitted to communion. They paid a fine for their offences, and so were read-mitted to communion by Bishop Ragnemod, who had charge of the church in Paris. A few days later the woman in question was summoned to trial, but she strangled herself with a rope.

An Adulterer's Punishment (1248)

Outside of the courtroom, popular reactions to adultery and other sexual misconduct could be harsh. The notion that a wronged husband could punish his wife's paramour, or a father his daughter's lover, endured from antiquity. In the rough and ready culture of the Middle Ages, popular justice could be swift and extremely harsh. In this case, the crowd's punishment went beyond the sentence a court would have delivered for seduction or rape. Although many legal codes prescribed castration, or even capital punishment, for rape, in practice such sentences were rarely handed down.

Source: Trans. J.A. Giles in Matthew of Paris, *English History,* vol. 2 (London: Henry G. Bohn, 1853), pp. 277-78; revised.

Although it may appear ridiculous, I do not think the following story ought to be passed over. In this same unlucky month, lest it be said that deplorable scandals only happened to those in religious orders, disgrace and irreparable damage happened to certain knights as well. For a certain knight from Norfolk, by the name of Godfrey de Millers, who was of noble birth and distinguished in military deeds, being wickedly led astray, at night secretly entered the home of the knight, John the Briton, so that he could have sexual relations with John's daughter. However, Godfrey was seized by some people hidden there, with the connivance of the trollop herself, who feared being a mistress, and he was thrown violently to the ground and seriously wounded. After this, he was hung from a beam, with his legs stretched apart. And when he was completely exposed to the will of his enemies, preferring to be beheaded, he was disgrace-fully mutilated by cutting off his genital member. Thus castrated and wounded, half-dead he was thrown out of the house. An angry clamor about this reached the king and the authors of this great cruelty were arrested. In the end, the said John the Briton was convicted and sentenced to be disinherited and exiled for-ever. The whore, however, concealing herself in impenetrable hiding places, could not be found, thus barely escaping plots on her life. As well, everyone who had been present when this enormous cruelty had been done, were dispersed in exile, banished as fugitives. Thus this inhuman and merciless crime involved many noble men in a lamentable calamity. Around the same time, a certain elegant cleric, the rector of a rich church, who surpassed all the knights living around him in giving many rich entertainments and occasions for hospitality, was entangled in a similar misfortune. However, the lord king, touched by compassion, and saddened to the point of sighs and tears, ordered it to be proclaimed as law, by the town crier, that no one should presume to mutilate the genitals of an adulterer, except in the case of his own wife.

Sexual Misbehavior (1475)

From the twelfth century onward the regulation of sexuality was of increasing concern to secular and ecclesiastical authorities. Secular officials were concerned that unregulated sexual behavior could harm the peace and order of their communities. Most sexual offences were brought before the ecclesiastical courts. The church was interested not only in the punishment of wrongdoers but also in the correction of sinners, so its sentences were as much penance for sins as they were punishments for crimes. The prevailing moral code tried to enforce premarital chastity and marital faithfulness on people whose behavior often strayed from these ideals. In such cases, miscreants would be arrested, witnesses called, and a trial held, as part of the mechanisms to control individual behavior and promote morality and social cohesion.

Source: Trans. Shannon McSheffrey from Greater London Record Office, MS DL/C/205, Consistory Court of London Deposition Book, 1467-76, fols. 262v-264r; printed with permission.

James Wolmere c. Agnes Henley: 17 February [1475]

Thomas Yonge of the parish of St. Sepulchre without Newgate, London, spurrier, where he has lived for ten years as a householder, illiterate, of free condition, forty-six years of age, sworn, etc., on the charges, etc. He says that he has known James Wolmere for the last ten weeks or thereabouts, Agnes Henley he does not know, John Rowland for two thirds of a year and not more, Elizabeth Rowland for a year and a half, and Joan Salman for six years …He says that John Rowland, Elizabeth [Rowland], and Joan [Salman] are poor and indigent as they are reputed amongst their neighbors, having only enough goods to sustain themselves, with the exception of Joan, who lives in part from the goods of her mother Elizabeth and in part from other means. And he says that the aforesaid Joan is a woman of ill fame, and is reputed as such in many places in the City of London …He says that the aforesaid Joan Salman was suspiciously arrested with a certain Walter Haydon, capper, on the Tuesday immediately following the last feast of St. Michael the Archangel, by a certain John Jonys, beadle of the ward of Farringdon Without, in a certain house situated in the Old Bailey, and she is reputed to be a woman of evil life and conversation in the said parish of St. Sepulchre. And the aforesaid Elizabeth Rowland was and still is reputed as a bawd because of the aforesaid arrest, because as it is commonly said, Elizabeth was the bawd between Walter Haydon and Joan Salman …And he says that as he himself saw on the day before the arrest, the aforesaid Elizabeth Rowland was in the same house where Joan Salman and Walter Haydon were later arrested, and it is from this that this witness knows that Elizabeth was the bawd and not otherwise …And he says that this witness guarded the door of the house when the said John Jonys, beadle, and William Rest went up to a certain chamber in the said house, and after John Jonys and

This nineteenth-century drawing depicts King Mark surprising his adulterous wife Iseult and her lover Tristan. He is portrayed killing Tristan as a punishment for adultery and betrayal.

William Rest came down again they told this witness as he was guarding the door that they had found Walter Haydon lying on a bed in the room and Joan Salman standing next to the bed.

William Reste, tailor, living in the Old Bailey in the parish of St. Sepulchre, London, where he has lived for seven years and more as a householder, illiterate, of free condition, forty-eight years of age or thereabouts, sworn, etc. He says that he has known James Wolmere for six weeks or thereabouts, Agnes Henley he does not know, John Rowland and Elizabeth his wife for a year, and Joan Salman for the same period of time ...He says that he was present in the said room on the aforesaid Tuesday when Joan Salman stood next to the bed with Walter Haydon lying on it, and when Walter and Joan were suspiciously caught there, John Jonys immediately took them to jail ...He says that Walter Haydon and Joan Salman were caught in the room as he said before around the hour of nine p.m. on that Tuesday.

Why did people want the woman's father to go to the tomb of St. Denis? Why did the woman hang herself? What are some examples of how adultery threatened familial honor? Why would a husband have more latitude than a father in the case of a woman's adultery? How might a woman's reputation influence the attitudes of the court? What do these cases suggest about privacy in medieval communities?

CHAPTER THREE:

MARRIAGE AND THE CHURCH

In the course of the early Middle Ages, the church had been successful at gradually assert-ing its jurisdiction over matters of marriage and sexual morality. These were viewed as inextricably linked to questions of sin and salvation. Adultery, fornication, and incest were serious sins so it was important for individual salvation to know that one's marriage was both legal and valid in the eyes of God. By the twelfth century, marriage was recog-nized as one of the seven sacraments and thus accorded special dignity that differentiated it from informal unions that were prevalent, especially among rural people.

Many of the church's teachings about marriage, however, were at variance with the practices of secular society and the social role that marriage played in establishing alliances and uniting families for economic or political purposes. In this atmosphere, repudiation and re-marriage were expedient. The church, however, taught that marriage was monog-amous and indissoluble. Moreover, the sacrament of marriage was achieved only through the freely exchanged consent of the spouses; the wishes of family or lords were theoreti-cally irrelevant.

The process by which the laws governing marriage were developed and disseminated was lengthy. By the beginning of the thirteenth century, the church had arrived at a com-prehensive law and theology of marriage; then began the complicated and slow process of disseminating that teaching and ensuring it was implemented in the lives of the laity. Evidence from fourteenth- and fifteenth-century ecclesiastical court records suggests that the laity continued to marry informally and to separate at their convenience. Now, how-ever, they were more likely to appear before a court that was intent on enforcing marriage law and regularizing practice.

23. THE THEOLOGY OF MARRIAGE: PETER LOMBARD'S *SENTENCES*

Over the centuries, various popes and church councils had rendered decisions pertaining to specific questions or controversial or problematic marriage cases. These decisions, while designed to provide solutions to specific cases, also established precedents. Moreover, these various decisions were often at odds with secular society's values and practices concerning marriage. The church used its authority and influence to promote its Christian under-standing of marriage, based on scripture and the teachings of the church fathers. By the twelfth century, there was a need for an organized, systematic, and definitive teaching on marriage. Two important works appeared that attempted to synthesize and systematize the myriad of previous teachings. The first was The Concordance of Disconcordant Canons, *better known as the* Decretum, *compiled by the Bolognese canon lawyer Gratian, ca. 1140. The second was* The Four Books of Sentences *written by the Parisian theologian Peter Lombard, ca. 1150.*

Both these writers addressed the theory and practice of marriage, its nature, how it was achieved, and the rules and regulations that governed it. Both affirmed the central tenets of the church's teaching: that marriage was monogamous and indissoluble. Both, too, discussed the conditions, such as consanguinity or immaturity, that impeded the for-mation of the marriage bond.

Where Gratian and Lombard differed, however, was on what constituted a valid, indissoluble marriage. Gratian argued that freely exchanged mutual consent was the only requirement for the formation of the marriage bond; physical consummation perfected that bond. Peter Lombard differed from Gratian on two important points. First, he down-played the role of sexual intercourse, noting that the Virgin Mary and Joseph had not consummated their union but must necessarily have been validly married. Second, Lom-bard refined the nature of the consent required, stating it must not only be exchanged freely but must be stated in words of the present tense (verba de presenti). *Promises to marry exchanged in words in the future tense* (verba de futuro) *did not form an indis-soluble bond. If the couple engaged in sexual intercourse subsequent to exchanging future consent, however, they were considered to be married.*

The significance of these teachings on the history of marriage should not be underes-timated. They formed the foundation for Christian practice that can still be observed. Moreover, by establishing the necessity of free and reciprocal consent, at least in theory, the church gave both men and women the possibility of autonomy from family and lords who wished to control their decisions. Thus, much of the individualistic nature of western mar-riage practices can be traced to these teachings developed in the twelfth century.

Source: Trans. Jacqueline Murray and Abigail Young from Peter Lombard, *Sententiae in IV libris dis-tinctae*, vol. 3, 3rd ed. (Grottaferrata: Collegii S. Bonaventurae, 1981), pp. 416–17, 419–20, 422–24, 427–28, 433–37, 439, 441, 446–47, 450, 462–69, 473–76, 508.

Book 4. Distinction 26

1.1 *Concerning the sacrament of marriage: the institution and cause of which is shown.* Although the other sacraments began after sin and on account of sin, it is read that the sacrament of marriage rather was instituted by the Lord, even before sin, not as a remedy but as an office....

2.1 *Concerning the twofold institution of marriage.* Moreover, the institution of marriage is twofold. The first was created in paradise, before sin, as an office, where the bed was unstained and marriages were honorable, from which Adam and Eve conceived without passion, gave birth without pain. The second was created outside paradise, after sin, as a remedy, in order to avoid illicit passions. The first was so that nature would be multiplied, the second so that nature might be excused and sin avoided. For, before sin, God said: "Go forth and multiply" (Gen. 1.28) and also, after sin, when almost every human being had perished in the flood (Gen. 9.1)....

2.3 If the first human beings had not sinned, they and their progeny would have joined without the urging of the flesh and the heat of lust. Just as some good deed is worthy of a reward, so their coitus would have been good and worthy of a reward. But, because of sin, the deadly law of concupiscence is inherent in our members, without which there is no carnal union. Their coitus is reprehensible and evil, unless it is excused by the goods of marriage....

5.2 That marriage is a good thing is shown not only by the fact that the Lord is said to have instituted marriage between our first parents, but also because Christ was present at a marriage at Cana in Galilee, and he commended it with a miracle, turning the water into wine (John 2.2-10). Also, afterwards, he forbade a husband to dismiss his wife, except for the reason of fornication (Matt. 5.32, Mark 10.11, Luke 16.18). Also, the Apostle Paul said: "A virgin does not sin if she marries" (1 Cor. 7.28). Therefore, it is established that marriage is a good thing. Otherwise it would not be a sacrament, for a sacrament is a holy sign.

6.1 *Of what marriage is the sacred sign.* Therefore, since marriage is a sacrament, it is both a sacred sign and the sign of a holy reality, that is of the union of Christ and the church, just as the Apostle Paul says. It is written, he says: "A man will leave his father and mother and cling to his wife, and they will be two in one flesh. Moreover, this is the greatest sacrament for I am speaking about Christ and the church" (Eph. 5.31-32). So that, between spouses, also, the union is made by consent of the souls and by the intermingling of the bodies. Thus, the church is joined to Christ by will and by nature, because she likewise wishes to be with him and he himself assumed the form of a human being. Therefore, the bride is joined to the bridegroom spiritually and bodily, that is by love and by conformity to nature. A sign of both of these unions is in marriage: for consent of the spouse signifies the spiritual union of Christ and the church, which happens through love, while the union of the sexes signifies that which happens by conformity to nature....

Book 4. Distinction 27

2. *What marriage is.* Therefore, nuptials or marriage is the marital union of a man and a woman, between lawful persons, maintaining an indivisible mode of life. "An indivisible mode of life" means that neither is able to profess continence or withdraw for prayer without the consent of the other, and that while they are alive, a conjugal bond endures between them, so that it is not licit for them to join with another, and each shall offer to the other that which belongs to each. Moreover, in this description only the marriage of lawful and faithful persons is included.

3.1 *Concerning the consent which makes marriage.* Moreover, the efficient cause of marriage is consent, not any kind but that expressed by words, not in the future tense but in the present tense. For if they consent in the future tense, saying I will take you as my husband, and I will take you as my wife, this consent does not make marriage. Likewise, if they consent in their minds and do not express it by words or by other sure signs, neither does such consent make marriage. Moreover, if consent were expressed in words, even though they did not will it in their heart, then that bond of the words with which they consented, saying I take you as my husband and I take you as my wife, makes marriage, provided that there was no coercion or deceit there....

4.1 *When marriage begins to exist.* But, in fact, they are spouses from that promise in which the marital agreement is expressed....

5.1 *According to some there is no marriage before sexual intercourse, but rather they are betrothed persons.* Some, nevertheless, assert that true marriage is not contracted before the bride is handed over and sexual intercourse occurs, nor are they truly spouses before sexual union occurs, but rather that from the first promise of betrothal the man is a bridegroom and the woman a bride, not a spouse. Moreover, they say that betrothed men and women are frequently called "spouses" not because they are but because they will be, since they have made a solemn promise between them concerning this matter. And on this account they claim that the words of the previous authorities must be understood in this way.

5.2 *On what reason they depend.* But they argue further that there is a great difference between a bride and a wife from this, that although a bride is allowed to choose to enter a convent before consummation, without consulting her bridegroom or even when he is unwilling, this done, the bridegroom is also allowed to marry another. But a married man or a married woman cannot preserve continence, except by mutual consent, nor enter monastic life, unless both of them equally profess continence....

7. And therefore they assert that from the first promises of betrothal they are called spouses, not because of their present state but because of their hope for the future, because from that pledge, which they owe to one another in turn, they are afterwards made spouses. Even the foregoing authorities, by whom it is asserted that consent makes marriage, are to be understood in this way, so that consent or the marriage agreement does not make marriage prior to consummation, but in consummation. For, just as the deflowering of virginity does not make marriage unless a marriage agreement occurs first, so neither the marriage agreement makes marriage before sexual intercourse occurs. Therefore, by the marriage agreement they become a betrothed couple before intercourse, but in intercourse they are made spouses. For the marriage agreement causes she who was formerly betrothed, in sexual intercourse to become a wife.

8. *The response to the aforesaid, with the conclusion of the foregoing points.* Moreover, thus we respond to them. Sometimes a betrothal occurs where there is a promise by a man and a woman to contract marriage, however, there is then no consent in the present tense. It is a betrothal having consent in the present tense, that is a marriage agreement, which alone makes marriage. Therefore, in that betrothal where there is a promise to contract marriage, they are only betrothed persons, not spouses, and it is permitted to such betrothed persons to profess continence and enter religious life without marital consent. But in that betrothal where there is consent in the present tense, marriage is contracted and from the first pledge of that betrothal they are called true spouses. And the learned speak variously about betrothed persons in accordance with this distinction of betrothal....

Book 4. Distinction 28

2.1 *Those things which pertain to the necessity and those to the propriety of the sacrament.* For in celebration of this sacrament, just as in others, there are certain things pertinent to the substance of the sacrament, such as present consent, which alone is sufficient to contract marriage. But there are certain things that are pertinent to the propriety and solemnity of the sacrament, such as the handing over of the bride by her parents, the blessing of the priest, and such like, without which the marriage occurs lawfully as to its power but not as to the propriety of the sacrament.

2.2 Therefore, without these things, they do not come together as lawful spouses but as adulterers and fornicators. So, too, those who marry in secret, they especially are fornicators, unless consent expressed in words of the present tense should support them, which consent makes a lawful marriage. For secret consent, expressed in words of the present tense, also makes marriage, although there it is not an honest contract. But consent does not ratify a marriage which was made in secret. For if one should dismiss the other, he or she is not forced to return and remain with his or her spouse by the judgment of the church, because a contract which was made in secret cannot be proved by witnesses. But if they, themselves, who consented to each other in secret, should voluntarily declare that same consent in public, then the proper consent supports them and lawful vows help them to ratify the marriage which previously had been contracted secretly. Therefore, consent expressed secretly by words supports them that a marriage occurred, but expressed publicly supports them to sanction and strengthen the marriage, and makes it possible for the church to judge concerning this, if need be.

3.1 *Concerning the very nature of that consent, whether it is to sexual intercourse, to cohabitation, or to something else.* This is asked since present consent makes marriage, of what nature that consent is, whether it is to sexual intercourse or to cohabitation or to both. If consent to cohabitation makes marriage, then a brother is able to contract marriage with his sister, a father with his daughter. If it is to sexual intercourse, then there was no marriage between Mary and Joseph. For Mary proposed to remain a virgin unless God ordered her to do otherwise, according to that which she is seen to have said to the angel: "How can this be since I do not know a man?" (Luke 1.34). That is, I have decided that I will not know a man. For it was not necessary for her to ask how she could have a son because she did not then know a man but because she had decided she would never do so. Bede, in his Commentary on Luke, said that she intended to remain a virgin. Therefore, if she afterwards consented to sexual intercourse, contrary to her intention, it would seem that she would have been guilty concerning the vow, even if it was not violated in deed.

3.2 *Behold what that consent was to.* Therefore, let us say that consent to cohabitation or to sexual intercourse does not make marriage, but rather consent to conjugal partnership, expressed according to words in the present tense, as when a man says, "I take you as my wife," not mistress, not servant, but spouse.

4.1 *Why woman was formed from the side of man.* Now, because she was not given as a servant or mistress, therefore, in the beginning she was neither formed from the highest nor the lowest, but from the side of man on account of the conjugal partnership. If she had been made from the highest, that is from the head, she would seem to have been created for domination. But if from the lowest, that is from the feet, it would seem that she ought to be subjected to servitude. But because she was intended neither as a mistress nor as a servant, she was created from the middle, that is the side, because she was intended for conjugal partnership.

4.2 Therefore, since they thus unite, so that the man says, "I take you as my spouse" and the woman says, "I take you as my husband" by these words, or others signifying the same thing, consent is expressed not to sexual intercourse or to physical cohabitation but to conjugal partnership, from which they ought to cohabit, unless, perhaps, they are separated bodily by a mutual vow to enter religious life, either for a period of time or for the rest of their lives.

Book 4. Distinction 29

1.1 *Coercion prevents marital consent, according to Pope Urban.* Moreover, marital consent ought to be free from coercion. For coerced consent, which ought not to be called consent, does not make marriage, as Pope Urban proves, writing to Sanchez, king of Aragon, in these words: "Concerning the marriage of your niece whom you have asserted by faithful promise that you intend to give to a certain knight in the present time of necessity, we decree, as fairness demands, that if, as is said, she has refused him completely as her husband, and if she persists in the same decision, so that she absolutely denies that she will ever marry that man, by no means shall you force her, unwilling and resisting, to be joined in marriage to that man."

1.2 *Concerning the daughter of Prince Jordanes.* Likewise: "But if what the legates of Prince Jordanes told us is established as true, that is that he himself coerced and sorrowing and his daughter weeping and resisting with all her might, he promised her in marriage to Rainald. Since the authority of the laws and canons do not approve of such a betrothal, lest this would seem very harsh to those ignorant of the laws and canons, thus we will temper our decision so that if the prince, with the consent of his daughter, should wish to complete that which was coerced, we will allow it. But if, however, four legates should hear both of the parties, and even if there is nothing on the part of Rainald which would further impede the union, let the legate accept from the same Jordanes an oath by which those things which have been said before may be confirmed. And we, following the writings of the canons and the laws, after this, will not prohibit his aforesaid daughter, if she wishes, from marrying another man 'in the Lord'."

1.3 From this it appears that marriage is to be made between persons consenting voluntarily, not between those resisting and unwilling. Nevertheless, those who are unwilling and forced to marry, if afterwards they cohabited for some length of time, without objection and complaint, with the ability to separate and the disposition to protest, they would seem to consent and that consequent consent supplies that which the preceding coercion took away....

Book 4. Distinction 30

2.1 *Concerning the marriage of Mary and Joseph.* Something ought to be added to the foregoing about the manner of that consent which occurred between Mary and Joseph. Certainly, it can be believed that not only Mary but also Joseph, for his own part, had decided to preserve virginity, unless God should order otherwise. And they thus consented to conjugal partnership, so that each would understand from the other, by the revelation of the spirit, that each wished to preserve virginity unless God should inspire otherwise. But they had not expressed this wish in words, but afterward they expressed it and they remained in virginity. Therefore, Mary consented to marital partnership but not to sexual intercourse unless God would specifically order it of her, by whose counsel she consented to marital union, because she wanted to preserve her virginity and so had not otherwise consented to marital partnership unless she had the familiar counsel of God....

3.1 *Concerning the final cause of marriage.* It has been shown what is the efficient cause of marriage. It follows to show from what cause marriage is usually contracted or ought to be contracted.

3.2 Therefore, the final cause for contracting marriage is principally the procreation of children. For, on account of this, God instituted marriage between the first parents, to whom He said: "Go forth and multiply." The second reason, after the sin of Adam, is to avoid fornication. Whence the Apostle Paul said: "On account of fornication let each man have his own wife and each woman her own husband" (1 Cor. 7-2). And there are other honest reasons such as the reconciliation of enemies and the reestablishment of peace. There are also other less honest reasons, on account of which it is sometimes contracted, such as the beauty of a man or woman which frequently impels souls inflamed by love to enter into marriage, so that they are able to satisfy their desire. Also, profit and the possession of riches is frequently a reason for marriage; and there are many others which it is easy for the diligent reader to discern....

Book 4. Distinction 31

5.1 *Concerning the excusing of intercourse which happens for the sake of these goods.* Therefore, when these three goods [faithfulness, sacrament, children] occur together in any marriage they can excuse sexual intercourse. For when spouses join for the sake of conceiving children, preserving the faithfulness of the marriage bed, intercourse is thus excused so that it has no blame. But when they come together because of incontinence, with the good of offspring lacking, even though marital faithfulness is preserved, the intercourse is not thus excused so that it bears no blame, but the fault is venial. Whence Augustine wrote in his book, *On the Good of Marriage*: "Marital intercourse for the sake of procreation has no guilt, however, marital intercourse for the sake of satisfying concupiscence, even though with one's spouse, on account of the faithfulness of the marriage bed, has venial guilt." Likewise: "The fact that married people, conquered by lust, use each other beyond what is necessary for procreating children, I count among those things for which we say each day: 'forgive us our trespasses'."

5.2 Moreover, where these goods are absent, that is faithfulness and children, it does not seem that intercourse can be free from blame. Whence in the *Sentences* of Sextus the Pythagorean it is read: "Every man who loves his own wife too ardently is an adulterer." Likewise, Jerome says: "A wise man loves his spouse judiciously not passionately. For the forces of sensual pleasures do not reign in him nor does he rush headlong to intercourse. Nothing is more filthy than to love a wife as if she were an adulteress. Those men who say that they have married their wives for the sake of bringing up children shall, in all events, imitate beasts and after the wife's belly has swollen, they should not destroy their children nor should they act like lovers to their wives, but like husbands." Likewise: "In marriage the acts of procreating children are conceded, however, the pleasures which are taken in the embraces of prostitutes are damned in a wife."...

8.1 *That not every pleasure of the flesh is as sin.* But perhaps someone should say that every carnal desire and pleasure which is in intercourse is bad and a sin because it is from sin and is disordered. And we say that that desire is always bad because it is filthy and a punishment for sin, but it is not always sin. For often a holy man experiences bodily pleasure in something, such as in resting after work, eating after hunger, however, such pleasure is not a sin unless it is immoderate. So, also, the pleasure which is experienced in marital intercourse, in which those three goods are present, is protected from sin....

Book 4. Distinction 34

1. *Concerning lawful persons.* Now it remains to consider which persons are lawful for purposes of contracting marriage. Lawful persons are judged according to the decrees of the fathers, which are diverse. For some were lawful marriage partners before the Law, others under the Law, others in the time of grace. Likewise, in the primitive church certain persons were lawful who now are not. But now there are those who are lawful or unlawful, those who are fully lawful, those who are partially. They are fully lawful who are not hindered by a vow of continence, or holy orders, or a blood relationship, or a different religion, or social condition, or natural frigidity, or some other reason. Persons are completely unlawful by vows, orders, blood relationship, and a different religion. They are partially lawful, that is neither fully lawful nor completely

unlawful marriage partners, by frigidity or social condition. For if such persons are joined unknowingly, they are able to remain together from whatever accidental cause and are divided by these deficiencies.

2.1 *Concerning the separation of frigid persons.* Concerning those who are unable to render the conjugal debt by reason of frigidity, the blessed Gregory the Great advised that they should remain together. But if the woman gives an excuse, saying, "I want to be a mother and bear children" he determined that both of them, along with seven oath-helpers, should swear that they had never joined physically and then let the woman contract a second marriage. But let the man who is frigid by nature remain without hope of marriage....

2.3 *From a letter of Gregory the Great*: Likewise: "Concerning those persons about whom you enquired, who claim that they are not able to be joined, trying their best physically, by reason of a frigid nature. [He advises:] Let that man, if he is not able to use her as a wife, hold her as a sister. [And he explains this:] But if they should wish to rescind the conjugal bonds, then let each remain unmarried. For if he is naturally unable to unite with this one, how can he be joined to another? Therefore, if the man wants to take another wife, the reason is clear: since the devil supplied the kindling of hate, he detested her and therefore he attempted to dismiss her on the basis of falsehoods. But if the woman should give an excuse and say: 'I want to be a mother and bear children,' then let each of them, swearing with seven oath-helpers, while touching the sacred relics, say that they never became one flesh by joining in sexual intercourse. Then it seems that the woman is able to contract a second marriage: 'I say human on account of the weakness of their flesh' (Rom. 6.19). But, let the man who is frigid by nature remain without a wife. If that man should join with another, then those who swore are guilty of the crime of perjury and after doing penance let them be forced to accept the first marriage."

2.4 This ought to be observed when both confess the same thing. But if the husband asserts that he rendered the debt to his wife and she differs, it is asked which of them ought to be believed. Thus, is was decided by the Council of Compendium: "If some man should take a wife and have her for some time, and that woman says that he has never joined with her, and that man says that he did so, the man's statement should stand because 'the man is the head of the woman'" (Eph. 5.23). This is established concerning a natural incapacity....

4.1 *It is added concerning the insane*, according to Pope Fabian: Also, while they are out of their minds, the insane are not able to contract marriage. Whence, Fabian said: "Neither an insane man nor an insane woman can contract marriage, but if there was a contract, let them not be separated."...

5.1 *Concerning those men who sleep with two sisters.* Also, concerning those men who sleep with two sisters or those women who sleep with two brothers, it seems that the canons censure them....

5.4 Whence, Gregory the Great said: "They who catch their wives in adultery cannot take another wife nor she another husband while both are alive. But if the adulteress happens to die, her husband can marry if he wishes, but the adulteress can never marry. Even if her husband dies let her lamenting, perform penance for all her days." This is done concerning that adultery which is committed with a relative of the husband or a relative of the wife.

6. *A wife ought not to be dismissed on account of some blemish or bodily deformity.* Also, this should be known, that it is not allowed for a man to dismiss his wife for some infirmity or physical blemish, and the converse, but the one ought to provide help to the other. *Wherefore, Augustine says in his book on the Lord's Sermon on the Mount:* "If anyone has a barren wife or one who is deformed in body, or weak in her limbs, or blind, or lame, or deaf, or anything else, whether she has been debilitated by disease or by labor and sorrow, no matter how very horrible it might be, (except for fornication) he shall sustain her in companionship and faithfulness.

Book 4. Distinction 35

1.1 *The husband and wife obey the same law.* This also ought to be noted, that when the Lord allowed a wife to be dismissed by her husband on account of fornication, the same license was not given to the woman. *Wherefore Jerome says in his letter to Oceanus on the death of Fabiola:* "The Lord decreed that a wife not be put away except for the cause of fornication, and if she were put away, that she should remain unmarried. Whatever is ordered for men consequently applies to women also, for it is not the case than an adulterous wife must be dismissed and an adulterous husband must be kept." Likewise, Jerome says: "Among us what is not allowed for women is equally not allowed for men and the same liability is condemned on equal terms." From this it is shown that a woman can remain with her husband despite his fornication, just as a husband with his wife.

1.2 *Whence Pope Innocent wrote:* "The Christian religion condemns adultery in either sex with equal reason. But women are not easily able to accuse their husbands of adultery. But men were accustomed to denounce more freely their adulterous wives before the priests. And, therefore, communion is denied to women when their crime has come out. Moreover, when a man's crime has been committed secretly, it is not easy for someone to be kept from communion by suspicions alone. He will be removed from the communicants if his deed is detected.

2. *That a man is not able to dismiss his fornicating wife unless he himself were devoid of sin.* But if it is asked whether an adulterer is able to dismiss an adulteress on account of fornication, we say an adulterous wife cannot be dismissed by her husband unless, indeed, he lived free from fornication, and the reverse....

3.1 *That they, who were separated by reason of fornication, are able to be reconciled.* If some man, free from fornication, dismissed his fornicating wife, he cannot be joined to another, but ought to remain continent or return to the dismissed wife; and so, too, concerning the woman. Whence the Apostle Paul said: "Those who are joined in marriage, not I but the Lord, order, a wife should not leave her husband, but if she leave, she should remain unmarried, or be reconciled to her husband" and concerning the husband he adds: "And let a man not divorce his wife" (1 Cor. 7.10-11)....

Book 4. Distinction 36

1.1 *If a wife can be separated from her husband on account of extreme circumstances, and the converse.* Now let us consider under what circumstances a marriage can be broken. To which we say, since a free woman is not denied the ability to marry a bondsman, but if he was not known to be of servile condition, he can freely be dismissed when his servitude has been discovered, according to this ruling from the Council of Vermaria: "If any freeborn man should take a bondswoman of another as his wife and he thought that she was a freewoman, if that woman herself is afterwards revealed to be a serf, if he is able to redeem her from servitude, let him; if he is not able, if he wishes, he may wed another. But if he knew she was a bondswoman and he approved, let him thereafter accept her as his lawful wife. Likewise, at the same council it was decreed: "If a freeborn woman should marry a bondsman, knowing that he was a serf, let her have him, because we all have one father in heaven. Let there be one law for man and for woman."

1.2 When it is stated "knowing he was a serf," it is to be understood that if she did not know he was a serf, she is not to be forced to remain with him. For if she were deceived about his status, she is not forced to remain with him by whose fraud she was deceived. But if the man knew the status of the woman, he cannot dismiss her, and the reverse....

2.1 *Concerning the union of a bondsman and a bondswoman of different lords.* It is also asked if the bondsman of one lord may marry the bondswoman of another lord, and whether there is marriage between them. At the Council of Chalon-sur-Saône it was decreed concerning this: "It is decreed by us that they who destroy the lawful marriages of serfs, on the basis of some powerful supposition, are not considering this: 'What God has joined together let no one separate'." Whence it seems to us that the marriages of serfs should not be destroyed, even if they have different lords, but remaining together in one bond of matrimony, let them serve their lords. And this ought to be observed in those cases where the marriage was legal and occurred with the approval of the lords.

2.2 Consider the end of this canon, where it seems to hint that without the approval of the lords a marriage is not able to be contracted between a bondsman and a bondswoman or, if contracted, it is not valid. However, it seems to some that a marriage can occur between them when the lords are unaware of it....

4.1 *Concerning the age for contracting marriage.* This also ought to be known, that boys before fourteen years old and girls before twelve are by law unable to enter matrimony. If, before the aforesaid age, they entered a union, they can be separated, albeit they were joined with the will and consent of their parents. But those who, joined in childhood, do not wish to abandon the union after reaching puberty but to remain joined, by this are rendered spouses and thereafter are unable to be separated.

4.2 Likewise, betrothals cannot be contracted before the age of seven. For they are contracted by consent alone which is not able to occur unless what is being done is understood by both parties.

4.3 We have described those two problems with the addition of some others, by which marriage can be dissolved, although it is not necessary that they always be dissolved. Now we must add the other things which make people completely unlawful marriage partners, and the first thing to consider is holy orders.

Book 4. Distinction 37

1.1 *In which orders marriage cannot happen.* Therefore, there are certain orders in which marriage is by no means able to be contracted and, if such a union should occur, it is dissolved: orders such as priest, deacon, and subdeacon. In other orders it is permitted to choose marriage unless they took up the religious habit or made a vow of continence....

Book 4. Distinction 42

7.1 *Concerning second, third, and subsequent marriages.* It ought also to be known that not only are first or second marriages licit but also third and fourth ones are not condemned....

What was the nature of conjugal intercourse before the Fall? What two things establish the marriage bonds? What is meant by "an indivisible mode of life"? What is the nature of the consent that makes marriage? What other things ought to occur in a lawful marriage? Why must consent be public? How did the marriage of Mary and Joseph influence the understanding of consent? What was the purpose or final cause of marriage? What were other acceptable reasons for marriage? less honest reasons? What are appropriate motives for sexual intercourse? Why were frigid persons not able to marry? What is the importance of the various teachings concerning the marriage of serfs? What was the legal age for marriage? Why do orders and vows of continence prohibit marriage?

24. A WOMAN'S VIEW OF MARRIAGE: HILDEGARD OF BINGEN'S *SCIVIAS*

Hildegard of Bingen (1098-1179) was one of the most remarkable women of the Middle Ages. She was a nun, ultimately becoming abbess of the community at Rupertsburg. She was widely read and both studied and wrote treatises on subjects as wide-ranging as medicine and music. She was an able administrator and gifted preacher, and some of the most prominent figures of the day, including Eleanor of Aquitaine and St. Bernard, were among her correspondents. Hildegard was also a mystic and experienced visions throughout her life. She recorded these visions in three books, the most famous of which is Scivias, in which God's voice is heard through Hildegard. In all of Hildegard's works, the great abbess brought her own unique interpretation and perspective to bear on important questions ranging from human physiology to theology and human salvation. Frequently, Hildegard's background in medicine and physiology is reflected in her discussions of human nature and sexuality; so, too, is Hildegard's perspective as a woman brought to bear. Hers is one of the few female voices surviving from the Middle Ages, and her writings, while certainly orthodox and reflecting the values and beliefs prevalent in the church, nevertheless present a uniquely female perspective as well.

Source: Trans. Columba Hart and Jane Bishop in Hildegard of Bingen, *Scivias* (New York: Paulist Press, 1990), pp. 77-84, 215, 474.

Vision Two

11. What things are to be observed and avoided in marriage

Because a mature woman was given not to a little boy but to a mature man, namely Adam, so now a mature woman must be married to a man when he has reached the full age of fertility, just as due cultivation is given to a tree when it begins to put forth flowers. For Eve was formed from a rib by Adam's ingrafted heat and vigor, and therefore now it is by the strength and heat of a man that a woman receives the semen to bring a child into the world. For the man is the sower, but the woman is the recipient of the seed. Wherefore a wife is under the power of her husband because the strength of the man is to the susceptibility of the woman as the hardness of stone is to the softness of earth.

But the first woman's being formed from man means the joining of wife to husband. And thus it is to be understood: this union must not be vain or done in forgetfulness of God, because he who brought forth the woman from the man instituted this union honorably and virtuously, forming flesh from flesh. Wherefore, as Adam and Eve were one flesh, so now also a man and woman become one flesh in a union of holy love for the multiplication of the human race. And therefore there should be perfect love in these two as there was in those first two. For Adam could have blamed his wife because by her advice she brought him death, but nonetheless he did not dismiss her as long as he lived in this world, because he knew she had been given to him by divine power. Therefore, because of perfect love, let a man not leave his wife except for the reason the faithful church allows. And let them never separate, unless both with one mind want to contemplate my son, and say with burning love for him: "We want to renounce the world and follow him who suffered for our sake!" But if these two disagree as to whether they should renounce the world for one devotion, then let them by no means separate from each other, since, just as the blood cannot be separated from the flesh as long as the spirit remains in the flesh, so the husband and wife cannot be divided from each other but must walk together in one will.

But if either husband or wife breaks the law by fornication, and it is made public either by themselves or by their priests, they shall undergo the just censure of the spiritual magisterium. For the husband shall complain of the wife, or the wife of the husband, about the sin against their union before the church and its prelates, according to the justice of God; but not so that the husband or wife can seek another marriage; either they shall stay together in righteous union, or shall both abstain from such unions, as the discipline of church practice shows. And they shall not tear each other to pieces by viperous rending, but they shall love with pure love, since both man and woman could not exist without having been conceived in such a bond, as my friend Paul witnesses when he says:

12. Words of the apostle on this subject

"As the woman is of the man, so is the man for the woman; but all are from God" (1 Cor. 11.12). Which is to say: woman was created for the sake of man, and man for the sake of woman. As she is from the man, the man is also from her, lest they dissent from each other in the unity of making their children; for they should work as one in one work, as the air and the wind intermingle in their labor. In what way? The air is moved by the wind, and the wind is mingled with the air, so that in their movement all verdant things are subject to their influence. What does this mean? The wife must cooperate with the husband and the husband with the wife in making children.

Therefore the greatest crime and wickedest act is to make by fornication a division in the days of creating children, since the husband and wife cut off their own blood from its rightful place, sending it to an alien place. They will certainly incur the deceit of the devil and the wrath of God, because they have transgressed that bond God ordained for them. Woe to them, therefore, if their sins are not forgiven! But although, as has been shown, the husband and wife work together in their children, nevertheless the husband and the wife and all other creatures come from the divine disposition and ordination, since God made them according to his will.

13. Why before the Incarnation some men had several wives

Before the Incarnation of my son, however, certain men among the ancient people had several wives at once, as they wished; they had not yet heard the open prohibition of my son, who when he came into the world showed that the right fruit of this union of husband and wife as long as they live is the fruit manifest in the union of Adam and Eve, a union to be exercised not by the will of man but by the fear of God. For it is better to have this right union, by the arrangement of the prudence of the church, than to crave fornication; but you humans ignore this, and pursue your lusts not only like humans but like beasts.

But let there be right faith and pure love of the knowledge of God between husband and wife lest their seed be polluted by the devil's art and divine vengeance strike them because they are biting and tearing each other to pieces and sowing their seed inhumanly with the wantonness of beasts. In such a case jealousy will torture them like a viper, and without the fear of God and without human discipline a defiled excess of seed will be stored up in them, and often, by the just judgment of God, this perversity of theirs will be chastised by having those born of them deprived of limbs and of health in their lives; unless I receive their penitence and show myself propitious to them. For if any shall call upon me in penitence for their sins, I will accept their penitence for the love of my son; for if anyone lifts a finger to me in penitence, that is, reaches out to me in penitence and groaning in his heart, saying, "I have sinned, Lord, before you!" my son, who is the priest of priests, will show me that penitence; for penitence which is offered to priests for the love of my son obtains the purgation of the sinners. Therefore, people who worthily do penance escape from the jaws of the devil, who, trying to swallow the hook of divine power, has grievously wounded his jaw; and now, therefore, faithful souls pass out of perdition and arrive at salvation. How?

Because the priests at the altar, invoking my name, will receive the confession of the peoples and show them the remedy of salvation. So, in order to find God propitious, let them not contaminate their seed by various vices, since those who emit their semen in fornication or adultery render their children, born of them thus, unsound. How? Can he who mixes mud or ordure with pure clay make a lasting vessel? Likewise, will he who contaminates his semen in fornication or adultery ever beget strong sons? But many work in different ways in their inmost being, and many of these become prudent toward the world and toward God. And with these the heavenly Jerusalem is filled; deserting vice and loving virtue, they imitate my son in chastity and in great works, carrying in their bodies, as much as they are able, his martyrdom.

But when I do not wish a person to have children, I take away the virile power of the semen, that it may not coagulate in the mother's womb; so also I deny the earth the power to bear fruit when by my just judgment I will to do so. But do you wonder, O human, why I let children be born in adultery and similar crimes? My judgment is just. For, since the fall of Adam, I have not found in human seed the justice that should have been in it, for the devil drove out this justice by the taste of the fruit. Therefore I sent my son into the world born of a virgin, so that by his blood, in which there was no carnal pollution, he might take away from the devil those spoils that he had carried off from humanity.

14. No human or angel but only the son of God could deliver Man

For neither a human being, conceived in sin, nor an angel, who has no covering of flesh, could save man, wallowing in sins and laboring under the heaviness of the flesh, from the power of the devil; but only he who, coming without sin, with a pure and sinless body, delivered him by his Passion. Therefore, though human beings are born in sin, I nevertheless gather them into my heavenly kingdom when they faithfully seek it. For no wickedness can take my elect from me, as Wisdom testifies, saying:

15. Words of Wisdom on this subject

"The souls of the just are in the hand of God; and the torment of death shall not touch them" (Wisd. 3.1). Which is to say: The souls of those who embrace the path of rectitude with devout affection are aided by the celestial helper; so that, because of the good works by which in the height of justice they strive for heaven, the torment of perdition does not break them, for the true light strengthens them in the fear and love of God. But after Adam and Eve were driven out of the place of delight, they knew in themselves the work of conceiving and bearing children. And falling thus from disobedience into death, when they knew they could sin, they discovered sin's sweetness. And in this way, turning my rightful institution into sinful lust, although they should have known that the commotion in their veins was not for the sweetness of sin but for the love of children, by the devil's suggestion they changed it to lechery; and, losing the innocence of the act of begetting, they yielded it to sin. This was not accomplished without the devil's persuasion; for that purpose he sent forth his darts, and it did not come to pass without his suggestion; as he said,

"My strength is in human conception, and therefore humanity is mine!" And, seeing that if man consented to him he would become a sharer in his punishment, he said again within himself: "All iniquities are against most powerful God, since he is certainly not unjust." And that deceiver put this as a great seal on his heart, that man, who had consented to him of his own accord, could not be taken away from him.

Therefore I took secret counsel within myself, to send my son for the redemption of humanity, that man might be restored to the heavenly Jerusalem. And no iniquity could withstand this counsel, for my son, coming into the world, gathered unto himself all who, forsaking sin, chose to hear and imitate him. I am just and righteous, not willing the iniquity that you, O human, embrace when you know you can do evil. For Lucifer and man each tried at the beginning of their creation to rebel against me and could not stand firm, but fell away from good and chose evil. But Lucifer laid hold of total evil and rejected all good, and did not taste the good at all, but fell into death. Adam, however, tasted the good when he accepted obedience, but he longed for evil, and in his desire accomplished it by his disobedience to God. Why this happened is not for you, O human, to investigate; mortal cannot know what there was before the creation of the world or what may happen after the last day, but God alone knows this, except insofar as he permits his elect to know it.

But that fornication, which is commonly done by people, is abominable in my sight, for I created male and female from the beginning in integrity and not in wickedness. Therefore those hypocrites who say it is lawful for them to commit fornication, with animal appetites, with whomever they wish, are unworthy of my eyes, because, despising the honor and loftiness of their rationality, they look to the beasts and make themselves like them. Woe to those who live so and persevere in this wickedness!

16. Blood relatives may not be united in marriage

I also do not wish the blood of relatives to be mingled in marriage, where the ardor of family love is not yet weakened, lest there arise shameless love in the relation of consanguinity; but let the blood of different families flow together, which feels no blood relationship burning within it, so that human custom may work there.

17. Example of milk

Milk that is cooked once or twice has not yet lost its flavor, but by the time it is coagulated and cooked the seventh or eighth time, it loses its qualities and does not have a pleasant taste except in case of necessity. And as one must not have sexual relations with a relative who is one's own spouse, so also one must abhor a sexual relationship with a relative related not to one but to one's spouse; let no human being join in such a coupling, which the church by its doctors, who established it in great responsibility and honor, has forbidden.

18. Blood relatives could marry in the Old, but not in the New Testament

Under the Old Testament people married their blood relatives by the precept of the law, but that was allowed because of their hardheartedness, so that they might be at peace among themselves and charity be strengthened in them; so that these tribes would not break my covenant by dividing and mixing with the pagans in marriage, until the time came when my son brought the fullness of charity, changing the joining of relatives in carnal bonds into marriages with different people in bashful modesty. Thus, since the bride of my son [the church] now possesses in holy baptism a bond of my fear and righteous justice, let such joinings of relatives be far from her; for the embraces of a man and woman related by blood would be wickedly enkindled into shameless fornication and ceaseless lust much more than those of unrelated people. I am explaining this by this person [Hildegard], to whom this human operation is unknown; she is receiving this explanation not from human knowledge, but from God. What next?

19. A man should be adult to marry and take only a wife of marriageable age

When a male is at the age of strength, so that his veins are full of blood, then he is fertile in his semen; then let him take in lawfully instituted marriage a woman who is also at the age of heat, that she may modestly receive his seed and bear him children in the path of rectitude.

20. On the avoidance of illicit and lustful pollution

But let not a man emit his semen in excessive lust before the years of his strength; for if he tries to sow his seed in the eagerness of lust before that seed has enough heat to coagulate properly, it is proof that he is sinning at the devil's suggestion. And when a man is already strong in his desire, let him not exercise his strength in that work as much as he can; because if he thus pays attention to the devil, he is doing a devilish work, making his body contemptible, which is entirely unlawful. But let the man do as human nature teaches him, and seek the right way with his wife in the strength of his heat and the vigor of his seed; and let him do this with human knowledge, out of desire for children.

But I do not want this work done during the wife's menses, when she is already suffering the flow of her blood, the opening of the hidden parts of her womb, lest the flow of her blood carry with it the mature seed after its reception, and the seed, thus carried forth, perish; at this time the woman is in pain and in prison, suffering a small portion of the pain of childbirth. I do not remit this time of pain for women, because I gave it to Eve when she conceived sin in the taste of the fruit; but therefore the woman should be cherished in this time with a great and healing tenderness. Let her contain herself in hidden knowledge; she should not, however, restrain herself from going into my temple, but faith allows her to enter in the service of humility for her salvation. But because the bride of my son is always whole, a man who has open wounds because the wholeness of his members has been divided by the impact of a blow shall not enter my temple, except under the fear of great necessity, lest it be violated, as the intact members of Abel, who was a temple of God, were cruelly broken by his brother Cain.

21. A woman shall not enter the temple after birth or defloration by a man

So a woman, too, when she bears offspring, may not enter my temple except in accordance with the law I give her, because her hidden members have been broken, that the holy sacraments of my temple may be unviolated by any masculine or feminine pain or pollution; because the most pure virgin bore my son, and she was whole without any wound of sin. For the place that is consecrated in honor of my only-begotten should be untouched by any corruption of bruise or wound, because my only-begotten knew in himself the integrity of the virgin birth. Therefore, let a woman who breaks the wholeness of her virginity with a man also refrain from entering my temple while injured by the bruise of her corruption, until the injury of that wound is healed, in accordance with the sure instruction of church teaching. For when his bride was wedded to my son on the wood of the cross, she kept herself hidden until my son commanded his disciples to teach the truth of the gospel throughout the whole world; but afterward she arose openly and publicly preached the glory of her bridegroom in the regeneration of the Spirit and water. So let a virgin who is joined to a husband do the same, namely remain hidden with modest shame until the time which church opinion appoints for her; and when she has given herself over to the love of her husband in her concealment, let her come forth openly.

22. *Those who have intercourse with the pregnant are murderers*

I do not want that work of man and woman to take place from the time when the root of a little child has already been placed in the woman, lest the development of that little child be polluted by excessive and wasted semen, until her purification after childbirth. After that it may be done again, in rectitude and not in wantonness, for the love of children. Thus the human race may procreate by honest human custom, and not as foolish people babble when they claim it is lawful to satisfy their lust at will, saying, "How can we contain ourselves so cruelly?" O humans, if you pay attention to the devil, he will incite you to evil and destroy you with his deadly poison; but if you raise your eyes to God, he will help you and make you chaste. Do you not desire chastity in your works rather than lust? The woman is subject to the man in that he sows his seed in her, as he works the earth to make it bear fruit. Does a man work the earth that it may bring forth thorns and thistles? Never, but that it may give worthy fruit. So also this endeavor should be for the love of children and not for the wantonness of lust.

Therefore, O humans, weep and howl to your God, whom you so often despise in your sinning, when you sow your seed in the worst fornication and thereby become not only fornicators but murderers; for you cast aside the mirror of God and sate your lust at will. Therefore the devil always incites you to this work, knowing that you desire your lustfulness more than the joy of children. Hear, then, you who are among the towers of the church! In your fornication do not accuse me, but consider yourselves; for when you despise me and run to the devil you do unlawful things, and therefore you do not wish to be chaste; as my servant Hosea says, speaking of the corrupted people ...

Vision Five

24. *Married people cannot become monastics unless both agree to do it*

If any layperson desires to renounce worldly things to bear the yoke of my liberty, let him come to me quickly, unless he is in the bonds of a fleshly union. This tie he may not rashly loose unless his consort wills it. How? Husband may not leave wife and wife may not leave husband for this purpose unless it is the will of both, and they both decide either to remain in the world or to separate from the world; for it cannot be that a whole person can remain well if one foot remains with his body and the other is cut off from it. So it is not fitting for a husband to worship the world while his wife deserts the world, or for a wife to reside in the world while her husband flees the world, if they wish to have glory in celestial life; for if this is done indiscreetly and foolishly, it will be called a robbery rather than an offering. So let those who are legally joined in a fleshly union live together with one mind, and not foolishly separate from each other without a dispensation or declaration from church authority, as is written again in the gospel ...

Vision Ten

3. Admonition to the married

But I do not reject the chaste coupling of legitimate marriage, which was set up by divine counsel when the children of Adam were fruitful and multiplied. But it is to be done for the true desire of children and not for the false pleasure of the flesh, and only by those to whom it is allowed and harmless by divine law, those allied to the world and not set apart for the Spirit. You should love the good you have from me better than yourself. You are heavenly in spirit but earthly in flesh; and so you should love heavenly things and tread the earthly underfoot. When you do heavenly things I show you a supernal reward; but when you seek to do what is unjust by the will of your flesh, I show you my martyrdom and the pains I endured for your sakes, that you may fight your wrong desires for love of my Passion.

You have been given great intelligence; and so great wisdom is required of you. Much has been given to you, and much will be required of you. But in all these things I am your head and your helper. For when heaven has touched you, if you call on me I will answer you. If you knock at the door, I will open to you. You are given a spirit of profound knowledge, and so have in yourself all that you need. And, this being so, my eyes will search you closely and remember what they find.

Therefore, I require of your conscience a wounded and sorrowful heart; for thus you can restrain yourself when you feel drawn toward sin and burn in it to the point of suffocation. Behold, I am watching you; what will you do? If you call upon me in this travail, with a wounded heart and tearful eyes and fear of my judgment, and keep calling on me to help you against the wickedness of your flesh and the attacks of evil spirits, I will do for you all that you desire, and make my dwelling-place in you.

According to Hildegard, what are the results of fornication or adultery? How did sexual intercourse become sinful? Why is fornication condemned? How does Hildegard's knowledge of physiology and medicine influence her ideas about marriage, sex, and procreation? How is Hildegard's female perspective reflected in her discussions of marriage and intercourse? In what ways are the teachings in her visions related to the doctrines of Peter Lombard's Sentences?

25. THE GOOD OF MARRIAGE:
ETIENNE DE FOUGÈRES

Etienne de Fougères (d. 1178) was chaplain to King Henry II of England. In 1168 he became bishop of Rennes but his association with Henry's court endured. He is best known for Le Livre des Manières, *written between 1173 and 1178. This poem, written in French, is one of the earliest examples of an estates poem, a poem that examines all of Christian society according to the various estates or orders of society. Etienne's poem examines various groups such as kings, knights, clergy, peasants, burghers, and women and the bonds that should exist between them to ensure the proper functioning of a healthy society. In the course of this examination, he identifies and criticizes instances of moral and social degeneracy that contribute to a decaying social order. One of the areas that Etienne considered to be potentially problematic is human sexuality. For Etienne, sexuality was a source of social disruption unless it was strictly controlled and regulated by the church, through the institution of marriage. He expounds upon disordered sexuality when he discusses women of the courtly ranks. He criticizes women for using cosmetics, seduction, adultery, abortion, and, significantly, for same-sex sexual activity. This litany of sexual misconduct, however, allows Etienne to highlight the joys of marriage including marital companionship, sexual fulfillment, and the rewards of child-rearing. His, then, is one of the few positive evaluations of marriage that counterbalanced literature promoting the superiority of a chaste mode of life.*

Source: Trans. Robert A. Clark from Etienne de Fougères, *Le Livre des Manières*, ed. R. Anthony Lodge (Geneva: Droz, 1979), ll. 973-1252; printed with permission.

Of ladies and lasses,
chambermaids, servants,
girls and maidens,
I've heard many a tale.

Countesses and queens
are much worse than simple maids
for they are the source of hatred,
quarrels and rapine.

Any fool for the asking
can have their love on the spot.
Behold: here are the seeds of war
that send people into exile and to the grave.

From ancient tales,
both Christian and pagan,

Nineteenth-century drawings of the funeral effigies of Henry II of England and Eleanor of Aquitaine. Their turbulent marriage captured the imagination of medieval contemporaries as much as modern observers.

> that are read in courts and synods,
> hear what evil high-born ladies do.
>
> Because of Helen of Troy
> ....
> Because of Delilah–may God never look upon her–
> Samson the strong lost his glory.
>
> The high-born lady who is coquettish
> argues and fights with her husband;
> she is dull and evasive towards him
> but burns for his inferior.

She considers herself high and mighty
if whole armies perish because of her;
she takes great pleasure in her lechery
and couldn't care less who laughs or cries for it.

Once the fire has been kindled
she prizes neither husband nor lord,
nor the whole world more than a strawberry!
Nor does she care what path she takes

as long as she can achieve her ends.
This is what she says to those who would reproach her:
she wants to take vengeance on her lord
who takes too much pleasure in mistreating her.

But by my faith! it's a vile kind of vengeance
When one heaps blame on oneself.
I'd sooner relinquish my case
than shame myself through vengeance.

Towards her husband she's sullen and mute
but what a change when she's with him!
for her lover she paints her face and changes
more than the sparrow-hawk fresh from molting.

For her companion in adultery
she seeks out the bile from next to the sheep's kidney
and tallow of white dog
to concoct her eye makeup.

A hundred curses may he have who lies about this!
From quicklime and yellow arsenic
they make a paste for hair removal,
but it doesn't smell like balm.

With the masks from her kit
she makes herself a beautiful woman from an ugly one;
from a whore she makes herself a maid,
from a wrinkled crone, a beauty.

The lady who adorns herself this way is a fool,
for God says so through the prophet
that such an appearance is not pleasing to him,
that he doesn't recognize her, nor did he make her so.

The woman who is a sorceress I consider
still crueler and more fierce:
she makes plasters in such a way
that many a good man lies in his bier.

She makes figures out of clay and wax
and says I don't know what charms,
for the devil can certainly kill
those whom the priest is accustomed to curse.

She torments her husband,
and poisons him
with the stem and tip of harmful herbs:
he will surely be dead before the hour of prime.

She kills the children carried by her daughters
when they have conceived in low couplings;
to kill them is nothing more to them
than to eat fat eels.

And there are those, so says Ovid,
who kill themselves most horribly
when they think they are killing their child,
and thus do they commit double homicide.

The rich lady who hates her distaff
and neither weaves nor spins nor unwinds her skein,
nor beats nor shakes the butter churn–
she sheds all cares,

except for making herself fine and pretty
and painting herself white or red,
and she says that her youth would go to waste
if she didn't apply herself to love.

She's good at loving her lover sweetly,
but as for her husband, he's bitter to her;
she's good at entreating her lover
and complaining often about her husband.

If her husband tries to discipline her
so that she can't reach her lover,
who might not hear her pretend to be sick
and be sick without any illness to complain of?

Then she yawns and stretches
and says that she has the shivers.
Her go-between comes and tells her
to have herself carried to a vigil.

She gets herself called to the vigil,
not for prayer but for play,
where she can find the one
who makes her deny God.

If she doesn't manage to find him
on the way there or on the way back,
she doesn't know what to do with herself.
She has to settle for sex with the lackeys.

Once she's coupled with them,
she says, "Such is my fate."
But such offspring is born in this way
by which noble blood is brought to an end.

The inheritance of her noble lord
falls into the hands of a bastard;
this is why young men now are not as great
as those of the old times.

If his heir is a bad apple, what can he do about it?
The offspring of a cat must hunt mice.
The offspring of a pig wallow in the mud
and the man is good, in turn, who is born of good parents.

The noble sons of noble fathers,
of good and noble mothers,
don't inflict heavy sorrows
but take pity on others' misfortunes.

There's nothing surprising about the "beautiful sin"
when nature prompts it,
but whosoever is awakened by the vile sin
is going against nature.

One must pursue [him] with dogs,
throw[ing] stones and sticks;
one should smite him with blows
and kill him like any other cur.

These ladies have made up a game:
with two bits of nonsense they make nothing;
they bang coffin against coffin,
without a poker stir up their fire.

They don't play at "poke in the paunch"
but join shield to shield without a lance.
They have no concern for a beam in their scales,
nor a handle in their mold.

Out of water they fish for turbot
and they have no need for a rod.
They don't bother with a pestle in their mortar
nor a fulcrum for their see-saw.

In twos they do their lowlife jousting
and they ride to it with all their might;
at the game of thigh-fencing
they pay most basely each other's share.

They're not all from the same mold:
one lies still and the other grinds away,
one plays the cock and the other the hen,
and each one plays her role.

I've told and related quite a lot to you
about the shameful acts of debased hearts;
but it won't be valued much
unless I speak to you of their goodness as well.

If Orhan and Organite were foolish women,
Tecle and Margaret were wise
and many another little woman
still living amongst us.

A woman who is good is a precious thing:
she never ceases to do good,
she draws high praise from everyone for her good speech,
and boldly gives good advice and does good deeds.

The man who insults women is a churl
whether he's from the town or the country,
and he gets women through some sort of trick.
And in the gospel

we often find mention of women,
and so it was intended for us that,
in our extreme perdition,
redemption was through a woman.

We had lost the City
of Heaven which was our inheritance,
and we were redeemed by him
in whom God took on humanity.

When God deigned to descend into her
and take on human flesh in a woman
and take away death and give back life,
well can we think and understand

that he raised woman up above man,
even if that man were St. Peter of Rome;
that noble lady is now above the angels,
she who took away the evil of the apple.

The abbot can bless monks,
and sanctifying nuns is the bishop's
ministry, according to custom.
And yet we also read in St. Paul

that a good wife is an ornament
to her lord, and she doesn't fail in her task
when she loves him and serves him in goodness
and gives him true counsel.

If a wife loves her husband,
she is not guilty before God or any man;
she can call his name out with confidence
and address all her troubles to him.

By the faith I owe St. Mary!
No joy is so sure
as that of husband and wife.
Never will their joy be taken from them.

They give each other such joy as they see fit,
and they don't care who may find them together.
Cursed be the joy that must be hidden away,
in which one trembles with fear!

What's sinful with a young girl
for whoever desires her in a lascivious way,
a man can do with his spouse
without incurring a heavy penance.

And the lady conceives and carries
and gives birth to a child, if she doesn't miscarry,
in which she finds pleasure and joy
and all her delight is a great comfort to her.

And her husband, as is his hope,
also takes great pleasure in his children,
and he looks forward to enjoying the fruits
when they have been raised and educated.

Children are a good thing to have
when they have understanding and wisdom;
their parents nurture their possessions for them.
But I know one thing for sure to be true:

that they drive their father and mother mad
when they kiss and embrace them:
for them they rob and steal,
for them they borrow and can't pay;

They work their bodies to exhaustion;
take and give sureties;
besiege and attack castles.
When they've done all that, they die and pass away.

Those who have children count their wealth,
dress poorly and fast even more;
and those who have none share their possessions
with the poor, very often and without regret.

The countess of Hereford
knows well if I'm right or wrong,
she who had children but who have all died;
now all her joy is with God.

She makes chapels, adorns altars,
shelters and houses the poor,
always rises and goes to bed
with a cheerful, not a mournful, countenance.

If she meets a dignitary,
a bishop, abbot, prior, or monk,
a hospitaler or a white canon,
she honors and serves him without making a fuss.

She offers them amices and albs
and chasubles of cloth from Trent,
which she cuts and sows with great application,
and she buys them with her own income.

She loves her husband loyally
and everyone treats her with great honor,
the oldest and the youngest,
the greatest and the most humble.

Women who are of good will
can take her as an example,
For their soft, white, and tender [skin]
will first be resplendent and then ash.

The most tender and the most pampered
will all too soon be withered and rotten;
then they won't find anyone to give them a smile,
to make them tarry or do them honor.

Neither in town nor in the market
will they be courted by anyone;
smooth and plucked eyelids
will be enclosed and shut away.

This is where shrieking,
Grumbling and sulking,
and adorning and combing
and washing and keeping oneself trim will end up.

Corporeal beauty is a fragile thing,
the only thing beautiful is the skin outside;
but anyone who could see inside the body,
then there would appear what treasure is within.

For if the outer skin is marred
through injury or disfiguring,
with bumps or with sores,
so perishes a woman's beauty.

May God maintain the good woman in the good,
bring the foolish woman back to the straight path and keep her there
and grant her that she keep herself there
so that peace and pardon may come to her.

What are the characteristics of a bad wife? How does adultery harm the nobility? What is "the beautiful sin"? What metaphors are used to describe the vile sin? Are they clear? What are the characteristics of a good marriage? What is the difference between sex and sexual desire inside and outside marriage? What role do children play in a good marriage?

26. ECCLESIASTICAL LEGISLATION: THE FOURTH LATERAN COUNCIL (1215)

In 1215, Pope Innocent III convened the Fourth Lateran Council. This was one of the most important ecumenical councils of the Middle Ages and brought together bishops, abbots, and other ecclesiastical officials from across Christendom. The council aimed at a thorough reform of church law and practice as it pertained to every level of society and every aspect of life. Thus, there were provisions to reform the clergy and enhance their education. There were also numerous canons directed toward the laity to ensure their orthodoxy and religious practices. Of particular importance were the provisions governing marriage. In many ways, the provisions of the Fourth Lateran Council were the culmination of the preceding process of articulating the fundamental doctrines of marriage including monogamy, exogamy, and indissolubility. The Council developed provisions to implement the church's teachings about marriage in a relevant and workable manner, at the parish level.

A nineteenth-century drawing of a medieval marriage. A bride and groom clasp hands and exchange consent while a priest conducts the wedding ceremony.

One of the major areas of reform was the definition of the degrees of consanguinity and affinity that prohibited the formation of a valid marriage bond. In the seventh century, these had been established to be seven degrees of relationship. This proved to be an insupportable burden on the laity, either because they could not find a suitable marriage partner beyond these relationships or because, in the absence of written records of births and marriages, there were no reliable witnesses to confirm or deny if a couple were distantly related. Furthermore, dynastic and politically advantageous unions were being made, despite the prohibitions, with the certain knowledge that the couple could easily separate should it be necessary in the future. Thus, these broad prohibitions threatened the very principles of exogamy and indissolubility.

Another strategy that the Council invoked to ensure the legitimacy of marriages was to prohibit clandestine marriages. By insisting on a public announcement of the impending nuptials by the reading of the banns three times, the church was providing an opportunity for those who might be aware of an impediment to come forward. In close-knit communities it was conceivable that the people could be unaware of their exact family tree. Oral tradition and the memories of village elders were among the few ways to reconstruct complicated kinship ties in the absence of written records. Thus, the church sought to ensure the integrity of marriages by requiring that they be public and open to community scrutiny.

Source: Trans. Norman P. Tanner, *Decrees of the Ecumenical Councils* (London: Sheed and Ward, 1990), vol. 1, pp. 257-59; reprinted with permission.

The Decrees of the Fourth Lateran Council (1215)

50. On the Restriction of Prohibitions to Matrimony

It should not be judged reprehensible if human decrees are sometimes changed according to changing circumstances, especially when urgent necessity or evident advantage demands it, since God himself changed in the New Testament some of the things which he had commanded in the Old Testament. Since the prohibitions against contracting marriage in the second and third degree of affinity, and against uniting the offspring of a second marriage with the kindred of the first husband, often lead to difficulty and sometimes endanger souls, we therefore, in order that when the prohibition ceases the effect may also cease, revoke with the approval of this sacred council the constitutions published on this subject and we decree, by this present constitution, that henceforth contracting parties connected in these ways may freely be joined together. Moreover the prohibition against marriage shall not in future go beyond the fourth degree of consanguinity and of affinity, since the prohibition cannot now generally be observed to further degrees without grave harm. The number four agrees well with the prohibition concerning bodily union about which the apostle says, that "the husband does not rule over his body, but the wife does; and the wife does not rule over her body, but the husband does;" for there are four humors in the body, which is composed of the four elements. Although the prohibition of marriage is now restricted to the fourth degree, we wish the prohibition to be perpetual, notwithstanding earlier decrees on this subject issued either by others or by us. If any persons dare to marry contrary to this prohibition, they shall not be protected by length of years, since the passage of time does not diminish sin but increases it, and the longer that faults hold the unfortunate soul in bondage the graver they are.

51. On the Punishment of Those who Contract Clandestine Marriages

Since the prohibition against marriage in the three remotest degrees has been revoked, we wish it to be strictly observed in the other degrees. Following in the footsteps of our predecessors, we altogether forbid clandestine marriages and we forbid any priest to presume to be present at such a marriage. Extending the special custom of certain regions to other regions generally, we decree that when marriages are to be contracted they shall be publicly announced in the churches by priests, with a suitable time being fixed beforehand within which whoever wishes and is able to may adduce a lawful impediment. The priests themselves shall also investigate whether there is any impediment. When there appears a credible reason why the marriage should not be contracted, the contract shall be expressly forbidden until there has been established from clear documents what ought to be done in the matter. If any persons presume to enter into clandestine marriages of this kind, or forbidden marriages within a prohibited degree, even if done in ignorance, the offspring of the union shall be deemed illegitimate and shall have no help from their parents' ignorance, since the parents in contracting the marriage could be considered as not devoid of knowledge, or even as affecters of ignorance. Likewise the offspring shall be deemed illegitimate if both parents know of a legitimate impediment and yet dare to contract a marriage in the presence of the church, contrary to every prohibition. Moreover the parish priest who refuses to forbid such unions, or even any member of the regular clergy who dares to attend them, shall be suspended from office for three years and shall be punished even more severely if the nature of the fault requires it. Those who presume to be united in this way, even if it is within a permitted degree, are to be given a suitable penance. Anybody who maliciously proposes an impediment, to prevent a legitimate marriage, will not escape the church's vengeance.

52. On Rejecting Evidence from Hearsay in a Matrimonial Suit

It was at one time decided out of a certain necessity, but contrary to the normal practice, that hearsay evidence should be valid in reckoning the degrees of consanguinity and affinity, because on account of the shortness of human life witnesses would not be able to testify from first-hand knowledge in a reckoning as far as the seventh degree. However, because we have learned from many examples and definite proofs that many dangers to lawful marriages have arisen from this, we have decided that in future witnesses from hearsay shall not be accepted in this matter, since the prohibition does not now exceed the fourth degree, unless there are persons of weight who are trustworthy and who learnt from their elders, before the case was begun, the things that they testify: not indeed from one such person since one would not suffice even if he or she were alive, but from two at least, and not from persons who are of bad repute and suspect but from those who are trustworthy and above every objection, since it would appear rather absurd to admit in evidence those whose actions would be rejected. Nor should there be admitted in evidence one person who has learnt what he testifies from several, or persons of bad repute who have learnt what they testify from persons of good repute, as though they were more than one and suitable witnesses, since even according to the normal practice of courts the assertion of one witness does not suffice, even if he is a person resplendent with authority, and since legal actions are forbidden to persons of bad repute. The witnesses shall affirm on oath that in bearing witness in the case they are not acting from hatred or fear or love or for advantage; they shall designate the persons by their exact names or by pointing out or by sufficient description, and shall distinguish by a clear reckoning every degree of relationship on either side; and they shall include in their oath the statement that it was from their ancestors that they received what they are testifying and that they believe it to be true. They shall still not suffice unless they declare on oath that they have known that the persons who stand in at least one of the aforesaid degrees of relationship, regard each other as blood-relations. For it is preferable to leave alone some people who have been united contrary to human decrees than to separate, contrary to the Lord's decrees, persons who have been joined together legitimately.

What were the degrees of prohibited relationship reduced to? How were these to be proved? What was meant by a clandestine marriage? What happened to children of a clandestine marriage or to those whose parents were related within the prohibited degrees?

27. EPISCOPAL LEGISLATION: THE STATUTES OF SALISBURY (1217-19)

In order to disseminate the reforms to marriage that had been legislated by the Fourth Lateran Council, bishops enacted local diocesan legislation. The Statutes of Salisbury, enacted between 1217 and 1219, were the earliest of these, and formed the basis of all subsequent English legislation. The bishop who enacted these statutes, Richard Poore, was a zealous reformer who was determined that the church's doctrines would have a practical effect at the parish level. Poore's statutes expand on the Lateran reforms and develop strategies to enforce them. They also reveal the ideas about marriage that the church was teaching to the laity, the very people who married and had children. Significantly, these regulations also reveal exactly how the rules and regulations governing marriage were to be taught to the laity. Priests were required to preach on these topics to their parishioners; they were to instruct people on the exact words necessary to form the conjugal bonds. Interestingly, while prohibiting clandestine or private marriage, the church at the same time ensured that people knew the exact words necessary to exchange consent and marry each other, without benefit of priest or witnesses. Thus, while trying to control marriage and enforce its jurisdiction, the church was also promoting the possibility of individual autonomy in matters of marriage. This Salisbury legislation shows the ultimate effect of the ideas of Gratian and Peter Lombard and the provisions of the Fourth Lateran Council when they were implemented at the parish level.

Source: Trans. J. Murray from F.M. Powicke and C.R. Cheney, eds., *Councils and Synods With Other Documents Relating to the English Church* (Oxford: Clarendon Press, 1964), vol. 2, pp. 85-90.

The Statutes of Salisbury (1217-19)

78. Concerning marriage cases

Likewise, we forbid either an archdeacon, a deacon, or a priest to presume to decide when a case is in doubt, without consulting the bishop, either pronouncing in favor or against a marriage, but let every doubt concerning marriage always be referred to the bishops.

79. Concerning Prohibited Marriages

Let priests admonish and forbid any man from making a contract of marriage with a woman whom he has defiled by adultery while her husband was alive, and this is so if the adulterer has promised the adulteress that he would marry her, while her husband was alive, or even if the adulterer or the adulteress herself had conspired in the death of her husband.

80. Concerning Recluses

Let every priest admonish recluses, if he should have any in his parish, lest he receive a young woman in his house at night, and similarly neither should a woman receive a young man, nor should a woman be enclosed without the testimony of the priest and of trustworthy men.

81. Concerning Fornication and Adultery.

Moreover, because a clamor has arisen to our ears, and we fear that it has risen to the ears of the lord Sabbahot, concerning fornications, adulteries, and incestuous sexual unions and other scandals frequently committed in prebends and prebendial churches which, by the admonition and order of the bishop, according to the statutes of the Council, ought to be corrected within a suitable period of time by the chapter, lest the blood of souls be looked for on our hands, by the strict authority of the Council, we order that (by the feast of St. John) those things which warrant correction, be corrected by the chapter. Otherwise, having God before our eyes, thereafter, in so far as the cure of souls requires, we will do what needs to be done to carry out the responsibilities of our office.

82. Concerning the Praise of Marriage

Let priests be eager to praise marriage, zealously and in various ways, by the dignity and goods of marriage itself, rendering detestable, by the contrary, the embraces of fornicators, confidently asserting marriage to be among the other sacraments, to have been created first and first instituted by the Lord himself in paradise. And since the goods of marriage are faith, children, and sacrament; the faith of the marriage bed, children for the worship of God, the sacrament of Christ and the church, it appears that in this life marriage is especially desirable, good, and privileged. For the children born of legitimate marriage are alone not excluded from dignities, as much ecclesiastical as civil, however, those born otherwise are rejected as if spurious.

83. Concerning the Reverence of Marriage

On account of this, we order that marriages be celebrated with honor and reverence, not with laughter and jokes, not in taverns, with public drinking or feasting. Nor should any man place a ring of reeds or another material, vile or precious, on young women's hands in jest, so that he might more easily fornicate with them, lest, while he thinks himself to be joking, he pledge himself to the burdens of matrimony. Moreover, do not let a promise of contracting marriage be given to anyone, except before a priest and three or four trustworthy people called together for this reason. But if it were done otherwise, not only would the pledge be held as nothing but also, even if sexual intercourse were to follow. Nevertheless, since they disturb the church of God exceedingly, and those contracting in such a way throw their souls into danger, we order that such people be sent to us, and we will send them to the Apostolic See, as disturbers of the peace of the church and people contemptuous of the laws of the church. And we direct that this statute be officially announced to the people every Sunday.

84. Concerning the Correct Form of Contracting

Likewise, we order that priests teach people contracting this form of words, in French or in English: "I, N[ame], accept you as mine." And similarly let the woman say: "I, N[ame], accept you as mine." For there is great power in these words and marriage is contracted by them. Nor let a priest presume to unite any persons in marriage without the banns being read out publicly and solemnly in church, three times, for which announcement being made absolutely no fee may be exacted. And if either person to be married is a complete stranger, let the priest in no way lend his authority to such a contract, unless it be proved to him beforehand that the people are able to contract legitimately. Similarly, if either of them is a stranger, let him or her have letters testimonial that he or she is able to contract legitimately and that the banns were read out three times in his or her parish.

85. Concerning Clandestine Marriages

Similarly, we prohibit clandestine marriages, directing that they be done publicly, before the church, in the presence of a priest called for that purpose. But if it were done otherwise, let it not be approved except by our special authority. Let a priest or other cleric who disdain to prohibit such unions or presumes to be present at them, be suspended from office for three years, in accordance with the statutes of the [Fourth Lateran] Council. And let him be punished more harshly if the degree of his guilt warrants it. But also, let appropriate penance be enjoined on those who should presume to be joined in such a fashion, even within a permitted degree.

86. Let Neither Sorcery nor Magic be Practiced in Marriages

Let sorcery and magic always be prohibited in marriages under pain of excommunication, and let everyone be held under such penalty, who hides impediments to marriage: vows, orders, consanguinity, affinity, disparate cult, compaternity. And only these four persons are excluded from marriage: godfather, godmother, godchild, spiritual brother or sister; that is to say the son or daughter of one's godfather. And let this serious warning be repeated frequently in every single parish.

87. Concerning the Marriage of Consanguines

Moreover, we prohibit a man from contracting with any woman who is a blood relation of his former wife, and similarly a wife with a blood relative of her former husband, up to the fourth degree. Likewise, a godson cannot contract marriage with the daughter of his godparent, whether she was born before or after the baptism took place.

88. Concerning the Provision of Pregnant Women

Likewise, let priests warn the pregnant women of their parish that when they realize the time of birth is beginning, they should arrange for themselves that they have water ready and at hand, and on account of the imminent danger, they speak with a priest concerning their confession, lest suddenly preoccupied, they are not able to have the opportunity to speak to a priest when they want.

89. Concerning the Entry of Married People into Religious Life

Likewise, let priests frequently teach the people and prohibit, under the pain of anathema, lest either spouse enter religious life, nor should he or she be received except by us or by our license. Likewise, let them teach women not to make vows except with the greatest deliberation and with their husband's consent and their priest's advice.

90. Concerning the Degrees of Marriage

In the General Council it was proclaimed that henceforth the prohibition of conjugal union should not exceed four degrees of consanguinity and affinity since this kind of prohibition of conjugal unions was generally not able to be observed, in the more distant degrees, without serious injury to souls. Whence, since now the prohibition of marriage is limited to the fourth degree, it is sanctioned that henceforth they who should presume to be united against this kind of prohibition, may not be defended by the length or duration of years, since the duration of time does not diminish but augments the sin. Moreover, we announce to you, by the authority of the Council, that regulations forbidding marriage contracts in the second and third degrees of affinity, and that the offspring born of a second marriage not be joined to a relative of the first husband, are abrogated and that such persons are permitted hereafter to contract marriage freely.

91. Concerning the Appropriate Time Period of Contracting

Likewise, when marriages are about to be contracted, they are to be proclaimed publicly in churches by priests, with a predetermined suitable period of time prescribed, so that a person who wishes or is capable can bring forward a legitimate impediment, and the priest may, nevertheless, investigate whether any impediment stands in the way. Moreover, when a probable conjecture appears against contracting marriage, let the contract be expressly forbidden until what ought to be done about it is clear from manifest evidence. But children born in the prohibited degree, even ignorantly, are absolutely considered illegitimate, having no protection from the ignorance of their parents since, by contracting in such a way, they appear not to lack knowledge or, at least, they affect ignorance. In the same way, an offspring is considered illegitimate if both parents, knowing of a legitimate impediment exceeding any prohibition, still presume to contract in the sight of the church. Moreover, if someone should bring forward a malicious impediment to impede a legitimate union, he or she will not escape ecclesiastical punishment.

92. Concerning the Evidence of Consanguinity in a Contract

Likewise it is decreed that in computing the degrees of consanguinity and affinity evidence based on hearsay is not valid unless serious people should appear in whom, rightly, there is confidence and they learned the things testified from their elders, before the suit was moved, and not on any account from one who could not be a reliable witness were he were alive, but from trustworthy people and those who are beyond any objection, since it would seem absurd enough to have admitted those whose authority would be refused.

Why should a priest preside at a marriage? What disabilities face illegitimate children? How and where should marriages not be celebrated? What sign of marriage does a man give a woman? How are those who marry clandestinely to be treated? What words form a marriage contract? How would people know this formula? What is necessary in order for a stranger to marry? What happens to priests who allow clandestine marriages?

28. THE PARISH PRIEST AND THE RULES OF MARRIAGE

The theories of marriage developed by theologians, and the laws governing marriage codified by canon lawyers and promulgated by popes and bishops and church councils, resulted in a highly complex set of rules and regulations. These rules, however, were extremely important to the daily life of ordinary people. They established the validity of a marriage, the legitimacy of children, and ultimately whether a couple were true spouses or bigamists, or guilty of incest or fornication. The implications were enormous; inheritances could be challenged and, at the highest reaches of society, international peace treaties could rise or fall according to the legitimacy of a marriage.

In the thirteenth century, in the wake of the reforms of the Fourth Lateran Council (1215), the need to make comprehensible the complex rules concerning marriage and the impediments to it was particularly acute. Parish priests needed to know how to compute the degrees of relationship or what other factors to consider when judging whether a couple could validly marry. To meet this need, little handbooks began to be written to present the rules of marriage in a simple and easy-to-read form. One of these, the Templum Dei *(The Temple of God), written between 1220 and 1230, presented the rules in a schematic form. This manual was written by Robert Grosseteste (ca. 1170-1253), who became bishop of Lincoln in 1235. Grosseteste was a reformer and devoted to enhancing the education of parish priests. This is but one of the many manuals he wrote, designed to aid priests in their administration of the sacraments.*

By presenting his material in diagrams, Grosseteste made the complex rules of marriage much more accessible. Thus, assessing the prohibited degrees of consanguinity was much simplified. So, too, the impediments to marriage were easier to understand. In particular, the charts clearly distinguish diriment impediments, those impediments which prohibited the formation of the conjugal bond and required a couple to separate, from simple impediments which forbade marriage but which allowed a couple to remain together in the event they went ahead in any case. It was through simplified manuals such as this one that the majority of priests would have learned about marriage and instructed the laity accordingly.

Source: Trans. J. Murray from Robert Grosseteste, *Templum Dei*, eds. Joseph Goering and F.A.C. Mantello (Toronto: Pontifical Institute of Mediaeval Studies, 1984), pp. 57-60.

16. Special Examination concerning Matrimony

1. Now we ought to turn to the sacraments, and especially the sacrament of orders, because of the great difficulty which is associated with them.

2. Matrimony is the legitimate union of a man and woman retaining an individual habit of life, sharing divine and human law.

3.

Frigidity—as one who is frigid naturally or by cunning, or is paralyzed, or mad, or a boy not yet seven years old, or a woman physically constricted.

Habit—as if someone puts on the habit of a religious, or solemnly takes vows in the presence of a prelate.

Order—as a subdeacon or above.

Relationship—as much carnal as spiritual.

Vows—if it was made solemnly it breaks [the marriage bonds]; if privately it only impedes it.

Condition—as if one marries a servant or a handmaiden or woman he previously knew in adultery, having made promises or plotted her spouse's death.

Disparate cult—as an unbeliever if he blasphemes or a believer who becomes an apostate.

Power—as one who marries from coercion or fear of death.

Error—as if he accepts A in the place of B and means to accept B.

Honesty—clearly public honesty: as if he makes a contract with her and does not know her, he is not able to contract with one of her relatives.

Conditions that impede and break marriage:

4.

ascending degrees:	great-great-grandfather	—great-great-grandmother	Also, note that those
	great-grandfather	—great-grandmother	unequally distant are said
	grandfather	—grandmother	to be separated by the
	father	—mother	more remote degree that separates them.

carnal relationship [consanguinity]:

son
father

(Let two notes be placed here.)

descending degrees:	first-son	—daughter	Also, note that in the
	second-grandson	—granddaughter	direct line there is no
	third-great-grandson	—great-granddaughter	ability to contract mar-
	fourth-great-great-grandson	great-great-granddaughter	riage regularly.

5.

Legal relationship:

Adoption: as if I adopt someone who is not legally independent, as my son or nephew or above.

Arrogation: as if I accept someone who is legally independent, as my son or nephew.

Affinity by marriage, without sexual union: this is not passed on and is called public honesty.

Affinity by sexual union: this is passed on in four degrees.

6.

Spiritual relationship:

by Baptism:

between the godfather and his wife with the godchild.

between the baptiser and his wife with the one baptised.

first degree

between the godfather and his wife with the father and mother of the godchild.

between the children of the godparents only with baptised person and not with the children of the baptiser.

second degree

by Penance: as, if you received a woman in penance, you are not able to take her as your wife.

by Confirmation: as, if you presented a man or woman at confirmation, you are not able to contract marriage with such a person.

7.

Affinity from sexual intercourse:

first:

between me and the relatives of a woman known carnally by me.

between my relatives and a woman known carnally by me.

This is passed on to the fourth degree.

second:

between me and a woman carnally related to one of my affines by primary affinity.

between a woman known carnally by me and a man joined carnally to one of her affines.

This is passed on in two degrees.

third:

between me and a woman known carnally by someone in the second type of affinity.

between one known carnally by me and someone joined carnally to any affine of hers to the same degree.

This is not passed on.

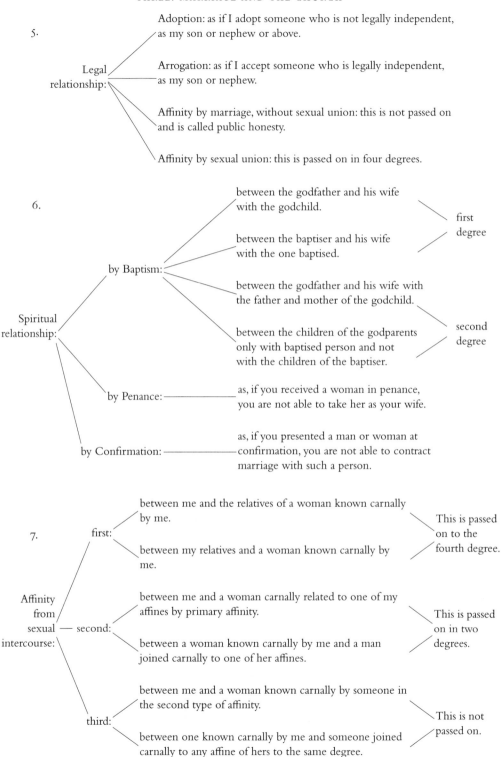

8.

Conditions that impede a contract but do not break it:

Uxoricide: because in this the delinquent ought to be punished.

Rape: because a man who raped a woman can marry her and no other afterwards.

Incest: that is he who is related to his wife in the first, second, or third degree.

Patricide: that is when someone kills his spiritual father or even another priest.

Adultery: that is when he committed adultery with a woman whom he later wants to marry.

Interdict: that is when it is forbidden to contract, especially with a virgin, such as during Lent and Advent.

9.

Things that impede seeking the conjugal debt:

Incest: as, if one of the spouses had sexual intercourse with the blood relative of the other.

Time, that is sacred time: such as on solemn days such as Lent and the like.

Status: as when your wife is pregnant, or after childbirth or during menstruation.

Cause: as when he wants to have intercourse solely for the cause of expending lust.

Chastity: when they contract marriage lest they be sought or solicited by others, but they live together in mutual chastity.

10.

Licit ends for contracting marriage:

Children: when they contract marriage for the sake of procreating children.

Honesty: when they contract marriage so that they will not fornicate.

Peace: when they contract marriage so that peace may be restored and confirmed

What circumstances impede a marriage? Who is the closest relative a person is permitted to marry? What is spiritual relationship? What circumstances prohibit a marriage but, should it take place, still permit an indissoluble marriage bond to be formed? What circumstances prohibit seeking marital intercourse? What are the appropriate reasons for a couple to marry?

29. HOW TO DISSOLVE A MARRIAGE

In the course of the twelfth century in particular, the church was active in disseminating and enforcing its doctrines on marriage, especially the principles of indissolubility. This met with resistance from secular society, particularly the elite who found it desirable to have a means to end unhappy, unfruitful, or otherwise undesirable unions. They wanted to continue to use marriage as a means to advance their individual and familial economic and political situations. Thus, they needed the flexibility to end unions that were no longer useful, in order to arrange new, advantageous ones. In order to circumvent the church's increasingly rigorous and successful enforcement of indissolubility, people utilized the various impediments to the formation of the marriage bond for their own ends. This was particularly true for the impediments of consanguinity and affinity, which defined the prohibited degrees of relationship so broadly that they could be invoked or ignored as was most expedient. It was relatively easy, in a period without accurate and authoritative records of births and marriages, for an unhappy spouse to discover a distant common ancestor who had been "inadvertently" overlooked during the course of the marriage negotiations. Ecclesiastical officials were well aware of the potential and actual abuse of consanguinity and affinity for secular ends. Some sought—usually unsuccessfully—to reconcile couples intent on separation; others actively colluded in fraudulent cases. Ultimately, in order to control this kind of abuse, the church narrowed the prohibited degrees of relationship at the Fourth Lateran Council (1215). The cases presented here occurred between 1148 and 1150 and were recorded by John of Salisbury (ca.1115/20-1180), in his Memoirs of the Papal Court. While ecclesiastical officials might try to reconcile unhappy spouses, their efforts were not always successful, as indicated by the case of Louis, king of France and Eleanor of Aquitaine. Not too long after their reconciliation, the couple did separate and Eleanor subsequently married Henry II, king of England.

Source: Trans. J. Murray from John of Salisbury, *Historia Pontificalis* in *Monumenta Germaniae Historica: Scriptores*, vol. 20, ed. G. H. Pertz (Hanover, 1868), pp. 521, 534, 536-37, 543-44.

6. Ralph, the count of Vermandois, had been excommunicated for three years because he did not want to take back his wife, whom he had unjustly repudiated. He was unable to receive absolution through the mediation of the king of France, when, at a recent meeting, he was seeking permission to depart for Jerusalem. Relying on the help and advice of the cardinal deacons, John Paparo and Gregory of St. Angelo, he obtained absolution, but not without the suspicion of bribery. For he swore an oath to follow absolutely the papal order, which previously he had always refused to do, but this time he knew, through the aforesaid cardinals, what the pope would command. Therefore, when, on the appointed day, the count and the wife whom he had rejected met in the palace at Rheims, as if to proceed with the case, the lord pope explained to everyone the reason he had absolved the count. Receiving a solemn oath according to the custom of the church, and because he was embarrassed to do

in front of the church what, however, he was doing: for he was rescinding the sentence of his predecessors Popes Innocent, Celestine, and Lucius, and it was believed a most equitable sentence which condemned the adultery which the count was alleged to have committed with the king's sister. It seemed better to seek the good will of the woman and her party, saying that he did that so that she would receive   reparations and finally she would be released from her suffering and troubles, and would have nothing to complain about. "You complain," he said, "that a hearing was denied to you and you were cheated and suffered violence from the opposing party. But we are reinstating your case so that you and your supporters are free to allege whatever you choose, just as the count has on his part." But she, believing that she had been invited there so that she would do what already had been decided, and not wanting to return to the count, who had given his heart to another, thanked him, saying she would gladly hear what the opposing side would say. Why say more? Bartholomew, bishop of Laon, and others came forward to swear with their hands on the gospels to the consanguineous nature of the relationship, which they had avoided doing on other occasions. But the pope prohibited the bishop to touch the sacred scriptures, saying it ought to suffice if the bishop gave his evidence having looked at the scriptures. Thus, the oath having been taken, the divorce was declared, and both of them were given the capacity to contract marriage "freely in the Lord." Moreover, the count was sentenced to return her dowry to the woman. But he replied that he had already returned it to Count Theobald, from which it was presumed by everyone that the parties had colluded....

23. In the year of grace 1149, the most Christian king of the Franks [Louis] arrived at Antioch, his armies having been crushed in the east. And there he was nobly received by Prince Raymond, brother of William, of happy memory, count of Poitiers. He was the queen's [Eleanor of Aquitaine's] uncle and owed faith, love, and reverence to the king for many reasons. But while they were detained there to console, refresh, and restore the survivors from the ruined army, the attentions paid by the prince to the queen, and his assiduous, practically unceasing conversation aroused the king's suspicions. Indeed, these were greatly increased when the queen wished to remain there when the king was preparing to leave. And the prince tried to keep her, if it would have pleased the king. When the king was quick to remove her from there, mentioning their consanguinity, she said it was illegal for them to remain together any longer because there was between them a relationship in the fourth and fifth degrees. Moreover, these words had been heard in France, before they had left, and Bartholomew of blessed memory, the bishop of Laon, had computed the degrees of relationship—but it was uncertain if the computation was true or false. From this the king was greatly disturbed. And although he loved the

queen deeply, almost excessively, nevertheless he agreed to divorce her if his counselors and the French nobility would permit it. There was one soldier among the king's secretaries, a eunuch, Terricus Gualerancius, whom the queen had always hated and was accustomed to laugh at, although he was faithful and on intimate terms with the king just as his father before him had been. He audaciously persuaded the king that he not allow her to linger any longer in Antioch both because in the name of their relationship guilt could be hidden, and because eternal shame threatened the kingdom of the Franks if, among the other misfortunes, it could be said the king was deserted and robbed of his wife. He said this either because he hated the queen or because he believed it, perhaps being moved by common rumor. Therefore, pulled away, she was forced to depart for Jerusalem with the king. And in each of their hearts their mutual anger grew and, although they hid it as they were able, the injury remained....

28. In the year of grace 1150 the king of the Franks returned. But returning, the galleys of the emperor of Constantinople lay in ambush, capturing the queen and others who were traveling in her ship. But the king was appealed to that he return to his brother and friend of Constantinople and force was already being prepared. But a galley of the king of Sicily, giving aid, freed the queen and extricated the king and accompanied them to Sicily with pride and triumph. For the king of Sicily planned all this, fearing the plots of the Greeks, and desiring an opportunity to show the devotion which he had for the king and queen of the Franks. Therefore, he hurried to them and leading a sufficient company, he accompanied the king to Palermo with the greatest honor. He was eager to honor both him and his followers with many gifts. And when he departed, he went with him through the whole of his kingdom right up to Ceprano, providing for all his needs at will. For this is the end and the boundary between the principality of Capua and Campania, which belongs to the demesne of the lord pope.

29. The cardinals and ministers of the church there ran to the king and, providing him with whatever he liked, they led him through Tusculum to the lord pope. He was welcomed by him with such kindness and devotion that it seemed to welcome not some mortal but an angel of the Lord. Having heard about the quarrel from each of them, he settled the strife between the king and queen, which had begun at Antioch. He forbade any further mention being made of their consanguinity and, confirming their marriage, he prohibited under threat of anathema, both orally and in writing, lest someone dare to impugn it, and ordered that it not be dissolved whatever the pretext. The face of the king showed him to be very pleased at this decree, because he loved the queen passionately, in an almost puerile way. The pope caused them to sleep in the same bed, which he had decorated with his own most precious hangings

and every day of their brief delay, by means of intimate discussion, he tried to restore love between them. He honored them with gifts and finally, in their send off, although he was a severe man, he was unable to contain his tears. And dismissing them, he blessed them and the kingdom of the Franks, which was held higher by him than all the other kingdoms of the world....

40. A certain count named Hugh, a Norman by birth, although he was born in Apulia, had for a long time been endeavoring to divorce his wife, who was born of the more noble line of Lombards and Romans and was related to Ptolemy of Tusculum. He presented himself to the lord pope, bringing with him the king of Sicily's governor and other officials and nobles from Apulia and Calabria, so that he might obtain the dissolution of his marriage. These governors are powerful officials who act in place of the princes in the cities and castles of that region. The bishops of that area also pursued vigorously the count's case, knowing this would please the king. The count had provided his case with lawyers and witnesses, and he had bribed the court so that in the deliberations on the judgment there were not two people who would argue against the divorce. The pope, having heard everyone's judgment but not revealing his own, returned to the courtroom in order to finish the case. Turning to the witnesses, he asked them which country they were from. They replied they were Normans and had come in order that they might present evidence of the truth and purge their kinsman from the crime and scandal of incest. They claimed they were related to both of the spouses. Again he asked how they knew of the alleged relationship and whether they were held in sufficient regard in Apulia that they ought to be heard in such a case. They replied that they had lived in Apulia a long time and were of such honesty that they had been admitted as witnesses in two divorces. Hearing this, the lord pope said, "We will not hear the same witness in more than one divorce case, much less will we hear you strangers, unsettled and suspect men, in a third. Therefore, imposing perpetual silence on you, under pain of anathema, by the authority of the apostles Peter and Paul, we prohibit you from again presuming to challenge any marriage. And since the testimony that we heard is not consistent and the truth of the matter has been made known to us fully from another, we confirm the marriage, and by apostolic authority we forbid that any bishop or any other person should dare to attack it." Thus, filled with tears, rushing from his seat, in the sight of everyone, great as he was, he prostrated himself at the feet of the count. His miter, slipping from his head into the dirt, was found under the feet of the astonished man, after the bishops and cardinals had raised him up. And thus the pope begged and urged him as much as a father's affection, an orator's facility, and the eminence of the Roman pontiff venerated by the faithful was able, that the count should receive his wife kindly, setting aside all rancor, not from the necessity to obey the law, but rather show-

ing the faith and affection of a spouse. He said, "My dearest son, so that you will do more freely and usefully what I ask, behold, I, the successor of Peter, the vicar of Christ, to whom, although unworthy, are handed the keys of the kingdom of heaven, will grant, if you agree that this my daughter, your wife will bring and confer on you an inestimable gift, that is forgiveness of your sins, so that whatever sins you hitherto commit will be disposed of by me on Judgment Day, so long as in the future you serve her faithfully." Everyone who was there was moved to tears, and the count himself, drenched with tears, promised he would obey with reverence and joy. Then, Eugenius ordered the count and the woman to approach him, and with his own hand he gave her to her husband saying, "Behold, I, Eugenius, bishop of the Apostolic See, in receiving and keeping this woman, by the grace of God grant you remission of all your sins, provided that you faithfully fulfil your promise." And taking a ring from his finger, he put it on the count's finger and added, "This ring, a symbol of faith and agreement, is a witness before God between you and me, that before the church I gave you a wife and you received her into your trust." And so they departed together. I was among those present, whence I took care to narrate these events most diligently for the glory of God and the honor of this great pope.

How did Ralph of Vermandois get his divorce (annulment)? What was his wife's reaction? Why might Eleanor have wanted to separate from Louis? What was the pope's reaction? Why? How genuine might the reconciliation between Hugh and his wife have been?

30. MARRIAGE LITIGATION IN FIFTEENTH-CENTURY LONDON

The responsibility for supervising marriage, enforcing matrimonial law, and judging contested cases was in ecclesiastical jurisdiction. The local bishop or his delegate, the official, would hear the disputes and court cases pertaining to marriage. Theirs were busy courts and their responsibilities were serious because marriage cases had a spiritual as well as legal, social, and economic dimension. That the church had been successful in its efforts to disseminate its complicated teachings on marriage is amply shown in the marriage litigation of the later Middle Ages. The fundamental principle that the freely exchanged consent of the man and woman was the only requirement for a valid marriage was seized upon by the laity. Men and women appear to have regularly married themselves through the informal and private exchange of consent; ecclesiastical requirements of the reading of the banns and the presence of a priest were ignored. This did not mean, however, that people married secretly. As these court cases reveal, couples might marry in the homes of friends or in public places such as taverns. The unions could be the result of negotiations, and involve friends and relatives who gathered specifically for that reason. The evidence also shows that people knew the exact words necessary for a valid marriage and that they sealed their vows with a kiss or a ring.

Yet, clearly, informal marriage could be problematic. There are suggestions that the distinction between marriage and betrothal, present and future consent, was imperfectly understood. Sometimes fame, the public recognition of a couple as husband and wife, was an important element in proving a valid marriage existed. Occasionally, there are hints that marriage was invoked to hide fornication or that simple fornication was used to defend oneself against an alleged but unwanted marriage.

It is always difficult to generalize from court cases. These were the problematic situations that ended up in court; the happy and contented marriages are not found in the public record. Two things should be noted. First, medieval people tended to go to court to have their marriages confirmed and declared valid, not to separate. Second, the informal nature of exchanges of consent led to many allegations of bigamy. Informality, and no doubt the promises that lovers whisper to each other, led to ambiguity and uncertainty. Consequently, it was left to the ecclesiastical courts to sort out exactly which marriages were valid. While the record of litigation allows glimpses into medieval life, it does so through the lens of legal formulae and the court scribe's report and summary of the testimony.

Source: Trans. Shannon McSheffrey from Greater London Record Office, MSDL/C/205, Consistory Court of London Deposition Book, 1467-1476, fols. 25r-26r, 30v-31r, 31v, 35v, 33r-36v, 41r-43r; London Public Record Office, Perogative Court of Canterbury 11/4, fol. 169r; printed with permission.

Richard Colyn c[ontra] Robert Arwom and Joan Deynes

8 July [1468], in the Old Palace
William Rokyston of Weston, Lincoln diocese, farmer, where he has lived for
twenty years, literate, of free condition, fifty years of age and more as he says,
sworn, etc. He says that he has known Joan Deynes for four years and Richard
Colyn for twelve years, but he does not know Robert Arwom. Questioned
further, after having first been warned of the danger of perjury, this witness says
that on Wednesday following the feast of Corpus Christi two years ago,
William Bakere of Walkeherne came to him in his house in the town of
Weston. On behalf of Richard Colyn, Bakere asked this witness to come the
next day to the town of Hadham to speak with Richard Colyn. So, on that
Thursday, this witness came to the town of Hadham where he found the said
Richard Colyn, Joan Deynes's mother, Joan Deynes herself, William Chapman,
and William Pynden ... all sitting in the hall of the inn at the sign of the
George, around the hour of eleven in the morning, eating bread and drinking
ale. After they all spoke together for about half an hour or so, Richard Colyn
and Joan Deynes left the hall together and entered the place called *le ʒerde* [the
yard] next to the hall. Richard and Joan talked alone there for about a quarter
of an hour. And then Richard Colyn called this witness, William Chapman,
William Pynden, and Joan Deynes's mother [to join them]. Before those people and none others, Richard asked the said Joan Deynes whether she wished
to keep the promise they had previously made between them, and she
answered that she did wish to keep that promise. And then and there, Richard
Colyn took Joan by the hand and said to her, "Here I Richard take you Joan as
my wife, and thereto I give you my faith." And then and there Joan said to
Richard, "And I Joan here take you Richard as my husband, and thereto I give
you my faith," and they kissed one another. This witness testifies to these
things from his own sight and hearing.... And he says that they contracted
with one another once in the presence of this witness, without any instruction.
And after this contract, this witness, Chapman, and Pynden went back into the
hall of the said inn and there they ate and drank, the landlady of the inn serving
them. And he heard that Joan Deynes's father was not at that time aware of the
said contract. He says also that he has not been instructed [about what to tes-
tify] nor corrupted and that he does not care who has victory in this case as
long as justice is served.

Anne Boteler alias Hope c[ontra] Robert Elyson

4 January [1469], in the Old Palace, by the Lord Official

Anne Horton of the parish of St. Giles Without Cripplegate, London, wife of Thomas Horton, of free condition, thirty years of age and more as she says, sworn, etc. on the statement, etc. She says that she has lived in the parish of St. Giles for five years and more, and before that time she lived in the parish of St. Andrew Cornhill for twelve years. She has known Anne Boteler alias Hope for sixteen years and more, and Robert Elyson for about two years. To the first and second articles of the statement, she says that around the feast of Christmas two years go, this witness used to go to Anne Boteler's house in the parish of St. Leonard Foster Lane on many occasions, and there [one day] she found the said Robert Elyson sitting in Anne's bedchamber and speaking with her. When Robert left, this witness asked Anne who Robert was and why he was frequenting her house in this way, and Anne answered by telling this witness that she wished to have Robert as her husband and he wished to have her as his wife. After this conversation, Robert and Anne, on many occasions around that Christmas, in Anne's bedchamber, discussed solemnizing marriage between them and purchasing wedding clothes for Anne. They said that they wanted the solemnization to be at dawn. This witness testifies to these things from her own sight and hearing, no one else being present there at that time.... She says that after these conversations between them, this witness frequently came into Anne's bedchamber at daybreak and saw Robert and Anne lying together nude in her bed, and that frequently, in the presence of Anne and this witness, Robert admitted that Anne was his wife, and Anne similarly in the presence of Robert and this witness also admitted that Robert was her husband.... To the fifth article, she says that in the parish of St. Leonard at that time there was public voice and fame that the said Robert and Anne had contracted marriage between them and that this marriage would be solemnized.

5 January [1469]

Robert West of the parish of Shoreditch, where he has lived for four years, and before that in the town of Wormeley in the County of Hertfordshire for [?] years, of free condition, fifty years of age, [sworn], etc. He says that he has known Anne Boteler for six years, and Robert Elyson since the previous July. Questioned further, he says that he knows only that, around the aforesaid month of July, Anne was working in his house as a chambermaid. During the period when she was working there, Robert [frequently?] came to the said house, and so this witness asked Anne why Robert came to the house. She answered that [he was her husband?]. And further, another day he asked Robert why he came to the house so frequently, and he answered that he loved

Anne before all other women, and he asked this witness whether he thought that she wished to have him as her husband. Immediately, this witness asked Anne, in the presence of Robert, whether she wished to have Robert as her husband, and she answered that she never wished to have him as her husband. And otherwise he has nothing to testify concerning the statement.

John Kyrkeby of the parish of St. John Zachary, London, lorimer [iron-worker], where he has lived for seventeen years, of free condition, forty years of age as he says, sworn, etc. He says that he first saw Anne Boteler on a certain day about six weeks ago and has not seen her since, and that he has known Robert Elyson well for twenty years. Questioned further, he says that on a certain day about six weeks ago, the said Anne came to this witness's house and asked him if he knew Robert, and he responded yes. Then Anne asked him whether he had ever heard Robert saying that he wanted to have her as his wife, and he said no. And otherwise he knows nothing regarding the contents of this statement.

23 January [1469], in the Old Palace
Robert Elyson, sworn, etc. concerning the charges, says on his oath that he never contracted marriage with Anne Boteler, nor ever admitted or recognized that he had affianced or contracted marriage with Anne, nor espoused her, nor gave her any goods nor received any from her for the sake of a contract of marriage or to contract with her. He also denies any fame [concerning the contract]. He admits, however, that he knew her [carnally] many times.

Robert Pope c[ontra] Lucy Braggis and John Randolf c[ontra] Lucy Braggis

Robert Pope c[ontra] Lucy Braggis

13 January [1469], in the Old Palace
William Love of the parish of St. George in Pudding Lane, embroiderer, parish clerk of the church of St. Botulph Billingsgate, has lived in the parish of St. George for six years and more, of free condition, thirty-five years of age as he believes, sworn, etc., concerning the statement, etc. He says that he has known Robert Pope for four years and Lucy Braggis for two years and more. To the first, second, and third articles of the said statement, he says that on a certain Sunday in February a year ago, Robert Pope and Lucy Braggis came to this witness's house in the afternoon about two o'clock. There, in the hall, after eating and drinking, Robert said to Lucy that they had discussed marriage many times and that he had come there that day to have a final answer from her about making such a contract with him. There and then, after some words

between them about the marriage, Robert took Lucy by the hand and asked her if she could ever find it in her heart to love him and relinquish all other men for the love of him, and whether she wished to have him as her husband. And she immediately responded that she could love him thus and relinquish all other men for love of him, and that she wished to have him as her husband. Then Robert, holding Lucy's hand, said to her, "And I love you in the same way, and I relinquish all other women for your love, and I will have you as my wife, by my faith." He kissed her and gave her a ring, putting the ring on her finger and blessing her, saying, "In the name of the father, and of the son, and of the holy spirit, Amen." ...Asked who was present there and heard these things, he said that there were no other people in the hall except for Robert, Lucy, and him, but he says that Agnes Hedy, his wife's daughter, and Joan Bakby, this witness's servant at that time, stood on the stairs leading from the hall to the chamber above, and the two women heard the contract from there, as they later told this witness. And he says that within two or three months after this, fame of this contract began to spread in the parish of St. George ...He says that they contracted sitting at the table in the hall, and they ate bread and drank beer; he happened to be there because Lucy sent Agnes Hedy to the church of St. Botulph so that he would come.... He says that he was an intermediary between them and worked to induce them to contract marriage with one another, asked to do so by both parties....

Alice Love, wife of William Love, of the parish of St. George in Pudding Lane, London, where she has lived for six years and more, forty years of age and more as she says, sworn, etc. She says that she has known Robert Pope for six and Lucy Braggis for five years. Questioned further, she says that on Ash Wednesday the previous year, in the church of St. George, in the morning, this witness had communication with the said Lucy and said to her that she had heard that she, Lucy, and Robert Pope had contracted marriage together and that she had asked God that they would long be united together and would be happy. And then Lucy told her that she had indeed contracted marriage with Robert. She gave to this witness a pair of coral [rosary] beads with *lez gaudiez* [large ornamental beads] of silver gilt, and asked this witness to give Lucy's best wishes to Robert and to give to him these beads. There was no one else present at the time and listening to this. And afterwards, within two or three months, Robert Pope gave to this witness in her home, in the presence of her husband, a silk belt decorated with silver and asked her to give his best wishes to Lucy, his wife, and to give to her the belt. And she gave Lucy the belt and Lucy received it happily. And she says that after that Ash Wednesday, around the following Easter, word that Robert and Lucy had contracted marriage together began to spread around the said parish.... And she says that she is not more fond of one party than of the other, nor is she a servant in Robert's household. She has had nothing for her work [in testifying] nor does she hope to have any. And she says that Agnes Hedy, her daughter, is of the age of 18 years and more....

Agnes Hedy, living in the parish of St. George in Pudding Lane, London, in the house of William Love examined above, where she has lived for five or six years, of free condition, eighteen years of age and more as she says, sworn, etc. She says that she has known Robert Pope for six and Lucy Braggis for four years as she says. Questioned further, she says that she agrees with the testimony of William Love regarding the words and contract between Robert and Lucy, and the day, hour, place, fame, and the putting on of the ring, all specified above by William Love. And she says that, at the time of the contract, this witness and Joan Bakby, at that time William Love's servant, stood on the stairway leading from the hall to the chamber above. She heard what was said between Robert and Lucy and saw and heard them contract marriage, and she believes that the said Joan Bakby heard the same words and contract as she says ...

26 January [1469], in the Old Palace

Joan Myghell, alias Bakby, wife of Michael Salours, of the parish of St. George in Pudding Lane, London, where she has lived with her husband for half a year and more, and before that time in the same parish with William Love for three years, of free condition, about eighteen years of age, sworn, etc. She says that she has known Robert Pope for about two years and Lucy Braggis for a year. Questioned further, she says that on the Friday after last Christmas, the said Robert Pope came to her in her house, and made her go with him to the tavern at the sign of the King's Head in Bridge Street to drink wine with him. Robert then asked her to act as a witness for his side and to say what William Love and Alice Love, witnesses examined above, were going to say and testify. And then this witness asked Robert what he wished her to testify, and he said that she should testify that Lucy Braggis is his wife, and she responded that she did not want to say that, because she never knew nor understood this, as she said. And otherwise concerning the contents of these charges she has nothing to testify.

Responses personally made by Lucy Braggis, 27 January [1469]....

Lucy Braggis, sworn, etc. concerning the charges, etc. She says that about two years ago, Robert Pope spoke with her many times about contracting marriage between them and desired to have her as his wife, and she said that before she could contract marriage with any man that she would want to deliberate and have the advice of her brothers. She says also that after this discussion, Alice Love gave to her a silk belt decorated with silver that had been Robert Pope's, but she only learned that it was Robert's later, when Alice told her, and at the time Alice gave her the belt she did not know that it belonged to him. She did not, moreover, receive the belt for the sake of contracting marriage with Robert, and she afterwards gave back the belt to Robert. And she says furthermore that another time this witness sent to Robert about two years ago a pair of coral beads through Alice Love, but she did not do it for the sake of marriage but because of the love and friendship that had existed between them before that time. And she says also that afterwards, around last Lent, Robert came to her to have a final answer from her about whether she wanted to have him as her husband, and she answered him that she had recently had a letter from her brothers in which they told her that they would provide her with another man that they wanted her to have as her husband, and so she then gave him her final answer, which was that she did not wish to have him as her husband....

Responses personally made by Robert Pope, 27 April 1469....
Robert Pope, sworn, etc. concerning the charges, etc. To the first charge, he says that once before the contract between him and Lucy Braggis this witness asked the said William Love to ask her whether she had contracted marriage with another man, and if she had not contracted, he asked Love if he would be an intermediary between him and Lucy, so that this witness could have her as his wife. And afterwards, after he had contracted with the said Lucy, the said William Love told this witness that he had asked her whether she had contracted with another man and she told him that she had never contracted with any man and that she wished to speak and drink with this witness. To the second charge, this witness says that because he was an alien that he does not have to answer to the contents of the charge. To the third charge, he says that the said William Love never promised him that he would have victory in the case.... To the fifth charge, he believes that the said Agnes Hedy at the time of her examination was of sufficient age and discretion to offer testimony, and that she and her testimony are trustworthy. To the sixth charge, he believes that the said Agnes was and is the stepdaughter of the said William Love....

John Randolf c[ontra] Lucy Braggis

16 May in the Old Palace . . .
John Bramanger, draper of the parish of St. Mary at Hill, London, literate, of free condition, forty-four years of age as he says, sworn, etc. concerning the statement, etc. He says that he has known John Randolf well for twelve years and Lucy Braggis since last Easter. To the first and second articles, he says that on a certain feast day last April, which one exactly he does not recall, in the afternoon, in a certain gallery that is otherwise called *a sumer parlour* in the

house of the Lady Cumbes in the parish of St. George in Pudding Lane in the city of London, this witness was present along with the said John Randolf and Lucy Braggis, William Gregory, and George Seman, where and when the said John Randolf asked this witness and the said William and George to bear witness concerning what was said and done there between them. And then the said John Randolf asked the said Lucy whether she was single and free from all bonds of matrimony and whether she had ever previously contracted marriage with any man, and she responded that she had never contracted marriage with any man. And then John Randolf asserted that he was also single and free from all bonds of matrimony and that he had not previously contracted with any woman. And then immediately John Randolf took Lucy by the hand and said to her, "I John take you Lucy as my wife, and thereto I give you my faith," and they unclasped their hands. And then the said Lucy took the said John by the hand and said to him, "And I Lucy take you John as my husband, and thereto I give you my faith," and they kissed one another. This witness testifies about these things from his own sight and hearing, as he says…. To the fourth article, he says that the aforesaid things about which he has testified were true and that he believes that there was and is public voice and fame about these things in the parish of St. George. To the interrogatories, he says that he does not care whether Robert Pope obtains victory and has Lucy as his wife or John Randolf or any other man, as long as justice is served….

George Seman of the parish of St. Stephen in Coleman Street, London, butler of the Lady Cumbes, illiterate, of free condition, fifty years of age and more as he says, sworn, etc. He says that he has known John Randolf for seven years and Lucy Braggis for about eight years…. To the questions, he says that this witness and the said Lucy Braggis are familiar servants and of the livery and in the employ of the Lady Cumbes….

Stephen Robert c[ontra] Angela Harewe, and Angela Harewe c[ontra] Stephen Robert

Stephen Robert c[ontra] Angela Harewe

18 February [1469]

William Clerke of the parish of Woodchurch [Kent], Canterbury diocese, gentleman, literate, of free condition, fifty years of age and more as he says, sworn, etc. concerning the statement, etc. He says that he has known Stephen Robert for twelve years and more, Angela Harewe for two years, and Anne Clyfford from the last feast of the nativity of St. John the Baptist. Questioned further, he says that on the day after the last feast of St. John the Baptist, about the middle of the day, he was present in the home of Alexander Clyfford in the town of

Bobbing [Kent], situated in Canterbury diocese, in a certain upper chamber. Gathered there were the said Stephen Robert and Anne Clyfford, Alexander Clyfford and his wife (the parents of the said Anne), Sir John Culpepyr, knight, Richard Culpeper, gentleman, John Edyngham otherwise called Engeham, Walter Roberd, William Salt, William Hochon, and others whom he does not now certainly recall. And then after many communications between the said Stephen and Anne and their other friends who were present there concerning contracting marriage between the said Stephen and Anne, Stephen took Anne by her right hand and said to her, "I Stephen Robert take you Anne Clyfford as my wife, and thereto I give you my faith," and they unclasped their hands. And then Anne took Stephen by the hand and said to him, "And I Anne take you Stephen Robert as my husband and thereto I give you my faith." This witness testifies about these things from his own sight and hearing. To the first question, he says …that he does not favor one party more than the other, but desires that justice will be done between the parties. To the second question, he says that he took as his wife the sister of the said Stephen Robert, who is now dead…. To the third question, he says that …this witness at that time and at other times solicited Stephen to contract marriage with the said Anne. To the fourth question, he says that the contracting parties, this witness, and the others present all wore gowns, but he cannot testify certainly as to their color, except that he recalls well that the said Richard Culpeper wore a gown of Kendale [green woolen cloth] and that at the time of the contract the said Stephen and Anne and the others present were standing…. To the sixth question, he says that he heard many times from the mother of the said Angela and from a certain man named Swanwyke that the said Stephen contracted marriage with the said Angela. But he cannot testify about the fame alleged in the interrogatory. To the seventh question, he says that he came to the City of London to take care of various items of business, and was asked by the said Stephen to offer testimony of the truth and because of this he has come to testify.

William Hochon of the parish of Woodchurch [Kent], Canterbury diocese, sherman, illiterate, of free condition, twenty-eight years of age and more as he says, sworn, etc. He says that he has known Stephen Robert for ten years, Anne Clyfford since the last feast of St. John the Baptist, and Angela Harew for two years as he says. Questioned further concerning the statement, he says that he agrees with the said William Clerk examined above….

Angela Harewe c[ontra] Stephen Robert

William Swanwyke of the parish of St. Alban's in Wood Street, London, where he lives and has lived for a year and more with William Brayn, illiterate, of free condition, thirty years of age as he says, sworn, etc. He says that he has known Angela Harewe and Stephen Robert for four years. Questioned further concerning the contents of the case, he says that on a certain day between the feast of Christmas a year ago and the following Lent, concerning which day he cannot be more specific, the said Stephen Robert came to this witness, who was then in the home of the said William Brayn, and told this witness that he had become betrothed to Angela Harewe. Because there had been no witnesses present for the said betrothal, he asked this witness to go with him to the said Angela and hear what would be said between them. And then the said Stephen entered into a certain lower parlor in the said house, where Angela was at that time, and this witness followed right after him. And then and there in that parlor, Stephen, sitting on a certain chest, said to Angela, who was also sitting on the chest, "I have brought with me William Swanwyke to hear what will be said between us." He took her by the hand and said to her, "Angela, will you have me as your husband?" And she answered and said to him, "By my faith, I will have you as my husband." And then immediately Stephen said to her, "And I by my faith will have you as my wife, and no other woman." And they unclasped their hands and kissed one another. This witness testifies about these things from his own sight and hearing. Asked who was present in that parlor at the time, he says that the said Stephen and Angela and this witness were present in the said parlor at the time that the words were spoken, and no one else. But he says that after this witness left the said parlor, Ralph Penne, Angela's brother, told him that he was standing outside the door of the said parlor and heard the words that were said between Stephen and Angela in the parlor. And he says moreover that in the parish of St. Alban there is public voice and fame that the said Stephen and Angela contracted marriage between them, and that it existed before the suit was brought before the court.... To the fourth question, he says that the said Stephen and Angela, at the time of the speaking of the said words, spoke loudly enough that anyone near the door outside the parlor could have heard and understood the aforesaid words....

Ralph Penne, brother of the said Angela Harewe, of the parish of St. Alban's aforesaid, in Wood Street, London, where he lives and has lived for three years with William Brayne, literate, of free condition, seventeen years of age as he says, sworn, etc. He says that he has known Angela his sister from the time that he had the discretion to know one person from another, and Stephen Robert from the feast of St. Michael a year ago. Questioned further, this witness says that on many occasions Stephen asked this witness to persuade Angela his sister to take the said Stephen as her husband. After this, on a certain day between Christmas a year ago and the beginning of Lent, but which day exactly he cannot recall, the said Stephen came to the home of William Brayne situated in the aforesaid parish, and entered a certain lower parlor in the house, where sat the said Angela, and William Swanwyke followed immediately after him into the room. This witness stood outside the parlor near the door, where he heard the words between Angela and Stephen as deposed by William Swanwyke above. But he says that at the time the words were spoken he did not actually see Angela, Stephen, or William Swanwyke in the parlor. He says that after this Stephen gave to this witness a gold ring that he was to convey to Angela, which he did, and Angela received the ring gratefully. As for fame [of the contract], he agrees with William Swanwyke the previous witness....

[...] March [1469], in the Old Palace

Stephen Robert, sworn, etc. concerning the case brought forth by the party of the said Angela, says that around the feast of St. Giles three years ago, this witness first knew the said Angela. On a certain day around the said feast, Angela came to the house of Agnes Robert, this witness's mother, situated in the town of Cranbrook [Kent], Canterbury diocese. There and then this witness, after conversing with the said Angela, asked her whether she could find it in her heart to love this witness. But she said that she did not know what sort of answer to give this witness at that time. He says also that at that time he so loved the said Angela that he freely wished to have her as his wife if he could have had the consent of his friends. And afterwards on many occasions in the house of Alice Brayn, the mother of the said Angela, situated in the parish of St. Alban's in Wood Street, London, this witness and the said Angela conversed about contracting marriage together. And on a certain day between the last feasts of Easter and Pentecost, this witness and the said Angela, in a certain parlor situated in the house of Alice Brayn, had communication concerning what goods Angela's mother would give to this witness for Angela's dowry if this witness took her as his wife. And then the said Angela answered that her brother had asked her mother about this, and that her mother had responded that she did not wish to give an answer to this without the advice of her husband William Brayn. And then William Swanwyke came into the parlor, and said to this witness in the presence of the said Angela, "This woman Angela loves you well." And this witness answered and said "I know this." Then immediately the said Angela said in the presence of the said William Swanwyke, "I Angela will never have any other man as my husband but you." And this witness said, "I do not know what response to give to you without the consent of my friends." And he said also that at that time he so loved the said Angela that he would have taken her as his wife, if he could have had the consent of his friends. Then four letters sent [to Angela] and a paper document, on which was depicted a shield with the image of an angel holding a harrow (in English *harewe*), written by the witness with his own hands, were shown to the witness, and two of these letters and the document were signed by the court scribe, Nicholas Parker. [The witness says also that many tokens were sent between them, but that he had never received a token from her nor sent one to her for the sake or in the spirit of having her as his wife.]

Will of John Roberd of Cranbrook, January 1461 [probated February 1461]

To all Christian people that this present writing comes to, John Roberd of Cranbrook sends greeting. Know you me, the said John, on the 20th day of January of the thirty-ninth year of King Harry the Sixth, to have ordained and made my last will in the form ensuing.... And if it happen that any of my said sons Walter or Stephen or both to be married within age of twenty-four years, that then my feoffees deliver livelihood to the furthering of him by the discretion of Robert Horne, John Engeham, and of William Saundys.... And I also will that Robert Horne have the governance and rule of my sons Walter and Stephen ...till my sons come to the age of twenty-four years as it is before rehearsed....

Why were the witnesses asked who else was present, where and when, and what people were doing when the couple exchanged consent? Why was it important for witnesses to remember what the man and woman had said? What role did friends and family play in contracting a marriage? What role did the church play in these cases? Why was bigamy a risk in medieval society?

CHAPTER FOUR:

MARRIAGE CEREMONIES, RITUALS, AND CUSTOMS

The basic outline of a marriage ceremony was summarized in the early Middle Ages, and by the thirteenth century the familiar liturgy was established. This ceremony, presided over by a priest, involved the handing over of the bride, the exchange of consent, the bestowing of a ring or another precious object on the bride, and the nuptial kiss. Although a dowry was not a liturgical requirement, it was necessary in practice and priests were instructed to enquire about it in order to avoid future complications. Marriage was seen as a process rather than a single act. The betrothal was agreed to, the dowry established, and the couple exchanged consent. A notary might be asked to draw up a legal agreement stipulating the dowry and other conditions. The celebrations were enhanced by popular practices designed to tease the couple, or to enhance their happiness and fertility. At all levels of society, the ceremony was followed by a feast or banquet as elaborate as finances would allow.

31. POPE NICHOLAS'S LETTER TO A BULGARIAN KING (866)

As Christianity spread across Europe it encountered various peoples with diverse social and cultural beliefs and practices which the church tried to reconcile and ultimately synthesize. Some of the correspondence between church officials in Rome and those in newly converted areas provide insights into how Christian doctrine was made to accommodate the customs of other peoples. As well, such correspondence shows the articulation of certain Christian doctrines at specific points in time. The letter of Pope Nicholas I, written in 866, in response to a series of questions posed by the Bulgarian king, Boris, is particularly important for understanding how the rules governing Christian marriage evolved in the west. Eighteen of the letter's 106 chapters address questions pertaining to marriage and sexual morality. Boris was uncertain about various aspects of Catholic dogma and sought clarification of a number of points of difference between Catholic teaching and those of the Greek Orthodox missionaries who were also proselytising among the Bulgarians. Nicholas's responses, which were to be expanded upon by his own emissaries, convey Christian teaching at a critical point in its development. Nicholas clarified the rules of consanguinity and reaffirmed the church's teaching about the appropriate times for sexual intercourse. For generations to come, canonists would cite this letter as the foundation of many aspects of the laws governing marriage. The letter, as well, provides early and important information about the rituals that accompanied marriage at its various stages. The customs of giving a wedding ring and covering the couple with a nuptial veil endured in western Christendom for centuries.

Source: Trans. J. Murray and A. Young from Ernest Perels, ed., "The Letter of Pope Nicholas to the Bulgarians" (Letter 99), in *Monumenta Germaniae Historica, Epistolae: Karolini Aevi*, vol. 6 (Berlin: Weidmann, 1925), pp. 568-600.

13 November 866

Not many of your questions require a response, nor did we think to spend much time on each one, because we intend to send to your country and to your glorious king, our beloved son, not only the books of divine law, whose author is God, but also, indeed, our suitable representatives, who will instruct you about each point, as time and reason dictate, to whom we have also entrusted books, which we anticipate will be necessary for them to have now....

2. Thus a person ought to love him as a father who receives him from the holy baptismal font. Nay, rather, just as the spirit is more outstanding than the flesh, because that is a spiritual clientage and adoption according to God, so also the spiritual father ought to be more loved in every way by his spiritual son. But there is no consanguinity between them and their sons, since the spirit does not know those things which are of blood relationship: according to

the Apostle Paul, "For the flesh is at war with the spirit and the spirit with the flesh, for these are turned against each other" (Gal. 5.17). However, between them there is another free and holy communion which ought not to be called consanguinity, but rather spiritual relationship. Whence, let us not think that there can be any conjugal relationship between them, in as much as the venerable Roman laws permit marriage to be contracted neither between those who by nature and those who by adoption are siblings. In fact, the first book of the *Institutes*, where it speaks about marriage, among other things, says: "Marriages cannot be contracted between persons who stand in the relationship of parent and child, for example, between a father and daughter, or a grandfather and granddaughter, or a mother and son, or a grandmother and grandson, and so on *ad infinitum*. And if such persons should be joined to each other, they are said to have contracted heinous and incestuous marriages. Indeed, this is so much the case that, even if they began to stand in the relationship of parent and child by adoption, they cannot be joined to each other in marriage. And so I cannot marry her who became my daughter or granddaughter by adoption. And below it states: "If someone became my sister by adoption, for as long as the adoption lasts clearly no marriage can take place between me and her." Therefore, if marriage is not contracted between them whom adoption unites, how much more ought they to cease from carnal union with one another, whom the regeneration of the holy spirit has bound together through the sacrament of heaven. Therefore, he is far more fittingly called the son of my father or my brother whom divine grace has chosen, rather than he whom human will has chosen as his son or my brother. And we more prudently reject the physical union, since the holy spirit has united us in his love, than either carnal necessity or the mutable decisions of some corruptible man.

3. To avoid excessive wordiness, we will not mention the custom, which you say the Greeks observe in companionate marriages, but we will endeavor to show you separately the tradition which the holy Roman Church received from ancient times, and continues to hold, in unions of this sort. In fact, in our country, when they contract a marriage alliance, neither men nor women wear on their heads a crown made of gold or silver or of some other metal, but after the betrothals are celebrated, which are the promised agreements of future marriage and which are by the consent of those who contract them, and those in whose power they are, and after the bridegroom solemnly promises the bride on his part, with pledges by means of his placing a ring of the finger of faith. And the bridegroom gives to her a dowry pleasing to both of them, along with a written copy of their agreement, in front of those people invited by both sides. Either soon after, or at an appropriate time, lest it be presumed that such a thing happen before the time defined by law, both are brought to conclude the marriage agreement. And indeed, first, by the hand of the priest,

they are made to stand in the church of the Lord, together with the offerings which they ought to offer to God. And, thus, in this way, at last, they receive the blessing and the heavenly veil, as an example that the Lord, placing the first people together in paradise, blessed them, saying: "Increase and multiply" (Gen. 1.28) and so on. In fact, also Tobias, before he had joined with his spouse, is described as having prayed with her to the Lord. Nevertheless, he who enters a second marriage does not receive that veil. But after this, leaving the church, they wear crowns on their heads which, by custom, are always kept in the church itself. And so, the marriage ceremony having been celebrated, they are directed to henceforth lead their life together as God wills. These are the laws of marriage; these, above the rest, which do not now come to mind, are the solemn covenants of marriages. However, we do not consider it to be a sin if these steps do not all occur together in the marriage ceremony, just as you say the Greeks claim, especially since so great a lack of property limits some people, so that no help is available to support them in these preparations. And on account of this, let their consent alone, from which their unions are made, be sufficient according to the laws. If, by chance, this consent alone is lacking in a marriage, then every other ritual celebrated, even including coitus itself, is in vain, as the great doctor John Chrysostom testified, who said: "Coitus does not make a marriage, but will." But now, as you asked, if the woman herself dies, can the man marry another woman? Know that it is in every respect possible, as the illustrious preacher the Apostle Paul advises, who says, "But I say to the unmarried and to widows: it is good for them if they remain thus, just as I also am. But if they are not continent, let them marry" (1 Cor. 7.8-9). And again, he says, "A wife is bound by the law as long as her husband lives, but if her husband dies, she is at liberty: let her marry whom she wishes, but only in the Lord" (1 Cor. 7.39). What is thus sanctioned concerning the wife ought also to be understood concerning the husband, because, on the other hand, often holy scripture speaks about man but nevertheless is understood to speak also about woman. For, behold, we say, "Blessed is the man who has not walked in the counsel of the ungodly" (Ps. 1.1) and again, "Blessed is the man who fears the Lord" (Ps. 111.1). Whence, we believe that not only a man but also a woman who did not walk in the counsel of the ungodly and who fears the lord, would not undeservedly be blessed....

9. You asked us whether you ought to take communion everyday during Lent.... One should continuously recall that one should always withdraw for prayer, and gather together for the sacrifices of the faithful, and that prophetic word of Isaiah: "On the day of your fast your will is found" (Isa. 58.3). For if, with the consent of spouses, an opportunity is also made for prayer at another time, when the body, by chance, is undefiled, how much more ought we to renounce every sensual pleasure and devote ourselves to chastity of mind and body, so than an occasion for prayer is properly available at the time when we

also give to God the tithes of our flesh, when we imitate the Lord himself in abstinence, when we deservedly deny ourselves not only unlawful things but even many things also lawful for us....

28. In the selected laws you will find what judgment ought to be made concerning someone who was caught with the wife of another man. Now, if the adulterer fled to a church, we resolve that it ought to be judged by the bishop what it is agreed that the sacred canons have determined or what it is clear that the holy bishops of the Apostolic See have decided.

29. Similarly, we also judge someone who has sexual intercourse with a female consanguine. But we direct that the contagion of such a great crime is certainly better left to the consideration and judgment of a priest....

39. You inquired about consanguinity between generations, so that you might know clearly which women in particular you ought to marry. But what the laws sanction concerning this we have already recalled and we think it worthwhile to mention again, summarily. The laws say: You are not allowed to have every woman as your wife, for we ought to refrain from marrying certain of them. For those persons are not able to contract marriage between them who are in the relationship of parents and children, such as between a father and daughter, or a grandfather and granddaughter, or a mother and son, a grandmother and grandson, and so on *ad infinitum*. Also, the same observation is made about those persons who are joined sideways across the degrees of relationship, but not to such an extent. For what the sacred canons, and especially the decrees of Pope Zachary, promulgate in this matter, we leave for your bishop to explain to you....

48. Whence we think that it can by no means be appropriate to marry or to give parties during the Lenten season. But what the sacred canons say about this, you will know by your bishop's teaching.

49. Moreover, you asked if you are first permitted to present to your spouses gold, silver, cattle, horses, and so on, as an endowment. Since it is not a sin and the laws do not forbid it, we ourselves do not prohibit it at all, and not only this but also it is conceded that whatever you did before baptism, you indeed now can still also do. For we know that Peter was a fisherman but Matthew was a tax collector, and after his conversion, Peter returned to fishing but Matthew did not return to the business of tax collection because it is one thing to seek a living by fishing and another to increase your money by the profits of tax farming. For there are many jobs which can scarcely, or not at all, be done without sin. Therefore, it is necessary that the soul, after conversion, does not return only to those activities which are implicated in sin. But if what someone did before conversion is without sin, there is also no blame in repeating this after conversion.

50. We entrust a decision about someone who has intercourse with his wife during Lent to be considered and determined by the judgment of your bishop,

or a priest appointed by him, who is able to know the practices of each one, and ought to discern and guide the cases of each one of you, weighing the persons and times. Moreover, it would be entirely possible to sleep with her, at the same time, without any contamination, if fire and straw could mix without harm, or if the sly deeds of devilish fraud were unknown. For when a man deals with a woman, it is difficult to avoid the wiles of the ancient enemy, which indeed were not lacking when the brother and sister, Amon and Thamar, were alone together for a very short space of time.

51. You asked if it was permitted to have two wives at the same time. If it is not allowed, you want to know where to find what to do. Neither does the origin of the human condition allow, nor any Christian law permit, a man to have two wives at once. For God, who made humanity, from the beginning made one male and one female only. He could have allowed the man to have two wives if he had wanted, but he did not. For it is written: "On account of this a man shall leave his father and mother and cling to his wife" (Gen. 2.24). It does not say to his wives. And elsewhere it says: "They shall be two in one flesh" (Gen. 2.24), that is male and female, and not three or more. And so, in the case in which two wives are found at one time, keeping the first wife, let him be forced to send away the more recent one, and moreover let him be compelled to undertake the penance which the priest of the place will assign. Finally, this is such a despicable crime that the sin of murder, which Cain committed against his brother Abel, was avenged by the flood in the seventh generation, but the crime of adultery, which Lamech first of all perpetrated in having two wives, is not remitted except by the blood of Christ, who came into the world in the seventy-seventh generation, according to the Gospel of Luke.

52. If you want to know what ought to be decided about those who made someone a eunuch, read the law books again....

59. We reckon that what you asked about trousers is pointless, for we do not desire that the external style of your clothes be changed but rather the values of the inner person in you. For we will examine not what you are wearing, except for Christ: "For as many of you as have been baptized in Christ, have put on Christ" (Gal. 3.27), but how successful you are in faith and good works. But because you asked candidly about this, clearly fearful lest you be accused of sin if you did even the least thing beyond the custom of other Christians, but we say, lest we seem to take something away from your desire, that in our books trousers have been ordered to be worn not as women use them, but as men do. But now, as you pass from the old man to the new, act in such a way that you pass from your earlier custom to our practice in every way, but only if it is agreeable. But whether you or your women either put off or put on trousers neither obstructs salvation nor does it serve to increase your virtues. Clearly, since we said that trousers had been ordered to be worn, it must be noted that

we wear trousers spiritually when we limit carnal desires by abstinence, for those places are bound by trousers in which the seat of lust is recognized. Perhaps, for that reason, after sin the first human beings, feeling illicit passions in their members, taking refuge in the leaves of the fig tree, wove girdles for themselves. But these are spiritual trousers which you were not able to wear until now, as I say with the Apostle Paul: "But you are not yet able, for you are still carnal" (1 Cor. 3.2). We have said a few things on this topic, although with God's help, we could say more....

63. Moreover, you asked if it were permissible for a man to sleep with or have intercourse with his wife on Saturday evening or on Sunday. To which, we reply, since, if worldly work ought to cease on Sunday, just as we have taught above, how much more ought every carnal pleasure and bodily pollution be completely avoided, especially since the name of the Lord's day plainly demonstrates that the Christian ought to do nothing on that same day, except what pertains to the Lord. Furthermore, what we understand about the day itself must be understood for the preceding evening. For it is one day which, having twenty-four hours, consists both of daytime and nighttime. For, unless one day continues in the absence as well as in the presence of the sun, what scripture says is worthless: "There was evening and morning one day" (Gen. 1.5). But now whether he ought simply to sleep with his own wife at that time, we have already briefly noted in the fiftieth chapter of these, our responses. Let me quote the Apostle Paul: "Furthermore, I say this to you as something beneficial, not as a snare, but for that which is decent, and gives you the power to serve the Lord without impediment" (1 Cor. 7.35).

64. How many days a husband should abstain from his wife after she has borne a child is shown clearly not by our ideas but by the words of Gregory of blessed memory, the Roman Pontiff and apostle to the English, who, writing to the bishop Augustine, whom he himself had dispatched to the Saxon settlement, said, among other things, "Her husband ought not to approach her, that is the wife's bed as long as she is nursing the child which is born. But a perverse custom has arisen in the behavior of spouses, that women disdain to nurse the children that they bear, and hand them over to other women to be nursed. Indeed, the reason why they despise nursing the children they bear, so long as they refuse to be continent, seems to be incontinence."...

68. You asked how many days after giving birth a woman can enter a church. We, following in the footsteps of our predecessor, the blessed Pope Gregory, have decided the same things which he said, writing among other instructions for a new people, just as we are doing now: "If a woman, in the very hour in which she gave birth, should enter a church, intending to give thanks, she has committed no sin. The pleasure of the flesh, not sorrow, is culpable. Moreover, the pleasure is in intercourse, for there is groaning in bringing

forth children. Whence also it was said to the first mother of everyone herself: "You will give birth in sorrow" (Gen. 3.16). Therefore, if we forbid an earnest woman to enter a church, we consider the penalty itself as a sin....

70. You decided to ask whether you ought to support and honor a priest who has a wife or to cast him out from you. We reply, since, although such men are reprehensible, yet it becomes you to imitate God who, as the gospel says: "Alone makes the sun to rise on the good and the evil and rains on the just and the unjust" (Matt. 5.45). Likewise, you ought not to send him from you, since the Lord did not sent Judas away from the ranks of the apostles, even though he was the false disciple. Indeed, you, who are a layman, ought not to judge priests of whatever sort they be, nor ought you to investigate anything about their lives, but whatever it is ought to be reserved to the judgment of the bishops in every respect.

71. To your query whether or not you ought to receive communion from a priest who either was caught in adultery or who was defiled merely by the rumor of this, we reply: no one, however polluted he may be, is able to pollute the divine sacraments, which are cleansing remedies for all contagions, nor is a ray of sunlight, passing through sewers and latrines, thereby contaminated. Consequently, whatever sort of priest he may be, he is not able to pollute what is holy. For that reason, communion ought to be received from him, even he who is reproved by the judgment of the bishops, since evil people harm only themselves by administering good things, and a burning wax torch offers harm to itself but brings light to others in the darkness and harms itself at the same time it helps others. Therefore, receive the mysteries of Christ without fear from every priest, since all are cleansed by faith. For this is the faith that conquers this world and because it is not a matter of the giver's faith but the receiver's. According to the teaching of St. Jerome, baptism is perfected in every soul, for believing is perfected in baptism and the body of Christ is made perfect in every priest. He again speaks in accordance with holy scripture, saying "Before you hear, lest you judge anyone, and before the proof of the accusation is advanced, suspend no one from your association because he who is accused is not immediately guilty, but he who is convicted is disgraced."...

87. You enquired whether anyone commits a sin who makes an unwilling widow undertake the monastic life as a nun. But concerning this it must be understood that there are some virtues without which we cannot enter eternal life, but there are others which are not required, except by someone who has taken vows. Indeed, without humility, chastity, and almsgiving and prayer no one is able to enter into eternal life and those, together with similar virtues, are the ones required of a person. But to take on the habit of a religious and to lead a life apart from the world is not required except from someone promising to do so to God. Whence, whoever brings force to bear on someone, so that he

assumes the monastic habit and a life apart from the world, this violent person does not escape sin. And, since what was done did not come about by the vow of the person choosing the monastic life, the one receiving the religious habit will have no reward from that, nor will the coercer fail to be judged for his cruelty....

96. Whatever your wife should think or do against you, or if she accuses you, she ought not be rejected or held in hatred, except for reason of fornication. According to the Apostle Paul, she should be loved just as Christ loves the church. But, as much as Christ is accused from the mouth of heretics and is blasphemed among the gentiles, he in any case tolerates them preaching wickedness and does not remove them from his merciful embrace when they have come to their senses.

What were the rituals and activities involved in a marriage ceremony? What did Pope Nicholas say about second marriages? Whose consent was necessary for a marriage to be valid? When and why should a husband and wife not sleep together? What does Nicholas say should happen to bigamists? What does Nicholas say about women wearing trousers? What does Nicholas advise concerning married clergy?

32. THE LEGEND OF ST. NICHOLAS AND THE THREE DOWRIES

St. Nicholas (d. 343) was born in Patras in the eastern Roman Empire. He became bishop of Myra and was widely admired for his holiness. The earliest life of Nicholas was written in the ninth century and includes the story of the three dowries. The cult of Nicholas was brought to the Latin west in the tenth century, by the Byzantine princess Theophano, who married the Holy Roman Emperor Otto II. In the late eleventh century, a band of Italian soldiers stole Nicholas' relics and took them to Bari. Thereafter, his cult flourished in the Italian peninsula. In the middle of the thirteenth century, Jacob de Voragine (ca. 1230-1298) included an account of Nicholas in his collection of saints' lives, the Legenda aurea (The Golden Legend). *This compilation of saints' lives was one of the most popular works of the Middle Ages. It was intended for the laity and was translated into various vernacular languages. St. Nicholas was consequently known across Europe for endowing the three destitute sisters to make them more attractive marriage partners. This was an act of charity the wealthy were urged to emulate. In the later Middle Ages it was not uncommon for wealthy people to provide dowries for poor girls as part of their charitable contributions in their last will and testament.*

Source: Trans. Granger Ryan and Helmut Ripperger in Jacobus de Voragine, *The Golden Legend* (New York: Longmans, Green, 1941), pp. 16-18; reprinted with permission.

December 6: St. Nicholas

Nicholas comes from *nicos*, that is, victory, and *laos*, that is, people, and means therefore a conqueror of the people, or, in other words, of all vices that are mean and common. Or it means a victory of the people, because he taught many peoples how to conquer vice and sin, by means of admonitions and examples. Or Nicholas comes from *nicos*, victory, and *laus*, praise; that is, conquering praise. Or it comes from *nitor*, brightness, and *laos*, people, and means brightness of the people; for in him was the power to make all clean and bright. For as Ambrose writes:"God's words make clean, true confession makes clean, and holy contemplation, and good works."

The life of St. Nicholas was written by certain doctors of Argos, a town in Greece, whence, according to Isidore, comes the name of Argolics, sometimes given to the Greeks. It is also said that this legend was first written in Greek by the Patriarch Methodius, and later translated into Latin by John the Deacon, who also added to it.

Nicholas, a citizen of the city of Patras, was born of rich and pious parents. His father was called Epiphanius, and his mother Joanna. His parents, after having brought him into the world, abstained from all contacts of the flesh and lived in godly love.

A nineteenth-century drawing of a stained glass window depicting scenes from the life of St. Nicholas. The top three panels portray the story of the three dowries.

On the very day of his birth, while he was being bathed, Nicholas arose and stood straight up in his bath. Throughout his infancy he took the breast only once on Wednesdays and Fridays. As a youth he avoided all the pleasures of his companions and spent his time visiting the churches; all the passages of the holy scriptures which he heard there, he committed to memory. Upon the death of his parents, being very rich, he looked for a way of using his wealth, not to win men's praise, but to promote God's glory.

Now one of his neighbors, a man of noble estate, was so poor that he was about to deliver his three daughters to prostitution in order to make a living from the profits of their shame. As soon as Nicholas heard of this, he was horrified at the thought of such a sin; and wrapping up a lump of gold in a cloth, he threw it through the window of his neighbor's house during the night, and then fled without being seen. When the man arose the next morning, he found the bundle of gold; and thanking God, he at once set about preparing the nuptials of his eldest daughter. Some time later, St. Nicholas did the same thing a second time. The neighbor, finding the gold, broke out in great paens of praise, and made up his mind for the future to watch, and find out who it was who thus came to the relief of his poverty. And when, a few days later, a quantity of gold twice as large was thrown into his house, he heard the noise which it made in falling. He set out in pursuit of Nicholas, who had taken flight, and begged him to stop, so that he could see his face. He ran so fast that he finally caught up with the young man, and so was able to recognize him. Throwing himself before him, he sought to kiss his feet; but Nicholas declined his thanks, and exacted a promise that the man would keep the secret of his deed until after his death.

How does this story illustrate the situation of poor families and of families with numerous daughters? What were the alternatives to marriage for a girl without a dowry? Was a dowry essential for marriage?

33. A BAD COURTSHIP AND A GOOD: *RUODLIEB*

Ruodlieb, a young honorable knight, is the hero of the Latin epic poem which bears his name. This anonymous poem was written in the mid-eleventh century and survives only in fragments. Gaps in the text often make the story difficult to follow. In the poem, the young knight, Ruodlieb, exemplifies the qualities of a Christian knight. His adventures reveal much about sexual morality and the customs and values governing marriage among the Germanic aristocracy at the time. In particular, it reveals the stages of marriage: betrothal, the handing over of the woman, and the wedding feast. More anomalous is the description of the bride's consent and her active role in the proceedings. This poem reveals the practice of marriage during a period when the ecclesiastical model was gaining increasing importance, but before the church had effectively systematized and codified its teachings. It also reflects the earlier custom of the man and woman exchanging property (dowries) upon marriage, rather than the later practice of the woman alone bringing a dowry to the marriage.

Source: Trans. C.W. Grocock, *The Ruodlieb* (Warminster: Aris and Phillips, 1985), pp. 29, 91-95, 105-31, 163-67, 175-87; reprinted with permission.

1. There once was a man, born of a noble family, who enhanced his innate nobility with his good behavior. He is said to have had many rich lords and frequently served them at their bidding, though he could win none of the honors he thought he deserved. Whatever any one of those masters gave him to do—avenging an enemy, or furthering their own interests—he wasted no time in energetically carrying it through. He frequently put his life at risk for these same liege-lords, whether in war, out hunting, or in every manner of deed. They gave him nothing—faithless fortune held them back—and they were always making promises, only to pretend that they had not.

He, however, could not overcome the hatred which rose up against him on account of those things, and he could not say what he ought to do about it; despairing that he could ever live anywhere in peace, he settled all his affairs, left them in his mother's charge, and at last left his home country for a foreign land. No-one went with him save his squire, who was to carry the pack laden with various items. The knight had taught him since he was a lad to endure hardship on his account....

5. "Poverty forces many a poor fellow to be a thief, it gives birth to envy in a man's family and friends, or even eggs his brother on to break the bonds of good faith. It is better for a man to be without wealth than to lose all feeling, and whoever is busy at prospering in godly wisdom will always have enough of silver and gold. He conquers whatever he wishes, because he is well-armed

within. But I remember having seen many who were absolutely stupid, who squandered all their riches through their stupidity and lived in abject poverty, and brought themselves low in their error. Riches did not help them—clearly, they harmed them. So then you can easily teach me such a word of wisdom that, if I follow it and do not treat it rashly, it will be as dear to me as if a man were to give me ten pounds. No-one can steal that from me, or plot against me and hate me because of it, and no robber will kill me in some narrow place. Wealth belongs in a king's chamber if it is very precious, whereas a poor man has enough if he has his strength and skill. I do not want money, but I thirst for the taste of wisdom."

The king listened to this, and then, getting up, said, "Come with me" and they walked into the inner chamber, allowing no-one to go with them. The king took his seat, with the exile, his vassal, standing before him, and then began to speak: "Now listen with all your heart to what I say to you, as a true friend speaks to a friend.

Never let a redheaded man be a close friend to you. If he becomes angry, he does not remember good faith, for his anger is terribly fierce and long-lasting. He will never be so good that there is no deceit in him, and you cannot avoid it—you will be stained by it yourself, for you will never be clean to your fingertips if you put them into pitch.

No matter how muddy the road has been trodden through a village, never leave the path and go across the fields, lest you are badly treated and lose your reins when someone snatches them, giving you a cheeky reply.

Wherever you see that an old man has a young wife, do not ask for accommodation for you on your journey; for though you are innocent, you will bring great suspicion on yourself. It may turn out that his fears will be raised, and her hopes; but ask for accommodation where a young man has an old widow for his wife: he will not fear, and she will not love you, and there you may sleep safely without suspicion.

If a neighbor asks you to lend him your mare to harrow his field, and it is pregnant and close to foaling, do not lend it, unless you want it to become ill, for if it levels the field it will lose its foal.

Do not let any kinsman be so dear to you that you become a burden to him by seeing him so often: you see, whatever happens frequently soon becomes wearisome to a man.

Never make your maidservant—even if she is very pretty—your consort, as if she were your wife, lest she despises you and answers you back haughtily, and lest she thinks she ought to be mistress of your household because she sleeps with you and sits at table with you. As she eats with you and lies with you at night, she will want to be the highest lady over all straightaway. Such happenings make a noble man a disgrace.

If you wish to marry a more noble wife in order to have children dear to you, then look for a woman whom you can know of—and nowhere except where your mother advises you! When you woo her, you should honor her in every way, and treat her gently, but be masterful to her, lest she should presume to have any quarrel with you; for there is no greater fault in men than when they are subjects of those whom they ought to govern. And even if she is of one mind with you on every subject, you must never reveal all your wishes to her, so that afterwards if she is reproved by you for doing wrong, and wishes to taunt you, she may have nothing to say which will diminish love and respect between you.

Let no sudden anger weigh so heavily on you that you cannot bear to pass the night without revenge, especially when the matter is doubtful, and not as related to you. You may well be glad the next day that you bridled your temper.

Never go to law with your lord or your master: even if they do not defeat you justly, they will do so by force; and do not lend them anything, because in truth you will lose it. When he asks you to lend him anything, then it is better that you give it to him, for he will find some fault for which he will take just as much from you: so both will be lost to you, and he will repay neither goods nor gratitude. He will say 'receive my thanks' when you are robbed by him, and you will bow your head to the Lord God and praise him that you have got away with your life, counting your losses as nought.

Furthermore, never let your journey to any place be in such haste that when you see a church, you pass on by without commending yourself to its saints and blessing them. Wherever bells are rung or mass is sung, get down from your horse and run there quickly, so that you may share in the catholic peace. This will not make your journey longer, but will rather shorten it for you, and you shall travel more safely and in less fear of an enemy.

Never refuse any man who begs you earnestly to break your fast for the godly love of Christ, for you do not break it, but fulfil his commands...."

6. They hurried on to the village, where they wanted to spend the night. The sun sank in the west, warning them to seek shelter. The redhead called a shepherd to come to them. He came over there, and the redhead asked him briskly, "Tell me the names of the local gentry: is there a rich man here who could be our host?" The shepherd said, "There are many here whom I know very well would not be so staggered if a count were to seek out one of them with a hundred armed men, that they could not give them honorable service. He would be a poor man who could not give ample hospitality to you and to stable your horses! Although there are many who are used to taking in guests, among them all none receives visitors so well as does a young man or as his little old widow-woman."

The redhead said, "What's a young man doing with an old widow? It's an old man who ought to have an old wife."

The shepherd said, "Nowhere could he have found a better one to marry. He was a very poor man before he married her. Now he is her master, he who once waited on her as a servant, and he fully deserves it, for he is a kind and godly man. Thanks be to God, who has shown such pity on a poor man."

Then the knight said, "Tell me what I ask you, good fellow, how it happened that a rich woman married a poor man."

Then he replied, "My lord, surely you have heard that 'an old ewe likes to lick the trough because it loves the salt'? ...The first husband she had lived a very hard life with her, for he was disagreeable, mean, and very rarely happy; men never saw him smiling or joking. He could scarcely tell what cattle, bees, or horses he had: he had no idea how many he had of each, yet both of them seldom fed on their own meat; they ate hard cheese, and drank whey. They sold whatever they had, and stashed the money away carefully. That charming young man came their way poor and naked; he went to this man, and first begged him for some bread. He gave him hardly a mouthful of rye bread; he took this, stood there politely, and ate it. When the table was removed, he made haste to take the dishes away so that a cat could not foul them or a dog dirty them, washed them scrupulously and then put them back in the cupboard. He made sure to set aside a spoon in a dish for the master, to set before him when he took his early or evening meal, and set down a knife and some salt with a spoon. If anything happened not to be well seasoned, he seasoned it with this, whether it was cabbage, or broth, or any kind of food. The old man made a mental note of this, even if he said nothing. The young man left out nothing he saw a need for. He watered the cattle and sheep, the pigs and the goats, he brought fodder to feed the horses, and did this all of himself—no-one gave him orders to. If anything else needed doing, he did it quite energetically, and when he had stayed with him like this for three days, the old fellow had given him nothing but a mouthful of bread to eat, and since he couldn't stand the hunger any longer, he bowed to him, for he wanted to leave for some other place. When he saw that he wanted to leave, this chap said to him, 'Stay here just two or three days now, till we can see what each other's habits are.'

The young chap agreed, and soon his bread ration got bigger: a quarter-loaf was given him in the morning, and another quarter in the evening. In the meantime, the old chap asked him if he knew any trade. 'Tell me if I could know a better trade than the one I do know, how to make many excellent dishes from cheap ingredients, herbs, or flour, and apart from these I ask only for milk, a little lard, and as much salt as will bring out the flavor. And there is one other thing, my lord, which it is imperative we have, and which you must not be annoyed about if it is told you by me.' 'Speak,' he said, 'I shall not be angry, whatever it is.' The lad said, 'Look at you, you seem wealthy to everyone, and your bread is utterly without taste. It's full of bran, dark, and bitter with darnel-weed. If you want to let me have a measure, or half, of any flour, to make some loaves, I shall present you with very many well-sifted loaves seasoned with parsley-seed and sprinkled with salt, some cakes smeared on top with lard, and other loaves, coronet-shaped and long straight ones. In making these, I shall not increase the number of loaves you have, and I shall most carefully put whatever falls out of the sieve in a bowl and I'll give it to your hens and your cackling geese. If ever I break bread and share it among the boys, I shall not give it to the servants in such a way as to make you look soft-hearted to them. In doing this I shall smarten up your whole house. You just stand there yourself, leaning on your fork and looking everything over.'

Seeing that the young man was very wise, this fellow gave him charge over all his property, to provide for his servants however he wished. He took such precautions and such care, too, that his master and his household lacked for nothing. He never took more for himself than the wages they had agreed on, and toiled often just to have clothes to wear. He served his lord in this way with the greatest of faith and without deceit for I don't know how long. Then that old villain died: no-one lived who was more unpleasant and sour than him. He was wept for at his burial by a few of his relations. Nothing stood against them then, and the widow became the lover of the young man. They kept it to themselves, but we saw them go to church together, and 'they who eat together will soon be in bed together.' By this time he was calling his lady 'mother' and she called him 'son.' The menservants and maidservants soon got used to calling him 'father,' and he for his part called them 'children.' We never saw a greater love, nor a couple so suited to one another. Their door, which before was shut to widows and orphans, is now always open wide to both rich and poor. You'll find suitable accommodation there if you want it, their home is large, it stands at the entrance to the village."

Then the foolish, overweening redhead said, "Is there an old man here who has a very beautiful wife?" This man said, "There is an elderly man, who had a very good wife. Sad to say, she died; he recently married again, and took himself a silly young woman, a shameless wench. She despises him, and so thinks it nothing to keep tricking him with her stupid lovers—but she is more wicked than they are."

7. He cut the bread up and shared it out among them, with what meat fell to them from the six dishes. Refreshed with these, the poor folk went home rejoicing, and the host said, "Whenever Christ sends someone to me, then I and my family should celebrate our own festival, just as we have been made glad by you this night. I consider that whatever comes from you is sent to me by God." He handed him a piece off the shoulder and some off the leg, cut it

into little pieces and shared it among all the servants, like the sacraments. After this, plenty of boiled and roast meat was set before the lord, and his drink poured into a walnut goblet carved from the hardest wood, finest spiced wine and mead; four golden rivers were carved on it, and the right hand of God was represented at the very bottom. A great lord had given it to him when he had stayed the night there. He never tasted of it unless the man who had been served from it handed it to him; it was kept for that purpose.

When the meal was over and water had been given to him, wine was brought to him. He drank some and handed it to his host; he gave it to his lady, and afterwards drank himself. The knight got up from the table and sat down a little, and relaxing thus he thought to himself how he could please the man. Finally he gave to the old lady his cloaks, so that she could wear them when she went to the holy church.

Let us not pass over what the redhead was doing in the meantime. When the knight went into that place where he found so many good things, the redhead asked him why he was going, "Where there's an old monkey," as he put it. The knight said, "Perhaps later you'll wish you had come with me. I have found what I wanted, but you shall get what you are looking for."

Many bystanders advised the redhead not to leave his companion, for he could not put up so well anywhere. But he hurried off and left him with a sneer, and hastened to see his niece, though he was to find only death.

He found the old man's gate well and truly bolted. The old man was standing in the yard, with his two children by him. Then the redhead knocked, and shaking the gate fiercely said, "Someone open the door now, don't leave me outside." The old man said, "Look through the fence, see who it is." A boy ran up and said, "There's a man shaking the gate and breaking it." The redhead said, "Open up, you keep asking as if you didn't know me." At this the young men were annoyed and extremely irritated. Frightened of the wicked man's strength, he ordered the gate to be opened to him. The impudent redhead rode shamelessly into the courtyard, not even laying aside his hat, and drew his sword like a madman as he jumped down from his horse, and threw the thong of its reins around a post. He stood before him in a very insulting manner. But gradually the redhead smiled, and said to the old man, "I'm amazed you don't speak, if you know me." "I don't know who you are," he said, "You go about things stupidly enough. I don't know who you are or what you want with us." "Your wife is my niece, and very close to me; allow me to meet with her alone." He said, "Do it," and ordered her to come to him. She came; when she saw him she burned with lust for him in her heart, smiled happily at him, and smiled to herself in her happiness at these things. "Your father and your mother send you every good wish. Later I shall speak to you alone — where you like — about something of a different kind."

Then they stood by the gate, and leaned against the fence. The redhead said, "Note first in your heart what I tell you, because our conversation must not be a long one: don't cry, don't laugh, keep a straight face lest that old dog senses our intentions: if you go along with me, you'll soon be free from him. For there is a young man here who is well endowed with every kind of good quality—he's not too short, not too tall, but of an average stature. He's fair-skinned, and his cheeks are all rosy; there's no-one more handsome than him in all the world. When he found out how beautiful you were and what troubles you endure every day, he was sad at heart and said to me, weeping, 'If you were ever faithful to me, dear comrade, go and tell that woman in her torment that if she wishes, I will rescue her and free her from her prison. When tomorrow she hears my melodious horn ring out, without speaking even to a woman whom she can trust, let her leave the courtyard unexpectedly and stand in the street until I come with many men to snatch her away. After this she will be my lady and shall do as she wishes.' Now send him what message you like, my darling niece."

She stood and listened to all this in a well-bred way, and her heart leapt for joy, but she said to him as though she was sad, "I shall do all this, be assured, and I give my word." The redhead took her right hand; by now his doubts had vanished. "For my wages I want you to sleep with me three times." "Do it ten times, if you can," she said, "or as many times as you like." "I shall make out that I wish to leave, and you forbid it."

He went back to the old man, and said, "Give me your counsel (to go)." He would willingly have done this, had he any authority over his wife. She asked him loudly not to let him depart. "Let him stay if he wants, and let him have whatever is ours!" She led his horse into the stable in a great hurry, and neither she nor the redhead gave it another thought: it could eat any grass it could find there.

The niece received him well as he entered the house. They sat down together straightaway and talked together very playfully, entwined their fingers together, and gave one another kisses.

The old man came in—no other was more serious than he—his face was all shaggy, and no-one was able to see what expression he wore because he was so very hairy, except for his nose, which was hooked and deeply-veined. His two eyes were dark, as if they had been dug out, and a forest of twisted hair overshadowed them. No-one could see where he had an opening in his face, his whiskers hung so long and thick. He ordered the servants to prepare enough for them to eat. Since their playing was distasteful to him, he sat between them and kept them apart with his own backside. They grew quiet a little, and were sad that he had sat between them. They leaned in front of him and talked, making many jokes. When he grew tired of this, he ordered the table to be laid, and said to his wife "That's enough: now show some decency. A woman should not be forward like this, and nor should a man. It isn't proper for her to flirt with a stranger in front of her husband."

He said this and got up as though going to the privy, and watched there through an auger-hole. The wretched redhead jumped into the master's chair, one hand caressed her breasts and the other her thighs, and she hid all this by spreading her fur cloak over her. The old man watched all this, peeping like a thief. When he came back, the man did not make way for him, for she would not permit it. He sat very angrily at the head of the table, and frequently urged his lady to hurry up and have the meal served. She mocked him, and laughingly delayed the dinner. He asked the servants if the dinner was ready. "You can eat as soon as you like," they said. "Now my lady, let us eat and go and lie down. It is time too that your dear friend had a rest; you've worn him out enough, now let him be."

8. (The priest) came and wanted to declare the holy faith to him. He had only the strength to groan over and over again, "I believe." He asked him if he was sorry for all the sins he had committed. He made it plain through nods and single words that he was sorry, and was then cleansed of all sin through the holy sacrament. With a sigh he committed his soul to the Lord, saying, "Holy Christ have mercy on me, a great sinner; forgive these people who have taken my life from me, and enable my children to do the same, I pray." He said this and no more, and soon afterwards he breathed his last.

When morning came the people assembled everywhere, and in front of the church itself there was a massive throng of the greater and lesser people of the region. The governor came when he had learned about the despicable crime, and when all those worthy to be seated had taken their seats, the governor said, "Here is terrible news: a man than whom there was none better has been struck down dead." Those sitting there wept and said, "Unless he is avenged, we know the same thing will happen again." He sent for the children and for the murderers themselves. When they arrived they stood in the governor's presence, the redhead grinning, the guilty woman gazing at the ground. When the governor saw him smiling he said, "It is a very bad thing that you should smile when you see us all weeping here. What kind of anger possessed you, to put him to death like that?" The redhead said, "He knocked my front teeth out for no other reason than I sat down near my niece." He said, "If that young girl is your niece, why did you ravish her and pile crime on crime?"

The redhead said, "Why did this wretch pull me towards her? You ask me why I did it? I wouldn't have if she hadn't made advances towards me!" She wept so much that a stream formed from her tears, and then great drops of blood flowed from her eyes. After she regained her strength she stammered out as best she could, "O you foul traitor, why do you lie about me like this? You are from the same mould as Adam, who put the blame on Eve. I made no advances to you, you villain, I had not seen you before! You deceived me with lying promises. I do not defend what I have done, I rather condemn what you have done, the exploit you've done at my behest. I confess, I do not want to be avenged. Governor, suspend the trial for a little while, while I accuse myself, while I condemn myself too. See, I stand here as my own judge, and will suffer of my own free will. If you want me to be hanged from a tall tree, shave off my hair, weave a long rope from it, so that I may be choked by that which often made me guilty. But I ask that you take my body down after three days and burn it, and throw the ashes into some water, lest the sun hides its ray or the air witholds its rain, lest hail is said to bring harm to the earth because of me. If you wish to shut me up in a box and drown me, write what I have done on the outside of the box, lest anyone who find me presume to give me burial; let them just break the box open and throw me into the water, so that I may more swiftly be eaten by fish and fierce crocodiles. If you want to thrust me into a burning smoky furnace, I shall step inside willingly, so that I may not be burned by the fires of hell. If you wish me to lose my life drowned in a sewer, for I am filthy through and through, and deserve such a punishment, I will jump in straightaway, because I would be happy at such an end, so that afterwards the stink of Tartarus would not last forever for me. Whatever even harsher punishment you find, I will willingly suffer it all, I deserved much worse."

She fell silent, and the governor said with pity in his voice, "This woman has judged herself; you say if it is enough in this case." All were weeping, and had great compassion on her. They said, "There is no need for the governor to ask any more in this instance." The advocates said, "We decree that her life be given her only if she repents of this foul deed." Her step-children were as gentle as lambs, and fell at the governor's feet, pleading that he should grant her life, pardon, and wholeness of body, and allow her to be mistress of her household as she was before. He promised this mercifully, but she refused it: "May they not call me mistress now, but rather murderer. If you wish me to live, I pray, at least take my wholeness from me. So that you do not disable me, cut off my nose and face either side, so that my teeth stand out foul and uncovered, so that afterwards no-one may give me kisses, and brand me with a cross on my forehead and on my two cheeks, which up to this glowed red as a rose, so that anyone will know that this was done to me because of my crime, and will say, 'Woe to you, what did you do to deserve that?', so this enormous guilt will not go unpunished in me." Then the governor put her in the care of the old man's children, so that she might be a mother and mistress to them and not, as before, a step-mother.

She cast off all her lovely clothes, and dressed in a tunic dyed black as soot.

She shaved her head and plaited little cords from this, with which she bound her tender breasts, so that the cords bit into her flesh until it became infected. A ragged cloth covered up her whole head, too, and so only her nose and eyes could be seen. She learned the psalter, and sang it for the soul of the old man. She would only eat when she could see a star, and then she ate burnt, black dry bread, and drank only three spoonfuls of plain water. She would walk barefoot through cold and heat, and slept on a bed covered only in straw with just a log there for a pillow. She got up before daybreak and kept watch at the old man's grave until she broke into a sweat and could no longer stand up; then she fell face down while she made a pool with her tears. Whether it snowed or rained, or whether the sun burned down in its heat, she went to that church as soon as the bell was rung, and did not return from there until it was daylight all around. Then she returned for a little while and washed her face, and the priest rang the bell to celebrate mass. Then she went back and afterwards stayed there until the ninth hour. She asked no authority for herself, but granted it all to the sons. She had what they gave her, and what they did not give her she did not ask for. She never smiled, played with no-one, and when others were smiling, weeping was sweet to her. No-one saw her angry, quarrelsome, or playful, until she left this life. When she had been entrusted to the sons, and had been taken up by them, the governor said to the people, "Say, what are we to do with the redhead, who committed this doubly lamentable crime amongst us?"

The redhead, sure of the death sentence, said, "I beg you, I have here a comrade; have him called here before you ask what punishment there should be for these evil deeds. He can tell you well enough what kind of man I am."

When, anxious to see him, they wanted to send for him, the knight's host said, "The man you want is ready standing here. He stayed with me last night, but that fellow didn't." They led him out, and the governor asked him as he stood there, "Tell me, noble knight, is this man here a friend of yours?"...

14. "Some of our dear relations are said to be on their way today by our pages, as I believe; when they come, they may be present while these things are made firm. Now you summon your daughter to you, and let your faithful comrades on both sides attend."

When the girl had come and the men were standing round about her, the court quickly filled with friends arriving. Ruodlieb welcomed them all and embraced them, asked them to eat and offered them plenty. When the tables had been removed, the ladies retired to their chambers and the daughter went in front of them; behind them walked those who carried their cushions, and many others who waited on them. She ordered wine to be brought to them to show their service to him; each one drank and passed the cup to his neighbor, until they handed the vessel back empty to the wine-steward. They bowed to her and left, returning to Ruodlieb and the lords.

Then Ruodlieb said, "Seeing that God has gathered you here, listen to me now and take care to assist me, so that this marriage which has been decided upon and entrusted to our care may now be established firmly. I desire that you here present should be witnesses to it for me. It is the case that this young nephew of mine and the young mistress fell in love with one another while playing at dice, and desire to be joined by the bond of matrimony." They all replied, "We must all consider this, that a man of such great nobility and wondrous virtue should not be disgraced, but should be snatched quickly from that shameful harlot, who truly deserves to be burned in the fire," and they praised the Lord God that in all this world there was ever a woman who could tear this witch away from him.

Then the young man stood up and thanked them all for showing such mercy to him, one and all, and said that he shuddered inwardly at the great shame of having disgraced himself because of that damnable prostitute. "Now you see that I have great need of a wife, and since we may most easily find her here, I wish this lady to be betrothed to me as my own, so you may be witnesses to this for me and, I pray, willing ones, when we exchange dowries, as is the custom."

They replied, "We will gladly assist you in this matter." Then Ruodlieb sent for those three ladies, who hurried there fretfully, the daughter in front. The company stood up before them in their honor. When all had taken their seats, they fell silent for a time, and then Ruodlieb stood up and asked them all to listen to him. Then he said that it was agreed by all relations and friends that this youth and this girl were burning with love for one another. They all asked him if he wished to take her as his wife, and with a smile on his face he replied, "I do." Then they asked her if she for her part wished willingly to take him as her lord; she too smiled a little, and then said, "Should I not want a slave vanquished in a game, whom I beat at dice with this agreement as our stake, that whether he won or whether he lost he should marry only me? I want him to serve me with all his might both night and day, and the better he does this, the dearer he shall be to me." Then there was a tremendous roar of laughter from everyone, because she had spoken so brazenly and yet in such a friendly way. When they saw that her mother did not oppose these things and that the families of both were well-matched in status and wealth, they took counsel and decided that they were well suited to one another, and that she should be betrothed to him in a lawful bond. The bridegroom drew his sword and scraped it along the stonework. A gold ring was fixed onto its hilt, and the bridegroom offered it to his bride, saying to her, "As this ring encircles the whole of your finger all around, so I bind my faith to you firmly and forever, and you must observe it towards me, or lose your head." She very wittily gave him the apt reply, "It is fitting for both to suffer the same judgment: why must

I keep better faith towards you than you towards me? Tell me, if you can defend this—was Adam allowed to have a mistress as well as Eve, since God made one of his ribs into a woman; when Adam shouted out that she was taken out from himself, tell me, where do you read that he was permitted two Eves? When you went off wenching, would you have liked me to be a whore for you? May it not be that I should be joined to you on this condition; be off with you, farewell, you may go wenching as much as you wish, but not with me. There are plenty in the world whom I can wed as well as you." So saying, she left him his sword and his ring. The young man said to her, "Let it be done as you wish, darling. If I ever do this, let me lose the goods I gave you, and let you have the right to cut off this head of mine." A smile passed over her lips as she turned back to him and said, "Let us be joined now on those terms, with no deceit." Her suitor said "Amen" to this and kissed her.

When they were thus united the people gave a roar of approval and praising God, they sang a wedding hymn. Ruodlieb gave the groom a leather coat beautifully edged with fur, and a cloak whose fringe rustled down to the ground. He also gave him a swift horse well equipped. He gave gifts to the bride who had wed his kinsman, too: he gave her three brooches to wear on her beautiful breast, two pairs of finely-wrought bangles, and likewise three rings set with jewels. He also gave her a cloak of ermine lined with scarlet cloth. The rest of the crowd gave them great wedding gifts of their own. But why should I worry how they got on together?...

16. "Farewell to an heir, if you do not have a son! What will happen, son, if you die without children? There will be a terrible dispute over our estates. I have no youthful vigor at all, for during the ten years that you spent with the Africans I was afflicted with woes every day and at every hour, grieving for you and managing our affairs, and if you had not come back I should soon have gone blind. But I grew young again when I knew that you were coming home, and now I keep a better hold on myself than my strength warrants. I should like us, if it is your desire too, to summon our vassals and our faithful friends, by whose counsel and faithful assistance you may find a woman to be a wife for you, whom you would know to be of such lineage on both sides that your offspring are not defective because of either line, and their behavior might not lessen your renown. May God point her out to you and join her to you!"

Ruodlieb very calmly spoke these words in reply to his mother: "Tomorrow we shall inform our relations and friends that they should come to us as quickly as they can. I shall not overlook the counsel that they give me, if you think it should be done; I shall rather accomplish what you want."

Messengers were sent and their friends assembled. When they came to him and were welcomed by him, Ruodlieb arranged their seats, for he knew well that each should sit in the place designated to him. He assigned one table to each two lords, and commanded one higher chair to be placed for his mother, so that she might look down on all those who were seated there and eat alone, so that in this way she could be seen to be mistress. By giving honor to his mother in this way, and holding her as his liege-lady, he earned praise from the people, but from the almighty a crown and everlasting life in heaven.

When she had eaten, he asked them to remove the tables, and the doors were closed. Two strong men guarded them, and they did not allow anyone in or out until that deliberation had come to a close.

Then Ruodlieb stood and asked them to be silent for a little, so that he could inform them for what reason he had summoned them. When they were silent he said, as his mother had persuaded him, "Now listen to me, my relations and friends! It is perfectly plain to you what great grief and what travail have affected my mother in her suffering, as bereft of my father and of myself she managed all our affairs. Now her health fails her, her limbs are weary, and she has not the strength now to do anything that she could do before. She has told me this frequently, and I shall see it for myself. And so she does not cease from advising me to take a wife. For this reason I sent to you to come to me now, so that each of you can think this over for himself and speak with me. Very few women are known to me, nor am I in a position to know where to turn with a happy outcome. You tell me what you would do in this matter, if you can find a wife for us who would not disgrace our family, but would enrich it with her fine manners and the noble breeding of her behavior."

They for their part replied, "We will willingly do this as best we can, so that we may see a dear son born of your line, your heir in manners and in the good qualities with which Christ has enriched and honored you." Each one agreed, and promised to do this. Then one of them stood up who knew these regions well, and the noble lords who lived there. He said, "I know one lady whose upright behavior, virtue, and nobility make her a match for you. I should like you to see her, so that having seen her you may admit that in all the world you have seen no young lady who strives so hard to do every good work, and who is such as would honor any man."

17. She herself brought some very fine wine in a wine-bowl, and sweet mead in golden cups, and standing before him she asked about the girls in his homeland, what reputation they had, whether they were beautiful or virtuous. He smiled and said, "Little do I know what you are asking me. There is nothing I have meddled in less than noting this kind of thing, what ladies do; I leave such a practice to the womanizer. If ever I pass by a place where I see ladies standing around, I bow to them and go where I intended. Now, what reply do you wish to make through me to Ruodlieb, my lady?"

She said, "Tell him that I send him now with a faithful heart as much love as the leaves which have just come, and as much passion as there are delights in birds, and as many honors as there are grasses and flowers."

He had little doubt but that she might well marry him. When he asked for leave to go, he was suddenly struck dumb; then as if covered in confusion he stammered as though very upset. "What has happened to me? How awful, how terrible! I am ashamed to say it: a worse thing never happened to any man; for he has sent you some little presents, all sealed up." He took from his boot a small box containing these gifts. She took it and retreated hastily from him to the window, where she stood and opened the box. When she saw that in it there was an exquisite cloth so carefully secured with a double pair of seals marked with his ring, she wondered greatly what it could be, broke the seals and undid the knots in the cloth. Then when she saw a purple cloth, tied up, she opened that, and found her headband and garters which she had dropped while the clerk was making love to her. When she saw them and remembered where she had lost them, she shuddered, her whole body grew pale, and she felt a chill. She doubted that the messenger was unaware of them; he was putting on a show, and she had just seen him acting most foolishly. "All the people have so far thought me a chaste woman," she mused: then she began to regain her strength of mind, went over to the envoy, and asked him if he knew what the gifts were that had been sealed up so, and if he had been there when Ruodlieb put them in the little box. He swore by him from whom no secrets are hidden that he did not know what the gifts were at all, and was puzzled why she had asked that; it had been sealed up when it had been entrusted to him.

Then she said, "Tell your relation, your friend, even if there were no man left alive anywhere except him, and even if he were to give me the whole world for my wedding gift, I do not wish to marry him: you tell him that truthfully." The envoy, who was saddened by this turn of events, said to the lady, "I am amazed as to why I have come under your suspicion. Do I not seem able to undo any deceit for you?" She said, "Be quiet now, and be off, without my blessing."

The messenger left and hastened back to Ruodlieb. As soon as he saw him he said to him with a smile, "I know that you have been well treated, and given food and drink; now relate how my requests were received. My gifts were well accepted, were they not? Out with it!" He said this with a smile, and shook with laughter. The messenger said to him that he would lose him as a friend if he asked him to be his messenger a second time. Ruodlieb passed over these remarks and said to him in a serious tone, "Now tell me, my kinsman, what did that young mistress say when you recounted my great passion to her?" "When I had told her most fully what you asked of her, she was quite speechless, and got ready a great meal for me, bringing plenty of wine, and mead too. When I asked her what she wished to reply to you, she said, 'Tell him that I send him with a faithful heart as much love as the leaves which have just come, and as much passion as there are delights in birds, and as many honors as there are grasses and flowers.' When I asked that leave be given me to depart I fell silent all of a sudden and then said, 'What is the matter with me?' pretending that I had forgotten something and not given her your gifts. She took them from me and went away rejoicing. After a little while she came back in a terrible temper and said, 'Tell me if you knew what these gifts are that you've brought!' I swore by the almighty who knows everything that I had never looked inside to see what they were, for it was sealed up, and it was obvious to me that I was not supposed to know. Then she said, 'Tell your kinsman, your friend, even if there was ever no man left alive anywhere except him, and he were to give me the whole world for my wedding gift, I do not wish to marry him — you tell him that truthfully.'"

"Now I think I need to ask another's hand," said Ruodlieb, "a lady who will not have a secret lover besides me."

But Ruodlieb's mother devoted herself in whatever way she could to Christ's poor, widows, orphans, and pilgrims, and by this she won a mighty blessing for Ruodlieb, for Christ showed her that he wished to raise him up. At a certain time she saw a pair of boars in her dreams, and a great crowd of swine with menacing tusks went along with them, as though they threatened to make war with Ruodlieb: but he cut off the head of each boar with his sword, and cut down all the swine that attacked him in a great slaughter. Then his mother saw a linden tree, broad and very high, at whose very top she saw Ruodlieb sitting on a couch, and around him in the branches stood an army as though ready for war. After a while a beautiful snow-white dove came carrying an ornate, bejewelled crown in its beak, and putting it on Ruodlieb's head it swiftly perched beside him and gave him loving kisses, which he accepted without refusal. His mother saw all these things in a vision and wondered what all that she had seen could portend. Although she knew that they pointed to honor, she did not become more proud because of them, but continued to be very humble, reckoning nothing to herself, but rather attributing to the gracious favor of the Lord whatever great honors he might grant to Ruodlieb.

Three days later, she told him what God had revealed to her, about the swine whose fierce heads he cut off, and about the carnage of the swine that accompanied those twin boars, how she saw him sitting at the top of a linden-tree, and his followers beneath him in the branches, and that the dove had flown to him carrying a crown, and sitting in his hands had offered him sweet kisses of love. "While I was looking at these things I suddenly woke up, and it annoyed me greatly that I had woken up. I know that that awakening means that I shall die before the end of these events comes to pass. My son, remember how often God in his goodness has helped you and saved you from death itself, and how by aiding you greatly in your exile he granted that you should return to your homeland with good health and wealth. Now I know that you are destined to win yet greater honors, and I am greatly afraid that the Lord has repaid us both in this way if we ever did things which pleased him. Beware of saying this, my son. For what can we do, who have nothing save what he gives us? But whether good or ill befalls you, give thanks to him."

What does this poem reveal about liaisons and marriages between people of different social statuses? What were the advantages for a young man to marry a widow? What does the tale of the redheaded man indicate about marriage and morality? How was a marriage negotiated? by whom? Who was present (or absent)? Where did it occur? Was mutual faithfulness the norm? What economic aspects of marriage are reflected in the poem? Do values vary according to social status?

34. THE LITURGY OF MARRIAGE

The Sarum Missal *contained the liturgy of the Church as it had developed and was practiced in the diocese of Salisbury in the first half of the thirteenth century. It was gradually adopted by other dioceses, and by the fifteenth century was followed across England, Wales, and Ireland. It became the authorized liturgical form for the Catholic Church in England and, after the Reformation, endured in the liturgical practices of the Church of England. The* Missal *provided outlines for the proper conduct of the sacraments, detailing the appropriate words and gestures at each point in the celebration. It did more, however, and provided priests with short theological and canonical rationales for various customs and practices. Thus, the Liturgy of Marriage incorporates a brief treatise on the inferiority of second marriages. It is important to note that unless specifically stated to be otherwise, the language of the liturgy was Latin rather than the vernacular. In the liturgy, the rules and ideas about marriage that were developed by earlier canonists and theologians are put into practice and given their practical application. Particularly noteworthy are the stages of the ceremony: the reading of the banns by the priest, the interrogation concerning impediments, the exchange of consent at the church door, the mass and nuptial blessing inside the church, and, finally, the blessing of the marriage bed.*

Source: Trans. Frederick E. Warren, *The Sarum Missal*, Part 2 (London: De La More Press, 1911), pp. 143-60; revised.

The question is asked when can matrimony be solemnized. First of all, sexual intercourse should not take place before the benediction has been pronounced over those marrying, and on solemn feast days sexual intercourse should be abstained from. This is the reason why the solemnization of marriage is prohibited during certain times, although engagements are not prohibited. Nevertheless, if a marriage is solemnized then, it would not be invalid. And so, note the times in which it is not lawful to solemnize a marriage....

That is to say, people must abstain from marriage from the first Sunday in Advent until the eighth day after the feast of Epiphany inclusive. The second time to abstain from marriage is from the beginning of Lent until the eighth day of Easter, that is until the day following the octave, which is called Low Sunday. Likewise, people must abstain from marriage from the Monday of Rogation Week, until after the octave of Whitsunday inclusive, that is, until the day after Trinity Sunday. At other times of the year, the solemnization of marriages can occur lawfully.

How to Solemnize a Marriage

The man and the woman are to stand before the door of the church or in the face of the church, in the presence of God, and the priest, and the people. Let

A nineteenth-century drawing of a royal marriage in the thirteenth century. This is based on an illustration by Matthew Paris.

the man stand to the right side of the woman and the woman to the left of the man. The reason for this is that woman was made from a rib from Adam's left side. Then the priest shall read out the banns, and afterwards, he shall say in their mother tongue in the hearing of everyone:

> "Behold, brothers, we are gathered here in the presence of God and the angels, and all the saints and in the face of the church, to join together two bodies, that is of this man and this woman,"

Here the priest shall look at both people,

> "so that from now on they will be one body, and that they be two souls in faith and in the law of God, so that they may together earn eternal life, and whatsoever they may have done before this,"

Then let the admonition be made to the people in their mother tongue, thus—

> "I admonish you all, by the Father and the Son and the Holy Spirit, that if there are any of you who know some reason why these young people are not able to be joined together legitimately, let him now confess it."

Let the same admonition be made to the man and woman, so that if they had done something secretly, or if they had made a vow of some kind, or if they know something about themselves, why they may not legitimately contract marriage, then let them confess it. If anyone should allege any impediment and provide a guarantee for proving it, let the marriage be deferred until the truth of the matter is ascertained. However, if no impediment is alleged, let the priest enquire about the woman's dowry. The priest should not betroth or consent to the betrothal of a man and woman before the third publication of the banns. The banns ought to be read out on three separate holy days, so that at least one ordinary day falls between every one of the holy days. After this, the priest shall say to the man, in the hearing of everyone, in their mother tongue:

> "N. do you wish to have this woman as your wife, and to love and honor her, to hold her and to keep her, in health and in sickness, just as a husband should a wife? And will you forsake all others on account of her, and keep yourself only to her, for as long as you both shall live?"

The man shall reply, "I will."
Likewise, the priest shall say to the woman:

> "N. do you wish to have this man as your husband, to obey and serve him, and to love and honor him, and to keep him in health and in sickness just as a wife should a husband? And will you forsake all others on account of him, and keep yourself only to him, for as long as you both shall live?"

The woman shall reply, "I will."
Then let the woman be given by her father or by a friend. If she is a girl, let her hand be uncovered; if a widow, covered. Let the man receive her, to be kept in God's faith and his own, just as he vowed in the presence of the priest. And let him hold her with her right hand in his right hand. And so let the man give faith to the woman, in words of the present tense, thus saying after the priest:

> "I, N. take you N. as my wedded wife, to have and to hold, for better, for worse, for richer, for poorer; in sickness and in health, till death us do part, and thereto I pledge you my faith" (withdrawing his hand).

Then, let the woman say after the priest:

"I, N. take you N. as my wedded husband, to have and to hold, for better, for worse, for richer, for poorer, in sickness and in health, to be bonnie and buxom, in bed and at board, till death us do part; and thereto I pledge you my faith" (withdrawing her hand).

Then, the man shall place gold or silver and a ring on the plate or book. And then the priest shall ask whether or not the ring had been blessed before. If it is answered no, then the priest shall bless the ring in this way:

Celebrant: "The Lord be with you."
Response: "And with your spirit."

"Let us pray. Creator and preserver of the human race, giver of spiritual grace, bestower of eternal salvation, you, Lord, send your blessing on this ring, so that she who will wear it may be armed with the strength of heavenly defense and it help her to eternal salvation. Through Christ our Lord."

Response: "Amen."
"Let us pray."

"Bless, Lord, this ring which we bless in your holy name, that whoever shall wear it, may abide in your peace and remain in your will, and live, and prosper, and grow old in your love, and let the length of her days be multiplied."

Then let holy water be sprinkled on the ring. If, however, the ring had been blessed before, then immediately after the man has placed the ring on the book, the priest, having received the ring, shall give it to the man. The man shall take it in his right hand with his three principal fingers, holding the bride's right hand with his left, and shall say after the priest:

"With this ring I you wed and this gold and silver I you give and with my body I you worship, and with all my worldly goods I you honor."

Then the groom shall put the ring on the bride's thumb saying, "In the name of the Father;" then on the second finger, saying, "and of the Son;" then on the third finger, saying, "and of the Holy Spirit;" and then on the fourth finger, saying "Amen." And let him leave the ring there because according to the *Decretum* c. 30, in that finger there is a certain vein running up to the heart, and inner love, which should always be fresh between them, is signified by the silver ring. Then, with their heads bowed, the priest shall pronounce the blessing over them.

"May you be blessed by the Lord, who made the world out of nothing."

Response: "Amen...."
Another prayer:

"May God the Father bless you, may Jesus Christ keep you, may the Holy Spirit enlighten you. May the Lord show his face to you and have mercy on you; may he turn his countenance to you and give you peace. And may he fill you with every spiritual blessing for the forgiveness of your sins, so that you may have eternal life and live for ever and ever."

Response: "Amen."
Here they shall go into the church, up to the step of the altar and, as they are going, the priest together with his ministers, shall say Psalm 128 ...
Then, with the groom and bride kneeling before the altar, the priest shall ask the congregation to pray for them, saying:
"Our Father, etc...."
Celebrant: "And lead us not into temptation."
Response: "But free us from evil."
Celebrant: "Save your servant and your handmaid."
Response: "My God, trusting in you."
Celebrant: "Lord, send them help from your holy place."
Response: "And out of Zion, defend them."
Celebrant: "Be for them, Lord, a tower of strength."
Response: "From the face of the enemy."
Celebrant: "Lord, hear my prayer."
Response: "And let my cry come to you."
Celebrant: "The Lord be with you."
Response: "And with your spirit."
"Let us pray...."
The prayer:

"God of Abraham, God of Isaac, God of Jacob, bless these young people, and sow the seed of eternal life in their minds, so that whatever they may learn that is useful for them, this let them desire to do. Through Christ, your Son, restorer of mankind. Who, with you, etc."

Response: "Amen."

"Let us pray."

The prayer:

> "Lord, look down from heaven and bless this union, and just as you sent your holy angel Raphael to Tobias and Sara, the daughter of Raguel, so deign, Lord, to send your blessing on these young people, so that they may remain steadfast in your will, and continue in your protection, and live, and prosper and grow old in your love, and let them be worthy and peaceful and the length of their days be multiplied. Through Christ etc."

"Let us pray."

The prayer:

> "Lord, look down propitiously on this your servant and on this your handmaid, so that in your name they may receive a heavenly blessing, and that they may see safe and sound the sons of their sons and daughters up to the third and fourth generation, and that they may persevere in your will and that the length of their days be multiplied. Through Christ etc."

"Let us pray."

The prayer:

> "May the omnipotent and merciful God, who by his power created our first parents Adam and Eve and by his own sanctification joined them; sanctify and bless your hearts and bodies, and unite you in the society and love of true affection. Through Christ etc."

Then the priest shall bless them, saying:

> "May omnipotent God bless you with every heavenly blessing; may he make you worthy in his sight; may he make abundant on you the riches of his glory; and teach you with the word of truth, so that you will be able to please him with body and mind alike."

Response: "Amen."

These prayers being finished, and the couple being brought into the presbytery, that is between the choir and the altar, on the south side of the church, and with the woman standing on the right side of the man, that is between him and the altar, let there begin *The Mass of the Trinity* ...

After the *Sanctus*, the groom and bride shall prostrate themselves in prayer at the step of the altar, a veil being held over them, which four clerics in surplices shall hold at the four corners, unless one or both of them shall have been married and blessed previously. Then the veil is not held over them, nor the sacramental blessing given.

Then, after the conclusion of the Lord's Prayer, before "The Peace of the Lord" is said, after the breaking of the Eucharist in the usual manner, and having left the host in three pieces on the paten, the priest, turning to them, shall say the following prayers in a reading tone, while they, meanwhile, kneel under the veil.

Celebrant: "The Lord be with you."

Response: "And with your spirit."

"Let us pray."

The prayer:

> "Be merciful, Lord, to our prayers and in your kindness assist the ordinances you instituted for the propagation of the human race, so that which is joined by your authority may be preserved by your help. Through Christ etc."

"Let us pray."

The prayer:

> "God, who by the power of your strength made everything from nothing, who, after everything was set in order, created for man, made in the image of God, the inseparable assistance of woman, so that woman should be created from man's flesh, teaching that what it had pleased you to make from one should never be lawful to separate."

Let the priest beware with regard to the following clause:

"God, who consecrated conjugal union to such an excellent mystery, so that in the union of marriage you signified the sacrament and union of Christ and the Church," because it is not said in second marriages.

> "God, by whom woman is joined to man and the union, ordained in the beginning, is granted your blessing which alone was not taken away by the punishment of original sin or the sentence of the flood, look graciously, we ask, on your servant who, joined in the union of marriage, seeks to be guarded by your protection. May the yoke of love and peace be upon her. Faithful and chaste, may she marry in Christ and remain an

emulator of holy women. Let her be amiable to her husband like Rachel, wise like Rebecca, long-lived and faithful like Sara. Let the father of lies acquire nothing over her from any of her actions. Bound to your faith and commandments, let her remain joined to one bed. May she flee illicit contacts. May she fortify her weakness with the strength of discipline. May she be serious and respectful, reverential and modest, learned in heavenly doctrine. May she be fruitful in child-bearing, excellent, and innocent. May she arrive at a welcome old age, and may she see her children's children up to the third and fourth generation. And may she reach the rest of the blessed and the kingdom of heaven. Through Christ etc."

It must be noted that the clause in the foregoing prayer, "God, who consecrated" up to "God, by whom woman is joined" is not said in second marriages, as stated above. For the man or woman entering a second marriage ought not to be blessed again by the priest, because as they have been blessed once, their blessing ought not to be repeated; because flesh which has been blessed attracts to itself flesh which has not been blessed. It is forbidden in the section concerning second marriages in *Decretals* 25 q.v.i. The blessing is not given at a second marriage for this reason, as blessed Ambrose thus testifies: "first marriages were instituted by the Lord, but second marriages are not permitted. First marriages are celebrated with every benediction; but second marriages are without any benediction...."

And this is true as much for a bigamous man as for a widowed woman, because blessed flesh draws to itself unblessed flesh. But all other benedictions ought to be said without distinction, according to the Roman Church, ...And it ought to be known that this question was discussed and determined in the sacred palace of the lord Pope, and was conveyed to England by Master John Haystede, in the year of our Lord 1321. And the cause of the discussion was because many priests had come together at that time at the Apostolic See, for the sake of obtaining absolution for indiscriminately bestowing blessings on second marriages. Therefore, a new regulation was established on this point....

Here it can be asked why second marriages are not blessed. To this, I say that a second marriage, although considered in itself has a sacramental nature, however, compared with the first sacrament, it has something of a sacramental defect, because it does not have the full signification, since it is not the union of one with one, as in the marriage of Christ and the Church. And it is by reason of this defect that the blessing is withheld from second marriages. But this must be understood when the second marriages are second on both the part of the man and the woman or on the part of the woman only. For if a virgin contracts with a man who has had another wife, nevertheless, the marriage is blessed. The signification is also preserved in another way, even in its order with regard to first marriages, because Christ, although he has one Church, nevertheless, has many persons espoused to him in that one Church. But the soul cannot be the bride of any other except Christ, because then it would be fornication with a demon and not spiritual marriage. And on account of this, when a woman marries a second time, the nuptials are not blessed on account of the defect of the sacrament.

After this, the priest shall turn to the altar and say, *The Peace of the Lord* and *O Lamb of God* in the usual way. Then, after the veil has been removed, the groom and bride shall arise from prayer and the groom shall receive the sign of peace from the priest and give it to the bride, kissing her. And neither of them are to kiss anyone else, but immediately a clerk, receiving the sign of peace from the priest, shall offer it to the others in the accustomed manner....

On the following night, when the groom and the bride have gone to bed, let the priest approach and bless the bed-chamber, saying
Celebrant: "The Lord be with you."
Response: "And with your spirit."
"Let us pray."
The prayer:

"Bless, O Lord, this chamber and all who dwell in it, that they may remain in your peace, and endure in your will, and live and grow in your love, and let the length of their days be multiplied. Through Christ etc."

The blessing over the bed alone:
Celebrant: "The Lord be with you."
Response: "And with your spirit."
"Let us pray."
The prayer:

"Bless this bedchamber O Lord, who neither slumbers nor sleeps, who watches over Israel, guard your servants resting in this bed from every fantasy and illusion of the demons. Guard them while awake, so that they may meditate on your commandments, while asleep so that they may think about you in slumber, and here and everywhere may they always be defended with the help of your protection."

Then let this blessing be said over those in the bed.:
"Let us pray."
The prayer:

"May God bless your bodies and your souls, and bestow His blessing on you, just as He blessed Abraham, Isaac, and Jacob."

Response: "Amen."
Likewise, another blessing over them:
"Let us pray."
The prayer:

"May the hand of God be over you and may He send His holy angel who will guard and tend you all the days of your life."

Response: "Amen."
Likewise, another blessing over them:
"Let us pray."
The prayer:

"The Father, the Son, and the Holy Spirit bless you, who are three in number but one in name."

Response: "Amen."
This done, the priest shall sprinkle them with holy water and dismiss them in peace, and so, depart.

When and why are marriages prohibited? Why would the priest enquire about the dowry? about impediments? What is the significance of the father handing over the bride? What does the ring signify? Why is it worn on a specific finger? Why are second marriages not blessed? Why did the priest bless the newlyweds' bed?

35. POPULAR CUSTOMS AND MARRIAGE CELEBRATIONS

While the church had many formal requirements for the rites surrounding marriage, there were also many popular practices which could accompany the celebration. Numerous moralists complained about the excessive feasting and drinking that could accompany marriage celebrations even among modest villagers. Friends and neighbors expected that a marriage would provide an opportunity for a community revel that occasionally degenerated into drunkenness and brawling. The most popular times of the year to marry were October and November, after the harvest and before Advent, and late December and January, a traditional period of revelry. At higher levels of society, marriages might be more sedate affairs but they, too, had their celebratory and customary aspects. They were also an occasion for gift-giving. These entries from the account books of King Edward II reflect something of what actually occurred during the nuptial ceremony and the costs associated with getting married. Given the royal origin of the account book, it reflects expenses at the highest social level in the early fourteenth century.

Source: Trans. Thomas Stapleton, "A Brief Summary of the Wardrobe Accounts of the Tenth, Eleventh, and Fourteenth Years of King Edward the Second," *Archaeologia* 26 (1836): 337–39; revised.

The Accounts of King Edward II

The marriage of the countess of Cornwall, niece of the king, in 1317:

In gifts distributed in the presence of our lord the king, in his chapel in Windsor Park, for the nuptials of Sir Hugh de Audley, junior and the countess of Cornwall, and those of John de Montacute and the daughter of Sir Theobald de Verdon, 13 shillings, 6 pence. And, on 28 April, in money thrown over the heads of Sir Hugh and the countess during the nuptials, by Sir Roger de Northburgh and Sir Robert de Wodehouse, 3 pounds.

On 9 February, in money thrown by the king's order, at the door of the king's chapel, within the manor of Havering-atte-Boure, during the solemnization of the marriage between Richard, son of Edmund, earl of Arundel, and Isabella, daughter of Sir Hugh le Despenser, junior, 2 pounds.

Delivered, for a veil to be spread over the heads of Richard de Arundel and Isabella, daughter of Sir Hugh le Despenser, junior, at their nuptial mass in the king's chapel, at Havering-atte-Boure, 9 February, one piece of Lucca cloth.

On 26 June, …in money thrown over the heads of Oliver de Bourdeaux and the Lady Maud Trussel, during the solemnization of their nuptials, at the door of the chapel within the park of Woodstock, 2 pounds, 10 shillings.

A nineteenth-century drawing of a medieval banquet similar to those which would celebrate a marriage.

A Royal Marriage Celebration (1252)

At the highest levels of society, marriages were arranged for many reasons, including the formation or confirmation of political ties and peace treaties. In these marriages, the views of the spouses were secondary to the affairs of state. Royal marriages, too, were a way for a king to entertain lavishly to impress his rivals, enemies, and friends alike with his evident wealth and largess. This account of the marriage of the king of Scotland to Margaret, the daughter of the king of England, which occurred in 1252, is remarkable for what it reveals about the lavish nature of royal weddings. It also betrays many values of feudal and royal society. Notable, too, in this account, is the onerous burden that was borne by those vassals who found themselves in the position of entertaining the king and his court.

Source: Trans. J.A. Giles in Matthew of Paris, *English History*, vol. 2 (London: Henry G. Bohn, 1853), 468–71; revised.

The King of Scotland Espoused Margaret, Daughter of the King of England

On the day after Christmas Day, which is the feast of St. Stephen, the king of Scotland espoused the daughter of the king of England. Because the unruly crowds of people rushed together and jostled so that they might be present and see such a marriage ceremony, the celebration of the marriage was performed secretly, in the early morning, before it was expected. Naturally, there assembled there a diversity of people, such a large multitude of English, French, and Scottish nobles, such a crowd of knights dressed in lavish clothing, taking pride in their silk and variegated ornaments, that the worldly and luxurious vanity, if it were described in full, would arouse amazement and boredom in those listening. There were also a thousand or more knights dressed in silken material, commonly called quaintise [a particularly fine and elegant material], and they appeared at the wedding on behalf of the king of England. And on the next day, casting off these, they again presented themselves to the court in new robes. On behalf of the king of Scotland, sixty or more knights dressed appropriately, and many of a rank equal to the knights, dressed similarly, presented themselves in the sight of everyone.

The King of Scotland did Homage to the Lord King of England on account of the Lands which he held from the King of England

Therefore, the king of Scotland did homage to the king of England on account of the lands which he held from the lord king of England, that is for that portion of the kingdom of England called Lothian, and the rest of his lands. But when the king of Scotland was called to do homage for the kingdom of Scotland, and to give fealty and allegiance to his lord, the king of the English, as his predecessors had done to the kings of England, as is clearly written in the chronicles of many areas. The king of Scotland replied that he had come there in peace and for the honor of the king of England, and by his command, so that he might be allied with him by means of the bonds of marriage, and not so that he might reply to so difficult a question. For he had not, he said, sought full consultation or advice on this matter with his nobles, as so difficult a matter required. But the lord king, when he heard this, did not wish by any disturbance to cast a shadow over so festive a celebration nor to trouble so young a king and his even younger bride, especially since the king of Scotland had come with the greatest joy when he was called to marry the king's daughter. Thus, for the time being, the king disguised his feelings, passing over it all in silence....

A Description of the Marriage Banquet

Therefore, celebrating joyfully, the kings and their nobles and their families spent Christmas with the greatest pleasure. If I were to describe fully the abundance and diversity of the menu, variety of the variegated clothing, the hilarity of the jesters, the number of guests, the description would seem exaggerated to the hearts and ears of those not present, and would give rise to ironical reactions. But, so that the rest may be understood by a useful comparison from one fact, more than sixty pasture cattle, a gift from the archbishop, formed the first and principal course at the banquet. The guests feasted alternately, now with one king, now with the other, who rivaled each other in preparing lavish meals, so that the illusory vanity of the world showed whatever it could of its brief and transitory joys to mortal humanity. Everyone dined for several days with the archbishop, who was, as it were, prince of the north and cheerful host of all, and he gave his advice to everyone in every case of failure or necessity. He effectually fulfilled everyone's needs, now by providing hospitality to travelers, at another time by pasturing horses, at other times by providing various household utensils, fuel for the fires, and gifts of money, so that because of this visit of his lord, in gifts of gold, silver, and silk he sowed on a barren shore 4,000 marks, which afterwards he never reaped. But, according to the circumstances, he needed to do these things so that the integrity of his reputation would be preserved, and the mouths of evil speakers would be closed.

Where did the marriages occur? Why did people throw money at the couple? What kind of entertainment accompanied the royal marriage? Why was this marriage arranged? Over how many days did the celebrations last?

CHAPTER FIVE:

HUSBANDS AND WIVES

For medieval people the focus of marriage and the center of the family were the marital couple, the husband and wife. How a man and woman should behave towards each other was a subject that theologians and moralists, poets and critics, writing as much in the vernacular as in Latin, put at the center of their reflections on marriage. The relationship between husband and wife was at once idealized and disparaged. It was a relationship believed to have been sanctified by God, one that could bring both spouses to grace and salvation. Yet it was a difficult relationship, too, given the centrality of sexual activity and the threat of sin that hovered over the couple. Writers equally recognized the potential difficulties that could assail two people meeting, cohabiting as virtual strangers, and yet facing the vicissitudes of making a living and raising a family. Marriage was at once an ideal state and one that provided numerous occasions for quarrels, betrayals, and misery.

36. AN EARLY CHRISTIAN VIEW OF HUSBANDS AND WIVES

The Clementine Homilies, written in the late first century in Greek, circulated with other apocryphal works attributed to Clement of Rome. The Homilies *comprise twenty religious and philosophical discourses that tell the story of a journey Clement allegedly made to Jerusalem and how while he was there he reputedly met St. Peter. The work presents much legendary material about Clement's own family and this provides the context for a discussion of the qualities desirable in a Christian husband or wife. While the* Homilies *did not significantly influence medieval writers, they are a useful early illustration of the values of the early Church which were inherited by the Middle Ages. They also provide a counter-balance to the more negative views of women, marriage, and sexual activity subsequently propounded by the church fathers.*

Source: Trans. Alexander Roberts and James Donaldson, "The Clementine Homilies," in *Ante-Nicene Fathers*, vol. 8 (Buffalo, NY.: Christian Literature Company, 1886), pp. 303–04; revised.

13. That same evening we all enjoyed the benefit of Peter's instruction. Taking occasion by what had happened to our mother, he showed us how the results of chastity are good, while those of adultery are disastrous, and naturally bring destruction on the whole race, if not speedily, then at least slowly. "And to such an extent," he says, "do deeds of chastity please God, that in this life he bestows some small favor on account of it, even on those who are in error; for salvation in the other world is granted only to those who have been baptized on account of their trust in him, and who act chastely and righteously. This you yourselves have seen in the case of your mother, that the results of chastity are in the end good. For perhaps she would have been cut off if she had committed adultery; but God took pity on her for having behaved chastely, rescued her from the death that threatened her, and restored to her her lost children.

14. "But someone will say, 'How many have perished on account of chastity!' Yes; but it was because they did not perceive the danger. For the woman who perceives that she is in love with anyone, or is beloved by anyone, should immediately avoid all association with him as she would avoid a blazing fire or a mad dog. And this is exactly what your mother did, for she really loved chastity as a blessing: therefore she was preserved, and, along with you, obtained full knowledge of the everlasting kingdom. The woman who wishes to be chaste ought to know that she is envied by wickedness, and that because of love many lie in wait for her. If, then, she remains holy through a steadfast persistence in chastity, she will gain victory over all temptations, and be saved. But, even if she were to do everything that is right, and yet should once commit the sin of adultery, she must be punished, as the prophet said.

15. "The chaste wife, doing the will of God, is a good reminiscence of his first creation; for God, being one, created one woman for one man. She is also still more chaste if she does not forget her eyes, and is not ignorant of the loss of eternal blessings. The chaste woman takes pleasure in those who wish to be saved, and is a pious example to the pious, for she is the model of a good life. She who wishes to be chaste, cuts off all occasions for slander; but if she is slandered by an enemy, though affording him no pretext, she is blessed and avenged by God. The chaste woman longs for God, loves God, pleases God, glorifies God; and to men she affords no occasion for slander. The chaste woman perfumes the church with her good reputation, and glorifies it by her piety. She is, moreover, the praise of her teachers, and a helper to them in their chastity.

16. "The chaste woman is adorned with the son of God as with a bridegroom. She is clothed with holy light. Her beauty lies in a well-regulated soul; and she is fragrant with ointment, even with a good reputation. She is arrayed in beautiful clothing, even in modesty. She wears about her precious pearls, even chaste words. And she is radiant, for her mind has been brilliantly lighted up. She looks into a beautiful mirror, for she looks into God. She uses beautiful cosmetics, namely, the fear of God, with which she admonishes her soul. The woman is beautiful, not because she has chains of gold on her, but because she has been set free from transient lusts. The chaste woman is greatly desired by the great king; she has been wooed, watched, and loved by him. The chaste woman does not furnish occasions for being desired, except by her own husband. The chaste woman is grieved when she is desired by another. The chaste woman loves her husband from the heart, embraces, soothes, and pleases him, acts the slave to him, and is obedient to him in all things, except when she would be disobedient to God. For she who obeys God is, without the aid of watchmen, chaste in soul and pure in body.

17. "Foolish, therefore, is every husband who separates his wife from the fear of God; for she who does not fear God is not afraid of her husband. If she does not fear God, who sees what is invisible, how will she be chaste, who does not come to the assembly to hear chaste-making words? And how could she obtain admonition? And how will she be chaste without watchmen, if she is not informed about the coming judgment of God, and if she is not fully assured that eternal punishment is the penalty for slight pleasure? Therefore, on the other hand, compel her even against her will always to come to hear the chaste-making word, even coax her to do so.

18. "It is much better if you will take her by the hand and come, in order that you yourself may become chaste; for you will desire to become chaste, so that you may experience the full blossoming of a holy marriage, and you will not hesitate, if you desire it, to become a father, to love your own children, and

to be loved by your own children. He who wishes to have a chaste wife is also himself chaste, gives her what is due to a wife, takes his meals with her, keeps company with her, goes with her to the word that makes chaste, does not annoy her, does not rashly quarrel with her, does not make himself hateful to her, furnishes her with all the good things he can, and when he does not have them, he makes up the deficiency by caresses. The chaste wife does not expect to be caressed, recognizes her husband as her lord, bears his poverty when he is poor, is hungry with him when he is hungry, travels with him when he travels, consoles him when he sorrows, and if she has a large dowry, is subject to him as if she had nothing at all. But if the husband has a poor wife, let him consider her chastity a great dowry. The chaste wife is temperate in her eating and drinking, in order that the weariness of the body, thus pampered, may not drag the soul down to unlawful desires. Moreover, she absolutely never remains alone with young men, and she suspects the old; she turns away from disorderly laughter, gives herself up to God alone; she is not led astray; she delights in listening to holy words, but turns away from those which are not spoken to produce chastity.

19. "God is my witness: one adultery is as bad as many murders; and what is terrible in it is this, that the fearfulness and impiety of its murders are not seen. For, when blood is shed, the dead body remains lying, and all are struck by the terrible nature of the occurrence. But the murders of the soul caused by adultery, though they are more frightful, yet, since they are not seen by people, do not make the daring a bit less eager in their impulse. Know, O humanity, whose breath it is you have to keep you in life, and you shall not wish that it be polluted. By adultery alone the breath of God is polluted. And therefore it drags him who has polluted it into the fire; for it hastens to deliver up its insulter to everlasting punishment."

What are the qualities of a chaste wife? What qualities should a husband cultivate? What view of sexual relations is presented? How is adultery regarded?

37. TERTULLIAN: *TO HIS WIFE* (CA. 200)

Tertullian (ca. 160-ca. 220) was the first of the great theologians who wrote in Latin. He lived in Carthage and likely converted to Christianity around the year 195. Tertullian was something of a rigorist and he promoted a strict form of asceticism. Yet, he was also a married man who exhibited great fondness for his wife, as this passage indicates. The treatise To His Wife, *written about the year 200, represents a more moderate understanding of marriage and chastity than is found in some of Tertullian's later works. In his discussion of second marriages, however, Tertullian sets out the fundamental issues that would continue to trouble theologians into the thirteenth century: the tensions between the imperative to chastity and marriage, and between the doctrine of monogamy and the practice of second marriages.*

Source: Trans. and ed. William P. Le Saint in Tertullian, *Treatises on Marriage and Remarriage: To His Wife an Exhortation to Chastity and Monogamy* (Westminster, MD.: Newman Press, 1951), pp. 10-22; reprinted with permission.

Book One: To His Wife: A Spiritual Legacy

I thought it would be well, my dearest companion in the service of the Lord, to give some consideration, even at this early date, to the manner of life that ought to be yours after my departure from this world, should I be called before you. I trust your own loyalty to follow the suggestions I shall offer. For if we pursue our purposes with such diligence when worldly issues are at stake, even drawing up legal instruments in our anxiety to secure each other's interests, ought we not to be all the more solicitous in providing for the welfare of those we leave behind us when there is question of securing their best advantage in matters concerning God and heaven? Ought we not, acting as it were before the event, bequeath them legacies of loving-counsel, and make clear our will respecting goods which constitute the eternal portion of their heavenly inheritance? God grant that you may be disposed to receive in its entirety the loving-counsel I now commit in trust to your fidelity. To him be honor, glory, splendor, grandeur, and power, now and forever.

This charge, then, I lay on you—that, exercising all the self-control of which you are capable, you renounce marriage after I have passed away. You will not, on that account, confer any benefit on me, apart from the good you do yourself. I would not want you to think that I now advise you to remain a widow because I fear to suffer hardship if you fail to preserve your person inviolate for myself alone. No, when the future time arrives, we shall not resume the gratification of unseemly passion. It is not such worthless, filthy things that God promises to those who are his own. Moreover, there is no promise given Christians who have departed this life that on the day of their resurrection they will be restored once more to the married state. They will, it is clear, be changed to the state of holy angels. For this reason they will remain undisturbed by feelings of carnal jealousy. Even that woman who was said to have married seven brothers in succession, will give no offence to a single one of all her husbands when she rises from the dead; nor does a single one of them await her there to put her to the blush. The teaching of our Lord has settled this quibble of the Sadducees. Yet it is still permitted us to consider whether the course of action I recommend is of advantage to you personally or, for that matter, to the advantage of any other woman who belongs to God.

Monogamy Blessed by God

2. Of course, we do not reject the union of man and woman in marriage. It is an institution blessed by God for the reproduction of the human race. It was planned by him for the purpose of populating the earth and to make provision for the propagation of mankind. Hence, it was permitted; but only once may it be contracted. For Adam was the only husband that Eve had and Eve was his only wife; one rib, one woman.

Now, everybody knows that it was allowed our forefathers, even the patriarchs themselves, not only to marry but actually to multiply marriages. They even kept concubines. But, although figurative language is used in speaking of both church and synagogue, yet we may explain this difficult matter simply by saying that it was necessary in former times that there be practices which afterwards had to be abrogated or modified. For the law had first to intervene, too, at a later date, the word of God was to replace the law and introduce spiritual circumcision. Therefore, the licentiousness and promiscuity of earlier days — and there must needs have been abuses which called for the institution of a law — were responsible for that subsequent corrective legislation by which the Lord through his gospel, and the apostle in these latter days did away with excesses or controlled irregularities.

3. But I would not have you suppose that I have premised these remarks on the liberty which was allowed in former times and the severity of later legislation, because I wish to lay the foundation of an argument proving that Christ has come into the world for the purpose of separating those who are joined in wedlock and forbidding the conjugal relationship, as though from now on all marriages were to be outlawed. This is a charge they must be prepared to answer who, among other perversions of doctrine, teach their followers to divide those who are "two in one flesh," opposing the will of him who first subtracted woman from man and then, in the mathematics of marriage, added two together again who had originally been substantially one. Finally, we do not read anywhere at all that marriage is forbidden; and this for the obvious reason that marriage is actually a good.

Celibacy Preferable to Marriage

The apostle, however, teaches us what is better than this "good," when he says that he permits marriage, but prefers celibacy—the former because of the snares of the flesh, the latter because the times are straitened. Hence, if we consider the reasons which he gives for each of these views, we shall have no difficulty in seeing that marriage is conceded to us on the principle that marry we may because marry we must. But what necessity proffers necessity cheapens. Scripture says that "it is better to marry than to burn;" but what sort of good, I ask you, can that be which is such only when it is compared to what is bad? Marriage, truly, is better because burning is worse! How much better it is neither to marry nor to burn!

In time of persecution it is better to flee from place to place, as we are permitted, than to be arrested and to deny the faith under torture. Yet, far happier are they who find courage to bear witness and to undergo martyrdom for the faith. It can be said that what is merely tolerated is never really good. Suppose I am doomed to die. If I quail at this, then it is good to flee. If, however, I hesitate to use the permission given, this itself shows that there is something suspect about the very reasons for which the permission is granted. Nobody merely *permits* that which is better, since this is something of which there can be no doubt; it is a thing which recommends itself by its own transparent goodness.

Nothing is to be sought after for the sole reason that it is not forbidden. When we come to think of it, even such things are, in a sense, forbidden because other things are preferred to them. To prefer the lofty is to exclude the low. Nothing is good just because it is not bad, nor is it, therefore, not bad simply for the reason that it does you no hurt. A thing that is good in the full sense of the word is to be preferred because it helps us, not merely because it does not harm us. You ought to choose things that are good for you rather than things which are merely not bad for you.

Every contest is a straining for the first prize. When a man comes in second, he has consolation, but he does not have victory. If we listen to the apostle, then, "forgetting the things that are behind," let us "stretch forth to those that are before," and be "zealous for the better gifts." Thus, although the apostle does not "cast a snare upon us," he does show us where our advantage lies when he writes: "The unmarried woman … thinks on the things of the Lord, that she may be holy both in body and in spirit. But she that is married is solicitous … how she may please her husband." In other places, also, the apostle is nowhere so tolerant of marriage that he fails to point out his own preference, and this is that we strive to follow his example. Blessed is he who is like Paul!

The Way of the Flesh

4. But we read that "the flesh is weak;" and this serves us as an excuse for pampering ourselves in a number of ways. We also read, however, that "the spirit is strong." Both statements are made in the same sentence. The flesh is of the earth, the spirit is of heaven. Now, why is it that, habitually seeking excuses for ourselves, we plead the weakness of our nature and disregard its strength? Should not the things of earth yield to the things of heaven? If the spirit, being nobler in origin, is stronger than the flesh, then we have no one to blame but ourselves when we yield to the weaker force.

There are two weaknesses in human nature which appear to make it necessary that those who have lost a spouse should marry again. First, there is the concupiscence of the flesh, and this has the strongest pull; second, there is the concupiscence of the world. We servants of God ought to scorn both weaknesses, since we renounce both lust and ambition.

Concupiscence of the flesh urges in its defense the right to exercise the functions of maturity; it seeks to pluck the fruits of beauty; it "glories in its shame;" it declares that woman's sex requires a husband to be her strength and comfort, or to protect her good name from ugly gossip.

But as for you, do you oppose against such specious arguments the example of those sisters of ours—their names are known to the Lord—who, having seen their husbands go to God, prefer chastity to the opportunities of marriage afforded them by their youth and beauty. They choose to be wedded to God. They are God's fair ones, God's beloved. With him they live, with him they converse, with him they treat on intimate terms day and night. Prayers are the dowry they bring the Lord and for them they receive his favors as marriage gifts in return. Thus they have made their own a blessing for eternity, given them by the Lord; and, remaining unmarried, they are reckoned, even while still on earth, as belonging to the household of the angels. Train yourself to imitate the example of continence furnished by such women as these and, in your love for things of the spirit, you will bury concupiscence of the flesh. You will root out the fleeting, vagrant desires which come of beauty and youth, and make compensation for their loss with the blessings of heaven which last forever.

The Way of the World

The concupiscence of the world which I mentioned has its roots in pride, avarice, ambition, and the plea that one is unable to get along alone. Arguments drawn from sources such as these it uses to urge the necessity of marriage; and, of course, it promises heavenly rewards in return; to queen it over another man's household; to gloat over another man's wealth; to wheedle the price of a wardrobe out of another man's pocket; to be extravagant at no cost to yourself!

Far be it from Christians to desire such things as these! We are not solicitous about how we are to be supplied with the necessities of life—unless we have no confidence in the promises of God. He it is who clothes the lilies of the field in such great beauty; who feeds the birds of the air, though they labor not; who bids us not to be concerned about the morrow, what we shall eat or what we shall put on. He assures us that he knows what is necessary for each of his servants. And this, certainly, is not a mass of jeweled pendants, nor a surfeit of clothing, nor mules brought from Gaul, nor porters from Germany. Such things do lend luster to a wedding, but what is necessary for us is, rather, a sufficiency which is consistent with sobriety and modesty. You may take it for granted that you will have need of nothing, if you but serve the Lord; indeed, all things are yours if you possess the Lord of all. Mediate on the things of heaven and you will despise the things of earth. The widow whose life is stamped with the seal of God's approval has need of nothing—except perseverance!

5. In addition to the reasons already advanced, some say that they wish to contract marriage because they desire to live on in their posterity and because they seek the bitter sweet which comes of having children. To us this is sheer nonsense. For, why should we be so anxious to propagate children since, when we do, it is our hope—in view, that is, of the straitened times which are at hand—that they will go to God before us. We ourselves desire, as did the apostle, to be delivered from this wicked world and received into the arms of our Lord.

Of course, to the servant of God posterity is a great necessity! We are so sure of our own salvation that we have time for children! We must hunt up burdens for ourselves with which, for the most part, even pagans refuse to be encumbered—burdens which are forced upon people by law, but of which they rid themselves by resorting to murder of their own flesh and blood; burdens, in sum, which are especially troublesome to us because they constitute a danger to the faith. Why did our Lord prophesy, "Woe to them that are with child and that give suck," if he did not mean that on the day of our great exodus children will be a handicap to those who bear them? This is what comes of marriage. There will be no problem here for widows, however. At the first sound of the angel's trumpet they will leap forth lightly, easily able to endure any distress or persecution, with none of the heaving baggage of marriage in their wombs or at their breasts.

The Christian Way

Accordingly, whether marriage be for the flesh or for the world or for the sake of posterity, the servant of God is above all such supposed necessities. I should think it quite enough to have succumbed once to any one of them and to have satisfied all such wants as these in a single marriage.

Are we to have weddings every day and, in the midst of nuptials, to be overtaken by the day of dread, even as were Sodom and Gomorrha? For in those places they were not just getting married and transacting business! When our Lord says that "they were marrying" and "they were buying," he wishes to stigmatize those gross vices of the flesh and the world which most withdraw men from the things of God—the one by the sweet seduction of lust, the other by greed for gain. And yet, these men were afflicted by blindness of this kind at a time when the end of the world was still far off. How shall we fare, if the vices God then found detestable keep us back from divine things now? "The time is short," Scripture says, "it remains that they who have wives, act as if they had none."

6. But now, if those who actually have wives are to put them out of their minds, how much more are those who have none prohibited from seeking a second time what they no longer have! Accordingly, she whose husband has departed this life ought to refrain from marrying and have done with sex forever. This is what many a pagan woman does in order to honor the memory of a beloved spouse.

When something seems difficult to us, let us think of those who put up with difficulties greater than our own. For example, how many are there who vow virginity from the very moment of their baptism! How many, too, who in wedlock abstain, by mutual consent, from the use of marriage! They have "made themselves eunuchs" because of their desire "for the kingdom of heaven." If they are able to practice continence while remaining married, how much easier is it to do so when marriage has been dissolved! For I rather imagine it is more difficult to sacrifice something we actually have than it is to be indifferent about something we no longer possess.

Examples of Pagan Virtue

A hard thing it is, truly, and arduous, that a Christian woman, out of love for God, should practice continence after her husband's death, when pagans use the priestly offices of virgins and widows in the service of their own satan! At Rome, for example, those women are called "virgins" who guard a flame which typifies the *unquenchable fire*, watching over that which is an omen of the punishment which awaits them together with the dragon himself. At the town of Aegium a virgin is selected for the cult of the Achaean Juno; and the women who rave at Delphi do not marry. Further, we know that "widows" minister to the African Ceres, women whom a most harsh insensibility has withdrawn from married life. For, while their husbands are still living, they not only separate from them but even introduce new wives to take their place— no doubt with the cheerful acquiescence of the husbands themselves! Such "widows" deprive themselves of all contact with men, even to the exclusion of kissing their own sons. Yet they become used to this discipline and persevere in a widowhood which rejects even those consolations which are found in the sacred bonds of natural affection. This is what the devil teaches his disciples. And they obey! As though on equal terms, the chastity of his followers challenges that of the servants of God. The very priests of hell are continent. For satan has discovered how to turn the cultivation of virtue itself to a man's destruction, and it makes no difference to him whether he ruins souls by lust or chastity.

Various Arguments Against Second Marriage

7. We have been taught by the Lord and God of salvation that continence is a means of attaining eternal life, a proof of the faith that is in us, a pledge of the glory of that body which will be ours when we put on the garb of immortality, and, finally, an obligation imposed upon us by the will of God. Regarding this last statement, I suggest that you reflect seriously on the following: if it is a fact that not a leaf falls to the ground unless God wills it, then it is equally true that no man departs this life unless God wills it. For it is necessary that he who brought us into the world should also usher us forth from it. Therefore, when God wills that a woman lose her husband in death, he also wills that she should be done with marriage itself. Why attempt to restore what God has put asunder? Why spurn the liberty which is offered you by enslaving yourself once more in the bonds of matrimony? "Are you bound in marriage?" Scripture says, "seek not to be loosed. Are you loosed from marriage? seek not to be bound." For, though "you sin not" in remarrying, yet, according to Scripture, "tribulation of the flesh will follow" if you do.

Hence, as far as such a sentiment is possible, let us be grateful for the opportunity offered us of practicing continence and let us embrace it immediately, once it is offered. Thus, what we were unable to do in marriage we will be able to do in bereavement. We ought to make the most of a situation which removes what necessity imposed.

The law of the church and the precept of the apostle show clearly how prejudicial second marriages are to the faith and how great an obstacle to holiness. For men who have been married twice are not allowed to preside in the church nor is it permissable that a "widow be chosen" unless she was the wife of but one man. The altar of God must be an altar of manifest purity and all the glory which surrounds the church is the glory of sanctity.

The pagans have a priesthood of widows and celibates—though, of course, this is part of satan's malevolence; and the ruler of this world, their *Pontifex Maximus*, is not permitted to marry a second time. How greatly purity must please God, since even the enemy affects it! He does this, not because he has any real affinity with virtue but because it is his purpose to make a mockery of what is pleasing to the Lord God.

Dignity of Chaste Widowhood

8. There is a brief saying, revealed through the mouth of the prophet, which shows how greatly God honors widowhood: "Deal justly with the widow and the orphan and then come and let us reason together, says the Lord." The two groups mentioned here have no human means of support whatever; they are dependent on God's mercy, and the Father of all takes it upon himself to be their protector. See how familiarly the widow's benefactor is treated by God! In what esteem, then, is the widow herself held when he who is her advocate will reason with the Lord! Not even to virgins themselves, I fancy, is so much given.

Although virgins, because of their perfect integrity and inviolate purity, will look upon the face of God most closely, yet the life a widow leads is the more difficult, since it is easy not to desire that of which you are ignorant and easy to turn your back upon what you have never desired. Chastity is most praiseworthy when it is sensible of the right it has sacrificed and knows what it has experienced. The condition of the virgin may be regarded as one of greater felicity, but that of the widow is one of greater difficulty; the former has always possessed the good, the latter has had to find it on her own. In the former it is grace which is crowned, in the latter, virtue. For some things there are which come to us from the divine bounty, and others we have of our own efforts. Those which are bestowed upon us by the Lord are governed by his generosity; those which are achieved by man are won at the cost of personal endeavor.

Safeguards of Chastity

Therefore, cultivate the virtue of self-restraint, which ministers to chastity; cultivate industry, which prevents idleness; temperance, which spurns the world. Keep company and converse worthy of God, remembering the quotation sanctified by the apostle: "Evil associations corrupt good manners." Chattering, idle, winebibbing, scandalmongering women do the greatest possible harm to a widow's high resolve. Their loquaciousness leads to the use of words offensive to modesty; their slothfulness engenders disloyalty to the austere life; their tippling issues in every sort of evil and their prurient gossip is responsible for inciting others to engage in the lustful conduct which such talk exemplifies. No woman of this kind can have anything good to say about monogamy. "Their god is their belly," as the apostle says; and so also is that which lies adjacent to it.

Here, then, my dearest fellow servant, is the counsel which even now I leave with you. And, really, although my words are superfluous after what the apostle has written on the subject, yet for you they will be words of consolation as often as, in thinking on them, you think of me.

Why does Tertullian argue that celibacy is preferable to marriage? Why were second marriages permissable under Jewish law? What were the secular arguments in favor of marriage? Why does Tertullian think widowhood was more difficult than virginity? What does he say about children? Why?

38. AN ANTI-MATRIMONIAL DIATRIBE

Much of the literature that was written to persuade men not to marry betrays the fiercely misogynistic views of their authors. A negative evaluation of marriage was frequently linked to and justified by an equally negative evaluation of women. Many clerics considered it far better to avoid women altogether and used this as the basis for anti-matrimonial polemics. One of the earliest, most influential writers to do so was St. Jerome (ca. 347–ca. 419). Jerome's polemical treatise Against Jovinian *(393) was so extreme that it embarrassed contemporaries such as Augustine, who was inspired to write* On the Good of Marriage *in reply. While Augustine's more moderate views influenced the subsequent theology of marriage, Jerome's virulent misogyny exercised tremendous influence throughout the Middle Ages. The following section, discussing the work of Theophrastus, shows how closely misogyny and condemnations of marriage were linked.*

Source: Trans. Henry Wace and Philip Schaff in St. Jerome, *Against Jovinian*, A Select Library of Nicene and Post-Nicene Fathers, vol. 6 (Oxford: James Parker and Company, 1893), pp. 383–84; revised.

Book I

47. I feel that in giving this list of women I have said far more than is customary in illustrating a point, and that I might be justly censured by my learned reader. But what am I to do when the women of our time press me with apostolic authority, and before the first husband is buried, repeat from morning to night the precepts which allow a second marriage? Seeing they despise the fidelity which Christian purity dictates, let them at least learn chastity from the heathen. A book *On Marriage*, worth its weight in gold, passes under the name of Theophrastus. In it the author asks whether a wise man marries. And after laying down the conditions—that the wife must be fair, of good character, and honest parentage, the husband in good health and of ample means—and after saying that under these circumstances a wise man sometimes enters the state of matrimony, he immediately proceeds thus: "But all these conditions are seldom satisfied in marriage. A wise man therefore must not take a wife. For in the first place his study of philosophy will be hindered, and it is impossible for anyone to attend to his books and his wife. Matrons want many things, costly dresses, gold, jewels, great outlay, maid-servants, all kinds of furniture, litters, and gilded coaches. Then come curtain-lectures all the night long: she complains that one lady goes out better dressed than she: that another is looked up to by all: 'I am a poor despised nobody at the ladies' assemblies.' 'Why did you ogle that creature next door?' 'Why were you talking to the maid?' 'What did you bring from the market?' 'I am not allowed to have a single friend, or companion.' She suspects that her husband's love goes the same

way as her hate. There may be in some neighboring city the wisest of teachers; but if we have a wife we can neither leave her behind, nor take the burden with us. To support a poor wife, is hard: to put up with a rich one, is torture. Notice, too, that in the case of a wife you cannot pick and choose: you must take her as you find her. If she has a bad temper, or is a fool, if she has a blemish, or is proud, or has bad breath, whatever her fault may be — all this we learn after marriage. Horses, asses, cattle, even slaves of the smallest worth, clothes, kettles, wooden seats, cups, and earthenware pitchers, are first tried and then bought: a wife is the only thing that is not shown before she is married, for fear she may not give satisfaction. Our gaze must always be directed to her face, and we must always praise her beauty: if you look at another woman, she thinks that she is out of favor. She must be called my lady, her birthday must be celebrated, we must swear by her health and wish that she may survive us, respect must be paid to the nurse, to the nursemaid, to the father's slave, to the foster-child, to the handsome hanger-on, to the curled darling who manages her affairs, and to the eunuch who ministers to the safe indulgence of her lust: names which are only a cloak for adultery. Upon whomsoever she sets her heart, they must have her love though they want her not. If you give her the management of the whole house, you must yourself be her slave. If you reserve something for yourself, she will not think you are loyal to her; but she will turn to anger and hatred, and unless you quickly take care, she will have the poison ready. If you introduce old women, and soothsayers, and prophets, and vendors of jewels and silken clothing, you imperil her chastity; if you shut the door upon them, she is injured and fancies you suspect her. But what is the good of even a careful guardian, when an unchaste wife cannot be watched, and a chaste one ought not to be? For necessity is but a faithless keeper of chastity, and she alone really deserves to be called pure, who is free to sin if she chooses. If a woman be fair, she soon finds lovers; if she be ugly, it is easy to be wanton. It is difficult to guard what many long for. It is annoying to have what no one thinks worth possessing. But the misery of having an ugly wife is less than that of watching a comely one. Nothing is safe, for which a whole people sighs and longs. One man entices with his figure, another with his brains, another with his wit, another with his open hand. Somehow, or sometime, the fortress is captured which is attacked on all sides. Men marry, indeed, so as to get a manager for the house, to solace weariness, to banish solitude; but a faithful slave is a far better manager, more submissive to the master, more observant of his ways, than a wife who thinks she proves herself mistress if she acts in opposition to her husband, that is, if she does what pleases her, not what she is commanded. But friends, and servants who are under the obligation of benefits received, are better able to wait upon us in sickness than a wife who makes us responsible for her tears (she will sell you enough to make a deluge for the hope of a legacy), boasts of her anxiety, but drives her sick husband to the distraction of despair. But if she herself is poorly, we must fall sick with her and never leave her bedside. Or if she is a good and agreeable wife (how rare a bird she is!), we have to share her groans in childbirth, and suffer torture when she is in danger. A wise man can never be alone. He has with him the good men of all time, and turns his mind freely wherever he chooses. What is inaccessible to him in person he can embrace in thought. And, if men are scarce, he converses with God. He is never less alone than when alone. Then again, to marry for the sake of children, so that our name may not perish, or that we may have support in old age, and leave our property without dispute, is the height of stupidity. For what is it to us when we are leaving the world if another bears our name, when even a son does not all at once take his father's title, and there are countless others who are called by the same name. Or what support in old age is he whom you bring up, and who may die before you, or turn out a reprobate? Or at all events when he reaches mature age, you may seem to him long in dying. Friends and relatives whom you can judiciously love are better and safer heirs than those whom you must make your heirs whether you like it or not. Indeed, the surest way of having a good heir is to ruin your fortune in a good cause while you live, not to leave the fruit of your labor to be used you know not how."

Jerome's Enduring Influence

Stories such as Jerome's discussion of Theophrastus on marriage were particularly useful to illustrate sermons. Consequently, they were copied over and over again, into collections compiled to assist preachers. First appearing in Latin, the stories or exempla *were eventually translated into the vernacular. As priests drew on these stories to enliven their sermons, they were one means by which misogyny and negative views about marriage were disseminated to and reinforced among the laity. What remains less certain, however, is how the laity, married or single, men or women, reacted to hearing such views propounded by their parish priest. This selection is from a fifteenth-century translation of a much earlier Latin collection of* exempla. *It illustrates how long Jerome's views continued to circulate in the western church and beyond.*

Source: Trans. J. Murray from *An Alphabet of Tales. An English Fifteenth-Century Translation of the* Alphabetum Narrationum *of Etienne de Besançon*, ed. Mary Macleod Banks (London: Early English Text Society, 1904), pp. 529-30.

It is Not Advantageous to Marry

In *The Book on Marriage,* Jerome tells of one Aurelius Theophrastus. In this book he asks if a wise man should take a wife. He says that, although she be ever so fair, or well brought-up, or have so honorable a father and mother, nevertheless, a wise man should not marry her, because Aurelius says it is impossible for a man to please both his wife and children. Women, he says, want to have gold and silver, and fashionable clothing, and a servant, and many other things. And this is all for nought because she will lie chattering and say that there are others who have better kerchiefs and are dressed more fashionably than she is. And if she is well-dressed and she encounters any people, she will say, "Look! I am the worst dressed in this whole town!" Also, she will say to her husband, "Why did you look at your neighbor's wife, and why did you speak with your neighbor's maidservant?" And when he comes from the market, she will say, "What have you brought? I may not have a friend nor a companion because of you, nor the friendship of another man but that I become suspect?" And therefore a man should not choose his wife after careful searching but take whoever comes along, whether she is fair, or ugly, or proud, or angry. Therefore, women should be examined before they are married. A horse, or an ass, an ox, or a cow, or a servant; all of these are examined before they are bought or hired, but a woman should not see a man before he weds her so that he is not displeased after they are married. And if you give her all your goods to keep, yet she will believe that you kept some for yourself, and thus she will suspect you and hate you and afterwards happily poison you. And if you bring craftsmen into the house, such as tailors or others, it is dangerous because of her lewdness. If you forbid her, it will cause her to trespass. Therefore, what benefit is there to guarding diligently a wife, when an unchaste wife may not be guarded. For necessity is the guardian of chastity and she who does not desire to sin may be called chaste. And if she is fair, other men will love her, and if she is ugly she will be proud and cause men to mock her, and it is very hard to keep well she, whom many men love, and it is very arduous to have a woman whom no man will cherish or have in his governance. Nevertheless, an ugly wife may be better guarded than a fair one, because there are always some people who will cast their eyes over her and fantasize about her.

Why did Theophrastus say a man should not marry? What are the moral and character flaws attributed to women? Why are children/heirs not sufficient reason to marry? How does Etienne de Besançon's version differ from Jerome's? How do both versions characterize marriage and women?

39. A GRIEVING HUSBAND: THE DEATH OF EINHARD'S EMMA

When Emma, the wife of Einhard, died in 836, his young friend, the monk Lupus of Ferrières, wrote him a brief note of consolation. Einhard responded with a letter full of unrelieved grief. We may not have enough information to assess the character and quality of the marriage of Einhard and Emma, but there is no mistaking his deep dismay at her death. What he grieved is another matter. Two business letters from Emma still survive in which we see her active in the running of his estates. The couple seems to have had no children and they left much of their property to the monastery of Lorsch.

Source: Trans. Paul E. Dutton in *Charlemagne's Courtier: The Complete Einhard* (Peterborough: Broadview Press, 1998), pp. 168-71; trans. from *Servati Lupi Epistulae*, ed. P.K. Marshall (Leipzig: Teubner, 1984), pp. 3-6.

Lupus writes to Einhard in early 836 after Emma's Death

Lupus [sends his greetings] to his most beloved teacher, Einhard.

I was shocked by the dreadful news of the death of your venerable wife. Now more than ever I wish I were with you to lighten the load of your sadness with my compassion or to console [you] with constant talk of impressions [on the subject of death] formed from [reading] the Bible. But until God renders this possible, I recommend that you reflect on the human condition, which we have incurred because of sin [that is, the First Sin], and that you endure with moderation and wisdom what has transpired. For you who have, with your vigorous mind, always risen above the seductions of good fortune, should not give in now to this bad fortune. Thus, after you have called on God, you should then demonstrate that strength of endurance, to which you would doubtless direct your own dear [friends] under similar circumstances.

I hope that you are well.

Einhard's Response to Lupus, in the first half of 836

Einhard [sends his] greetings to his Lupus.

The overwhelming pain that I received from the death of she who was once my most devoted wife and most recently my dearest sister and companion has banished and driven out of me all enthusiasm and concern for my own affairs or those of my friends. Nor does [this pain] seem likely to end, since [my] memory so stubbornly dwells on the nature of her death that it cannot be completely torn away from it. On top of that, what constantly adds to that pain and makes an already sore wound worse is, without doubt, that my prayers were unable to accomplish anything and the hope I had placed in the merits and intervention of the martyrs [Marcellinus and Peter, whose relics were placed in Einhard's church at Seligenstadt] entirely misled [me in] my expectations. Thus, in my case, the words of those consoling me, which normally relieve the sadness of others, instead cause the wound in my heart to become raw and open once again, since these people tell me to endure calmly misfortunes they are not experiencing themselves and they advise me to be happy over a situation in which they cannot show [me] any reason for joy or happiness. For what human being full of reason and sound mind would not weep over his fate and count himself unhappy and the most pitiful [of all humans], when, overcome by toubles, he learns that the one he had believed would support his prayers [that is, Christ or the saints] had turned against him and was unmoved?

Do these [troubles] not seem to you [to have been] of the kind that could provoke sighs and tears in [such] a small and puny man, that could force him to moaning and wailing, and even cast him into an abyss of despair? And they would certainly have cast [me down there to stay] if I had not, propped up by the power of divine mercy, turned at once to discover what greater and better men had proclaimed ought to be believed and followed in matters and misfortunes of this sort. Outstanding doctors [of the church] were within reach [in my library] and they were not to be spurned, but rather to be listened to and followed in every way: namely, the glorious martyr Cyprian and those brilliant interpreters of Sacred Scipture Augustine and Jerome. Inspired by their opinions and wholesome arguments, I tried to lift up a heart pulled down by heavy sadness, and I purposely began to ponder how I ought to feel about the death of that dearest partner of mine, whose mortal life rather than her [true] life I saw come to an end.

I even attempted to see if I could bring about by myself through reason what the long passage of time normally achieves, namely, that the wound with which the sudden blow of an unexpected death struck my mind should begin to form a scab and to heal with the medicine of my own mind's consolation. But the immensity of the wound makes treatment difficult. Although extremely beneficial things are advised by those doctors [of the church], acting as the most skilled and gentle physicians, in order to alleviate a heavy pain, the wound which continues to bleed is still not prepared to heal.

You may well be astonished by this and say that the pain arising from an event of this sort ought not to last so long, as if it is [ever] in the power of the one suffering to say when it should end, since he neither knew in advance nor had the capacity to know when the suffering would begin. It, nevertheless, seems that the size and length of one's pain and sorrow can only be measured in terms of the [individual] losses suffered. Since I am acutely aware of my loss every day in every action, in every affair, in every matter of the house and household, and in all the necessary assignments and arrangements pertaining to [my] divine and human duties, how can that wound which has leveled so many and such great misfortunes upon me not reopen and grow sore again, rather than heal over and become solid [skin], when it is so often touched upon?

For I suppose (and I doubt that the supposition deceives me) that this pain and anxiety, which came upon me because of the death of my dearest partner, will be with me forever until that point in time, which God granted me for purposes of living this wretched earthly life, is brought to its appointed end. Nevertheless, this experience has so far been good for me rather than harmful, since it slows and holds back, as if with bit and reins, my spirit, which was rushing after pleasure and success, and reminds me of death's approach. The ease and forgetfulness of old age had seduced me into hoping and longing for a long life. I see [now] that I do not have much longer to live, but how much longer that may be is utterly unknown to me. But I most assuredly know that a newborn child can die soon and that an old man cannot live long. And so I believe it would be far more useful and blessed for me to pass the brief and uncertain period of time [left to me] in mourning rather than joy. For if, according to Scripture, those will be blessed and happy who lamented and mourned in this life, then those on the contrary, who do not fear to end their days in constant and unending joy, will end up unhappy and wretched.

I give thanks and am grateful for your kindness, especially since you deigned to console me with your letter. For you could give no greater or surer sign of your affection for me than to hold out a comforting hand to one who had laid down sick and to urge me to rise up. For you were not able to neglect one who was laid low in his mind and weighed down by grief.

Farewell, dearest and most beloved son.

How did Einhard try to cope with the loss of his wife? Whom or what does he blame for her death? What was his great disappointment? How does he characterize the nature of their bond? What does he regret now that Emma is gone? Is the letter about Einhard or Emma, that is, can we form any impression of her from it? Can we moderns penetrate or understand the emotional and rhetorical character of a personal letter of this sort?

40. THE MARRIAGE OF GUIBERT OF NOGENT'S PARENTS

Around the year 1115 Guibert, abbot of Nogent, wrote his memoirs. He included an account of his parents' marriage and his mother's years as a widow. Guibert's father was a knight from the area of Clermont, his mother from a somewhat higher social strata. Guibert's mother was twelve years old when they contracted the marriage, as permitted by canon law. Although Guibert described his father as a youth, this does not indicate his age so much as his unmarried status. Their marriage was unconsummated long enough that it disturbed members of the family. Eventually, there were a number of children born to the couple, of whom Guibert was the youngest. Less than a year after Guibert's birth, his father died. His father's nephew became the head of the family and he tried to encourage Guibert's mother to remarry, a suggestion she rejected. Guibert's memories of his parents, and particularly his mother, were tempered by his years in the cloister and his desire to use his memoirs to present to his monks worthy examples of people striving for God. Even Guibert's didactic reinterpretation of his parents' relationship, however, could not hide the strains, especially sexual strains, in their marriage.

Source: Revised. John F. Benton, *Self and Society in Medieval France. The Memoirs of Abbot Guibert of Nogent (1064?-c.1115)* (New York: Harper Torchbooks, 1970), 63-75; reprinted with permission.

12. After these lengthy accounts I return to you, my God, to speak of the conversion of that good woman, my mother. When hardly of marriageable age, she was given to my father, a mere youth, by the provision of my grandfather, since she was of the nobility, had a very pretty face, and was naturally and most becomingly of sober mien. She had, however, conceived a fear of God's name at the very beginning of her childhood. She had learned to be terrified of sin, not from experience but from dread of some sort of blow from on high, and— as she often told me herself—this dread had so possessed her mind with the terror of sudden death that in later years she grieved because she no longer felt in her maturity the same stings of righteous fear as she had in her unformed and ignorant youth.

Now, it so happened that at the very beginning of that lawful union conjugal intercourse was made ineffective through the bewitchments of certain persons. It was said that their marriage drew upon them the envy of a stepmother, who had some nieces of great beauty and nobility and who was plotting to slip one of them into my father's bed. Meeting with no success in her designs, she is said to have used magical arts to prevent entirely the consummation of the marriage. His wife's virginity thus remained intact for three years, during which he endured his great misfortune in silence; at last, driven to it by those close to him, my father was the first to reveal the facts. In all sorts of ways, his kinsmen endeavored to bring about a divorce, and by their constant pressure upon my father, who was then young and dull-witted, they tried to induce him to become a monk, although at that time there was little talk of this order. They did not do this for his soul's good, however, but with the purpose of getting possession of his property.

When their suggestion produced no effect, they began to hound the girl herself, far away as she was from her kinsfolk and harassed by the violence of strangers, into voluntary flight out of sheer exhaustion under their insults, and without waiting for divorce. She endured all this, bearing with calmness the abuse that was aimed at her, and if out of this rose any strife, she pretended ignorance of it. Besides this, certain rich men, perceiving that she was not in fact a wife, began to assail the heart of the young girl; but you, O Lord, the builder of inward chastity, did inspire her with purity stronger than her nature or her youth. Your grace it was that saved her from burning, though set in the midst of flames, your doing that her weak soul was not hurt by the poison of evil talk, and that when enticements from without were added to those impulses common to our human nature, like oil poured upon the flames, yet the young maiden's heart was always under her control and never won from her by any allurements. Are not such things solely your doing, O Lord? When she was in the heat of youth and continually engaged in wifely duties, yet for seven whole years you kept her in such continence that, in the words of a certain wise man, even "rumor dared not speak lies about her."

O God, you know how hard, how almost impossible it would be for women of the present time to keep such chastity as this; whereas there was in those days such modesty that hardly ever was the good name of a married woman sullied by evil rumor. Ah! how wretchedly have modesty and honor in the state of virginity declined from that time to this our present age, and both the reality and the show of a married woman's protection fallen to ruin. Therefore coarse mirth is all that may be noted in their manners and naught but jesting heard, with sly winks and ceaseless chatter. Wantonness shows in their gait, only silliness in their behavior. So much does the extravagance of their dress depart from the old simplicity that in the enlargement of their sleeves, the tightness of their dresses, the distortion of their shoes of Cordovan leather with their curling toes, they seem to proclaim that everywhere modesty is a cast away. A lack of lovers to admire her is a woman's crown of woe, and on her crowds of thronging suitors rests her claim to nobility and courtly pride. There was at that time, I call God to witness, greater modesty in married men, who would have blushed to be seen in the company of such women, than there is now in brides. By such shameful conduct they turn men into greater braggarts and lovers of the market place and the public street.

What is the end of all this, Lord God, but that no one blushes for his own levity and licentiousness, because he knows that all are tarred with the same brush, and, seeing himself in the same case as all others, why then should he be ashamed of pursuits in which he knows all others engage? But why do I say "ashamed" when such men feel shame only if someone excels them as an example of lustfulness? A man's private boastfulness about the number of his loves or his choice of a beauty who he has seduced is no reproach to him, nor is he scorned for vaunting his love affairs before you. Instead, his part in furthering the general corruption meets with the approval of all. Listen to the cheers when, with the inherent looseness of unbridled passions which deserve the doom of eternal silence, he shamelessly noises abroad what ought to have been hidden in shame, what should have burdened his soul with the guilt of ruined chastity and plunged him in the depths of despair. In this and similar ways, this modern age is corrupt and corrupting, distributing evil ideas to some, while the filth thereof, spreading to others, goes on increasing without end.

Holy God, scarcely any such thing was heard of in the time when your handmaid was behaving as she did; indeed, then shameful things were hidden under the cloak of sacred modesty and things of honor had their crown. In those seven years, O Lord, that virginity which you in wondrous fashion prolonged in her was in agony under countless wrongs, as frequently they threatened to dissolve her marriage with my father and give her to another husband or to send her away to the remote houses of my distant relatives. Under such grievous treatment she suffered bitterly at times, but with your support, O God, she strove with wonderful self-control against the enticements of her own flesh and the inducements of others.

I do not say, gracious Lord, that she did this out of virtue, but that the virtue was yours alone. For how could that be virtue that came of no conflict between body and spirit, no straining after God, but only from concern for outward honor and to avoid disgrace? No doubt a sense of shame has its use, if only to resist the approach of sin, but what is useful before a sin is committed is damnable afterward. What prostrates the self with the shame of propriety, holding it back from sinful deeds, is useful at the time, since the fear of God can bring aid, giving holy seasoning to shame's lack of savor, and can make that which was profitable at the time (that is, in the world) useful not for a moment but eternally. But after a sin is committed a sense of shame which leads to vanity is the more deadly the more it obstinately resists the healing of holy confession. The desire of my mother, your servant, O Lord God, was to do nothing to hurt her worldly honor, yet following your Gregory, whom, however, she had never read or heard read, she did not maintain that desire, for afterward she surrendered all her desires into your sole keeping. It was therefore good for her at that time to be attached to her worldly reputation.

Since the bewitchment by which the bond of natural and lawful intercourse was broken lasted seven years and more, it is all too easy to believe that, just as by prestidigitation the faculty of sight may be deceived so that conjurers seem to produce something out of nothing, so to speak, and to make certain things out of others, so reproductive power and effort may be inhibited by much less art; and indeed it is now a common practice, understood even by ignorant people. When that bewitchment was broken by a certain old woman, my mother submitted to the duties of a wife as faithfully as she had kept her virginity when she was assailed by so many attacks. In other ways she was truly fortunate, but she laid herself open not so much to endless misery as to mourning when she, whose goodness was ever growing, gave birth to an evil son who (in my own person) grew worse and worse. Yet you know, almighty one, with what purity and holiness in obedience to you she raised me, how greatly she provided me with the care of nurses in infancy and of masters and teachers in boyhood, with no lack even of fine clothes for my little body, so that I seemed to equal the sons of kings and counts in indulgence.

And not only in my mother, O Lord, did you put this love for me, but you inspired with it other, far richer persons, so that rather because of the grace you granted me than under the obligations of kinship, they lavished on me careful tending and nurture.

O God, you know what warnings, what prayers she daily poured into my ears not to listen to corrupting words from anyone. Whenever she had leisure from household cares, she taught me how and for what I ought to pray to you. You alone know with what pains she labored so that the sound beginning of a happy and honorable childhood which you had granted might not be ruined by an unsound heart. You made it her desire that I should without ceasing burn with zeal for you, that above all you might add to my outward comeliness inner goodness and wisdom. Gracious God, gracious Lord, if she had known in advance under what heaps of filth I should blot out the fair surface of your gifts, bestowed by you at her prayer, what would she have said? What would she have done? How hopeless the lamentations she would have uttered! How much anguish she would have suffered! Thanks to you, sweet and temperate creator, "Who has made our hearts." If, indeed, her vision had pierced the secret places of my heart, unworthy of her pure gaze, I wonder if she would not there and then have died.

13. After introducing these comments by way of anticipation, let us return to what we left farther back. I have learned that this woman had such a fear of God's name, even while she was serving the world, that in her obedience to the church, in almsgiving, in her offerings for masses, her conduct was such as to win respect from all. Full belief in my story will, I know, be made difficult by a natural suspicion that the partiality of a son has exaggerated her virtues. If to praise one's mother be thought a cautious, disingenuous way of glorifying one-

self, I dare to call you to witness, O God, who knows her soul, in which you did dwell, that I have truthfully asserted her surpassing merit. And indeed, since it is clearer than daylight that my life has strayed from the paths of the good and that my pursuits have always been an affront to any sensible person, of what avail will the reputation of my mother or father or ancestors be to me when all their grandeur will be squeezed out of their wretched offspring? I, who through lack of will and deed fail to make their behavior live again, am riding posthaste to infamy if I claim their praise for myself.

While she was still a young married woman, something happened which gave no slight impulse to the amendment of her life. The French in the time of King Henry were fighting with great bitterness against the Normans and their Count William, who afterward conquered England and Scotland, and in that clash of the two nations it was my father's fate to be taken prisoner. It was the custom of this count never to hold prisoners for ransom, but to condemn them to captivity for life. When the news was brought to his wife (I put aside the name of mother, for I was not yet born, nor was I for a long time after), she was struck down half dead with wretched sorrow; she abstained from food and drink, and sleep was still more difficult through her despairing anxiety, the cause of this being not the amount of his ransom but the impossibility of his release.

In the dead of that night, as she lay in her bed full of deep anxiety, since it is the habit of the devil to invade souls weakened with grief, suddenly, while she lay awake, the enemy himself lay upon her and by the burden of his weight almost crushed the life out of her. As she choked in the agony of her spirit and lost all use of her limbs, she was unable to make a single sound; completely silenced but with her reason free, she awaited aid from God alone. Then suddenly from the head of her bed a spirit, without doubt a good one, began to cry out in loud and kindly tones, "Holy Mary, help her." After the spirit had spoken out in this fashion for a bit, and she had fully understood what he was saying and was aware that he was thoroughly outraged, he sallied forth burning with anger. Thereupon he who lay upon her rose up, and the other met and seized him and by the strength of God overthrew him with a great crash, so that the room shook heavily with the shock of it, and the maidservants, who were fast asleep, were rudely awakened. When the enemy had thus been driven out by the divine power, the good spirit who had called upon Mary and routed the devil turned to her whom he had rescued and said, "Take care to be a good woman." The attendants, alarmed by the sudden uproar, rose to see how their mistress was and found her half dead, with the blood drained from her face and all the strength crushed out of her body. They questioned her about the noise and heard about the causes of it from her, and they were scarcely able by their presence and talk and by the lighting of a lamp to revive her.

Those last words of her deliverer—nay, your words, O Lord God, through the mouth of your messenger—were stored up forever in the woman's memory and she stood ready to be guided to a greater love, if with God's help the opportunity should occur later. Now, after the death of my father, although the beauty of her face and form remained undimmed, and I, scarcely half a year old, gave her reason enough for anxiety, she resolved to continue in her widowhood. With what spirit she ruled herself and what an example of modesty she set may be gathered from the following event. When my father's kinsmen, eager for his fiefs and possessions, strove to take them all by excluding my mother, they fixed a day in court for advancing their claims. The day came and the barons were assembled to deliver justice. My mother withdrew into the church, away from the avaricious plotters, and was standing before the image of the crucified Lord, mindful of the prayers she owed. One of my father's kinsmen, who shared the views of the others and was sent by them, came to request her presence to hear their decision, as they were waiting for her. Whereupon she said, "I will take part in this matter only in the presence of my Lord." "Whose Lord?" said he. Then, stretching out her hand toward the image of the crucified Lord, she replied, "This is my Lord, this is the advocate under whose protection I will plead." At that the man reddened and, not being very subtle, put on a wry smile to hide his evil intent and went off to tell his friends what he had heard. And they, too, were covered with confusion at such an answer, since they knew that in the face of her utter honesty they had no just grounds, and so they ceased to trouble her.

Shortly after that, one of the leading men of that place and province, my father's nephew, who was as greedy as he was powerful, addressed the woman in the following terms: "Madame," said he, "since you have sufficient youth and beauty, you ought to marry, so that your life in this world would be more pleasant, and the children of my uncle would come under my care to be brought up by me in a worthy fashion, and finally his possessions would devolve to my authority, as it is right they should." She replied, however, "You know that your uncle was of very noble descent. Since God has taken him away, Hymen shall not repeat his rites over me, my lord, unless a marriage with some much greater noble shall offer itself." Now, the woman was quite crafty in speaking of marrying a greater noble, knowing that could hardly, if at all, come to pass. Consequently, since he bristled at her talk of a higher noble, she, who was wholly set against nobles and commoners alike, put an end to all expectation of a second marriage. When he set down to overweening pride her talk of a greater noble, she replied, "Certainly either a greater noble or no husband at all." Perceiving the resolution with which the lady spoke, he desisted from his designs, and never again sought anything of the kind from her.

In great fear of God and with no less love of all her kin and especially of the poor, this woman wisely ruled our household and our property. That loyalty which she had given her husband in his lifetime she kept unbroken and with double constancy to his spirit, since she did not break the ancient union of their bodies by a substitution of other flesh on his departure, and almost every day she endeavored to help him by the offering of the life-bringing sacrifice. Friendly to all the poor in general, to some in her great pity she was generous and courtly to the full extent of her means. The sting of remembering her sins could not have been sharper if she had been given up to all kinds of wickedness and dreaded the punishment of every ill deed that is done. In plainness of living there was nothing she could do, for her delicacy and her customary sumptuous diet did not accord with frugality. In other matters her behavior was completely unexpected. I personally have both seen and made certain by touch that although on certain occasions she wore outer garments of rich material, next to her skin she was covered with the roughest haircloth. Although her delicate skin was completely unaccustomed to it, she wore this cloth throughout the day and even went to bed in it at night.

She never or hardly ever missed the night offices, while she regularly attended the assemblies of God's people in holy seasons, in such fashion that scarcely ever in her house was there rest from the singing of God's praises by her chaplains, who were always busy at their office. So constantly was her dead husband's name on her lips that her mind seemed to turn on no other subject, and in her prayers, in giving alms, even in the midst of ordinary business, she continually spoke of the man, because she could do nothing without thinking of him. For when the heart is full of love for someone, the mouth shapes his name whether one wants to or not.

14. Passing over those matters in which she showed her goodness, but not her most admirable qualities, let us proceed with what is left. When I had passed about twelve years, as I was told, after my father's death, and his widow had managed her house and children while wearing a laywoman's clothes, she now made haste to bring to happy birth a resolve with which she had long been in labor. While she was still pondering this idea, discussing it with no one but that master and teacher of mine whom I discussed before, I heard a certain devil-possessed dependent of hers, who was rambling on under the devil's influence about other matters, shouting out these words, "The priests have placed a cross in her loins." Nothing indeed could have been truer, although I did not then understand what he was intimating, for thereafter she submitted not to one but to many crosses. Soon afterward, while her intention was still unknown to anyone but the person I have mentioned, who was then a sort of steward in her house and who himself a little later followed her in her conversion by renouncing the world, she saw the following vision in a dream: she seemed to be marrying a man and celebrating her nuptials, much to the amaze-

ment and even stupefaction of her children, friends, and kinsfolk. The next day when my mother went into the country for a walk attended by the man who was my teacher and her steward, he explained what she had seen. My mother did not need to be a skilled interpreter in such matters. One look at my master's face, and without speech from him she knew that the vision pointed to the subject of their many conversations about the love of God, to whom she longed to be united. Making haste with what she had begun and overcome by the burning zeal within her, she withdrew from the life of the town in which she lived.

At the time of this withdrawal, she stayed with the owner's permission at a certain manor belonging to the lord of Beauvais, Bishop Guy. This Guy was a man of courtly manner and noble birth, in person well-fitted for the office he held. After conferring notable benefits on the church of Beauvais, such as laying the first stone of a church for regular canons dedicated to St. Quentin, he was charged before Archbishop Hugues of Lyon, the papal legate, with simony and other crimes by those who owed their training and advancement to him. Because he did not appear when summoned, he was declared deposed by default, and, being at Cluny and afraid of the sentence pronounced against him, he retired into the monastery there. Since he seemed to cherish my mother and my family and loved me most of all with a special affection, as one who had received from him every sacrament of benediction except that of the priesthood, when members of my mother's household asked him to allow her to live for a while in his property adjoining the church of that place, he gladly consented. Now, this manor, named Catenoy, was about two miles distant from our town.

While staying there, she resolved to retire to the monastery of Fly. After my master had had a little house built for her there near the church, she then came forth from the place where she was staying. She knew that I should be utterly an orphan with no one at all on whom to depend, for great as was my wealth of kinsfolk and connections, yet there was no one to give me the loving care a little child needs at such an age; though I did not lack for the necessities of food and clothing, I often suffered from the loss of that careful provision for the helplessness of tender years that only a woman can provide. As I said, although she knew that I would be condemned to such neglect, yet your love and fear, O God, hardened her heart. Still, when on the way to that monastery she passed below the stronghold where I remained, the sight of the castle gave intolerable anguish to her lacerated heart, stung with the bitter remembrance of what she had left behind. No wonder indeed if her limbs seemed to be torn from her body, since she knew for certain that she was a cruel and unnatural mother. Indeed, she heard this said aloud, as she had in this way cut off from her heart and left bereft of succor such a fine child, made worthy, it was asserted, by so much affection, since I was held in high regard not only by our own family but by outsiders. And you, good and gracious God, did by your sweetness and love marvelously harden her heart, the tenderest in all the world, that it might not be tender to her own soul's harm. For tenderness would then have been her ruin, if she, neglecting her God, in her worldly care for me had put me before her own salvation. But "her love was strong as death," for the closer her love for you, the greater her composure in breaking from those she loved before....

Why did Guibert's parents not consummate their marriage immediately? Why did their relatives want them to divorce? What happened to Guibert's father? What did Guibert's mother dream? What might it have meant? Why did the family want her to marry again? Why did she refuse? Why does Guibert refer to himself as an orphan? Why did Guibert's mother abandon him? Why do we never learn her name? How did Guibert regard his father?

41. CAUTIONARY TALES

Much of the information about marriage in the Middle Ages comes from theoretical liter-ature, that is from the writings of theologians, canon lawyers, and moralists who sought to portray the ideals of marriage or the rules governing it. The private relationships between husbands and wives are particularly obscure. One type of literature that reveals some-thing of the popular attitudes toward marriage and the relationships between husbands and wives can be found in collections of exempla. Exempla *are stories that were gath-ered together for preachers to use to illustrate their sermons. While these collections were assembled in the high Middle Ages and continued to be used into the later Middle Ages, many of the stories can be traced to the early Middle Ages. Consequently, they had some-thing of a universal relevance or appeal, rather than reflecting the values and attitudes of a specific time or place. Nevertheless,* exempla *are useful because they indicate the vision of marriage that was presented to the laity by their parish priest in his Sunday sermon. These* exempla, *from the vernacular sermons of the great thirteenth-century preacher Jacques de Vitry, indicate that ambivalent ideas about marital relations and the sexual nature of men and women could coexist.*

Source: Trans. J. Murray from Jacques de Vitry, *The Exempla or Illustrative Stories from the Sermones Vulgares* (New York: Burt Franklin, 1971), pp. 93-95, 104-05, 107, 117.

Domestic Violence

225. I heard about a certain man who, drunk with the cup of Babylon, took a plowshare and tied it in a sack and began to beat his wife vigorously. But, as she was crying out vehemently because her bones were breaking, the neighbors ran together to her. That worthless man said to them, "Behold how that miser-able woman screams because I am beating her with my sack." When she and her relatives brought her husband to court because he had mistreated his wife, he swore in front of the judge that he had beat her with a sack and he had not touched her except with the sack. He had his neighbors as witnesses, who had seen the sack from the outside but had not perceived the plowshare in it. So the husband escaped the hand of the judge and led his wife, with her broken bones, back home.

Danger to Pregnancy

226. I heard about a certain drunk who, when he returned from the tavern and had intercourse with his pregnant wife, killed the child in his mother's womb from his fetid and vinous breath. As a result, the woman brought forth a still-born child.

229. I heard about certain men who bother their pregnant wives when they are near childbirth, because the men do not want to and are unable to abstain from their pregnant wives for a short time. As a result, the child in the mother's womb is killed and deprived of baptism. Cursed be that desire which snatches the soul of its son from God. We do not say, however, that a man commits a mortal sin every time he exceeds moderation in knowing his wife, as long as he knows her in the appropriate time, place, and manner.

A Wife's Deceit

248. I heard about a certain evil woman whose husband believed her in every particular, so that, when she wanted to go to her lover, she said to her husband: "You are sick. Stay in my bed and sweat and take care not to get up until I tell you." Then, closing the door of the room and taking the key with her, she went away and did not return until evening. The man, believing that he was sick, did not dare to get out of bed until his wife returned and said: "Friend, you can get up because I see that you are cured of the illness."

One day, when she said to her lover that she loved him more than her husband, he replied: "I will believe this is true if you will give to me your husband's best tooth."

The woman, returning to her husband, began to cry and feign sadness. Her husband said to her: "What's wrong? Why are you crying?" She replied: "I dare not say." "I want you to tell me," he said. And when he repeatedly insisted, she finally said: "Such an odor is emitted from your mouth that I am quite unable to bear it." That man, amazed and grieving, said: "Why didn't you speak to me? Can I not do something to effect a cure?" His wife said to him: "There isn't any remedy unless you have the tooth which is emitting the odor extracted."

And so, at his wife's encouragement, he had a good and healthy tooth extracted which she showed to him and immediately took the tooth away and gave it to her lover. It is not easy believing a wife nor accepting the advice of an adulterer.

A Woman's Deceit

255. I heard about a certain woman who complained before a judge about a young man who, as she said, had done violence to her and overpowered her. The young man denied this. The judge said to him: "Give her 10 silver marks so that you can make satisfaction for the violence you did to her." The money having been received, she went away rejoicing. Then the judge said to the young man: "Follow her and steal the money from her." She began to resist strenuously and shout so that men came running and the youth was unable to

steal the money from her. Moreover, when the youth and the woman were brought before the judge, the judge said: "Woman, you have what you sought. Why did you shout so strenuously now?" She replied: "Lord, because this man wanted to steal my money from me. But I resisted strenuously and shouted so that he wasn't able to prevail." The judge said to her: "Return the money to the young man because if you had fought him off so strenuously before and shouted in this way, he would never have been able to overpower you. But you love money more than chastity." And so the young man left the judge with the money.

A Mother's Lament

281. I heard about a certain woman who, weeping and grieving copiously, sought her priest, a devout man. When he asked her what she wanted, she replied: "Lord, you know that my daughter has always lived honestly and guarded her virtue. A certain man, our neighbor, solicited her and, when he was by no means able to persuade her to consent to him, he left angry and said: "I will say such things about you that you will never have honor." And he began to defame her everywhere and to say that he had had carnal relations with her. Thus, my daughter was criticized and defamed, so that before many men wanted to join in marriage with her, now I can scarcely even find a pauper or a very humble man who wants to contract marriage with her." Behold how evil and detestable such men are, and worse than thieves, for it is more tolerable to lose a possession than a reputation.

What does the story about the wife who was beaten suggest about social attitudes toward domestic violence? What do the stories reveal about married life and marital sexual activity? How are husbands and wives characterized?

42. A SERMON ON THE IDEAL HUSBAND

While there was a great deal of material written in the Middle Ages that both criticized the shortcomings of wives and presented the qualities of an ideal wife, this was not the case for husbands. There are very few reflections on what qualities were desirable in a husband, or what constituted a good father, especially from the perspective of a wife (as opposed to her family and kin). The qualities of an ideal spiritual husband, described in sermon literature, provide insights into the qualities that society might have deemed desirable in a husband. This passage is extracted from Adam of Picardy's Sermon on the Second Sunday after Epiphany, *which was delivered on 19 January 1282.*

Source: Trans. J. Murray from "The Image of the Ideal Husband in Thirteenth Century France," by Nicole Bériou and David L. d'Avray, in idem, *Modern Questions about Medieval Sermons. Essays on Marriage, Death, History and Sanctity* (Spoleto: Centro Italiano di Studi sull'Alto Medioevo, 1994), pp. 61–64.

"Marriage was made in Cana in Galilee," etc. (John 2.1). Concerning marriages it must be noted that marriages are threefold. First, there are carnal marriages, as when a man is joined to a woman by marriage, and this happens legitimately or illegitimately, that is by adultery, and nothing more will now be said about these. There are other spiritual marriages which are twofold because either the soul is married to Christ by means of merit, or it is married to the devil by means of sin. And these two kinds of marriage are made by consent. Now, concerning these, it ought first to be noted that, just as in carnal marriage, there are certain conditions required in the bridegroom and the bride, and there are also other things which can and ought to impede marriage; so it happens in these spiritual marriages. It is these two things we are to discover and consider.

First, therefore, it ought to be known that in carnal marriage six conditions are required in the bridegroom and similarly in spiritual unions. The first condition befitting in a bridegroom is beauty. For when a bridegroom is handsome, then he is very pleasing. Moreover, God is extremely beautiful. Whence Psalm 44.3 states: "He is beautiful beyond the sons of men." And in the Song of Songs it says: "My beloved is fair and comely, etc." And, therefore, he adorns greatly the soul betrothed to him. And, moreover, any soul ought to be betrothed to Christ by love and consent. On the other hand, however, the devil is extremely filthy because, "His face is made blacker than coals" (Lam. 4.8), as is said about him and, therefore, he disfigures and deforms and denigrates the soul betrothed to him. Whence it is written in Lamentations 1.6: "All her beauty has departed from the daughter of Sion." Therefore, we ought not to marry our souls to him, but to the beautiful bridegroom.

The second condition required in a bridegroom is physical prowess or fortitude. For let no one wed freely a feeble and impotent man. Certainly, God is the most powerful, no rather all powerful. Whence, Psalm 23.8 says, "The Lord is strong and powerful; the Lord is powerful in battle." But the devil is feeble and impotent, the sign of which is that he is conquered by a small stick, that is by devout prayer and good works of this kind. Whence Augustine wrote: "Prayer is a scourge to demons, a protection for the person praying and a solace to the angels." Therefore, if we do not want to have this filthy and evil husband, we can flee and overcome him by devout prayer. Likewise, Pope Gregory wrote: "The enemy is weak who can only conquer one who is willing." Therefore, we ought not to wed our souls to such a bridegroom, but to Christ who is so powerful, and we will have strong assistance from him.

The third condition befitting and required in a bridegroom is that he be rich. Indeed, this is now more necessary than all the preceding conditions. Now, God is extremely wealthy because he has every treasure and the whole world and every good proceeds from him, just as the Apostle James says. Whence, it is written in Psalm 23.1: "The earth and its plenitude is the Lord's, etc." Whence anyone's soul ought to be given to him as bride, because he endows her greatly and adorns her with innumerable riches, namely with virtues, and he makes her wealthy in eternity. Moreover, he leads his bride, with an extremely beautiful and charming company, into a very beautiful place, that is heaven, so that there the nuptials might be completed. But the devil is extremely poor because he is an exile from paradise and, therefore, he does not have a place where he can take his bride, except into the most filthy, unclean, and horrid place, and with a filthy company. And he often beats her and treats her badly, just as he did to that wealthy banquet guest, whose bed was immediately prepared in hell, he betrothed his soul to the devil through gluttony and avarice because he was proud and avaricious and gluttonous; and he denied to Lazarus the scraps falling from his table. Moreover, afterwards that man sought from Lazarus a drop of water to cool his burning tongue. Behold how the devil repaid him for his merit and the betrothal of his soul, just as is found in the gospel. And Pope Gregory said this: "If he was thus attacked, who did not give his own possessions, how will it be for the one who takes what is someone else's?" Therefore, we ought not to betroth our souls to him.

The fourth condition that is required in a bridegroom is that he be of good birth. Thus is God, because all those who do good deeds are of his lineage and are his sons. Whence the just man serves God as a freeman, but the devil, on the other hand, is ignoble, nor does he have anyone good or noble in his lineage. For he was an exile and ejected from paradise, therefore, we ought not to wed our souls to him, but rather to God.

The fifth condition is that he be kind and gentle, for God is extremely kind and gentle. For he at least gives temporal goods as much to the unjust as to the just, and sometimes more, and also spiritual goods, such as health and happiness, as it appears in the case of evildoers and usurers, who are almost never sick, from which his kindness is clear. Whence in the Gospel of Matthew 11.29 it is written: "Learn from me because I am gentle and humble of heart." And because of this we ought to behave so that our souls are wed to him and not to the devil, for that one is extremely iniquitous. Whence Pope Gregory said: "It is very hard to serve such a lord who cannot be pleased by any service." Furthermore, it is noted that, according to Bernard of Clairvaux, the devil has six daughters whom he marries to anyone. The first is pillage whom he marries to soldiers; the second, usury, to burghers; the third, deceit, to merchants; the fourth, pride, to clerics; the fifth, hypocrisy and envy, to monks; but lust he marries to no one. For this is a pestilence common to everyone, one who enters into military camps or the nobility, who infiltrates the walls of monks, penetrates the rooms of clerics, troubles the elderly, disturbs youths, so that there is no one "who hides himself from her heat (Psalm 18.7)."

The sixth condition required is that he be wise. Thus is God because he is the font of all wisdom and prudence, whence Psalm 146.5 says: "Of his wisdom there is no number." But the devil is extremely stupid, for he loves evil more than good and is oblivious to every good. Therefore, one ought not to be married to him, but to the one who sees everything and from whom nothing is hidden. Thus, therefore, on account of these six conditions, our souls ought to be wed to God.

What qualities or conditions are desirable in a bridegroom? Why would wealth be considered so important? What does this sermon indicate about the importance of birth and lineage in medieval society? How is lust distinguished?

43 · A POPULAR VIEW OF MARRIAGE: *THE VISION OF PIERS THE PLOWMAN*

The Vision of Piers the Plowman, *attributed to William Langland, was written in the last half of the fourteenth century. It was an immensely popular poem and was widely read in the fourteenth and fifteenth centuries. Indeed, the poem's central character Piers, a poor plowman who exhibited great Christian virtue, became a legendary figure, so popular he was invoked during the Peasants' Revolt in 1381. This poem was written in the period following the trauma of the Black Death (1348). It was written in English and provides a biting and satiric commentary on the ills of the day. Significantly, it attacks the corruption of church and state alike. The poem exhibits sympathy for the plight of the poor, especially in rural areas. In this extract, many of the abuses of marriage are criticized and marriage motivated by affection rather than economics is encouraged.*

Source: Trans. J. F. Goodridge in William Langland, *Piers the Ploughman* (Harmondsworth: Penguin Books, 1959), pp. 146-49; reprinted with permission.

A nineteenth-century drawing of a medieval German illustration of peasant life. For those who worked the land, marriage was an economic partnership of husband and wife. All worked to support their family.

To live in true marriage is also Do-well; for married men must work and earn a living and keep the world going. All the confessors of the church, the kings and knights, the emperors and peasants, the virgins and martyrs, spring from marriage, and all arose out of one man. And woman was created as an agent to assist in this work; and thus marriage was made first by the consent of the father and the advice of friends, and then by the mutual agreement of the two partners. So marriage was established, and God himself made it; the heaven of wedlock is here on earth, and he himself was its witness.

But I believe that all traitors, thieves, liars, wasters, and other such idle wretches were conceived out of wedlock, or else in a forbidden time as Cain was by Eve. For the Psalm says of such sinners —

> Behold, he labors with mischief:
> He has conceived sorrow, and brought forth ungodliness.

And all Cain's progeny came to an evil end. For God sent an angel to Seth saying, "I command that your issue be wedded only with your issue, and never with Cain's." But some ignored God's command and coupled Cain's children with Seth's. Then God was angry with his creatures and said, "I will destroy man whom I have created ... for I regret that I have made them." And he came to Noah and said, "Go at once and build a ship of planks and timbers, and board it quickly with your wives and three sons; and stay there till forty days have passed, when the flood will have washed clean away all the cursed blood that Cain has engendered. The beasts, too, shall curse the day that Cain was born, for they shall all die for his misdeeds, on every hill and valley, and the birds of the air besides — all but two of each kind, which shall be saved in your wooden ark." Thus the children paid for their forefather's guilt, and for him they had to suffer.

Yet in one respect the gospel contradicts this, for it is written, "The son shall not bear the iniquity of the father, neither shall the father bear the iniquity of the son." But it seems to me that if the father is a liar and a scoundrel, the son will in part inherit his father's faults. Graft an apple on an elder, and I doubt if your apple will be sweet; and it is even less likely that the son of a villein should be without some touch of his father. — "Do men gather grapes of thorns, or figs of thistles?"

So, through this accursed Cain, misery first came into the world — all because they contracted marriages against the will of God. For all who marry off their children so, are bound to suffer for it. And nowadays, to tell the truth, there are many unnatural marriages, for many marry only for money, and these marriages produce such wretched offspring as those whom the Flood destroyed. Good men should marry good women, even if they have no money. For Christ said, "I am the truth and the life, and can raise whom I will." I think there is nothing more unseemly, than to give a young girl to a doddering old man, or to marry for money some aged widow who will bear no children, except in her arms! For since the plague hundreds of couples have married, yet the only fruit they have brought forth are foul words; they live in jealousy, without happiness, and lie in bed quarreling, so that all the children they get are strife and nagging! If they went to try for the Dunmow flitch, they would- n't stand a chance without the devil's help; and unless they were both lying there'd be no bacon for them.

So I warn all Christians never to seek to marry for wealth or rich relations. But bachelors should marry spinsters, and widowers widows. And see that you marry for love, and not for property, then you will gain God's grace and find money enough to live on.

Every layman who cannot keep himself chaste should be wise enough to get married, and so remain free from sin. For the pleasure of lechery is a bait from hell. While you are young and your weapon is virile, slake your lust in marriage if you want an excuse for it. —

"While you are strong, do not give your strength to harlots, For it is written in the gates, a harlot is the entrance of death."

And once married, be careful to observe the proper times — not as Adam and Eve did when Cain was engendered. There should be no love-making at forbidden times, nor should you ever come together unless both man and wife are clean in life and soul, and in perfect charity. Then your marriage will be pleasing to almighty God; for he himself ordained marriage, and said in the scriptures: "To avoid fornication, it is good for every man to have his own wife, and every woman her own husband."

But those born out of marriage are generally vagabonds — swindlers, foundlings, imposters, and liars. Lacking the grace to earn a living or gain peo- ple's affection, they turn beggars and waste whatever they lay hands on. To spite Do-well, they do evil and serve the devil, with whom they will dwell when they die, unless God gives them grace to amend their ways....

According to the vision, how is a marriage made? What are the differences in the charac- ter of legitimate and illegitimate children? How do children acquire their personalities and qualities? Who are proper spouses? What are inappropriate reasons to marry? When and why should a couple avoid intercourse? How has society, and consequently marriages, become so degenerate?

44. ST. BERNARDINO ON MARRIAGE

St. Bernardino of Siena (1380-1444), a Franciscan friar, was one of the most gifted and popular preachers of the Middle Ages. He traveled across Italy, preaching in the public squares because the churches could not hold the large audiences he drew. Perhaps because Bernardino himself was an orphan, many of his sermons focused on marriage and family life and the problems and dilemmas that could arise from these intense emotional relationships. Bernardino illustrated his sermons with lively exempla, *many of which survive in the original Italian. These stories provide insights into the family, the household, and the relationships of its members. Bernardino's sermons, focused on the daily life of ordinary people, present a balanced view of marriage and family. His audience included married lay people, which in part accounts for the absence of the clerical misogyny found in more theoretical literature. In Bernardino's sermons there is a mingling of authority and tradition with experience that reflects the dynamic society in which he lived.*

Source: Trans. Ada Harrison, *Examples of San Bernardino* (London: Gerald Howe, 1926), pp. 55, 112-14, 117-19, 123-26, 140-41.

A Bachelor Establishment

Do you know how a man lives that has neither wife nor house-keeper to look after him? O, I will tell you, because I know. If he is rich, and has grain in his storehouse, the sparrows eat it and the rats. And the same with his wine and his oil. Do you know also how he sleeps in his bed? He sleeps in it as it were in a ditch, and once he has put on the sheet he doesn't move it off again until it rots. The same way in the room where he eats. There it's all melon-rind, bones, scrapings of salad, everything lying about the floor, from which nothing is ever swept. And what is the table like? Well, the cloth's laid on it, and doesn't come off it until it falls to pieces. He cleans the dishes up bit by bit. The dog licks them, and washes them that way. And the plates? All covered with grease. Do you know how he lives? He lives like a beast. And I say that no man can live well alone like that. The woman is the one who knows the care of the house. That she does understand.

Choosing a Wife

Do you wish your wife to be faithful to you? Then you keep faith with her. There are many who want to take wives, and cannot find them. Do you know why? Because the man will say: I want a wise woman, while all the time he himself is a fool. That is not right. Fool must wed with fool. And you, what kind of a wife do you want? O, a tall one, you say. And you are a snippet. That's no good. There is a certain country where the women find husbands according to their height. And there was a man of this country who wished to take a wife, and wanted to see her first. So he was taken to her house by her brothers, and they showed her to him barefooted, without a hat, and when they measured her she was taller than any other girl in the place. Finally they asked him: well, do you like her? And he answered: yes, I like her very much. But the girl, seeing he was such a little nobody, said: well, I don't like you. And that was a good one for him.

Well, to return to our subject. How do you want your wife to be? You want her honest. And you yourself are dishonest. Again, what kind of a wife do you want? A temperate one. And you yourself are never seen outside the tavern You won't find one to your taste. And you, what wife do you want? An industrious one. And yet you waste the whole day. What do you want? A peaceable wife. And you are a man who would pick a quarrel with a straw if it pricked your foot in the road. And what wife do you want? An obedient one. And yet you have never obeyed your mother or your father or any other person. You don't deserve one. Finally, what wife do you want? O, one that is good and beautiful and wise, in fact one that has all the virtues. Well, I tell you that if you want such a one so you must be yourself, for if you expect her to be virtuous, good, and beautiful, be sure she will expect the same of you.

On Dowries

You give your daughter to a man for his wife, and neither he who takes her, nor his father nor his mother thinks whence come the fine things she brings with her. If they were wise, that would be their first thought: Whence come these fine things, these gowns and these garments, that are her dowry? For many times, aye! and most times, they come from thieving and usury, and the sweat of peasants, and the blood of widows, and the marrow of babes and orphans. If you were to take one of these fine gowns and crush it and twist it, you would see drip from it the blood of living creatures. Alas! you do not think what cruelty you do, to dress in the clothes another man has earned for you while he is dying of cold.

The Wedding Ring

The ring is the heart, and the finger is faith. The woman that wears a ring on her finger, that ring that she carries, what does it mean? It means that she should keep faith with her husband, with mouth, with heart, and with deed; and every time she breaks faith she lies in her throat. Is there no one here that has fallen, no wife of ill repute? O, when you fall from the way, then the ring that you wear tells no truth, for you show that you have broken faith with your husband. Your heart is not faithful to him, and when you have dealings with a courtesan your mouth is not faithful to him, and when you fall into sin you are not faithful to him in deed. You see that, though you carry the ring, the sign of faith, you deny it. For neither in word, nor in deed, not in thought do you keep faithful.

Forbearance to Wives

O, how precious is the fruit of a good woman. You have it written in the scriptures, "*Ex fructibus eorum, cognoscetis eos,* By their fruits you shall know them." How do you know when a pear-tree is good — you know, a garden pear? By its fruit. And so with a vine, and a fig. You know them by their fruit; and so I say of all trees. So you will know by the fruit of a woman whether she is good or not. When a woman is good, and has children, that is the noblest fruit there can be in the world, if they are good. For you know this is the tree God planted, the noblest thing that could ever be. O, to see a fine boy-child! You never could see a lovelier fruit. The tree, you know, was planted in so precious a place, that is the earthly paradise, and was set there by the hand of God himself. Yet there are many who do not even worry whether their children are boys or girls, and there are many who have children and do not value them at all. And when they see them do some childish folly, they don't know how to put up with it, so little discretion have they.

Some there are who can far better suffer a hen, that lays them a fresh egg every day, than their own wives. And sometimes the hen breaks a jug or a cup, and yet they don't get angry with it or beat it, through their desire not to miss its fruit, that daily egg. O foolish creatures men are, that they cannot suffer a single ill word from their wives, that bear them such more noble fruit. For as soon as your wife speaks a word that doesn't please you, Up! you take your stick, and begin covering her with blows. And the hen that clacks the whole day long and never ceases — you have any amount of patience with her, simply for the sake of having that little egg. Many fastidious men, seeing their wives sometimes not so neat and dainty as they should be, at once belabor them for it, and yet you see the hen drop filth even on your table, and you have patience with her. Consider, O hasty man, consider the noble fruit of your wife, and bear with her. It is not right to beat her for every little thing.

The Vanity of Woman

Have you heard of the taverner who sells two kinds of wine at a time, one finer than the other, and gives the good one to his friends and those that drink often in his house and the other to the country louts? Just so does the vain woman do. She sells her best wine out of doors and in church, to those that stare at her, and the other she sells to her poor lout of a husband. When she goes to church she is dressed up, tricked out and garlanded like my Lady Esmeralda, and at home she is like a slut. What shame should you feel for your conduct in the privacy of your house, let alone among all the crowd. For it is your duty to be neater and better dressed when you are alone with your husband than among the greatest throng in church. And often you like to show yourself like a lion abroad, when at home you are nothing better than a silly sheep.

The Treacherous World

Think how the world deceives on every side. As you see it in great things, so it is in small. Take this example, O you woman who has a greedy husband. Sometimes your husband is greedy and anxious for fine tit-bits and likes a rich stew. So he will go to the butcher and choose a piece of fine fat veal and buy it. Then he takes it home and says to his wife: make me a dish of good stew. When she has made it, she dishes it up, and brings it to table, and by misfortune, with the very first bits that the greedy husband puts in his mouth he swallows a fly that had fallen into the pot. O, O, O, that is a moral for us. How many there are who have found themselves in great estate and then have come to nothing. How many have rich pleasures in their grasp, and then when they seem to have everything the fly falls. There is no tit-bit you can find in the world that is perfect. You see, and this often and often, how the bride comes to her husband. She is dressed up, decked, adorned, combed, and perfumed. Wait a minute! Ask her husband's mother what she thinks. Yes, she comes finely decked out; she has jewels, a wreath on her head, and a golden ring. So she comes to the house of her husband, and when she has been there a little, the old mother says to her son: Your wife says this and that. She tells me that she wants to be mistress of the house, and do everything her own way, and nothing mine at all. O, it's true what the proverb says: the ass comes from the mountain, and drives the horse from its stall. There where she hoped to be helped, respected, and loved, she finds hatred beginning to grow. O, where is that happy time you had once? How long did it last? Not long. There was a fly in the ointment. I tell you there is nothing good in this world. Do you want to have it plainer still? Which one of you is contented, man or woman? Has anyone ever had his happiness, and there was no fly in it? Not one of you, not one of you there is that does not know the pricks of the world. Troubles are the pricks of the world; therefore do not trust to it. It is treacherous. If a man were wise he would pin his faith to God rather than to the world, saying, I know that the world is not to be trusted. It is full of falseness, fair of promise, and evil in result.

How does a bachelor live? What personal qualities did Bernardino think important when choosing a spouse? How did Bernardino characterize good wives? How did Bernardino characterize husbands? What kind of relationship did he portray between mother-in-law and daughter-in-law? How would the congregation likely have responded to these sermons? Were they effective?

45. THE FIFTEEN JOYS OF MARRIAGE

The Fifteen Joys of Marriage *was written in French around the year 1400. The author of this satire is unknown, but internal evidence suggests he may have been a cleric. Certainly, the poem follows in the tradition of misogynist invective that character-ized much literature about women and marriage written by the medieval clergy.* The Fif-teen Joys *is a satirical critique of marriage. It presents marriage as a snare into which unsuspecting men were lured by manipulative women. Once caught, the hapless husband is at the mercy of his conniving wife and ungrateful family and household. Yet, like all satire,* The Fifteen Joys of Marriage *also reflects something of society and the perils and hardships of married life. Whether, in fact, the work can be read as a veiled compli-ment to women, as the author alleges, must be left to the discretion of the individual reader.*

Source: Trans. Brent A. Pitts, *The Fifteen Joys of Marriage* (New York: Peter Lang, 1985), pp. 4-5, 31-37, 67-75, 103-07, 131-32; reprinted with permission.

... Now whereas certain pious souls meditating on the Virgin Mary and con-templating the great joys she must have experienced in the holy mysteries of the Annunciation, Nativity, and Assumption of Christ (to name just a few), have set these down in Fifteen Joys (in whose name and honor several good Christians have also composed lovely, pious prayers to the Blessed Virgin), I, too, meditating and pondering the married state—a servitude I've never expe-rienced personally since God has seen fit to put me in another kind of bondage, deprived as I am of a freedom I can never recover—I, too, have con-cluded that marriage entails fifteen pitfalls, based either on what I've seen myself or heard from people who ought to know. Although married folk con-sider them joys, pleasures, and delights, and believe no other joys can compare, it seems to me that, rationally speaking, these fifteen joys of marriage are rather the greatest torments, afflictions, griefs, and misfortunes on earth; no other tor-tures, with the possible exception of mayhem, could measure up. Still I don't condemn them for marrying; rather, I approve and consider they're doing the right thing. After all, we're only born into this world to do penance, suffer affliction, and mortify the flesh so as to win paradise, and it seems to me that a fellow could find no harsher penance than submission to the pains and tor-ments described below. Yet there's another side to this: since they reckon these torments as joys and delights, and become as calloused to them as an ass to its burden, they seem perfectly content; thus one wonders whether in their case this form of penance has any real merit. And so, having observed these pains that they take for joys, and considered the divergence of their opinion and that of yours truly and several others, I've taken great delight watching them swim about in the snare where they're so inextricably caught, and composing these Fifteen Joys of Marriage to console them. Now I've consumed time, ink, and paper for the sake of others yet unmarried, and surely won't dissuade them from entering the net, nor is that my intention. Yet perhaps a few will come to regret their decision when it's too late, thus they'll have these joys forever, till the end of their miserable days.

The Fourth Joy

The fourth joy of marriage is when the husband has been married for six, seven, nine years or ten (either more or less), has five or six children, and has known all the bad days, terrible nights, and misfortunes discussed above, or a few of them, all of which have caused him many a fitful sleep. Already his youthful ardor has grown quite cold, and it's high time for him to call it quits if he can. After all, he's so downtrodden, so weary and worn out from domestic chores and travail, he no longer cares about anything his wife says or does. On the contrary, he's as calloused to it all as an old mule that, by instinct, seems immune to the goad and scarcely plods faster than its accustomed gait.

The poor fellow observes and beholds one, two, or three of his daughters who are ready or even eager to wed—a condition easily diagnosed, for such girls are still playful and sporting. And though perhaps the good fellow is short of cash, the girls and other children will still have to have dresses, stockings, slippers, slips, food, and other items. He'll have to keep his daughters presentable, and for three principal reasons: first, so they'll receive earlier proposals from a number of suitors; second, because if the good fellow refuses to outfit them, he'll lose in the bargain, for his wife has gone this road before and won't put up with his stubbornness; third, because girls are by nature light-hearted and fun-loving and desire always to be teasingly attired, so perhaps if he fails to set them up adequately, they'll find another way (one I'll not reveal) to have their pretty outfits. And yet, hounded on all sides by the great responsibilities he must shoulder, the good fellow himself will be so shabbily dressed, he'll no longer care about living. He wouldn't mind so much, for—like the fish in the snare—he'd still have comfort enough if they'd just let him suffer in peace, but they shorten his life besides.

So, too, with the good fellow who's entered the net of matrimony by means of the torments I've described, and countless others besides: when he encounters the trials set forth above and realizes what the future holds, as I've said, he cares no more about living; he's completely disspirited, like a worn-out nag that no longer reacts to spurs or other prods. Despite this, the husband has to trot and roam all over the countryside to keep an eye on his land or his goods, according to his position. Perhaps he has two old nags to ride, or one, or none at all. Now he has to go six or ten leagues away for certain business dealings; another time he must travel twenty or thirty leagues to a hearing, or else he's off to court for a ruinous lawsuit he's enmeshed in, a case pending since his great-granddaddy's day. His boots are at least two or three winters old; they've been overhauled so many times that now they're quite run-over. They stand a full foot shorter than when he bought them: the tops, which once reached his knee, now stop at mid-shin. And then there's his set of antique spurs, one of which has lost its rowel, that dates from old King Lothair's time. He owns a special outfit, too, that's a good five or six years old, but he doesn't normally wear it except on holidays or when he dresses up; it's an old-fashioned frock, though, for a new style has come along since his was made up. Whatever dramatic presentations or musical entertainments he witnesses, he can't get his mind off domestic affairs; thus his preoccupation spoils his pleasure in anything he sees. He lives on a shoestring during these trips; his horses, too, if indeed he has any. His ragtag squire wears an old sword captured by the master at the battle of Flanders or elsewhere, and a frock that obviously was cut without benefit of its wearer's presence, or at least it wasn't made to order, for the shoulder seams sag way too low. He carries some old saddlebags where his master stowed his armor at the battle of Flanders, or perhaps he has other garb according to his position.

In brief, then, the good fellow does his best and gets by as frugally as possible, for there are plenty back home to squander his money. He knows precious little about litigation, and when he's been mercilessly fleeced by lawyers, sergeants, and court clerks, he heads for home as soon as he can. Because of his yearning for home, and also to avoid the expense of a roadside inn, perhaps he finally arrives home at an hour midway between dusk and dawn. He finds no supper, for his wife and the entire household are sound asleep. He takes it all in stride, though, for he's quite accustomed to such treatment. As for myself, I believe God tests only those whom he knows and trusts to be meek and docile enough to bear those trials patiently; thus he tempers the wind to the shorn lamb. But should the good fellow arrive home a bit earlier, worn out, weary, harrassed, and worried, burdened by his affairs and anticipating a family welcome—although he knows from past experience what to expect—instead he'll find his wife ranting and raising the roof. Remember, too, that whatever the good fellow might request, his servants will just shrug him off: they're all partial to the wife, who's won them over completely; if they ever annoyed her, they'd have to look elsewhere for work, for they know the lady means what she says. Thus the husband's only wasting his time when he tries to get service, as long as the wife's against it. Should the master's poor squire request something for himself or for his horses, he'll be so maligned and rebuked, he won't dare protest.

Thus the good fellow, who's easy-going and doesn't want to make a scene or upset his family, takes it all in stride. Though shivering with cold, he sits across the room from the fire while his wife and children huddle round the hearth. Perhaps he observes his wife's behavior: ill-tempered and out of sorts,

she takes no notice of him, not lifting even a finger to have his supper prepared. Instead she scolds and snipes, and this gets under the poor fellow's skin,
though he answers not a word. Now it often happens that because of his
hunger and fatigue, and because of his wife's outrageous behavior (she leads
him to believe the pantry's bare), the poor fellow tries to stand up to her, complaining, "Really, wife, you can't see past your own nose! Here I'm tired and
worn out, I haven't eaten or drunk all day, I'm soaked to the skin, and still you
show no concern for me, whether by fixing my supper or otherwise!"

"My word," she retorts, "you pulled a fast one! When you took the squire
along on your trip, I had no one to put my flax and hemp in water for steep-
ing, so I lost more at that, by God, than you'll recoup in four years. What's
more, I told you ages ago, damn it, to get that hole mended in the chicken
coop. Now the marten has eaten three of my laying hens, and you can imagine
how much that'll set us back. By God, if you live to see the day, you'll be the
poorest man in your family."

"Wife, don't say such things. Heaven be thanked, we always have enough to
get by. Besides, there are some fine folks in my family."

"How's that? In your family? Mother Mary, I'm sure I've never met them! I
can scarcely think of one who's worth his salt!"

"By God, woman," he says, "there are some good folks just the same."

"And what good are they to you?"

"What good?" asks the husband. "Well, what good are yours to me?"

"What good are my folks to you?" the wife replies. "By God, you'd be in a
sorry mess if they weren't!"

"Good Lord," he says, "let's drop the subject for now."

"You'd better!" she warns. "They'd back you into a corner if you said that to
their face."

Then the good fellow shuts up, for perhaps he's afraid she'll report his
remarks to her relatives — after all, she does come from a better family than he.

Then one of the children begins wailing, and perhaps it's the husband's
favorite child. The wife takes a switch and begins beating the child soundly,
more to spite the husband than for any other reason. Then the poor husband
says, "Woman, stop beating him!" and makes to get angry.

"Ha! the devil you say, you never take the trouble to discipline them, so you
can hardly protest! I'm after them day and night! A plague take them all!"

"Oh, woman," he answers, "what a terrible thing to say!"

"Ah, sir," complains the wetnurse, "you don't know the trouble your wife
has, and the trials they put us through just keeping them fed."

"I swear, sir," adds the maid, "you should be ashamed coming home as you
do, expecting us to bow and scrape when you blow in. You're just inviting
trouble."

"What trouble is that?" he asks. "My word, that's not so."

Then the entire household is against him and, assailed on all sides (as usual), the good fellow knows quite well he can't prevail. He often goes off to bed without supper or fire, soaked through and catching a cold to boot; or if he does have supper, it'll be a miracle, and for sure he'll dine in such ease and comfort! Then he's off to bed where he listens all night to the children's bawling; the wife and nurse let them cry just to gall him. Thus he spends his night worrying and fretting, and he counts it all for joy since he wouldn't have it otherwise. And so he is and will always remain till the end of his miserable days.

The Seventh Joy

Now the seventh joy of marriage is when the bachelor finds a very good, well-behaved, and genteel woman; but then again, perhaps she's a horny wench who'd never turn a cold shoulder to a juicy proposition. Now don't forget, there's a universal in marriage to the effect that every wife, whatever her status, and whether she's honorable or otherwise, believes and esteems her husband to be the world's most paltry and least potent practitioner of the secrets of love.

Then, too, it often happens that the young man, who's lusty and full of sap, marries a good and honorable young woman, and that they guzzle as much as they can of love's pleasures for one, two, three years or more, till at last their youthful ardor cools. Yet the wife's appetites don't wane as soon as her mate's, whatever his station in life, for she doesn't have all his troubles, toil, and tribulation; why, even if he did nothing but play and romp, he'd still run down sooner than his wife. Now it's quite true that a woman is sorely beset for so long as she's pregnant or bearing children, and that during childbirth she suffers untold grief and pain. But all this is nothing compared to the travail a reasonable man must endure when pondering any of his important undertakings. And as for the discomfort of pregnancy or childbirth, it impresses me not a bit more than that of a hen or goose laying an egg as big as my fist, and this through a hole too small for my pinkie just a moment before. One process is just as great as the other in Nature's scheme. Thus you'll see the hen remain plumper than the cock, despite the fact that she lays daily; for the rooster is so stupid, he spends the whole day scratching for food to bill-feed his mate, while her sole concerns are eating, gabbling, and resting easy. And the same holds true for good, respectable husbands, I say it to their credit.

Later on it happens that the good fellow becomes quite racked and exhausted: he has constant toil and trouble, and his thoughts are always elsewhere. He's no longer inclined to bedtime sport, or only seldom enough to gratify his wife; or perhaps he's not as adroit as before, in which case he drops it altogether. Thus the wife must do without, although she's as lusty as ever in

this regard. And because the wife's portion dwindles with each passing day, all
the pleasures, delights, and loving looks they'd exchanged in younger years
when the husband was nimbler, are now transformed into brawling and contention. As her dosage is gradually diminished, they begin to fight, and when
her portion is no longer sufficient (supposing, now, that she's a good and honorable woman with no inclination to wrongdoing), still she persists in believing
her husband less lusty than others; her suspicions are all the more justified since
he's the only man she's ever had, and he can't satisfy her. Now, logically, man
must satisfy woman—either that, or Nature hasn't justly proportioned things. I
believe further that if one man couldn't satisfy a woman, then God and the
church would have ordained that she have two, or as many as she needs.

Now certain women sometimes undertake to determine whether other
men are as inept as their husbands; after some preliminary experimentation,
perhaps they believe it more than ever. For perhaps the woman takes a lover
who can only fulfil her on the sly, catch-as-catch-can; but then she is love-
starved and responds marvelously despite the danger. If she'd thought her husband paltry and inept before, now her suspicions are confirmed, for present
pleasures are always more vivid than past delights; experience, after all, is a great
teacher. Then again, perhaps the bachelor marries a sensual wench who's quite
susceptible to other men's advances, and who has the same opinion of her husband as the woman just described; for perhaps she's rubbed bellies with a few
whose prowess is vastly superior to hubby's. He doesn't bother with it much
nowadays, for he knows very well she'll be around when he feels the urge.

Now remember that men think just the opposite of what's commonly said,
for whatever sort of wife they have, they generally believe her superior to any
other. You'll find exceptions, of course, but only among desperate, half-crazed
profligates with little or no intelligence. Thus it's not unusual to see husbands
praising their wives and extolling their virtues: to hear them tell it, no wife
could match theirs nor offer so many good features, such fine physical charms
or healthy animal drive. For her part, once her husband has died the widow
remarries right away, sometimes waiting scarcely a month before taking on her
next mate, just to see if he's as wretched and weakly as the first. It also happens
sometimes that she's neither faithful nor loyal to him. Her behavior ruins their
existence; her loose living jeopardizes everything as she squanders the money
her husband earns by the sweat of his brow, according to his position, and lav-
ishes it in countless ways: this much for her lover, that much for her bawdy
procuresses, and this much again for her confessor, a Gray or White Friar who
pockets a hefty fee for yearly absolution (these folk are the pope's right-hand
men).

Our good fellow, the husband, watches his p's and q's, avoiding great
expense; he keeps close tabs on whatever income, pension, stores, and expenses

he might have, according to his position. Now when he's tallied down to the penny and then counted once again, he finds his affairs awry and becomes quite concerned. Then when he's gone to bed, he takes it up with his wife, whom he loves more than himself, saying, "Honestly, my love, I don't know what's amiss, but I can't tell where our goods are going, whether money, grain, wine, or other. As for myself, I always keep such a tight rein on our affairs, I don't dare buy myself even a new frock."

"Truly, dear, I'm just as amazed as you. I can't imagine what's happening either, for I'd say I manage and conduct our interests as well and as smoothly as can be."

Thus the good fellow doesn't know where he stands. When poverty overtakes him, he still doesn't know what's happened except to conclude and say to himself that he's just unlucky, that Lady Fortune has beset him and now has the upper hand. Nor will he ever believe slander against his wife, thus he'll never find anyone, except perhaps by chance, who'd let on about it. After all, only an idler would raise the subject, and thereafter he'd be the worst enemy the husband could have.

Then again, it sometimes happens that the husband has a close friend who sees the wife's mismanagement and feels duty-bound to warn the husband to beware for his household, without breathing a word more, or perhaps he'll spell out the entire situation. The husband will be astonished at first, and then gloomily go his way. His wife will know by his expression that something's amiss, and perhaps she'll even guess that the friend has spilled the beans, for he's accused her once before. She'll come off quite nicely, though, God willing. For now, the good fellow doesn't let on; instead, thinking to test her, he says, "My dear, I must make a twelve-league journey."

"Whatever for, sweetheart?" she asks.

"I have to tend to this or that," he says.

"I'd rather you sent a servant instead."

"No, I'll have to go myself or risk a loss," he says, "but I'll return in two or three days."

Then off he goes, pretending to set out on his journey. Instead he hides in the woods, choosing a good spot from which to observe goings-on in the house. Suspecting the revelation to her husband, the lady sends word to her lover not to come under any circumstances, for she's taking no chances. Thus she keeps so much to the straight and narrow that, thank God, her husband will never find out.

When he's spied and listened well, the good fellow pretends to return from his journey. He arrives in a jolly mood, for he now believes his friend's story a lie; besides, how could he think that this woman who makes over him, who kisses and hugs him so tenderly and calls him "my love," would ever do such a

[loves his wife more than himself
blinds him to her actions/motives]

thing? Thus he's sure there's nothing to the report. Now when he's alone with his wife, he remarks, "Truly, my sweet, I've had some upsetting news of late."

"Lordy, sweetheart, I'm sure I don't know what it could be, but then it's true you've been sulky for a good while now. I was frightened to death you'd taken losses, or that a relative had been killed or captured by the English."

"You're way off," he says. "It's much worse than that."

"Mother Mary!" says she. "Then what can it be? Come on, out with it!"

"All right, then! One of my friends told me that So-and-so was sleeping with you, and a good many things besides."

The lady crosses herself and feigns astonishment, then smiles and says, "Cheer up, my love! Goodness, honey, I wish all my sins were as easily disproved as this." Then she places her hands on his head and declares, "My love, I'll go one better: the devil take all beneath my hands if ever a man's lips (save yours and our cousins'—with your consent, of course) touched mine. Tush! tush! Is that all? My dear, I'm so relieved you told me, for I feared it was something else. I'm quite sure I know who started these lies; I only wish to God you knew the reason why! My word, would you be shocked, he claims such friendship for you! All in all, though, I'm relieved he's opened this can of worms."

"Eh? What's that?"

"Not to worry, dear! You'll find out soon enough."

"No, really," he insists, "I want to know."

"By God, my love," says she, "it made me fume when you invited him so often, but I put up with it because you claimed such fondness for him."

"Come now," he says, "tell me."

"Truly, sweetheart, you don't have to know."

"But I want to know, so out with it."

Then she kisses and hugs him ever so sweetly, and says, "Oh, my love, my sweet husband! The backstabbers are trying to turn you against me!"

"Who, sweetheart? Tell me who!"

"O God, my love, my precious, it's your treacherous friend, the one who told you those lies! For better than two years he's pressed me to step out on you, but I've turned him down flat, though he pursued me relentlessly. Why, when you thought he was visiting for friendship with you, in truth he came just for lechery! He wouldn't leave off until lately when I vowed and declared I'd tell you, for he meant nothing to me. But I'm sure of myself and didn't want to come between you; besides, I kept thinking he'd hold his tongue. Alas! It's not his fault he hasn't shamed you!"

"Mother Mary, so he's the traitor! I'd never have suspected …"

"By God, milord, if he ever sets foot in this house, or if I hear that you've spoken with him, I'll file for divorce! But, my word, you needn't worry on my account; God willing, I'll not begin such shenanigans now! And I beg God on bended knee that if ever I feel the urge, lightning will strike me dead on the spot! Alas, sweet lover," she says, snuggling up to him, "I'd be a wicked old thing to do such mean, lowdown things to you of all people, my handsome, good, sweet, and gentle husband, you whose every desire is attuned to mine! May God shorten my days if ever I become so lewd! And I beg and pray you, my love, keep that man away from our house, the one your treacherous friend accused me of sleeping with—devil take my soul, though, if he even once got close! Just the same, though, I never want him anywhere near me." Then she begins sobbing. The good fellow comforts her, solemnly swearing to do everything she's said except to bar his house to the accused, for he's done no wrong. While he vows he'll never believe such stories nor listen to such babble, in truth he'll always be gnawed by misgivings and feel hurt in his heart.

Now here's the conclusion: the friend who reported to the husband, and who told him with his best interests at heart, will henceforth be the husband's worst enemy. Thus the husband is reduced to bestiality; he'll chew his cud and be transformed into a beast, with nary a hint of magic. Now he has real troubles: he's caught fast in the snare, and now his wife will kick up her heels more than ever. No one ever accuses her, though, for the good fellow wouldn't believe the tales anyway. And the real culprit, the traitor who'd been pointed out to him from the start, will be the best friend he could want. Old age will overtake him and perhaps he'll sink into poverty, never to recover. Such are the joys he's found in the net of matrimony! He becomes a laughingstock: one calls him Old Johnny Cuckold, another points at him in the street, another says it's a great misfortune for such a fine fellow as he. Still another remarks that it makes no difference, that such are the rules of the game, and that the husband is a dull sort, anyway. Finer folk will turn him out and steer clear of him. Thus he lives in the sorrow and pain that he counts for joys, and there he'll always remain till the end of his miserable days.

The Twelfth Joy

The twelfth joy of marriage is when—after repeated passes about the snare— the young man finally discovers the opening, enters, and finds just the woman he was seeking. Perhaps he would have done better to find another, but he wouldn't want that for anything; seems to him he's better matched than anyone, and that his mate was made in heaven. To his mind, there's none like her: he thrills to the sound of her voice and revels in her manner and wisdom, though perhaps she talks only stuff and nonsense. And perhaps the young man tends to jump to her beck and call, acting only on her advice, so that whenever anyone has dealings with him, he says, "I'll discuss it with my wife" (or "with the lady of the house"). If she wants something done, it's done; if she's against it, it's not, for the good fellow is so henpecked, he's as docile as a plow ox. Now he's ripe!

If he's a nobleman and the prince requires his service, then he'll serve if his wife so desires. Perhaps he'll say, "My dear, I must go off."

"Go off? And whatever for? You'll spend a fortune, get yourself killed, and then the children and I will be in a fine predicament!"

In short, if she's against it, he won't go; he'll have to save face and defend his honor as best he can! Or else if she wants, she sends him out of the house to any place she sees fit. If she scolds him, he never talks back, for however wrong she may be, it seems to him that she's right and knows best. Henceforth he'll perform great exploits, now that his wife is at the helm. Now the world's wisest woman has about as much sense as I have gold in my eye or a gorilla has tail; her intelligence fails her before she's finished half her task or said half her speech. In such a case the man already has suffering aplenty and things go badly for him, provided she behaves respectably. But if she doesn't, and this is frequently the case, then you can imagine his suffering, and what conniving, low-down, dirty tricks she deals him: first she shoos him off to bed before he's ready; or if she has some secret rendez-vous, she wakes him at midnight, reminding him of some urgent affair; or else she sends him on a pilgrimage she's suddenly promised to make, complaining that her side's begun to hurt. And off he'll go, come hail or high water!

And if it happens that the wife's lover, who knows his way around the house, is watching for a chance to speak with her and just can't be patient, he'll come over at night, enter the grounds and steer toward cellar or shed, always on the lookout for a way to see her. Or else he's so desperate, he bursts into the very bedroom where hubby lies sleeping, for a lusty rogue loses all control and follows his heart's command in satisfying his desire. This is why we often observe that if a lover is seen or nabbed for poor timing and his lady loses face as a result, the woman is so brazen that when she sees his efforts on her behalf, she'll risk death before refusing him, and the fire of lust burns even hotter. Now sometimes when the lover gets inside the house, as I've said, the dog smells him and begins baying. But the wife convinces the husband it's only rats, saying she's known the dog to growl that way before. Should the good fellow discover the mystification, he'll think nothing of it, believing his wife's just looking out for his interests. In brief, he's caught fast in the snare! She has him rock the children and take them out to play; why, she even makes him hold the yarn spools when she does her Saturday spinning.

As if this weren't enough already, now a new tribulation descends: his country goes to war, and the entire population must withdraw to the cities and castles. But the good fellow can neither leave his home nor abandon his wife; then, too, perhaps he's captured, led off ignominiously, beaten, and forced to pay a huge ransom. Now he really has problems! And to avoid certain recapture he retires to a castle, but first he must zigzag through the woods and grope through hedges and thickets, so that he emerges ragged and bruised. Screaming and scolding, his wife welcomes him home; she blames him for all the troubles and turmoil, as if he could arrange a truce between the two warring kings. To make matters worse, she refuses to remain at home, so the good fellow has to scurry to cart the family to the city or castle, and God knows the grief he has loading and unloading wife and children, packing and loading trunks, finding an inn, and unpacking when at last they arrive safely within the fortress walls — there's not a man alive who could say! You can imagine, too, what distress he endures, how he slaves, and how he's bombarded with endless chatter, for his wife can only vent her frustration on him. The husband braves wind and rain, trotting off now by day, now by night, on foot or on horseback, according to his means, first here, now there, always searching for food and other essentials. In brief, he'll never rest his weary bones; rather he'll know only the tribulation and trouble to which he was born. And if it happens that he gets so fed up with his wife's nagging that he tries to retort, or attempts some other resistance, then he'll have double trouble, for surely he'll be humiliated and vanquished in the end; he'll be more subservient than ever before, for now he's waited too long to begin his revolt. You might guess, too, that the children are ill-mannered and ill-taught; the good fellow hardly dares touch them. They get everything they want, of course; whatever they do is well done — why, they almost put out his eye once while throwing stones at play. Then when the war is over, the whole cartload has to be hauled back home, where the torture begins anew.

Now the good fellow falls prey to old age. Since he's less esteemed than before, he'll be pushed aside like an aging falconer too old to set his hand to another trade. The wife marries off her daughters as she sees fit: perhaps she finds poor matches for them, and neither the daughters nor their husbands have a tittle of respect for the good fellow. He becomes gouty and can't remedy the misfortunes he's suffered. Then the good fellow weeps for his mistakes in the net where he's caught, and from which he'll never escape; rather he'll remain forever in pain and wailing. Nor would he dare have a mass said for his soul, for he loves his wife more than his own salvation, and his only will entrusts his soul to her care. Thus he spins out his life in sadness and languor, and there he'll surely remain till the end of his miserable days.

Conclusion

Now this is the end of the Fifteen Joys of Marriage. I call them "joys" because married folk just can't fathom the things I've mentioned above; they consider them great bliss, and it seems they'd not have it otherwise. As for myself, though, I hold such things to be the greatest woes possible here on earth. Now if the ladies complain that I haven't attributed or assigned these joys (which I consider woes) to them as I have to men, I beg their pardon. Still and all I haven't wronged them since everything here is to their praise and honor, and also since in principle the above-mentioned things apply equally to men, as I've said. I haven't stated outright or even tried to imply that all the above joys, or even two or three of them, apply for every husband, but I can say for a fact that there's no married man, however wise, crafty, and cunning he may be, who won't have at least one or perhaps several of these joys.

Wherefore we may reasonably conclude that the man who willfully accepts these shackles must bear the consequences as well. Now I don't mean to suggest that a man's wrong to marry, but for a fact I don't consider this coupling a joyous or happy affair. They should try at least to avoid becoming so beastly, for each one can see well enough what happens to the others; O yes, they're all too eager to poke fun at them and play their jokes, but once they've tied the knot themselves, they end up more hobbled and hogtied than the rest. Thus, each should refrain from mocking the others, for to my knowledge there's none exempt from the joys I've described. Still, each believes his own case special, imagining he's immune to the joys and luckier than the others; the more he persists in such fallacy, though, the more bridled he really is. I can't say I know why, except perhaps to note that that's just the way the game is played. Now if you ask me how to remedy the situation, my answer is that a feasible solution exists — it's difficult, but at least there is a remedy. Just now, though, I prefer not to elaborate; but if you came to ask in person, I'd tell you exactly what I think. For the present I'll keep it under my hat, for some lady, gentlewoman or other might hold it against me, although in truth it's all to their honor, as I've said. After all, anyone who truly understands what I've written here will see that the husband doesn't always get the short end, and that's a credit to the ladies....

What evidence suggests the author might have been a cleric? How does a wife control her husband? Who has the more difficult role, the husband or wife? Why? How is marital sexuality characterized? How could this work be understood "to honor ladies"?

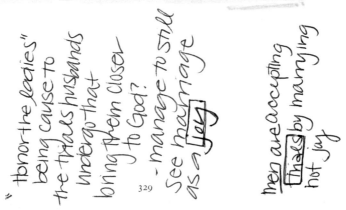

honor the ladies" being cause to the that's husbands undergo that bring them closer to God?

– manage to still see marriage as a joy

329

men are accepting that by marrying hot joy

CHAPTER SIX:

MARRIAGE AND FAMILY

In matters of marriage, medieval people were required to navigate between two connecting and sometimes contradictory value systems: that of the church and that of secular society. Moreover, how people lived and coped with daily life suggests that there was a significant distance between theoretical portrayals of marriage and lived reality. Economic, political, and social concerns frequently overshadowed emotional considerations. In many social groups women and men married without really knowing their spouse. In other groups, spouses may have grown up together or been friends or neighbors. Some marriages were happy, others profoundly unhappy. Violence and deceit were not unfamiliar in courtship and marriage. Both church courts and secular courts could be involved with problems ranging from domestic violence to cases of illegitimacy.

46. MARRIAGE AMONG THE FRANKS

One of the most valuable sources for information about the culture and society of the early Middle Ages is The History of the Franks *written by Gregory, bishop of Tours (539-594). Gregory provides remarkable insights into the rough-and-tumble world of the Frankish Kingdom in the sixth century. Although they had formally converted, the Franks were barely Christianized and older Germanic customs co-existed with those of their new religion. Nowhere is this more evident than in the areas of marriage and family life. Ecclesiastical authorities were powerless to impose Christian morality. Gregory records the excesses and breaches of church law by the Franks with an air of weary resignation. Polygamy and concubinage were common. Incestuous marriage, especially with affines, was practiced, and divorce was a male prerogative. These practices made for complicated family arrangements, arrangements that were frequently linked to the complex political maneuvering that characterized the Frankish state.*

Source: Trans. Lewis Thorpe in Gregory of Tours, *The History of the Franks* (Harmondsworth: Penguin Books, 1974), pp. 197-98, 218-23, 255; reprinted with permission.

4.3 King Lothar had seven sons by his various wives. By Ingund he had Gunthar, Childeric, Charibert, Guntram, Sigibert, and a daughter called Chlothsind; by Aregund, who was the sister of Ingund, he had Chilperic; and by Chunsina he had Chramn. I had better tell you how he came to marry the sister of his own wife. When he had already married Ingund and loved her with all his heart, she made the following suggestion to him: "My lord, you have already done what you wished with me, your handmaiden, and you have taken me to bed with you. To complete my happiness, listen now to what I have to say. I ask you to choose for my sister, who is also a member of your household, a competent and wealthy husband, so that I need not be ashamed of her, but rather that she may be a source of pride to me, so that I may serve you even more faithfully." Lothar was too much given to woman-chasing to be able to resist this. When he heard what Ingund had to say, he was filled with desire for Aregund. He went off to the villa where she lived and married her. When he had slept with her, he came back to Ingund. "I have done my best to reward you for the sweet request which you put to me," he said. "I have looked everywhere for a wealthy and wise husband whom I could marry to your sister, but I could find no one more eligible than myself. You must know, then, that I myself have married her. I am sure that this will not displease you." "You must do as you wish," answered Ingund. "All I ask is that I may retain your good favor." Gunthar, Chramn, and Childeric died during their father's lifetime. I shall describe Chramn's death in a later chapter. Alboin, king of the Longobards, married Lothar's daughter Chlothsind.

4.25 The good King Guntram first made Veneranda his mistress and took her to bed with him. She was the servant of one of his subjects. By her he had a son called Gundobad. Later on Guntram married Marcatrude, the daughter of Magnachar. He packed his son Gundobad off to Orleans. Marcatrude had a son of her own. She was jealous of Gundobad and encompassed his death. She sent him poison in a drink, so they say, and killed him. Soon after Gundobad's death she lost her own son by the judgment of God. As a result the king was estranged from her and he dismissed her. She died not long afterwards. Then Guntram married Austrechild, also called Bobilla. He had two sons by her, the elder called Lothar and the younger Chlodomer.

4.26 King Charibert married a woman called Ingoberg. He had by her a daughter, who eventually married a man from Kent and went to live there. At that time Ingoberg had among her servants two young women who were the daughters of a poor man. The first of these, who wore the habits of a religious, was called Marcovefa, and the other Merofled. The king fell violently in love with the two of them. As I have implied, they were the daughters of a wool-worker. Ingoberg was jealous because of the love which the king bore them. She made a secret plan to set their father to work, in the hope that when Charibert saw this he would come to despise the two girls. When the man was working away Ingoberg summoned the king. Charibert came, hoping to see something interesting, and, without approaching too near, watched the man preparing wool for the royal household. He was so angry at what he saw that he dismissed Ingoberg and took Merofled in her place. He had another woman, the daughter of a shepherd who looked after his flocks. Her name was Theudechild and he is said to have had a son by her, but the child was buried immediately after his birth....

Next King Charibert married Marcovefa, the sister of Merofled. They were both excommunicated as a result by St. Germanus the bishop. The king refused to give up Marcovefa: but she was struck by the judgment of God and died. Not long afterwards the king himself died in his turn. After his death Theudechild, one of his queens, sent messengers to King Guntram, offering her hand in marriage. The king replied in these terms: "She may come to me and bring her treasure with her. I will receive her and I will give her an honorable place among my people. She will hold a higher position at my side than she ever did with my brother, who had died recently." Theudechild was delighted when she heard this. She collected all her possessions together and set out to join Guntram. When he saw her, Guntram said: "It is better that this treasure should fall into my hands than that it should remain in the control of this woman who was unworthy of my brother's bed." He seized most of her goods, left her a small portion, and packed her off to a nunnery at Arles. Theudechild bore ill the fasts and vigils to which she was subjected. She sent messengers in secret to a certain Goth, promising him that, if he would carry her off to Spain and marry her there, she would escape from the nunnery with what wealth remained to her and set off with him without the slightest hesitation. He immediately promised to do what she asked. She once more collected her possessions together and made them into bundles. As she was about to make her escape from the nunnery, she was surprised by the vigilant abbess. The abbess, who had caught her red-handed, had her beaten mercilessly and locked her up in her cell. There she remained until her dying day, suffering awful anguish.

4.27 King Sigibert observed that his brothers were taking wives who were completely unworthy of them and were so far degrading themselves as to marry their own servants. He therefore sent messengers loaded with gifts to Spain and asked for the hand of Brunhild, the daughter of King Athanagild. This young woman was elegant in all that she did, lovely to look at, chaste and decorous in her behavior, wise in her generation, and of good address. Her father did not refuse to give her to Sigibert, but sent her off with a large dowry. Sigibert assembled the leading men of his kingdom, ordered a banquet to be prepared, and married Brunhild with every appearance of joy and happiness. She was, of course, an Arian, but she was converted by the bishops sent to reason with her and by the king who begged her to accept conversion. She accepted the unity of the blessed Trinity and was baptized with the chrism. In the name of Christ she remains a Catholic. When he saw this, King Chilperic sent to ask for the hand of Galswinth, the sister of Brunhild, although he already had a number of wives. He told the messengers to say that he promised to dismiss all the others, if only he were considered worthy of marrying a king's daughter of a rank equal to his own. Galswinth's father believed what he said and sent his daughter to him with a large dowry, just as he had sent Brunhild to Sigibert. Galswinth was older than Brunhild. When she reached the court of King Chilperic, he welcomed her with great honor and made her his wife. He loved her very dearly, for she had brought a large dowry with her. A great quarrel soon ensued between the two of them, however, because he also loved Fredegund, whom he had married before he married Galswinth. Galswinth was converted to the Catholic faith and baptized with the chrism. She never stopped complaining to the king about the insults which she had to endure. According to her he showed no respect for her at all, and she begged that she might be permitted to go back home, even if it meant leaving behind all the treasures which she had brought with her. Chilperic did his best to pacify her with smooth excuses and by denying the truth as convincingly as he could. In the end he had her garrotted by one of his servants and so found her dead in bed. After her death God performed a great miracle. A lamp suspended on a cord burned in front of her tomb. One day, without anyone touching it, the cord broke and the lamp fell to the stone floor. The hard stone withdrew at the point of impact and the lamp penetrated it just as if it had been made of soft material, and there it stood embedded up to its middle without anything being broken. Everyone who saw this knew that a miracle had occurred. King Chilperic wept for the death of Galswinth, but within a few days he had asked Fredegund to sleep with him again. His brothers had a strong suspicion that he had connived at the murder of the queen and they drove him out of his kingdom. Chilperic had three sons by one of his earlier consorts, Audovera: these were Theudebert, about whom I have told you already, Merovech, and Clovis. I must return now to what I was describing to you.

5.2 Chilperic sent his son Merovech to Poitiers with an army. Merovech disobeyed his father's orders and marched on Tours, where he spent the holy days of Easter. His army did great damage to the entire neighborhood. Under the pretext of visiting his mother Audovera, he next moved to Rouen. There he joined Queen Brunhild and made her his wife. When Chilperic heard that in defiance of custom and canonical law Merovech had married his uncle's widow, he was bitterly angry and marched to Rouen quicker than I can say the word. As soon as Merovech and Brunhild learned that Chilperic had decided to separate them, they sought sanctuary in the church of St. Martin, which is built of wooden planks high on the city walls. The king arrived and did all in his power to persuade them to come out. They knew that he was up to no good and they refused to believe him, but he swore that insofar as it was God's will he would not try to separate them. When they heard his solemn oath, they came out from the church. Chilperic kissed them both and received them according to their rank. He had a meal with them and set off for Soissons a few days later, taking Merovech with him.

Why did Lothar marry Aregund? Why did Marcatrude kill Gundobad? Why was Charibert excommunicated? What does the fate of Galswinth indicate about a wife's position? Why did Chilperic object to Merovech's marriage? Was this credible?

47. COUNTING FAMILIES IN THE NINTH CENTURY

For the early Middle Ages, it is difficult to find evidence that reveals the private lives of the common folk. The rural peasantry, in particular, was not literate and only infrequently came to the notice of the literate elites. Even when they do appear in the surviving documentation, they do not speak with their own voices nor reveal much about their emotional lives or familial attachments. One source, however, that does allow access to this social group, is surveys of landed estates. Inventories that survive from the ninth century list not only real estate, but also the people who worked the land and owed services and dues to their lords. The famous Polyptych *of Saint-Germain-des-Prés records a survey of over 2,000 households made between 801 and 820. These households comprised more than 10,000 individuals. The survey reveals the size of various households, the relationship between the people who lived together, and how much land and other property they held. The basic nature and structure of these agrarian families are intriguing and subject to different sorts of analysis. The slaves mentioned were, in fact, lower-level serfs, while* lidi *and* coloni *were people of intermediate status between slave and free. The term* polyptych *is derived from the many folds in the documents.*

Source: Trans. Paul E. Dutton, *Carolingian Civilization* (Peterborough: Broadview Press, 1993), pp. 183-87; reprinted with permission.

II. Brief Concerning Neuillay

At Neuillay there is a manse [farm unit] that belongs to the lord; it has an abundance of other buildings. It has there ten small fields containing 40 bunuaria in land, which can be sown with 200 modia of oats; nine arpents of meadow-land from which 10 loads of hay can be collected. There is a forest there, which is, according to estimation, 3 leagues in length, 1 league in width, in which 800 pigs can be fattened.

1. Electeus a slave and his wife, a colona by the name of Landina, who are dependents of Saint-Germain, live at Neuillay. He holds half a farm that has 6 bunuaria of arable land, a half arpent of meadow. He plows four perches of winter wheat and thirteen of spring wheat. He spreads manure on the lord's fields, and does nothing else nor owes anything, because of the service that they provide.

2. Abrahil a slave and his wife, a lida by the name of Berthidlis, are dependents of Saint-Germain. These are their children: Abram, Avremarus, Bertrada. And Ceslinus a lidus and his wife a lida by the name of Leutberga. These are their children: Leutgardis, Ingohildis. And Godalbertus a lidus. These are their [his]

children: Gedalcaus, Celsovildis, Bladovildis. These three [families] live in Neuillay. They hold a farm having 15 bunuaria of arable land and 4 arpents of meadow. They do service in Anjou and in the month of May at Paris. For the army tax they pay 2 sheep, 9 hens, 30 eggs, 100 planks and as many shingles, 12 staves, 6 hoops, and 12 torches; and they take 2 loads of wood to Sûtré. They enclose 4 perches with stakes in the lord's court, 4 perches with hedge in the meadow, and as much as necessary at harvest time. They plow 8 perches with winter wheat, 26 perches with spring wheat. As well as their labor and service, they spread manure on the lord's fields. Each of them pays 4 denarii on his head.

3. Gislevertus a slave and his wife a lida by the name of Gotberga. These are their children: Ragno, Gausbertus, Gaujoinus, Gautlindis. And Sinopus a slave and his wife a slave Frolaica. These are their children: Siclandus, Frothardus, Marellus, Adaluildis, Frotlidis. And Ansegudis a slave. These are their [her] children: Ingalbertus, Frotbertus, Frotlaicus, Frotberga. These three [families] live in Neuillay. They hold 1 farm having 26 bunuaria of arable land and 8 arpents of meadow. They pay like the above.

4. Maurifius a lidus and his wife a colona by the name of Ermengardis. Ermengildis is their son. And Gaudulfus a lidus and his wife a lida by the name of Celsa. Gaudildis is their son. These two [families] live in Neuillay. They hold 1 farm having 28 bunuaria of arable land and 4 arpents of meadow. They pay like the above.

5. Ragenardus a slave and his wife a colona by the name of Dagena. Ragenaus is their son. And Gausboldus a slave and his wife a lida by the name of Faregildis. These 2 [families] live in Neuillay. They hold 1 farm having 11 bunuaria of arable land and 4 arpents of meadow. They make [payment] like the above.

6. Feremundus a slave and his wife a colona by the name of Creada. And Feroardus a slave and his wife a lida by the name of Adalgardis. Illegardis is their daughter. And Faroneus a slave. And Adalgrimus a slave. These four [families] live in Neuillay. They hold 1 farm having 8 bunuaria of arable land and 4 arpents of meadow. They make [payment] like the above.

7. Gautmarus a slave and his wife a lida by the name of Sigalsis. These are their children: Siclevoldus, Sicleardus. That one lives in Neuillay. He holds a quarter of a farm having 1 and a half bunuaria of arable land and 1 arpent of meadow. He pays a quarter of what a whole farm pays.

8. Hildeboldus a slave and his wife a lida by the name of Bertenildis. These are their children: Aldedramnus, Adalbertus, Hildegaudus, Trutgaudus, Bernardus, Bertramnus, Hildoinus, Haldedrudis, Martinga. And Haldemarus a slave and his wife a colona by the name of Motberga. These are their children: Martinus, Siclehildis, Bernegildis. These two [families] live in Neuillay. They hold half a farm having 6 bunuaria of arable land and a half arpent of meadow. They return half of what is owed by a whole farm.

9. Bertlinus a lidus and his wife a colona by the name of Lantsida. These are their children: Creatus, Martinus, Lantbertus. He lives in Neuillay. He holds a quarter of a farm having 3 bunuaria of arable land and 2 arpents of meadow. He does service. He ought to pay a quarter of what a whole farm pays, but to look after this debt he takes care of the pigs.

10. In Neuillay there are 6 and a half inhabited farms; another half a farm is uninhabited. There are 16 hearths [families]. For the army tax they pay 12 sheep; in head tax 5 *solidi* and 4 *denarii*; 48 chickens, 160 eggs, 600 planks and as many shingles, 54 staves and as many hoops, 72 torches. They take 2 cart-loads to the wine harvest, and 2 and a half in May, and half an ox.

11. These are the slaves: Electeus, Gislevertus, Sinopus, Ragenardus, Gausboldus, Feremundus, Gedalbertus, Faroardus, Abrahil, Faroinus, Adalgrimus, Gautmarus, Hildevoldus. They pay with torches and by carrying.

12. These are the lidi: Maurifius, Gaudulfus, Bertlinus, Ceslinus, Gedalbertus.

13. These are the female slaves: Frotlina, Ansegundis, Alda, Framberta. They keep the chickens and make cloth, if wool is supplied to them.

14. These are the female lidae: Berthildis, Leutberga, Gotberga, Celsa, Faregildis, Sigalsis, Bertenildis. They pay 4 *denarii* in tax.

15. Ragenardus holds 1 bunuarium from the lord's property. Gislevertus holds, apart from his farm, 2 fruitful fields.

18. Brief Concerning Coudray-sur-Seine

1. In Coudray there are 11 and a half free farms that pay each year 5 and a half oxen for the army tax, 33 chickens, 165 eggs.

2. There is in Coudray a farm belonging to the lord having 60 bunuaria of arable land in which 175 modia of wheat can be sown; 14 arpents of vineyards in which 230 measures of wine can be collected; 10 arpents of meadow in which 40 loads of hay can be collected; 25 bunuaria of woods.

3. Gerbertus a colonus and his wife a colona by the name of Adalgundis are dependents of Saint-Germain. They have living with them 2 children with these names: Bismodus, Gerberga. He holds 1 free farm having 11 bunuaria of arable land and 2 arpents of vineyards. He pays to the army tax a half an ox, 2 measures of wine in pannage; and he plows 7 perches. In payment he makes 1 arpent of wine; 3 chickens, 15 eggs. Manual labor, wood-cutting, cartage services, handiwork, as much as is required. Payment for wood due: 1 foot.

4. Teutgrimus a colonus and his wife a colona by the name of Ingberta are dependents of Saint-Germain. Teutberga is their daughter. He holds 1 free farm having 6 bunuaria of arable land and 1 arpent of vineyards. He pays as above.

5. Hiltbertus a colonus of Saint-Germain and his wife a slave hold a free farm having 12 bunuaria of arable land and [2] arpents of vineyards. He pays as above.

6. Amalgis a colonus and his wife a free woman by the name of Ardelindis are dependents of Saint-Germain. Odilelmus a colonus and his wife a slave by the name of Ermengardis are dependents of Saint-Germain. They have living with them 2 children with these names: Leudricus, Gisloina. These two [families] hold 1 free farm having 2 bunuaria of arable land and 2 arpents of vineyards. This farm pays the same as above.

7. Sicharius a colonus of Saint-Germain and his wife a free woman by the name of Solisma. Sicharia is their daughter. Ermbradus, [a dependent] of Saint-Germain, and his wife [a dependent] of Saint-Germain, have living with them 5 children by these names: Hildebertus, Godalbertus, Madalgarius, Ermbrada, Elia. These two [families] hold 1 free farm having 11 and a half bunuaria of arable land and 2 arpents of vineyards. This farm pays the same as above.

8. Sicboldus a colonus of Saint-Germain and his wife a free woman by the name of Ercamberta. Agebertus a colonus of Saint-Germain. These two [families] hold 1 free farm having 11 bunuaria of arable land and 2 arpents of vineyards. This farm pays the same as above.

9. Godebertus a lidus. Mattheus a colonus of Saint-Germain and his wife a colona by the name of Cristiana. These two [families] hold 1 free farm having 7 bunuaria of arable land, 1 arpent of vineyard, and 3 parts of an arpent.

10. Ermenulfus a colonus of Saint-Germain. Ingulfus a colonus of Saint-Germain. These two hold 1 free farm having 7 bunuaria of arable land and 2 and a half arpents of vineyards. This farm pays the same as above.

11. Airbertus a colonus of Saint-Germain. Adalradus a colonus and his wife a colona by the name of Frotlindis are dependents of Saint-Germain. These two [families] hold 1 free farm having 10 bunuaria of arable land and 2 arpents of vineyards. This farm pays [the same as above].

12. Edimius a colonus and his wife a colona by the name of Electa are dependents of Saint-Germain. Frothardus a colonus of Saint-Germain has his mother with him. These two [families] hold 1 free farm having 5 bunuaria of arable land and 1 and a half arpents of vineyards. This farm pays [the same as above].

13. Ermenoldus a colonus and his wife a colona by the name of Walda are dependents of Saint-Germain. They have living with them 2 children with these names: Sicrada, Sigenildis. Teutgarnus a colonus and his wife a colona by the name of Ermentrudis are dependents of Saint-Germain. Melismus is their son. These two [families] have 1 free farm having 11 bunuaria of arable land and 1 arpent of vineyard, and 2 parts of an arpent.

14. Airoardus a colonus of Saint-Germain holds half a farm having 5 bunuaria of arable land and 1 arpent of vineyard. He makes other payments as if that of half a farm.

How large were these rural households? What were the relationships between members of the household? Would all the inhabitants be listed? Who might have been left out and why? What patterns of naming emerge in the various families? What kind of economic activities did the household undertake?

48. SPIRITUAL MARRIAGES

In the Middle Ages marriage was both a social and spiritual institution. As an institution it had existed long before the appearance of Christianity and was the fundamental unit of society and central to family and inheritance customs. The procreation of legitimate offspring required marriage and marriage occurred to ensure the generation of legitimate offspring. The early church fathers' suspicion of women's sexual potential and their elevation of virginity as a higher mode of life resulted in many believers, especially women, rejecting marriage and the sexual activity it implied. Social convention and parental will, however, frequently required such people to marry, despite their individual wishes. As a result, a phenomenon developed in which couples who were legitimately and legally married cohabited but remained in perpetual chastity. The couple might reach an agreement not to consummate their marriage on their wedding night or they might agree to chastity after years of marriage and having raised their children. The clergy were at once in awe of such unions and suspicious of them. They saw the ability of a man and woman to cohabit in chastity as a sign of great grace but they were also suspicious about the average person's ability to withstand sexual temptation. Such chaste unions were found throughout the Middle Ages from the fourth through the sixteenth century.

Source: Trans. Lewis Thorpe in Gregory of Tours, *The History of the Franks* (Harmondsworth: Penguin Books, 1974), pp. 95–97; reprinted with permission.

The Marriage of Injuriosus and Scholastica (Sixth Century)

1.47 At the same time a certain Injuriosus, who was a wealthy man sprung from a senatorial family in Clermont-Ferrand, asked for the hand in marriage of a young woman in similar circumstances. The dowry had been handed over and he arranged a day for the wedding. Each of the two was an only child. The day of the ceremony arrived and the marriage service was duly performed. According to the custom the two were placed in the same bed. The young woman was greatly distressed: she turned her face to the wall and wept bitterly. Her husband said to her: "Tell me what is the matter. Tell me, I beg you." She remained silent and he said again: "I beg you, in the name of Jesus Christ, the son of God, be sensible and tell me what is making you so sad." She turned to him and answered: "If I were to weep every day of my life there would still not be enough tears to wash away the great grief which fills my heart. I had determined to preserve my poor body for Christ, untouched by intercourse with man. Now to my great sorrow I am deserted by him and I have not had the strength to achieve what I wanted so much; for on this day, which I could have wished never to see, I have lost that which I have preserved from the beginning of my life. I am forsaken by the sempiternal Christ, who promised me heaven as my dowry, for now it is my fate to be the consort of a mortal man. In place of the roses which shall never wither, the remains of my own faded roses disfigure rather than adorn me. At the moment when, beside the river of the Lamb, with its four separate streams, I should have put on the stole of purity, this wedding-gown brings me shame instead of honor. What is the use of our talking any longer? How unhappy I am! I should have had heaven as my reward, instead I am plunged into hell. If this was to be my fate, why could not the very first day of my life have also been my last? How I wish that I could have passed through death's dark portal before I had even sucked my mother's milk! If only the kisses of my gentle nurses could have been bestowed upon my dead body! The things of this world are loathsome to me, for my eyes are fixed on the hands of the redeemer, which were pierced to bring life to the world. I no longer see diadems glittering with precious jewels, but in my mind I gaze upon his crown of thorns. I have nothing but scorn for your vast estates and and your lands which spread so far and wide, for it is the joys of paradise for which I yearn. Your sun-drenched rooms are hateful to me when I gaze at our Lord sitting in majesty above the stars." As she raved on and the tears ran down her face, her young husband was moved with compassion. "Our parents are the most nobly-born in Clermont," he said. "We are their only children, and they have planned this marriage for us to produce children, so that when they are dead no heir from outside our families may claim the succession." "This earthly existence of ours is of no value," she replied. "Wealth is of no value, the pomp and circumstance of this world is of no value, the very life which we enjoy is of no value. We should look instead to that other life which is not ended when death finally comes, which is not dissolved by any illness, which is not closed by any accident, but where man lives for ever in eternal bliss, in a radiance which never fades, and, what is more than all this, where he is translated to cohabit with the angels and enjoys a happiness which is eternal, rejoicing in a meditation which lasts for ever, in the presence of our Lord himself." "Your sweet words have brought eternal life to me," answered her husband, "and this shines on me like a bright star. If you are determined to abstain from intercourse with me, then I will agree to what you want to do." "It is difficult for a man to make such a compact with women," she answered. "All the same, if you can agree that we shall remain unsullied in our human existence, then I will share with you the dowry which is promised to me by my spouse, the Lord Jesus Christ, to whom I have vowed myself as handmaiden and bride." Her husband crossed himself and said: "I will do what you ask." Hand in hand they went to sleep, and for many years after this they lay each night in one bed, but they remained chaste in a way which we can only admire, as was revealed when the time came for them to die. When her life's journey was over and the young woman had gone to join Christ, after he had performed all her funeral rites and had placed her in the tomb, her husband said: "I thank you, Lord Jesus Christ, master, and eternal God, for granting that I may hand back to your loving care this treasure as unsullied as when I received her from your hands." As he spoke, she smiled up at him. "Why do you say that," she said, "when no one asked you to?" Not long after she was buried her husband followed her. Although their two tombs were placed by different walls, a new miracle occurred which proved their chastity. When morning dawned and the people came to visit the place, they found the tombs side by side, although they had left them far apart. This shows that when heaven unites two people the monument which covers their buried corpses cannot hold them apart. Down to our own times the inhabitants of the place have chosen to call them "The Two Lovers." I have told their story in my *Book of Miracles*.

The Marriages of Queen Etheldreda (Seventh Century)

Source: Trans. J.A. Giles, *The Venerable Bede's Ecclesiastical History of England* (London: Henry G. Bohn, 1847), pp. 204-07; revised.

4.19 King Egfrid married Etheldreda, the daughter of Anna, king of the East Angles, whom we have frequently mentioned, a very religious man and exceptional in mind and deed. Previously, another man had married her, that is Tonbert, the chief of South Gyrwe. But he died shortly after the marriage and she was given to the aforesaid king. Although she lived with him for twelve years, nevertheless she preserved the glory of perfect virginity, just as Bishop Wilfrid of blessed memory told me when I inquired, because some people questioned it. He told me that he was a sure witness of her virginity. Indeed, Egfrid had promised he would give him many lands and much money if he could persuade the queen to consent to the conjugal act, because he knew the queen loved no one more than the bishop himself. Nor should it be doubted that the same thing could also happen in our time, which true histories tell us happened several times in earlier periods, with the assistance of the same Lord, who has promised to remain with us until the end of the world. And also, the divine miracle whereby her flesh, being buried, would not be corrupted, is a sign that she had remained uncorrupted by contact with a man.

For a long time she had been asking the king to permit her to relinquish the cares of the world and to serve the only true king, Christ, in a monastery. Finally, and with difficulty, she prevailed and entered the monastery of the Abbess Ebba, who was the aunt of King Egfrid, which was at a place called Coldingham. She received the veil and habit of a nun from Bishop Wilfrid. A year afterward, she herself became abbess in the region called Ely. There she built a monastery and began, by her deeds and the example of her heavenly life, to be the virgin mother of many virgins dedicated to God. It is reported about her, that from the time she entered the monastery, she never wore linen but only woolen clothing, and she would rarely wash in a hot bath, except just before one of the great feasts, such as Easter, Pentecost, and Epiphany, and then she did so last of all, after the other handmaidens of Christ who were present had washed, with the assistance of her and her attendants. Moreover, she rarely ate more than once a day, except on great feast days, or some other urgent occasion. She always remained in the church at prayer from matins until daybreak, unless she was prevented by serious illness. Some also say that, by the spirit of prophecy, in the presence of all, she not only foretold the plague from which she would die, but also the number of those of her monastery who would be snatched from this world. She was taken to the Lord, in the midst of her flock, seven years after she had been made abbess. As she had ordered, when her turn came, she was buried among them in a wooden coffin.

She was succeeded in the office of abbess by her sister Sexberga, who had been the wife of Erconbert, king of Kent. After her sister had been buried for sixteen years, she decided to exhume her bones, put them in a new coffin, and move them into the church. Accordingly, she ordered some of the brothers to look for a stone from which to make a coffin. They went on board a ship, because the area of Ely is surrounded on all sides by water or marshes, and has no large stones. They came to a small abandoned city not far from there, which is called in the English language Grantchester. Presently, near the city walls, they found a white marble coffin, beautifully made, and neatly covered with a lid made of the same stone. Concluding that God had caused their journey to be successful, they gave him thanks, and brought it to the monastery.

When her grave was opened, the body of the holy virgin and bride of Christ was brought into the light, it was found to be as uncorrupted as if she had died and been buried on that very day, as the aforementioned Bishop Wilfrid and others who knew about it can testify. But the physician Cynefrid, who was present at her death and when she was taken out of the grave, gave more certain proof and related that when she was ill she had a large tumor under her jaw. "I was ordered," he said, "to cut open that tumor in order to drain out the poisonous matter in it. When I did this she seemed to be somewhat easier for two days, so that many thought she would recover from her illness. But, on the third day, the former pains returned and she was snatched out of the world and exchanged pain and death for everlasting life and health. And when, after so many years, her bones were to be taken out of the grave, a tent was built over it and the whole congregation stood around it singing, the brothers on one side and the sisters on the other. The abbess with a few others went in to take up and wash the bones. All of a sudden, we heard the abbess cry out loudly from within, 'Glory be to the name of the Lord!' Not long after they called me in, lifting the door of the tent; then I saw the body of the holy virgin, raised from the grave and laid on a bed, as if she were asleep. Drawing the veil from her face, they showed to me the incision I had made, healed, so that, to my astonishment, instead of the gaping wound which she had when she was buried, there were only vestiges of a scar. Besides this, all the linen cloths in which her body had been wrapped, appeared whole and as fresh as if they had been wrapped around her chaste limbs that very day." It is reported that when she suffered from the tumor and the pain in her jaw, she was delighted with that sort of illness and used to say, "I know that I deserve to bear the weight of my sickness on my neck, because I remember, when I was very young, I bore the unnecessary weight of jewels. Therefore, I believe that our good God would have me endure the pain in my neck, so that I might be absolved from the guilt of my needless levity. Now, instead of gold and precious jewels, a burning red tumor juts out on my neck." It also happened that from the touch of the linen, devils were expelled from the bodies of possessed people, and sometimes other illnesses were cured. The coffin in which she was first buried is reported to have cured some who suffered from eye diseases who, praying with their heads touching the coffin, presently were delivered from the pain or dimness in their eyes. They washed the virgin's body, dressed it in new robes, brought it into the church, and laid it in the new coffin that had been brought, where it is held in great veneration to this day. The coffin was found to fit the virgin's body wonderfully, as if it had been made specifically for her; and the place for the head seemed to be cut and shaped exactly to fit her head.

Who arranged Injuriosus's marriage? Why? Why did Scholastica not want to consummate their marriage? How was their chastity proven? How was Etheldreda's virginity proven? What other things did Etheldreda do that show how pious she was?

49. A REBELLIOUS WIFE

Marriage was considered an hierarchical relationship, and since the time of St. Paul the church had preached the necessity for wives to be subordinate and obedient to their husband. Frankish women, however, were independent and resourceful, qualities necessary to survive in a tumultuous and violent society. Furthermore, ties to one's natal family were strong and marriage did not necessarily mean a shift in familial loyalties. Consequently, women could and did challenge their husband's rule. The story of Ingritude and Berthegund illustrates the pull of conflicting loyalties and the volatility of familial relationships in the early period of medieval history.

Source: Trans. Lewis Thorpe in Gregory of Tours, *History of the Franks* (Harmondsworth: Penguin Books, 1974), pp. 518-21; reprinted with permission.

9.33 About this time Ingritude who had founded a nunnery in the forecourt of St. Martin's church, went to the king to complain about her daughter (Berthegund). This was the nunnery in which also lived Berthefled, King Charibert's daughter. The moment Ingritude set out, Berthefled left in her turn and moved to Le Mans. She was a woman who ate and slept a lot, and she had no interest at all in the holy offices.

I propose to tell you the tale of Ingritude and her daughter from the beginning. Years before, when, as I have explained to you, Ingritude first founded her convent for young women inside the forecourt of St. Martin's church, she sent a message to her daughter, saying: "Leave your husband and come, so that I can make you abbess of the community which I have brought together." As soon as Berthegund received this stupid message, she came to Tours with her husband. She entered her mother's nunnery, saying to her husband: "Go back home and look after the children, for I don't propose to return with you. No one who is married will ever see the kingdom of heaven." The husband came to me and told me what his wife had said to him. I went to the nunnery and read aloud the relevant portion of the Nicene Creed, which runs as follows: "If any woman abandons her husband and scorns the married state in which she has lived honorably, saying that no one who is married will ever see the kingdom of god, let her be accursed." When Berthegund heard this, she was afraid of being excommunicated by God's bishops, so she left the convent and went back home again with her husband.

Three or four years passed. Then Ingritude sent another message to her daughter, asking her to come back. One day when he was away from home, Berthegund loaded some boats with her own possessions and those of her husband, and set out for Tours with one of her sons. Her mother was unwilling to keep her there, because the husband kept asking her to return. She was worried, too, about the charge to which Berthegund had exposed them both by her illegal act. She therefore packed her off to Bertram, bishop of Bordeaux, who was Berthegund's brother and Ingitrude's son. The husband followed Berthegund to Bordeaux, but Bertram said to him: "You married her without her parents' consent, and therefore she is no longer your wife." This was when they had been married for nearly thirty years! The husband visited Bordeaux several times, but Bishop Bertram refused to give his sister up. When King Guntram came to the town of Orleans, as I have told you in a previous book, the husband sought an audience and made a bitter attack on Bishop Bertram. "You have taken away my wife and her servants," he said. "What is more, and this ill becomes a bishop, you have seduced some of my women-servants and my wife has had intercourse with some of your men." The king was very angry and forced Bishop Bertram to promise to give Berthegund back to her husband. "She is a relation of mine," the king said. "If she has done anything wrong in her husband's home, it is for me to punish her. If she has done nothing wrong, why should her husband be humiliated in this way by having his wife taken away from him?" Bishop Bertram gave his promise. "I admit that my sister came to me after many years of married life," he said. "It was out of brotherly love and affection that I kept her with me as long as she wished to stay. Now she has left me. He can come to fetch her and take her away whenever he wishes, for I shall not stand in his way." That is what he said, but in secret he sent a messenger to Berthegund, telling her to take off her secular clothes, do penance, and seek sanctuary in St. Martin's church. All this she did. Then her husband arrived with a number of his men to force her to leave the church. She was wearing the habit of a nun and refused to go with her husband, for she said that she had taken a vow of penitence.

Meanwhile Bishop Bertram died in Bordeaux. Berthegund then came to her senses. "What a fool I have been," she said, "to listen to the advice of my stupid mother! Now my brother is dead, my husband has left me, and I am cut off from my children! How unhappy I am! Where shall I go, and what shall I do?" She thought things over for a while and then she went to Poitiers. Her mother wanted to keep her with her, but she was unable to do so. A quarrel then arose between them, and they kept on appearing before the king, Berthegund trying to establish a claim to what her father had left and Ingitrude asking for the estate of her late husband. Berthegund produced a deed of gift from her brother Bertram, saying: "My brother gave me this, and that, too." Her mother would not recognize the deed and tried to claim everything for herself. She sent men to break into her daughter's house and steal everything, including the deed of gift. By doing this Ingitrude put herself in the wrong, and at her daughter's request, she was forced to restore what she had taken. Maroveus, one of my fellow bishops, and I received letters from the king, ordering us to try to pacify the two of them. Berthegund came to Tours and appeared in our court, and we did all we could to make her listen to reason. Her mother took no notice of us. She went off to the king in a raging temper, determined to disinherit her daughter from all share in her father's property. She pleaded her case in the king's presence, without her daughter being there, and the judgment given was that one quarter should be restored to Berthegund, but that Ingritude should receive three quarters, to share with her grandchildren, whom she had from another son. The priest Theuthar, who had been one of King Sigibert's referendaries but had since entered the church and joined the priesthood, came at King Childebert's command to make the division. However, Berthegund refused to accept the judgment, and so the division was not made and the quarrel continued.

What did the Nicene Creed forbid? Why? What was the pretext to declare the marriage null? Why did Berthegund leave her husband? What was at the root of the quarrel between mother and daughter?

50. AN UNHAPPY MARRIAGE: GODELIEVE OF GHISTELLE

The life of St. Godelieve was written by the monk Drogon in 1084 as part of the process leading up to the elevation of her relics and the official recognition of her sanctity. In this, the church was merely following the popular recognition of the young woman's sanctity that had followed on her murder in 1070. The life of Godelieve tells the story of an unhappy wife whose husband and in-laws took an immediate dislike to her. Abandoned and abused by her husband and his family and servants, Godelieve endured a domestic martyrdom that ended only with her murder at her husband's orders. The vita *of Godelieve opens a window on the practice of marriage and the individual and social expectations that accompanied it. As well, it is possible to see how canon law was developing and how the church was gradually extending its jurisdiction over marriage. Godelieve's marriage was negotiated by her parents alone. It was an unhappy union but an indissoluble one that appeals to father, lord, or bishop could not annul. In the end, the long-suffering wife was freed from her marriage only by death, but popular sympathy was such that her friends and neighbors declared it a kind of martyrdom.*

Source: Trans. Jacqueline Murray and Abigail Young from Maurice Coens, "La Vie ancienne de Sainte Godelieve de Ghistelles par Drogon de Bergues," *Analecta Bollandiana* 44 (1926): 125-37.

Here Begins the Prologue of Drogon's Life of St. Godelieve

To Lord Radbod, by the grace of God bishop of Noyon-Tournai, Drogon, monk and unworthy priest, wishes you the good that surpasses every good.

The fame of your name and your nobility, most blessed father, is well and worthily remembered in many places. Indeed, you live in the knowledge of letters, you are zealous for the needs and utilities of your neighbors, as was Martha, and equally you occupy yourself with the word of the Lord, sitting at his feet, as did Mary. These characteristics, when they are found usefully in one person, are cultivated by students of wisdom, so that they rejoice that what seems lacking in themselves, according to the divisions of the grace of God, is, clearly granted by a good creator, present in a brother. Nor indeed is that done unjustly. For the singular seed of charity reigns in them, which chooses for its neighbor, without a doubt, what it desires for itself. Truly, most excellent bishop, when I perceive that you are considered excellent, according to the agreement and praise of many people, I reflect diligently in my heart that it is right that you, who are exalted by the great gift of all virtues, should give counsel to me in my thinking and sustain me when I slip. For I was compelled by the repeated urging of many of the faithful, to begin the martyrdom of holy Godelieve, which is beyond my powers; first treating from which parents she was born, then, nubile, to which man she was betrothed, then by whose plots and by whom and in what way she was martyred. And so these things, insofar as they were true, worthy of relating, and apt for recollection, I described equally in a document and sent it to you, dearest father, so that, by your authority, if indeed you judge it worthy, they might remain established and confirmed and, by your pontifical decree, they might be valid to whomever they should come. But yet, venerable father, before my words are read by many people, first you yourself read them carefully, such as they are, prune what is superfluous, make clear what is not, so that your work makes evident what they try to say, so that they may be clearer. But, indeed, we heard that these events, which we recorded, were so from those who even today are alive and testify that they saw these things. For that reason, let no one at all criticize me, because, even if I were silent, holy authority shouts out that many had also done this. Truly, I shall leave it to your judgment, and the judgment of the wise, if I am criticized by some about these matters, and I shall begin my story as well as I am able.

Goodbye. Here ends the prologue.

Here begins the life or passion of the same saint, which is on the third Kalends of August [30 July].

1. The kindness of the omnipotent God calls both sexes to his mercy. Now he causes this one to come to his kingdom by various sufferings of tribulations; now he crowns that one with victorious endurance; now he rewards another, who is strong in the peace of the church, the increase of virtues, and the love of God and his neighbor, with a worthy reward. Moreover, when all are crowned, these ones with roses, those with white lilies, he remains for everyone the eternal and highest good, and is considered as one by them, although it is agreed that he is varied in the quality of merits, according to the divine goodness, to these in martyrdom, to those by the sum of peace. For also, in heaven, the palm of victory awaits the martyrs and eternal glory awaits the confessors, but how much and of what kind we can scarcely imagine what to say, nor can the human heart, the soul, or the mind consider. But, when the faithful soul, unconquered and persevering, is protected from the many plots of a cunning enemy, she is crowned by the greater glory, the more constant she was found in the face of abusive treatment. Here she places the shield of humility, while on either side she strengthens herself with an impenetrable breastplate of endurance. In fact, also, when the rest of the virtues join themselves to these others, they exalt the humble mind, strengthened by them, they make her an inhabitant of heaven. And when she enjoys eternal glory, her ashes and bones in the ground are venerated far and wide, with miracles. But now, to come to

the point, here an orderly account should commence, which will show the story of the life of St. Godelieve, and the time and place of her suffering.

2. Therefore, she was born in the Boulonnais district, specifically in the city which is called Boulogne-sur-Mer, coming from well-born parents, her father, Heinfrid, and her mother, Odgive. Moreover, being reared in the tender years of her childhood, she began to be devoted to God, obeying her parents, now preparing for every suffering, now living her young life as clean and right-eously as possible. And so, in this way, she arrived at adolescence and then at full marriageable age. She was sought by many men because she was strong in virtuous behavior, truly gentle and humble in her action, and sweet and affable in prudent speech. Among others, there was one, Bertolf by name, powerful, of high birth and wealth, whose dower was more pleasing to both parents than the other suitors. So the girl was betrothed to him according to the law of marriage. But, on the very same day that he took his bride home, mentally assaulted by the enemy, he began to hate her. Meanwhile, moreover, he began to regret his undertaking, sometimes also to blame himself on account of what he had done. Not only do bad words corrupt good behavior, as is the saying of the apostle, but also bad behavior renders the mind of a bad person worse when it is stirred up by the curses of reproaches. For also, he was driven to hatred by the words of his mother, who ought to have rejoiced in the manner of a good mother, at the good fortune of her married son.

3. To be sure, the saying of certain secular wisdom, that all mothers-in-law hate daughters-in-law, has some truth in it. They are weakened in this vice, as they wish their sons to be married, however, they begrudge both them and the women that they marry. For thus speaking metaphorically: "Surely, dear son," she said, "you were able to find crows enough in your own country that you should want to bring home a crow from another country? What did you do? What would make you want to do such a thing? Surely in this matter you ought to have taken the advice of your mother and of others who advise you, equally as you took your father's advice? And what made you want to do it? In fact, you will find you cannot correct this erroneous deed since you decided to make the mistake." Thus, upset by these and other of his mother's words, he was burdened by sadness and this great sickness of his soul grew of itself greater day by day. For, now alone in his mind, now sharing the advice of his friends, he would complain: "I have troubled my mother's spirit by my marriage." He said, "No, rather I have lost myself by not taking better advice." Moreover, his bride had black eyebrows, black hair, and white skin, which is welcome and very pleasing in a woman and is oftentimes held in honor. For she was also of the best appearance to the beholder, cheerful so that you would think that she would rejoice with you when happy and would seem nothing but compassion-ate for you when sad.

4. But that same Bertolf did not want to be present at his wedding but, as if concentrating on other and more beneficial business, on account of its usefulness, he acted in a certain way, now going to the market, now meeting with friends who lived elsewhere. And, indeed, he did this in order that he might be absent, lest he see her whom he hated. Although unwilling, his mother celebrated the wedding, taking the place of the groom. She brightened a gloomy face, hiding the poison she was carrying in her mind. Through three full days her son was absent, while the marriage rites were celebrated by his mother and people hostile to the match. After the third day, Bertolf returned and Godelieve, sent away from her own home, with her husband, along with the household, went to live at his father's house. The newly married bride, not deserving this, deserving a better husband, sat at home, governing the household, now with the distaff and spindle, now with the loom, she relieved the sadness in her heart. She spent her nights alone. She poured out prayers, not without tears, that God would grant her husband a better disposition. When her husband saw this, he began to discuss with his parents how he could discredit her by his mode of life, because clearly she was a shame to him and a detriment to his way of life. For now, also, the father, himself, pitied the son (if indeed this can be called pity) and, along with his son, he hated Godelieve. A servant was suggested to him, who would serve her badly and who would bring her one loaf a day, at the stated hour, and nothing else. But the woman of God gave thanks to God for the loaf she received. She would take it, distributing half to the poor, receiving the other half to nourish her own body. For, as a part of her martyrdom, she saw that her servants abounded in wealth and had both meat and plenty of food to eat. But she had only bread with salt to eat and water, once a day. For her husband said to the servant waiting on her that she would accept nothing else and if he did something other than what was ordered, he would be punished.

5. Nor yet did the hostile husband rest, but he planned greater trials, he prepared more cruelties, he who tortured the servant of God and who made her brighter in the eyes of almighty God and humankind. He said, "That which I have given to my wife seems to be much too much. Anything more is a loss to me. Now, let half of the whole loaf of bread be taken away and reserved for general need. Let only the other part be given to her. And so I shall take from her the pretext of charity by which she grows strong. I will take away her mind, so that she is able to think neither about God nor herself." In fact, the husband thought this; he spoke and declared the deed equally with the word. And she received what was given, and gave thanks to the Lord for such quantity. She also used to pray this prayer: "You, God, who is creator of everything, be, I beseech you, a help for my weakness. Behold with what kind and how many miseries I am afflicted. Although, my pious Lord, the quantity of my

portion is reduced by my husband, however, it scarcely diminishes in me the feeling of good will. And let the pauper also accept this half. Indeed, even let it be given to you through this pauper." Thus she spoke and distributed a piece of the half of the loaf of bread to a pauper. O, disposition of a pious will, o endurance, one and the same persevering in this woman! You always endure in the same way in opposing circumstances. Your husband cursed you; you blessed him. He envied you this; you reconciled God to him, in both your prayers and your mind, if a good God could be reconciled with an impious man. In fact, he also wished death for you; he threatened it. You always prayed to God that he might live.

It was especially difficult for her to live on so small a ration, but she did not want to break that promise which she had once made to God. People in her region, rejoined to her by affinity, felt compassion for her in this situation. They distributed bread, meat and fish, and those things given for the use of humanity, by which also she lived, while the reasons for her distress were there to see in the washing of the rags with which she covered her body. Nor ought it be left unsaid that everyone, present or absent, sided with her, having compassion, even also those who only knew her by name. For God gives this to every single one of his faithful, that the good part of human beings shall love him, so that light may thus gather and be joined with light. It would be like a monster if two opposites were joined in her.

6. But his own party favored Bertolf, his adherents contriving to give him evil advice. They incited Bertolf to commit a crime against the innocent woman, he who, on his own, was quite ready, willing, and able to do so. Because of such injuries by her husband or many, or even the most, by her whole household, Godelieve was forced to flee from her husband himself, needy, even with bare feet, to depart from her own country and, with only one companion along, to return to her native land and her father. There she was asked about the injustice of her husband and about the injuries of her household, if indeed they had united against her out of their love for their lord and had hurled curses against the pious wife. Then, finally, her father, having compassion for the misfortunes of his daughter, gave her shelter for however long, until by holier advice, he might foster a more useful plan which would be a particular honor for his cause and of more use to his daughter. Finally, finding what seemed better to him, he approached Count Baudouin, recounting in order the causes of the injuries that had happened to him and his daughter, making it clear at the end how her husband had forced her to flee. But the count sent him to the bishop in whose diocese Bertolf resided. Naturally, he who was prudent and prepared was to consult on the cause of every necessity to any person. The count said, "It is the bishop's role to rule Christendom, to correct any things that are outside the path of holy order. But it falls to me to

aid in those things which he cannot solve on his own. Episcopal authority compels him first to look after his own flock. But if he will not obey or slights the bishop's jurisdiction, then I will come to the matter, in so far as it is in me, I shall consider your needs." What more is there to dwell on? The worthless man was forced to take Godelieve back. He solemnly swore that he would not mistreat her. He received her back with a legal right and led her home again with him. But, as the first time, she resided alone in her house. She prayed to the almighty God that he would deign to console her, who also consoled his servants.

7. As a matter of fact, some people, certain of the then friends of the said Bertolf, declared their longstanding anger and enduring hatred towards this woman. They slandered her in this, that she did not become gentler or softer by God's instructions, nor by the authority of the bishop, nor by the orders of the prince against her, but that neither the condition of human union nor worldly rumor would soften her fierce mind. The woman dear to God met those people hurling curses with sweet words and the handmaid of God forbade her husband to be cursed. "It is a crime and a sin," she said, "to speak a little ill, moreover, it is held a great sin to curse. For this, as I have heard, the apostle commanded: 'Bless your persecutors; bless and do not curse them.' By which, let anyone contain his speech from curses of every kind and his tongue from slander. For the very act of hearing of this is a sin to me, far less shall I, myself, utter curses. For thus God poured forth his grace and tenderness on my heart. Let such hatreds be distant to me and let my husband nurture me as his own." While some people, commiserating the harshness of her misfortune, lamented for her because of her miseries, she, full of divine grace, consoled herself. She showed a happy face and smiling mouth, because the spirit dwelling in her mind rendered her ever cheerful. For, in adversity, she adhered to the Lord, she loved his laws, embracing them all with total devotion, which precepts, although she served him, she loved because of their merit. For her name showed this very fact, because, in the Germanic language, it means "dear to God."

8. Moreover, it is wonderful to remember and it is worthy to inscribe on the pages that, although some were lamenting the causes of her misfortunes and were saying that she was alone, she, who neither had nor would have the pleasures of the body, nay, rather would not even enjoy the delights of this world (for lovers judge these things according to the mind of this same world; indeed, those who are earthly are followers of earthly things), nevertheless, laughing at the frivolousness of the words, with a modest countenance, invincible both in faith and hope, met these complainers with a brief speech. She replied from a ready spirit, "Truly, I by no means worry about the pleasures of the body and I count as little the riches of the transitory world. For whatever we see, whatever

we have, whatever we want to have but don't yet have, is transient. For not even a person endures. For even in one fleeting hour such a one passes away and, according to the sum of truth, all flesh is comparable to the flowering plant which now blooms and, after a very little time, cut down, it withers." Then, inspired by the spirit of prophecy, here she added these things that follow to what came before: "One should not say, nor hope, that I am unhappy, although I am battered by these ills in the raging sea of life and I am afflicted, as you claim, by unhappiness. As a matter of fact, I should be praised above all the women of all Flanders who are alive today, and I will appear to all as more wealthy than I now imagine. He will do this for me, who is thought to be most powerful, who enriches whom he wishes with his virtues, and raises the wretched from the dust of this unhappiness." And so, saying such things, she declared herself to be comforted by the Holy Spirit and her mind eased and fortified with heavenly consolation. And, moreover, she knew beforehand that she would be regarded an inhabitant of heaven through those things which she was about to endure. In fact, persevering to the end, she would be distinguished by the good works of her virtues. I am witness to the common faith of humankind, I who prepare these accounts, whatever they may be. I have both known and seen that monks, who were practiced in the gift of highest chastity, endowed with the zealousness of good will, in the height of virtue, resisting whatever is contrary to good, are edified by her sweet exhortation and more ready of mind to avoid vice. For this sort of grace dwelt in her, given by divine mercy, so that whoever talked with her would feel compassion for the one who had endured or was enduring unworthy things; he would rejoice when he realized that she was stepping on her adversities as if she were superior.

9. Now, let what has been said about her life suffice. Henceforth, let the pen describe how she passed from this life to God. And so, when every trick and every deceitful contrivance of the aforesaid Bertolf had come to naught, by the grace of God, so that neither by hunger, nor by his cunning device, was he able to make the holy woman die, he began to worry, then to be disturbed and, frequently, agitated by his thoughts. And, seething inside with unbridled spurs of anger, and now and then muttering, turning over in his mind such confused thoughts as: "Can no such human device be found which will be an aid to my purpose? For I live, and I live unhappily so long as I see all my cleverness to be overcome. I am wasting away because she lives. While she lives, there is no life in my body. For hunger did not oppress her, nor did a long fast wear out her body. As a matter of fact, she flourishes safe and, by as much more as she is oppressed and worn down by hardships, so much more brightly her youthfulness shines forth. And, if in this way, an opportunity for my plan does not succeed, another will be found, tried, and shall be taken up. She can perish either by sword or by fire or by water, or even by some other torment that our cus-

tom may find." He was excited by these frenzies and he was moved by this understanding to wound and savage his own mind without a weapon, before he could touch her with any torment. Then, he called two serfs, specifically Lantbert and Hacca. He sought their advice about what he might be able to try on her, about which kind of torments he would inflict, to kill her. They replied as seemed best to them. They offered more useful advice and encouraged him. They set a day; they devised the type of torment by which she might more easily die and the deed be done more secretly. Moreover, they also set a time and they set out what time of day or night might be more useful or secret for doing this.

10. Now, the day came, or rather the time was established, on which it would be made clear what and what sort of woman full of God she was, and on which she would be rewarded by glory in heaven, she whose heart was shining with divine grace from heaven, which grace her virtue, as endurance, signified with humility. Truly, on that night on which they planned, by the deceit of criminals, to kill her, before sunset, her husband came home to her. First, he kissed her with a false mouth, embracing her, feigning a smile on his mouth, who nurtured poison in his breast. Then, he did that which he was unaccustomed to do with her. He sat beside her, as if with a cheerful face or a happy heart. Therefore, both of them were seated on the couch. Since she was afraid to approach her husband, and since she showed reverence to him in not a few ways, as seemed proper to do, he drew her to him by the hand, relieving her fear with gentle words, then, having begun with words of this kind, he spoke to the servant of the Lord: "It is not a little sad to me that I am so fierce towards you and that I seem to be thought of such stubborn mind that you are not accustomed to my presence nor to soft words nor the shared pleasures of carnal desire. But, indeed, I do not know what sent misfortune between us. I do not know what discord alienated my mind, so that I became a stranger to you and seem scarcely in command of my affections. As it seems to me, this is caused by the devil. For he injures the hearts of mortal people, now inciting envy in one, now hatred in another. Truly, I want to put an end to this distance between us and to nurture you as a dear wife, and so, by gradually putting away hatred, to join our minds and our bodies as one." O, heart infected with every evil! O, venomous tongue of man! You imitate Judas, the betrayer of the Lord; in wickedness that man gave a false kiss to the gentle lamb. You offered kisses to your wife and, with a cunning heart, you comforted an innocent woman. Judas betrayed the king and lord of all to hateful crowds, for a reward. You betrayed your wife to serfs whom you intended to reward with some present. Therefore, if we may compare great things to little ones, and the lowest to the highest, then an equal punishment, an equal weight will befall you on account of your wickedness. "I have found," he said, "a woman, who boasted she was able to bind us together in firm love, then to cause us to love each other all the

time, so that nowhere on earth would two spouses love each other so greatly. Indeed, I entrusted that business to the serfs, Lantbert and Hacca. These will lead the woman to you. Trust all of this to them. For that reason, therefore, I am mentioning this matter to you ahead of time, lest it be unknown to you, lest you refuse, indeed, lest you be worried." When the underhanded husband had finished this, she replied, "I am the Lord's servant. I commit my whole being to him. But, at least, I will agree if it can be done without involving any wickedness." O, happy woman devoted to God! You made God your counselor ahead of anyone else, and, so, he cares for you. You feared for yourself, lest by magic he be separated from you. For this reason, you chose marriage, lest you lose the Lord, who joins people in marriage. When she had stated the aforesaid things, she fell silent. But Bertolf, getting up from the couch on which he was sitting and mounting a horse, went to spend the night at Bruges, waiting there until the death of his wife was announced to him, so that he would be reckoned innocent of committing the crime.

11. Then, the sun setting, night fell. Everyone took refreshment and, overcome by sleep, rested, when, behold! Lantbert and Hacca appeared, rousing the lady from her sleep. "Get up, lady," they said, "for we come, anxious about your business and we bring the woman about whom our master spoke to you. Behold! she stands in front of your gates, already waiting a long time for you. Quick! Get up! Hurry! lest you miss this opportunity." First, she protected herself with the sign of the holy cross. Then she commended herself totally to God. And when she was about to get dressed, these men immediately prevented it. "With bare feet;" they said, "with loose hair; come only in your shift. So, thus, this business will certainly benefit you. Now, in the silent middle of the night, and before dawn, indeed, it must be done to you." Soon, she added to their replies: "I commend myself to the Almighty. I am his creature. He, the most merciful, will see what is done to me. Moreover, then, I give myself to your care." And, getting up, she continued on her way with them. But, what they did, or what they said once or twice, was frivolous, a great evil, and a trick. Indeed, it did not seem worth noting. But, the third time, when she was also deceived by them, they stretched a noose around her neck and, with their hands, they also strangled her with all their strength, lest screaming, she be heard. And when they realized that she was already unconscious, they submerged her in water, so that if any life or breath survived, that element would extinguish it. And, by the wondrous disposition of God, it happened that if anything was made unclean by exposure to life on earth, by this element it would be rendered cleansed and bright.

12. Afterwards, the business of her enemies was finished. For, likewise, they carried her to her own bed, rearranged her, putting her in her clothes. And, while the sun was ascending to the highest heavens, the household was murmuring together about what might have prevented their mistress from rising.

For she had been accustomed to get up either before dawn or soon after sunrise, to bustle about, to give orders to the others, and to go to church. Why, they wondered; however, they did not want to wake up the lady, believing her to be detained either by illness or by sleep. But, when the day was already somewhat advanced, someone entered her room to try to wake her up but, because she was dead, she couldn't be awakened. The word spread. The neighbors came to view the body but no wound, no sign of a sword was found on her whole body. But, finally, bruises appeared on her neck, where the evil henchmen had stretched the noose. Some claimed she had died a natural death, others murmured otherwise. And how she was viewed by them determined what they thought. On the same day, she was quickly buried. And, since bread, which might be distributed for the good of her soul, was in short supply, they went to correct it and purchased grain. And the same grain benefitted the purchaser. For, indeed, it increased both in itself and when made into flour, so that it surpassed all measurement, and the customer marveled at the occurence of this sign. Praise to you, Lord! For your honor she was as generous to the poor as she was able, while alive; you graciously demonstrated that in this miracle also.

13. As a matter of fact, as well, part of the ground there, where she was killed, was changed into white rocks, so that the Lord could demonstrate her merit, and so that he could reveal to all the faithful the place of her death. So, this happened. Certain people, from devotion to the saint, took earth from there and brought it home, which, afterwards, they were amazed, was turned into jewels. I, myself, who am writing this, coming as a witness, saw the same jewels and, because of this, I blessed the name of the Lord. Almighty God also changed another element to the glory of his honor, so that he made public what happened and, at the same time, how great was the merit of the woman drowned there. For anyone with a fever, anyone suffering from some illness, approaching there, drank the very same water, immediately rejoiced to have received for themselves the desired cure from her merits. Similarly, at her tomb, the Lord often demonstrated how high she stood in heaven, since he distinguished that same tomb, indeed, rather her body, with heavenly signs. Truly, we will say a little concerning much and we will bring public testimony of the signs, so that by these anyone may easily believe how greatly the daughter of the Lord flourishes in the glory of heaven.

14. Now, a father brought his son, crippled from birth, to her tomb, praying that he would deserve to be healed by her merit. Truly, after some time, the crippled boy was straightened, whom, indeed, the father brought back home healthy. Moreover, that boy was called Algotus. Because he was a boy, he was getting ready to be instructed in letters. But, when he became strong in body, he received holy orders, gradually rising to the diaconate.

15. A certain lame woman lay before the gates of the monastery of St. Trudo for nine years, waiting in that same place with others, where she might be healed. Truly, many having been healed, many having been straightened, she alone continued, so that the merit of the tomb would be revealed far and wide, by God's providence. At last, hearing reports of the memory of holy Godelieve, she had herself brought to the place and praying there, she awaited the Lord's mercy. Truly, indeed, waiting there only a short time, she was cured, made healthy, and happy, she returned to her native land on her feet, safe and sound. And this happened in a wondrous way. For she demonstrated the same piety towards the needy which had distinguished the saint while she was alive.

16. A certain man, on the sabbath day, at a time during which such work was not allowed, collected grain in the field. Kernels of grain stuck to his hand. With his other hand, he tried to brush off the grain but he was by no means able. Realizing that he wished to remove the grain but was unable, you would have seen him, with one hand trying to help the other, but more and more grains adhered. Soon, recognizing that he was guilty of the deed, he came to the tomb of the dead woman already frequently discussed. He flung himself on the ground to pray. The prayer not yet finished, he stretched out his fingers, then the grains fell from the hand and the palm was visible.

17. A solemn feast day was approaching which was highly regarded by the people. A priest, standing nearby after mass, was giving orders so that it would be observed by everyone and no one should do any work on it. A woman of the same town, hearing and giving little consideration to the instructions of the priest, considered it of little importance. She prepared a dye in an earthenware vat and took up a stick so that she could stir it. Suddenly, the stick adhered to both her hands. She struggled, now by stretching out, now by drawing back her arms but nothing worked. The story of the miraculous event spread: her household appeared; her neighbors came running. Some of the bystanders tried to wrest it from her hands; some of them were afraid to touch it. Finally, forced by her punishment, she sought out the tomb of her helper, praying on the ground, seeking the merit of God's holy woman. Between her tears and words of prayer, first the fingers, then the hand were all of a sudden freed from the stick. The stick fell, the woman healed, returned to her home.

How did Drogon learn the details of Godelieve's life? Why was Bertolf chosen to be Godelieve's husband? Where were the couple to live? When did the couple marry? Who participated in the ceremony? How did Godelieve react to how she was treated? How did Godelieve's father receive her when she returned home? Why was Godelieve's father sent to the bishop? Did Bertolf and Godelieve consummate their marriage? How did Bertolf propose that the couple overcome their marital difficulties? What does the story of Godelieve suggest about marriage and about a wife's options?

51. A LORD ASSERTS HIS RIGHTS:
GERALD OF AURILLAC

An individual's status as free or servile had an important effect on the shape of a medieval person's life. Serfs or villiens were tied to their land and owed traditional dues and services to their manor lord. Special fines were levied by the lord for granting his permission for a servile woman to marry (in England called the merchet*). Similarly, servile women who gave birth to an illegitimate child or were caught fornicating could also be fined. Related to these kinds of fines is the idea that a lord's rights extended to the body of his tenants and that he could demand sexual access to his female serfs. It is a highly problematic belief, however, given how little concrete evidence is available. Furthermore, villiens were not the equivalent of slaves who were owned by their masters. Rather, they were people in an economic and legal relationship, albeit a highly restrictive one, with their lord. Both parties had legal obligations and protections that would render* droit de seigneur *highly improbable. Nevertheless, if indeed such a practice did occur in the early Middle Ages, there may be a faint echo of it found in the life of Gerald, count of Aurillac (d. 909) written by Odo of Cluny (879-942). Gerald was a noble who tried to live a Christian life while remaining in the world. His* vita *is filled with examples such as this one which illustrate how the life of Christian chastity could be at odds with the privileges and responsibilities of secular rulers.*

Source: Trans. J. Murray from Odo of Cluny, *Vita S. Geraldi Comitis confessoris* in *Acta Sanctorum*, 13 October, vol. 6 (Paris, 1868), pp. 304-05.

The old deceiver tested the virtue of the youth, and finding I do not know what of the divine in him, flared up in envy, and for this, as much as he was able, took trouble to overpower him by all the tricks of temptation. But Gerald had already learned to flee to the bosom of divine tenderness in prayer and to refute his tests through the grace of Christ. But the enemy, insatiably envious, having learned by experience that he was unable to dominate him through the pleasure of the flesh, roused the winds of war against him through wicked men, as we said above, so that through them he could attack the altar of his piety in his heart, into which he himself was by no means able to intrude. Let us return to his youth—the most ingenious enemy was ardently inflamed against his chastity, which the chaste youth himself dearly loved. For it was new and unusual to him, that some young boy should have totally avoided the destruction of his modesty. Therefore, he insistently suggested to him sexual desire which is his first and greatest strength for leading astray humankind. When Gerald had thoroughly resisted this, the enemy was tortured that he had not been able to introduce this, at least, to the doors of his heart. Therefore, he repeated an ancient trick and returned to the instrument of deception by which Adam and his posterity used often to be deceived; I am speaking about woman. It is said he brought a certain young girl to his attention. While Gerald incautiously considered the color of her clear skin, soon he began to weaken at its attractiveness. O, if on the spot he had understood what was hidden under the skin! Because the beauty of the flesh is certainly nothing except the disguise of the skin. He turned away his eyes but the image impressed on his heart through them remained. And so he was in anguish, seduced and scorched by a blinding fire. At last vanquished, he sent to the girl's mother to tell her that he would come in the night. Following the messenger, he violently hurried to the death of his soul. But meanwhile, just as captives accustomed to their chains, groaning, remember their original freedom, Gerald sighed and remembered the customary sweetness of divine love. Although with weak intent, he asked God that that temptation would not completely devour him. Coming to the arranged place, the girl entered the room. Because it was cold he stood beside the fireplace, facing her. Now divine grace looked on Gerald. For then the girl seemed to him deformed, so that he would not believe her to be the one he had seen, although her father assured him she was. But understanding that this did not happen without divine will, that the same young girl should not have the same attractiveness in his eyes, he immediately gathered himself to Christ's mercy. Disturbed and sighing deeply, he mounted his horse and with no reluctance, made haste to leave hurriedly, giving thanks to God. Perhaps too much cold attacked him who had allowed himself to burn for the whole night, so that clearly an icy severity would punish a tepid pleasure. Moreover, he immediately ordered the father to give the girl in marriage. By legal witness, Gerald gave her her freedom and granted her a certain small piece of land. Perhaps, suspecting his weakness, he had her marriage hastened. This was why, as an act of charity, he gave her the gift of her freedom, lest her marriage be delayed. But you who were to become a cedar of paradise, how could you be so agitated? Certainly, so that you might learn how you might be on your own. For also your patron, that is the prince of the apostles, to whom afterwards you committed yourself and everything of yours, would not have known himself well enough, unless the moment of temptation had taken him by surprise. But now you experienced what a man is like on his own and how he can be by the grace of God: do not disdain to have compassion on the fragility of your supplicants. Moreover, we know that it is not unusual for the saints to be tempted. For they are born with vices inherent in their corrupt nature, that is so that wherever they struggle, struggling they may overcome, and overcoming they may be crowned. Moreover, there is a difference between he who, receiving the pleasure of vice, succumbs and he who, fighting against it, overcomes and rather occupying his mind with the pleasure of virtue drives out the poison of perverse pleasure, which perhaps he has devoted himself to for a time, with the antidote of pious supplication. And the youth, more prudent from experiencing this danger, like someone in a slippery place, after hitting his foot, proceeded more cautiously, being sufficiently careful that the eyes should announce nothing to his heart, from which death might enter his soul through its windows.

What was Gerald's weak spot? What were the implications of this for women's role in society? What social status did the girl hold? What are the implications of Gerald's visit? What effect would Gerald's subsequent actions have had on her life?

52. DUPLICITOUS WIVES AND ILLEGITIMATE HEIRS

In the twelfth century, the church was trying to enforce its various teachings on marriage, with greater or lesser success. The task of enforcing these regulations fell to the local clergy, that is, the bishops and their parish priests. There were, however, few mechanisms for enforcement at this early date, aside from moral suasion, excommunication, and threats of punishment in the afterlife. While bishops might carry a great deal of authority and be respected, nevertheless, some people were sufficiently confident or obstinate to resist their rulings. This is the case in this anecdote taken from the life of St. Hugh. Hugh of Avalon, a Carthusian monk, became bishop of Lincoln in 1186. His hagiographer, Adam of Eynsham, was a friend and confidant and incorporated personal insights into his life of the holy man. This passage reveals how the bishop, although widely recognized for his holiness and rectitude, was unable to impose his will on the recalcitrant. It also demonstrates how the secular and ecclesiastical views of marriage could sometimes be in conflict and how the church could use spiritual means to enforce secular ends. In this period the issue of an individual's status as free or servile remained important. It was generally believed that if one unwittingly married a serf, the union could be dissolved and that serfs should not marry without their lord's consent. The issue of legitimacy also loomed large. Men feared the introduction of "strangers" into their lineage and jealously guarded their wife's chastity. These concerns were reflected in secular laws which barred illegitimate children from inheriting and canon laws which excluded illegitimate men from ordination to the priesthood.

Source: Trans. Decima L. Douie and Hugh Farmer, *The Life of St. Hugh of Lincoln* (London: Thomas Nelson, 1962), vol. 2, pp. 20–27; reprinted with permission.

Book 4, Chapter 5: *How the wife of a certain knight in order to defraud her brother-in-law pretended to be pregnant and passed off another woman's child as hers, and how some of the participators in such a crime died as a result of the bishop's excommunication.*

There was in the county of Lincoln a knight already advanced in years, whose wife was barren. His brother, an honorable and worthy knight, was by hereditary right his lawful heir if he died without children. His wife disliked the brother and having never concealed her feelings, feared that if she were left a widow he would be her guardian. As she had no child of her own, with serpentine guile and wickedness she passed off another child as hers, in order to shut him out of the inheritance. With a belly swollen and big with deceit, she fastened a cushion over her womb, to pretend that she was pregnant, but in reality her crime was all that she had conceived. The knight to whose prejudice the malicious and cunning device had been planned, seeing that he was being tricked, but unable either to prove or prevent it, brought the matter to the notice of his friends, and pressed them for their advice, but received no satisfactory answers.

Meanwhile the woman took to her bed, and groaned as if she were in travail. She produced a newborn female infant which she had procured from a woman in a village in the neighborhood, and brought it up with as much care as if it had been really her own. She summoned the true mother, and made her foster-mother to her own child. These events occurred not far from Lincoln just when Easter was approaching. The knight who had been defrauded by a woman's guile came to the bishop accompanied by certain men of repute who had already heard rumors of the malicious fraud, and told the whole story which aroused the suspicions of all who heard it. Nobody yet knew for certain to whom the female infant belonged or how her reputed mother had obtained her with the intention of disinheriting him.

The righteous and holy man was greatly roused when he heard about it and immediately summoned the husband of the wicked woman to his presence. When he came he interrogated him privately, charged him with it, and rebuked him, trying hard to make him confess his guilt. He, however, fearing the scoldings of his shameless wife more than the wrath of God, and ensnared by her crafty tongue, at first denied his complicity in the crime. At last under pressure from the bishop, who bluntly told him that the general belief was that, since he was so old and sickly, the child could not possibly be his and that he was unlikely to be unaware of his wife's wiles. At length, being driven into a corner he gave himself away, saying, "For a long time, owing to my bad state of health, I have had very little intercourse with my wife. I should like, if you will allow me, to learn the truth about this from her. Tomorrow morning I will let you know whatever I find out, and will be ready to take your counsel on what can best be done about everything which transpires from my investigations." The bishop then let him depart with a final warning. "Know," he said, "that tomorrow we shall launch a solemn and terrible sentence of excommunication against the perpetrators of this evil deed and their abettors, if you do not do what you have promised." After this dismissal he returned home and gave the barren mother a full report of his conversation with the bishop.

The brazen woman's reaction was to abuse him so vigorously that the unhappy man was dissuaded from returning to his faithful counselor. Reluctantly yielding to his tyrant, whom contrary to the order of nature he had long been accustomed to obey, he stayed at home, and added the sin of deceit to his former error. The following day was the most holy and glorious feast of our Lord's Resurrection, and the bishop, having preached to the people, described the whole business to them, making plain the seriousness of the crime, and asserting that he must bring the full weight of his episcopal authority to bear upon such an offence. Having informed them of the enormity of committing such a sin not only against one's own brother but against any of one's neighbors, since it meant that he and his descendants would irrevocably lose their rights, he said that that kind of sin was of such immense seriousness as to cause the eternal death of its perpetrators. He then excommunicated all who had dared by means of the fictitious birth described to deprive the knight, who has already been frequently mentioned, of his inheritance.

Satan did not long delay to exercise his cruel sway over those delivered over to him by the sentence of this holy man. On the following night he suddenly claimed and seized the soul of the man who had connived at his wife's wickedness by concealing it, instead of rebuking and correcting it. He was found dead in the bed on which he had lain down to enjoy, as he thought, a quiet rest. Let this be a lesson to those who are led into crime and sin by the weaker sex which should be subject to them, and are not forewarned by the example of our first parent, whose wife, beguiled by the serpent, brought upon him and his descendants the awful fate of exile from paradise, and death. Truly, as the wise man said, "No head is more cunning than that of the serpent, and no iniquity more iniquitous than that of a woman." Woe to the sinner whom fate unites with her!

Both these sayings are obviously applicable to this woman, whose rage and fury were so strong and persistent that the tragic loss of her husband did not deter her from carrying out her wicked device against her hated brother-in-law. She continued to maintain her lie, in spite of the anathema which was so well deserved, and claimed the inheritance for her child. The lawful heir thus being excluded from his brother's estate, the child and her lands were given by the king to a certain youth, the brother of Hugh de Neville, the chief forester of the kingdom. Although she was not yet four years old, he decided that their marriage should be solemnly celebrated, fearing that something might prevent his acquisition of her inheritance.

When this was reported to the bishop, as he had frequently issued constitutions forbidding the marriage of those who had not yet reached the years of discretion, he now gave a special order forbidding any priest or devout Christian to be present at the wedding. In this matter he was considering alike the eternal and temporal security of many people and the claims of justice, for he thought that such a marriage before the truth had been fully sifted through investigations in the law courts would be to the prejudice of the parties concerned.

Immediately afterwards, the bishop having set out for Normandy on account of certain business with the king, the relatives and friends of the young man assembled in a remote village, and there, taking advantage of either simplicity or the greed of the parish priest, married him to the child publicly in the church, thus uniting a peasant of unfree birth to a noble. Their lust to acquire what legally belonged to someone else was so great, that neither the servile condition of the bride, nor the obvious risk of damnation could deter them from the ill-omened marriage. As soon as the bishop returned from abroad, they informed him of what had taken place. He suspended the priest who had celebrated the marriage, and sequestered his benefice, and publicly excommunicated all those who had flouted his prohibition, and who had contumaciously refused to appear before him in defiance of the law.

In the meantime, the maid of the false mother who had sought for and procured the child of another mother, being conscience-stricken, came first to the penitentiary and sub-dean of the church of Lincoln, Master William de Bramfeld of pious memory, and then by his advice to the bishop, to whom, shedding abundant tears, she made known exactly what had occurred. The bishop then, now having full information about everything, kept to himself for the time being what had been revealed to him secretly. On the next day, however, he ordered that the sentence he had already launched should be published every Sunday in the churches of the neighborhood.

A little while after this had been done, the wretched woman whose machinations were responsible for this evil act came at last to her senses, and began to feel misgivings about the horrible sin she had committed. Finally, she had the excellent idea of coming to the bishop, bringing with her the maid who had been her confidant and partner in sin. She first with many tears confessed her guilt to him in private, and then again in the presence of many honest men including the writer, declaring amid her sobs that she had betrayed her husband, and cheated her brother-in-law, the former to his death and the latter out of his lawful inheritance. All these things were reported by the bishop to the archbishop of Canterbury, who was then justiciar of the whole kingdom, as well as to the brothers and friends of the despoiler of the property of another person, and to almost all the nobles and barons of the Curia Regis.

In spite of this, the husband of the girl who was the innocent cause of the wrong, and his counselors kept possession of what they had wrongfully acquired, declaring that according to the laws of England a child was regarded as legitimate whom the husband of a woman had recognized as legitimate during his lifetime. On this pretext the legitimate heir was prevented from entering into his inheritance. Meanwhile, however, more out of respect for the bishop than because the story was generally known, no definite judicial sentence was given against him.

This indefatigable champion of justice again crossed the sea to Normandy. At the time of his departure he openly declared on more than one occasion that if the knight took her to wife as he intended, he should realize that he had united himself to a serf, and would not enjoy her for very long. These crafty men devised a scheme by which a day was fixed for the parties on which the case was to be settled at London without the possibility of further postponements.

Therefore Adam de Neville, the girl's husband, went hastily to London with a great company of relatives, and on the night before the day on which the judges had promised that the land would be irrevocably adjudged to him, for up till then he had only had the custody of it, lodged at no great distance from the city. Whilst his counselors and supporters were in the city discussing earnestly with the justices the wording of the verdict, he went joyously to bed somewhat intoxicated, and died unexpectedly in his sleep, and alone and unprepared, for he had expected nothing of the kind, appeared before the tribunal of a more impartial judge to receive retribution for his crimes. It is to be feared that there to his shame he heard from the lips of the most just judge the sentence so often given by his loyal spokesman. Whenever the holy man heard the name forester formerly strange and unknown to him, and from every side the growing number of complaints from their victims, he used to say, making a pun on their barbarous name, "These men are aptly and very properly called foresters, for they will remain outside the kingdom of God."

This man being thus removed and snatched away from the world by God, his widow, although still too young for wedlock, was given with another's patrimony to one of the king's chamberlains. He also died, but after the saint's departure from this world, and then the wretched girl was surrendered to a third husband, much more wicked than her former ones, who on account of the innumerable outrages committed by him against various churches, had many times been excommunicated. His past deeds proclaim in no uncertain manner what his future fate will be unless he takes warning. The woman who was responsible for the whole business, ended a life passed for some time in misery and distress by a tragic death.

Why did the couple have no children? Were there other possible reasons? Why did the woman want to avoid the brother-in-law inheriting the estate? Why was the fraud such a serious matter? Did the bishop react appropriately? Why did the bishop object to the marriage between the daughter and Adam de Neville? Why did the author? How were children recognized to be legitimate? How and why did class distinctions play such a large part in this case?

53. THE LEGITIMATION OF CHILDREN

Although both secular society and the church agreed that sexual activity should be regulated and, in theory, confined within legal marriage, in practice these prohibitions were not always observed. At all levels of society there are examples of sexual activity outside of marriage, activity which frequently resulted in the birth of illegitimate children. Illegitimacy could bring disgrace upon the parents. In particular, a bondswoman could be fined by her lord for fornication and both partners might be punished. The children of such unions, however, also faced penalties. Canon law forbade ordination to an illegitimate man, although this was frequently excused by dispensation. Secular law stipulated that only legitimate children should inherit. In order to mitigate somewhat these liabilities, the church allowed such children to be legitimized by their parents' subsequent marriage. In the course of the marriage ceremony the children joined their parents under the nuptial veil. This passage describes events that occurred in the late twelfth century.

Source: Trans. Elisabeth M.C. Van Houts, *The Gesta Normannorum Ducum of William of Jumièges, Oderic Vitalis, and Robert of Torigni* (Oxford: Clarendon Press, 1995), vol. 2, pp. 267, 269; reprinted with permission.

The Deeds of the Norman Dukes

8.36. Because we have referred to Countess Gunnor on account of Roger of Montgomery's mother, her niece, I should like to write down the story as reported by people of old of how Gunnor came to be Duke Richard's wife. One day when Duke Richard was told of the celebrated beauty of the wife of one of his foresters, who lived in a place called Equiqueville near the town of Arques, he deliberately went hunting there in order to see for himself whether the report he had learned from several folk was true. While staying in the forester's house, the duke was so struck by the beauty of his wife's face that he summoned his host to bring his wife, called Sainsfrida, that night to his bedchamber. Very sadly the man told this to Sainsfrida, a wise woman, who comforted him by saying that she would send in her place her sister Gunnor, a virgin even more beautiful than her. And thus it happened. Once the duke perceived the trick he was delighted that he had not committed the sin of adultery with another man's wife. Gunnor bore him three sons and three daughters, as is set out above in the book containing the deeds of this duke. When, however, the duke wished his son Robert to become archbishop of Rouen, he was told by some people that according to canon law this was impossible, because his mother had not been married. Therefore Duke Richard married Countess Gunnor according to the Christian custom and during the wedding ceremony the children, who were already born, were covered by a cloak together with their parents. Thereafter Robert could be appointed archbishop of Rouen.

How did Richard and Gunnor meet? How did social status influence their relationship? Why did Richard finally marry Gunnor? How was the legitimization of the children symbolized?

54. FEUDAL MARRIAGE

Among the feudal nobility marriage was a highly important economic and political mat-
ter; it was a means of forging alliances and increasing wealth not only for the two fami-
lies, but also for their overlords. Marriage was closely controlled by parents, extended fam-
ilies, and feudal lords. The desires and wishes of the spouses, both male and female, were
of little concern. Because of the political implications of marriage, lords insisted on final
approval of the choice of a spouse for a vassal and his children and widow, to ensure the
union did not in any way disadvantage him. Similarly, granting permission to marry,
fining those who married without license, and selling the right to arrange a marriage were
all lucrative sources of income for a feudal overlord. In particular, arranging a marriage to
a wealthy heiress was a useful way of rewarding retainers and ensuring their loyalty.
Often, however, such marriages disparaged heiresses who were forced to marry men
beneath their social rank. Arranging the remarriage of the widows of vassals was an
equally lucrative and useful practice. On their part, vassals tried to preserve their rights by
insisting that widows and children not be disparaged and forced to marry a social inferior.
The tension between the vassals' interests and those of the lord are evident in the provi-
sions of the Magna Carta *which the barons forced the king to accept, and in the king's*
continuing attempts to control marriage and wardship.

The *Magna Carta* (1215)

Source: Trans. J.C. Holt, *Magna Carta*, 2nd ed. (Cambridge: Cambridge University Press, 1992), pp. 451, 453, 455, 467; reprinted with permission.

2. If any of our earls or barons, or others holding of us in chief by knight service shall die, and at his death his heir be of full age and owe relief, he shall
have his inheritance on payment of the ancient relief, namely the heir or heirs
of an earl 100 pounds for a whole earl's barony, the heir or heirs of a baron 100
pounds for a whole barony, the heir or heirs of a knight 100 shillings at most
for a whole knight's fee; and anyone who owes less shall give less according to
the ancient usage of fiefs.

3. If, however, the heir of any such person has been under age and in wardship, when he comes of age he shall have his inheritance without relief or fine.

4. The guardian of the land of such an heir who is under age shall not take
from the land more than the reasonable revenues, customary dues and services,
and that without destruction and waste of men or goods. And if we entrust the
wardship of the land of such a one to a sheriff, or to any other who is answerable to us for its revenues, and he destroys or wastes the land in his charge, we
will take amends of him, and the land shall be entrusted to two lawful and prudent men of that fief who will be answerable to us for the revenues or to him
to whom we have assigned them. And if we give or sell to anyone the wardship

of any such land and he causes destruction or waste, he shall lose the wardship and it shall be transferred to two lawful and prudent men of the fief who shall be answerable to us as is aforesaid.

5. Moreover so long as the guardian has the wardship of the land, he shall maintain the houses, parks, preserves, fishponds, mills, and the other things pertaining to the land from its revenues; and he shall restore to the heirs when he comes of age all his land stocked with plows and wainage such as the agricultural season demands and the revenues of the estate can reasonably bear.

6. Heirs shall be given in marriage without disparagement, yet so that before a marriage is contracted it shall be made known to the heir's next of kin.

7. After her husband's death, a widow shall have her marriage portion and her inheritance at once and without any hindrance; nor shall she pay anything for her dower, her marriage portion, or her inheritance which she and her husband held on the day of her husband's death; and she may stay in her husband's house for forty days after his death, within which period her dower shall be assigned to her.

8. No widow shall be compelled to marry so long as she wishes to live without a husband, provided that she gives security that she will not marry without our consent if she holds of us, or without the consent of the lord of whom she holds, if she holds of another....

15. Henceforth we will not grant anyone that he may take an aid from his free men except to ransom his person, to make his eldest son a knight, and to marry his eldest daughter once; and for these purposes only a reasonable aid is to be levied....

54. No one shall be taken or imprisoned upon the appeal of a woman for the death of anyone except her husband.

What concerns are shown about the conduct of guardians? What safeguards were included governing the marriage of heirs? Why would widows have been particularly vulnerable to coercion to remarry from an overlord? Why was it so important that a widow not remarry without the lord's consent? What was in the king's interest, what in the baron's?

Royal Concerns about Marriage

Source: Trans. J.A. Giles in *Matthew Paris's English History* (London: Henry G. Bohn, 1852), vol. 1, pp. 47-48, 117; revised.

An Unauthorized Marriage (1237)

Around the same time, the king's anger was again kindled against the earl of Kent, Hubert de Burgh, because Richard, earl of Gloucester, still a boy in the king's custody, secretly was joined in marriage to Margaret, Earl Hubert's daughter, without the king's permission or sanction. For the king had intended, it was said, to unite in marriage the same youth, the earl of Gloucester, along with all his lands and honors, with a certain relative of William, bishop-elect of Valencia, a native of Provence. Finally, however, with the intercession of a great many people, and because Earl Hubert declared that he had not known about this nor had it been arranged by him, and on his promising a sum of money to the king, the king's indignation subsided.

An Arranged Marriage (1238)

In the year of Our Lord 1238, which was the twenty-second year of his reign, King Henry III held his court in London, at Westminster, where, on the day after Epiphany, which was a Thursday, Simon de Montfort solemnly espoused Eleanor, the daughter of King John, sister of King Henry III, and widow of William Marshal, earl of Pembroke. The ceremony was performed and the Mass celebrated by Walter, chaplain of the royal chapel of St. Stephan at Westminster, in the king's small chapel which is in a corner of his chamber, with the king, by his own hand, giving the bride to the said Simon. Simon received her gratefully because of his disinterested love, her own beauty, the rich honors that she brought with her, and the lady's excellent royal lineage. She was the legitimate daughter of a king and queen; the sister of a king, an empress, and a queen, so that the children of such a noble lady would have sprung from royal roots.

Why was the king angry about the earl of Gloucester's marriage? How was he placated? Why was Simon happy to marry Eleanor? What do these cases indicate about marriages among the nobility?

Feudal Agreements

Source: Trans. Oliver J. Thatcher and Edgar Holmes McNeal, *A Source Book for Mediaeval History. Selected Documents Illustrating the History of Europe in the Middle Age* (New York: Charles Scribner's Sons, 1905), pp. 371-72.

An Agreement between Blanche of Champagne and King Philip II (1201)

Blanche's Letter to Philip

I, Blanche, countess palatine of Troyes. Be it known to all, present and future, that I have voluntarily sworn to my lord, Philip, king of France, to keep the agreements contained in this charter ...

I have voluntarily sworn that I will never take a husband without the advice, consent, and wish of my lord, Philip, king of France, and that I will place under his guardianship my daughter and any child of whom I may be pregnant from my late husband, Count Theobald. In addition, I will turn over to him the fortresses of Bray and Montereau, and give him control of all the men who dwell there and all the knights who hold fiefs of the castles, so that if I break my promise to keep these agreements, all the aforesaid men shall hold directly of my lord, Philip, king of France; and they shall all swear to aid him even against men and against every other man or woman. The lord of Marolles shall put himself and his castle also under the control of the king, and similarly all the knights who hold fiefs of Provins, and all the men of Provins, and all the men of Lagny and Meaux, and all the knights who hold fiefs of these places ... I will do liege homage to my lord, Philip, king of France, and I will keep faith with him against all creatures, living or dead.

Philip's Letter to Blanche

In the name of the holy and undivided Trinity, amen. Philip, by the grace of God king of France. Be it known to all, present and future, that we have received Blanche, countess of Troyes, as our liege woman, for the fief which our beloved nephew and faithful subject, Theobald, former count of Troyes, held from us ... We have sworn to her that we will keep the agreements written in this charter in good faith, as to our liege woman; namely, that we will protect and nourish her daughter whom she has placed in our ward, in good faith and without deceit, and that we will not give her in marriage until she reaches the age of twelve years. After she has reached that age, we will provide her with a husband in accordance with the desires and advice of ourself, our mother, the lady Blanche, and the barons whose names are written here, or of the persons who hold their fiefs, if they have died. These are the barons: William, archbishop of Rheims; Odo, duke of Burgundy; Guy of Dampierre; Gualcher of Châtillon, etc.

What does Blanche promise Philip? Why is it important? What does Philip promise Blanche in return? Whose advice will be sought concerning the daughter's marriage?

Control of Marriage

Source: Trans. A.E. Bland, P.A. Brown, and R.H. Tawney, *English Economic History. Select Documents* (London: G. Bell, 1921), pp. 29-31; modernized.

A License for a Widow to Marry, 1316

The king to all who read this, greetings. Know that by a fine of 100 shillings which our beloved John de la Haye has paid to us on behalf of Joan, who was the wife of Simon Darches, deceased, who held from us as tenant in chief the honor of Wallingford, we have given a license to Joan so that she may marry whomever she wishes, provided that he has given his allegiance to us. Witness, the King at Westminister, 11 July.

Marriage of a Widow without License (1338)

The king, to his beloved and trustworthy William Trussel, his escheator on this side of the Trent, greetings. Whereas Millicent, who was the wife of Hugh de Plescy, deceased, who held from us as tenant in chief, recently took an oath in our Chancery that she would not marry without our license. She has now married Richard de Stonley, without having obtained our license. We refuse to leave such contempt unpunished and wish to take measures for the injury done to us in this matter. We command that without delay you take into our hands all the lands and tenements in your jurisdiction which Richard and Millicent hold as the dower Millicent inherited from the aforesaid Hugh. You shall answer to us, at our Exchequer, for the issues resulting from this, until we see fit to order otherwise. Witness, the king at the Tower of London, 6 May.

Wardship and Marriage (1179-80)

Otto de Tilli renders account of 400 pounds to have the wardship of the land of his grandson. Let his daughter be given in marriage at the king's will. In the treasury are 100 pounds. He owes 300 pounds.

Adam, son of Norman and William, son of Hugh de Leelai renders account of 200 marks for marrying Adam's daughter to William's son, with the king's good will. In the treasury there are 50 marks. They owe 100 pounds.

Grant of an Heir's Marriage (1320)

The king, to all who read this, greetings. Know that by a fine of 6 pounds which our beloved clerk, Adam de Lymbergh has paid to us, we have granted to him the marriage of John, son and heir of Joan de Chodewell, deceased, late one of the sisters and heirs of Philip le Brode, deceased, who held lands from us as tenant in chief. The said John is underage and in in our wardship. [The marriage is to be] without disparagement. In witness whereof etc. Witness the king at Odiham, 26 March. By the council.

And orders are given to Richard de Rodeney, the king's escheator on this side of the Trent, to deliver the heir, John, to the said Adam, to be married in the aforesaid manner. Witnessed as above.

What are the king's concerns in these orders? Why would someone pay for the privilege to marry freely? Were male and female heirs treated differently?

55. A FRAUDULENT MARRIAGE AGREEMENT
(1280)

Because marriage had such important economic consequences and was one of the ways by which men could increase their land holdings, it was a high stakes game. Individuals could go to great lengths to secure the hand and the land of widows and heiresses, including by means of fraud, as this case demonstrates. The details of the case tell us much about how a couple might negotiate marriage and the issues that might preoccupy them. Allegations of a previous marriage contract were common in medieval courts. They most frequently appear in cases where one spouse claimed a prior contract as a reason for not being returned to a spouse who alleged he or she had been deserted. Unfortunately, the uneven survival of medieval records means that we do not know when or if Agnes might have received restitution of her land.

Source: Trans. G.O. Sayles, *Select Cases in the Court of King's Bench under Edward I* (London: Selden Society, 1972), pp. 20-23; reprinted with permission.

The lord king sent his writ to his treasurer and chamberlains in these words:

Edward by the grace of God king of England, lord of Ireland and duke of Aquitaine, to his treasurer and chamberlains, greeting. Because for some definite reasons we want to be certified upon the record and process of a suit, which was before Ralph of Hengham and his fellows, lately appointed our justices to hold pleas before us, between Agnes of Sparkford and William of Patney, with respect to certain trespass done to the same Agnes by the aforesaid William, so it is said, we command you that, having examined the rolls of the aforesaid Ralph which are in our treasury and your custody, you should without delay send us under the seal of our exchequer that record and process with everything concerning them, and this writ. Witness myself at Westminster the fifth day of June in the eighteenth year of our reign [1290].

He also sent his writ to Walter of Wimborne in these words:

Edward by the grace of God etc. to his beloved and faithful Walter of Wimborne, greeting. Because for definite reasons we want to be certified upon the record and process of a certain inquisition, taken before you a long time ago at Ilchester between William of Patney and Agnes of Sparkford with respect to tenements in Uphill and Crediton, we command you to have the record and process of the aforesaid inquisition with everything concerning them before us a fortnight after Trinity wherever etc. And you yourself in your own person are then to be there to show your warrant whereby you took the aforesaid inquisition and to do and receive further what justice shall advise. And you are to have there this writ. Witness myself at Westminster the twenty-eighth day of May in the eighteenth year of our reign [1290].

Pleas Before the Lord King ... in the eighth year of King Edward's reign [1280].

Somerset

Agnes of Sparkford complains of William of Patney that, whereas he had treated with that Agnes concerning a marriage to be contracted between them and that he should make her his wife, and the same Agnes, by reason of the marriage to be contracted between them, enfeoffed that William of all her land, to wit, of two carucates [plow-land] of land with appurtenances in Uphill and Crediton, and put him in good and peaceful seisin [possession], that William as soon as he had had good seisin did not allow the aforesaid Agnes to enter the aforesaid land and refused to contract marriage with her, but alleged to her that he had contracted with another and made her his wife a long time ago, wherefore she says that she is wronged and has suffered loss to the value of three hundred pounds, and thereof she produces suit.

And William comes and denies force etc., and says that there never was any agreement between them, but he says that the same Agnes of her good and spontaneous will enfeoffed that William of the aforesaid land for two hundred marks of silver, for which he made full satisfaction to the same Agnes, and that it is so he asks for enquiry to be made by the country. And the aforesaid Agnes likewise. Therefore the sheriff is ordered to cause to come before Walter of Wimborne at Ilchester on Saturday after the Feast of St. Matthias the Apostle [2 March 1280] ...

Afterwards on the aforesaid day came the aforesaid Agnes and likewise William before the aforesaid Walter. The inquisition came by the underwritten, to wit, Ralph de Lucy, Ralph of Brent, William le Rok', William Wynegod, Thomas Jordan, Thomas Averay, Adam of Barrow, Robert of Tetton, John Page, William Mancel, William le Jouster, and Hugh Cobe, who said on their oath that the aforesaid William came to the aforesaid Agnes and made her to understand that he would willingly make her his wife, and she gave him her consent. And afterwards, some days having elapsed, he again treated with her about contracting a marriage between them, but he said to her that it would be hard for him to marry her unless he could be certain about the land of the aforesaid Agnes, if he should happen to survive her. And the aforesaid Agnes, on that account of the marriage to be contracted between them, enfeoffed him with the aforesaid land and put him in seisin [possession]. And that William, having such a seisin, alleged to the aforesaid Agnes that it would be necessary for her to stay elsewhere until he had exercised his seisin and he fixed his term to her, faithfully promising her that, when the fixed term had gone by, he would bring her back to the aforesaid lands and there would marry her. Believing him, she thus departed and, when the term fixed for her had gone by, because the aforesaid William did not come to her as he had promised her, the aforesaid Agnes came to the aforesaid land with the intention of entering it, and she asked the aforesaid William to keep his promise to her about making her his wife. And the aforesaid William did not allow her to enter the aforesaid land, and he said to her that he could not make her his wife because he had someone else as his wife whom he had previously espoused a long time ago. The jurors also say that the aforesaid William, in order to color his deed, inserted in his charter of enfeoffment that he had given the aforesaid Agnes for the aforesaid enfeoffment two hundred marks, but they say that, whatever he paid of the aforesaid money to the same Agnes, this was all from the goods and chattels of the aforesaid Agnes, because the aforesaid Agnes had entrusted herself, her land, and goods and her chattels to the aforesaid William as to him whom she believed she would have as her husband. And they expressly say on their oath that for such reason of a marriage to be contracted between them she enfeoffed the aforesaid William of the aforesaid land and not for any other reason, and that the aforesaid William was culpable in that he could not have made the marriage discussed between them effective. Therefore afterwards, before Ralph of Hengham, Nicholas of Stapleton, and Walter of Wimborne at Westminster, it was awarded that the aforesaid Agnes should recover her seisin of the aforesaid lands etc., and that the aforesaid William be committed to gaol. And order was sent to the sheriff that by the oath etc. he should diligently enquire concerning damages etc. Afterwards a fortnight after St. John the Baptist's Day the sheriff returned the inquisition, which says that the aforesaid Agnes had damages by reason of the aforesaid deceit to the value of forty marks etc. And because the aforesaid William has lands in the counties of Somerset and Southampton, therefore order is sent to the sheriffs of Somerset and Southampton etc. that from the lands and chattels etc.

Afterwards came Ralph of Hengham into the bench and into the presence of Gilbert of Thornton and Roger Brabazon, and recorded that the aforesaid Agnes came to the queen at Clarendon and made a complaint against a certain William of Patney concerning this, that he tricked her out of her land in that he took enfeoffment from the aforesaid Agnes, that is to say, of two carucates of land with appurtenances in Uphill and Crediton, by reason of a marriage to be contracted between them, and this marriage could not be duly performed because of a legal impediment contracted on the part of the aforesaid William. And on this there came the lord king himself who clearly understood that deed, and at once ordered speedy justice to be done to the aforesaid Agnes. And the aforesaid William, who was present in court, was immediately attached and came before him and Walter of Wimborne. And questioned about the aforesaid deed, he said that he ought not to answer for his free tenement without the king's writ. And this same matter was shown to the lord king, who said that in such a case he ought to reply without any writ, especially since he was found in his court. And afterwards the aforesaid William put himself on an inquisition of his country, as is found above in the aforesaid Walter's record. Asked who took the inquisition and who gave the judgment, he says that the aforesaid Walter took the inquisition and likewise gave the judgment. And because it is found in the aforesaid Walter's record that the aforesaid judgment was given in the presence of Nicholas of Stapleton, it is said to William of Winchester, son and heir of the aforesaid William, that he should sue out a writ to the aforesaid Nicholas so that he might certify the king a fortnight after St. John the Baptist's Day wherever etc. concerning the aforesaid record.

Afterwards Nicholas of Stapleton sent word that he knew nothing and never knew anything about the record or process nor about the judgment on the aforesaid inquisition because no record ever reached him, as appears on the dorse of the king's writ addressed to the aforesaid Nicholas and sent back to him, and this writ remains among the writs of precept of the eighteenth year of the present king's reign.

Afterwards the lord king ordered Gilbert of Thornton and his fellows to hear and determine the aforesaid suit. And the aforesaid William of Patney came. And there came Hugh of Cressingham and Humphrey of Waldon in the name of the queen who holds the aforesaid tenetments. And the aforesaid William is told to speak against the aforesaid queen if he wants to say anything thereon. And he did not say anything against the same queen. Yet by consent of the aforesaid Hugh and Humphrey, day is given to the aforesaid William and likewise to the aforesaid Hugh and Humphrey before the king in the next parliament etc.

What does this case reveal about courtship and the motives for marriage? Why did William not marry Agnes? How well did Agnes know William before their exchange of promises?

56. MARRIAGE CASES IN VILLAGE COURTS

Just as feudal lords endeavored to control marriage and inheritance among the highest ranks of medieval society, so, too, on manors lords tried to exercise control over the marriages of their villeins. Indeed, the very requirement to pay a fine to the lord upon marriage was a clear indication that the family held land by customary tenure and that the person was a bondsman or bondwoman rather than free. In England, the fine a woman paid to the lord for permission to marry was called the merchet. *The courts were also concerned with the maintenance of public order and morality. They punished adulterers and fornicators and levied a fine called the* leyerwite *on unmarried women who had lovers or bore children. The manor courts' records reveal the richness of life on the local level and indicate how complex patterns of marriage and remarriage could result in complicated questions of inheritance. The elderly might also use the manor courts to register their retirement arrangements. Aging villagers could surrender the use of their land to younger folk, sometimes their children, sometimes not, in exchange for life maintenance. The fines levied by manor courts went to the lord of the manor, although the juries of local villagers exercised an important role in applying customary law and serving as the community's collective memory. The records surviving from English manor courts provide a window onto the vibrant life of medieval village society.*

Source: Trans. F.W. Maitland, *Select Pleas in Manorial and Other Seignorial Courts, vol. 1, Reigns of Henry III and Edward I,* Selden Society (London: Bernard Quaritch, 1889), pp. 12, 15-16, 24-25, 27-29, 32, 40-41, 75, 92-94, 97-98, 120-21, 126-27, 173-74; revised.

Wretham, Norfolk. The Friday after the feast of St. Michael, 1247

Gilbert, Richard's son, gives 5 shillings for a license to take a wife. Pledge, Seaman. The term [for payment], the Feast of the Purification.

The following women were violated and therefore they must pay the *leyer-wite*: Botild, Alfred's daughter (fine 6 pence); Margaret, Stephen's daughter (fine 12 pence, pledge Gilbert, Richard's son); Agnes, Seaman's daughter (fine 12 pence, pledge the said Seaman); Agnes, Jor's daughter (fine 6 pence, pledge Geoffrey Franklain); Magot, Edith's daughter (fine, 6 pence).

Ruislip, Middlesex. The Saturday after the Purification of the Blessed Virgin, 1248

Richard Guest gives 12 pence and if he recovers will give 2 shillings to have a jury of twelve lawful men to decide whether he had the greater right to a certain headland at Eastcot which Ragenilda widow of William Andrews holds, or the said Ragenilda. Pledges for the fine, John Brook and Richard of Pinner. And the said Ragenilda comes and says that she is not able to bring the land into judgment because she has no right in it except by reason of the wardship of the son and heir of her husband, who is under age. And Richard is not able to deny this. Therefore, let him await [the heir's] coming of age.

Weedon Beck, Northamptonshire. The court held on St. Luke's day, 1275

William Fleming gives 4 pounds to the lord for a license to contract marriage with the widow Susan. Pledge, Richard Serjeant ...

The full court declares that if any woman shall have completely left the lord's domain and contracted marriage with a free man, then the said woman is well able to return and recover whatever right and claim she has in any land. But if she was married to a serf, then she cannot do this while the serf is alive, but after his death she is well able to do so.

Atherstone, Warwick. The court held on the Sunday after the feast of St. Luke, 1275

Dulcia gives the lord 12 pence to have a judgment of the court about her dower. Pledges, Hugh Tulluse, Thomas Lucas.

Bledlow, Buckinghamshire. The court held on the feast of St. Philip and James, 1275

Hugh Churchyard contracted marriage without a license; fine 12 pence ...

Henry Cross gives the lord 4 shillings for a license to marry; pledge, Robert Serjeant.

Cottisford, Oxford. The court held on the Tuesday after Trinity Sunday

Isabella Warin gives the lord 4 shillings for a license to marry for her daughter Mary; pledge, John Serjeant.

Tooting, Surrey. The court held on the Saturday after the feast of St. Martin, 1280

It is presented by the unanimous verdict of the whole court that if anyone should contract marriage with a woman who has the right in any land according to the custom of the manor and is in possession of it, by the will of the lord, and the said woman surrenders her right and her possession into the hands of the lord and he, whom she married, receives that right and possession from the hands of the lord, in such a case the heirs of the woman are forever barred from the land and let the right to it remain with the husband and his heirs. Therefore, let William Wood, whose case falls under this rule, hold his land in the aforesaid manner. And for making this inquest, the said William gives the lord 6 shillings, 8 pence.

Ruislip, Middlesex. The court held on the Saturday after Quasimodo Sunday, 1280

The tenements of Lucy Mill are to be seized into the lord's hands because of the adultery which she has committed and the bailiff is to answer for them.

The chief pledges present that Cristina, daughter of Richard Malevile, has married at London without the lord's license; therefore, let the said Richard be held accountable. He has paid a fine of 12 pence. Likewise, Alice Berde has done the same; therefore, let the said Alice be held accountable.

PÉGARD.

A nineteenth-century drawing of a stone house that was a common type of peasant dwelling in rural Moravia from the tenth through fourteenth centuries.

Weedon Beck, Northamptonshire. The court held on the Friday after the feast of St. Denis in the year 1288

Richard Loverd renders into the lord's hands one cottage with appurtenances and Emma Loverd, daughter of the said Richard, renders one acre of arable land and Hugh Coverer is put in possession of the same and he gives the lord 5 shillings for entry; and for a license to contract marriage with the said Emma. And Hugh will keep the said Richard in board as well as he keeps himself and every year will give him one garment and one pair of linen hose and one pair of boots and slippers.

Weedon Beck, Northamptonshire. The court held on the Monday after the feast of the Invention of the Holy Cross, in the nineteenth year of Edward I (1291)

William Clerk renders into the hands of the lord a half virgate of land which once was Ivo's, for the use of his daughter Juliana. Afterwards, at the wish of the said Juliana, the said William is put in possession of the said land, to hold the land for the rest of his life, with the intention that after William's death Juliana shall be his nearest heir, to have and hold the said half virgate of land, according to the custom of the manor. And if Juliana shall die without an heir borne of her body, the said land shall revert to the heirs of the aforesaid William. And William gives the lord 10 shillings for having the aforesaid matters recorded and enroled in full court.

Atherstone, Warwickshire. The court held on the Wednesday after the feast of the Invention of the Holy Cross in the nineteenth year of Edward I (1291)

Agnes, formerly the wife of Walter Muck, makes a demand against Reginald Miller for a third part of a burgage as her reasonable dower, which, as she says, the said Reginald unjustly deprives her; and she puts this before the court. And the aforesaid Reginald comes and defends against her claim of injury and her right, and he says that the custom of the manor of Atherstone is such that when any married woman comes into full court with her husband and they render a tenement into the lord's hands to the use of a purchaser, then after the husband's death, the wife will recover no dower from the tenement so rendered and sold in court. And Reginald puts before the court that such is the custom of the manor and that the said Agnes thus came into full court with her husband and rendered into the lord's hands all right and claim which she had or in some way might have, in whole or in part, of the said burgage, to the use of the said Reginald. And the said Agnes freely concedes such is the custom, but she says that she never in full court rendered into the lord's hand her right which she had in the said burgage; and this she puts before the court. And twelve jurors of the court, that is, Adam Clerk, Thomas Julian, Hugh Churchyard, Ralph Stace, Ralph Smith, John Agnes's son, Ralph Baker, Walter Douce, Ralph Baker the younger, John Bover, Robert Woderowe, Thomas Lucas, and Robert Muck, say upon their oath that the aforesaid Agnes did come to full court and did render into the lord's hands all right and claim which she in any way might have in the said burgage. And therefore they say upon their oath that she has no right, according to the custom of the manor of Atherstone, to demand a third part of the said burgage. Therefore, it is considered that the said Reginald be without a day [in court] and that the said Agnes be held at the lord's pleasure.

Court of Broughton on the Tuesday after a month from Easter in the year 1294

Cecilia Moyllard was bound to appear in court and has a postponement until the feast of St. Michael to show the charter by which she says she is enfeoffed of the tenement in Barford of which her minor daughter Isabella is heir after the death of her father.

Elton. Court held on the day of St. Clement, 1278

And they say that Maggie Carter has born a child out of wedlock with Richard son of Thomas Male. They are both fined 6 pence.

And Agnes daughter of Philip Saladin has raised the hue against Thomas Morborne, who attempted to have sexual intercourse with her ...

And Agnes Cuttyle has born a child out of wedlock—she is a pauper ...

Moreover, they say that Jordan Mustard, born the lord's bondsman, remains at Alwalton where he has married a wife of the homage of the Abbot of Peterborough and he has there a half-virgate of land of the villanage of the said abbot. Therefore, it is ordered to Reginald Page and his tithing group to produce Jordan, etc....

It is presented by the said jurors that Reginald, Benet's son, wrongfully refuses to be one of the twelve jurors, alleging that he is a freeman. However, his sister Alice paid a fine with Stephen of Elton, then farmer [of the manor] for a license to marry, and his sisters Cristiana and Athelina likewise paid a fine with William of Wald, then a farmer. Therefore, the said Reginald is in mercy for his contempt, [fine] 6 pence.

They also say that William of Barnwell wrongfully alleges himself to be free, on account of which he refuses to be one of the jurors, however he ought to pay the *merchet* at the lord's will if he has a daughter whom he wishes to give in marriage. And thus did John the Freeman, ancestor of Elias the Freeman. He gave the *merchet* for his daughter who married one Roger Crudde at Nassington. Therefore William [is fined] 6 pence.

View of the Frankpledge at Gidding on the Tuesday before the feast of St. Andrew in the nineteenth year of King Edward and the fifth year of Abbot John, before William of Washingley (1290)

The chief pledges being sworn say that Richard Dyer, a married man, was convicted in the chapter of adultery with a certain woman ... and so lost the chattels of the lord. Therefore, he is in mercy. The lord's fine is forgiven; pledge, Martin Walter's son ...

And they say that John Monk still continues his lust with Sarah Hewen, wife of Simon Hewen, and is constantly attending various chapter courts where frequently he loses the lord's goods because of his adultery with Sarah, as has often been presented before now, nor will he be chastened. Therefore, he was in the stocks. And afterwards he paid the fine with one mark, with John Lach, John Beneathton, Walter King, Simon Bayllon, Walter Franklain, and John of Cottenham as pledges. And all the said pledges undertake that if the said John at any time hereafter is again convicted of adultery with the said Sarah, they will bring him back and put him back in the stocks until they have some other command from the lord or his steward.

The court at King's Ripton ... in the twenty-third year of King Edward and the ninth of Abbot John (1295)

Joan daughter of William of Alconbury appeared against the Abbot of Ramsey in a plea of land and the said Abbot is represented by Thomas Clerk, his attorney. And the said Joan demands eight acres of land against the lord Abbot as her right, because when in the churchyard of King's Ripton before the whole parish, the said Joan rendered into the hands of the Abbot William the said eight acres of land with appurtenances to the use of William her father. She was then under age, so that the said rendering was of no effect; and she prays that this be investigated.

And the lord Abbot, by his attorney, says that the said Joan was of full age when she surrendered the said land to the said William, according to the custom of the manor, and the said William was in good and peaceful possession for seven years and more and afterwards surrendered the said land to the use of William Chaplain ... who died without an heir, so that the said Abbot holds the land as forfeit for lack of an heir, and he prays that this be investigated.

Whence an inquest is made and the jurors say upon their oath that the said Joan was of full age according to the usage of the manor when she surrendered the said land. The age of majority of women is thirteen and a half years and the age of majority for men is fourteen and a half years. They say that the said Joan has no right in the said land but it is land properly forfeited to the lord Abbot. Therefore, it is considered that she take nothing by her writ, and be held accountable for her false complaint. She is pardoned because she is poor.

Court of King's Ripton held on the Thursday after the Translation of St. Benedict in the twenty-ninth year of King Edward and the fifteenth of Abbot John (1301)

Roger of Kellow, an outsider, who married Catherine, the daughter of Thomas Reeve of King's Ripton, who is by birth a native of the said village, comes and demands in court, in the name of Robert and Nicholas, his sons born from the body of Catherine by a lawful marriage, the 6 acres of land lying in the fields of King's Ripton which William the chaplain, son of Bartholomew Carpenter, lately deceased, purchased and held from the lord, according to the custom of the manor. And afterwards William gave and granted these lands to the said Robert and Nicholas, the legitimately begotten sons of the said Roger and Catherine, by an agreement made between the parties on the Monday in the middle of Lent in the twenty-eighth year of King Edward [1300]. In affirmation of this gift and grant the said chaplain, who was impeded by grave infirmity so that in no way could he come to the lord's court, handed over the whole of the said land, for the use of the said boys, into the hands of Thomas Cooper, then the custodian of the manor of King's Ripton, just as the custom is in the said village, until some one should come and hold the lord's next court. So, it was intended that Roger and Catherine should, at their own expense, cultivate the said land during the lifetime of the said chaplain and sow it with his seed and deliver to him the crop which grew on it. And every year, as long as the said chaplain should live, they would provide him with one good coat of colored cloth or of good russet, and if he should live for three or four years or more from the date of this agreement, the said Roger and Catherine, besides the coat, would pay him in the first year 40 shillings, in the second year 26 shillings 8 pence, in the third year 13 shillings 4 pence, and in the fourth year nothing and nothing in any subsequent year. The said agreement was fully satisfied for the said chaplain from the Monday in Mid-Lent [in the twenty-eighth year of the reign] until the Nativity of the Blessed Virgin Mary [September 8] following, on which festival the said chaplain died. But, before his death, he assigned and in his testament bequeathed all his purchased land to the said Robert and Nicholas, legitimately begotten sons of Roger and Catherine, which it was lawful for him to do (as Roger says) and for all other natives of the manor. Therefore, Roger of Kellow says that the said Robert and Nicholas, his sons begotten lawfully of the said Catherine, are nearer to have that land than anyone else, and he demands that this be investigated ... [The jurors say] that none of them was present when the chaplain made his testament, and they know nothing about it and will not make any statement about this point at present. And so leaving their business undone, and in great contempt of the lord and his bailiffs, they left the court. And therefore it is ordered that the bailiffs cause a fine of 40 shillings to be levied for the use of the lord from the property of the said jurors.

Court of Brightwaltham held on the Wednesday before the feast of St. Margaret in the twenty-fourth year of King Edward (1296)

Henry Morcock, John his brother, John Jocelyn, William of Mescombe, William his brother, Thomas Chaffinch, William at Cross, John Guyot, John Pope, Adam Scot, Geoffrey William, John Aurey, Geoffrey Jordan, Thomas Bayge, Roger Smoker, William Sket, William at Kepe, Ralph Tailor, Richard Young, Robert Osmund, John Bysouthwood, John Woodward, Roger Chapman, Roger Bysouthwood, Warin Bysouthwood, being sworn, say upon their oath that one Alan Poleyn held a certain tenement in Conholt on servile condition and he espoused a woman called Cristina and had by her a son, Elias by name. On Alan's death the said Cristina held the whole of that tenement according to the custom of the manor. Afterwards she married one Richard Aleyn, who had by her a son named Randolph. Afterwards Elias, the son and heir of the said Alan Poleyn, hearing how his mother had lost all right that she had in that tenement, because she had married without the lord's permission, came to the lord's court and demanded that the tenement of his father, whose heir he was, should be rendered to him as his right and inheritance, according to the custom of the manor, and was admitted thereto, as by right he ought to have been admitted. Nevertheless, by the lord's consent and of his own will, he granted that Cristina his mother might hold a certain portion of the same tenement for the rest of her life. And the said Cristina enfeoffed her son Randolph of that portion of the land *de facto*, although she could not do it *de iure*; and then she died. Then the said Randolph, being in possession of that portion, married one Edith and had by her a son named John and then Randolph died. After his death Edith married one Robert Tailor, who being in possession of the said tenement surrendered to the lord in full court all the right that he had in the said portion of the said tenement. After this, Hugh Poleyn, son and heir of the said Elias, son of Alan, came and demanded to be admitted to the whole of the tenement, and paid a fine for an inquest in the lord's court as to the right that he had in the tenement. Then an inquest was held and decided upon oath administered to it that Alan Poleyn, who had espoused one Cristina, begot Elias, and that on Alan's death Elias his son and heir married one Juliana and had by her a son, Hugh the petitioner, and that the said Hugh had sufficient right to the said tenement, nor was there any nearer heir. Then the said Hugh was admitted to the said tenement, according to the custom of the manor, and paid a fine for his entry, and so on. Wherefore they say expressly that the said Edith who now demands the said portion of the said tenement, nevertheless had no right at all in her demand. Therefore it is considered that the said Hugh, who now holds the land, should hold it in peace and that the said Edith is accountable for her false claim.

What kind of property cases came before the courts? What could happen to a woman's land if she gave her husband possession of it? What kind of punishments were levied for fornication? adultery? marrying without permission? What were the terms of the retirement agreements recorded? Why was Agnes Cuttyle not fined? How was Reginald's status as a bondsman proven?

57. HOUSING AND HOUSEHOLDS

In the later Middle Ages the quality of housing available to families improved markedly at all levels of society. In the countryside houses were increasing in size. Also, they might have a timber frame which was sturdier than the traditional wattle-and-daub construction. Houses also began to have two or more rooms and occasionally a second story for sleeping. Hearths replaced open fires and the introduction of chimneys meant houses were much less smoky. In towns, too, houses were improved by the introduction of chimneys and the addition of glass windows which let in more light. The wealthy also had more access to creature comforts such as beds with hangings, blankets, and sheets.

Whether a new family were being established through marriage or a family needed to move, in the city and countryside finding a suitable house could be a complicated matter. Deeds of ownership needed to be arranged. In cities and towns it was necessary to establish the exact boundaries of a dwelling and what land and appurtances were included in the transfer. Medieval notaries went to considerable length to ensure clarity in contracts, whether for buying a house, repairing or extending an existing structure, or building a new abode. These leases and permits reveal many aspects of urban housing, including building materials and the ever-present risk of fire. Although slate and tile replaced thatch for roofs by the end of the Middle Ages, fire continued to be a threat to urban life.

Source: Trans. Henry Thomas Riley, *Memorials of London and London Life in the XIIIth, XIVth, and XVth Centuries* (London: Longmans, Green, 1868), 46–47, 65–66, 125, 183–85, 452–53; revised.

Specifications for building a house, 1308

Simon of Canterbury, carpenter, appeared before the Mayor and Aldermen on the Saturday after the Feast of St. Martin the Bishop [11 November], in the second year of the reign of King Edward, son of King Edward. He acknowledged that before the next Easter, he would build at his own proper rates, down to the locks, for William of Hanigtone, pelterer, a hall and room with a chimney, and one larder between the hall and the room; and one solar above the room and larder; also, one recess with a window at the end of the hall, beyond the high bench, and one step with a porch, from the ground to the door of the hall, outside of that hall; and two enclosures as cellars, opposite to each other, beneath the hall; and one enclosure for a sewer, with two pipes leading to the said sewer; and one stable, between the hall and the old kitchen, twelve feet in width and ? feet in length, with a solar above the stable, and a garret above the aforesaid solar; and at one end of the solar, there is to be a kitchen with a chimney; and there is to be a room with a bay window, eight feet in width, between the hall and the old chamber. And if he shall not do so, then he agrees ... etc. And the said William de Hanigtone acknowledged that

A nineteenth-century drawing of a fifteenth-century town house in King's Lynn. Methods of building and levels of domestic comfort increased at the end of the Middle Ages, for well-off towndwellers.

he was bound to pay Simon for the aforesaid work, the sum of 9 pounds, 5 shillings, 4 pence sterling, half a hundred of Eastern marten-skins, fur for a woman's hood valued at 5 shillings, and fur for a robe for him, the said Simon.

Agreement made for plastering the hall of John de Bretagne, earl of Richmond, 1317

On Thursday the Feast of St. Dunstan [10 May], in the tenth year of the reign of King Edward, son of King Edward, Adam the Plastrer came and acknowledged a certain document to be his deed, the tenor of which is as follows:

Know all men that I, Adam the Plastrer, citizen of London, am bound and obligated to Sir John de Bretagne, earl of Richmond, to find plaster of Paris, at my own expense, good and sufficient and without fault, proper for the hall of the said earl. Also, I will competently, at my own expense, plaster and complete the said hall, and will repair the walls of the same with the said plaster, well and fittingly, inside and out, as well as the flues, to the top of the roof, in such a manner as befits the repair of the aforesaid hall. All this I will do for twenty-four pounds sterling, which our Lord the earl has paid to me in advance. To perform faithfully this work within eight weeks, I do bind myself and all my goods, moveable and immoveable, namely my lands, houses, and tenements, that are within the City of London ... Given at London, on the Thursday before the Feast of Pentecost, in the tenth year of the reign of King Edward, son of King Edward.

Grant of a permit to build a raised extension, 1381

To all persons who shall see or hear these present letters, the Mayor, Aldermen, and the Citizens of the City of London, greetings. Know that we have granted to Sir Robert Knolles, knight, our dear and well beloved fellow citizen, and to Custance, his wife, permission to make a raised extension of the height of fourteen feet, extending from the house of the said Sir Robert and Custance, his wife. [This may be constructed] on the west side, to another house belonging to them on the east side, beyond Seething Lane in the Parish of All Hallows Berkingchurch, near to the Tower of London. The said Sir Robert and Custance, his wife, their heirs and assigns are to have and to hold this structure for ever, they rendering annually to the Chamberlain of the Guildhall of the same city, for the time being, on behalf of the citizens, one red rose, at the Feast of the Nativity of St. John the Baptist [24 June]. In witness of this, the Common Seal of the city is set to these Letters Patent, Sir William Walworth, knight, being the Mayor of the City of London, and Walter Doget and William Knyghtcote, sheriffs of the same city. Given at London, the 23rd day of July, in the fifth year of the reign of King Richard the Second.

Agreement to indemnify the City against fire, 1302

Thomas Bat came before John le Blund, Mayor of London, and the aldermen, on the Friday before the Feast of St. Hilary [13 January] in the thirtieth year of the reign of King Edward, son of King Henry, and bound himself, and all his rents, lands, and tenements, to keep the City of London indemnified from peril of fire and other losses which might arise from his houses covered with thatch, in the Parish of St. Laurence Candlewick Street. And he agreed that he would have the said houses covered with tiles about the next Feast of Pentecost.

And in case he should not do this, he granted that the mayor, sheriffs, and bailiffs of London should cause the said houses to be roofed with tiles and [paid for] out of the proceeds of his aforesaid rents.

Conveyance of a dwelling-house in Broad Street, 1331

This indenture witnesses that whereas Edmund Crepin, son of Walter Crepin, late citizen of London, has given, and has confirmed by his deed of enfeoffment, to John de Yakeslee, tentmaker to our Lord the king of England, all of that principal dwelling-house which he, the same Edmund, had in the Parishes of St. Peter Cornhill, St. Benedict Fynke, and St. Martin de Otessyche, in the Wards of Cornhill and Broad Street, in the City of London. This includes the great gate of the house facing towards Cornhill, and the solar above that gate. This also includes another great gate of the same house, facing towards Broad Street, along with the entrance and exit to and from the aforesaid dwelling, as much by the great gate facing Cornhill as by the gate facing Broad Street. This also includes all the other appurtenances whatsoever pertaining to the same house within the two said gates. Sir Oliver de Ingham, knight, has hitherto held the said house from the said Edmund and has inhabited that dwelling. It is situated, in breadth, between the tenement of William de Manhale, the tenement of Agnes Rikeman, the tenement of Sir Henry de Coventry, the late Rector of the Church of St. Bridget in Fleet Street, and the tenement which John de Totenham, carpenter, holds from the said Edmund, the tenement of the Friars of St. Austin in London, which Thomas Lyoun holds for the term of his life, and the tenement of the late Henry de Shorne, towards the west. The house extends lengthwise from the king's highway of Cornhill, and from the tenements of the said Edmund, towards the south, as far as the tenement which the aforesaid John de Totenham, carpenter, holds from Edmund, and the king's high street of Broad Street, towards the north. This is the manner in which the aforesaid principal dwelling-house is divided by the boundary markers recently placed there, and it is separated from the other tenements of the said Edmund, located around it.

The whole of the aforesaid principal dwelling-house, with the two gates, and with the solar above the said great gate built facing Cornhill, free entrance and exit by the two great gates, and all the other appurtenances of the same house within the same two gates, in any manner belonging to him, the said John de Yakeslee, his heirs and assigns is to have and to hold, as the chief lords of that fee, by the services due unto them and accustomed for the same, for ever, as is contained more fully in the deed of feoffment, which the aforesaid Edmund has made to the said John de Yakeslee, and sealed with his seal. In witness whereof, the aforesaid Edmund, for himself, and the aforesaid John for himself, have each interchangeably set his seal to this indenture; John de Pulteney, then being mayor of the City of London, John de Mockinge and Andrew Aubrei, sheriffs of the same City, John Hauteyn, alderman of the Ward of Broad Street, and Henry de Gisorz, alderman of the Ward of Cornhill.

Witnessed by Hugh de Waltham, John Pyntel, and others. Given at London, on the Sunday after the Feast of St. John Port Latin [6 May].

What kinds of rooms were found in the houses described in these agreements? How were the boundaries of the house and property identified? What kinds of materials were used to build houses?

58. DOMESTIC VIOLENCE

In medieval society, marriage was very much a partnership between husband and wife. Both were important contributors to the well-being of the family and its economic prosperity. In villages, both husband and wife were needed to work the land. In cities, a craft shop required the labor of the whole family. Among the wealthy and powerful, wives were the administrators of great estates, responsible for feeding, clothing, and supervising retainers and servants. Not all marriages were happy, however, and folk tales and moralists both suggest domestic violence was not uncommon. In towns and villages when domestic violence escalated to murder, the cases were investigated by the coroner. The reports of the coroners, who investigated accidental and violent deaths, provide eloquent testimony to the brutality that could overtake some marriages. While wives were far more likely to be brutalized and perish at the hands of their husbands, folk literature suggests, and the coroners' records confirm, that women sometimes acted violently toward their spouses. Nevertheless, despite these kinds of cases, the values of medieval society did not condone domestic violence. Social pressure was brought to bear on abusers and in extreme cases the church sanctioned separation a mensa et thoro (from bed and board). This allowed a woman to separate from her abusive husband and receive financial support from him. Separation, however, did not always protect a woman from her husband, as some of these cases indicate.

Source: Trans. Charles Gross, *Select Cases from the Coroners' Rolls 1265-1413,* Selden Society (London: Bernard Quaritch, 1896), pp. 13, 15, 38, 45-46, 70; reprinted with permission.

Eaton, 5 May, 1269

It happened in the liberty of Eaton on Sunday next before Port Latin Day in the fifty-third year [that Richard, son of Robert of Staplehoe, came to Wilden at night to the house of his wife Ivette and induced her to go with him to her father's house in Staplehoe. On the way to that place he killed her and threw her body into a well, called Whitewell. Robert of Leigh found her the next morning and raised the hue; he produced two pledges].

Inquest was made before Simon Read, the coroner, by four neighboring townships, Eaton, Colmworth, Wilden, Wyboston, and Staplehoe; they say as is aforesaid. They also say that Richard has no chattels. It is ordered that Richard be arrested. Englishry was presented by Walter Baker of Alboldesle, her father, and Hugh, Christian's son, her uncle on the mother's side ...

Ravensden, 29 March, 1271

It happened in the vill of Ravensden on the night of Sunday next before Easter Day in the fifty-fifth year that Walter Bedell of Renhold came to the house of his wife Isabel, Reginald's daughter, in Ravensden, and asked her to come with him to the grange of Renhold to get a bushel of wheat which he wished to give her, and she went with him. And when they reached the meadow called Longmead, he at once struck her over the left ear, evidently with a knife, giving her a wound three inches in length and to the brain in depth; afterwards he threw her into the water of a brook called Ravensbrook. And on the following Monday Matilda, her mother, Reginald's wife, first found her dead; she raised the hue, and the hue was pursued. And she produced pledges: Roger Newbond and Walter Alfred of Ravensden. Richard Smith, the first neighbor, produced pledges: Walter Alfred and Hugh White. William Engaine, the second neighbor, produced pledges: John Savage and Richard Smith.

Inquest was made before Ralph of Goldington, the coroner, by four neighboring townships, Goldington, Renhold and Ravensden as one township, Bolnhurst, and Wilden; they say as is aforesaid, and they know nothing else. They were asked about his chattels, and they say that he had a lamb at Wilden, which is appraised at twelve pence; it is delivered to the township of Wilden.

Bedford, 31 August, 1276

Pleas of the crown presented at the county court of Bedford on Monday next after the feast of the Decollation of St. John in the fourth year of King Edward

Hundred of Manshead. A woman killed her husband. Inquest was made before the coroner by four vills. She sought sanctuary, confessed her crime before the coroner and the four vills, and abjured the realm; the port of Dover was assigned to her; her chattels were appraised.

Essex, Little Coggeshall, 10 April, 1371

It happened that Agnes, wife of John Driver of Little Baddow, was found dead there [at Little Coggeshall] on Thursday of Easter week in the forty-fifth year of King Edward the Third. John Growel, who first found her dead body, notified the four nearest neighbors, that is, Edmund Fuller, Walter Trew, John Steer, and Richard Hayward, and they notified Thomas Peacock, the king's bailiff of that hundred, who notified John of Gestingthorpe, one of the coroners of the county, and he came to Coggeshall on the following Friday of that week to view the body of Agnes. And John Growel, the finder, showed the body to [the coroner], and the latter viewed it and felt it, and made inquest concerning her death on the oath of Thomas Lavender, John Mile, Roger Fuller, Adam Sprott, John Clerk, John Fabyan, John Westwood, John Strogel, John Wheeler, Henry Stork, Richard Draper, and John Russell. And they say on their oath that on Palm Sunday of the aforesaid year John Driver, son of

Emma of Baddow and husband of the said Agnes, took his wife Agnes with him to a certain well filled with water in the field of Coggeshall called West-field, and there he beat her on the head and neck, and so ill-treated her that he almost killed her. Then, believing her to be dead, he threw [her] into the well, so that her whole body was under water except her neck and head. And Agnes thus lay in the water until Good Friday, when John Growel found her lying in the aforesaid position and still alive. He notified the neighbors, and they took her from the well and carried her to the house of Margery Rush in the afore-said vill, where she lay alive and lingered until the following Thursday in Easter week, and then she died of the said injuries. Thus John Driver feloniously killed the aforesaid Agnes.

Barnack, 20 September, 1314

It happened at Barnack on Friday next before the feast of St. Matthew the Apostle in the eighth year of King Edward that John Baker of Pilsgate died in his house at Pilsgate, having confessed and partaken of the communion; and he was buried without view of the coroner. And on the same day R. de Vere, the king's coroner in Northamptonshire, came there and caused John's body to be disinterred, and he found a wound on John's head, which seemingly had been made with an axe. Inquest was made before the said R. de Vere by four neigh-boring townships, that is, Barnack, Pilsgate, Walton, and Bainton. [They say that John was beating his wife Emma, and she raised the hue. Her brother came, and, with her assent wounded John with an axe, which was worth a penny. Emma and her brother were arrested and placed in charge of the bailiffs of the abbot of Peterborough].

Why did the husbands lure the wives away from the house before killing them? What role did women's natal family play in these cases? the neighbors? Where were bodies hid-den? Who prosecuted the cases?

CHAPTER SEVEN:

CHILDBIRTH

Childbirth was a central event in a married woman's life and one of the most dangerous experiences she would face. Given the central role that procreation was given in the theology of marriage and the importance to secular society of the generation of legitimate heirs, it is significant that attitudes toward childbirth were ambivalent. For many clerics childbirth was a graphic reminder of women's role in the Fall from Paradise. The blood of childbirth and menstruation were polluting, and sexual intercourse was prohibited at these times. Although some ecclesiastical authorities tried to counteract more rigorous assertions about women's "uncleanness," these notions nevertheless persisted, especially among the celibate clergy. Medical writers, less encumbered by moral stereotypes, were concerned with the health of both mother and child. Medical advice to ensure a safe delivery was supplemented by special prayers for women at this most dangerous time. St. Margaret and the Virgin Mary were considered to have the care of women in labor as part of their particular concerns. Childbirth had a social dimension as well. The birth of an heir cemented the lineage, ensured peaceful continuity of the line, and was an occasion for rejoicing among greater and lesser folk alike. For women, the role of mother, especially mother of an heir, was coveted. Moreover, childbirth was a particularly female activity. Women friends and relations, female servants and midwives, would attend the laboring mother-to-be. Consequently, lying-in was a social event, accompanied by food, drink, and story-telling.

59. GREGORY THE GREAT ON SEX, CHILDBIRTH, AND PURITY

In the year 597, Pope Gregory the Great sent a mission to England to convert the Anglo-Saxons to Christianity. A letter reputed to have been sent by Gregory to his emissary, Augustine of Canterbury, addresses a number of questions of doctrine and practice that Augustine was supposed to have encountered while in England. These questions and answers were incorporated by the Venerable Bede, in his History of the English Church and People, *in 731 C.E. Gregory's advice became the foundation for subsequent teaching on Christian morality, especially pertaining to appropriate marital intercourse. In this section, the church's teaching on childbirth and sexual activity in marriage is developed. The blood taboos that had traditionally restricted women's access to the sacraments were significantly modified and those times during which sexual relations were forbidden were clarified. Significantly, the letter discussed the customs and ideas about ritual purity as they pertained to both men and women. Although it is now certain that the letter was not actually written by Gregory the Great, throughout the Middle Ages it circulated under his name. This lent the letter greater authority than it would otherwise have received.*

Source: Trans. J.A. Giles in *The Venerable Bede's Ecclesiastical History of England* (London: Henry G. Bohn, 1847), pp. 45-50; revised.

Book I. Chapter 27

Augustine's Eighth Question: Should a pregnant woman be baptized? And how long after she has given birth may she enter a church? And after how many days may a newborn receive the sacrament of holy baptism, lest death should intervene and prevent it? How long after a woman gives birth may her husband have intercourse with her? Is it lawful for her to enter the church or receive the sacrament of communion when she is menstruating? Or can a man who has had intercourse with his wife enter the church before he has washed with water? All these things need to be known by the ignorant English people.

Gregory's answers: I do not doubt that these questions have been asked of you, my brother, and I think that I have already given you the answer. But I believe that you want me to confirm the responses that you yourself would give. Why shouldn't a pregnant woman be baptized, since fruitfulness of the flesh is no offence in the eyes of God? For when our first parents sinned in paradise, they forfeited the immortality which they had received, by the just judgment of God. Because, therefore, almighty God would not destroy the whole human race on account of its faults, he deprived man of his immortality for his sin, and, at the same time, from his great goodness, he preserved man's power to propagate the race after him. How, then, can that which has been preserved for the human race by the free gift of almighty God, exclude anyone from the grace of holy baptism? It is very foolish to imagine that a gift of grace could be in opposition to this mystery, by which all guilt is removed.

When a woman has delivered, after how many days may she enter a church? You know from reading the Old Testament that she should stay away for thirty-three days for a male child and sixty-six days for a female child. Now you must know that this ought to be understood symbolically. For if she enters the church at the very hour she that she is delivered, to give thanks, she is not guilty of any sin. It is the pleasure of the flesh, not its pain, that is at fault. But it is in carnal copulation that there is pleasure whereas there is pain in bringing forth a child. Whence it was said to the first mother of all: "In sorrow you shall bring forth children." If, therefore, we forbid a woman that has given birth to enter the church, we make a crime of her very punishment.

It is by no means forbidden to baptize either a woman who has given birth or her newborn child, even at the very hour of delivery, if there is a danger of death, because, while the grace of the holy mystery is to be provided with discretion for the living and cognizant, so it is to be offered without delay to the dying, lest, while another time is sought to confer the mystery of redemption, even with a short delay, the person to be redeemed should die.

Her husband should not approach her until the infant is weaned. A bad custom has sprung up in the behavior of married people, that is, that women disdain to nurse the children to whom they have given birth, and give them to other women to nurse. This practice seems to have been devised solely because of incontinence because, as they will not be continent, they will not nurse the children which they bear. Those women, therefore, who, from this evil custom, give their children to others to bring up, must not have sexual relations with their husbands until the time of purification has passed. For even in the absence of childbirth, women are forbidden to have sexual relations with their husbands during menstruation, so much so that sacred law condemns to death any man who approaches a woman during her menstrual period. Yet the woman, nevertheless, must not be forbidden to enter the church while she is menstruating, because this superfluity of nature cannot be considered a crime, and it is not just that she should be refused admittance to a church for that which she suffers against her will. For we know that the woman who suffered from the issue of blood, humbly approaching behind our Lord's back, touched the hem of his garment and her infirmity immediately left her. If, therefore, she who had an issue of blood might commendably touch the garment of our Lord, why may not a woman who is menstruating lawfully enter the church of God? But, you will say, "Her infirmity compelled her, but those about whom we are speaking are bound by custom." Consider, then, dearest brother, that all we suffer in this mortal flesh, through the infirmity of nature, is ordained by the just judgment of God after the Fall. To be hungry, to be thirsty, to be hot, to be cold, to be weary is from the infirmity of our nature. And what is it to seek food against hunger, drink against thirst, clothes against the cold, rest against weariness than to seek a remedy for our infirmities? And so for a woman the flow of menstrual blood is an infirmity. If, therefore, it was a commendable presumption in the woman who, in her infirmity touched our Lord's garment, why may not that which is permitted to one infirm person, be granted to all women who are infirm through the weakness of their nature?

She must not, therefore, be forbidden to receive the mystery of holy communion at these times. But if any one, from profound reverence, does not presume to receive communion, it is laudable; yet, if she receives it, she is not to be judged. For it is the part of noble minds to acknowledge their faults in some way, even when there is no fault, because often what is done without fault nevertheless originates in a fault. Therefore, when we are hungry it is no sin to eat, yet being hungry results from the sin of the first people. Similarly, women's menstruation is not sinful because it happens naturally. However, because our nature itself is so depraved that is seems to be polluted even without the consent of the will, the fault proceeds from sin, and human nature itself recognizes what it has become by judgment. And let humanity, who committed sin wilfully, unwillingly bear the guilt of that offence. And therefore let women consider this for themselves, and if, during their monthly menstrual period, they do not presume to approach the body and blood of the Lord, they are to be commended for their laudable consideration. But, when they are carried away by love of the same mystery to receive it, according to the usual custom of religious life, they are not to be prevented, as we said before. For, as in the Old Testament the outward deeds are observed, so in the New Testament what is done outwardly is not so diligently regarded as what is thought inwardly, in order that it be punished by a subtle determination. For as the law forbids the eating of many things as unclean, yet the Lord said in the gospel, "It is not that which goes into the mouth that defiles a person but that which comes out of the mouth that defiles a person" (Matt. 15.11). And soon after he said, "Evil thoughts proceed out of the heart" (Matt. 15.19). From this it is clearly seen that that is shown by almighty God to be polluted which proceeds from the root of a polluted thought. Whence the Apostle Paul also says, "To the pure all things are pure, but to them that are defiled and unbelieving, nothing is pure" (Tit. 1.15). And later, declaring the cause of that defilement, he adds, "For even their mind and conscience is defiled." Therefore, if no food is unclean to him who has a clean mind, why should that which a clean-minded woman suffers according to nature, be imputed to her as uncleanness?

A man who has intercourse with his own wife ought not to enter the church unless he has washed with water, nor ought he to enter immediately although washed. The law commanded the ancient people that when a man had intercourse with a woman he ought to wash himself with water, and not enter the church before sunset. This can be understood spiritually, because a man has intercourse with a woman when his mind is joined in thought of the delights of illicit concupiscence. For unless the fire of concupiscence is driven from his mind, he ought not to be considered worthy of the company of his brothers while he thus bears the vileness of depraved desire. Although several different nations have different opinions concerning this issue and seem to observe different rules, it was however always the custom of the Romans from ancient times, after intercourse with his own wife to seek purification by washing and for a short time to abstain reverently from entering a church. Nor in saying this do we reckon marriage to be sinful, but because it is not possible to have lawful intercourse without the pleasure of the flesh, it is proper to abstain from entering a holy place, because the pleasure itself cannot be without sin. For he was not born from adultery or fornication who said, " Behold, I was conceived in iniquity and in sin my mother gave birth to me" (Ps. 50.7). He knew himself to have been conceived in iniquity and lamented that he was born in sin because the tree bears in its bough the moisture it drew from the root. In these words, however, he does not call the intercourse of married people sinful, but only the desire for intercourse. Indeed, there are many things which are lawful and legitimate and yet we are to some extent defiled in doing them. As very often, by being angry we correct faults and at the same time disturb our own peace of mind. And though what we do is right, yet it is not to be approved that our mind should be disturbed. For he who said, "My eye was disturbed with anger" (Ps. 6.8), had been angry at the vices of those who had offended. Now, since only a tranquil mind can rest in the light of contemplation, he grieved that his eye was disturbed by anger because, while he was correcting evil deeds below, he was obliged to be distracted and disturbed from the contemplation of the highest things. Anger against vice is, therefore, commendable and yet harmful because he thinks that by his mind being agitated, he has incurred some guilt. And so intercourse is lawful when it is for the sake of children, not for pleasure, and carnal union must be for the sake of conceiving children and not to satisfy vices. But if any man approaches his wife not moved by lustful desire, but only for the sake of conceiving children, such a man is certainly to be left to his own judgment, either as to entering the church or to receiving the body and blood of the Lord, for he who being placed in the fire cannot burn, is not to be forbidden by us to receive. But when it is not the love of conceiving children but of pleasure that dominated the act of coitus, the couple have cause to lament their deed. For the holy

preaching allows them this, and yet fills the mind with fear of that very concession. When the Apostle Paul said, "Let him who cannot contain himself have
his own wife," he took care to add, "But I say this by way of indulgence, not as
a commandment" (I Cor. 7.6). For that which is lawful is not granted by way
of indulgence because it is right, therefore, that which he said he indulged, he
showed to be an offence.

It should be considered seriously that when God was to speak to the people
on Mount Sinai, he first commanded them to abstain from women. And if so
much purity of body was required there, where God spoke to the people by
means of a subject creature, that those who were to hear the words of God
were not to join with women, how much more ought women who receive the
body of almighty God preserve themselves in purity of the flesh lest they be
burdened with the very greatness of that inestimable mystery? For this reason,
the priest said to David, concerning his men, that if they had abstained from
women, they should receive the shewbread, which they would not have
received at all if David had not first declared them pure with regard to women.
Then a man who, after marital intercourse, has washed with water, is also able
to receive the mystery of holy communion, since it is lawful for him, according
to what has been said before, to enter the church.

*Why did women stop nursing their infants? When were a husband and wife prohibited
from having sexual relations? Why were there questions about when a woman was
allowed to enter a church? When was a man considered unclean? Distinguish the pollution believed to be caused by menstruation from that caused by intercourse. Why/how are
they different? What are the legitimate reasons for sexual relations? The illegitimate
ones? Was this letter an attempt to accommodate, for missionary purposes, the pagans of
England?*

60. A MEDICAL DISCUSSION OF CHILDBIRTH

Pregnancy and childbirth were a normal and expected part of a married woman's life. Yet childbirth was also the most dangerous process a woman could experience. Moreover, a woman might have upwards of ten pregnancies in her married life. The mortality rate for mothers and their newborns was very high, prompting priests to exhort midwives to know the proper formula for baptism. If the newborn, or partially born, child were about to die the midwife could baptize it in extremis. Childbirth was a female affair with neither the father nor a male physician being present. The birth was presided over by a midwife and the mother's female relations and friends. Midwives were often highly skilled in the practical aspects of childbirth. As well, they were knowledgeable in the use of herbal remedies and the practice of folk medicine. Some of the potions recommended to induce labor might also function as abortifacients, and consequently midwives were often subject to clerical criticism. This selection is from an early fifteenth-century English treatise on obstetrics and gynecology. The instructions for difficult births are remarkably detailed and amply indicate the dangers associated with childbirth. Many of the potions and ointments that are recommended can be traced back to the medical writers of antiquity.

Source: Trans. Beryl Rowland, *Medieval Woman's Guide to Health: The First English Gynecological Handbook* (Kent, OH: Kent State University Press, 1981), pp. 123, 125, 127, 129, 131, 133, 135, 137, 139; reprinted with permission.

The tenth chapter is concerned with the sicknesses that women have in childbearing. Sicknesses that women have bearing children are of two kinds, natural and unnatural. When it is natural, the child comes out in twenty pangs or within those twenty, and the child comes the way it should: first the head, and afterward the neck, and with the arms, shoulders, and other members properly as it should. In the second way, the child comes out unnaturally, and that may be in sixteen ways, as you will find in their proper chapters, and the first is as follows:

When the child's head appears, as it were, head first, and the rest of the child remains inside the uterus. The remedy for this is that the midwife, with her hand anointed with oils, that is, wild thyme oil, pure lily oil, or oil of musk, as is necessary, put her hand in and turn the child properly with her hands from the sides of the uterus. And [see that] the orifice of the womb is so well anointed that the child can come forth in right order.

The second mode of unnatural childbirth occurs when the child comes out with his feet jointly together, only the midwife can never bring the child out when it comes down like this. But when the child begins to come out in this way, the midwife with her hands anointed with oil must put them in and push him up again and so arrange him that he can come forth in the most natural manner, so that he does not flatten his hands in the sides of the uterus.

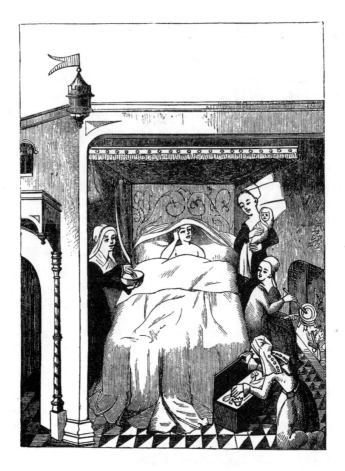

A nineteenth-century drawing of a medieval birthing chamber. Female friends and relatives attended births and assisted the midwife and cared for the new mother.

The third unnatural mode is if the child's head is so bulky and large that he cannot emerge: the midwife should then push him back and anoint the orifice, that is, the mouth of the privy member with fresh May butter or with common oil, and then the midwife's hand, oiled first and then put in and the orifice enlarged, brings the child forth by the head.

In the fourth mode of unnatural childbirth, the woman in labor shall be placed in a short, narrow, high-standing bed, with her head off the bed, and the midwife, with her hand anointed with oil, thrusts her hand in after the child who is in an unnatural position, turns him correctly, and then brings him forth; but the bed that the woman should lie in must be made hard.

The fifth mode of unnatural childbirth is when the child extends his hand first, his head is turned back, and the mouth of the privy member is narrow or shut; then, with the inducement of the hands of the midwife, the orifice should be enlarged, and the child's hand put in again so that the child does not die as the result of the midwife's error. We prescribe that the midwife put her hand in, turning the child's shoulders toward the back and hands properly down at the side. And then take the head of the child; then slowly bring him forth.

The sixth mode of unnatural childbirth is when the child extends both his hands with his two shoulders, with his hands one on one side and one on the other, and the head is turned back in a reversed position into the side. The midwife with her hand shall put the child in again, as we said in the adjoining chapter, that is, she should put his hands to his sides, take the child's head, and gently bring him forth. If he has a small head, and if he throws out his hands first, the midwife should arrange for the head to come to the mouth of the privy member, and so by her hands she shall bring him forth by the grace of God.

The seventh mode of unnatural childbirth occurs when the child first throws out his right foot, and the midwife will never deliver him in this way unless she first applies her fingers and puts the child up again; and after that, she must put in her hand and align that foot with the other foot to get both feet in the right position if possible, and the child's hands to his sides, and his feet as they should be, and then bring the child forth.

The eighth mode of unnatural childbirth occurs when the child puts out both feet and the rest of the child is left bent up in the body, as we said previously. The midwife with her hand shoved in should carefully arrange the child, and so bring him out, as I said previously.

The ninth mode of unnatural childbirth occurs when the child displays first one hand and one foot and covers his face with the other hand. The midwife places the fingers of one hand on the groin of the woman in labor, and with the other hand puts the child in again, as we have demonstrated before, and so brings the child forth if possible.

The tenth mode of unnatural childbirth occurs when the child presents first his feet apart, one hand between his feet, and his head hanging backward. The midwife with her hand put inside should correct the position of the child, placing one hand by the other down at his sides, adjusting the head in the best way, arranging the feet properly, and then bring the child forth.

The eleventh mode of unnatural childbirth occurs when the child's neck comes out first; then the midwife with her hand should push him up again by the shoulders, raise the child aloft, bring him down to the orifice, and so fetch him out.

The twelfth mode of unnatural childbirth occurs when the child first presents his knees bent; then the midwife shall push him back in again; the midwife should put her hands on both sides in the woman's groin and then, with her own hand annointed with oil put inside, correct the position of the knees. And she should take the child by the shoulders and so gently bring him out backward. And so, when the postion of his feet has been corrected and he has been put up in the right position, then bring him forth by the grace of God and the midwife's skill.

The thirteenth mode of unnatural childbirth occurs when the child first presents his thighs and comes forth with his buttocks first; then the midwife with her hand should put the child in again by the feet, and then bring him forth to the orifice, and deliver him smoothly.

The fourteenth mode of unnatural childbirth is if the child's head and the soles of his feet come together; we instruct the midwife in such circumstances to push her hand into the privy member so that the child be taken and carried upward into the womb again; then the child should be grasped by the head and brought out.

The fifteenth mode of unnatural childbirth occurs when the child lies prostrate or else upright, and his feet and his hands are over his head. Then the midwife with her hand inside should straighten the child with her fingers; then, as far as she can, let the head come forward, and so bring the child out.

The sixteenth mode of unnatural childbirth occurs when there is more than one child, as happens every day, and they all come to the orifice at once; then let the midwife put one back again with her fingers while she brings out one of the children. And then afterward, another, so doing that the uterus is not constricted nor the children brought to grief, as often happens.

In order to deliver a woman of a child and to kill it if it cannot be brought out: take rue, savin, southernwood, and iris, and let her drink them. Also take 2 drachms each of the juice of hyssop, and of dittany, and 2 scruples of quicksilver, and this medicine is proved to be effective. Also take 4 drachms each of the juice of iris and bull's gall, 2 drachms of suitable oil, mix all of these together, put it in a pessary, give it to the woman, and this medicine will bring out all the decomposed matter of the womb. And it will deliver a woman of a dead child, and of her secundines, and it brings on menstruation. Again, give to the pregnant woman 2 drachms of asafetida 3 times daily, and let the stomach and back be anointed with oil and gall, and afterward let oil, ox gall, and asafetida be placed in the vulva with a feather.

And the sicknesses that women have in childbearing come sometimes from the sickness of the child, and that may be because the child has grown considerably in his mother's womb before she has caught the dropsy; and this the midwife may well know, and the woman also. And sometimes the sickness comes through the frailty of the woman because she is not strong enough to deliver the child. And this may be in two ways: because of the great sickness that the woman has had and that has greatly weakened her; or because of the great anxiety of the woman, and if this is the first time that she has conceived for twelve years. Sometimes it comes from the blocking of the womb. And that may be due to two reasons: because fatness stops the mouth of the womb and holds back the blood that she should have been purged of before children were conceived; or sometimes it is because the child is dead in its mother's womb. And the signs are as follows: they feel no stirring or movement of the child inside; on the second day of labor the mouth smells evil; they feel much pain and distress about the navel; the face and the entire body waste away; they want things that are harmful to them; they wake a lot and sleep little; they have a great trouble in making water and going to the privy, and also they have great discomfort about the genitals. And if the child does not come out as it should, the midwife can help well enough without any other medicines, as I have previously described. But if her sickness be any of the ones that I have mentioned, make her a bath of mallows, fenugreek, linseed, wormwood, southernwood, pellitory, fennel, and mugwort boiled in water, and let her bathe in it for a good time. And when she comes out of the bath, see that she is anointed from the navel downward to the privy member with butter, deute, and ointment of Aragon, both in front and behind. And afterward make her a fumigation underneath of 1_ ounces of spikenard and 1 ounce of roots of costmary. And also when she comes from the bath, if she is a rich woman, give her 1 ounce of the juice of the balsam tree in warm wine; if she is a poor woman, boil roots of costmary and artemisia in wine, add to it 2 ounces of bull's gall, and let her drink the mixture when she comes from the bath. Or mix 2 ounces of borax with wine and give her that to drink; or give her 3 drachms each of the juice of dittany, hyssop, half a scruple of mercury, and this medicament will cast out the child alive or dead, and even more successfully if it is given with a pill of myrrh, according to Rhazes' instruction; take 2 ounces of myrrh, 2½ ounces of lupins, 8 drachms each of rue leaves dried with wild mint, thyme, that is, woodruff, mountain willow, asafetida, orchis, juice of panax, galbanum, aromatic gum, and some good malmsey as required. Make pills like small tablets, each weighing 2 drachms. Give her one of them with an infusion of junipers in wine, for these are good for difficult births, to bring out the secundines and destroy the mola of the womb. If these cannot be obtained, make a plaster of artemisia boiled in water and plaster the woman with it from the navel to the privy member, for it makes a woman quickly give birth to a child, whether it is alive or dead in her womb, and it draws out the secundine. But let it not remain there very long, for it will draw out the uterus also. A fine, valuable powder for women who are in labor and for pangs afterward: take 3 drachms of the pods of cassia fistula, an ounce of savory, and another ounce of hyssop; powder all these together and give it to the woman in the juice of vervain warmed. And this potion when drunk causes her to be quickly delivered, and it draws out the secundine. It also makes a woman who is stopped up to have her purgation straightaway. Also, cyclamen spread under a woman while she is in labor makes her give birth quickly.

The juice of vervain does the same thing when drunk. Alternatively, let her drink an eggshell full of the juice of leek or dittany, and mallows. These and savin also have great power to deliver a woman of her child. And the water from a man's skin that he has washed his hands in also has the same power. Signs that a woman is about to give birth are much stirring and movement in the womb, and sometimes all of the womb moves up to the stomach, causing the woman to have a great desire to give birth; and she feels very heavy about the navel, and the child bestirs itself vigorously to pass from its mother. Then have her nostrils stopped, so that the vital spirits can go down to the uterus, and encourage her with her burden. And have her put on a girdle of hart's skin. And if she faints, have sweet-smelling things placed at her nose, and rub the soles of her feet and the palms of her hands with sharp, biting things, such as vinegar and salt. Balm, that is, juice of the balsam tree made in the manner of a suppository, causes a woman to be delivered of a child; it draws out the secundine also, but it causes her to be barren ever after. And the juice of rue and artemisia causes a woman quickly to be delivered of her child though it is dead in her womb. It is also helpful to make the patient sneeze with pepper powder and castory powder by throwing them up her nose. And a drink of savory juice causes a woman quickly to be delivered of her child, and if the herb is plastered on her womb it makes the child come out alive or dead. A precious stone called jasper has great power to help women in childbirth. Also, for a woman who has a dead child in her womb, give the juice of a beech tree mixed with honey, make a plaster of wormwood, and fasten it to her left hip. Woman's milk and oil drunk together make a woman give birth. Another prescription: half a drachm each of savin, gladiola, that is, iris, southernwood, rue, dittany, hyssop, savory; let them be well crushed in 3 ounces of the best white wine and drunk, and she will be quickly delivered.

What risks did women face in childbirth? What is the significance of a potion that could bring on both childbirth and menstruation? What is the significance of the potion made of water from a man's skin?

61. DESCRIPTION OF A BIRTHING CHAMBER

Christine de Pisan (1365-1430?) wrote a number of important and remarkable treatises including The City of Ladies *and* The Treasure of the City of Ladies, *also known as* The Book of Three Virtues. *Christine was married to the physician of the king of France. Her husband died suddenly and very young, leaving Christine with children and a mother to support. As a result of this tragedy, Christine became a professional writer, patronized by luminaries in the French court and supporting herself and her family by her writing. One of Christine's major concerns was the status and reputation of the female sex, which she believed was unfairly maligned by male writers imbued with conventionalized misogyny.* The City of Ladies *presents a catalog of virtuous women. Its sequel,* The Treasure of the City of Ladies, *is a practical guide to the kinds of things women needed to know to live in the world. Christine divided her discussion according to rank, addressing servants and prostitutes as well as queens and noble women. Her discussion of the kinds of challenges that confronted widows clearly reflects Christine's own unhappy personal experience. This passage, from her advice to women of the merchant class, indicates how Christine believed each person should live according to her rank. She describes the chamber in which a pretentious bourgeois woman was preparing to give birth, an occasion which was both momentous and decidedly social.*

Source: Trans. Sarah Lawson in Christine de Pisan, *The Treasure of the City of Ladies* (Harmondsworth: Penguin Books, 1985), p.154; reprinted with permission.

3. Of the wives of merchants

... But now let us say something about merchants' wives. Was this not truly a great extravagance for a wife of a grocer? Even as a merchant, the husband is not like those of Venice or Genoa who go abroad and have their agents in every country, buy in large quantities and have a big turnover, and then they send their merchandise to every land in great bundles and thus earn enormous wealth. Such ones as these are called "noble merchants." But this one we are describing now buys in large quantities and sells in small amounts for perhaps only a few pennies, more or less, although his wife is rich and dresses like a great lady. Not long ago she had a lying-in before the birth of her child. Now, before one entered her chamber, one passed through two other very fine chambers, in each of which there was a large bed well and richly hung with curtains. In the second one there was a large dresser covered like an altar and laden with silver vessels. And then from that chamber one entered the chamber of the woman in childbed, a large and well-appointed room hung from floor to ceiling with tapestries made with her device worked very richly in fine Cyprus gold.

In this chamber was a large, highly ornamented dresser covered with golden dishes. The bed was large and handsome and hung with exquisite curtains. On the floor around the bed the carpets on which one walked were all worked with gold, and the large ornamented hangings, which extended more than a hand span below the bedspread, were of such fine linen of Rheims that they were worth three hundred francs. On top of this bedspread of tissue of gold was another large covering of linen as fine as silk, all of one piece and without a seam (made by a method only recently invented) and very expensive; it was said to be worth two hundred francs and more. It was so wide and long that it covered all sides of this large, elaborate bed and extended beyond the edge of the bedspread, which trailed on the floor on all sides. In this bed lay the woman who was going to give birth, dressed in crimson silk cloth and propped up on big pillows of the same silk with big pearl buttons, adorned like a young lady. And God knows what money was wasted on amusements, bathing, and various social gatherings, according to the customs in Paris for women in childbed (some more than others), at this lying-in! Although there are many examples of great prodigality, this extravagance exceeds all the others, and so is worth putting in a book! This thing was even reported in the queen's chamber! …

What did Christine de Pisan think about how this woman prepared for childbirth? Why would the woman (and her husband) think this preparation was appropriate? What kind of activities might accompany a lying-in?

62. PRAYERS FOR WOMEN IN CHILDBIRTH

The fears and dangers surrounding childbirth were numerous and justified. Childbirth was the most dangerous experience a woman faced and both mother and child would be at risk if the birth were difficult. Women themselves evoked the Virgin Mary and St. Margaret, the patron saint of childbirth. The church, as well, developed a formal liturgy and prayers of supplication for women in childbirth. These prayers reveal much about ecclesiastical attitudes toward birth and how mother and child were valued.

Source: Trans. Frederick E. Warren, *The Sarum Missal*, Part 2 (London: De La More Press, 1911), pp. 161–65; revised.

Mass in honor of the glorious Virgin for pregnant women or women laboring in childbirth

Kind virgin of virgins, holy mother of God, on behalf of your devoted hand-maids, present their earnest prayers to your Son, you who are the kind assistant to women in labor....

Prayer

O, most merciful Father, hear the entreaty of your servant on behalf of your poor handmaidens who are now, or will be in the future, in labor, most humbly entreating your majesty that, as by your providence you decreed them to conceive, so by your blessing you would go before them, to bring matters quickly to a conclusion, to the praise of your holy name, through the intercession of glorious virgin....

Gradual

Behold, a virgin conceived and for us gave birth to a son whose name was called Jesus.

V[ersicle]. Who descended into the virgin's womb as rain into a sheep fleece. And just as the sun through a shut door, he has come to us from a virginal womb.

Alleluiah. V[ersicle]. To your assistance, O Mary, poor women in labor flee. I entreat you not to despise them in their necessity, but, virgin ever blessed, free them from every danger.

Sequence

O, Mary, handmaid of Christ, mother of God, hear a poor sinner truly sighing unto you, lest infants be in danger in their mother's womb.

Who, not being baptised, ensnared in the net of original sin, descend together into limbo, which is part of hell.

And so, Mary, succor the wretched little children, who, on account of the heavy cloud [of sin] of Adam, the first man, are there forever deprived of the vision of God.

O the abyss of God's many judgments, who although they perish without guilt, however, do not perish without cause.

How pernicious, therefore, was Eve's bite of the forbidden fruit, by which death was thus established on her posterity.

But, O how happy and joyous, O Mary, was the dialogue between you and the angel, by which life came forth for the whole world.

But your most blessed childbirth, free from pain, seems to outshine all others.

Through which the curse of Eve was dissolved, and equally a blessing was bestowed on all women.

To whom, therefore, other than to you, consoler of all women, shall desperate pregnant women, groaning with tears, flee?

Hear them, immaculate Virgin, and do not let your only begotten child regard the sins of our parents.

But mercifully hear the wailing of the little ones, lest forever they should be plunged into the fearful punishment of hell.

And then, after they have been regenerated by the water of holy baptism, deem them worthy to lead to eternal joy....

Offertory

Hail Mary, consoler of women in childbirth, full of grace, helper of infants, because the Lord is with you, be their protector, so that you may be called blessed above women, and the fruit of your womb may be extolled by all Christians, as blessed above all.

Secret

O most tender Christ Jesus, who in your consideration deigned to be born into the world, without contact with pain, from the virginal womb of your gracious mother, through a gate most holy and closed, mercifully agree to arrange that the fruit of your handmaidens come into this world in such a way healthy and whole, that they merit to be reborn with you at the baptismal font. Who lives, etc....

Communion

In childbirth, O Mary, let the sun of your mercy shine, by which shining other lights, after God, are as if nothing.

After Communion

Most blessed Spirit, through whom all things were made, we pray that you agree to hear your handmaids on whose behalf we present these prayers to your tender mercy, as they hope to be delivered by your auspicious holy assistance, so, by the intercession of the most blessed mother of God, you will deign to pour forth the light of your grace on their speedy delivery. Who with the Father, etc.

What fears are expressed in these prayers? What happens to unbaptised children who die in childbirth? Why? How was Mary's childbirth distinguished from the birth experience of other women?

63. REJOICING FOR A SAFE DELIVERY

Childbirth was an experience that united women across social divides. Its pain and its dangers affected rich and poor alike. The mortality rate was extremely high. The anxiety reflected in the foregoing prayers for a safe delivery would give way to joy and celebration when both mother and child were safe and healthy. This was particularly true if the birth was of political significance, for example, of an heir to the throne. This letter from Queen Isabel, wife of Edward II, announces the birth of her son and the king's heir in the year 1312. The joy that resulted was more focused on the political nature of the birth and the fact that the succession to the throne was secure, which in turn signaled political stability for the kingdom, than on the simple survival of mother and child.

Source: Trans. Henry Thomas Riley, *Memorials of London and London Life in the XIIIth, XIVth, and XVth Centuries* (London: Longmans, Green, 1868), pp. 105-07; revised.

A letter from Queen Isabel, announcing her safe delivery of a son, with an account of the rejoicing this occasioned.

Isabel, by the grace of God, queen of England, lady of Ireland, and duchess of Aquitaine, to our well beloved mayor and aldermen and the people of London, greeting. Since we believe that you would gladly hear good news about us, we thus wish to inform you that by the grace of our Lord, we have given birth to a son on the 13th day of November, with both ourselves and the child being safe. May our Lord preserve you. Given at Windsor, on the above date.

The bearer of this letter was John de Falaise, the queen's tailor; and he came on the Tuesday right after the Feast of St. Martin [11 November], in the sixth year of the reign of King Edward, son of King Edward [1312]. But, given that news had already been brought by Robert Oliver on the previous Monday, the mayor and aldermen and the majority of the people of London, who were gathered together in the Guildhall at Vespers, sang and danced and showed great joy at the news. They went through the city with blazing torches and with trumpets and other musical instruments.

And on the next Tuesday, early in the morning, it was cried throughout the city that the day was a holiday and there was to be no work done or business conducted. Everyone was to dress up as well as he could and go to the Guildhall at the hour of Prime. When they were ready, they would go with the mayor, along with the other good people of London, to St. Paul's and there give praise and bring offerings to the honor of God, who had shown them such favor on earth, and to show respect for this child that had been born. And after this, they were to return together to the Guildhall, to do whatever might be ordered.

And the mayor and the aldermen assembled at the Guildhall, together with the good people. From there they went to St. Paul's where the bishop, on that very day, chanted Mass with great solemnity, and they made their offering. After Mass, they led carols in the Church of St. Paul, to the sound of trumpets, and then each person returned home.

On the following Wednesday, the mayor, with the assent of the aldermen and the people, gave to the said John de Falaise, bearer of the aforementioned letter, ten pounds sterling and a silver cup weighing four marks [32 ounces]. The next morning, this same John de Falaise sent back the present because he considered it too small.

On the following Monday, the mayor was richly dressed and the aldermen attired in similar finery, and the drapers, mercers, and vinters were dressed up. They rode on horseback to Westminster and there made offerings and then returned to the Guildhall, which was excellently decorated and hung with tapestries, and there they dined. After dinner, they went singing and dancing throughout the city for the rest of the day and a great part of the night. On the same day, the Conduit in Cheap ran with nothing but wine, for all those who chose to drink there. And at the Earl of Gloucester's Cross, right near the Church of St. Michael in West Cheap, there was a pavilion which extended into the middle of the street. In this a tun of wine was set for all those who passed by and who wished to have a drink.

On the Sunday after Candlemas [2 February] in the same year, the fishmongers of London were richly dressed and they arranged for a boat to be decorated in the guise a great ship, with all the rigging that belongs to a ship. It sailed through Cheap as far as Westminster, where the fishmongers came, well mounted, and presented the same ship to the queen. On the same day, the queen started on her way to Canterbury on pilgrimage and the fishmongers, all richly dressed, escorted her through the city.

Who was involved in the celebration? How and for how long did the people celebrate? What does this indicate? Why was the celebration so elaborate? Why did the Queen go to Canterbury?

CHAPTER EIGHT:

PARENTS AND CHILDREN

In the Middle Ages there was not the same focus on the family, the ménage of parents and children, as is found in modern western society. Family, familia, was a social institution that was porous and flexible and could expand and contract at different times of life. A bishop's or king's familia would include servants and retainers, clerics and warriors, along with a large number of relatives. In a village or modest urban craft shop, enterprises that depended on the work of husband, wife, and children, the household might include servants, apprentices, unmarried adult children, an elderly parent, or an orphaned relative. Even medieval theologians and canon lawyers tended to focus on marriage and the relationship between husband and wife, while having little to say about parents and children as a specific and distinct family group.

Nevertheless, despite the flexibility and size of the household and the absence of lengthy discussions by writers, the Middle Ages, too, recognized the existence of a special bond between parents and children. These relationships were intense, emotional, and enduring. Just as parents nurtured their young children, so children would be responsible for their aging parents. Childhood itself was perceived as a special and distinct time of life. It was a period free from the cares of adulthood. Equally, however, it was the time during which the adult was formed. Thus, it was incumbent upon parents and teachers to ensure children were properly cared for and raised to be upright and responsible adults. Sometimes the bonds between parent and child were intense, sometimes they frayed. Nevertheless, children who were orphaned were considered particularly vulnerable. Bereft of their parents' care, society as a whole had a responsibility to protect them.

415

64. BIBLICAL ADVICE ON PARENT/CHILD RELATIONS

When medieval people turned to the Bible for models of familial behavior, they were greeted by a certain ambivalence. From the very point when humanity had been created in the form of Adam and Eve, primacy had been given to the marital relationship rather than the bonds between parents and children. In Genesis, it is stated that a man shall leave his mother and father and cling to his wife (Gen. 2.25). Paul, too, directed most of his teaching to the husband and wife. One of the exceptions to the scriptural generalizations that children honor their parents is found in the lyrical celebration of parents and children in the book of Ecclesiasticus.

Source: *The Holy Bible, Douay Rheims Version* (Baltimore: John Murphy, 1899; rpt. Rockford, IL: Tan Books, 1971); modernized.

Ecclesiasticus 3.1-19

1. The children of wisdom are the church of the just: and their generation, obedience, and love.

2. Children, hear the judgment of your father, do so that you may be saved.

3. For God has made the father honorable to the children: and seeking the judgment of the mothers, has confirmed it on the children.

4. He who loves God will obtain pardon for his sins, and will keep himself from sin, and his prayers will be heard.

5. And he who honors his mother is like one who stores a treasure.

6. He who honors his father will have joy in his own children, and his prayers will be heard.

7. He who honors his father will enjoy a long life: and he who obeys the father, will be a comfort to his mother.

8. He who fears the Lord, honors his parents, and will serve them as if they who brought him into the world were his masters.

9. Honor your father, in word and deed, and with patience,

10. So that a blessing may come upon you from him, and his blessing may remain in the end.

11. The father's blessing establishes the houses of his children: but the mother's curse uproots the foundation.

12. Do not glory in the dishonor of your father, for his shame is no glory to you.

13. For the glory of a man is from the honor of his father, and a father without honor is the disgrace of the son.

14. Son, support your father in his old age and do not trouble him during his life;

15. And if his mind fails, have patience with him, and do not despise him when you are in your prime, for supporting your father will not be forgotten.

16. For good shall be repaid to you for the sin of your mother.

17. And in justice you will be edified, and on the day of affliction you will be remembered: and your sins will melt away as the ice in the fair warm weather.

18. Of what an evil reputation is he who forsakes his father: and he is cursed by God who angers his mother.

What will happen to a child who honors his or her parents? What should children do for elderly parents?

65. JEROME ON THE EDUCATION OF GIRLS

In 385 St. Jerome, having been pushed out of Rome for his ascetic extremism, settled in Bethlehem. He lived there along with the wealthy Roman matron Paula and her daughter Eustochium. Paula founded a community for like-minded women nearby. In 403 Jerome wrote a letter to Laeta, Paula's daughter-in-law, who had just given birth to her own daughter, whom she named Paula. Laeta had sought Jerome's advice about how best to raise her young daughter. Jerome's reply contains something of a treatise on early Christian child-rearing, including advice on how to teach children to read and write. Jerome also managed both to rejoice at the birth of the little girl and to extol the superiority of the ascetic life of virginity. He also suggests that Laeta send her daughter Paula to Bethlehem to be raised by her aunt Eustochium and Jerome himself, a suggestion that Laeta did in fact accept. This letter shows a softer side to Jerome, who was known for his misogyny and harsh criticism of marriage and other worldly attachments.

Source: Trans. Henry Wace and Philip Schaff in St. Jerome, *To Laeta*, A Select Library of Nicene and Post-Nicene Fathers, vol. 6 (Oxford: James Parker and Company, 1893), pp. 190-91, 193-95; revised.

For, in answer to your prayers and those of the saintly Marcella, I wish to address you as a mother and to instruct you how to bring up our dear Paula, who was consecrated to Christ before her birth and vowed to his service before her conception. Thus in our own day we have seen repeated the story told to us in the Prophets, of Hannah, who though at first barren afterwards became fruitful. You have exchanged a fertility bound up with sorrow for children who shall never die. For I am confident that having given to the Lord your first-born, you will be the mother of sons. It is the first-born that is offered under the Law. Samuel and Samson are both instances of this, as is also John the Baptist who when Mary came in leaped for joy. For he heard the Lord speaking by the mouth of the Virgin and desired to break from his mother's womb to meet Him. As Paula has been born in answer to a promise, her parents should raise her in a way suitable to her birth. Samuel, as you know, was nurtured in the Temple, and John was trained in the wilderness. The first, as a Nazarite, wore his hair long, drank neither wine nor strong drink, and even in his childhood talked with God. The second shunned cities, wore a leather girdle, and ate locusts and wild honey. Moreover, to typify that penitence which he was to preach, he was clothed in the hide of the hump-backed camel.

4. Thus must a soul be educated which is to be a temple of God. It must learn to hear nothing and to say nothing but what belongs to the fear of God. It must have no understanding of unclean words, and no knowledge of worldly songs. Its tongue must be steeped while still tender in the sweetness of psalms.

EIGHT: PARENTS AND CHILDREN

Boys, with their wanton thoughts, must be kept away from Paula. Even her maids and female attendants must be separated from worldly associates, for if they have learned some mischief they may teach it to her. Get a set of letters for her, made of boxwood or of ivory, and call each by its proper name. Let her play with these, so that even her play may teach her something. And let her not only grasp the right order of the letters and turn their names into rhymes, but constantly disarrange their order and put the last letters in the middle and the middle ones at the beginning so that she may know them all by sight as well as by sound. Moreover, as soon as she begins to use the stylus on the wax tablet, and while her hand is still faltering, either guide her soft fingers by laying your hand upon hers, or else have simple copies cut upon a tablet so that her efforts, confined within these limits, may keep to the lines traced out for her and not stray outside of these. Offer prizes for good spelling and encourage her with little gifts such as delight children of her age. And let her have companions in her lessons to excite emulation in her, that she may be stimulated when she sees them praised. You must not scold her if she is slow to learn but rather employ praise to excite her mind, so that she may be glad when she excels others and sorry when she is excelled by them. Above all, you must take care not to make her lessons distasteful to her lest a dislike for them, conceived in childhood, continue into her mature years. The very words which she tries bit by bit to put together and to pronounce ought not to be haphazard ones, but words specially selected and purposefully chosen, for example, those of the prophets or the apostles, or the list of patriarchs from Adam on, as given by Matthew and Luke. In this way, while her tongue will be well-trained, her memory will likewise be developed.

Again, you must choose for her a teacher of approved years, life, and learning. A man of culture will not, I think, blush to do for a kinswoman or a highborn virgin what Aristotle did for Philip's son when, descending to the level of a servant, he consented to teach him his letters. Things must not be despised as of small account if, in their absence, great results cannot be achieved. The very rudiments and first beginnings of knowledge sound differently in the mouth of an educated person and of an uneducated. Accordingly, you must see that the child is not led astray by the silly coaxing of women to form a habit of shortening long words or of decking herself with gold and purple. Of these habits one will spoil her conversation and the other her character. She must not, therefore, learn as a child what afterwards she will have to unlearn. The eloquence of the Gracchi is said to have been largely due to the way in which, from their earliest years, their mother spoke to them. Hortensius became an orator while still on his father's lap. Early impressions are hard to eradicate from the mind. When wool has been dyed purple who can restore it to its previous whiteness? An unused jar retains the taste and smell of what was in it for a long time afterwards. Greek history tells us that the imperious Alexander, who was lord of the whole world, could not rid himself of the tricks of manner and bearing which in childhood he had caught from his governor Leonides. We are always ready to imitate what is evil; and faults are quickly copied where virtues appear unattainable. Paula's nurse must not be intemperate, or loose, or given to gossip. Her foster-mother must be respectable, and her foster-father of grave demeanor. When she sees her grandfather, she must leap into his arms, put her arms round his neck, and, whether he likes it or not, sing "Alleluia" in his ears. She may be hugged by her grandmother, smile at her father to show that she recognizes him, and thus endear herself to everyone, so that the whole family will rejoice in the possession of such a rosebud. She should be told at once who her other grandmother and her aunt are; and she ought also to learn in what army she is a recruit, and under what captain she is called to serve. Let her long to be with those absent and encourage her to make playful threats of leaving you for them.

5. Let her very dress and clothing remind her to whom she is promised. Do not pierce her ears or paint her face, consecrated to Christ, with white lead or rouge. Do not hang gold or pearls about her neck or load her head with jewels, or by reddening her hair make it suggest the fires of hell. Let her pearls be of another kind which she may sell hereafter and buy in their place the pearl that is "of great price."...

8. Let her not take her food with others, that is, at her parents' table; lest she see dishes she may long for. Some, I know, hold it a greater virtue to disdain a pleasure which is actually in front of them, but I think it a safer self-restraint to avoid what will certainly tempt you. Once as a boy at school I read the words: "It is hard to blame what you allow to become a habit." Let her learn even now not to drink wine "wherein lies excess." But as, before children come to a robust age, abstinence is dangerous and trying to their tender bodies, let her have baths if she require them, and let her drink a little wine for her stomach's sake. Let her also be supported on a diet of meat, lest her feet fail her before they commence to run their race. But "I say this by way of concession, not by way of command" (1 Cor. 7.6); because I fear to weaken her, not because I wish to teach her self-indulgence. Besides, why should not a Christian virgin do wholly what others do in part? The superstitious Jews reject certain animals and products as food, while in India, the Brahmans and in Egypt, the Gymnosophists subsist completely on porridge, rice, and apples. If mere glass repays so much labor, must not a pearl be worth more labor still? Paula has been born in response to a vow. Let her life be like the lives of those who were born under the same conditions. If the grace accorded is in both cases the same, the pains bestowed ought to be so, too. Let her be deaf to the sound of the organ, and not even know the uses of the pipe, the lyre, and the harp.

9. And let it be her task daily to bring to you the flowers which she has culled from Scripture. Let her learn by heart so many verses in Greek, but let her be instructed in Latin also. For, if the tender lips are not from the beginning shaped to this, the tongue is spoiled by a foreign accent and its native speech debased by alien elements. You yourself must be her mistress, a model on which she may form her childish conduct. Never, either in you nor in her father, let her see what she cannot imitate without sin. Remember both of you that you are the parents of a consecrated virgin, and that your example will teach more than your precepts. Flowers are quick to fade and a baleful wind soon withers the violet, the lily, and the crocus. Let her never appear in public unless accompanied by you. Let her never visit a church or a martyr's shrine unless with her mother. Let no young man greet her with smiles, no dandy with curled hair pay compliments to her. If our little virgin goes to keep solemn, all-night vigils, let her not stir a hair's breadth from her mother's side. She must not single out one of her maids as her special favorite or confidante. What she says to one all ought to know. Let her choose for a companion not a handsome well-dressed girl, able to warble a song with liquid notes but one pale and serious, sombrely attired and with the hue of melancholy. Let her model be some aged virgin of approved faith, character, and chastity, apt to instruct her by word and by example. She ought to rise at night to recite prayers and psalms; to sing hymns in the morning; at the third, sixth, and ninth hours to take her place in the line to do battle for Christ; and, lastly, to kindle her lamp and offer her evening sacrifice. In these occupations let her pass the day, and when night comes let it find her still engaged in them. Let reading follow prayer and prayer again succeed reading. Time will seem short when employed on so many and varied tasks.

10. Let her learn too how to spin wool, to hold the distaff, to put the basket in her lap, to turn the spinning wheel, and to shape the yarn with her thumb. Let her put away with disdain silken fabrics, Chinese fleeces, and gold brocades. The clothing which she makes for herself should keep out the cold and not expose the body which it professes to cover. Let her food be herbs and wheaten bread with one or two small fish now and then. And so that I may not waste more time giving precepts for the regulation of appetite (a subject I have treated at length elsewhere) let her meals always leave her hungry and able immediately to begin reading or chanting. I strongly disapprove — especially for those of tender years — of long and immoderate fasts in which week is added to week and even oil and apples are forbidden. I have learned by experience that the ass toiling along the highway makes for an inn when it is weary. Our abstinence may turn to gluttony, like that of the worshipers of Isis and Cybele, who gobble up pheasants and turtle-doves piping hot so that their teeth may not violate the gifts of Ceres. If perpetual fasting is allowed, it must

be regulated so that those who have a long journey before them may hold out through it; and we must take care that we do not, after starting well, fall halfway. However, in Lent, as I have already written, those who practice self-denial should spread every stitch of canvas, and the charioteer should for once slacken the reins and increase the speed of his horses. Yet there will be one rule for those who live in the world and another for virgins and monks. The layperson in Lent consumes the lining of his stomach, and living like a snail on his own juices, makes ready a paunch for the rich foods and feasting to come. But with the virgin and the monk the case is different; for, when these give the rein to their steeds, they have to remember that for them the race knows no intermission. An effort made only for a limited time may well be severe, but one that has no such limit must be more moderate. For, whereas in the first case we can recover our breath when the race is over, in the second we have to go on continually and without stopping.

11. When you go a short way into the country, do not leave your daughter behind you. Leave her no power or capacity of living without you, and let her feel frightened when she is left to herself. She should not converse with worldly people nor associate with virgins indifferent to their vows. She should not be present at the weddings of your slaves nor take part in the noisy games of the household. As regards the use of the bath, I know that some are content with saying that a Christian virgin should not bathe along with eunuchs or with married women, with the former because they are still men, at all events in mind, and with the latter because pregnant women offer a revolting spectacle. For myself, however, I wholly disapprove of baths for a virgin of full age. Such a one should blush and feel overcome at the idea of seeing herself undressed. By vigils and fasts she mortifies her body and brings it into subjection. By cold chastity she seeks to put out the flame of lust and to quench the hot desires of youth. And by deliberate squalor she hastens to spoil her natural good looks. Why, then, should she add fuel to a sleeping fire by taking baths?

12. Let her treasures be not silks or gems but manuscripts of the holy scriptures; and in these let her think less of gilding and Babylonian parchment and arabesque patterns, than of correctness and accurate punctuation. Let her begin by learning the psalter, and then let her gather rules of life out of the proverbs of Solomon. From the Preacher let her gain the habit of despising the world and its vanities. Let her follow the example set by Job of virtue and of patience. Then let her pass on to the gospels, never to be laid aside when once they have been taken in hand. Let her also drink with a willing heart the Acts of the Apostles and the Epistles. As soon as she has enriched the storehouse of her mind with these treasures, let her commit to memory the Prophets, the Heptateuch, the books of Kings and of Chronicles, and the rolls of Ezra and Esther. When she has done all this she may safely read the Song of Songs, but not

before. Were she to read it at the beginning, she would fail to perceive that, although it is written in carnal words, it is a marriage song of a spiritual bride. Not understanding this, she would be hurt by it. Let her avoid all apocryphal writings, and if she is led to read such not by the truth of the doctrines which they contain but out of respect for the miracles contained in them. Let her understand that they are not really written by those to whom they are ascribed, that many mistakes have been introduced into them, and that it requires infinite discretion to look for gold in the midst of dirt. Let her always have Cyprian's writings in her hands. She may go through the letters of Athanasius and the treatises of Hilary without fear of stumbling. Let her take pleasure in all those books which show a due regard for the faith. But if she reads the works of others, let it be rather to judge them than to follow them.

13. You will answer, "How shall I, a woman of the world, living at Rome, surrounded by a crowd, be able to observe all these injunctions?" In that case do not undertake a burden to which you are not equal. When you have weaned Paula as Isaac was weaned and when you have clothed her as Samuel was clothed, send her to her grandmother and aunt. Give up this most precious of gems, to be placed in Mary's chamber and to rest in the cradle where the infant Jesus cried. Let her be brought up in a monastery; let her learn to avoid swearing; let her regard lying as sacrilege; let her be ignorant of the world; let her live the angelic life. While in the flesh let her be without flesh, and let her think that all human beings are like she is. To say nothing of its other advantages, this course of action will free you from the difficult task of minding her, and from the responsibility of guardianship. It is better to regret her absence than to be forever worrying about her. For you cannot help but worry as you watch what she says and to whom she says it, to whom she bows and whom she likes best to see. Hand her over to Eustochium while she is still an infant and her every cry is a prayer for you. She will thus become her companion in holiness now, as well as her successor hereafter. Let her gaze upon and love her, let her "from her earliest years admire" one whose language and bearing and dress are an education in virtue. Let her sit on her grandmother's lap, and let her grandmother repeat to her the lessons that she once taught to her own child. Long experience has shown her how to rear, to preserve, and to instruct virgins; and daily woven in her crown are the mystic hundred rewards of the highest chastity. O happy virgin! Happy Paula, daughter of Toxotius, who through the virtues of her grandmother and aunt is nobler in holiness than she is in lineage! Yes, Laeta, if you could only see with your own eyes your mother-in-law and your sister, and realize the mighty souls which animate their small bodies. Such is your innate desire for chastity that I cannot doubt but that you would go to them even before your daughter, and emancipate yourself from God's first decree of the Law to put yourself under his second dispensation of

the gospel. You would count as nothing your desire for other children and would offer up yourself to the service of God. But because "there is a time to embrace, and a time to refrain from embracing" (Eccl. 3.5), and because "the wife does not have power over her own body" (1 Cor. 7.4), and because the apostle says "Let every man remain in the state to which he was called" (1 Cor. 7.20) in the Lord, and because he that is under the yoke ought to run so as not to leave his companion in the mire, I counsel you to pay back in full in your children what in the meantime you defer paying in your own person. When Hannah had once offered in the tabernacle the son whom she had vowed to God, she never took him back; for she thought it unbecoming that one who was to be a prophet should grow up in the same house with her who still desired to have other children. Accordingly, after she had conceived and given birth to him, she did not venture to come to the temple alone or appear before the Lord empty-handed, but first paid Him what she owed; and then, when she offered up that great sacrifice, she returned home. And because she had borne her firstborn child for God, she was given five children for herself. Do you marvel at the happiness of that holy woman? Imitate her faith. Moreover, if you will only send Paula, I promise to be both tutor and foster-father to her. Old as I am, I will carry her on my shoulders and train her stammering lips, and my charge will be a far grander one than that of the worldly philosopher, for while he only taught a king of Macedon who was one day to die of Babylonian poison, I shall instruct the handmaid and spouse of Christ who one day must be offered to her Lord in heaven.

How will Laeta be rewarded for bringing up Paula as a Christian? How were children taught to read and write? What else should Paula learn? What kind of family life does Jerome portray? What kinds of things are allowed to a child to ensure that he or she grows up strong and healthy? What must be avoided? Why does Jerome discourage baths? Why does Jerome encourage Laeta to send Paula to him? Did Jerome think of Paula as a normal child?

66. FRANKISH PARENTS' GRIEF

Gregory of Tours recorded not only the political but also the personal events that affected the Frankish kingdom in the sixth century. He is frequently unflinching in his observation and description of the harshness, even cruelty, that characterized so much of life in this violent period. But Gregory also reveals the importance of family relationships and indicates that they could and did have an intense emotional component. His poignant description of the loss of children to the plague shows the tenderness and helplessness that confronted the parents of ill children. Even those whose lives were immersed in violence, such as Chilperic and Fredegund, are shown to have loved their children and grieved at their death. Children and the elderly, as the most vulnerable members of society, were the first to succumb to the ravages of plague, disease, or starvation. Familiarity with death, however, did not seem to lessen grief, as Fredegund's extreme reaction suggests. Fredegund's desperate search for answers and the reason for the outbreak of the plague also indicates the helplessness of parents who had no means by which to cure their children.

Source: Trans. Lewis Thorpe in Gregory of Tours, *The History of the Franks* (Harmondsworth: Penguin Books, 1974), pp. 296-98, 364-66; reprinted with permission.

5.34 A most serious epidemic followed these prodigies. While the kings were quarreling with each other again and once more making preparations for civil war, dysentery spread throughout the whole of Gaul. Those who caught it had a high temperature, with vomiting and severe pains in the small of the back: their heads ached and so did their necks. The matter they vomited up was yellow or even green. Many people maintained that some secret poison must be the cause of this. The countryfolk imagined that they had boils inside their bodies; and actually this is not as silly as it sounds, for as soon as cupping-glasses were applied to their shoulders or legs, great tumors formed, and when these burst and discharged their pus they were cured. Many recovered their health by drinking herbs which are known to be antidotes to poisons. The epidemic began in the month of August. It attacked young children first of all and to them it was fatal: and so we lost our little ones, who were so dear to us and sweet, whom we had cherished in our bosoms and dandled in our arms, whom we had fed and nurtured with such loving care. As I write I wipe away my tears and I repeat once more the words of Job the blessed: "The Lord gave, and the Lord has taken away; as it has pleased the Lord, so is it come to pass. Blessed be the name of the Lord, world without end" (Job 1.21).

In these days King Chilperic fell ill. When he recovered, his younger son, who had not yet been baptized in the name of the Holy Ghost, was attacked in his turn. They saw that he was dying and so they baptized him. He made a momentary recovery, but then Chlodobert, his older brother, caught the disease. When their mother Fredegund realized that he, too, was at death's door, she repented of her sins, rather late in the day, it is true, and said to the king: "God in his mercy has endured our evil goings-on long enough. Time and time again he has sent us warnings through high fevers and other indispositions, but we have never mended our ways. Now we are going to lose our children. It is the tears of paupers which are the cause of their death, the sighs of orphans, the widow's lament. Yet we still keep on amassing wealth, with no possible end in view. We still lay up treasures, we who have no one to whom we can leave them. Our riches live on after us, the fruits of rapine, hated and accursed, with no one left to possess them once we are gone. Were our cellars not already over-flowing with wine? Were our granaries not stuffed to the roof with corn? Were our treasure-houses not already full enough with gold, silver, precious stones, necklaces, and every regal adornment one could dream of? Now we are losing the most beautiful of our possessions! Come, then, I beg you! Let us set light to all these iniquitous tax-demands! What sufficed for King Lothar, your father, should be plenty enough for our exchequer, too." As she said this, the queen beat her breast with her fists. She ordered to be placed before her the tax-demands which had been brought back by Mark from her own cities, and she put them on the fire. She spoke to the king a second time. "What are you waiting for?" she asked. "Do what you see me doing! We may still lose our children, but we shall at least escape eternal damnation." King Chilperic was deeply moved. He tossed all the files of tax-demands into the fire. As soon as they were burnt, he sent messengers to ensure that no such assessments should ever be made again. Meanwhile their youngest son wasted away before the onslaught of the disease and finally died. With broken hearts they carried him to Paris from their estate at Berny, and buried him in the church of St. Denis. As for Chlodobert, they placed him on a stretcher and carried him to the church of St. Medard in Soissons. They set him down before the saint's tomb and made vows for his recovery. He died in the middle of the night, worn to a shadow and hardly drawing breath. They buried him in the church of the holy martyrs Crispin and Crispinian. The whole populace bewailed his death: they walked behind his funeral cortège, the men weeping and the women wearing widows' weeds as if they were escorting their own husbands to the grave. From this time onwards King Chilperic was lavish in giving alms to cathedrals and churches, and to the poor, too....

6.34 Once again legates arrived from Spain. They brought gifts, and in conference with King Chilperic they arranged that his daughter Rigunth should marry Recared, the son of King Leuvigild, according to the agreement made some time earlier. The contract was confirmed, all the details were settled and the ambassador set off for home. King Chilperic then left home and traveled some way towards Soissons, but on the journey he suffered yet another bereavement. His son, who had been baptized only the year before, fell ill with dysentery and died. This is what the ball of fire presaged, the one I described above as emerging from a cloud. They were all prostrate with grief. They turned back to Paris and buried the child there. They sent after the ambassador and called him back, for clearly what they had just planned would now have to be deferred. "I can hardly think of celebrating my daughter's wedding when I am in mourning because I have just buried my son," said Chilperic. For a time he considered the idea of sending another daughter to Spain instead, Basina, whom he had shut away in the nunnery in Poitiers, her mother having been Audovera. She was unwilling, and the blessed Radegund backed her up. "It is not seemly," she said, "for a nun dedicated to Christ to turn back once more to the sensuous pleasures of this world."

6.35 While these things were going on, it was announced to the queen that her little son Theuderic, who had just died, had been taken from her by witchcraft and incantations, and that Mummolus the Prefect, whom she had long hated, was involved in this. The truth seems to have been that, when Mummolus was at supper in his own home, someone from the court was lamenting that a child very dear to him had recently died of dysentery. The Prefect answered: "I always keep by me a certain herb which has this property, that, if anyone who is attacked by dysentery drinks a concoction of it, he is immediately cured, however desperately ill he may be." This was reported to Queen Fredegund, and she was furious. She had a number of Parisian housewives rounded up, and they were tortured with the instruments and the cat [a whip], and so compelled to act as informers. They confessed that they were witches and gave evidence that they had been responsible for many deaths. They then added something which I find quite incredible: "We sacrificed your son, O Queen, to save the life of Mummolus." Fredegund then had these poor wretches tortured in an even more inhuman way, cutting off the heads of some, burning others alive, and breaking the bones of the rest on the wheel. She went to stay with King Chilperic for a while in their manor at Compiègne, and while there she revealed to him all that she had been told about the Prefect. Chilperic immediately sent his men to seize the person of Mummolus. He was interrogated, loaded with chains, and put to the torture. Then his hands were tied behind his back, he was suspended from a rafter and he was questioned about these sorceries. He denied that he knew anything of them. He did admit one thing: that he had often received from these women unguents and potions which were supposed to bring him into the good favor of the king and queen. As they took him down, he called one of the torturers to him and said: "Tell the king, my master, that what you keep doing to me causes me no pain." When the king heard this, he said: "It must be true then, that he is a sorcerer, if the punishment which we are giving him does not hurt him." Mummolus was extended on the rack and then flogged with treble thongs until the torturers were quite exhausted. After this splinters were driven beneath the nails of his fingers and toes. So things continued: finally, at the very moment when the sword was about to cut off his head, Queen Fredegund granted him his life. There followed an indignity which was perhaps worse than death itself. All his property was sequestered; and he was placed on a cart and packed off to Bordeaux, which was his native city. On the way he had a stroke. He had just enough strength to reach his destination, but he died almost immediately afterwards.

The queen now collected together anything that had belonged to her dead son and burned it, all his clothes, some of them silk and others of fur, and all his other possessions, whatever she could find. It is said that all this filled four carts. Any object in gold or silver was melted down in a furnace, so that nothing whatsoever remained intact to remind her of how she had mourned for her boy.

To what did Fredegund attribute the plague? What attitude to children is evident in these accounts? Is there a difference between how sons and daughters are discussed?

67. AN UNHAPPY CHILDHOOD:
GUIBERT OF NOGENT

Guibert of Nogent wrote his Memoirs *in 1115 when he was about sixty years old. He discussed at length his memories of his childhood and the stories he had been told about his birth and infancy. Guibert was born into the lesser aristocracy and might well have led a life of arms and been involved in worldly affairs. His mother's difficult labor and his own fragility in infancy led to his life as a Benedictine monk. Deprived by death of his father's guidance, Guibert was raised by a religious mother and an ill-educated tutor. Even at a distance of half a century, the painful memories of his childhood still wounded the adult Guibert. He was raised without playmates. Isolated from the world and subject to unceasing demands from his tutor, Guibert was also effectively abandoned by the mother he adored. This passage provides a picture of the harsh educational practices that medieval people believed would instill both good morals and good learning. It also reveals the enduring pain of one man's childhood.*

Source: Revised John F. Benton, *Self and Society in Medieval France. The Memoirs of Abbot Guibert of Nogent (1064?-c.1115)* (New York: Harper Torchbooks, 1970), pp. 40-42, 44-50; reprinted with permission.

1.3 To this woman, as I hope and believe truest to me of all whom she bore, you granted that this worst sinner should be born. In two senses I was her last child, for while the others have passed away with the hope of a better life, I am left with a life of utter despair. Yet, through her merit next to Jesus and his mother and the saints, while I still live in this evil world there remains to me the hope of that salvation which is open to all. Certainly I know, and it is wrong to disbelieve, that, as in the world she showed me greater love and brought me up in greater distinction (with a mother's special affection for her last-born), she remembers me the more now that she is in the presence of God. From her youth she was full of God's fire in Zion, since the concern she had for me in her heart did not cease whether she was asleep or awake. And now that she is dead, the wall of her flesh being broken away, I know that in Jerusalem that furnace burns with greater heat than words can express, the more that, being filled there with the Spirit of God, she is not ignorant of the miseries in which I am entangled, and, blessed as she is, she bewails my wanderings when she sees my feet go astray from the path of goodness marked out by her recurrent warnings.

O Father and Lord God, who gave being to me (I who am bad in such manner and measure as you know) from her so truly and really good, you also granted me hope in her merit, a hope which I should not dare to have at all if I were not for a little near you relieved of the fear of my sins. Likewise you brought into my wretched heart perhaps not hope so much as the shadow of hope, in that you vouchsafed to me birth, and rebirth also, on the day that is the highest of all days and best-loved by Christian people. My mother had passed almost the whole of Good Friday in excessive pain of childbirth (in what anguish, too, did she linger, when I wandered from the way and followed slippery paths!) when at last came Holy Saturday, the day before Easter.

Racked by pains long-endured, and her tortures increasing as her hour drew near, when she thought I had at last in natural course come to birth, instead I was returned within the womb. By this time my father, friends, and kinsfolk were crushed with dismal sorrowing for both of us, for while the child was hastening the death of the mother, and she her child's in denying him deliverance, all had reason for compassion. It was a day on which, with the exception of that solemn office which is celebrated exclusively and at its special time, the regular services for the household were not taking place. And so they asked counsel in their need and fled for help to the altar of the Lady Mary, and to her (the only Virgin that ever was or would be to bear a child) this vow was made, and in the place of an offering this gift laid upon the gracious Lady's altar: that should a male child be born, he should be given up to the religious life in the service of God and the Lady, and if one of the inferior sex, she should be handed over to the corresponding calling. At once a weak little being, almost an abortion, was born, and at that timely birth there was rejoicing only for my mother's deliverance, the child being such a miserable object. In that poor mite just born, there was such a pitiful meagerness that he had the corpse-like look of a premature baby; so much so that when reeds (which in that region are very slender when they come up—it being then the middle of April) were placed in my little fingers, they seemed stouter in comparison. On that very day when I was put into the baptismal font—as I was so often told as a joke in boyhood and even in youth—a certain woman tossed me from hand to hand. "Look at this thing," she said. "Do you think such a child can live, whom nature by a mistake has made almost without limbs, giving him something more like an outline than a body?"...

1.4 After birth I had scarcely learned to cherish my rattle when you, gracious Lord, henceforth my father, did made me an orphan. For when about eight months had passed, the father of my flesh died. Great thanks are due to you that you allowed that man to depart in a Christian state. If he had lived, he would undoubtedly have endangered the provision you had made for me. Because my young body and a certain natural quickness for one of such tender age seemed to fit me for worldly pursuits, no one doubted that when the proper time had come for beginning my education, he would have broken the vow which he had made for me. O gracious provider, for the well-being of us both you determined that I should not miss the beginning of instruction in your discipline and that he should not break his solemn promise for me.

And so with great care that widow, truly yours, brought me up, and at last she chose the day of the festival of the blessed Gregory for putting me in school. She had heard that that servant of yours, O Lord, had been eminent for his wonderful understanding and had abounded in extraordinary wisdom. Therefore she strove with bountiful almsgiving to win the good word of your confessor, that he to whom you had granted understanding might make me zealous in the pursuit of knowledge. Put to my book, I had learned the shapes of the letters, but hardly yet to join them into syllables, when my good mother, eager for my instruction, arranged to place me under a schoolmaster.

There was a little before that time, and in a measure there was still in my youth, such a scarcity of teachers that hardly any could be found in the towns, and in the cities there were very few, and those who by good chance could be discovered had but slight knowledge and could not be compared with the wandering scholars of these days. The man in whose charge my mother decided to put me had begun to learn grammar late in life, and he was the more unskilled in the art through having imbibed little of it when young. Yet he was of such character that what he lacked in letters he made up for in honesty.

Through the chaplains who conducted the divine services in her house, my mother approached this teacher, who was in charge of the education of a young cousin of mine and was closely bound to some of my relatives, at whose court he had been raised. He took into consideration the woman's earnest request and was favorably impressed by her honorable and virtuous character, but he was afraid to give offence to those kinsmen of mine and was in doubt whether to come into her house. While thus undecided, he was persuaded by the following vision:

At night when he was sleeping in his room, where I remember he conducted all the instruction in our town, the figure of a white-headed old man, of very dignified appearance, seemed to lead me in by the hand through the door of the room. Halting within hearing, while the other looked on, he pointed out his bed to me and said, "Go to him, for he will love you very much." When he dropped my hand and let me go, I ran to the man, and as I kissed him again and again on the face, he awoke and conceived such an affection for me that putting aside all hesitation, and shaking off all fear of my kinsfolk, on whom not only he but everything that belonged to him was dependent, he agreed to go to my mother and live in her house.

Now, that boy whom he had been educating so far was handsome and of good birth, but he was so eager to avoid proper studies and unsteady under all instruction, a liar and a thief, as far as his age would allow, that he never could be found in productive activity and hardly ever in school, but almost every day played truant in the vineyards. Since my mother's friendly advances were made

to him at the moment when the man was tired of the boy's childish folly, and
the meaning of the vision fixed still deeper in his heart what he had already
desired, he gave up his companionship of the boy and left the noble family to
which he was attached. He would not have done this with impunity, however,
if their respect for my mother, as well as her power, had not protected him.

1.5 Placed under him, I was taught with such purity and checked with such
honesty from the vices which commonly spring up in youth that I was kept
from ordinary games and never allowed to leave my master's company, or to eat
anywhere else than at home, or to accept gifts from anyone without his leave;
in everything I had to show self-control in word, look, and deed, so that he
seemed to require of me the conduct of a monk rather than a clerk. While
others of my age wandered everywhere at will and were unchecked in the
indulgence of such inclinations as were natural at their age, I, hedged in with
constant restraints and dressed in my clerical garb, would sit and look at the
troops of players like a beast awaiting sacrifice. Even on Sundays and saints'
days I had to submit to the severity of school exercises. At hardly any time, and
never for a whole day, was I allowed to take a holiday; in fact, in every way and
at all times I was driven to study. Moreover, he devoted himself exclusively to
my education, since he was allowed to have no other pupil.

He worked me hard, and anyone observing us might have thought that my
little mind was being exceedingly sharpened by such perseverance, but the
hopes of all were disappointed. He was, in fact, utterly unskilled in prose and
verse composition. Meanwhile, I was pelted almost every day with a hail of
blows and harsh words while he was forcing me to learn what he could not
teach.

In this fruitless struggle I passed nearly six years with him, but got no reward
worth the time it took. Yet otherwise, in all that is supposed to count for good
training, he devoted himself completely to my improvement. Most faithfully
and lovingly he instilled in me all that was temperate and modest and outwardly refined. But I clearly perceived that he had no consideration or restraint
in the trial he put me to, urging me on without intermission and with great
pain under the pretense of teaching me. By the strain of undue application, the
natural powers of grown men, as well as of boys, are blunted, and the hotter the
fire of their mental activity in unremitting study, the sooner is the strength of
their understanding weakened and chilled by excess, and its energy turned to
apathy.

It is therefore necessary to treat the mind with greater moderation while it
is still burdened with its bodily covering. If there is to be silence in heaven for
half an hour, so that while it continues the unremitting activity of contemplation cannot exist, in the same way what I may call perseverance will not stay
fresh while struggling with some problem. Hence we believe that when the

mind has been fixed exclusively on one subject, we ought to give it relaxation from its intensity, so that after dealing in turn with different subjects we may with renewed energy, as after a holiday, fasten upon that one with which our minds are most engaged. In short, let wearied nature be refreshed at times by varying its work. Let us remember that God did not make the world without variety, but in day and night, spring and summer, winter and autumn, he has delighted us by temporal change. Let everyone who has the name of master see in what manner he may moderate the teaching of boys and youths, since such men think their students should be treated like old men who are completely serious.

Now, my teacher had a harsh love for me, for he showed excessive severity in his unjust floggings, and yet the great care with which he guarded me was evident in his acts. Clearly I did not deserve to be beaten, for if he had had the skill in teaching which he professed, it is certain that I, though a boy, would have been well able to grasp anything that he taught. But because he stated his thoughts poorly and what he strove to express was not at all clear to him, his talk rolled ineffectively on and on in a banal but by no means obvious circle, which could not be brought to any conclusion, much less understood. He was so uninstructed that he retained incorrectly, as I have said before, what he had once learned badly late in life, and if he let anything slip out (incautiously, as it were), he maintained and defended it with blows, regarding all his own opinions as firmly established. I think he certainly should have avoided such folly, for indeed, a learned man says, "before one's nature has absorbed knowledge, it is less praiseworthy to say what you know than to keep silent about what you do not know."

While he took cruel vengeance on me for not knowing what he did not know himself, he ought certainly to have considered that it was very wrong to demand from a weak little mind what he had not put into it. For as the words of madmen can be understood by the sane with difficulty or not at all, so the talk of those who are ignorant but say that they know something and pass it on to others will be the more darkened by their own explanations. You will find nothing more difficult than trying to discourse on what you do not understand, so that your subject is obscure to the speaker and even more so to the listener, making both look like blockheads. I say this, O my God, not to put a stigma on such a friend, but for every reader to understand that we should not attempt to teach as a certainty every assertion we make, and we should not involve others in the mists of our own conjectures.

It has been my purpose here, in consideration of the poorness of my subject to give it some flavor by reasoning about things, so that if the one deserves to be reckoned of little value, the other may sometimes be regarded as worth while.

1.6 Although he crushed me by such severity yet in other ways he made it quite plain that he loved me as well as he did himself. With such watchful care did he devote himself to me, with such foresight did he secure my welfare against the spite of others and teach me on what authority I should beware of the dissolute manners of some who paid court to me, and so long did he argue with my mother about the elaborate richness of my dress, that he was thought to guard me as a parent, not as a master, and not my body alone but my soul as well. As for me, considering the dull sensibility of my age and my littleness, I conceived much love for him in response, in spite of the many weals with which he furrowed my tender skin, so that not through fear, as is common in those of my age, but through a sort of love deeply implanted in my heart, I obeyed him in utter forgetfulness of his severity. Indeed, when my master and my mother saw me paying due respect to both alike, they tried by frequent tests to see whether I would dare to prefer one or the other.

At last, without any intention on the part of either, an opportunity occurred for a test which left no room for doubt. Once I had been beaten in school— the school being no other than the dining hall of our house, for he had given up the charge of others to take me alone, my mother having wisely required him to do this for a higher wage and a better position. When my studies, such as they were, had come to an end about the time of vespers, I went to my mother's knee after a more severe beating than I had deserved. And when, as often happened, she began to ask me repeatedly whether I had been whipped that day, I, not to appear a telltale, entirely denied it. Then against my will she threw off my inner garment (which is called a shirt or *chemise*) and saw my little arms blackened and the skin of my back everywhere puffed up with the cuts from the twigs. Grieved to the heart by the very savage punishment inflicted on my tender body, troubled, agitated, and weeping with sorrow, she said: "You shall never become a clerk, nor any more suffer so much to get an education." At that, looking at her with what reproach I could, I replied: "If I had to die on the spot, I would not give up studying my lessons and becoming a clerk." I should add that she had promised that if I wished to become a knight, when I reached the age for it she would give me the arms and equipment of knighthood.

When I had declined all these offers with a good deal of scorn, she, your servant, O Lord, accepted this rebuff so gladly, and was made so cheerful by my disdain of her proposal, that she repeated to my master the reply with which I had opposed her. Then both rejoiced that I had such an eager longing to fulfill my father's vow. I was eager to pursue my lessons more quickly, although I was poorly taught. Moreover, I did not shirk the church offices; indeed, when the hour sounded or there was occasion, I did not prefer even my meals to that place and time. That is how it was then: but you, O God, know how much I afterward fell away from that zeal, how reluctantly I went to divine services, hardly consenting even when driven to them with blows. Clearly, O Lord, the impulses that animated me then were not religious feelings begotten by thoughtfulness, but only a child's eagerness. But after adolescence had exhausted itself in bringing forth wickedness within me, I hastened toward the loss of all shame and that former zeal entirely faded away. Although for a brief space, my God, good resolve, or rather the semblance of good resolve, seemed to shine forth, it came to pass that it soon vanished, overshadowed by the storm clouds of my evil imagination.

How did Guibert's family behave during his difficult birth? What was Guibert like as a child? How was Guibert educated? Was this a good way to bring up a boy? What did Guibert think of his teacher? Did his teacher also fail as a tutor or chaperone? What role did physical punishment play in child-rearing and education? How did Guibert really feel about his mother? his childhood?

68. THE IDEALS OF CHILDHOOD

Saints' lives are a useful source for understanding medieval views of childhood. Most such lives include discussions of the saint's parents and upbringing. These were not ordinary children, however, and the hagiographer's intention was to show how, even in childhood, the saint's remarkable holiness was evident. Nevertheless, bearing this in mind, it is possible to find in saints' lives reflections of the ideal child: how a "perfect" child would behave. Similarly, it was also common for adolescent saints to go through a period of rebellion or of conflict with their parents and family. These features are found in the life of St. Anselm, written by his friend Eadmer. Anselm of Bec became archbishop of Canterbury in 1093. He died in 1109. Eadmer no doubt had the opportunity to talk to Anselm about his childhood. This selection also includes an important discussion of Anselm's ideas about child-rearing. In the early Middle Ages, it was common for families to dedicate a child to religious life. Children of both sexes, from families of any social status, could be placed in religious houses as oblates up to the age of ten. This decision was binding on the child and meant a lifelong commitment. Thus, children of all ages were found in religious communities across Europe, and these children needed to be nurtured and educated. The practice of oblation declined markedly in the twelfth to fourteenth centuries, although religious communities continued to serve as types of boarding schools and orphanages.

Source: Trans. R.W. Southern in Eadmer, *The Life of St. Anselm, Archbishop of Canterbury* (Oxford: Clarendon Press, 1979), pp. 3-7, 20-21, 37-39; reprinted with permission.

1.1 *Concerning the life and character of the parents of Anselm, Archbishop of Canterbury*

Being now about to commit to writing an account of the life and conversation of Anselm, archbishop of Canterbury, I first invoke the help of God's great mercy and majesty. I shall then say something briefly about the place of Anselm's birth and the character of his parents, so that the reader may know from what root came the qualities which later shone forth in the child. His father, then, was called Gundulf; his mother Ermenberga; both of them of noble birth, so far as worldly dignity goes, and living spaciously in the city of Aosta. This city is on the border of Burgundy and Lombardy, and Ermenberga was born there. Gundulf was a Lombard by birth and became a citizen of Aosta by adoption. Though they were both affluent, and bound together in marriage, yet they were somewhat different in character. Gundulf was given up to a secular way of life, was careless of his goods and lavish in his munificence, so that he was regarded by some not only as generous and good-hearted, but even as prodigal and spendthrift. Ermenberga however was prudent and careful in the management of her household, both spending and saving with discretion, and performing well the offices of a mother of a family. Her ways were upright and blameless and in a true sense guided by reason. Such was her life; so she persevered till death; so she was found worthy to die. But Gundulf, almost on the day of his death, turned from the world and became a monk, in which condition he died.

1.2 How Anselm while yet a boy saw himself in a vision fed with the whitest of bread at God's command

Now Anselm, their son, when he was a small boy lent a ready ear to his mother's conversation, so far as his age allowed. And hearing that there is one God in heaven who rules all things and comprehends all things, he—being a boy bred among mountains—imagined that heaven rested on the mountains, that the court of God was there, and that the approach to it was through the mountains. When he had turned this over often in his mind, it happened one night that he saw a vision, in which he was bidden to climb to the top of the mountain and hasten to the court of the great king, God. But then, before he began to climb, he saw in the plain through which he was approaching the foot of the mountain, women—serfs of the king—who were reaping the corn, but doing so carelessly and idly. The boy was grieved and indignant at their laziness, and resolved to accuse them before their lord the king. Then he climbed the mountain and came to the royal court, where he found God alone with his steward. For, as he imagined, since it was autumn he had sent his household to collect the harvest. The boy entered and was summoned by the Lord. He approached and sat at his feet. The Lord asked him in a pleasant and friendly way who he was, where he came from, and what he wanted. He replied to the question as best he could. Then, at God's command, the whitest of bread was brought him by the steward, and he refreshed himself with it in God's presence. The next day, therefore, when he recalled to his mind's eye all that he had seen, like a simple and innocent boy he believed that he had been in heaven and that he had been fed with the bread of God, and he asserted as much to others in public. So the boy grew and was loved by all. His ways were upright and made him greatly to be loved. He went to school, he learnt his letters, and in a short time made great progress.

1.3 How, in order to become a monk, he asked God for an illness, and his request was heard

He had not yet reached the age of fifteen, when he began to revolve in his mind how he could best form his life according to God's will, and he came to the conclusion that there was nothing in the life of men superior to the life of a monk. In his desire to follow this life, he came to an abbot who was known to him and asked him to make him a monk. But the abbot, when he discovered what he wanted, refused to do as he wished without his father's knowledge, for fear of offending him. Then Anselm, persisting in his resolve, prayed that God might find him worthy of some sickness, so that thus, if by no other means, he might be received into the monastic order as he desired. Wonderful to relate, God heard his prayer and sent him straightway a considerable weakness of body—thus making known to him how much in other things also he might be confident of being heard with pity. Being thus sharply attacked by illness, he sent to the abbot, told him that he feared he was going to die, and begged to become a monk. Again the abbot's fear prevented what he asked: or rather it did so, so far as the human eye could see. But God, who knows the future and is not deceived, did not wish his servant to be tied up in the habits of that place, because in the bosom of his mercy he had certain other men tucked away, whom—as later became clear—he designed in the future to be formed according to his will by Anselm's help. After this the youth regained his health, and he resolved that with God's help he would in the future do what he was at that time unable to perform.

1.4 How he left his native land because of his father's great hostility to him

From that time, with health of body, youth, and wordly well-being smiling upon him, he began little by little to cool in the fervor of his desire for a religious life—so much so that he began to desire to go the way of the world rather than to leave the world for a monastic life. He gradually turned from study, which had formerly been his chief occupation, and began to give himself up to youthful amusements. His love and reverence for his mother held him back to some extent from these paths, but she died and then the ship of his heart had as it were lost its anchor and drifted almost entirely among the waves of the world. But almighty God, foreseeing what he was going to make of him, stirred up for him a hateful and domestic strife, lest in enjoying a transitory peace he should lose his soul. That is to say, he stirred up in his father's mind so keen a hatred against him that he persecuted him as much, or even more, for the things he did well as for those which he did ill. Nor could he soften his father by any degree of humility, but the more humble he showed himself towards his father, the sharper did he feel his father's anger towards him. When he saw that this was becoming more than he could bear, he feared that worse might come of it, and he chose rather to renounce both his patrimony and his country than to bring some disgrace upon either himself or his father by continuing to live with him. He gathered together those things which were necessary for the journey, and left his country, with a clerk as his companion and servant. As they were crossing Mount Cenis, he grew weary and his strength failed him, being unequal to the toil. He tried to revive himself by eating snow, for there was nothing else at hand which he could eat. His servant was grieved to see this and began to make a careful search in the bag which was carried on the ass's back to see if by chance there was anything to eat. Soon, against all expectation, he found some bread of exceptional whiteness and, having eaten and been refreshed, Anselm set out once more on the road with renewed strength....

1.11 *The reason for his giving more attention to the training of young men than of others*

Nevertheless his chief care was for the youths and young men, and when men asked him why this was, he replied by way of a simile. He compared the time of youth to a piece of wax of the right consistency for the impress of a seal. "For if the wax," he said, "is too hard or too soft it will not, when stamped with the seal, receive a perfect image. But if it preserves a mean between these extremes of hardness and softness, when it is stamped with the seal, it will receive the image clear and whole. So it is with the ages of men. Take a man who has been sunk in the vanity of this world from infancy to extreme old age, knowing only earthly things, and altogether set in these ways. Converse with such a man about spiritual things, talk to him about the fine points of divine contemplation, show him how to explore heavenly mysteries, and you will find he cannot see the things you wish him to. And no wonder. He is the hardened wax; his life has not moved in these paths; he has learnt to follow other ways. Now consider a boy of tender years and little knowledge, unable to distinguish between good and evil, or even to understand you when you talk about such things. Here indeed the wax is soft, almost liquid, and incapable of taking an image of the seal. Between these extremes is the youth and young man, aptly tempered between the extremes of softness and hardness. If you teach him, you can shape him as you wish. Realizing this, I watch over the young men with greater solicitude, taking care to nip all their faults in the bud, so that being afterwards properly instructed in the practice of holy exercises they may form themselves in the image of a spiritual man."...

1.22 *Concerning the discretion which he taught a certain abbot to practice toward boys who were being educated in his school*

On one occasion then, a certain abbot, who was considered to be a sufficiently religious man, was talking with him about matters of monastic discipline, and among other things he said something about the boys brought up in the cloister, adding: "What, I ask you, is to be done with them? They are incorrigible ruffians. We never give over beating them day and night, and they only get worse and worse." Anselm replied with astonishment: "You never give over beating them? And what are they like when they grow up?" "Stupid brutes," he said. To which Anselm retorted, "You have spent your energies in rearing them to good purpose: from men you have reared beasts." "But what can we do about it?" he said; "We use every means to force them to get better, but without success." "You force them? Now tell me, my lord abbot, if you plant a tree-shoot in your garden, and straightway shut it in on every side so that it has no space to put out its branches, what kind of tree will you have in after years when you let it out of its confinement?" "A useless one, certainly, with its branches all twisted and knotted." "And whose fault would this be, except your own for shutting it in so unnaturally? Without doubt, this is what you do with your boys. At their oblation they are planted in the garden of the church, to grow and bring forth fruit for God. But you terrify them and hem them in on all sides with threats and blows that they are utterly deprived of their liberty. And being thus injudiciously oppressed, they harbor and welcome and nurse within themselves evil and crooked thoughts like thorns, and cherish these thoughts so passionately that they doggedly reject everything which could minister to their correction. Hence, feeling no love or pity, good-will or tenderness in your attitude towards them, they have in future no faith in your goodness but believe that all your actions proceed from hatred and malice against them. The deplorable result is that as they grow in body so their hatred increases, together with their apprehension of evil, and they are forward in all crookedness and vice. They have been brought up in no true charity towards anyone, so they regard everyone with suspicion and jealousy. But, in God's name, I would have you tell me why you are so incensed against them. Are they not human? Are they not flesh and blood like you? Would you like to have been treated as you treat them, and to have become what they now are? Now consider this. You wish to form them in good habits by blows and chastisement alone. Have you ever seen a goldsmith form his leaves of gold and silver into a beautiful figure with blows alone? I think not. How then does he work? In order to mould his leaf into a suitable form he now presses it and strikes it gently with his tool, and now even more gently raises it with careful pressure and gives it shape. So, if you want your boys to be adorned with good habits, you too, besides the pressure of blows, must apply the encouragement and help of fatherly sympathy and gentleness." To which the abbot replied: "What encouragement? What help? We do all we can to force them into sober and manly habits." "Good," said Anselm, "just as bread and all kinds of solid food are good and wholesome for those who can digest them; but feed a suckling infant on such food, take away its milk, and you will see him strangled rather than strengthened by his diet. The reason for this is too obvious to need explanation, but this is the lesson to remember: just as weak and strong bodies have each their own food appropriate to their condition, so weak and strong souls need to be fed according to their capacity. The strong soul delights in and is refreshed by solid food, such as patience in tribulation, not coveting one's neighbor's goods, offering the other cheek, praying for one's enemies, loving those who hate us, and many similar things. But the weak soul, which is still inexperienced in the service of God, needs milk,—gentleness from others, kindness, compassion, cheerful encouragement, loving forbearance, and much else of the same kind. If you adapt yourself in this way according to the strength and weakness of those under you, you will by the grace of God win them all for God, so far at least as your efforts can." When the abbot heard this, he was sorrowful, and said, "We have indeed wandered from the way of truth, and the light of discretion has not lighted our way." And he fell on the ground at Anselm's feet confessing himself a miserable sinner, seeking pardon for the past, and promising emendment in the future....

What perspectives on child-rearing are presented here? Which was more effective? Did Anselm's own childhood influence his views on how best to treat children?

69. INTRAFAMILIAL CONFLICT

For much of the Middle Ages, the pressure on land and competition for employment meant that young people could not marry until they had the economic means to support a new household or until they inherited from their parents. Another option that was quite common, especially among the rural peasantry, was a form of retirement planning. Parents might surrender their land to a child, usually the male heir, in return for a set annuity. This, then, would provide the economic foundation necessary for the child to marry. Not all such arrangements were satisfactory, however, and intergenerational tension could result in the impoverishment of the retired parents. So, too, inheritance practices could lead to difficulties between siblings or relatives by marriage. Tension between family members, either vertically across generations or horizontally across the extended family, could destroy domestic harmony, or lead to hardship and suffering, or even death. These issues were addressed in tales and fables and sermon exempla. These stories were designed to inform, inspire, and warn the audience. Preachers used them to great effect to enliven their sermons and convey moral lessons in a compelling fashion. Many collections of these stories appeared in the earlier thirteenth century, such as those compiled by Odo of Cheriton and Caesarius of Heisterbach. They were used for generations to come, however, and Caesarius' collection was translated into many vernacular languages.

Source: Trans. H. Von E. Scott and C.C. Swinton in Caesarius of Heisterbach, *Dialogue on Miracles* (London: George Routledge, 1929); vol. 1, pp. 432-33; vol. 2, pp. 280-81; reprinted with permission.

5.22 Of a man who dealt treacherously with his mother and was punished in the neck by a serpent

There was a young man, a layman, born on the banks of the Moselle, named Henry, if I remember rightly, who deceived his simple mother in the following way, with words which were indeed honeyed, but with an intention which was poisonous. "Mother," he said, "I beg that you will solemnly renounce all your property, to wit, all your fiefs and freeholds and allow me to take them over, so that by the aid of these riches I may be able to marry a more honorable wife. Everything I possess is yours, and I will provide for you most honorably."

His mother, who did not perceive the guile of the serpent in her son, consented to his request and resigned all the income of her possessions. To make a long story short, the wife was brought home and the mother was driven out. And when she fell into want and daily complained to him, he shut his ears that he might not hear his mother's laments.

One day when sitting at table with his wife, he heard the voice of his mother as she knocked at the door, and said: "Listen, the devil is once more making a disturbance here," and he said to the servant: "Go and put this chicken in the sideboard until she goes away"; and when this was done and she was admitted, after begging her son to have pity on her, she was driven out with a great storm of words. Then he said to the servant: "Now you can bring back our chicken." But the servant, when he opened the chest, saw not a chicken but a coiled up serpent on the dish; so he came back terrified and told his master what he had seen. Whereupon he sent a maid-servant and she said that she had seen the exactly the same thing. He, thinking that they were mocking him, said angrily: "Even if it be the devil himself I'll fetch him out"; and getting up from the table he bent over the sideboard to take up the dish, and immediately the serpent leapt upon his neck, and that he might properly punish the vice of duplicity made a double coil of himself round the man's throat. And so when he sat down to eat, the serpent shared his food, and as often as food was taken away from him, or any instrument brought by which he might be detached, he so tightened his hold on his victim's neck, that his face swelled and his eyes started out of his head.

Novice—Rightly does he seem to me to have been punished by means of a serpent, because as the devil deceived Eve by a serpent, so by the same means did he deceive his simple mother.

Monk—You judge rightly. It is now thirteen years, more or less, since these things happened. For this same Henry was carried in a carriage through our province to various shrines of saints, and many people saw him. And his mother, having compassion on his pains, followed him with maternal affection. About the same time the vice of duplicity and cunning, being duly found out, was terribly punished by Philip, king of France, of whom we spoke above.

11.54 Of the death of Bernard of Munster who killed his sister's husband

Scarcely two years ago a certain citizen of Munster died, leaving his house and a good deal of money to his only son. He, by riotous living with harlots and in taverns, squandered the whole of his personal property. Moreover he sold his house to his sister's husband and going away spent the price of it in a short time. Compelled by necessity he returned to his sister's husband, who for the sake of his wife and the property sold to him, kept him with him. Treated at first with consideration but later with neglect, in indignation he left him and asked to have the house he had sold given back, complaining he had been cheated. Unable to get it fairly or by threats, he killed him in the middle of the market place with an axe and flying immediately to the church of St. Paul, where the clergy were celebrating service, he began to cry out: "Defend your liberties, my masters." And this they did. The good men came to him and were willing to take him under their protection, desiring to arrange matters between him and the friends of the slain man through pity for him. At first he agreed to this, but presently taking counsel with himself, he said: "I will not go out; be absolved from the oath you took." After a little one of his companions called out and said: "Come out, Bernard, come out; there is excellent wine sold at such and such a tavern." Following them he was soon after betrayed and taken. Asked why he had left the church, he replied: "Its pavement seemed to grow so hot under my feet that I could not bear it." When he was placed on the wheel and scholars came in the morning saying: "Bernard, are you still alive?" for he had been a man of letters, he replied: "I am still living," and presently he added: "Last night I saw that plain full of devils." But they could get no word or sign of penitence from him.

An Aged Father and His Son

Source: Trans. John C. Jacobs, *The Fables of Odo of Cheriton* (New York: Syracuse University Press, 1985), p. 153; reprinted with permission.

109. Against all who fail to honor their fathers

Another fellow had an aged father who suffered from chronic coughing. "This crude peasant," the son complained, "why he's debilitating us all with his hacking and spittle. Wrap him up in this old sheep skin and dump him out—someplace far from here." And the father died from the cold because he had nothing adequate to wear.

This cruel son had a little boy of his own. And his young son got a hold of an old hide and hung it up on the wall. Now his father asked just what he planned to do with it. "I'm saving it for you to use when you get old," answered the boy, "since that's what you did for your own father. So from you, I'm learning what's necessary to handle *your* old age." In Ecclesiasticus 8.7 we read: "Do not despise a man in his old age, for we all will grow old."

Why did the son need his mother's property? What does the story about the cruel son say about the relationship between mothers-in-law and daughters-in-law? Is this realistic or stereotypical? What responsibility did the good husband have for his irresponsible brother-in-law? Was it based on law or custom? What attitudes toward the elderly do these stories reveal?

70. PARENTS, CHILDREN, AND CHILD-REARING

Bartholomaeus Anglicus (Bartholomew the Englishman) wrote one of the most influential medieval encyclopedias, On the Properties of Things (De Proprietatibus Rerum) *(ca.1240). It was widely read and was translated from Latin into six languages. Its enduring importance is attested to by John of Trevisa's translation into English in the fourteenth century. A discussion of the "ages of man" allowed Bartholomew the opportunity to discuss different age groups: infant and child (both boys and girls), along with the duties and responsibilities of their care givers: mother, father, nurse, and midwife. He refers throughout to his sources, the great Greek philosopher Aristotle, Constantine the African who translated many medical works from Greek into Latin, and the etymologist Isidore of Seville. Bartholomew did not simply repeat his sources, however, but rather incorporated a great deal of practical information, perhaps gained from his own personal observation. In* On the Properties of Things *it is possible to glimpse something of how children were regarded, their proper upbringing, and the duties and responsibilities of various members of a family. Bartholomew also discusses the roles of various care-givers such as wet-nurses and midwives.*

Source: Trans. J. Murray from *On the Properties of Things. John Trevisa's Translation of Bartholomaeus Anglicus* De Proprietatibus Rerum. *A Critical Text* (Oxford: Clarendon Press, 1973), pp. 298-305, 309-11.

Book Six. Concerning the Ages of Man

Chapter 4. Concerning Infants

The little child is conceived and bred from seeds with contrary qualities, and if it is male, his place is in the right side of the womb and if it is female, in the left side. He is fed and nourished in the mother's womb by menstrual blood. From the beginning, man takes his nourishment from such vile and unstable matter, by the natural working and the assistance of the virtue of the heat that the mother draws out. All the members are shaped little by little, not all at once. Christ alone was shaped and formed at once in his mother's womb when he was consigned therein, as Augustine says. When the soul enters the infant, life is infused therewith and feelings also, and the child feels naturally the surrounding small skin. And when that skin breaks the child moves and with that movement the mother's womb contracts and is sorely pained. When nature has finished the creation and shaping of the child, if he is whole and sound, then in the eighth or ninth month or tenth month, she forces him to come out of the womb and, in the process of coming out, he is surrounded with a skin that is called the second skin. And in the birthing the mother's womb is labored with hard spasms, and that happens if the child is coming out too quickly. Then, when he comes out into the air, if it is too hot or too cold, then he becomes miserable and sad, so that he shows openly his natural misery by crying and weeping. The newborn child's skin is tender, soft, pliable, and unstable. Therefore, various medicines and foods are necessary for the child. So says Constantine, who also says that children that come out of the womb should be washed in roses pounded with salt, so that the members may be comforted and delivered and cleansed of sticky wetness. Then the roof of the mouth and the gums should be rubbed with a finger dipped in honey, to cleanse and comfort the inner part of the mouth, and also to excite and stimulate the child's appetite with the sweetness and sharpness of the honey. And he should be bathed frequently and anointed with oil of myrtle or roses and all the limbs should be anointed with this oil, and especially the limbs of male children because their limbs are harder and firmer than the limbs of females because of their exertion. Also, he directs that they should sleep in dark places so that their sight can be gathered and united, for a place that is too bright separates and divides the sight of a small eye that is still tender, and often makes children squint. And they should not be set in light that is too bright lest the spirit of sight be separated and diffused.

Above all, it is necessary to guard against bad milk and corrupt nourishment and food. Children should not be fed with such because from the mucus of the milk comes bad sores and harsh pains such as blemishes, blisters, and pimples in the mouth, vomiting, fevers, cramps, diarrhea, sweating, and other symptoms. And if the child is sick, medicine shall be given to the nurse and not to the child. And the nurse shall be ruled by a good diet so that the strength of the nurse be in place and supply and fulfill the defect in the child, as Constantine advises. For, from the good disposition of milk comes the good disposition of the child, and the contrary. Because, from the nurse's corrupt milk and the softness of the child's nature and also the ease and speed of transforming the milk into humors, flesh, and blood come unnatural previous afflictions in the little child's body. And because of the softness of the child's limbs, they may easily and quickly curve and bend and take various shapes, and therefore children's members and limbs should be bound with strips of fabric and other similar bands so that the limbs might not be crooked nor evil-shaped ... Likewise, because children consume a great deal of food, they need a great deal of sleep to call the natural heat to the inner organs to cause the good digestion of meat and drink. And, therefore, by the movement of the sort that nurses are accustomed to rock children in their cradles, to encourage the natural heat with easy, moderate movement, and to bring the child gently and pleasantly to sleep, by dispersing the vapors in his brain. Also, they are accustomed to sing lullabies and other cradle-songs to please the child. For this reason, Aristotle says that a child has a large brain in comparison with his body. Therefore, the top part of the child is heavier than the bottom part and therefore, when he begins to walk, a child crawls on hands and feet and then, afterwards, he lifts up his body a little, for the top part decreases and becomes lighter and the lower part grows and increases and becomes heavier. Then the age of first childhood, that is up to seven years old, ends with the beginning of second childhood, that is between seven and fourteen years old.

Chapter 5. Concerning Boys.

A child who is between seven and fourteen years old is called *puer* (boy) in Latin, from the word *puritas,* meaning "cleanness and purity," as Isidore of Seville says. For the child is properly called a boy when he has been weaned from milk and has left the breast and teat, and knows good and evil. Therefore, he is able to receive correction and knowledge, and then he is placed under tutors to learn, and is compelled to receive knowledge and discipline. Children of this age are of a hot and moist complexion, and in such children the movements of Venus do not have great mastery because of the narrowness of the passages before they arrive at the year of puberty, that is, when the lower beard first grows in the pubic area. Therefore, because of the purity of natural innocence, such children are called boys (*pueri*), as Isidore says. Then such children have soft flesh, flexible and pliable bodies, are agile and light in movement, are quick to learn songs, and are carefree. They lead their life without cares or worries and value only their own pleasure and enjoyment, and fear no peril worse than a beating with a stick. And they love an apple more than gold. In the time of puberty or when the lower beard grows, they are not ashamed to be seen naked and bare. They care little when they are praised or shamed or blamed. Because of the increasing of the body's heat and of the humors they are easily and quickly angry and quickly calmed and forgiving. Because their bodies are tender they are easily hurt and injured and they do not endure hard work well. Because of the increasing of the hot humors that have mastery in them, they move swiftly and are changeable and unstable. And because of the great heat, he desires huge amounts of food, and so is easily disposed to various sicknesses and maladies because of overindulging in meat and drink. And children that have been born from an ill father or mother inherit that illness, as happens to the children of leprous parents or those with gout, who often infect their children.

Boys are distinguished from men by their voice and face. Therefore Aristotle says that in children the voice does not change before they begin thinking of Venus. When a child's voice changes it is an indication of puberty, and they then are able to beget children. Small children often have bad manners and vices, think only of the here and now, and take no heed of things to come. They love games and vanities. They forsake most things of value, and on the contrary, prize those things of little or no value. They desire what is bad and harmful to them. They bear the likeness more of a child than a man and moan and groan more over the loss of an apple than the loss of their inheritance. Any good deed that is done for them quickly passes from memory. They covet everything they see and plead and grab for it. They love talking to children such as themselves, and avoid the company of adults. They cannot keep secrets but discuss everything they see and hear. They laugh suddenly and they cry suddenly. They are always yelling and chattering and laughing and making faces; they are scarcely quiet while they sleep. When they have been scrubbed clean, immediately afterwards they are again filthy. When their mothers wash and comb them, they kick and squirm and push with their hands and feet and resist with all their might. A boy thinks only about his own appetite and does not understand moderation. They are always asking to eat and drink and scarcely get out of bed before they demand food.

Chapter 6. Concerning Girls

A female child is called girl (*puella*), from the word for clean and pure as the pupil of the eye, as Isidore of Seville says. Among everything that is loved in a girl, chastity and purity are loved the most. Men shall notice girls because they are of a hot and moist complexion. Girls' bodies are soft and small and supple and fair. Their demeanor is modest and timid and joyful and their clothing is dainty. As Seneca says, suitable clothing befits a chaste girl. Girl (*puella*) denotes an age of unblemished virtue, as Isidore says. For we commonly used to call girls maidens. And a maid is called a virgin (*virgo*) and has that nature from a green age, just as a stick (*virga*) is said, as it were, to be green. As well, a maid is called a virgin because of her cleanness and her uncorrupted state because she does not know the real passions of women, as Isidore says. Aristotle says that every woman generally has wavier and softer hair than a man, and a longer neck. A woman's complexion is fairer than a man's and her face is cheerful, gentle, bright, and amiable. Her body is small and from the shoulders to the navel is narrow, and wider from there to the knees, and longer down to the soles of the feet. Her fingers and the extremities of her other limbs are subtle and pliant. She has a light, easy gait with small steps. She has a swift wit. She is merciful but also envious, bitter, deceitful, easily led, and quick to the pleasures of Venus. Therefore, Aristotle says that in all species of animals, the female is weaker than the male, except for female bears and leopards, which are crueler and stronger than the males. And in other species, the females are more easily taught and are more deceitful and more preoccupied with nursing and feeding and caring for their young. A woman is more gentle than a man (she weeps more easily than a man), and is more envious and more amorous. And there is more malice in a woman than in a man. She has a weak nature, tells more lies, is more modest, and slower in working and moving than a man, according to Aristotle.

Chapter 7. Concerning Mothers

The mother is called mother (*mater*) because she offers her breast to feed her child and is occupied with nursing and caring for her child. The child is fed in the mother's womb with menstrual blood, but when the child is born nature sends that blood to the breasts and turns it into milk to feed the child, and so the child is better and more naturally fed with the milk of his own mother than with other milk. The mother conceived with pleasure but labors and brings forth her child with sorrow and woe, and she loves her child tenderly and embraces him and kisses him and busily feeds and nurses him. Moreover, after the mother is pregnant she does not menstruate because, Aristotle says, the blood turns into the child's nourishment. A mother is less troubled if she is carrying a male child than if she is carrying a female child, and so her color is fairer and her bearing lighter, as both Aristotle and Constantine say. Near the time of birth the mother is more troubled and tormented carrying the child.

Aristotle and Galen both say that it is a sign that a woman is pregnant if she craves various things, changes color and becomes pallid under her eyes, her breasts grow large and round, and her womb drops because the weight of the child stretches the mother little by little. Mothers have nausea and vomit, and are heavy and do not move easily. In labor with the child they cry out as if near death; this is especially so for young women with small and narrow limbs. The more woe and sorrow a woman has in labor, the more she loves that child when he is born, and cares and feeds and nurtures him and the more she holds and nurtures him. Look for a discussion of the obstacles to a woman conceiving and nourishing a child above, in the Fifth Book, in the discussion of the mother and breasts. Also, there is a more detailed discussion of miscarriages and their causes.

Chapter 9. Concerning Nurses

A nurse has her name from nourishing because she is appointed to nourish and to feed the child. Isidore says the nurse takes the place of the mother in the feeding and nourishing of the child. And she necessarily behaves like a mother,

A nineteenth-century drawing of a medieval illustration of nurses with their young charges. Medieval infants were swaddled to ensure that their limbs grew straight and were not deformed.

so that the nurse is happy if the child is happy and sad if the child is sad. She picks him up if he falls and gives him milk if he weeps, and kisses him when he lies down, and gathers him up and holds him tight when he sprawls. She washes and cleans him when he soils himself, and she feeds him with her fingers when he refuses to eat. And, because he cannot yet speak, the nurse speaks slowly and sounds out the words, to teach him more easily how to talk. If he is sick, she gives him medicine to make him better. She picks him up and carries him, sometimes on her shoulders, sometimes in her arms, sometimes in her lap, and rocks him back and forth if he cries and wails. She chews up his food in her own mouth and prepares it for the toothless child, so that he can swallow it more easily. And so she feeds him when he is hungry and soothes him with whistling and lullabies when he goes to sleep. She swaddles him in linen cloths and corrects and straightens his limbs and binds them with swaddling bands to keep the child from being deformed, with crooked limbs. She bathes and anoints him with fine ointments.

Chapter 10. Concerning Midwives

A midwife is a woman who has the skill to help a women who is in labor with a child, so that she can give birth to her child with less woe and sorrow. And because the child should be born with less labor and woe, she soothes and anoints the mother's womb and helps and comforts her in this way. She takes the child out of the womb and ties his umbilical cord at four inches long. She washes the blood off the child with water and rubs salt and honey on him to dry up the humors and soothe his limbs and wraps him in linen cloths.

Chapter 14. Concerning Fathers

The father is the head and source of procreation, and the father desires to perpetuate his nature in his children and to preserve in his children the nature that he cannot preserve in himself, as Constantine says. In the process of procreation he pours out his own essential fluids into the generation of children but his own nature is never lessened in the pouring out of his essential fluids. And he engenders children who are like him in nature and shape, especially if the virtue of the father surpasses that of the mother in the seed, as Aristotle says. Therefore, the father is diligent about the procreation of children and naturally loves his child so much that he gives up his own food in order to feed his child. And that is generally the case among all kinds of animals except a few which have abandoned natural instincts and do not occupy themselves with looking after their offspring but rather push them away, as Aristotle says of the eagle that pushes away his chicks and beats them off with his wings, beak, and claws. A man loves his child, and feeds and nourishes him, and sets him at his own table when the child is weaned. He teaches the child with words and chastises him with beatings and sets him to learn under the supervision of guardians and tutors. The father does not praise the child lest he be proud. He loves most the son that is most like him and often observes and watches over him. He gives to his children clothing and food and drink appropriate to their age. He purchases land and provides an inheritance for his children, and makes sure it increases. He tills the land and leaves it to his heirs.

The father is called father (*pater*), from the Latin word for "feeding" (*passendo*), because he feeds his children in their youth and is fed by them in his old age, as happens naturally among the ravens. As Aristotle says of such birds, the young feed the old when they cannot fly to get their own food. Therefore, the gift and reward of a long life is promised to him that worships and supports his father and mother, as Ambrose says. Because it is written: "Honor your father and your mother so you may live long on the earth" (Ex. 20) and "He who honors his father shall have a long life (Ecc. 3) ... And so children shall honor their father, support and respect him, praise and obey him....

The child comes from the essence of the father and mother, and takes food and nourishment from them, and cannot live or flourish without their help. The more the fathers loves his child, the more he will be occupied in teaching and chastising him and keeping him more strictly under his correction and knowledge. And the one the father loves the most, it seems he does not love at all because he reproves him and beats him often lest he be attracted to bad habits and vices. And the more the child is like the father, the more he is loved by the father. The father is ashamed if he hears any bad reports about his children. The father's heart is sorely troubled if any rebelliousness is found in his children. The feeding and upbringing of children is the most important occupation of loving parents. The inheritance is kept for the children, in hope of offspring. Often, the child is punished and disinherited by law for injuring and despising his father; no unkindness is worse than the unkindness of evil children, if they do not help their father and mother in time of need, as they were once helped by them. Often, from respect for the father and mother, people honor the child and give him gifts. The law requires that the eldest son have a larger portion of the inheritance. Sometimes, because of a wrong done to the father by the eldest son, the inheritance, rights, and name of the eldest son is taken away and given to another son who is more worthy to have them....

Why were parents advised to swaddle their infants? How does Bartholomew explain childhood illnesses? What does Bartholomew say about boys? How does this differ from his discussion of girls? What is the role of the mother? How does this differ from the role of the father? How does the information that Bartholomew presents differ from the kind of information found in his sources?

71. A HAPPY CHILDHOOD: JEAN FROISSART

Jean Froissart (1337-1410) was the most important chronicler of the Hundred Years'
War. He was born in Valenciennes in north-eastern France and was educated in the
manner of most urban children. His parents expected he would enter the family business.
He had fond memories of the carefree days of his boyhood. His discussion also provides
an important catalog of the kinds of games that medieval children played. Certainly, the
strictness of formal education is apparent, but so, too, are happy recollections of growing
up. Froissart shows the easy interaction of children, both boys and girls, in the streets and
playgrounds and in the schools of later medieval cities.

Source: Trans. Edith Rickert, Jean Froissart, "*L'Espinette amourouse*," in *Chaucer's World* (New York:
Columbia University Press, 1948), pp. 96-98; reprinted with permission.

In my boyhood I was one who liked too well to have a good time; and I still
do.... When I was only twelve years old I was very eager for dances and carols,
to hear minstrels and lively talk. And I always liked those who loved dogs and
birds. And when they sent me to school ... there were little girls there of my
own age, and I, innocent as I was, gave them pins or an apple or a pear or a little glass ring, and it seemed to me wonderful when they were pleased.

I was never tired of playing the games children play when they are under
twelve. For one thing, in a brook I made a little dam with a tile. And I took a
small saucer and made it float down. And in a hollow by a brook ... I often
built a mill out of two tiles. Then we played with bits of paper and got our
coats and hats and shirts wet in the brook. Sometimes we made a feather fly
down the wind, and I have often sifted earth with a shell onto my coat, and I
was a clever fellow at making balls. Many a time I amused myself making a
pipe of straw, and I was very good at chasing butterflies. When I caught them,
I tied threads to them; then when I let them go, I could make them fly as I
pleased. Dice, chess, tables, and other grown-up games I did not care about, but
I liked to make mud pies, round loaves, cakes, and tartlets, and I had an oven of
four tiles where I put this stuff....

And when Lent came I had under a stool a great storehouse of shells for
which I would not have accepted any money. And then of an afternoon, with
the shell which had holes in it, I played with the children of our street; and
when we threw it into the air, I would say to them, "Toss it high...." And when
the moon was bright, we played at "Pinch Me," and in the spring I was very
cross when they interfered with my playing. We played games called "Follow
the Leader," and "Trot-trot Merlo," and pebbles [marbles?], and Hockey[?], and
"Heads or Tails," I seem to remember; and when we were together, we all ran
... and played "Robber Enguerrand" and "Brimbetelle" [swinging?] and

A nineteenth-century drawing of medieval boys at play.

"Deux Bastons qu'on Restelle" [stilts?]. And I have often made of a stick a horse called Grisel. We used to make helmets of our hats; and often, before the girls, we beat one another with our caps. Sometimes we played at "The King Who Doesn't Lie," at bars [prisoners' base], at "Little Lamb," at "Take Me Away from Colinet," and at "I Tell on Who Strikes Me." And we played "L'Esbahi" [surprise?], and also at charades (or riddles), at "Avainne" [oats?], at Hide-and-Seek, at "Erbelette" [Little Grass?], "Aux risées," at "Strike the Ball," at "Reculées" [retreat?], at Mule, at "Who Can Jump Highest?" at "The Cart of Michaut," then at "La Coulee belee" [Run, Sheep, Run], which one makes a gay dance of, at "Hare and Hounds," at "Cluignette" [winking?], at the "Sotte buirette" [silly face?], at "Cow's Horn in the Salt," and throwing leaden pennies or pebbles against a fence. And then we rolled nuts; the boy who missed lost his temper. I amused myself night and morning with a spinning top; and I've often made soap bubbles in a little pipe, two or three or four or five. I loved to watch them. With such games—there were still others—I have often tired myself out.

When I was a little wiser, I had to control myself, for they made me learn Latin; and if I made mistakes in saying my lessons, I was beaten; and when I was beaten or afraid of being beaten, I did better. Nevertheless, away from my master I could never rest till I fought with the other boys; I was beaten and I beat, and I was so knocked about that often my clothes were torn. I went home and there I was scolded and beaten again, but to be sure one gets used to all that, for I never had the less fun for it. But when I saw my companions passing before me down the street, I dropped everything and ran after them to play.

How did going to school influence Froissart? How did he relate with girls? with boys? How did he remember being disciplined?

72. THE INSTRUCTION OF CHILDREN

Concern for the upbringing of children and their good moral conduct was not limited to ecclesiastical writers and moralists. The common folk themselves were concerned that their children grow up to be honorable adults. These two fifteenth-century vernacular works, originally written in verse, show the kinds of concerns that parents felt. They present a realistic view of life, the situations that would confront children and the choices they would have to make as they reached adulthood, married, and started their own households and families. These works were written in the urban milieu of London and reflect the values of the emerging middle class. They offer insight into the qualities expected in a husband or wife as well as the prevalent ideas of bourgeois comportment.

Source: Trans. Edith Rickert, *The Babee's Book: Medieval Manners for the Young* (London: Chatto and Windus, 1923), pp. 31-47; revised.

How the Good Wife Taught Her Daughter

The good wife taught her daughter,
Frequently and often,
To be a good woman.
She said: Daughter, dear to me,
Something good you now must hear,
If you will prosper.

Daughter, if you will be a wife,
Look wisely that you work;
Look lovely and in good life,
Love God and holy church.
Go to church whenever you may,
Don't spare yourself on account of rain,
For you will fare best on that day;
To commune with God is necessary.
He will necessarily thrive,
Who lives well all his life,
My dear daughter.

Gladly give both your tithes and your offerings,
To the poor and bedridden—take care you are not reluctant.
Give from your own goods and do not be too miserly,
For seldom is the house poor where God is steward.

Well is he proved
Who the poor have loved,
My dear child.

When you sit in church, bend over your beads;
Do not chatter with a gossip or with a friend.
Do not deride either old or young,
But carry yourself and speak well.
Through your fair conduct
Respect for you will increase,
My dear child.

If any man offers to court you, and would marry you,
Do not scorn him, whoever he may be;
But tell your friends and do not conceal it.
Do not sit near him where sin might be committed,
For a slander raised in error
Is hard to quell,
My dear child.

The man you shall marry before God, with a ring,
Love him and honor him most of all earthly things.
Answer him meekly and not like a shrew,
So you may soften his mood, and be his dear darling.
A fair word and a meek word
Softens anger,
My dear child.

Be fair of speech, be glad and in a mild mood,
True in word and deed, and have a clear conscience.
Keep free from sin, from villainy, and from blame;
And do not behave so that anyone can shame you,
For he who leads a good life,
Often has won his full reward,
My dear child.

Be of modest appearance, wise, and cheerful,
Do not change your countenance whatever you may hear.
Do not behave as a giddy girl, for that will accomplish nothing.
Do not laugh too loud nor yawn too wide.
But laugh softly and mildly,

And do not be too wildly cheerful,
My dear child.

And when you go on your way, do not go too fast,
Do not toss your head, nor shrug your shoulders,
Do not talk too much, hold yourself above swearing,
For all such manners come to an evil end.
For he that acquires an evil name,
Has a foul reputation,
My dear child.

Do not go into the town, gazing about,
From one house to another, seeking amusement;
Nor should you go to the market to sell your cloth,
And then to the tavern to bring your credit low.
For they who haunt taverns
Soon change prosperity for poverty,
My dear child.

And if you are in any place where good ale is prevalent,
Whether you are serving it or sitting down,
Partake of it moderately, so that you will not incur blame,
For if you are often drunk, it brings you shame.
For those who are often drunk—
Soon are no longer prosperous,
My dear child.

Do not go to wrestling or cock-shooting,
As if you were a strumpet or a gadabout,
Stay at home, daughter, and love your work;
And so you shall, my dear child, grow rich sooner.
It is for evermore a happy thing,
For a man to be served from his own store,
My dear child.

Do not acquaint yourself with each man who goes by on the street,
Though if any man speaks to you, swiftly greet him;
Do not stand by him, but let him depart on his way,
Lest by his villainy he should tempt your heart.
For all men are not true

Who can speak sweetly,
My dear child.

Also, beware accepting gifts out of covetousness;
Unless you know another reason, quickly decline them;
For with gifts many men soon overcome women,
Although they were as true as steel or stone.
Indeed, she is bound
Who takes a fee from any man,
My dear child.

And wisely govern your house, and serving maids and men,
Do not be too harsh or too gentle with them;
But pay attention to what most needs to be done,
And set your people at it, both promptly and soon.
For things are ready when they're needed
If the deed is already done,
My dear child.

And if your husband is away from home, do not let your folk work poorly,
But notice who does well and who does nothing;
And he who does well, reward him well for his time,
But he who does the other, treat him as a wretch.
A deed already done
Soon lets another be done,
My dear child.

And if your time is short and your need is great,
Then like a housewife set to work with speed;
Then will they all do better who stand about you,
For work is sooner done that has many hands.
For many hands and people
Makes heavy work light;
And after your good service,
Your name shall be enhanced,
My dear child.

Whatever your household does, you must supervise them,
And as much as you can, in the end,
If you find any fault, make them amend it immediately,
As much as they have time and space, and can be restrained.

To compel a deed to be done, if there is no time,
Is but a tyranny, without temperance and grace,
My dear child.

And make sure that everything is well when they leave their work,
Do not forget to take the keys into your custody
And be careful who you trust; and do not accept any excuse,
For much harm comes to those who do not beware.
But, daughter, be wise, and do as I teach you,
And trust no one more than yourself, for no sweet words,
My dear child.

And give your household their wages on payday,
Whether they still live with you, or they have moved away.
Be generous to them from the goods you have in store,
And then they shall speak well of you, both the young and the old.
Your good name to your friends
Lends great joy and gladness,
My dear child.

And if your neighbor's wife has on rich attire,
Do not mock her on that account, nor let jealousy burn you like a fire,
But thank God in heaven for what he may give you,
And so you shall, my daughter dear, live a good life.
He has ease in his power,
Who thanks the Lord every hour,
My dear child.

Be housewifely on working days,
For pride, rest, and idleness take away prosperity;
But when the Holy Day arrives, be well dressed,
The Holy Day is for worship, and God will cherish you.
Keep in mind to worship God always,
For much pride comes from the wicked day,
My dear child.

When you are a wife, also be a neighbor,
Then love your neighbors well, as God has commanded you.
It is fitting for you to do so,
And to do to them as you would have done to you.

If any discord happens, night or day,
Do not make it worse, mend it if you can,
My dear child.

And if you are a rich wife, then do not be too harsh,
But welcome sweetly your neighbors who come to you
With meat, drink, and an honest countenance, as you can offer,
To each man according to his degree, and help the poor as necessary.
And also perhaps it may happen,
Please well your neighbors who dwell beside you,
My dear child.

Daughter, beware, whatever happens,
Not to make your husband poor from spending or from pride.
A man must spend as he can who has only modest goods,
For as a wren has veins, men must let their blood.
His prosperity grows thin,
Who spends all he earns,
My dear child.

Do not borrow too eagerly, nor take your wages first,
This may make more need, and end by being worse.
And do not make yourself seem rich with other men's goods,
Therefore never spend a penny more.
For though you borrow quickly,
It must be paid again at last,
My dear child.

And if your children rebel and will not bow low,
If any of them misbehave, neither curse them nor scold;
But take a switch and beat them in a row,
Until they cry for mercy and they understand their guilt.
Dear child, by this teaching
They will love you even more,
My dear child.

And take care that none of your daughters is ruined;
From the very time that they are born,
Be diligent and plan for their marriage,
And give them in marriage, as soon as they are of age.

Maidens are fair and amiable,
But they are unstable in love,
My dear child.

Now I have taught you, daughter, as my mother did me;
Think about it night and day, so that this lesson is not forgotten.
Be moderate and humble, as I have taught you,
Then whatever man you wed will never regret it.
Better you were never born
Than you weren't taught this wise lesson,
My dear child.

Now prosperity and good fortune be yours, my sweet child [near or far]!
Of all our ancestors that ever were or are,
Of all the patriarchs and prophets that ever were alive,—
May you have their blessing, and well may you thrive!
For it is well for that child
Who is not defiled with sin,
My dear child.

May you have the blessing of God, and of his shining mother;
Of all the angels and archangels and every holy person!
And may you have the grace to travel your road directly,
To the bliss of heaven, where God sits in his might!
Amen.

How the Wise Man Taught His Son

Listen, young lords, and you shall hear how the wise man taught his son. Listen carefully to this and learn it if you can, for this song was written with good intent to make men true and steadfast, and a thing well begun often makes a good ending.

There was a wise man who taught his son, while he was yet a child of tender years, meek and fair to look upon, very eager for education, and with a great desire to do everything good; and his father taught him well and properly, by good example and fair words.

He said: my son, take care every morning, before you do worldly things, to lift up your heart to God, and pray as devoutly as you can for the grace to lead a good life, and to escape sin both night and day, and that heaven's bliss may be your reward.

And, my son, wherever you go, do not be full of stories; beware what you say, for your own tongue may be your enemy. If you say anything, take care where and to whom, for a word spoken today may be repented seven years later.

And, son, whatever manner of man you are, do not give yourself to idleness, but busy yourself every day according to your estate. Beware of rest and leisure: these nourish sloth. To always be busy, more or less, is a very good sign of honesty.

And, son, I warn you also not to desire to hold office, for then it cannot be otherwise than you must either displease and hurt your neighbors, or else perjure yourself and not do what your office demands; and earn yourself ill-will, here and there, a hundred times more than thanks.

And, son, as far as you are able, do not be involved in evil pursuits, nor bear false witness in any man's cause. It would be better for you to be deaf and dumb than to enter wrongfully into a case. Think, son, on the dreadful doom that God shall deem us at the last!

And, son, I'll warn you of something else, on my blessing, beware of tavern-haunting, and of the dice, and flee all lechery, lest you come to an evil end, for it will lead astray all your wits and bring you into great mischief.

And, son, do not sit up too late at night, or have late suppers, though you are strong and healthy, for with such excess your health shall worsen. And debates arise from staying up late, and from sitting and drinking endlessly, therefore beware and go to bed early and sleep.

And, son, if you would have a wife, do not choose her for her money, but inquire wisely about all her life, and pay attention that she is meek, courteous, and prudent, even though she may be poor, and such a woman will do you more good service in time of need than a richer wife.

And if your wife is meek and good, and serves you well and pleasantly, do not be so insane as to burden her too grievously, but rule her with a fair and light hand, and cherish her for her good deeds. For a thing unskillfully overdone causes needless grief to grow, and it is better to have a meal's meat of homely fare with peace and quiet, than a hundred dishes with grudging and much care. And therefore learn this well, that if you want a wife to ease your life, do not marry her for her riches, though she might endow you with lands.

And do not displease your wife, nor call her villainous names, for it shames you if you malign a woman; and in doing so you are not wise, for if you defame your own wife, no wonder that another should do so! Soft and fair will tame alike hart and hind, buck and doe.

On the other hand, do not be too hasty to fight or chide, if your wife comes to you at any time with a complaint about a man or child; and do not be avenged until you know the truth, for you might make a stir in the dark, and afterwards you both may regret it.

And, son, if you are well at ease and regarded warmly by your neighbors, do not get new-fangled ideas, or be hasty to change, or to flit; for if you lack wit and are unstable, and men will speak of it and say: "This fool can stay nowhere!"

And, son, the more goods you have, the more you should be meek, and humble, and do not boast a lot; it is wasted for by their boasting men know fools.

And take care that you pay what you owe, and set not great store by other's riches; for death takes both high and low, and then—farewell, all that there is! And therefore live by my counsel, and take the example of other men, how little their goods avail them when they are lying in their graves; and a stranger marries his wife, and all that there is is his.

Son, avoid deadly sin, and try to enter Paradise. Make amends for your trespasses and distribute your goods to the poor, make friends of your enemies, and strive to gain salvation for your soul, for the world is false and frail, and every day grows worse. Son, set nothing by this world's wealth, for it fares as a ripe cherry. And death is always, I believe, the most certain thing that there is; and nothing is so uncertain as to know the time of death. Therefore, my son, think about this, about everything I've said, and may Jesus, who for us wore the crown of thorns, bring us to his bliss.

Amen.

What was the Good Wife's advice about courtship? What kind of entertainment and socializing occupied people? What are the qualities of a good housewife? What advice is offered on child rearing? How does the Wise Man's advice compare with that of the Good Wife? How should a husband and wife behave toward each other?

73. THE CARE OF ORPHANS

Given the high mortality rate during the Middle Ages, owing to a diversity of vicissitudes and dangers including war, disease, and childbirth, many children were at risk of losing one or even both parents. Guardianship was not necessarily a straightforward issue: it involved not only the care and education of the orphan, but also the administration of the child's inheritance, and, ultimately, included decisions pertaining to the child's marriage. In the event of the father's death, the wardship or guardianship of the children frequently was assigned to the children's mother, or their mother and a male friend or relation together. The absence of the mother as guardian sometimes indicates that she predeceased her husband. Other times, however, a male relative or even a family friend was the preferred guardian. This was one way that fathers might seek to ensure that their children were cared for by influential people who could help them in the world or who would increase rather than squander their inheritance. Guardians were required to supervise the child's estate and could charge legitimate expenses against it. The fact that guardianship could be lucrative, and a ward's inheritance a source of temptation, is attested to by the frequency with which guardians were required to give sureties for the responsible and upright administration of their wards' estates.

Source: Trans. Henry Thomas Riley, *Memorials of London and London Life in the XIIIth, XIVth, and XVth Centuries, A.D. 1276-1419* (London: Longmans, Green, 1868), pp. 117-18, 170, 248-49, 446-48; modernized.

The Wardship of the Son of William le Fullere is granted to Andrew Horn, fishmonger (1315)

The wardship of William, son of William le Fullere the elder, one year of age, was delivered and granted to Andrew Horn, fishmonger of London, with the agreement of the nearest friends of the child and of the mayor and aldermen, on the Tuesday before the Feast of St. Laurence [10 August], in the 9th year [of the reign of King Edward the Second (1315)], along with ten pounds sterling left to the child by the forenamed William le Fullere. This was done on the understanding that the aforesaid Andrew should maintain the child and provide proper and sufficient food and clothing and everything else necessary for him, from the profits arising from the said moneys, until the child reaches the age of majority. And when the child comes of age, Andrew was to account fully for the same ten pounds.

And he found surety for this, namely Reginald de Herbyzon who, along with the said Andrew, that is each of them individually, bound all his goods, both moveable and immoveable, into whosoever's hands they might come.

The Wardship of John, son of Robert Fitz-Walter (1328)

The wardship of John, son of Robert Fitz-Walter, was granted and delivered by Hamon de Chiggewelle, mayor, and the aldermen, to Johanna, wife of the late Robert; together with the tenements of the same John, which the said Robert owned in the City of London, until John reaches the full legal age. John de Writelee and Thomas de Maryns stood surety for this, on the Monday before the Feast of the Translation of St. Thomas the Martyr [7 July].

The Wardship of Isabel de Hakeneye; with Inventory of her plate and jewels, 1350

The wardship of Isabel, daughter of Richard de Hakeneye, late alderman of London, was delivered and granted to Richard, son of the aforesaid Richard de Hakeneye, brother of the said Isabel, on the Monday after the Feast of St. Valentine [14 February], in the 24th year of the reign of King Edward the Third etc., by Walter Turk, mayor, the aldermen, and Thomas de Waldene, chamberlain. Also granted were various pieces of silver plate and jewels, in weight and value assessed at 20 pounds, 10 shillings, 3 pence, which had been left to Isabel by the will of Alice, the wife of the aforesaid Richard de Hakeney, and mother of the same Isabel, along with 43 pounds sterling in ready money. This was full payment of Isabel's portion [of the estate] left to her by the will of her father Richard, as well as by the will of her mother, Alice. Also included with this was one messuage and three shops in the Parish of St. Agnes in Aldresgate, in London, which are of no value beyond the deductions on them. — The wardship was granted to her brother Richard, on the understanding that he shall answer to Isabel when she reaches the age of majority, concerning the silver plate [and jewels], worth 20 pounds, 10 shillings, 3 pence in weight and value, and concerning the said 43 pounds, where and when he is summoned by the aldermen and chamberlain. He shall also account for the profits that in the meantime accrued from the said 43 pounds. The aforesaid Richard shall be paid for his reasonable outlays and expenses, disbursed in the meantime for the maintenance of the said Isabel. Furthermore, in the meantime, it shall not be lawful for the said Richard to marry the aforesaid Isabel to anyone, without the assent of the mayor and aldermen.

And the said Richard bound himself, his heirs and executors, and all his goods, moveable and immoveable, wherever they might be, to do all this well and faithfully, And for greater surety concerning this, John, son of John de Horwode, Gosselin, son of Gosselin de Cleve of London, Thomas, son of Robert de Hakeneye of London, present in court, bound themselves, jointly and individually, in the same manner and form as the aforesaid Richard had bound himself.

The particulars as to the silver plate and jewels left to the said Isabel in the will of the aforesaid Alice, are set forth as follows, namely:

First, two silver pots, in weight and value, 100 shillings. One enameled pot, with a lid, weight 4 pounds, 5 shillings. One enameled cup with a lid, weight and value, 68 shillings, 4 pence. Another enameled cup, weight and value, 100 shillings. Three silver-plated cups, with three lids, weight and value 38 shillings. One silver water-pot, weight and value, 28 shillings, 4 pence. One silver foot for a cup, weight and value, 10 shillings, 7 pence. Twelve silver spoons, weight and value, 13 shillings. Three silver buckles, with two clasps, weight 12 shillings. Five rings, value 5 shillings. Sum total, 20 pounds, 10 shillings, 3 pence.

Account of the moneys expended by a Guardian upon his Ward, 1380

Account of John Bryan, citizen and fishmonger, delivered on the first day of December in the 4th year [of the reign of King Richard the Second], in the Chamber of the Guildhall of London, in front of the auditors appointed by William Walworth, the mayor at the time; for the time that he was the guardian of the body and chattels of Alice, daughter of John Reigner, blader, an orphan of the said city; at the request of Richard Fraunceys, fishmonger, Alice's husband, who was present at the time.

He charges himself with 100 marks received for the use of the said Alice, and with the profit from it for five years, at 4 shillings on the pound annually, according to the custom of the City, amounting to 100 marks. Sum total: 200 marks.

He claims an allowance of one half of such increase, namely 2 shillings on the pound annually for five years, for his trouble overseeing the same, according to the custom of the City, making 50 marks. For Alice's board, at 8 pence per week, making 34 shillings, 8 pence annually, in total, 8 pounds, 13 shillings, 4 pence. For her clothes, both linen and woollen, and bed, 13 shillings, 4 pence annually, totaling 3 pounds, 6 shillings, 8 pence. For ointment and medicines for Alice's head, and for her education, shoes, and other small necessities, 13 shillings, 4 pence annually, totaling 3 pounds, 6 shillings, 8 pence. For his expenses pertaining to a plea in the Courts of the bishop of London and of the archbishop, for Alice's marriage contract, 4 pounds, 13 shillings, 4 pence. Sum total, 53 pounds 6 shillings, 8 pence.

Account of the moneys expended by a Guardian upon her Ward, 1381

Account of Agnes, widow of Adam Fraunceys, of the moneys expended during time she had the guardianship of Paul, son of Thomas Salesbury, knight, rendered in the Chamber, on the 29th day of May, in the 4th year etc., in front of the auditors appointed by William Walworth, the mayor at the time.

For the clothing of the said Paul and of his servants, bedding and other furnishings of his chamber, and for schooling, books, silver girdles, riding, and the other necessities for four years: 50 pounds, 3 shillings, 9 and a half pence. For the table of Paul and his servants for the same time, at 5 shillings per week: 52 pounds.

What kinds of relatives were named guardians? When might a guardian be asked to account for the ward's property? What kinds of expenses could a guardian charge? Who authorized guardianship?

CHAPTER NINE:

BEYOND CHRISTENDOM

During the Middle Ages, western Europe was a remarkably homogeneous culture. Despite regional identities, a myriad of jurisdictions, shifting boundaries, and internal political tensions, Europe nevertheless was Christendom, united by religion and distinct from non-Christians. From antiquity, Jews and Christians had lived side by side, although Christian hostility toward their Jewish neighbors increased throughout the period. During periods of ecclesiastical reform, the Crusades, or other crises, the Jews frequently faced legal constraints or violence and massacres. Medieval Christians were also familiar with followers of Islam, both as rivals for control of the Holy Land and as neighbors on the Iberian Peninsula.

Too frequently the tensions between these three religious groups mask their coexistence. The very fact that Christian rulers promulgated laws forbidding miscegenation—sexual relations—between Christians and Jews or Muslims indicates that there was a certain degree of interaction between these communities.

Jewish, Christian, and Muslim ideas about marriage bear remarkable similarities, as well as decided differences. The practice of divorce permitted by Jewish and Muslim law was at variance with the Christian teaching of indissolubility. More troubling for Christian observers, however, was the Muslim approval of polygamy, considered to be proof of lasciviousness. At the other extreme, however, were the values and attitudes of some heretical groups living in Europe. Cathars and similar sects taught that marriage and sexual relations were best avoided. If a person could not maintain chastity, it little mattered who one's sexual partner was. Thus, although the medieval church successfully developed and disseminated a unitary teaching on marriage, people were nevertheless exposed to a variety of different beliefs.

74. LAWS REGULATING CONTACT BETWEEN JEWS, MUSLIMS, AND CHRISTIANS

Despite the impression that in the Middle Ages western Europe was an exclusively Christian society, in fact, Christians did come into contact with peoples who embraced other religious beliefs. In the Iberian Peninsula, in particular, Christians, Jews, and Muslims lived side by side and interacted on a daily basis. In order to reduce what were seen as dangerous activities—especially miscegenation—Christian rulers enacted laws to restrict interaction between Christians and members of other faiths. The following laws, from fifteenth-century Valladolid, reflect the kinds of regulations that were enacted throughout the Middle Ages. It was common at the time to refer to Muslims living in Iberia as Moors.

Source: Trans. John Edwards, *The Jews in Western Europe: 1400-1600* (Manchester: Manchester University Press, 1994), pp. 88-91; reprinted with permission.

The Laws of Valladolid, 1412

4. Also that no male or female Jew or Moor, whether inside their houses or outside them, shall eat or drink among Christians ... or Christians ... among Jews ... or Moors.... Also that Jews ... or Moors ... should not have Christian squires or household servants, serving lads or lasses, to do them service or [be at] their command, or do any domestic task in their houses or cook food for them or do any domestic task for them on the Sabbath day, such as lighting the fires and fetching wine for them, and similar services, nor should they have Christian nursemaids to look after their children, nor should they have [Christian] livestock-drivers or gardeners or shepherds, nor should they approach or attend the celebrations or weddings or burials of Christians, nor should they become the godmothers or godfathers of Christians, nor should Christians be godparents to them, nor should they go to their weddings or burials or have any dealings with them concerning the above, on pain of 2,000 *maravedis*....

10. Also that no male or female Jew or Moor should dare visit a Christian in his or her illnesses or give them medicines or potions, nor should Jewish or Moorish men bathe in a [public] bath with the said Christian men, nor should they send them presents of puff pastries or spices, or baked bread, or dead birds or any other dead meats or dead fish, or fruits or other dead things to eat. And anyone who goes against this and does the contrary, whether Jew or Moor, shall pay 300 *maravedis* for each offence.

11. Also that no Christian woman, whether married or single, or a girl-friend or a prostitute, should dare to enter into the enclosure in which the said Jews and Moors live, by night or by day. And any Christian woman who does enter inside, if she is married, shall pay, for each offence of entering the enclo-

sure, 100 *maravedis*, and if she is single, or [someone's] girlfriend, she should lose the clothes she was wearing, and, if she is a prostitute, she should be given a hundred lashes by the justices and thrown out of the city, town, or village in which she lives....

13. Also that no male Jews of my kingdoms and lordships, after ten days from now, should wear hoods with straps hanging down [a sign of nobility and authority at the time], unless they are strips no longer than a few inches made like a cone [symbol of a trickster] or horn, sewn all round up to the point [of the hood]; also that they should wear over their [other] clothes tabards with flaps, and that they should not wear capes, and that they should wear their customary red badges as they do now, on pain of losing all the clothes they have on.

14. Also that all the Jewish and Moorish women of my kingdoms and lordships, after the said ten days have passed, should wear large cloaks down to their feet, without fine silk decoration and without feathers, and [should wear] headgear without gold [decoration], and should cover their heads with the folds of the aforesaid cloaks. And anyone who does the contrary shall thereby lose the clothes she is wearing, down to her undershirt, for each offence....

18. Also that from now on none of the Jews and Moors of my kingdoms and lordships should cut their beards or have them cut with a razor or scissors, but instead should wear them long, as they grow; neither should they trim or cut their hair; and that they should go about as they used to do in former times. And anyone who does the contrary should be given a hundred lashes and in addition should pay a hundred *maravedis* each time he does it.

The Laws of Valladolid, 1432

Inasmuch as in many communities, may their Rock and Savior guard them, there are dishonest and harmful rules and customs concerning the manner and dress of women, and their jewels, which are excessive and beyond what is proper: They wear very costly and flashy clothes, [including] both rich materials and rich objects, such as trains and gold and silver, jewels and pearls, and rich adornments of fur, and many other things, which are the cause of much ill, [because] heads of families spend money and get into debt, so that in this way envy and hatred grow once more between the [Christian and Jewish] peoples, and they even think that they may rise to great wealth, in place of their poverty and misery, and abandon [the Jewish community]; yet, from time to time decrees are made for this reason against us, and, furthermore, we have never been considered entirely innocent, and it is right that we should make strong laws concerning this and should be strict in this matter.

Therefore we announce that no woman who is not a marriageable girl or a fiancée in the year of her marriage, should wear a saucy dress of gold cloth, or Chinese silk or taffeta, or silk, or fine leather, nor should she wear decoration of fine [woolen] cloth, or Chinese silk, nor should she wear jewelery made of gold or pearls, or a band of pearls on the top of her forehead, or a train measuring more than a foot in length from any of her clothing.

And this statement is not to be understood to apply to the clothes which may be worn during festivals, or the reception of a lord or lady, or for dances or similar occasions things — things that everyone is involved in. And inasmuch that there is great diversity amongst [Jewish] communities in matters of dress [so] that it would not be possible to make general laws, let it be sufficient to declare all the details which ought to be included in [such a law]. Therefore, we order that communities should make an ordinance among themselves on the aforementioned subject for the period of this law [of Valladolid], so that [Jewish] people may show restraint and realize that we are in the diaspora [expelled from the Land of Israel] because of our sins: and if they have the wish to be strict [with these women] beyond what is ordained here, they may do so.

Also, if, when anyone gets married or has a wedding, or has a child born to him [sic], as in other celebrations of that kind, they spend excessively, we agree that [local] communities should rule on the matter in the way that seems fitting to them, and in conformity with necessity and the situation.

What was the social function of Jews and Muslims wearing distinctive clothing? Why were there regulations against Jews or Muslims employing Christians? Why were Christian women restricted from contact with Jewish or Muslim men? Why were there no similar regulations restricting Christian men from contact with Jewish or Muslim women?

75. MARRIAGE CASES IN THE JEWISH COMMUNITY

When difficult problems arose in the medieval Jewish community requiring the interpretation of the law, questions were submitted to rabbis. These rabbis presented their answers in the form of responsa, *written responses to both theoretical and practical questions. These* responsa *provide insights into the life of the Jewish community living in Christian Europe. The following* responsa, *written by Rabbi Meir of Rothenburg, examine questions pertaining to marriage and family life in the Jewish community during the thirteenth century. It should be remembered, however, that these* responsa *represent the difficult cases and situations that were referred to the rabbis for resolution. In this they are similar to cases that went before Christian ecclesiastical courts. Thus, the* responsa *do not reflect the happy and harmonious marriage and family life. Nevertheless, they do reveal the rules, beliefs, and values upon which Jewish marriage and family life was based. The* ketubah, *which is frequently mentioned, was the portion of the husband's estate a Jewish woman was entitled to receive when widowed or divorced.*

Source: Trans. Irving I. Agus, *Rabbi Meir of Rothenburg: His life and his works as sources for the religious, legal and social history of the Jews of Germany in the thirteenth century* (New York: Ktav Publishing House, 1970), vol. 1, pp. 240-41, 279-81, 283-85, 300-02, 307-10, 319-20, 322-24, 326-31, 338-39, 368-70, 381, 383-85; reprinted with permission.

169. Q. A vowed to abstain from having intercourse with his wife. He stipulated, however, that such vow be void if it involve a violation of the law.

A. If A did not procure his wife's consent to his abstention, prior to making the vow, it is void. If he did procure his wife's consent thereto, the vow is binding unless A be released from it by three laymen.

R. Meir adds that he can not release A from his vow unless A personally appear before him, for he can not release a person from a vow through a messenger.

240. Q. L had been married to A, a person of blemished descent. After A died, no one wanted to marry L. [She maintained, however, that she had originally been granted permission to marry A, and demanded that the stigma attached to her because of her marriage to him be removed from her. May this be done?]

A. It is true that I have known a woman who was reported to have received permission to enter upon martial relations with a Gentile. I have also heard in France that some women were permitted to have marital relations with Gentiles. I failed, however, to inquire for the reasons that prompted the granting of such permission. I, for my part, can find no justification for granting permis-

A nineteenth-century depiction of a medieval Jewish community consulting
its rabbi. Jewish men tended to wear beards.

sion to a woman who wants to live with a Gentile merely in order to gratify
her carnal desires.

242. Q. A, of priestly lineage, saw his wife L go to a secluded place with a certain young man. They stayed there only for a short time, for L's mother walked
toward them with a lighted candle. On another occasion, while lying in bed
late at night, A heard, on the other side of the wall, the heavy breathing of his
wife and the young man as they were arduously embracing each other, which
to him was clearly indicative of consummated sexual intercourse. The same
incident was repeated on another night. On these occasions L was late coming
to bed. Next morning, however, when A rebuked L for her lewd conduct, she
protested vigorously. Nevertheless A was convinced that his wife committed
adultery and was, therefore, forbidden to him. A had always loved and catered
to L, but she had never returned that love, and had never submitted to him
willingly.

Rabbi Hezekiah b. Jacob, to whom the question was first submitted, ruled
that L be forbidden to A.

A. One judge is not at liberty to permit what another has prohibited. Were I present at the time when Rabbi Hezekiah received the query, I would have argued the case with him. A woman is not forbidden to her husband unless either: a) the husband is jealous of a certain man, and warns her against private meetings with this man, and the wife disregards this warning in the presence of witnesses; or b) they actually be found in a position indicative of fornication. But, heavy breathing itself is no indication that illicit sexual intercourse took place. Therefore, I shall wait till Rabbi Hezekiah recuperates from his illness, whereupon I shall discuss this matter with him.

246. R. Isaac left his wife Sarah in the month of *Adar* of the year 5031 (1271), and traveled to a distant place in search of sustenance for his family. Next year he learned that his wife had played the harlot and had thus become pregnant. He returned home, and in the month of *Ab* of the year 5032 (1272) he appeared before us and asked us to investigate his wife's conduct during his absence, since she bore a child in the month of *Adar* of the same year (1272), twelve months after he had left her. Sarah asserted, however, that she was pregnant when her husband left her. Therefore we, the undersigned, wrote to R. Shealtiel and his two sons, who lived in the same village with Sarah, and they testified in writing that Sarah bore a child twelve months after R. Isaac left her. The signatures and seals of the deponents have been attested to by reliable witnesses. Then, a person appeared before us because of the ban (proclaimed against all those who knew anything relating to this case and did not appear as witnesses) and testified that on the evening of *Shabuot* of the previous year (1271) he went to Sarah's home in order to recite the *kiddush* in her presence, and found Gentiles, loafers, who caroused with her, caressed and embraced her. We concluded, therefore, that she must have become pregnant at that time. Other persons testified to have seen her on *Purim* of this year (1272) in the last stages of pregnancy. On previous occasions, however, in the month of *Elul,* she violently protested that she was not pregnant, and cursed and abused those who had said to her that she was pregnant. Moreover, before the evil report reached the town, Sarah's father appeared before us and asked us to allow him to put his daughter to death by drowning her. When asked for his reasons, he stated that a daughter of his (meaning Sarah) was an incorrigible harlot, who bore a bastard daughter by a Gentile and then killed her child. When asked whether he tried other means of controlling her, he answered that whenever he reproved her she threatened to apostatize altogether and pleaded that she was not the first woman who ever sinned. She had left the house on a number of occasions but was persuaded to return by the entreaties of her mother. The father feared lest she turn to evil and, therefore, asked for permission to kill her. However, we did not permit him to carry out his design. We sent the testimony to Rothenburg to the great luminary, Rabbi Meir. Since the Rabbis of

Erfurt who are near us, and those of Wurzburg, who are far from us, as well as Rabbi Meir of Rothenburg, all agree to allow R. Isaac to divorce Sarah even against her will, the divorce has been given in our presence. Signed: Moses Azriel b. Eleazar hadarshan, Eleazar b. Yehiel, Ephraim b. Joel.

R. Meir's opinion was as follows:

The testimony of R. Shealtiel and his sons is of no consequence for two reasons. a) They are related to each other; their testimony is that of a single witness, and, therefore, insufficient. b) The foetus could have lingered in the mother's womb for twelve months. Sarah's giving birth to a child twelve months after her husband left her, is, therefore, no proof of her depravity. The testimony of the other witness regarding Sarah's indecent behavior on the evening of *Shabuot,* being the testimony of a single witness, does not deprive Sarah of her right to her *ketubah.* If R. Isaac believes the aforementioned witness or if he takes the word of his wife's own father, he must divorce Sarah even against her will. If she renders it impossible for him to divorce her, he may marry another woman without divorcing Sarah as a warning to all indecent and depraved women. But he must pay Sarah her *ketubah.* However, if Sarah admits her guilt, or acknowledges the truth of the testimony regarding her indecent conduct on the evening of *Shabuot,* or if she cannot satisfactorily explain why she denied her being pregnant in the month of *Elul* of the previous year, or answer all other questions regarding her conduct, she loses her right to her *ketubah* and is entitled only to whatever is left of the valuables she had brought with her upon her marriage.

268. Q. In the presence of witnesses Leah asked A to betroth her. While she was in a yard not owned by her, A threw a ring into her lap for the purpose of betrothal. The witnesses, although they saw Leah shake her dresses in order to brush the ring away, did not see whether or not the ring actually fell into her lap. Does Leah need a divorce from A?

A. Had the witnesses seen the ring fall into Leah's lap, she would need a divorce in spite of her claim that she never intended to become A's wife and that she was joking when she asked him to betroth her. For we would, then, be concerned only with facts and not with her thoughts and unexpressed intentions. But, since the witnesses did not see the ring fall into Leah's lap, and the yard where the incident took place did not belong to Leah, she needs no divorce, for no betrothal took place. R. Meir adds: If my teachers agree with my decision, all will be well. But if they do not agree I shall subscribe to whatever they decide to do. However, I should prefer not to be strict in this matter and not to require Leah to obtain a divorce, lest A become rebellious and refuse to divorce her, and lest he travel to a distant land and thus render it impossible for the unfortunate woman ever to marry again.

269. Q. Without any previous courting A gave money or presents to Leah saying they were tokens of love. The witnesses testify that A did not speak to Leah about marriage while he gave her the money, and that she did not express her consent.

A. If there are witnesses that A proposed to Leah on a previous occasion and that she accepted his proposal, she is betrothed to A, even though A did not expressly say he was betrothing her. When there are no such witnesses, but both A and Leah admit that they had a previous understanding between them, or that at the time A gave the money to Leah they both intended the money to bind them in betrothal, Leah is betrothed to A. Moreover, the mere statement of A to Leah that he gave her the money as a token of love may constitute a betrothal, and therefore, Leah needs a divorce from A before she can marry another.

273. Q. B sent A to betroth Leah as his wife on his [B's] behalf. A came to Leah's town, invited the important persons of the community, showed them proof that he acted as B's agent, and appointed witnesses, but when he came to betroth Leah as B's wife, he said: "You are hereby betrothed to me," instead of "You are hereby betrothed to B." When the witnesses objected, A said that it was a slip of the tongue, that he did not intend to betroth Leah as his wife, especially since he was married already and that he would not violate the prohibition of polygamy by Rabbenu Gershom. He, therefore, repeated the ceremony and betrothed Leah to B. Must A divorce Leah before she may marry B?

A. No, A is to be believed that he did not intend to betroth Leah as his wife, and his unintentional act is not valid.

R. Meir adds: I wrote you my opinion but I do not want you to rely on it to free Leah without a divorce until you have inquired of the Rabbis of the surrounding territory and of the Rabbis of France. If they agree with me you may accept the above decision; but if they do not agree with me, their opinion is to take precedence over mine.

275. Q. A betrothed L with a copper ring.

A. Since A said: "I betroth thee with this ring," and not "with this ring of gold," the betrothal was valid.

276. Q. A betrothed L with a ring which the witnesses to the betrothal, and a goldsmith, declared that it was made of gold. Half a year later, however, it was discovered that the ring was made of copper.

A. Since L relied on the opinion of the witnesses as to the quality of the ring, and since this opinion was erroneous, the betrothal was void, for a false statement made by the witnesses to a betrothal should have the same force as such a statement made by the groom. In practice, however, I should not dare release L without a divorce.

This Responsum is addressed to: "my teacher Rabbi Jonathan."

277. If a minor betroths a woman, his act is of no consequence, even rabbinically.

279. Q. Are a bride and a bridegroom permitted to live in the same house after betrothal?

A. They are not permitted to live in the same house because there may be occasions when no chaperones are about, and a person is not permitted to cohabit with his betrothed before they are actually married. Moreover, there is danger lest familiarity may breed contempt.

282. Q. A demands that his wife leave her home town and live with him in another place. She, however, refuses to do so.

A. A husband may force his wife to move from one town to another of approximately the same size; and from one home to another, similar to it within the same country. He cannot, however, force her to move from a town to a city or from a city to a town, from a poor home to a rich home or vice versa. The *Tosephta* rules that a woman who has married a man must move to his home wherever it be, but you should not follow this ruling in practice, since the Palestinian Talmud apparently opposes this view.

283. Q. Regarding the three countries into which Palestine is divided in reference to the laws of marriage, to the effect that a husband may not force his wife to move from one country to another, what is considered a country nowadays?

A. France, England, Germany, and Bohemia, are to be considered separate countries in reference to the laws of marriage, since a different language is spoken in each of these lands. It is indeed reasonable to assume that only territories within which a different language is spoken are to be considered as different countries in the above sense. Were we to consider Saxony, Franconia, Alsace, the Rhine province, and Bavaria, separate countries, then Palestine, a land of four hundred miles by four hundred miles, would have had to be considered a land containing more than three countries.

286. Q. Does the clause of the *Ketubah*: "and I will labor, honor, nourish, and sustain thee" provide that a husband may be coerced into hiring out as a laborer in order to support his wife?

A. A number of legal proofs have been marshaled to the effect that a husband may be forced to work in order to support his wife; but none is conclusive. However, I have observed that great teachers in France forced husbands to hire themselves out in order to support their wives, and I am content to follow my teachers.

288. Q. While A was absent in a foreign country, his wife borrowed money for her sustenance. Upon his return, A refused to pay his wife's debts claiming that she could have supported herself by her work.

A. Biblical law requires that a husband must provide his wife's sustenance; therefore, A must pay whatever his wife borrowed for her sustenance.

291. Q. Leah, a married woman, borrowed money from her father to buy herself clothes. Leah's father demands the money from A, Leah's husband. The latter, however, refuses to pay his wife's debt.

A. If Leah bought herself clothes in accordance with the rank of his, or her, family and borrowed the money from her father as a personal loan, A must pay that debt. But, if Leah's father gave her money and hoped that A would repay him, A is free from the obligation of repayment. Even in the former case, if A claims that his father-in-law owed him an equal sum of money, he [A] is under no obligation to pay, but must take an oath to support his claim. If Leah bought excessive clothes, A is under no obligation to pay for them.

293. Q. A has two sons and several daughters, some under six years of age, and some older. These children possess property of their own which they received as gifts. Must A nevertheless provide them with food and sustenance? Your pupil is inclined to think that A is under no obligation to do so, since feeding one's children is considered by the Talmud to be a charitable act, and A's children need no charity.

A. Your reasoning is correct as far as the older children are concerned, but does not apply to those under six years of age, for as the Rabbis decreed that a husband must provide his wife with food and sustenance even if she has property of her own, they also decreed that a father feed his children until they reach the age of six, even though they have property of their own.

297. Q. A often strikes his wife. A's aunt, who lives at his home, is usually the cause of their arguments, and adds to the vexation and annoyance of his wife.

A. A Jew must honor his wife more than he honors himself. If one strikes one's wife, one should be punished more severely than for striking another person. For one is enjoined to honor one's wife but is not enjoined to honor the other person. Therefore, A must force his aunt to leave his house, and must promise to treat his wife honorably. If he persists in striking her, he should be excommunicated, lashed, and suffer the severest punishments, even to the extent of amputating his arm. If his wife is willing to accept a divorce, he must divorce her and pay her the *ketubah*.

298. Q. A often beats his wife. She begged him to promise not to beat her any more, but he refused to make any such promise. Even when she appeared in the synagogue to demand that A pay the debts she had contracted in order to pay for her sustenance [probably during a period of separation], A stubbornly refused to promise that in the future he would refrain from beating her.

A. A must pay for his wife's sustenance since by his action he has shown that he had not decided to desist from his shameful practice. One deserves greater punishment for striking his wife than for striking another person, for he is enjoined to respect her. Far be it from a Jew to do such a thing. Had a similar case come before us we should hasten to excommunicate him. Thus, R. Paltoi Gaon rules that a husband who constantly quarrels with his wife must remove the causes of such quarrels, if possible, or divorce her and pay her the *ketubah*; how much more must a husband be punished, who not only quarrels but actually beats his wife.

299. Q. L claims that her husband is impotent.

A. The law considers such a claim by a wife to be valid, on the assumption that a woman would not dare present against her husband claims he knows to be false. Nowadays, however, there are many impudent and brazen women, and the above assumption is no longer true. Moreover, in this case there is reason to believe that L is lying since her husband has had children with a former wife. Even though he might have weakened since, we can put no trust in L's words. Therefore, we must not force the husband to grant L a divorce, but we ought to persuade him to do so.

300. Q. A is impotent. His wife demands that he divorce her.

A. We may force A to divorce his wife, especially if she has no children.

302. Q. A has been dripping blood for the past four years. During that period he refrained from sexual intercourse with his wife on the ground that his doctors forbade him to have intercourse as it endangered his life. Is A to be considered a rebellious husband and hence should three denars per week be added to his wife's *ketubah* for the period of his abstention?

A. Since A was forced by illness to refrain from intercourse with his wife, he is not to be considered a rebellious husband. A rebellious husband is one who refuses to live with his wife because he is angry with her or because he hates her. A person who is physically unable to live with his wife, however, is not considered a rebellious husband. A, however, must divorce his wife and must pay her the *ketubah,* since he is in the same category as a leper for whom coitus is harmful. Although A's sickness does not disable him permanently and is curable, we do not compel his wife to wait indefinitely in the hope that he might be cured. Thus Maimonides rules that under such circumstances a woman must wait only six months. Although we have compared A to a leper for whom coitus is harmful, nevertheless we should not force A by flagellation to divorce his wife, but should only resort to persuasion. We should merely tell him the law requires him to divorce his wife and pay her the *ketubah;* should he refuse to do so, he would be called "transgressor." Whether A divorces her or not, however, we force him to pay his wife the *Ikkar ketubah* and her dowry, but we do not force him to pay her the additional jointure since some authorities hold the opinion that under the circumstances she is not entitled to the additional jointure. Should A's wife aver that she does not believe that A's doctors told him to refrain from sexual intercourse, and insist that he is a rebellious husband, he would have to take an oath in support of his assertions. Should A refuse to take the oath, we would have to add to his wife's *ketubah* three Tyrian denars per week for the entire period of his abstention. I have sufficient proof to support my view that the three denars prescribed by the Mishnah mean Tyrian denars. Should A admit that he had refrained from sexual intercourse with his wife because he was angry with her and that he had lied about both his sickness and the advice of his doctors, and should he declare that he now desires to resume marital relations with her, the aforementioned amount would be added to her *ketubah* and she would be required to resume her marital duties. Regardless of what happened in the past, A may now claim that he is well and that he is able to live normally with his wife, since the truth of his claim is bound eventually to be proven or disproven.

303. Q. A wife refused to have conjugal relations with her husband for a long time, with the result that she lost her *ketubah* according to Mishnaic law. She repented and wanted to resume marital relations with her husband, but the latter refused. Must he pay for her sustenance?

A. When the woman lost her rights to the money she was entitled to under the *ketubah* she also lost her other rights enumerated therein, and her husband is under no obligation to support her any longer.

304. Q. L rebelled against her husband. She refused, however, to accept her divorce from him, stating that she disliked him and wanted to cause him pain and annoyance. Nevertheless, heretofore they had lived in harmony.

A. L should be persuaded to forego her *ketubah* and accept her divorce. Should she refuse to forego her *ketubah,* her husband should be permitted to marry another woman. L should remain a deserted wife tied to her husband until she consents to forego her *ketubah* and accept her divorce. We cannot permit a situation wherein L's husband would be prevented from fulfilling his duty of propagation. Were we to allow L's conduct to go unpunished, great misfortune would ensue, for the daughters of Israel would turn to mischief.

312. Q. A says that he was on good terms with his wife when she went to her mother's home for her baby to be delivered, and that as now she refuses to return to him, somebody must have persuaded her to rebel against him. He, therefore, demands that his wife resume her marital duties. The trustee of A's wife states that A used to beat his wife even during her menstruation period and that he caused her so much pain and humiliation that he became repulsive to her.

A. A's wife cannot be compelled to live with A, even though she had children with him, ["for we cannot force anyone to live with a snake"], nor can A be forced to divorce her. They are to remain apart until either A's wife consents to resume her marital duties, or A consents to divorce her. Meanwhile, A must return to his wife whatever is left of her dowry.

313. Q. A rebellious wife who refuses to live with her husband admits that she has never allowed her husband to come near her. What should be done to her?

A. Since the women of our generation are loose in their manner of life, we do not permit the husband to remarry while she is forced to remain single till old age, which procedure was recommended by R. Eleazar b. Nathan, and we do not require a waiting period of twelve months till the divorce be granted. Therefore, the elders of the community should endeavor to persuade both parties to a speedy divorce without resorting to coercion of either party. Upon the granting of the divorce the woman should receive only what she actually brought in as dowry, but not the full fifty pounds of dowry written in her *ketubah;* for when the husband received her dowry and evaluated it at fifty pounds, though actually it was worth less, he did so because he wanted to marry her and live with her. Now that she refuses to live with him she loses the extra value placed on her dowry, the additional jointure promised her by the husband, as well as the 200 *zuzin* prescribed by the Talmud. Though in this country the same amount of dowry is written in the *ketubah* of a rich as in that of a poor bride, irrespective of the amount she actually brings in, in order not to shame the brides who bring in a small dowry, this rebellious wife is not entitled to collect the full amount written in her *ketubah,* since she never lived with her husband.

347. Q. A widow seized the property of her late husband. She kept it for years; some of it she squandered, and some of it she gave away as presents. Now the orphans demand that she take an oath regarding her management of the aforesaid property.

A. The orphans are justified in their demand that the widow take an oath regarding the property she has squandered or given away. Although the Yerushalmi rules that a widow who seized the property of her late husband is not required to render an accounting, Ritzba (R. Isaak b. Abraham) is of the opinion that this ruling of the Yerushalmi applies only when the widow is expected eventually to take an oath regarding her *ketubah.*

349. Q. A widow demands her *ketubah* and a creditor demands his money from an estate. Who has priority in collecting from the estate?

A. The creditor has priority over the widow. Moreover, even when the estate consists of assets only to satisfy one of the claimants, the creditor is paid in preference to the widow. In our times, since the creditor as well as the widow collects from unencumbered movables, the creditor has priority over the widow in collecting from such movables.

368. Q. A left two daughters, one of whom is married. May his widow collect money for her sustenance from the possessions of A's married daughter?

A. A's married daughter must support his widow, or pay her the *ketubah* only from the valuables she inherited from A, but not from any gifts she received from him during his life, unless such gifts were made *causa mortis* [in anticipation of his death].

374. Q. Witnesses testified that A's wife had committed an act forbidden to her by ban and oath. Moreover she brought forward a scoundrel who was in love with her and who threatened to kill A should he mistreat her. Is A permitted to divorce his wife against her will? Is she entitled to her *ketubah?*

A. A is enjoined to divorce his wife since she disregarded a ban and an oath and thus transgressed against Mosaic law. The ban of Rabbenu Gershon against divorcing one's wife without her consent, was not directed against those husbands who perform meritorious deeds by divorcing their wives. However, since A's wife claims that she was not forewarned of the consequences of her deed, and A can produce no witnesses to prove that she was so forewarned, she will be entitled to collect her *ketubah* after receiving her divorce.

377. Q. A, who fell sick, gave a bill of divorce to his wife on the condition that it be valid from the time of its delivery if he should die as a result of that sickness. A died as a result of that sickness and the people did not allow his wife to touch him, weep over him, or even walk after his hearse, claiming that such action on her part would invalidate her divorce.

A. The people were wrong. It is not within the province of a wife to invalidate her divorce.

What sexual values and ethics are presented in the responsa? *How did the Jewish authorities treat adultery? When could Jewish couples divorce? What role did consent play in Jewish betrothal and marriage? What actions were involved in a betrothal? What kind of relationships and responsibilities are portrayed between parents and children? husbands and wives? How did the Jewish community react to domestic violence? What is the most significant difference between the medieval Christian and Jewish laws of marriage?*

76. A JEWISH MERCHANT'S LETTER

One of the features that characterized the medieval Jewish community was its high rate of mobility. Jewish traders traveled across Europe and as far away as India. Such journeys were dangerous and lengthy; the return trip to India could take over two years. Such absences could put strain on marital relationships and lead to insecurity and uncertainty for the family remaining at home. These included loneliness and insecurity on the part of both the spouses. The reference to the wife's legal rights on the Sabbath refers to the requirement under Jewish law that a husband visit his wife once a week for sexual relations. This letter, found in the great cache of documents illuminating medieval Jewish life known as the Cairo Geniza, was written by a Jewish merchant in India to his wife who was left behind in Egypt. It shows how mercantile considerations and personal concerns were closely interwoven. The writer's wife is not mentioned by name in accordance with prevailing standards of decency.

Source: Trans. S.D. Goiten, *Letters of Medieval Jewish Traders* (Princeton: Princeton University Press, 1973), pp. 221–26; reprinted with permission.

In (your name!) ...

Would I try to describe the extent of my feelings of longing and yearning for you all the time, my letter would become too long and the words too many. But he who knows the secrets of the heart has the might to bring about relief for each of us by uniting us in joy.

Your precious letters have arrived; I have read and scrutinized them, and was happy to learn from them that you are well and healthy and that you have escaped from those great terrors, the like of which have not been experienced for many generations. Praise be to God for your deliverance and for granting you respite until you might be recompensed in a measure commensurate with your sufferings.

In your letters you alternately rebuke and offend me or put me to shame and use harsh words all the time. I have not deserved any of this. I swear by God, I do not believe that the heart of anyone traveling away from his wife has remained like mine, all the time and during all the years—from the moment of our separation to the very hour of writing this letter—so constantly thinking of you and yearning after you and regretting to be unable to provide you with what I so much desire: your legal rights on every Sabbath and holiday, and to fulfill all your wishes, great and small, with regard to dresses or food or anything else. And you write about me as if I had forgotten you and would not remember you had it not been for your rebukes, and as if, had you not warned me that the public would reprove me, I would not have thought of you. Put this out of your mind and do not impute such things to me. And if what you think or say about my dedication to you is the product of your mind, believing that words of rebuke will increase my yearning—no, in such a way God will not let me reach the fulfillment of my hope, although in my heart there is twice as much as I am able to write. But he is able to have us both reach compensation for our sufferings and then, when we shall be saved, we shall remember in what situation we are now.

You rebuke me with regard to the ambergris [a prized perfume or medicine]. You poor ones!!! Had you known how much trouble and expense I have incurred to get this ambergris for you, you would have said: there is nothing like it in the world. This is the story: after I was resurrected from the dead and had lost all that I carried with me I took a loan of [...] dinars and traveled to countries beyond al-Ma'bar. I checked my accounts and found [ ] with "the decimals." I took them and paid to one of our co-religionists who traveled back from al-Ma 'bar to Aden ... and for it he bought for you....

This was my way of life from the moment I left you until I arrived in Aden (and from there to India) and from India back to Aden: day and night I was constantly drinking, not of my free will, but I conducted myself in an exemplary way and if anyone poked fun in foul speech in my presence, I became furious with him, until he became silent, he and others. I constantly fulfilled what God knows, and cured my soul by fasting during the days and praying during the nights. The congregations in Aden and in India often asked me to lead them in prayer, and I am regarded by them and regard myself as a pious man.

Now in one of your letters you adjure me to set you free, then letters arrived from the old man [her late father] saying the same. Later Ma 'ānī ("Eloquent") b. al-Dajājī ("Seller of Fowl") met me and told me that you came to his house before he set out on his travel. You had given him nutmeg paste as a collateral on a loan of 100 dirhems, but he released 20 dirhems to you. Please let me know whether this is correct, in which case I shall return this sum to him. He reported also that you had asked him to return to you letters which your late father—may God have mercy on him—had sent with him, but he had said to you: "I have already packed them away on the boat." Then you said that these letters were not written with your consent and you asked him not to deliver them to me. On this Ma 'ānī had replied: The judge might have meanwhile sent a message demanding something from the elder, in which case the delivery of these letters might be useful to him.

Now, if this [divorce] is your wish, I cannot blame you. For the waiting has been long. And I do not know whether the Creator will grant relief immediately so that I can come home, or whether matters will take time, for I cannot come home with nothing. Therefore I resolved to issue a writ which sets you free. Now the matter is in your hand. If you wish separation from me, accept *the bill of repudiation* and you are free. But if this is not your decision and not your desire, do not lose these long years of waiting: perhaps relief is at hand and you will regret at a time when regret will be of no avail.

And please do not blame me, for I never neglected you from the time when those things happened and made an effort to save you and me from people talking and impairing my honor. The refusal was on your side, not on mine. I do not know whether [asking for a divorce] is your decision or that of someone else, but after all this, please do not say, you or someone else: this is our reward from him and our recompense. All day long I have a lonely heart and am pained by our separation. I feel that pain while writing these lines. But the choice is with you; the decision is in your hand: if you wish to carry the matter through, do so; if you wish to leave things as they are, do so. But do not act after the first impulse. Ask the advice of good people and act as you think will be the best for you. May God inspire you with the right decision.

[Best regards to my sister] and her husband, the illustrious elder Abu 'l-Fadā'il, the scholar, to Ma'ānī, the scholar, and his son. I have exerted myself for him to a degree that only God knows. The elder Abu 'l-Khayr ("Mr. Good") agreed to pay him 10 mithqāls (Egyptian dinars), which the elder Abu 'l-Makārim ("Noble Character") will deliver to him.

Convey my greetings to the elder Abū Ishāq, the son of your paternal uncle, to his mother, to the elder Abu 'Imrān and his children, to the daughter of your paternal uncle, and to all those whom you know, my most sincere regards.

I sent you 7½ mann of nutmeg, which is better than anything found in the Kārim and worth more than other sorts of it by 1 dinar; 11 mann of good galingale; two futa cloths for the children; 2½ of celandine and 25 of odoriferous wood; fourteen pieces in number.

How did the husband seek to placate his wife? What concerns of hers does he seem to be answering? Why might other people have tried to persuade the wife to seek a divorce?

77. A JEWISH FATHER'S ADVICE: ELEAZAR OF MAINZ

The ethical will was a literary genre common to Jewish communities across medieval Europe. Through these wills, fathers conveyed to their sons and daughters their hopes, dreams, and advice on how to lead a proper and honorable life. They combine both conventional and idealized values with insights into the individual's circumstances. The ethical will of Eleazar of Mainz, who died in 1357, was addressed to both his sons and daughters. It describes the behavior he considered appropriate and the values that governed Jewish family life. As well, it conveys something of the problems and concerns that preoccupied the Jewish community living in Christian Europe in the wake of the Black Death.

Source: Trans. Israel Abrahams, *Hebrew Ethical Wills,* Part 2 (Philadelphia: Jewish Publication Society of America, 1948), pp. 208-18; reprinted with permission.

These are the things which my sons and daughters shall do at my request. They shall go to the house of prayer morning and evening, and shall pay special regard to the Tephillah and the Shema. So soon as the service is over, they shall occupy themselves a little with the Torah, the Psalms, or with works of charity. Their business must be conducted honestly, in their dealings both with Jew and Gentile. They must be gentle in their manners, and prompt to accede to every honorable request. They must not talk more than is necessary, by this will they be saved from slander, falsehood, and frivolity. They shall give an exact tithe of all their possessions; they shall never turn away a poor man empty-handed, but must give him what they can, be it much or little. If he beg a lodging over night, and they know him not, let them provide him with the wherewithal to pay an inn-keeper. Thus shall they satisfy the needs of the poor in every possible way.

My daughters must obey scrupulously the rules applying to women; modesty, sanctity, reverence, should mark their married lives. They should carefully watch for the signs of the beginning of their periods and keep separate from their husbands at such times. Marital intercourse must be modest and holy, with a spirit of restraint and delicacy, in reverence and silence. They shall be very punctilious and careful with their ritual bathing, taking with them women friends of worthy character. They shall cover their eyes until they reach their home, on returning from the bath, in order not to behold anything of an unclean nature. They must respect their husbands, and must be invariably amiable to them. Husbands, on their part, must honor their wives more than themselves, and treat them with tender consideration.

If they can by any means contrive it, my sons and daughters should live in communities, and not isolated from other Jews, so that their sons and daughters may learn the ways of Judaism. Even if compelled to solicit from others the money to pay a teacher, they must not let the young, of both sexes, go without instruction in the Torah. Marry your children, O my sons and daughters, as soon as their age is ripe, to members of respectable families. Let no child of mine hunt after money by making a low match for that object; but if the family is undistinguished only on the mother's side, it does not matter, for all Israel counts descent from the father's side.

Every Friday morning, they shall put themselves in careful trim for honoring the Sabbath, kindling the lamps while the day is still great, and in winter lighting the furnace before dark, to avoid desecrating the Sabbath (by kindling fire thereon). For due welcome to the Sabbath, the women must prepare beautiful candles. As to games of chance, I entreat my children never to engage in such pastimes. During the leisure of the festival weeks they may play for trifling stakes in kind, and the women may amuse themselves similarly on New Moons, but never for money. In their relation to women, my sons must behave continently, avoiding mixed bathing and mixed dancing and all frivolous conversation, while my daughters ought not to speak much with strangers, nor jest nor dance with them. They ought to be always at home, and not be gadding about. They should not stand at the door, watching whatever passes. I ask, I command, that the daughters of my house be never without work to do, for idleness leads first to boredom, then to sin. But let them spin, or cook, or sew.

I earnestly beg my children to be tolerant and humble to all, as I was throughout my life. Should cause for dissension present itself, be slow to accept the quarrel; seek peace and pursue it with all the vigor at your command. Even if you suffer loss thereby, forbear and forgive, for God has many ways of feeding and sustaining his creatures. To the slanderer do not retaliate with counterattack; and though it be proper to rebut false accusations, yet is it most desirable to set an example of reticence. You yourselves must avoid uttering any slander, for so will you win affection. In trade be true, never grasping at what belongs to another. For by avoiding these wrongs — scandal, falsehood, money-grubbing — men will surely find tranquility and affection. And against all evils, silence is the best safeguard.

Now, my sons and daughters, eat and drink only what is necessary, as our good parents did, refraining from heavy meals, and holding the gross liver in detestation. The regular adoption of such economy in food leads to economy in expenditure generally, with a consequent reluctance to pursue after wealth, but the acquisition of a contented spirit, simplicity in diet, and many good results. Concerning such a well-ordered life the text says: "The righteous eats to the satisfaction of his desire." Our teachers have said: "Method in expenditure is half a sufficiency." Nevertheless, accustom yourselves and your wives, your sons and your daughters, to wear nice and clean clothes, that God and man may love and honor you. In this direction do not exercise too strict a parsimony. But on no account adopt foreign fashions in dress. After the manner of your fathers order your attire, and let your cloaks be broad without buckles attached.

Be on your guard concerning vows, and cautious as to promises. The breach of one's undertakings leads to many lapses. Do not get into the habit of exclaiming "Gott!," but speak always of the "Creator, blessed be he;" and in all that you propose to do, today or tomorrow, add the proviso, "if the Lord wills, I shall do this thing." Thus remember God's part in your life.

Whatever happiness befall you, be it in monetary fortune or in the birth of children, be it some signal deliverances or any other of the many blessings which may come to you, be not stolidly unappreciative, like dumb cattle that utter no word of gratitude. But offer praises to the Rock who has befriended you, saying: "O give thanks to the Lord, for he is good, for his mercy endures for ever. Blessed are you, O Lord, who are good and dispenses good." Besides thanking God for his bounties at the moment they occur, also in your regular prayers let the memory of these personal favors prompt your hearts to special fervor during the utterance of the communal thanks. When words of gratitude are used in the liturgy, pause to reflect in silence on the goodness of God to you that day. And when you make the response: "May your great name be blessed," call to mind your own personal experiences of the divine favor.

Be very particular to keep your houses clean and tidy. I was always scrupulous on this point, for every injurious condition, and sickness and poverty, are to be found in foul dwellings. Be careful over the benedictions; accept no divine gift without paying back the giver's part; and his part is man's grateful acknowledgment.

And O, my sons and daughters, keep yourselves far from the snare of frivolous conversation, which begins in tribulation and ends in destruction. Nor be you found in the company of these light talkers. Judge you rather every man charitably and use your best efforts to detect an honorable explanation of conduct however suspicious. Try to persuade yourselves that it was your neighbor's zeal for some good end that led him to the conduct you deplore. This is the meaning of the exhortation: "In righteousness shall you judge your neighbor." To sum up, the fewer one's idle words the less one's risk of slander, lying, flattery—all of them, things held in utter detestation by God.

On holidays and festivals and sabbaths seek to make happy the poor, the unfortunate, widows and orphans, who should always be guests at your tables; their joyous entertainment is a religious duty. Let me repeat my warning against gossip and scandal. And as you speak no scandal, so listen to none, for if there were no receivers there would be no bearers of slanderous tales; therefore the reception and credit of slander is as serious an offence as the originating of it. The less you say, the less cause you give for animosity, while "in the multitude of words there is no transgression wanting." Always be of those who see and are not seen, who hear and are not heard. Accept no invitations to banquets, except to such as are held for religious reasons: at weddings and at meals prepared for mourners, at gatherings to celebrate entry into the covenant of Abraham, or at assemblies in honor of the wise. Games of chance for money stakes, such as dicing, must be avoided. And as I have again warned you on that head, again let me urge you to show forbearance and humility to all men, to ignore abuses levelled at you, but the indignant refutation of charges against your moral character is fully justifiable.

Be of the first ten in synagogue, rising betimes for the purpose. Pray steadily with the congregation ...

I beg of you, my sons and daughters, my wife, and all the congregation, that no funeral oration be spoken in my honor. Do not carry my body on a bier but in a coach. Wash me clean, comb my hair, trim my nails, as I was wont to do in my life-time, so that I may go clean to my eternal rest, as I went clean to synagogue every sabbath day. If the ordinary officials dislike the duty, let adequate payment be made to some poor man who shall render this service carefully and not perfunctorily. At a distance of thirty cubits from the grave, they shall set my coffin on the ground, and drag me to the grave by a rope attached to the coffin. Every four cubits they shall stand and wait awhile, doing this in all seven times, so that I may find atonement for my sins. Put me in the ground at the right hand of my father, and if the space be a little narrow, I am sure that he loves me well enough to make room for me by his side. If this be altogether impossible, put me on his left, or near my grandmother, Yuta. Should this also be impractical, let me be buried by the side of my daughter.

What value did Eleazar place on education? What were his ideas about marriage? What personal qualities did he want his children to cultivate? What should their houses be like? How should they conduct themselves?

78. ISLAMIC TEACHINGS ON MARRIAGE AND THE FAMILY

Little is known about the private lives of individuals in the areas that embraced Islam during the period of the European Middle Ages. This is in part because the activities within the household were considered to be in the private women's sphere and thus were relegated to oral tradition rather than incorporated into the formal language of the masculine public sphere. The ideological foundations and rules that governed marriage and the family were set out in the Quran, which records God's revelations to his prophet Muhammad (ca. 570-629). The teachings of the Quran were, of course, subject to considerable variation when applied in different times and places. The paucity of private sources, however, makes it difficult to assess how these teachings were implemented in daily life. The teachings about marriage and family are found in a number of sections of the Quran and includes a discussion of Muhammad's own marriage.

Source: Trans. N.J. Dawood, *The Koran* (Harmondsworth: Penguin, 1956, 1997), 11, 32-35, 60-65, 74, 78, 246, 248-49, 295-99, 396-97; reprinted with permission.

Part 2. The Cow

In the Name of God, the compassionate, the merciful

This book is not to be doubted. It is a guide for the righteous, who believe in the unseen and are steadfast in prayer, who give in alms from what we gave them; who believe in what has been revealed to you [Muhammad] and what was revealed before you, and have absolute faith in the life to come. These are rightly guided by their Lord; these shall surely triumph....

You shall not wed pagan women, unless they embrace the faith. A believing slave-girl is better than an idolatress, although she may please you. Nor shall you wed idolaters, unless they embrace the faith. A believing slave is better than an idolater, although he may please you. These call you to the fire; but God calls you, by his will, to paradise and to forgiveness. He makes plain his revelations to mankind, so that they may take heed.

They ask you about menstruation. Say: "It is an indisposition. Keep aloof from women during their menstrual periods and do not approach them until they are clean again; when they are clean, have intercourse with them whence God enjoined you. God loves those that turn to him in penitence and strive to keep themselves clean."

Women are your fields: go, then, into your fields whence you please. Do good works and fear God. Bear in mind that you shall meet him. Give good tidings to the believers....

Those that renounce their wives on oath must wait four months. If they change their minds, God is forgiving and merciful; but if they decide to divorce them, know that God hears all and knows all.

Divorced women must wait, keeping themselves from men, three menstrual courses. It is unlawful for them, if they believe in God and the last day, to hide what God has created in their wombs: in which case their husbands would do well to take them back, should they desire reconciliation.

Women shall with justice have rights similar to those exercised against them, although men have a status above women. God is mighty and wise.

Divorce may be pronounced twice, and then a woman must be retained in honor or allowed to go with kindness. It is unlawful for husbands to take from them anything they have given them, unless both fear that they may not be able to keep within the bounds set by God; in which case it shall be no offence for either of them if the wife redeems herself.

These are the bounds set by God; do not transgress them. Those that transgress the bounds of God are wrongdoers.

If a man divorces his wife, he cannot remarry her until she has wedded another man and been divorced by him, in which case it shall be no offence for either of them to return to the other, if they think that they can keep within the bounds set by God.

Such are the bounds of God. He makes them plain to men of knowledge.

When you have renounced your wives and they have reached the end of their waiting period, either retain them in honor or let them go with kindness. But you shall not retain them in order to harm them or to wrong them. Whoever does this wrongs his own soul....

If a man has renounced his wife and she has reached the end of her waiting period, do not prevent her from remarrying her husband if they have come to an honorable agreement. This is enjoined on every one of you who believes in God and the last day; it is more honorable for you and more chaste. God knows, but you know not.

Mothers shall give suck to their children for two whole years if the father wishes the sucking to be completed. They must be maintained and clothed in a reasonable manner by the child's father. None should be charged with more than one can bear. A mother should not be allowed to suffer on account of her child, nor should a father on account of his child. The same duties devolve upon the father's heir. But if, after consultation, they choose by mutual consent to wean the child, they shall incur no guilt. Nor shall it be any offence for you if you prefer to have a nurse for your children, provided that you pay her what you promise, according to usage. Have fear of God and know that God is cognizant of all your actions.

Widows shall wait, keeping themselves apart from men, for four months and ten days after their husbands' death. When they have reached the end of their waiting period, it shall be no offence for you to let them do whatever they choose for themselves, provided that it is decent. God is cognizant of all your actions.

It shall be no offence for you openly to propose marriage to such women or to cherish them in your hearts. God knows that you will remember them. Do not arrange to meet them in secret, and if you do, speak to them honorably. But you shall not consummate the marriage before the end of their waiting period. Know that God has knowledge of all your thoughts. Therefore take heed and bear in mind that God is forgiving and lenient.

It shall be no offence for you to divorce your wives before the marriage is consummated or the dowry settled. Provide for them with fairness; the rich man according to his means and the poor man according to his. This is binding on righteous men. If you divorce them before the marriage is consummated, but after their dowry has been settled, give them the half of their dowry, unless they or the husband agree to waive it. But it is more proper that the husband should waive it. Do not forget to show kindness to each other. God observes your actions....

You shall bequeath your widows a year's maintenance without causing them to leave their homes; but if they leave of their own accord, no blame shall be attached to you for any course they may deem reasonable to pursue. God is mighty and wise. Reasonable provision shall also be made for divorced women. That is incumbent on righteous men....

Part 4. Women

In the Name of God, the compassionate, the merciful

You people! Have fear of your Lord, who created you from a single soul. From that soul he created its spouse, and through them he bestrewed the earth with countless men and women.

Fear God, in whose name you plead with one another, and honor the mothers who bore you. God is ever watching you.

Give orphans the property which belongs to them. Do not exchange their valuables for worthless things or cheat them of their possessions; for this would surely be a grievous sin. If you fear that you cannot treat orphans with fairness, then you may marry other women who seem good to you: two, three, or four of them. But if you fear that you cannot maintain equality among them, marry one only or any slave-girls you may own. This will make it easier for you to avoid injustice.

Give women their dowry as a free gift; but if they choose to make over to you a part of it, you may regard it as lawfully yours.

Do not give the feeble-minded the property with which God has entrusted you for their support; but maintain and clothe them with its proceeds, and speak kind words to them.

Put orphans to the test until they reach a marriageable age. If you find them capable of sound judgment, hand over to them their property, and do not deprive them of it by squandering it before they come of age.

Let not the rich guardian touch the property of his orphan ward; and let him who is poor use no more than a fair portion of it for his own advantage.

When you hand over to them their property, call in some witnesses; sufficient is God's accounting of your actions.

Men shall have a share in what their parents and kinsmen leave; and women shall have a share in what their parents and kinsmen leave: whether it be little or much, they shall be legally entitled to a share.

If relatives, orphans, or needy men are present at the division of an inheritance, give them, too, a share of it, and speak kind words to them.

Let those who are solicitous about the welfare of their young children after their own death take care not to wrong orphans. Let them fear God and speak for justice.

Those that devour the property of orphans unjustly, swallow fire into their bellies; they shall burn in a mighty conflagration.

God has thus enjoined you concerning your children:

A male shall inherit twice as much as a female. If there be more than two girls, they shall have two-thirds of the inheritance; but if there be one only, she shall inherit the half. Parents shall inherit a sixth each, if the deceased have a child; but if he leave no child and his parents be his heirs, his mother shall have a third. If he have brothers, his mother shall have a sixth after payment of any legacy he may have bequeathed or any debt he may have owed.

You may wonder whether your parents or your children are more beneficial to you. But this is the law of God; surely God is all-knowing and wise.

You shall inherit the half of your wives' estate if they die childless. If they leave children, a quarter of their estate shall be yours after payment of any legacy they may have bequeathed or any debt they may have owed.

Your wives shall inherit one quarter of your estate if you die childless. If you leave children, they shall inherit one-eighth, after payment of any legacy you may have bequeathed or any debt you may have owed....

If any of your women commit a lewd act, call in four witnesses from among yourselves against them; if they testify to their guilt confine them to their houses till death overtakes them or till God finds another way for them.

If two men among you commit a lewd act, punish them both. If they repent and mend their ways, let them be. God is forgiving and merciful....

Believers, it is unlawful for you to inherit the women of your deceased kinsmen against their will, or to bar them from re-marrying, in order that you may force them to give up a part of what you have given them, unless they be guilty of a proven lewd act. Treat them with kindness; for even if you dislike them, it may well be that you dislike a thing which God has meant for your own abundant good.

If you wish to replace one wife with another, do not take from her the dowry you have given her even if it be a talent of gold. That would be improper and grossly unjust; for how can you take it back when you have lain with each other and entered into a firm contract?

You shall not marry the women whom your fathers married: all previous such marriages excepted. That was an evil practice, indecent and abominable.

Forbidden to you are your mothers, your daughters, your sisters, your paternal and maternal aunts, the daughters of your brothers and sisters, your foster-mothers, your foster-sisters, the mothers of your wives, your step-daughters who are in your charge, born of the wives with whom you have lain (it is no offence for you to marry your step-daughters if you have not consummated your marriage with their mothers), and the wives of your own begotten sons. You are also forbidden to take in marriage two sisters at one and the same time: all previous such marriages excepted. Surely God is forgiving and merciful. Also married women, except those whom you own as slaves. Such is the decree of God. All women other than these are lawful for you, provided you court them with your wealth in modest conduct, not in fornication. Give them their dowry for the enjoyment you have had of them as a duty; but it shall be no offence for you to make any other agreement among yourselves after you have fulfilled your duty. Surely God is all-knowing and wise.

If any one of you cannot afford to marry a free believing woman, let him marry a slave-girl who is a believer (God best knows your faith: you are born one of another). Marry them with the permission of their masters and give them their dowry in all justice, provided they are honorable and chaste and have not entertained other men. If after marriage they commit adultery, they shall suffer half the penalty inflicted upon free adulteresses. Such is the law for those of you who fear to commit sin: but if you abstain, it will be better for you. God is forgiving and merciful.

God desires to make this known to you and to guide you along the paths of those who have gone before you, and to turn to you with mercy. God is all-knowing and wise.

God wishes to forgive you, but those who follow their own appetites wish to see you stray grievously into error. God wishes to lighten your burdens, for man was created weak....

To every parent and kinsman we have appointed heirs who will inherit from them. As for those with whom you have entered into agreements, let them, too, have their share. Surely God bears witness to all things.

Men have authority over women because God has made the one superior to the other, and because they spend their wealth to maintain them. Good women are obedient. They guard their unseen parts because God has guarded them. As for those from whom you fear disobedience, admonish them and send them to beds apart and beat them. Then if they obey you, take no further action against them. Surely God is high, supreme.

If you fear a breach between a man and his wife, appoint an arbiter from his people and another from hers. If they wish to be reconciled, God will bring them together again. Surely God is all-knowing and wise....

Serve God and associate none with him. Show kindness to parents and kindred, to orphans and to the destitute, to near and distant neighbors, to those that keep company with you, to the traveler in need, and to the slaves you own....

Believers, do not approach your prayers when you are drunk, but wait till you can grasp the meaning of your words; nor when you are unclean — unless you are traveling the road — until you have washed yourselves. If you are sick or on a journey, or if, when you have relieved yourselves or had intercourse with women, you can find no water, take some clean sand and rub your faces and your hands with it. Gracious is God and forgiving....

To God belongs all that the heavens and the earth contain. God encompasses all things.

They consult you concerning women. Say: "God has instructed you about them, and so have the verses proclaimed to you in the book, concerning the orphan girls whom you deny their lawful rights and refuse to marry; also regarding helpless children. He has instructed you to deal justly with orphans. God has knowledge of all the good you do."

If a woman fears ill-treatment or desertion on the part of her husband, it shall be no offence for them to seek a mutual agreement, for agreement is best. People are prone to avarice. But if you do what is right and guard yourselves against evil, know then that God is cognizant of all your actions.

Try as you may, you cannot treat all your wives impartially. Do not set yourself altogether against any of them, leaving her, as it were, in suspense. If you do what is right and guard yourselves against evil, you will find God forgiving and merciful. If they separate, God will compensate both out of his own abundance: God is munificent and wise....

They consult you. Say: "Thus God instructs you regarding those that die childless and without living parents. If a man die childless and he have a sister, she shall inherit the half of his estate. If a woman die childless, her brother shall be her sole heir. If a childless man have two sisters, they shall inherit two-thirds of his estate; but if he have both brothers and sisters, the share of each male shall be that of two females."

Thus God makes plain to you his precepts so that you may not err. God has knowledge of all things.

Part 24. Light

In the Name of God, the compassionate, the merciful

A chapter which we have revealed and sanctioned, proclaiming in it clear revelations, so that you may take heed.

The adulterer and the adulteress shall each be given a hundred lashes. Let no pity for them cause you to disobey God, if you truly believe in God and the last day; and let their punishment be witnessed by a number of believers.

The adulterer may marry only an adulteress or an idolatress; and the adulteress may marry only an adulterer or an idolater. True believers are forbidden such marriages.

Those that defame honorable women and cannot produce four witnesses shall be given eighty lashes. Do not accept their testimony ever after, for they are great transgressors—except those among them that afterwards repent and mend their ways. God is forgiving and merciful.

If a man accuses his wife but has no witnesses except himself, he shall swear four times by God that his charge is true, calling down upon himself the curse of God if he is lying. But if his wife swears four times by God that his charge is false and calls down his curse upon herself if it be true, she shall receive no punishment....

Enjoin believing men to turn their eyes away from temptation and to restrain their carnal desires. This will make their lives purer. God has knowledge of all their actions.

Enjoin believing women to turn their eyes away from temptation and to preserve their chastity; not to display their adornments (except such as are normally revealed); to draw their veils over their bosoms and not to display their finery except to their husbands, their fathers, their husbands' fathers, their sons, their step-sons, their brothers, their brothers' sons, their sisters' sons, their women-servants, and their slave-girls; male attendants lacking in natural vigor, and children who have no carnal knowledge of women. And let them not stamp their feet when walking so as to reveal their hidden trinkets.

Believers, turn to God in penitence, that you may prosper.

Take in marriage those among you who are single and those of your male and female slaves who are honest. If they are poor, God will enrich them from his own bounty. God is munificent and all-knowing.

Let those who cannot afford to marry live in continence until God shall enrich them from his own bounty. As for those of your slaves who wish to buy their liberty, free them if you find in them any promise and bestow on them a part of the riches which God has given you.

You shall not force your slave-girls into prostitution in order that you may enrich yourselves, if they wish to preserve their chastity. If anyone compels them, God will be forgiving and merciful to them....

Part 33. The Confederate Tribes

... Prophet, say to your wives: "If you seek this nether life and all its finery, come, I will make provision for you and release you honorably. But if you seek God and his apostle and the abode of the hereafter, know that God has prepared a rich recompense for those of you who do good works."

Wives of the prophet! Those of you who clearly commit a lewd act shall be doubly punished. That is easy enough for God. But those of you who obey God and his apostle and do good works shall be doubly recompensed; for them we have made a rich provision.

Wives of the prophet, you are not like other women. If you fear God, do not be too complaisant in your speech, lest the lecherous-hearted should lust after you. Show discretion in what you say. Stay in your homes and do not display your finery as women used to do in the days of ignorance. Attend to your prayers, give alms, and obey God and his apostle.

Women of the household, God seeks only to remove uncleanness from you and to purify you. Commit to memory the revelations of God and the wise sayings that are recited in your dwellings. Gracious is God and all-knowing.

Those who submit to God and accept the true faith; who are devout, sincere, patient, humble, charitable, and chaste; who fast and are ever mindful of God—on these, both men and women, God will bestow forgiveness and a rich recompense.

It is not for true believers—men or women—to order their own affairs if God and his apostle decree otherwise. He that disobeys God and his apostle strays far indeed.

You [Muhammad] said to the man whom God and yourself have favored: "Keep your wife and have fear of God." You sought to hide in your heart what God was to reveal. You were afraid of man, although it would have been more proper to fear God. And when Zayd [Muhammad's adopted son] divorced his wife, we gave her to you in marriage, so that it should become legitimate for true believers to wed the wives of their adopted sons if they divorce them. God's will must needs be done.

No blame shall be attached to the prophet for doing what is sanctioned for him by God. Such was the way of God with those who went before him (God's decrees are preordained); who fulfilled the mission with which God had charged them, fearing God and fearing none besides him. Sufficient is God's reckoning.

Muhammad is the father of no man among you. He is the apostle of God and the seal of the prophets. Surely God has knowledge of all things....

Believers, if you marry believing women and divorce them before the marriage is consummated, you are not required to observe a waiting period. Provide well for them and release them honorably.

Prophet, we have made lawful for you the wives to whom you have granted dowries and the slave-girls whom God has given you as booty; the daughters of your paternal and maternal uncles and of your paternal and maternal aunts who fled with you; and any believing woman who gives herself to the prophet and whom the prophet wishes to take in marriage. This privilege is yours alone, being granted to no other believer.

We well know the duties we have imposed on the faithful concerning their wives and slave-girls. [We grant you this privilege] so that none may blame you. God is ever forgiving and merciful.

You may put off any of your wives you please and take to your bed any of them you please. Nor is it unlawful for you to receive any of those whom you have temporarily set aside. That is more proper, so that they may be contented and not vexed, and may all be pleased with what you give them.

God knows what is in your hearts. Surely God is all-knowing and gracious.

It shall be unlawful for you [Muhammad] to take more wives or to change your present wives for other women, though their beauty please you, unless they are slave-girls whom you own. God takes cognizance of all things.

Believers, do not enter the houses of the prophet for a meal without waiting for the proper time, unless you are given leave. But if you are invited, enter; and when you have eaten, disperse. Do not engage in familiar talk, for this would annoy the prophet and he would be ashamed to bid you go; but of the truth God is not ashamed. If you ask his wives for anything, speak to them from behind a curtain. This is more chaste for your hearts and their hearts.

You must not speak ill of God's apostle, nor shall you ever wed his wives after him; this would surely be a grave offence in the sight of God. Whether you reveal or conceal them, God has knowledge of all things.

It shall be no offence for the prophet's wives to be seen unveiled by their fathers, their sons, their brothers, their brothers' sons, their sisters' sons, their women, or their slave-girls. Women, have fear of God; surely God observes all things.

The prophet is blessed by God and his angels. Bless him, then, you that are true believers, and greet him with a worthy salutation.

Those who speak ill of God and his apostle shall be cursed by God in this life and in the life to come. He has prepared for them a shameful punishment.

Those who traduce believing men and believing women undeservedly shall bear the guilt of slander and grievous sin.

Prophet, enjoin your wives, your daughters, and the wives of true believers to draw their veils close round them. That is more proper, so that they may be recognized and not be molested. God is ever forgiving and merciful....

Part 65. Divorce

In the name of God, the compassionate, the merciful

Prophet (and you believers), if you divorce your wives, divorce them at the end of their waiting period. Compute their waiting period and have fear of God, your Lord. You shall not expel them from their homes, nor shall they go away, unless they have committed a proven lewd act. Such are the bounds set by God; he that transgresses God's bounds wrongs his own soul. You never know; after that, God may bring about some new event.

When their waiting term is ended, either keep them honorably or part with them in honor. Call to witness two honest men among you and give your testimony before God. Whoever believes in God and the last day is exhorted to do this. He that fears God, God will give him a means of salvation and will provide for him whence he does not reckon: God is all-sufficient for the man who puts his trust in him. God will surely bring about what he decrees. God has set a measure for all things.

If you are in doubt concerning those of your wives who have ceased menstruating, know that their waiting period shall be three months. The same shall apply to those who have not yet menstruated. As for pregnant women, their term shall end with their confinement. God will ease the hardship of the man who fears him.

Such is the commandment which God has revealed to you. He that fears God shall be forgiven his sins and richly recompensed.

Lodge them in your own homes, according to your means. You shall not harass them so as to make life intolerable for them. If they are with child, maintain them until the end of their confinement; and if, after that, they give suck to the infants they bore you, give them their pay and consult together in all reasonableness. But if you cannot tolerate each other, let other women suckle for you.

Let the rich man spend according to his wealth, and the poor man according to what God has given him. God does not charge a man with more than he has given him; God, after hardship, will bring ease....

What were appropriate dress and conduct for a respectable woman? What issues were considered when divorcing? How were Muhammad's own marriages and family characterized? How did the norms governing Muslim marriage differ from those of Christianity? Judaism? What rules governed polygamy? What social circumstances might polygamy have addressed? How were wives and children protected? How are slaves discussed?

79. CHRISTIAN MISUNDERSTANDING OF ISLAMIC TEACHINGS ON MARRIAGE

The spread of Islam across the Mediterranean basin meant that by the mid-ninth century Christians and Muslims contacted each other in the Iberian Peninsula, southern Italy, and the Holy Land, among other areas. Despite this contact, Christian Europeans tended to have a distorted view of Muslim religion. One area in which misunderstanding endured was marriage. This may in part be attributed to some of the profound differences between Islamic and Catholic teachings: the Islamic practices of polygamy and divorce were particularly problematic for Christians. Such teachings were diametrically opposed to the doctrines that the Catholic Church had developed and disseminated over the centuries, doctrines which had been adopted across Christendom by the twelfth century. Europeans, especially those living in northwestern Europe, who did not have any direct contact with Muslims, had a sketchy knowledge of Islamic beliefs and practices, especially those pertaining to marriage and to the prophet Muhammad's own life and conduct. This cross-cultural misunderstanding is reflected in the account of the appearance of Muhammad and the rise of Islam written by the prolific chronicler, Matthew of Paris (ca.1200-1259).

Source: Trans. J.A. Giles in Matthew of Paris, *English History* (London: Henry G. Bohn, 1852), vol. 1, pp. 14-18, 22-24; revised.

Concerning a letter sent to the pope about the laws of Muhammad

About the same time a letter was sent to the lord pope, Gregory IX, from eastern lands, by preachers who were traveling in those parts. And when the false doctrine, no rather the madness of Muhammad, the prophet of the Saracens, who was described in the letter, came to the world's attention, it excited everyone's derision and mockery....

Concerning Muhammad's upbringing

This man, who is called Muhammad the Ishmaelite, when he had been orphaned upon the death of his father, Abdimenef, was taken charge of by a man named Hebenabecalip, a man who attended to the idols at a placed called Clingua and also at Aliguze, who nourished him and raised him. When he had arrived at the age of youth, he became a hired hand to a certain woman named Adige, the daughter of Hulaith. This woman gave him an ass for his service, so that she could receive payment for the goods which he would bring to areas of Asia. At last, he secretly joined with this same woman in coitus and married her, and he grew very rich from her money. Elated by this, he began to boast excessively and endeavored to establish himself as ruler over all the tribes and his own people, and would have presumed to be called their king had not some more noble and stronger than himself opposed his usurpation. Then he declared himself a prophet sent from God, and that all the people ought to believe his words. Those Arab people, rustic and uncivilized, who had never seen a prophet, believed him. There was also a certain apostate, who had lapsed into heresy and was excommunicated, who taught the same beliefs and wrote his doctrines. And this said Muhammad drew into his company whatever thieves and brigands he was able. When a large group had gathered, he stationed them in secret out-of-the-way places so that they could rob merchants coming and going from Asia. One day, he was coming from the cities of Jerveth and Matham, when he found on the road a camel belonging to a man named Abige Heli, son of Hyesem, which he immediately seized, and fled to the city of Macta. The citizens of Macta, however, not considering him a prophet, insulting him, ejected him from the city as an imposter and cursed him as a predator and robber of travelers. He then went to a certain desert city, where the people were partly Jewish and partly pagans, idolaters, poor and ignorant. There, Muhammad, along with his followers, built a temple in which he could present his fictions to the simple people....

Concerning Muhammad's adultery and his lust

Muhammad had a servant named Zeid, whose wife, named Zemah, was very beautiful, whom Muhammad himself loved greatly. This servant, Zeid, however, knowing this and being aware of his master's lustfulness, said to his wife, "Take care that my master does not see you, for if he should see you, I will immediately repudiate you." One day, however, when the servant was absent, Muhammad came to his house calling for him. When he did not answer, Muhammad continued knocking at the door so long that the woman, becoming annoyed, replied, " Zeid is not here." Arriving later, Zeid saw his wife talking with his master. When the lord had left he said to her, "Did I not tell you that if my master were to see you or speak with you I would repudiate you?" At once, he threw her out of his house. However, Muhammad immediately received her. Fearing lest he be reviled for adultery, however, he pretended that a letter had come to him from heaven, in which God ordered him that it should be proclaimed as law among the people that when any man repudiate his wife, and another man receive her, she should be the wife of the man who received her. And to this day this is the law among them, and it originated from the aforesaid situation.

Concerning this repudiated adulteress and Muhammad's wives

A certain man named Galy, the son of Abytalip, reproved Muhammad for his adultery, particularly because he loved this adulteress most of all his wives. "O, prophet," he said, "on account of that woman whom you are keeping, you incur opprobrium from everyone." He, however, conquered by lust, did not dismiss her but mitigated his adultery with false arguments. Moreover, Muhammad had fifteen wives: two were free women, the rest were servants. The first was Adige, daughter of Ulaith. The second was the aforesaid repudiated adulteress. The third was Zoda, daughter of Zunga. The fourth was Aza, daughter of Gomar. The fifth was Mathezelem; to this wife he granted whatever she liked best as a dowry. The sixth was Zeinahy, daughter of Gnar; to this one he swore in anger that he would not come to her for a month, but overcome by lust, breaking his oath, he had intercourse with her before the term was up. The seventh wife was Zeinaph, daughter of Urynaph; the eighth, Abbap, daughter of Abifiziel; the ninth Mamuona, daughter of Alfaritalim; the tenth, Geotheria, daughter of Alimisitasy; the eleventh, Zafia, a Jew who was formerly called Anazalia, daughter of Haby; the twelfth, Aculevia, daughter of Fantima; the thirteenth, Umaia, daughter of Aldacal; the fourteenth the daughter of Annomen, named Halaeydia; and the fifteenth was Malicha, daughter of Gathial. The servants were Miriam, daughter of Ibrasus, his son, and Ramath, daughter of Simeon....

Concerning the marriage of Saracens

According to their law, a man may have three or four wives, if he has sufficient property for this. At any rate, the wives ought to be free women, but they may have as many servants and concubines as they are able to provide for and govern, contrary to what is written in Genesis: "They shall be two in one flesh;" it does not say three or four. Likewise, Lamech, who first introduced polygamy, was rebuked by God and punished more severely than the first murderer. If a wife should displease any one of them, or if some contention, dispute, or hatred should arise between them, immediately a divorce is effected both for the husband and the wife, and each dismisses the other freely. But if, after dismissing his wife, a man regrets it and wishes her to be restored to him, unless she has previously joined with another man and she herself consents to return, he is in no way allowed to receive her as his wife; this is so, because there is not legitimate marriage among them. Indeed, they pay their dowries not according to the law but according to the custom of the heathens. They have no doctrinal guidance in this and they are joined with no nuptial blessing.

Concerning their superstition

They join in coitus, especially during periods of fasting, believing they please God more. They fast only one month a year, and then from morning until night. From nightfall until morning they do not stop eating. On fast days, they ought not to pray with an empty stomach; but then they especially have sexual intercourse with their wives, as if they will receive far greater reward. If someone is ill during a period of fasting or is troubled in any way, or is on pilgrimage, he is allowed to eat, and to resume fasting when he is healthy. Moreover, during fasts they diligently eat meat and all sorts of rich food except wine. They do not have intercourse with pregnant women, but only prior to conception, asserting it an honorable motive and there ought not to be intercourse except for the purpose of conceiving children....

The end of the letter sent to the pope about the pseudo-prophet Muhammad

... Indeed, the aforesaid Muhammad taught and wrote in his book, the *Quran*, which the Saracens use and consider authentic just as Christians do the gospels, that the first and chief commandment of God, in importance as well as in temporal order, is "Increase and multiply." Whoever transgresses this sins irremediably. Hence, so that the Saracen people may be increased, like horses and mules having no understanding, Muhammad ordered and enjoined that they should have as many wives, along with concubines, as they can support and the Saracens can use and abuse them at will. And if someone should have fewer than he could provide for and govern, having regard for his property, he is accused of transgressing the law and of avarice and more are assigned to him by the decision of the authorities. Thus, Muhammad thought little of angelic virginity, as if it were sterility, and disparaging continence, he condemned it as barrenness, not considering that the Lord gave only one Eve to one Adam as a helpmate and for the procreation of children. Thus, therefore, Muhammad, by multiplying wives, established polygamy, and not being admonished by the example of Lamech, that man of blood who first introduced bigamy. Afterwards he paid for his crime, was reproved by the Lord, and was erased from the face of the earth by the flood. Hence it is that the weak and effeminate Saracens wallow in lust and uncleanness, according to the orders of their filthy prophet Muhammad, who introduced this custom so that he could propagate and increase his people and lineage, and thus strengthen his law by their very numbers ...

How did Matthew of Paris explain the remarriage of divorced women? On what basis did Matthew criticize Muslim marriage in general and polygamy in particular?

80. THE CATHARS' REJECTION OF MARRIAGE

In the eleventh and twelfth centuries the increasing popularity of heresies posed a severe challenge to the Catholic Church. The Cathars, in particular, were a threat as they competed with traditional Christianity for the hearts and minds of the common folk, especially in southern France and northern Italy. The Cathars were antimaterialist and believed that human spirits were trapped in physical bodies. They rejected marriage and procreation and embraced virginity. These beliefs were considered so serious a threat to Christian marriage that an affirmation of the sanctity of marriage was included in the canons of the Fourth Lateran Council (1215). The exact beliefs of the Cathars, however, remain shrouded because their own writings have not survived. Rather, information about them comes from descriptions by their enemies, clerics who wrote and preached against heresy. Included here are extracts from an investigation of an heretical group at Monforte, in Italy, and from James Capelli's treatise against the Cathars, written in the mid-thirteenth century. James was a Franciscan friar whose treatise against the Cathars is characterized by a sense of balance and the absence of the slanders of more excessive and hostile writers. The testimony found in the registers of Jacques Fournier, who interrogated the inhabitants of Montaillou, a village in which Cathar beliefs endured longer than elsewhere in Europe, provides insight into how heretical beliefs were understood at the village level and how they were incorporated into people's lives. The testimony of Béatrice de Planissoles, reporting on her conversations with her lover, the heretical priest Pierre Clergue, shows a more libertine side to Cathar beliefs.

Source: Trans. Walter L. Wakefield and Austin P. Evans, *Heresies of the High Middle Ages. Selected Sources* (New York: Columbia University Press, 1991), pp. 86–88, 305–06; trans. Patrick J. Geary, *Readings in Medieval History* (Peterborough: Broadview Press, 1989), pp. 545–46; reprinted with permission.

The Heretics at Monforte (ca. 1028)

At this time, when Bishop Aribert had visited nearly all the suffragans of the cities of the blessed Ambrose, for the sake of whom he had traversed Italy, exhorting them to all good works, he came at length to Turin, accompanied by a large number of devoted clerics and a troop of brave knights. When he had established himself there for several days, preaching to the bishop and clergy of the city and the people of the whole town with prophetic and apostolic admonitions, as was fitting in so great a man, he heard of a strange heresy which had recently taken root in the citadel above the place called Monforte.

Now when Aribert had heard of this, he ordered that one of the heretics from the stronghold be brought before him so that he might obtain more precise knowledge of the matter. The man [Gerard], having been brought into his presence, stood with eager countenance ready to answer all the questions, his mind fully prepared for suffering, happy if he were to end his life in the severest torture. Then Aribert, on seeing the fellow to be imbued with so much fixity of purpose, began to question him earnestly and in due order about the life, customs, and faith of these people. So, after permission was given to him and silence was enjoined, Gerard arose, saying: "To God omnipotent — the Father, the Son, and the Holy Spirit — I give boundless thanks that you take the pains to examine me so carefully. And may he who knew you from the beginning in the loins of Adam grant that you live unto him and die unto him and be glorified, reigning with him forever and ever. I will lay bare to you my life and the faith of my brethren in the same spirit in which you inquire into them. We esteem virginity above all else, although we have wives. He who is a virgin keeps his virginity, but he who has lost it, after receiving permission from our elder, may observe perpetual chastity. No one knows his wife carnally, but carefully treats her as his mother or sister. We never eat meats. We fast continually and pour forth prayers unceasingly; our leaders pray always, day and night, in turn, that no hour may pass without prayer. We hold all our possessions in common with all men. None of us ends his life without torments, that we may thus avoid eternal torments...."

When Gerard had said these and other things with extreme cleverness, to some persons they seemed to be great and terrible. Notwithstanding, Bishop Aribert, recognizing his astuteness and evil genius from certain phrases he had uttered, commanded him to make clear exactly what he and his associates believed ...

Aribert: "Why do you take wives except to beget offspring, whence stems the human race?" He replied, "If the whole human race should agree not to experience corruption, the race would be begotten like bees without coition...."

James Capelli, *Summa against the Heretics* (ca. 1240)

The Protests of the Heretics That in Matrimony No One Can Be Saved

Having discussed the sacrament of the eucharist, we turn to the subject of matrimony. Now matrimony is the legitimate union of man and woman who seek an inseparable community of life under faith and worship of one God. Against this the ferocious rabies of the heretics foams out false phrases full of idle superstition. They babble that no one can ever be saved in matrimony. Indeed, these most stupid of people, seeking the purity of virginity and chastity, say that all carnal coition is shameful, base, and odious, and thus damnable. Although spiritually they are prostituted and they pollute the word of God, they are, however, most chaste of body. For men and women observing the vow and way of life of this sect are in no way soiled by the corruption of debauchery. Whence, if any one of them, man or woman, happens to be fouled by fornication, if convicted by two or three witnesses, he forthwith either is ejected from their group or, if he repents, is reconciled by the imposition of their hands, and a heavy penitential burden is placed upon him as amends for sin. Actually, the rumor of the fornication which is said to prevail among them is most false. For it is true that once a month, either by day or by night, in order to avoid gossip by the people, men and women meet together, not, as some lyingly say, for purposes of fornication, but so that they may hear preaching and make confession to their presiding official, as though from his prayers pardon for their sins would ensue. They are wrongfully wounded in popular rumor by the many malicious charges of blasphemy from those who say that they commit many shameful and horrid acts of which they are innocent. And, therefore, they vaunt themselves to be disciples of Christ ... They are all bound by their superstitious and false religion, as we said, to the vow of continence. Hence, the devil, having suggested to them that they condemn marriages, they call all other persons sensuous and lewd, and thus they are cast out from the chaste body of the Church and lose the reward of their continence....

The Testimony of Béatrice de Planissoles (1320)

(7 August, 1320, in the Chamber of the bishop before the bishop and Gaillard de Pomiès)

About 21 years ago, a year after the death of my husband, I wanted to go to the church of Montaillou to confess during Lent. When I was there, I went to Pierre Clergue, the rector, who was hearing confessions behind the altar of St. Mary. As soon as I had knelt before him, he embraced me, saying that there was no woman in the world that he loved as much as me. In my surprise, I left without having confessed.

Later, around Easter, he visited me several times, and he asked me to give myself to him. I said one day that he so bothered me in my home that I would rather give myself to four men than to a single priest because I had heard it said that a woman who gave herself to a priest could not see the face of God. To which he answered that I was an ignorant fool because the sin is the same for a woman to know her husband or another man, and the same whether the man were husband or priest. It was even a greater sin with a husband he said, because the wife did not think that she had sinned with her husband but realized it with other men. The sin was therefore greater in the first case.

I asked him how he, who was a priest, could speak like that, since the church said that marriage had been instituted by God, and that it was the first sacrament instituted by God between Adam and Eve, as a result of which it was not a sin when spouses know each other. He answered, "If it was God who instituted marriage between Adam and Eve and if he created them, why didn't he protect them from sin?" I understood then that he was saying that God did not create Adam and Eve and that he had not instituted marriage between them. He added that the Church taught many things which were contrary to truths. Ecclesiastics said these things because without them it would inspire neither respect nor fear. Because, except for the gospels and the Lord's Prayer, all of the other texts of scripture were only *"affitilhas,"* a word in the vernacular which designates what one adds on one's own to what one has heard.

I answered that in this case ecclesiastics were throwing the people into error.

(8 August, 1320, in the Chamber of the bishop before the bishop and Gaillard de Pomiès)

Speaking of marriage, he told me that many of the rules concerning it do not come from divine will who did not forbid people to marry their sisters or other persons related by blood, since at the beginning brothers knew their sister. But when several brothers had one or two pretty sisters, each wanted to have her or them. The result was many murders among them and this is why the church had forbidden brothers to know their sisters or blood relatives carnally. But for God the sin is the same whether it is an outside woman, a sister, or another relative, because the sin is as great with one woman as with another, except that it is a greater sin between a husband and wife, because they do not confess it and they unite themselves without shame.

He added that the marriage was complete and consummated as soon as a person had promised his faith to the other. What is done at the church between spouses, such as the nuptial benediction, was only a secular ceremony which had no value and had been instituted by the church only for secular splendor.

He further told me that a man and a woman could freely commit any sort of sin as long as they lived in this world and act entirely according to their pleasure. It was sufficient that at their death they be received into the sect or the faith of the good Christians to be saved and absolved of all the sins committed during this life. Because, he said, Christ said to his apostles to leave father, mother, spouse, and children, and all that they possessed, to follow him, in order to have the kingdom of heaven. Peter answered Christ, "If we, who have left everything and followed you, will have the kingdom of heaven, what will be the share of those who are ill and cannot follow you?" The Lord answered Peter that his "friends" would come and impose their hands on the heads of the ill. The ill would be healed and healed, they would follow him and have the kingdom of heaven.

The rector said that these "friends of God" were the good Christians, whom others call heretics. The imposition of the hands that they give to the dying saves them and absolves them of all their sins.

To prove that it was better for the world if brothers married sisters, he told me, "You see that we are four brothers. I am a priest and do not want a wife. If my brothers Guillaume and Bernard had married Esclarmonde and Guillemette, our sisters, our house would not have been ruined by the need of giving them a dowry. It would have remained whole. With a wife who would have been brought into the house for Raimond, our brother, we would have had enough spouses and our house would have been richer. It would therefore have been better if the brother married the sister or the sister the brother, because when she leaves her paternal house with great wealth in order to marry an outsider, the house is ruined."

And with these opinions and many others, he influenced me to the point that in the octave of St. Peter and St. Paul I gave myself to him one night in my home. This was often repeated and he kept me like this for one and one half years, coming two or three times each week to spend the night in my house near the chateau of Montaillou.

I myself came two nights to his house so that he could unite himself with me. He even knew me carnally Christmas night and still this priest said the mass the next morning, although there were other priests present.

And when, on this night of the Nativity, he wanted to have relations with me, I said to him, "How could you want to commit so great a sin on so holy a night?" He answered that the sin was the same to have intercourse with a woman on any other night or on Christmas night. Since this time and many others he said mass the morning after having known me the night before without having confessed since there was no other priest and since I often asked him how he could celebrate the mass after having committed such a sin the night before, he answered that the only valid confession is one which one makes to God, who knows the sin before it is committed, and who alone can absolve it....

What were the Cathar beliefs about virginity and marital chastity? Why did they condemn marriage? What did Pierre argue about sexual sin? about marriage? What was his rationale for favoring incestuous marriages?

INDEX OF TOPICS

SOURCES

The Author of this book and the Publisher have made every attempt to locate the authors of copyrighted material or their heirs or assigns, and would be very grateful for information that would allow them to correct any errors or omissions in a subsequent edition of the work.

CHAPTER ONE

Augustine. *The Good of Marriage.* Trans. Charles T. Wilcox in *Treatises on Marriage and Other Subjects.* Fathers of the Church Vol. 27 (1955), pp. 12-14, 16-17, 19-20, 24-26, 31, 33. Reprinted by permission of the Catholic University of America Press, Washington, DC.

Augustine. *The City of God.* Trans. Gerald G. Walsh and Grace Monahan. Fathers of the Church Vol. 14 (1952), pp. 450-54. Reprinted by permission of the Catholic University of America Press, Washington, DC.

The Burgundian Code: Book of Constitutions or Law of Gundobad. Trans. Katherine Fischer Drew (Philadelphia: University of Pennsylvania Press, 1972), pp. 17, 31-33, 40-41, 44-46. Copyright © 1949, 1976 University of Pennsylvania Press. Reprinted by permission.

The Laws of the Kings of England from Edmund to Henry I. Ed. A.J. Robertson (Cambridge: Cambridge University Press, 1925), 163, 173, 177, 201, 203, 209, 211, 213. Reprinted by permission of the publisher.

CHAPTER TWO

"Charlemagne's daughter and her lover." New translation by Paul E. Dutton from *Chronicon Laureshamense.* Ed. K.A.F. Pertz in *Monumenta Germaniae Historica: Scriptores Vol 21* (Hanover: Hahn, 1869). Printed by permission of Paul E. Dutton.

Andreas Capellanus. *The Art of Courtly Love.* Trans. John Jay Parry (New York: Columbia University Press, 1990), pp. 27-36, 141-50. © 1990 by Columbia University Press. Reprinted by permission of the publisher.

Samuel Rosenberg *et al., Songs of the Troubadours and Trouvères* (New York: Garland, 1998), 64-65, 68-69. Reprinted by permission of the publisher.

The Goliard Poets: Medieval Latin Songs and Satires. Trans. George F. Whicher (1949), 163-65, 190-93, 218-19. Copyright © 1949 by George F. Whicher. Reprinted by permission of New Directions Publishing Corporation.

Early Medieval French Lyrics. Ed. Claude Colleer Abbott (London: Constable, 1932), pp. 29, 31, 33, 63, 71, 73. Reprinted by permission of the publisher.

Medieval Ages: Specimens of European Poetry from the Ninth to the Fifteenth Centuries. Ed. Angel Flores (New York: Dent, 1963), pp. 142-44, 179-80. Reprinted by permission of the Estate of Angel Flores, c/o The Permissions Company.

The Lais of Marie de France. Trans. Robert Hanning and Joan Ferrante (Durham, NC: Labyrinth Press, 1978), pp. 60-69. Reprinted by permission of the Baker Book House Company.

The Owl and the Nightingale. Trans. J.W.H. Atkins (Cambridge University Press, 1922), 152, 155, 169 81. Reprinted by permission of Cambridge University Press.

The Story of Abelard's Adversities. Trans. J.T. Muckle (Toronto: Pontifical Institute of Medieval Studies, 1975), pp. 26-40. © 1964 by the Pontifical Institute of Medieval Studies. Reprinted by permission of the publisher.

The Letters of Abelard and Heloise. Trans. Betty Radice (Harmondsworth: Penguin Classics, 1974), pp. 113-18, 133-34, 145-48. Copyright © Betty Radice, 1974. Reprinted by permission of the Penguin Books.

Dante Alighieri. *The Divine Comedy, Vol 1: Inferno*. Trans. Charles S. Singleton (Princeton, NJ: Princeton University Press, 1970), pp. 47-57. Copyright © 1970 by Princeton University Press. Reprinted by permission of Princeton University Press.

Greater London Record Office. MS DL/C.205 Consistory Court of London Deposition Book 1467-76, fols 25r-26r, 30v-31r, 31v, 35v, 33r-36r, 41r-43r, 262v-264r. Trans. Shannon McSheffrey. Reprinted by permission of the translator and the Diocese of London.

CHAPTER THREE

Peter Lombard. *Sententiae in IV Libris Distinctae* (Rome: Frati Editori di Quaracchi, Fondazione Collegio san Bonaventura), multiple excerpts. Trans. J. Murray. Used by permission of the publisher.

Hildegard of Bingen. *Scivias*. Trans. by Mother Columba Hart and Jane Bishop (New York: Paulist Press, 1990), pp. 77-84, 215, 474. Copyright © 1990 by the Abbey of Regina Laudis of the Strict Observance, Inc. Used by permission of Paulist Press.

Etienne de Fougères, "The Good of Marriage." *Le Livre des Manières*. Ed. R. Anthony Lodge (Geneva: Droz, 1979), ll. 973-1252. Trans. Robert L.A. Clark. Reprinted by permission of Robert L.A. Clark.

Robert Grosseteste. *Templum Dei*. Ed. Joseph Goering and F.A.C. Martello (Toronto: Pontifical Institute of Mediaeval Studies, 1984), 58-60. Copyright © 1984 by the Pontifical Institute of Mediaeval Studies, Toronto. Trans. J. Murray.

Decrees of the Ecumenical Councils. Ed. Norman P. Tanner (London: Sheed and Ward, 1990), pp. 257-59. Reprinted by permission of Georgetown University Press.

Prerogative Court of Canterbury 11/4, fol 169r. Custodian: Public Record Office, The National Archives, Richmond, Surrey, UK. Trans. Shannon McSheffrey. Reprinted by permission of Shannon McSheffrey.

CHAPTER FOUR

Jacobus de Voragine. *The Golden Legend*. Trans. Granger Ryan and Helmut Ripperger (New York: Longmans, Green, 1941), pp. 16-18. Copyright © 1941 Princeton University Press. Reprinted by permission of Princeton University Press.

CHAPTER FIVE

Tertullian. *Treatises on Marriage and Remarriage: To His Wife, an Exhortation on Chastity and Monogamy*. Trans. William P. LeSaint (Westminster, MD: Newman Press, 1951), pp. 10-22. Reprinted by permission of Paulist Press.

Charlemagne's Courtier: The Complete Einhard. Trans. Paul E. Dutton (Peterborough, ON: Broadview Press, 1998), pp. 168-71. Reprinted by permission of the translator and publisher.

Self and Society in Medieval France: The Memoirs of Abbot Guibert of Nogent. Ed. John F. Benton (New York: HarperCollins, 1970), pp. 40-42, 44-50, 63-69, 72-75. Copyright © 1970 by John F. Benton. Reprinted by permission of HarperCollins Publishers, Inc.

William Langland. *Piers the Ploughman*. Trans. J.F. Goodridge (Harmondsworth: Penguin Classics, 1955; revised edition 1968), pp. 146-49. Copyright © J.F. Goodridge 1959, 1966. Reprinted by permission of Penguin Books.

The Fifteen Joys of Marriage. Trans. Brent A. Pitts (New York: Peter Lang, 1985), 4-5, 3137, 67-75, 103-07, 131-32. Reprinted by permission of the publisher.

CHAPTER SIX

Gregory of Tours. *The History of the Franks*. Trans. Lewis Thorpe. (Harmondsworth: Penguin Classics, 1974), pp. 95-97, 197-98, 218-23, 255, 294-95, 296-98, 364-66, 518-21. Copyright © Lewis Thorpe, 1974. Reprinted by permission of Penguin Books.

"Counting families in the ninth century" from *Carolingian Civilization*. Trans. Paul A. Dutton (Peterborough, ON: Broadview, 1993), 183-87. Reprinted by permission of the translator and publisher.

Maurice Coens, "La vie ancienne de sainte Godline de Ghistelles." *Analecta Bollandiana* 44 (1926), 101-37. Trans. J. Murray and A. Young. Used by permission of the Société des Bollandistes, Brussels.

The Life of St. Hugh of Lincoln. 2nd ed. Ed. Decima L. Douie and Hugh Farmer (London: Thomas Nelson, 1962), 20-27. Reprinted by permission of the publisher.

The Gesta Normannorum Ducum of William of Jumièges, Uderic Vitalis and Robert of Turigni. Vol. 2 (Oxford: Clarendon Press, 1995), 267-69. Reprinted by permission of the publisher.

Magna Carta. 2nd ed. Trans. J.C. Holt (Cambridge University Press), various excerpts. Reprinted by permission of the publisher.

Thatcher, Oliver J. and Edgar Homes McNeal. *A Source Book for Medieval History* (New York: Scribners, 1905), 371-72. Reprinted by permission of the publisher.

Select Pleas in Manorial and Other Seignorial Courts, Vol. 1: Reigns of Henry III and Edward I. Ed. F.W. Maitland (London: Bernard Quartich, 1889), multiple excerpts. Reprinted by permission of the Selden Society.

Select Cases from the Coroners' Rolls (1265-1413). Ed. Charles Gross (London: Bernard Quartich, 1896), multiple excerpts. Reprinted by permission of the Selden Society.

CHAPTER SEVEN

Medieval Woman's Guide to Health: The First English Gynecological Handbook.
Trans. Beryl Rowland (Kent, OH: Kent State University Press, 1981),
123, 125, 127, 129, 131, 133, 135, 137, 139. Reprinted by permission of
Kent State University Press.

Christine de Pisan. *The Treasure of the City of Ladies.* Trans. Sarah Lawson.
(Harmondsworth: Penguin Classics, 1985), p. 154. Copyright © Sarah
Lawson, 1985. Reprinted by Permission of Penguin Books.

CHAPTER EIGHT

Eadmer. *The Life of St. Anselm, Archbishop of Canterbury.* Ed. and trans. R.W.
Southern (Oxford: Clarendon Press, 1979), 3-7, 20-21, 37-39.
Reprinted by permission of Oxford University Press.

The Dialogue on Miracles. Trans. H. von E. Scott and C.C. Swinton Bland
(Routledge, 1919). Vol. I: 432-33. Vol II: 280-81. Reprinted by permission of the publisher.

The Fables of Odo of Cheriton. Ed. and trans. John C. Jacobs (Syracuse, NY:
Syracuse University Press, 1985), 153. Reprinted by permission of the
publisher.

On the Properties of Things: John Trevisa's translation of Bartholomaeus Anglicus De
Proprietatibus Rerum, *A Critical Text.* Ed. M.C. Seymour (Oxford:
Clarendon Press, 1973), 298-305, 309-11. Trans. J. Murray. Used by
permission of Oxford University Press.

Jean Froissart. "L'espinette amourouse." In *Chaucer's World,* ed. Edith Rickert
(New York: Columbia University Press, 1948), 96-98. Reprinted by
permission of the publisher.

CHAPTER NINE

The Jews in Western Europe: 1400-1600. Trans. and ed. John Edwards (Manchester: Manchester University Press, 1994), 88-91. Reprinted by permission of the publisher.

Irving A. Agus. *Rabbi Meir of Rothenburg.* Vol 1 (New York: KTAV Publishing,
1970), multiple excerpts. Reprinted by permission of the publisher.

Letters of Medieval Jewish Traders. Trans. S.D. Goiten (Princeton: Princeton University Press, 1973), 221-26. Copyright © 1973 by Princeton University
Press. Reprinted by permission of Princeton University Press.

Hebrew Ethical Wills, Part Two. Ed. Israel Abrahams (Philadelphia: Jewish Publication Society of America, 1948), 208-18. Used by permission of the Jewish Publication Society, © 1948.

The Koran. Trans. N.J. Dawood (London: Penguin Classics 1956; fifth revised edition 1990), multiple excerpts. Copyright © N.J. Dawood, 1956, 1959, 1966, 1968, 1974, 1990. Reprinted by permission of Penguin Books.

Heresies of the High Middle Ages: Selected Sources. Trans. Walter L. Wakefield and Austin P. Evans (New York: Columbia University Press, 1991), 86-88, 305-06. Reprinted by permission of the publisher.

Readings in Medieval History. Ed. Patrick J. Geary (Peterborough, ON: Broadview Press, 1989), 545-46. Reprinted by permission of the publisher.

READINGS IN MEDIEVAL CIVILIZATIONS AND CULTURES

series editor: Paul Edward Dutton

BORN of a desire for a richer, multi-layered approach to the political, social, religious, economic, and intellectual history of the Middle Ages, Readings in Medieval Civilizations and Cultures seeks to supply readers--both scholars and students--with collections of translated primary sources including many to which they would not normally or easily have access. Each volume includes both standard texts and lesser-known ones that reveal important and intriguing aspects of various periods of the Middle Ages and the issues at play.

I.

Carolingian Civilization: A Reader, ed. and trans.
Paul Edward Dutton (1993)

II.

Medieval Popular Religion: A Reader,
ed. and trans. John Shinners (1997)

III.

Charlemagne's Courtier: The Complete Einhard,
ed. and trans. Paul Edward Dutton (1998)

IV.

Medieval Saints: A Reader,
ed. Mary-Ann Stouck (1999)

V.

From Roman to Merovingian Gaul: A Reader,
ed. and trans. Alexander Callander Murray (2000)

VI.

Medieval England, 1000-1500: A Reader,
ed. Emilie Amt (2000)

VII.

Love, Marriage, and Family in the Middle Ages: A Reader,
ed. Jacqueline Murray (2001)

Inquiries about the series and its future volumes should be sent to
Broadview Press:
P.O. Box 1243, Peterborough, Ontario, Canada K9J 7H5